THE
FINAL
SUPERSTITION

THE
FINAL
SUPERSTITION

A Critical Evaluation
of the Judeo-Christian
Legacy

JOSEPH L.
DALEIDEN

Prometheus Books

59 John Glenn Drive
Amherst, NewYork 14228-2197

Published 1994 by Prometheus Books

98 97 96 95 94   5 4 3 2 1

Library of Congress Cataloging-in-Publication Data

Daleiden, Joseph L.
    The final superstition : a critical evaluation of the Judeo-Christian legacy /
Joseph L. Daleiden.
        p.   cm.
    Includes bibliographical references and index.
    ISBN 0-87975-896-1 (alk. paper)
    1. Christianity—Controversial literature. 2. Judaism—Controversial
literature. I. Title.
BL2747.D35   1994
200—dc20   94-15700
                                                                              CIP

Printed in the United States of America on acid-free paper.

To Salman Rushdie and those courageous men and women throughout history who have risked their livelihood and, oftentimes, their lives challenging religious authoritarianism.

Contents

7

Acknowledgments

I gratefully acknowledge the encouragements and useful criticism of several people, including Walter Buckman, Mitch Vogel, Jim Peipmeier, and Professor Delos McKown. While acknowledging their valuable comments, I hold them in no way responsible for the conclusions I have drawn.

John Baldy did an exceptional job proofing the text to correct my penchant for split infinitives and numerous other grammatical errors.

Bobbie White and my daughter Carolyn had the nearly impossible task of typing the first draft from my illegible scribbling. My daughters, Carolyn and Denise, and my wife, Peg, were kind enough to read drafts to ensure that the content was comprehensible to persons not versed in theology or the history of religion. Their encouragement is much appreciated. As for my son, Rob, who was too young at the time to contribute to this volume, I offer my apologies for having been too busy with my own homework to give him much help with his. But on second thought, knowing my lack of patience, that probably was to our mutual advantage.

Finally I wish to thank the editors at Prometheus Books, Steven L. Mitchell and Eugene O'Connor, for their many thoughtful suggestions and scrupulous editing.

Preface

This started out to be a book on economic policies. However, I soon realized that Robert Heilbroner was correct in contending that all economics is ultimately derived from philosophy. It is no mere coincidence that Adam Smith, the father of modern economics, was a moral philosopher by training. By definition, the science of economics is concerned with the production, distribution, and consumption of goods and services to meet the unlimited wants of humankind. But as soon as we consider the concept of distribution we enter the realm of ethics.

In seeking to model human behavior economists have forgotten that it is a function of many underlying variables that are culturally and temporally different. One of the primary variables is the value system or ethic that is dominant at any given time. Not only does the prevailing ethical theory affect the behavior of citizens within a society, but, equally important, it colors the perception of the economists who are attempting to understand and influence that behavior. One of the major discoveries of quantum physics is that the mere act of observing can affect the outcome of an experiment at the subatomic level. Just as the observer and the thing observed cannot be totally separated in the science of physics, the values of economists cannot but affect their interpretation of observed economic phenomena.

It is apparent, therefore, that economic policy be based on a clearly defined statement of ethical principles. Ethical theory, however, is in its turn implicitly based on a philosophy of human nature, different concepts of which lead to different conclusions about human goals (purposes, ends— I use the terms interchangeably) and the legitimate means by which a person may attempt to achieve those goals. In Western societies the prevailing philosophy of human nature is heavily influenced by the Judeo-Christian theological tradition. Hence, it becomes necessary to review that tradition to determine whether it provides a legitimate view of humankind upon

11

which to base an ethical theory and, ultimately, socioeconomic policies.

Although I have spent a great portion of my life studying religion in its various forms, I was not excited about the prospect of undertaking a critical evaluation of the Judeo-Christian tradition—for two reasons. First, with the resurgence of Christian fundamentalism, it did not seem to be a particularly propitious time to write a book questioning the validity and value of that tradition. And second, it has been my experience that any serious attempt to discuss the subject of religion or philosophy leaves most people either infuriated or bored to death.

Nevertheless, after due reflection, I concluded that precisely because fundamentalism is so pervasive, there was sufficient reason once again to expose the dark side of the Judeo-Christian tradition. Not that it hasn't been done many times before but, for reasons that I'll take pains to explain, the true history of Western religions is constantly being swept aside in favor of more expeditious myths.

The second problem—namely, writing on religion in a style that would be sufficiently entertaining to hold a reader's interest—I found even more perplexing. What reader would be encouraged to take the journey with me into the oftentimes labyrinthine world of theology and philosophy? Surely not those zealots who are so committed to their religious beliefs that even an examination of their belief systems is considered sacrilegious. No amount of reason or logic could persuade them. However, there does appear to be a large number of people who are not committed to suppressing their intellectual integrity in blind adherence to an unexamined system of beliefs. This is especially true of many (although, sadly, not nearly enough) college students who have adopted their religious views without being aware of the large body of historical research that calls into question the motivations and integrity of the founders of many of the popular religions of our time. Few are aware of the origins of the biblical writings, or have devoted any time to critically evaluating the messages that such works convey. I find this to be especially true of those who are able to quote passages of the Bible to suit every occasion.

Even college students who have taken courses in theology have often been denied exposure to the cogent arguments that question the divinity of Jesus or the concept of a divine creator. Worse still, disingenuous theology professors often provide an atheistic strawman which can be easily disposed of without coming to grips with the real contradictions of theism. I experienced this sort of ruse firsthand in the theology and philosophy courses I took in college. Virtually every serious philosopher who questioned Christian metaphysics was given short shrift. It wasn't until after I left the university that I was able to begin my real education.

Having determined that my audience should be those individuals who are still willing to engage in rational discussion, my final decision was to adopt a style that, although considered by some to be outrageous, might help achieve what historian Barbara Tuchman claims must be the first goal of every writer: to get the reader to turn the page.

The idea of using the dialectical approach is far from original. It has been used since the time of Plato. Moreover, many of the books of the Old Testament report dialogues between their heroes and Yahweh. So there is some precedent for my approach, which is a conversation between God and Joe (indicated in the dialogue sections as **G** and **J**, respectively) followed by a straightforward exposition in the final chapters. The concept of God which I employ in my dialogue is the one with which I was raised: an eternal supreme being, creator of the universe, perfect in power, knowledge, and goodness, who responds to the prayers of humankind and ultimately sits in judgment of us all.

Some may be offended by my treatment of their deeply revered beliefs. It is not my intention to offend or to destroy the psychological comfort which belief in God and immortality offers to many persons. Rather, I hope to forcefully demonstrate that beliefs which are thousands of years old, and stem from an age when humankind was by and large ignorant and savage, need to be carefully scrutinized for validity and relevance in today's society. If we are to formulate a sound ethic and just and effective socioeconomic policies, we must, wherever possible, remove all myths and falsehoods embedded in our theories. I hope to create sufficient doubts regarding religious beliefs that people will pause before attempting to translate their theological doctrines into public policy. As I will amply demonstrate, it is the true believers, who attempt to back their beliefs with the power of the state, who have caused so much misery throughout history. Doubt encourages tolerance.

Given this rationale, I ask the reader to accompany me on a mental excursion, back through the accumulated religious traditions of Western society. The trip won't always be easy; for some it may become too painful to continue. It is extremely difficult—some would argue impossible—to discard beliefs which have been learned from parents and which are woven into the fabric of our culture. Yet the further progress of our society requires that we perceive as clearly as possible the reality of the world as it actually exists, rather than a world of myths, no matter how intoxicating those myths may be. In the long run, history has shown that intellectual hallucinogens will wreak havoc with any society. The purpose of this volume is to clear away the sediment of thousands of years of myths and deliberate falsehoods in an effort to reach a bedrock of truth regarding Western society's Judeo-Christian beliefs.

It is my hope that future volumes will explore several hypotheses regarding human behavior and the ethical theories derived from them. Are we free to choose, or is our behavior determined solely by our genetic and environmental conditioning? Can education make a major difference in the way people behave? Can specific socioeconomic policies be devised that will modify behavior in a way that increases the happiness of all, or is human society so complex that we would all be better off in the long run relying on the evolutionary forces of social Darwinism? Admittedly, these difficult questions have puzzled philosophers and scientists for centuries, so it would be presumptuous of me to believe that I have *the answer*. However, by adopting an eclectic approach I hope to provide some new insights to these age-old questions.

I also intend to convey my thoughts on the major socioeconomic policy issues facing the United States in the twenty-first century. The specific policies recommended will be grounded in the propositions developed earlier and the results of recent economic research. It is to be expected, however, that this discussion will raise many more questions than it answers. Nonetheless, it is my hope that it will focus the discussion and provide an agenda for research that may shed light on some of the seemingly unsolvable problems our society faces.

Note: For dating purposes, instead of B.C. (Before Christ) and A.D. (*Anno Domini*), I have adopted the nondenominational forms used in biblical scholarship, B.C.E. (Before the Common Era) and C.E. (Common Era).

Introduction

G: Why have you requested this dialogue? I'll tell you why: you are doing it because of your well-known rejection of authority. Since I am the ultimate authority figure, you are going to attempt to reject me. You haven't changed much since you rebelled against your father as a teenager.

J: Who would have thought God was Freudian? I really would like to get on with the purpose of this discussion, if you don't mind.

G: Wait, I haven't yet agreed to participate. Why this format? It's certainly not original.

J: I know, but I explained my reasons in the Preface.

G: You are wasting your time. Who will want to read the scribblings of an obscure economist who doesn't have degrees in either philosophy or theology?

J: I don't recall any of the ancient Greek philosophers receiving Ph.Ds.

G: But they spent their entire lives studying.

J: Exactly, and so have I. More importantly, I have the benefit of 2,000 years of additional thinking by the world's greatest minds.

G: Assuming you understand any of it. . . . I can see exactly where you are heading. I know all the arguments you will use and the conclusion you will draw. Why go through with this futile charade?

J: The same reasoning can apply to my life or the entire history of man. Why did you bother to create the world if you knew how everything would turn out? But I prefer to consider that question later. Any other objections?

G: Yes. Your conclusion stinks.

J: That is not a very Godly statement.

G: I'm trying to be concise.

J: Very well. Anything else?

15

G: Don't you find it just a little disingenuous for you to be putting words in my mouth? You know I'm not really talking to you. This whole conversation is a concoction of your perverse imagination.

J: Au contraire, Mon Dieu. You are the true God—the only God, as I shall conclusively demonstrate to anyone with the courage and fortitude to follow this dialectic to its inescapable conclusion. In some ways this dialogue is not unlike the conversations Jeanne d'Arc had with her voices, or for that matter any of your followers who tell me they talk to you through prayer or meditation.

G: It is not the same. My followers are open to receive my word. You are biased.

J: If your followers receive your word unadulterated by their own biases, why are there so many different interpretations of what you have said? I'm afraid that doesn't wash.

G: Of course people can, by virtue of their free will, interpret or distort my word to serve their own ends. But that does not mean I have not revealed to them the Truth.

J: Ah ha! The Divine Word. But where do I find your words? In the Old Testament? The New? The Koran? The Rig Veda? The Upanishads? The Bhagavad Gita? The Mishnah? The Nihongi? The Tao Te Ching?

G: My truth is revealed in the study of many of the sacred works of antiquity.

J: Of what value are these works if everyone who reads them comes away with a different interpretation?

G: I have sent divinely inspired prophets and teachers to interpret them for humankind.

1

Cult Religions and Fundamentalists: Prophets from the Barnum School

Never give a sucker an even break.

—W. C. Fields

J: It would appear that you certainly sent a host of divine messengers. Since the dawn of history there has been no shortage of people who declared that they spoke for the gods. The result has been the creation of perhaps 1,000 religions throughout the ages, including about eighty Christian sects. Each of these religions has been propagated by people who professed to have an exclusive knowledge of the intentions and desires of the gods. From the most primitive shamans, to the oracles at Delphi, to the prophets of the Old Testament, down to the present-day Evangelists and religious leaders, the field of divine interpreters has been overflowing with men and women jostling for recognition by the masses. Not surprisingly, since the benefits to be reaped include the adoration of followers and substantial power and riches.

G: You cannot ignore the fact that many religious leaders have suffered martyrdom in bearing witness to their faith.

J: Not as often as the myths would have us believe. More often than not, it was their followers who endured the martyrdom or, when they had the power to do so, inflicted martyrdom on all those who refused to adopt the beliefs of the faithful. History provides ample evidence, as I will show, that those who claimed that they were sent as messengers to reveal the word of God were frequently frauds and charlatans of the lowest sort. The situation today is indicative of the historical tradition as well: most of the aspiring prophets and messiahs subscribe whole-heartedly to old P. T. Barnum's dictum, "There's a sucker born every minute, and two to take him." These religious con artists find no shortage of pigeons: the poor and the sick, the ignorant and the uneducated, the alienated and the distressed.

G: Are we to believe that all those who seek to spread belief systems are charlatans? And their followers merely dupes?

J: I don't claim that all religious leaders are dishonest; some may simply be ignorant zealots or persons possessed by an overactive imagination. Let's review the evidence. I'll start with a review of the newer arrivals on the religious scene, some of the self-proclaimed prophets of the last two centuries who have spawned the fastest-growing religions in America today: Jehovah's Witnesses, Seventh-Day Adventists, Christian Scientists, and Mormons.

Jehovah's Witnesses

Almost anyone who lives in a large metropolitan area has had a Jehovah's missionary knock on the door. Immediately one is struck by their sincerity; their clean-cut look, their enthusiasm, and their total ignorance of other religions, philosophy, science and just about anything else that isn't written in the Bible.

G: They are not all so ignorant.

J: No, not all. But a short review of the history of the Jehovah's Witnesses leads one to question how any person could be so naive as to swallow this incredible belief system.[1] The sect was founded by Charles Taze Russell in the latter half of the nineteenth century and its believers were originally known as Russellites. Like many who wrestled with the problem before him, Russell was stymied by the incongruity of a merciful God who sentenced his created children to an eternal hell if they dared to disobey his commands. Russell began studying the Bible to find a way out of this paradox which has never been successfully resolved by Christian theologians. Having little formal education, Russell used a literal interpretation and a great deal of imagination to construct a theology that denied death entirely, at least for the elect. After Russell's death in 1914, his successor, Joseph Franklin Rutherford, coined the slogan of the Witnesses: "Millions Now Living Will Never Die."

G: Catchy phrase, I like it.

J: Like so many sects, the basis of the Witnesses' theology lies in the belief that the Second Coming of Christ is to occur very soon. Russell examined the chronology of the Bible and, ignoring the conflicting genealogies contained in the New Testament, concluded that there were fourteen generations from Abraham to David, fourteen generations from David to the Babylonian captivity, and fourteen generations from the captivity to Christ. Then, by the most excruciating and absurd calculations he concluded that the Second Coming was to occur in 1874. When Christ didn't show up as predicted, Russell went back to his calculations and came up with a new forecast of Christ's return: 1914. This was enough to keep the faithful in line for another forty years, until just about the time of his death. Russell's calculations are indicative of the level of sophistication of his theology. The calculations are based on a variety of unrelated quotes from the Bible. Starting with the Book of Revelations' reference to a "woman clothed with the sun" who would be protected from a great red dragon for 1,260 days (Rev. 12:1, 3, 6), Russell multiplied by two (why not?). The resulting 2,520 days are next transformed to years because the prophet Ezekiel had been told to lie on his right side for forty days to symbolize the number of years of Jerusalem's punishment. The resulting number of years are then added to an incorrect date Russell assumed for the victory of Babylon over Jerusalem.

G: I don't think I follow that.

J: I would have little respect for your divine logic if you could. It is, obviously, nothing but gibberish designed to fool only the most gullible. Jumping around the Bible taking numbers from here and there, a person could come up with any date he wants.

When 1914 ushered in a world war instead of the predicted Second Coming, Russell, true to type, remained undaunted. With considerable moxie, Russell proclaimed to his disappointed (but not disillusioned) followers that the Lord did indeed come in 1914 but wasn't yet ready to reveal himself. Just when would he inaugurate his new kingdom? A 1966 Witness publication, still enthralled with the numbers game, announced:

> Six thousand years from man's creation will end in 1975, and the seventh period of a thousand years of human history will begin in the fall of 1975 A.D. . . . It would not be by mere chance or accident . . . for the reign of Jesus Christ . . . to run parallel with the seventh millennium of man's existence.[2]

Alas, it turned out to be another failed prophecy; the sinful world continues rolling along.

But cold reality has little influence on true believers; the Witnesses still cling to the belief that it is only a matter of time before this evil world will be destroyed in the final battle of Armageddon. And who will be saved? Not the mass of humanity who are destined to perish, both body and soul. Only the Witnesses can be saved, and these are of two classes. The elite are the 144,000, most of whom have already passed to a spiritual existence. The best that the remaining 99 percent of the Witnesses can hope for is an eternal physical life here on earth under the reign of Christ. Still that isn't so bad. Most of the Jehovah's Witnesses are at the bottom of the socioeconomic heap today and after Armageddon the rest of the heap will have been blown away. No wonder the prospect of an ultimate thermonuclear conflagration makes the Witnesses tremble with anticipation.

G: Aren't you being a little harsh with these well-meaning, if somewhat simple, people? They devote their lives to trying to convert others to share in their salvation. You have to admire their self-sacrificing efforts.

J: Who was it who said that the road to hell was paved with good intentions? It isn't enough that people desire to do good if the results are bad. And the belief of the Witnesses often does cause great harm, especially to their own members. To begin with, like most cultists who believe they possess the true faith, the Witnesses have little tolerance for other beliefs. They label as a "false and misleading conception" the "belief in the Fatherhood of God and the brotherhood of man, that all men are God's children and therefore have a common bond and union in Him however differently they may conceive Him."[3] They believe that, "Woman is merely a lowly creature whom God created for man as man's helper."[4] They are opposed to knowledge and true learning. The Watchtower Society recommends the following for its libraries:

> *Watchtower* and *Awake,* bound volumes from past years and older publications of the society. . . . Encyclopedias, atlases or books on grammar may be useful but we don't recommend purchasing them. It is not necessary to include books on health, genetics, politics, science, mathematics, etc. . . . It is inadvisable to have books on spiritism, mysticism, higher criticism, evolution or fiction.[5]

Note how they slip in the inadvisability of having books on higher criticism (those which provide a critical analysis of the Bible) and evolution, the two disciplines that would certainly undermine their mythical world.

The Witnesses' slavish devotion to the literal interpretation of the Bible has led to a more deadly belief: their refusal to accept blood transfusions for themselves or their children. A passage in the Acts of the Apostles repeats the Old Testament prohibition against ingesting blood: ". . . you are to abstain from meat that has been sacrificed to idols, from blood, from anything that has been strangled, and from fornication" (Acts 15:2–29). Obviously eating has nothing to do with transfusions, but such distinctions escape zealots. Blood is blood, the context is irrelevant to the Witnesses. And lives are lost as the result of this ignorance.

G: That is a sad fact. But for many persons who have little meaning in their lives, the Witnesses can provide a focal point, a sense of purpose.

J: So can any cult, which is exactly why they are potentially dangerous. The focus might be contrary to the best interests of society as well as the individual. We might forgive the silliness of a religion whose members profess that demons are everywhere, even in the gift of a "possessed" pair of gloves unwittingly given by a friend.[6] But a religion whose members "are three times more likely to be admitted to a psychiatric hospital than the general population"[7] is certainly not doing its membership any good. After reviewing his findings, medical researcher John Spencer concluded that "either the Jehovah's Witnesses sect tends to attract an excess of prepsychotic individuals who may then break down, or else being a Jehovah's Witness is itself a stress that may precipitate a psychosis."[8] In either case I would suggest that a person who feels an overwhelming need to join a religious organization would do better seeing a psychiatrist than joining this group.

G: Arguably, there are many religious organizations that are far better at fulfilling my will and the needs of man.

J: Are there? Let's examine another popular religious cult in the United States, the Christian Scientists.

G: I think they would resent your calling them a "cult."

J: Probably so. The term appears to be related to the size of the following. Yesterday's disreputable cult is today's respected religion.

Christian Science

As a child I often wondered at the variety of strange church names and one in particular: The Church of Christ, Scientist. I had never read that Jesus was a scientist in any sense of the word. It wasn't until much later that I realized the founder of this organization, Mary Baker Eddy, never understood the meaning of the word. However, like science fiction author L. Ron Hubbard, whose work of pseudoscience resulted in establishing the Church of Scientology, Mrs. Eddy recognized that simply using the word *science* would give her ideas the flavor of objective truth. And, like

Hubbard, Mrs. Eddy's teachings are based neither on science nor on a consideration of the truth. As a religious movement Christian Science is a prime example of how otherwise decent and intelligent people can be motivated to commit acts which, if committed in circumstances other than under the auspices of a religious belief, would be considered the most heinous of crimes.

G: Quite a severe charge.
J: But not unwarranted, as I'll demonstrate. Confronted with the historical dilemma of theism, Mrs. Eddy attempted to reconcile her belief in the goodness of God with the existence of evil, suffering and death. She could not accept the ancient belief that God is also responsible for all evil as well as good. Therefore, employing the logic that only a true believer can command, she concluded that since it was obvious that God was real, then evil, suffering, and death must be unreal—mere illusions caused by man's sinful nature. According to Mrs. Eddy:

> The starting point of Christian Science is that God, Spirit, is All-in-All, and that there is no other might or mind. Spirit is immortal truth; matter is mindless error. . . . Spirit is God, and man is his image and likeness. Therefore, man is not material, he is spiritual.[9]

What this dubious metaphysics has to do with science is anyone's guess, but when expounded in her 1875 book *Science and Health,* it quickly gathered a number of adherents. At the time, medicine was still at a relatively primitive stage, with many quacks and con artists who preyed on the ill and the suffering. Even reputable doctors knew nothing about the role of bacteria and viruses as the causes of disease. Without the benefits of antibiotics, there was no effective treatment for even influenza. Take a perfectly healthy looking person, watch him suddenly catch influenza and die within a few weeks, and you might very easily believe that there was a spiritual rather than physical cause. As further evidence of the spiritual nature of disease, Mrs. Eddy could point to the examples in the gospels where Jesus cured by merely forgiving sins. Despite the lack of any true science to support her beliefs, it is not surprising that her doctrine found supporters. Faith healing is one of the most primitive and enduring forms of religion, practiced by shamans and magicians back in prehistoric times.

If Mrs. Eddy had simply attempted to supplement medicine with faith, as do most religious sects, there would be no great harm. However, she went further and decided that since disease was an illusion to begin with, any form of medical treatment was false and demonstrated a lack of faith in the goodness of God and spiritual essence of man. The result was a modern horror: the church of Mrs. Eddy is opposed to drugs, immunizations, therapeutic diets (such as for diabetes), chest x-rays, fever thermometers, taking pulses, etc. The list is extensive. There are, however, notable exceptions. If Mrs. Eddy had a medical problem, she sought appropriate help and then wrote that into the law of her church. Mrs. Eddy needed eyeglasses, so optometrists were acceptable. Mrs. Eddy needed dental work, so dentistry is permitted. Mrs. Eddy used a hypodermic needle to relieve pain, so her followers can do that as well. The primary prohibitions seem to be aimed at those ailments which, because they were invisible to the naked eye, were thought to be "illusions." That we can now "see" bacteria and viruses and understand how they attack the body is of no consequence to Christian Scientists. All of Mrs. Eddy's writings are believed to be divinely inspired revelations and she ruled that they could not be changed without her approval. (Why a divine revelation would need to be changed at all seems not to have bothered her sense of logic.)

G: If Mrs. Eddy was the dogmatic crackpot you suggest, isn't it remarkable that a substantial number of influential and otherwise intelligent people still adhere to her creed?

J: The reasons people subscribe to this particular religion are, for the most part, the same as the reasons others subscribe to any religious belief, and I will spend some time on that subject in a later chapter. For now I would simply submit that most people develop their religious beliefs at their mothers' knees. If their peer group shares those beliefs, and there is no pressing need to question them, the beliefs will be maintained throughout a person's life. In the case of Christian Science, however, there are two other special reasons.

First, precisely because many of the Christian Science adherents are rich and powerful, they have gained governmental recognition for their religion in a manner that appears to be an endorsement. For example, in forty-eight states the church has won religious exemptions from immunizations.[10] Ironically, it is because such a large portion of the U.S. population does receive immunizations that the Christian Scientists are generally not subject to contagious diseases. In many states they have won exemptions from metabolic testing of newborn babies, silver nitrate drops, premarital and postnatal blood tests, and from studying about disease in public schools.[11] Furthermore, although Christian Science practitioners are unqualified to even recognize most serious illnesses, let alone treat them, many insurance companies will reimburse fees charged by Christian Science practitioners. This, of course, is just good business; practitioners are much cheaper than doctors and hospitals. And it makes no financial difference to the medical insurer whether the patient lives or dies (in fact, quick deaths save the medical insurers money). The result of this unwarranted toleration by government and the insurance industry is to effectively legitimize the bogus belief system of Christian Science.

G: You choose to ignore the fact that faith can heal. There is incontrovertible evidence for this conclusion.

J: That's a perfect lead in to the second reason that belief in Christian Science lingers on. The idea that faith heals, like all half truths, has an element of validity. Since many of the ills people have are psychosomatic, simply believing that a treatment will effect a cure may result in a cure. There is nothing supernatural about that. As any doctor knows, a placebo can be quite effective for a number of psychological maladies; and a competent psychologist can "cure" bad backs, headaches, and a variety of intestinal disorders.

The problem is that for the more serious diseases faith is not enough, and this is where Christian Science can work great evil. Take the case of fifteen-month-old Matthew Swan.[12] When he developed a severe fever his well-intentioned parents called the most prominent Christian Science practitioner in Detroit for treatment. For two weeks his parents were assured that their son was being healed, but were warned that their fear or "false parental thoughts" were hampering treatment. When their baby gnashed his teeth in delirium, his parents were told that they should "take the positive interpretation of the evidence" that their baby might be "planning some great achievement" while "gritting his teeth." When the practitioner began to suspect that the child's illness may indeed be serious, she suggested that the convulsions might be due to a broken bone in the boy's neck. This allowed the practitioner to recommend taking Matthew to a hospital, because Christian Science permits the setting of broken bones by a doctor. Unfortunately, it was too late. The diagnosis was advanced meningitis. What was the practitioner's reaction? She feigned outrage when she learned that the child was receiving medical care for a disease rather than a broken bone and refused to pray for him any longer. Matthew died after a week in intensive care.

G: Most tragic. But you can't condemn an entire religious movement because of one unfortunate instance.

J: This is not an isolated case. Nor is Christian Science the only religious group that is guilty of such negligence. It is endemic to fundamentalist faith-healing cults. It is outrageous that the state and federal governments are guilty of complicity in these tragedies. If nonreligious parents denied medical treatment for their children there is no doubt that they would, and should, be held accountable for child abuse and, if warranted, manslaughter. Although no one doubts the good intentions of the religious believer, the consequence for the child is the same. It should, therefore, be the responsibility of federal, state, and local governments to protect children from ignorant and superstitious parents, just as they would from any other child abuser. In 1974, however, the U.S. Department of Health, Education and Welfare caved in to the intense lobbying of Christian Scientists. Possibly because some top HEW officials were Christian Science members, the "religious immunity" provision was added to the Code of Federal Regulations.[13] The clause exempted parents who withhold medical treatment from a child for religious reasons from charges of negligence.[14] The results of this law were disastrous, extending as it did not only to the Christian Scientists, but to all religious cults. In Indiana alone, many children whose parents belonged to the ultra fundamentalist Faith Assembly Church died, and the state prosecutor claimed that the law prevented him from filing any charges.[15]

Every attempt to repeal the clause was met with a barrage of Christian Science lobbyists raising the emotional cry of religious freedom. With a staunch ally in Senator Orrin Hatch, the Christian Scientists were able to uphold the clause. The ultimate result was that appendicitis, kidney infection, diarrhea, even dehydration continued to result in deaths of young children which could have easily been avoided. It was not until the mid-1980s that the U.S. Department of Health and Human Services issued new regulations with regard to child abuse which defined failure to provide medical care as neglect and required states to override parental judgment "whenever the child's health warranted it." Yet the deaths continued. In October 1990 a federal appeals court in Florida upheld the conviction of a Christian Science couple who failed to provide medical care for their child, who subsequently died. Such is the legacy of a religion founded in an era when medical science was largely unknown, and whose membership is dogmatically locked into that ignorance.

Seventh-Day Adventists

J: Shall we move on to the next group of spokespeople for God?

G: Why not? You obviously feel you are on a roll. I only wish to interject that throughout history there have been persons who, through self-delusion or purposeful deceit, have claimed to speak for me. That does not mean that I have no legitimate representatives. It just means that the believer must exercise some discretion in choosing whom to follow.

J: What an interesting acknowledgment. Must *caveat emptor* be stamped on each religious creed? Well if Mary Baker Eddy was guilty of self-delusion, the same cannot be said of Ellen White, the cofounder of the Seventh-Day Adventist Church. Mrs. White was a young follower of William Miller, the prophet who predicted that Christ would return to earth on October 22, 1844. (It seems that predicting the Second Coming has been the favorite pastime of Christians ever since Christ himself erroneously predicted "there are some of those standing here who will not taste death, till they have seen the Son of Man coming in his kingdom" (Matt. 16:28). The accuracy of specific predictions has never been the strong point of prophets, as I shall demonstrate in a later chapter.) When the day of the "great disappointment" came and went, as usual, a few die-hard devotees began the excruciating process of rationalizing the error. Mrs. White, along with her husband, James White, and a friend Joseph Bates, at last fastened upon a truly novel idea—the Sanctuary Doctrine. As summarized by Douglas Hackleman, the editor of *Adventist Currents,* this doctrine states that "in 1844, Christ as high priest, moved from the first apartment of the heavenly sanctuary—where his activities had been analogous to the daily ministrations of Israel's priests—to the most holy place of the heavenly sanctuary, where on October 22, 1844, he began a work of 'investigative judgment.' "[16] Since then, Christ has been busy examining the records of his followers throughout history to see which of them have merited salvation.

G: Where in the world, the reader may ask, did they come up with a theory like that?

J: Why, Ellen White was informed of it in frequent visions! So we have yet another prophet who claimed to speak for God. According to Mrs. White, "the many volumes of my books" were "what God has opened before me in vision—the precious rays of light shining from the throne."[17] Elsewhere she specifically states that "the words I employ in describing what I have seen are my own, unless they be those spoken to me by an angel, which I always enclose in marks of quotation."[18] Such avowed integrity! What a shock it is to learn that this divine oracle had a nasty little habit of plagiarism.

G: Quite a charge. You can, no doubt, substantiate it?

J: Without a doubt. Take the case of the statement of Mrs. White to which I just referred. It was taken from a letter of Mrs. White's in which she first asks "What voice will you acknowledge as the voice of God?" and then proceeds to paraphrase, without reference, two paragraphs in Daniel March's book *Night Scenes in the Bible*.[19] At least sometimes Mrs. White demonstrated good taste in her choice of authors from whom to steal. Her inspired description of the Fall was obviously borrowed from John Milton's *Paradise Lost*.[20]

G: Perhaps a mere coincidence?

J: You know better. Mrs. White received a copy of Milton's classic work—and according to her son, she had read it—just before she published her first volume on the Fall.

The Adventists are noted for their many hospitals and, unlike the Christian Scientists, demonstrate great concern for physical health. This is a direct result of the interest of James and Ellen White, the latter contending that "the great subject of health reform was opened before me in a vision,"[21] and elsewhere, "I had never seen a paper treating upon health" before her June 1867 vision.[22] In her article on the subject Mrs. White claimed, "I have had a great light on this subject of health reform. I did not seek this light; I did not study to obtain it; it was given to me by the Lord to give others."[23] When it was noted that her views were very like those written in the publication "Laws of Life" by Drs. Trall, Jackson, and others, Mrs. White denied ever having seen an article on the subject and contended that it was only after her own vision that her husband "was aroused upon the health question."[24] Yet it was discovered that six months before the date of Mrs. White's alleged vision, her husband had become much interested in health as indicated by articles he ran in his *Adventist Review and Sabbath Herald*, which included an article by none other than Dr. James Caleb Jackson. Much more evidence could be provided. Douglas Hackleman compares, side by side, Ellen White's writings with the passages she obviously plagiarized. Her own son admitted his mother's "habit" of borrowing, but apparently did not realize it was so pervasive. Other Adventists became disillusioned with Mrs. White when she claimed to see in visions things that they personally had told her.[25]

Not only did Ellen White appropriate other people's ideas, but she failed to follow her own dictums when they were inconvenient. Although she chastised those who digressed even occasionally to eat meat, she wrote, in one of her rare moments of originality, of dining on wild duck while on vacation in the Rocky Mountains. In fact, her estate acknowledges that she ate meat much of her life.

This overwhelming evidence proves that the foundress of the Adventist religion did not speak for God, but was a fraud, a hypocrite, and a liar; and her husband must have known as much and so is equally guilty, at the very least, of complicity. What, then, was the reaction of Mrs. White's church to the discovery of the true nature of their founders? As in all such instances throughout history, the totally predictable response was to circle the wagons in defense of the myth against the onslaught of truth. Ronald Numbers, a professor in the church's School of Medicine was the first to drag the skeleton from the closet and blow the whistle on Ellen White. He was, of course, fired. In 1982, Walter Rea published his book *The White Lie*[26] and was promptly relieved of his church post. Ronald Greybill, an associate secretary of the White estate, wrote a manuscript in 1983 supporting the findings of Numbers and Rea. When the church tried to suppress Greybill's manuscript, it was leaked worldwide. Exit Greybill. The list goes on. I haven't heard what happened to Douglas Hackleman yet. Perhaps he'll survive; sooner or later the church will realize what so many other religious institutions have learned: The truth or falsity of a doctrine of a religion is irrelevant to the vast majority of the membership. The reason for following a specific belief is much more psychological than rational. Again, we must hold this discussion for later. We set out to determine if any person can be judged to speak for God, and we came up wanting in the first three cases. Next we'll examine one of the fastest-growing religions, both in terms of membership and political power.

Church of Jesus Christ of the Latter Day Saints—The Mormons

There are many unimpeachable sources which provide overwhelming evidence to the true nature of the founder of Mormonism. It amply demonstrates that if there ever is established a hall of fame for the world's greatest charlatans, Joseph Smith, the founder of the Mormons is a shoo-in. A handsome, charismatic con artist, he wrote the book on how to flimflam a gullible public. To understand how Smith was able to perpetuate his scheme, it is important to appreciate the nationalistic fervor that characterized the United States during the first fifty years of its existence. For the thousands of migrants who continued to pour into our young nation, it was the promised land. All that these uneducated optimists needed was a messiah to forge a new religion in the New World. Like the immigrants, Joseph Smith had fertile ground to till—in the immigrants themselves.

Smith was well suited for the task. He had an active imagination and a gift for creating make-believe worlds. His mother relates that as a child he enjoyed telling elaborate stories about ancient civilizations with complete descriptions of "their dress, mode of traveling, and the animals upon which they rode; their cities, their buildings with every particular; their mode of warfare; and also their religious worship."[27] Add to this Smith's upbringing by parents who frequently had "visions," throw in a touch of larceny, and you have all the makings of a great religious leader.

G: Larceny?

J: You heard right. It is embarrassing for present-day Mormons to discover that on March 20, 1826, Joseph Smith was found guilty of pretending to find buried treasure by means of "glass looking." The charge of Smith's arrest had long been denied by his loyal followers, but in 1971 the records of Smith's arrest and conviction were uncovered.[28]

It was a common superstition in Smith's time that precious metals could be discovered by certain "gifted" people using a "seer stone"— a sort of crystal ball. Smith convinced a local deacon that he could put the stone in his hat and see down into the earth. After a month of false leads, which were excused on the basis that the demons who guarded the treasure kept moving it deeper, the sons of the gullible deacon were concerned that he was squandering his life savings on this fast-talking confidence man. They had Smith arrested.

The next time Smith used his seer stone, he had his scam better thought out. In 1830, the twenty-five-year-old Smith claimed to have used his seer stone to translate a group of golden plates written in "reformed Egyptian" and given to him by an angel named Moroni. He alleged that the plates were written by the Hebrew ancestors of the American Indians. Why the ancient Hebrews wrote in Egyptian is anyone's guess.

According to Smith, the plates tell the story of two groups of immigrant peoples who left the Middle East to sail to the New World 2,000 years before Columbus. The first group, the Jaredites who came from the tower of Babel, destroyed each other completely. The next wave of immigrants were the Nephites and Lamanites who arrived here around 600 B.C.E. The Lamanites "dwindled in unbelief" and "God did cause the skin of blackness to come upon them." Because of the curse they became "dark and loathsome, . . . an idle people full of mischief and subtlety,"[29] as contrasted to the hardworking and peaceful Nephites. (No wonder racism was a hallmark of the Mormon tradition until very recently.)

According to the wondrous tale of Smith, in 34 C.E., Jesus Christ visits America, performs a few miracles for the Nephites, tells a revised version of the Sermon on the Mount, picks twelve more apostles and departs. By about 421 C.E., the wicked Lamanites have destroyed the poor Nephites. One of the last survivors, Moroni, Son of Mormon, the creator of the plates, seals up the record to await the man who is destined to reestablish true Christianity in the world, Joseph Smith. Such was the origin of the sacred Book of Mormon upon which a new religion was grounded.

G: How could anyone believe such a preposterous tale?

J: As we shall see, it is no more unbelievable than the first five books of the Bible. Moreover, many historians of Smith's time, upon viewing the similarities between the Aztec and Egyptian cultures, and not knowing that there was a time when the people of Asia could walk across the Bering Strait to Alaska, theorized that the Indians might be descendants of the so-called Lost Ten Tribes of Israel. Joseph Smith no doubt was familiar with Ethan Smith's work, *A View of the Hebrews,* published shortly before the Book of Mormon, in which Smith described Indian inscriptions as "hieroglyphic records and paintings."[30] In fact, virtually all the elements in the Book of Mormon were stolen from somewhere else, including Smith's father's own dreams,[31] eighteen chapters of Isaiah, and hundreds of direct quotes from the King James version of the New Testament.

When Smith was challenged as to the authenticity of his golden plates, he contended that a facsimile he prepared had been given to Professor Charles Anthon of Columbia University, who vouched for their authenticity. However, Professor Anthon declared in a letter that the whole story was "perfectly false." He described the paper he was brought as "all kinds of crooked characters . . . prepared by some person who had before him at the time a book containing various alphabets."[32]

A month before Smith's death some men brought him six more brass plates covered with "hieroglyphics." Smith pronounced the plates genuine and began translating them. He contended that "they contain the history of a person . . . a descendant of Ham through the lions of Pharaoh, King of Egypt, and that he received his kingdom from the ruler of heaven and earth."[33] Shortly after Smith's death, the men who had given him the plates confessed that they were a "humbug" manufactured with meaningless etchings simply to entrap and expose Smith as a fraud. Unlike the first set of plates which were "taken away by an angel," the infamous "Kinderhook" plates are still with us as a testimony to the true character of Joseph Smith. As Decker and Hunt point out in their book *The God Makers,* "only a bogus prophet translates bogus plates."[34]

G: Weren't there supposed to have been eleven witnesses to the original plates?

J: Yes, only three of which remained in Smith's church and another three who professed to have seen the plates "in an angelic vision." Of those three, Martin Harris claimed he traveled to the moon and later set what may be the all-time record for religious conversions, personally changing his religion no less than thirteen times.[35] The other two witnesses had later visions which caused them to renounce Smith's religion.

G: Smith certainly was the most audacious prophet of all time.

J: With the possible exception of one other.

G: Surely you don't mean . . .

J: Precisely.

G: But that's blasphemy.

J: Yes, but blasphemy by whom? Me, or the one who claimed to be the Son of God, or those who have alleged that he claimed to be the Son of God? But that discussion will have to wait a while. To return to Smith: being a self-proclaimed representative of God, and handsome to boot, made him very attractive to the women of his church and he was soon seducing his friends' wives. When one of his apostles, Orson Pratt, was told by his wife that Smith had propositioned her, Pratt was abject. In fact, the whole congregation was becoming agitated by Smith's amorous adventures. But Smith's sharp-witted response was to test the credulity of his flock even further. He declared that years earlier God had revealed to him that it was a solemn obligation of Mormons to take many wives (apparently even if they were someone else's). According to Smith, polygamy was now essential for the attainment of the ultimate goal of godhead. Amazingly, this blatant prevarication smoothed the feathers of Orson Pratt (maybe he hoped to get in on the action, or more likely, couldn't bear the shattering of his mythical world), and he was back in the church.

The crisis successfully sidestepped, Smith moved in quickly to demand, on the basis of "revelation," the wives of every one of his apostles.[36] One poor woman, who found Smith's charm and theology insufficient to overcome her scruples, begged to remain with her husband. Smith magnanimously accepted a daughter instead.[37]

After Smith's death, Brigham Young carried on this noble tradition, telling a follower named H. B. Jacobs that, "The woman you claim for a wife does not belong to you. She is the spiritual wife of brother Joseph, sealed to him. I am his proxy, and she in his behalf with her children, are my property."[38] Brigham learned well his lesson from Joseph Smith.

G: Isn't some of what you have related merely hearsay?

J: Perhaps, but there is ample evidence to prove that Smith was a womanizer, a liar, and a hypocrite. In the Mormon's Official History of the Church, he is quoted as having denied having more than one wife even after professing his earlier revelation that the Lord told his first wife, Emma, to accept his many other wives or be damned.[39] In 1844 Smith and his brother publicly condemned an elder of the church for preaching polygamy because they were afraid of arousing the anger of local citizens. But at the same time they advocated "plural wives" in secret.[40] It was easy to see how Smith could get tripped up in his lies, because in an effort to justify his promiscuity, he reported his revelations long after they supposedly occurred. Smith's wife never believed him and eventually rejected his dogma and his church. But most of his sheeplike followers bleated their approval.

The second president of the Mormon Church, Brigham Young, was no better than the first. After being accused by a young woman of trying to seduce her into marrying him on the assurance that Smith had a revelation authorizing such secret marriages, he swore that the woman was lying. That occurred in Illinois where polygamy was a crime. Later, in the safety of Utah, Brigham Young could denounce monogamy as "the source of prostitution and whoredom."[41] As for the law, Young could boast, "I live above the law and so do this people."[42]

By 1890, however, the legal situation had changed. Utah was now subject to federal law and the state Supreme Court ruled that it would approve any statute outlawing polygamy. The Mormon leadership suddenly had a new revelation: plural marriage was no longer required by God's command. This inconstancy of Divine revelation has been quite common in the history of Mormonism. The most recent example concerns equal rights for minorities. Although it has been a racist organization for most of its history, passage of the Civil Rights Act forced the Mormon Church to rethink its doctrines on the position of blacks. Consequently, in 1978 the Mormon leadership went up to their temple to receive a new revelation from God permitting blacks to become priests. (Why a black should want to belong to an organization that institutionalized racism for years is a mystery.)

G: Doesn't it show that the Mormons are capable of adapting to social realities? I view this flexibility as one of the religion's redeeming qualities.

J: True, but shouldn't adaptation be unnecessary for a church guided by Divine inspiration? Or did you only recently change your mind regarding equal rights for minorities?

G: Don't be ridiculous. It just takes a while for the message to get through to some groups.

J: You mean, only after the courts or legislature have threatened punitive action. While history has amply shown that a dogmatic approach to truth is a great evil, for the Mormons truth is malleable in the extreme. As one of their later presidents, Spenser W. Kimball, put it: "Modern revelation is what President Joseph Smith says it is unless President Spenser W. Kimball says differently."[43] Since the Book of Mormon's publication in 1930, it has undergone over 4,000 changes.[44]

But let's finish the glorious career of the Mormon founder. Smith was not content with control over his happy band of gullible fanatics. He had an even grander scheme. He would "not only govern over all people in a religious capacity but in a political capacity."[45] And by "all people" Smith meant the entire world, an ambition still shared by the Mormons down to the present day. In 1838, Smith initiated a policy of "spoiling the gentiles." He formed an army of marauders who, in the name of God, began plundering non-Mormons. Smith told his men to think of him as a general and he planned to take St. Louis by that winter. The Missouri militia had a different idea and, when he met an overpowering force, Smith quickly surrendered his army. His men were charged with treason, murder, arson, burglary, robbery, larceny, and perjury.[46]

Simply being run out of Missouri did little to dampen Smith's grand illusion. By 1844 we find the irrepressible Smith as mayor of Nauvoo, Illinois, and intent on running for President of the United States. By this time not all the Mormons were still enamored with their fanatical leader. When a group of dissidents published an exposé of Smith's amorous adventures, he had their press smashed. When law officials came to arrest him, Smith called out the Nauvoo militia to stop them. This prompted the governor of Illinois to send state troops to take custody of Joseph and his brother Hyrum. While Smith waited in the local jail, a mob stormed the jail house. A gun battle ensued and the prophet, who only a few months earlier had predicted that "he could not be killed within five years of that time,"[47] was shot and thrown out a second story window. An inglorious end to the life of Joseph Smith of whom the Mormon's Doctrines of Salvation state, "[There is] no salvation without accepting Joseph Smith."[48] Naturally, Smith is revered today by the Mormons as having been martyred for bravely propagating the word of God.

G: It would seem that just knowing what an incredible fraud and charlatan their founder was would cause today's Mormons to leave their church in droves. Yet the religion thrives. There must be something about his teachings that touches a responsive nerve in many people to account for the continued growth of that organization.

J: Well, it is easy to see the attraction of Mormonism in its early days. The polygamy doctrine attracted some, and the promise of predestined supremacy for the church fired up the fanatics. Most religious organizers have discovered that to be successful, you have to make some incredible promises to be fulfilled in the not too distant, but oftentimes receding, future. Moses promised a land of milk and honey, and the later Judaic prophets promised victory over Israel's enemies. The early Christians were promised the imminent Second Coming of Christ. Later, to mitigate their initial disappointment, the emphasis was switched from the kingdom of Christ on earth to the kingdom of heaven. Eternal life, or at least escape from death, is the promise of virtually every major religion. Smith topped them all. He promised not only the coming sovereignty of his church on earth—originally it was scheduled for February 14, 1891—but he also promised the opportunity for all Mormons to become gods—not just to live with God, but to become coequals! With regard to their preordained national conquest, Church Elder Lunt stated in 1884, "We look forward with perfect confidence to the day when we will hold the reins of the U.S. government . . . after that we expect to control the continent."[49]

Although their timetable has shifted somewhat, that still is the Mormons' goal. They believe that it will be accomplished either by their domination over American politics, or by their rise to power after a nuclear confrontation with Russia. That is why there is a strong survivalist element among Mormons: many have stockpiled food, water, and weapons. They must have been severely disappointed with the end of the Cold War.

As for becoming gods, the theological reasoning behind it is too complex and convoluted to bother recounting here. Suffice it to say that it involves progressing through a number of secret rites (which only about 30 percent of the Mormons complete) which leads to initiation into the Temple. In the Temple the initiate ultimately learns the secret greeting by which one day God will recognize him and accept him into the fraternity of the gods. The new god will get his own world which he can rule over in the same manner as the Judeo-Christian God is said to rule over this one.

G: What do you mean, "this one"? I rule all worlds.

J: Better explain that to the Mormons, perhaps through another revelation. Returning to the initiation, I might mention that it can also be performed in the name of a deceased ancestor, thus giving him a chance at godhead as well. This is one of the reasons for the Mormons' preoccupation with genealogy.

Unfortunately for women, they can't make godhead on their own; they must hope to be "married for eternity" to some man who makes the grade. The result of this nonsensical belief is that, contrary to common opinion, Utah has a divorce rate higher than the U.S. average. Women leave their temporal husbands to find men who can guarantee them an eternal career as a god's wife. On the other hand, men drop skeptical wives who might jeopardize their chance to become gods.

Upon examination, the Mormon rituals turn out to be no more than a bastardized version of the old Masonic rites. It was with considerable embarrassment that Dr. Reed C. Durham, Jr., a past president of the Mormon History Association, admitted that the story invented by Joseph Smith of how he found the gold plates—the very foundation of Mormonism—appears to have been a plagiarized version of the Masonic legend of Enoch. Enoch was also given gold and brass plates engraved with hieroglyphics recounting the history of the world and mysteries of God.[50] It should come as no surprise to learn that many of the early Mormons, including Joseph Smith, were also Masons at one time.

When one reads that Joseph Smith taught that the moon was inhabited by people who dressed like Quakers and lived to be a thousand years old—to which Brigham Young added that the sun was also inhabited[51]—one is tempted merely to dismiss the Mormon cult as a silly farce. But the consequences of Mormonism, if it continues to gain adherents and political power, are nothing to laugh about. Like most religions, Mormonism is the antithesis of reason and the scientific method of acquiring knowledge. For the Mormons truth is determined by feeling: "and if it is right I will cause that your bosom shall burn within you; therefore you shall feel that it is right."[52] It's difficult to see how one who follows this dictate can distinguish truth from heartburn. But the command is essential for religions based on emotion. To think for oneself would mean the death of belief. The hallmark of Mormonism is unquestioning, fanatical obedience. The words over the Mormon headquarters would not be out of place in any fascist organization: "The Course of Wisdom is the Course of Obedience."[53] President Herbert C. Kimball exhorted, "If you are told by your leader to do a thing do it. None of your business whether it is right or wrong."[54] The Mormon Home Teachers convey the message to Mormons throughout the world: "When our leaders speak the thinking has been done."[55] Unquestioning obedience is the ultimate Mormon virtue. Is it any wonder that people like Decker and Hunt express concern at the disproportionate representation of Mormons in the federal government, particularly the CIA, FBI, and military?[56]

Until 1930, the leaders of the Mormon Church attempted to enforce their absolute control over individual members through blood oaths. Brigham Young stated that, "any man or woman who violates the covenants made with God will be required to pay the debt. The blood of Christ will never wipe that out, your own blood must atone for it."[57]

G: Let's be fair, the threat of blood retaliation has long ago been abandoned by the Mormons.

J: Thanks to secular laws. But the threat of social ostracism still exists and is equally effective at maintaining the membership roles. Talk to non-Mormons living in Utah and they will tell you that they are very much aware of not belonging to the "club." For a Mormon businessman to leave the church, either by expulsion or choice, can have serious, potentially fatal consequences for his business. As for holding a major political office in that state, if you are not a Mormon you can forget it.

G: All right, I think you've made your case. I see no need to defend religious cults that lie outside the mainstream of the Judeo-Christian tradition.

J: Many of the potentially worst consequences have been mitigated by protection in the federal Bill of Rights. Mormons are opposed to women's rights, birth control, and abortion (for the Mormons, every embryo is a potential god). The results are predictable: one-half of all babies born in Utah have teenage mothers, 50 percent of whom are unmarried.[58] Utah's divorce rate is higher than the U.S. average, in part due to the early marriages, in part because the need to find a suitable mate for eternal bonding. The child murder rate is five times the national average and the state ranks thirteenth in child abuse.[59] Mormons are opposed to alcohol but the use of licit and illicit drugs is greater for Mormons than non-Mormons. The frustration with their oppressive religion is manifested even in the Mormon dietary habits: 46 percent of all adults in Utah are overweight compared to the national average of 19 percent.[60] Such are the benefits of Mormonism.

For the sake of its followers, we can only hope that the Mormon leadership's demonstrated willingness to abandon the more harmful doctrines enunciated by Joseph Smith, Brigham Young, and the early church presidents will permit Mormonism to make progress in the area of human rights, and develop a more socially responsible doctrine. Take just one instance where reform is essential: birth control. If the rest of the country had the birth rate of the Mormons, the American population would eventually overtake that of China.

G: Isn't that a bit far-fetched?

J: Only because the vast majority of Americans are indeed more responsible. However, the issue is whether the majority must tolerate the actions of those who are not.

Before leaving this discussion of the Mormons, I wish to make note of one new, and potentially sinister, development—the alliance of Mormons and Moonies called Causa International. I find it particularly ludicrous that Mormons and Moonies, both the epitome of intolerance and dictatorial leadership, try to present themselves as the defenders of freedom. But we can see that their alliance is only natural. Sun Myung Moon, who in 1990 embarrassed his spiritual comrades by declaring that he was Jesus Christ making his long-awaited return, sounds very much like past Mormon presidents when he proclaims, "I am your brain. Every people or organization that goes against the Unification Church will gradually come down and die."[61] Moon was sentenced to jail for tax fraud. As expected, instead of being disillusioned, his followers simply contended that he was being persecuted for his religious beliefs. Let's not forget that Joseph Smith also spent time in jail and it didn't disenchant his followers either.

G: I think it should be pointed out that despite the intentions of their founders, which at times have no doubt been questionable, most of the followers have been sincere, well-intentioned people.

J: My purpose is not to judge the followers. I seek only to answer the question, can any of these religious leaders legitimately claim to speak for you, God? In reviewing the "prophets" who founded the religions discussed thus far, the evidence is that, at best, they were deluded, and at worst they were outright frauds. Today there are dozens of fundamentalist sects in this country led by men and women who claim to be God's spokespersons. Let's take a moment to examine the practices of some of these fundamentalist evangelists. I'll begin with the so-called faith healers.

Faith Healers and Fundamentalists

G: Obviously you are going to deny that I can grant special persons the power to heal in My name. But every night you can turn on your television and witness first hand hundreds of such healings. People climb out of wheelchairs, throw away canes and walkers, and run across the stage. Others who have suffered for years with pain in their backs or stomachs feel instant relief. Still others proclaim they have been cured of cancer, arthritis, and diabetes after their doctors have pronounced them incurable despite treatment with the latest medical technology. Surely you cannot claim that all these thousands of people are part of some massive conspiracy.

J: No. They are simply the victims of a racket as old as humankind.

Today we laugh at the portrayal of the patent medicine salesman of earlier times. But they were such dangerous quacks and frauds that laws were passed to protect the gullible and the desperate from exploitation.

G: Why do you assume that faith healers are dishonest?

J: I don't merely assume. Let's examine the evidence. The Committee for the Scientific Examination of Religion (CSER)—a group of philosophers, scientists, psychologists and at least one magician, James Randi—has conducted an extensive investigation into the practices of some of the nation's most popular faith healers. The results of his investigations are published in Randi's book *The Faith Healers.*[62]

    The results would be humorous were they not so disturbing. Take the case of Peter Popoff. He uses the practice common to faith healers of "calling out," whereby he calls out the name of an individual, details the nature of the affliction, and may even provide the names of relatives or the individual's street address to demonstrate that he is indeed inspired by God. He then pronounces the person cured—a remarkable demonstration. But when magician James Randi and a group of investigators infiltrated one of Popoff's performances, they became skeptical of a small hearing device he wore in his ear. Later, by means of an electronic scanner receiver, they were able to intercept the messages being transmitted to Popoff from his wife, who carried the transmitter in a huge handbag. She would mingle among the audience asking questions and recording their answers. Then during his healing act, she would prompt her husband on the names, ailments, and personal data on the poor unsuspecting believers.

G: Of course I deplore such deception. But is Popoff doing any real harm?

J: Harm? Not only might his deception result in people not seeking the medical help they need, but Popoff actually persuades his followers to discontinue their medications. On one occasion he asked his audience to "break free of the devil" by throwing their medications onto the stage. Afterward, the investigators discovered perscriptions for digitalis, nitroglycerine tablets, oral diabetes medication, and many unidentified pills.[63] Encouraging people to discard potentially life-sustaining drugs can only be described as reprehensible. But for this chicanery Popoff was rewarded by his deluded followers with an estimated $1.4 to $2 million a month!

G: I find such heartless exploitation carried out in My name despicable.

J: Then why don't You stop it? Popoff is by no means the only one who practices such deception. He is just the most inept. W. V. Grant uses a more artful approach similar to that used by the mentalists Kreskin and Joseph Dunninger. Like Popoff, Grant and his associates mix with the audience before the performance to glean information about some of the afflicted persons which Grant can use during his performance. However, instead of using electronic devices, Grant memorizes the details on five or six petitioners from notes made by him and his staff beforehand. After calling out and "curing" these sufferers, he leads the audience in a hymn during which he sneaks a peak at the notes on the next group he will call out. The actual notes he used to record details on his victims were found in the trash after one of Grant's performances.[64] Also thrown into the garbage were the prayer cards which Grant promised to take with him and pray over for six days, as well as many checks for $3 to $5—amounts too small to bother cashing.

G: But didn't Grant actually effect cures for some of the people?

J: The CSER investigators attempted to follow up on those supposedly cured by Grant. Here is a sampling of their results:[65]

• A woman who rose from her wheelchair was found not to be confined to a wheelchair in the first place. It turns out that Grant supplies many of the more feeble-looking of his walk-in audience with wheelchairs.

• The physician of a woman claimed to have been cured of Parkinson's disease contends that her condition "is slowly but continuously progressive."

• A woman with diabetes and high blood pressure who was supposedly "healed" by Grant had been urged to discontinue her medication. Later she suffered cardiac arrest and experienced a diabetic crisis.

• A man supposedly cured of throat cancer through the power of prayer was discovered also to have undergone radiation treatment and surgery.

• None of the three doctors who supposedly diagnosed a women with throat cancer could be found. But she "knew" she had throat cancer because of the "bad taste in her mouth."

• A blind woman who demonstrated her newfound sight by grabbing Grant's nose was found still to be blind. She could make out blurs before and after this "miraculous cure."

The examples are limited only by the resources of the investigators. In the case of Grant, as with the other faith healers investigated, not a single validated cure of an organic illness could be found. Grant's petitioners suffer from psychosomatic or organic illnesses. The psychosomatic conditions frequently respond to any placebo, as medical doctors all know. But for those who suffer from a real organic illness Grant has no healing power. They leave sadly disillusioned, and frequently much worse off physically and financially.

To describe just one sad example: A young girl on a portable oxygen tank was wheeled in. After declaring that her heart and lungs were diseased, Grant "healed" the girl and then told her to remove the tube from her nose, get up, and run across the stage. She did so, praising Jesus all the way. Five minutes later as attention was drawn elsewhere, the girl was again back in her wheelchair and having a difficult time breathing even with the oxygen.[66] There are not many dramatic failures like the one just mentioned, because Grant passes by those who appear to be legitimately crippled or paralyzed, to focus instead on those with psychosomatic illnesses or other diseases where a change in condition would not be immediately apparent.

Grant practices another form of deception common to faith healers and other fundamentalist evangelists. He inflames his audience by claims of outrageous atrocities on the part of the "godless."[67] Despite his easily exposed misinformation about having attended fictional colleges where he turned down scores of nonexistent football scholarships, Grant's gullible followers unquestioningly swallow his every word.[68] Such is the true power of faith. And is it profitable! Grant's take for his deplorable deceit is estimated at $10 to $20 million annually, all tax-free because the money is considered a "donation" to a religious organization.

G: No doubt there are unscrupulous people in the world, but that doesn't mean that all faith healers are. Isn't it just possible that some faith healers could be sincere and well meaning, although mistaken as to their powers?

J: Possibly. I read in the *Catholic Digest* of a Sister Briege McKenna who professes to have healing powers as evidenced by certain anecdotal instances of cures.[69] But such healers are never subject to verification by the usual validation methods that any medical treatment most undergo. As for healing, the body's natural recuperative powers will overcome disease for some people, or at least put it in remission for a time. Then there is the noted placebo effect whereby a certain number of people will respond to any treatment, even a sugar pill, which they believe will be effective. This is of course particularly noticeable when the illness is psychosomatic (which makes it none the less real).

G: Well then, perhaps there is a role for faith healers.

J: Emphatically not! Even if they are well-intentioned, they run the risk of encouraging an ill person to fail to seek knowledgeable medical treatment. If a placebo is really all that is called for, it is far preferable for a doctor to make that diagnosis than some well-intentioned but medically ignorant faith healer. At best faith healing is returning to the age of the shaman and witch doctor. Moreover, it would appear that the majority of faith healers are far from well-intentioned.

Another so-called faith healer, Ernest Angley, was actually imprisoned for a while in 1984 in Germany. When a Swiss woman died of a heart attack during one of his healing sessions, the Germans, who take a dim view of his kind of deceit, charged him with fraud and practicing medicine without a license. When he was released on bond Angley skipped bail and beat a hasty retreat to the United States where his kind of chicanery can be practiced with impunity.[70]

Back in the tolerant United States, Angley's faith healing skills were insufficient to prevent the death of his own wife, aptly named Angel. Always able to exploit every tragedy, Angley won the sympathy of his congregation by telling them how he had promised his wife that he wouldn't selfishly stand in the way of the Lord taking her to heaven. We can only surmise that Angel was grateful for her husband's thoughtfulness, and you much relieved that Angley was not going to thwart Your Divine Will.

G: If such people are the blatant fakers you suggest, why don't their followers see through the deception? Surely there can't be that many unsuspecting dupes?

J: P. T. Barnum knew better. So did Benjamin Franklin, who said, "There are no greater liars than quacks, except for the patients."[71] Aside from simple gullibility, there is a psychological motivation for their followers to continue to believe despite all evidence to the contrary. As explained by Joseph E. Barnhart, individuals will overlook an evangelist's obvious chicanery and failures "because they as fellow participants in the magic working ritual, sense themselves to be an essential part of the same hypnotic drama the evangelist is caught up in. To condemn him is to condemn themselves. To defend him is to defend themselves."[72] We have all been in the situation where we find ourselves stanchly defending a position we know to be wrong rather than admit our error. No one wants to admit, even to himself, that he was foolish.

To avoid charges of chicanery leveled at him by his colleagues, one of the deans of the faith healers, Oral Roberts, has shifted his tactics in recent years. His television ministry places more emphasis on entertainment and healing financial illness than on the old-fashioned healing gambits. Roberts now also advocates the latest in medical treatment to supplement his faith healing. A nice touch: it removes the problem of any potential bad press, improves his rate of success immeasurably, and still lets him take credit for the cures. However, Roberts went on to make one of the all-time outrageous claims, declaring that You, God, told him that unless he raised over $4 million in 1987,

You would have to take him from this world. Considering the awful place this world is in the eyes of evangelists, one would think his followers would have held back their contributions just to give old Oral the opportunity to gain his everlasting reward, but they didn't. He actually raised the money!

By far the smoothest TV evangelist is the polished, Yale-educated Pat Robertson. His technique is the essence of simplicity. Through his TV program he employs a variation of what the old mind reading magicians used to call "cold readings," that is, he claims to see someone suffering from a particular illness and predicts that they will be cured through his prayer. Given his millions of viewers it is an absolute certainty that some will have the illness and, even in the case of a serious illness such as cancer, we would expect a certain percentage to enter a state of remission or even be cured through natural means. Like other so-called healers, Robertson doesn't report his failures. He does, however, show videotaped reenactments of "miracles" that have occurred.

G: It is indeed a shame that some evangelists take advantage of people's faith.

J: It is much more than a merely "a shame." Pat Robertson tried to use his popularity as a lever to pursue his political ambitions. As such, his religious movement has become a threat to our democracy. The wall of separation between church and state, which has worked so well for so long, is now beginning to buckle from the onslaught of those who would turn this country into a "Christian nation" with their spiritual leaders holding the keys to power.

G: Don't you think you are exaggerating the danger just a bit?

J: Not in the least. It is not just cult groups, such as the Mormons, who dream of control, but the Christian fundamentalists like Tim LaHaye, Jerry Falwell, and Pat Robertson. Their primary goal is to tear down the "wall of separation" between church and state so carefully constructed by the framers of the First Amendment to the Constitution two hundred years ago.

These charismatic religious leaders have demonstrated their power to persuade their followers to vote as directed. They are dangerous, power-hungry opportunists who seek to control the American political process. According to LaHaye, "The only individuals who can lead the moral majority . . . are the millions of Church people. However, they will not follow politicians; they respond only to the leadership of their pastor-shepherds."[73] Here we again see the hallmark of fundamentalist Christianity: mindless, sheeplike submission of the congregation to the dictates of their minister-masters. Jerry Falwell sounds no different than Joseph Smith and the Rev. Moon when he declares, "The Church should be a disciplined, charging army. . . . Christians, like slaves and soldiers, ask no questions."[74]

G: I admit that extremists are a little unnerving.

J: A little? According to Gerard T. Straub, a disillusioned disciple of Robertson's, "Pat's mission is to legislatively remove evil from our government and society by seeking political control. He wants to be God's policy worker in America."[75] What type of man is this who pretends he is qualified to speak for God? In the opinion of Straub, "Pat is a pompous pope of the video Vatican of Christian broadcasting and he rules his empire with absolute authority and does not tolerate debate, discussion, or dissent, because these are the stepping stones to doubt."[76]

G: Isn't that a little strong? Can we really accept the opinion of a man who obviously has an axe to grind with Robertson?

J: With good reason. Straub admits that while he was under the sway of Robertson's charismatic personality, he stole the questions which "Today Show" host Tom Brokaw had prepared for an interview with Robertson. Pat did not hesitate one second to grab the pilfered questions and prepare his "spontaneous" answers to the unsuspecting Brokaw. Such a lack of integrity is, however, small potatoes to the faith healing he perpetrates weekly on his TV show.

We saw an inkling of the power of the religious right in the 1992 presidential election when they effectively dictated the Republican party platform. Had it not been for the poor economy, there is every indication that George Bush would have been reelected on an essentially fundamentalist platform. We may get some idea of their ultimate goals by listening to the words of Robertson's fundamentalist brothers: Tim LaHaye states flatly that, "no humanist is qualified to hold any government office in America."[77] Ed McAteer says he would, "go to the extreme and prohibit the teaching of evolution altogether, since it is contrary to the word of God."[78] Paul Weyrich admits, "We're radicals working to overthrow the present structure in this country—we're talking about Christianizing America."[79] And Gary North explains the real reason why the fundamentalists are attacking the public school system in the United States:

So let us be blunt about it: we must use the doctrine of religious liberty to gain independence for Christian schools until we train up a generation of people who know that there is no religious neutrality, no neutral law, no neutral education, no neutral civil government. Then they will get busy in constructing a Bible-based social, political, and religious order which finally denies the religious liberty of the enemies of God.[80]

Undaunted by the Republicans' failure in the general election, fundamentalists fully intend to press on in their efforts to take over the nation's school boards. They know that voter apathy in school elections can permit as little as 6 percent of the general population to determine the outcome. Citizens for Excellence in Education (CEE), a California-based fundamentalist group headed by Robert Simonds, claims to have elected 1,965 school board members since 1989. They hoped to gain 3,100 more seats in 1992. They are very clear about their objective. Linda Steele, a CEE activist, told the *Wall Street Journal* that the group plans "to take over the school boards and debunk the myth of separation of Church and State."[81]

G: Evangelical leaders such as LaHaye, Weyrich and North don't represent the majority of Christians or their priests and ministers. Most religious leaders do not seek political power.

J: Perhaps not personally, but they do seek to change the laws of the nation to conform to their particular theology at the expense of the beliefs of all others. To cite just a few examples, in recent years there has been an organized attempt on the part of the various Christian sects to:

- amend the Constitution to authorize government-sponsored group prayer in public schools;

- tax all citizens to pay for sectarian private schools;

- establish the theological position that the legal definition of a person be applied to a zygote;

- censor textbooks on sexuality, or those which discuss any other subjects in a manner they find objectionable;

- replace scientific teaching with the theological belief of creationism; and

- repeal the Fourteenth Amendment, which applies the Bill of Rights to state and local governments.[82]

The irony is that those Christians who work so hard to abridge the liberties of us all are willing to die for the word "freedom." They simply have no idea what the concept of freedom means. The great jurist, Supreme Court Justice Louis Brandeis, warned, "The greatest dangers to liberty lurk in insidious encroachment by men of zeal, well meaning but without understanding."[83]

History has shown time and again just how dangerous zealous men can become when the state fails to check their aspirations. We will pursue this topic shortly. For now let me conclude this discussion with this thought. Fundamentalism is not unique to America. We find it on the rise in virtually every country in the world today. In South America, Protestant fundamentalist sects are growing at such a rapid rate that they have already threatened the Catholic Church's hegemony in the region and may surpass it in absolute numbers within twenty to thirty years. They are supported by the wealthy class who fear the new liberation theology promoted by reform-minded priests. Ironically it is also embraced by the Indian peasants who resent the Church's traditional support of their Spanish conquerors.

It is not only Christian fundamentalism that is growing. In the Middle East, the resurgence of Islamic fundamentalism is represented most dramatically by the rise to power of the ayatollahs and the spread of Shiite terrorism which threatens to assassinate any Arab leader who does not seek to reestablish Muslim fundamentalism. Egypt's Anwar Sadat was but the first to be killed. In Israel, Orthodox Jews have sought to make their religious observances binding on all citizens. In India, some Hindu sects have reverted to the ancient practice of burning the widows of the deceased, while Sikh fundamentalists have launched an all-out terrorist war against the Hindu "infidels." In Japan, the Sōka Gakkai* movement is attempting to establish itself as a national religion. Finally, throughout Latin and South America cult groups are springing up: they combine an odd conglomeration of Indian and Christian myths. Almost all of these fundamentalists movements, like that in the United States, try to tie their religious objectives to a nationalistic cause. And all, without exception, represent a threat to the cause of freedom and world peace.

G: I wish to make it clear that none of these reactionary religious forms can legitimately claim to represent My Divine Will.

J: That takes us back to the question asked at the outset: How is anyone to determine who does, in fact, speak for You?

We have reviewed four cult religions founded by "prophets" who alleged that they spoke for You. The evidence is overwhelming that at best they were deluded, and at worst they were conniving oppor-

---

*The Sōka Gakkai movement believes that the thirteenth-century religious leader Nichiren was an incarnation of the eternal Buddha. Nichiren taught that national prosperity and security could be achieved only by rigorous adherence to orthodox Buddhist law.

tunists. We have also reviewed the intentions of some of the more well-known faith healers and fundamentalists who claim that they are Your agents. They have been discovered to be driven by a desire for wealth, power, and political ambition. Their number could be multiplied many times. There are dozens of small fundamentalist sects in this country led by men and women who contend that they are inspired by You. More often than not these cult leaders prey on the ignorance and superstition that seems to be growing in America. In the recent past they held out the specter of an inevitable nuclear confrontation with the Soviet Union to lend credence to their apocalyptic prophecies. With the demise of the USSR, they have shifted emphasis to the increase in crime and family dissolution as evidence of a moral decay that only a return to religious traditions can correct.

Our society is being conditioned to accept a doomsday scenario as inevitable. Quite naturally, then, like the cancer victim who has just been informed of his certain death, the tendency is to clutch at straws. No one is more susceptible to a con than a desperate person, and we are fast becoming a nation of desperate men and women. A study of history shows that throughout the ages, in all parts of the world—both East and West—during times of political turmoil new religions pop up like mushrooms after a rain.

The latest fad in American religion is a straightforward, unabashed, neo-Calvinistic appeal to greed. Attempting once again to capitalize on a trend, churches such as the Assemblies of God have picked up on the "me-first" spirit of the eighties, and promise that faith in God can ensure earthly riches as well as those in the hereafter. Despite the embarrassment caused by evangelists such as Jim Bakker and Jimmy Swaggart, the Assemblies of God are growing faster than ever. Portraying God as sort of a cosmic Santa Claus, they encourage people to pray not for world peace or brotherhood or justice, but for personal wealth. From multi-million-dollar pulpits where congregations are entertained with laser lights, state-of-the-art sound systems, and special effects, brainless Yuppie followers are encouraged to pray for top-paying jobs and high-priced cars. The results have been gratifying to the ministers who watch their collections swell.[84]

The worst of the new religious cults have proven extremely dangerous and, ironically, the danger is most often to their own members. Two thousand years ago, the fanatic Judaic sect at Qumram set the example with their mass murder and suicide. More recently, the extreme harm that such cult leaders can cause was exemplified by the slaughter Reverend Jim Jones and David Koresh visited upon their own people. No less repulsive are the many instances of child abuse and neglect being brought to light among fundamentalist cults in this country. Such abuse exists not only in fanatical sects such as the House of Judah or Church of God of the Union Assembly.[85] The failure of Jehovah's Witnesses and Christian Scientists to obtain basic medical treatment for their children is equally criminal and was recognized as such in a 1944 Supreme Court decision which stated "The right to practice religion freely does not include the liberty to expose the community or the child to communicable disease or the latter to ill health or death."[86] It matters not that the parents may have good intentions, the outcome for a child denied a life-saving blood transfusion is the same as if he or she were deliberately murdered.[87]

Not all fundamentalist ministers intend to deceive. However, I have yet to hear or read one who does not fit the description that Delos McKown gives of the preacher in his novel *With Faith and Fury*:

> He has no historical sense whatsoever, and he does not really respect the biblical text either. He doesn't really try to find out what was meant by those who first delivered those words to those who first received them. He just roams up and down the bible ripping out any and all verses that seem to cohere with with whatever tack he happens to be on, but without any understanding of the times, places, worldviews, and circumstances in which the textual materials developed. Things that are meant allegorically, he takes literally, and things that are meant literally, he twists into metaphor. . . . And misrepresent, my God! how he misrepresents positions that are not his own, including the Bible's. Then he attacks his own misrepresentations hip and thigh, boldly, bravely; and those boobies in the pews think that righteousness has triumphed again.[88]

Most of these latter-day Elmer Gantrys appear to oppose the most basic liberty of Americans, freedom of speech. Or, more precisely, they hold that freedom of speech should extend only to their opinions, not to anyone else's. Although they seek to force the public schools to teach fundamentalist theological beliefs under the guise of science (such as creationism), in their own schools and universities they censor the reading of their students like a Russian Commissar. When Jerry Falwell disapproved of the book written by one of the faculty members at Falwell's Liberty Baptist College ("Liberty," what an ironic choice of names), he ordered it removed from the bookstore and banned from the campus.[89] Another faculty member had his copies of some Jewish tracts confiscated. Students are told to stay out of art museums and theaters and not to read books.[90] Such an attack on the First

Amendment would not have surprised our Founding Fathers since, as I mentioned before, they were well acquainted with the abuses of organized religion. It is only the logical consequence when people believe that their ministers speak for You.

G: You build a very convincing argument for distrusting religious leaders who contend they speak for Me, and offer no reliable evidence to support their contention. However, that does not disprove that some religious leaders do in fact represent My Will.

J: Well then, let's leave the cults and turn to one of the major religions of the world. Does the pope speak for You?

2

Papal Authority and the Catholic Church: A Dictator by Any Other Name Is Much More Palatable

> There is only one, holy, Catholic and apostolic Church outside of which there is neither salvation nor remission of sin.
>
> —Pope Boniface VIII (1302)

G: Does the pope speak for Me? For Catholics, yes. And to others who listen to his teachings of love as well.

J: Yes, I have often heard popes use the word "love" in their sermons and encyclicals. The present pope, John Paul II, expouses love for all humankind, and he, like all his predecessors, is no doubt sincere. But a close examination of the teachings and practices of past popes reveals that the price for their love is intellectual submission, obsequious obedience, and blind trust.

G: And what is wrong with obedience to your Creator? To Me? In demanding obedience to their rulings on faith and morals the popes are acting as My representatives on earth. They are inspired to articulate My commands.

J: But how can anyone know they are inspired? Simply because the popes allege it to be so? We have just seen that many other religious leaders make that same claim and they have all been shown to be bogus prophets. Furthermore, it seems to me that investing a mere man with the authority to speak for You is taking a terrible chance. The man may become the most inhumane despot imaginable. It bothers me that people kneel and kiss the pope's hand (it used to be the pope's

49

foot) like Caligula, and the pope wears the purple and white garments of the Roman emperors. Even his title, Supreme Pontiff, was once held by the emperors of Rome. In the Roman religion sacrifices were made by the college of Pontifices headed by the Pontifex Maximus. Caesar Augustus assumed the title when he sought to establish a state religion. That the popes adopted the title of Pontiff is not, therefore, surprising, since they, too, sought to wed the power of religion to the power of the state.

The attempt to emulate Roman emperors is not accidental. And it is so very dangerous. I recall the words of a character in Jean Paul Sartre's novel *The Reprieve,* who fervently declares, "One voice, one sole voice in all the world. He speaks for me, he thinks for me, he decides for me."[1] The person referred to is Adolph Hitler, but it is the same sentiment that all true believers express whether the object of their unquestioning devotion is Joseph Stalin, Benito Mussolini, the Ayatollah Khomeini, Sun Myung Moon, Joseph Smith, or Pat Robertson. Investing any man with absolute authority is to beg for tyrannical abuses of the most horrible nature.

G: How dare you compare the papal representatives of Christ with such false prophets as Sun Myung Moon or mass murderers like Joseph Stalin?

J: Well, let's look at the similarities between the pope and Reverend Moon. Both men profess to have a special, unique relationship with You. Both head autocratic organizations which tolerate no dissent. Both operate large power bases (but Moon's is obviously small potatoes next to that of the pope). Both appeal most strongly to the uneducated and disenfranchised of the world. Both seek special economic privileges such as freedom from taxation; the pope also seeks federal aid to his schools. Both seek to incorporate their religious beliefs into the political process.

As to the fairness of comparing past popes to fanatics such as Hitler or Stalin, I hasten to point out that I am not evaluating the popes' intentions. The popes may have been motivated by the highest regard for the spiritual welfare of humankind. Nevertheless, they have been responsible for the greatest atrocities imaginable, and the present pope's opposition to contraception and the reproductive rights of women is contributing to the misery in the world—all in Your name. J. M. Robertson has estimated that from the first crusade launched by Pope Urban II in 1095 to the fall of Acre, in what is now Northern Ireland, in 1291, nine million lives were lost.[2] This may be an overestimation, but the number is certainly in the millions and represents only the beginning of the carnage which places the Catholic Church in the same league with the Third Reich and the purges of Stalin or Mao. Before the crusades against the "heathens" were concluded, the popes began an internal crusade against heretics within Christendom. The resulting Inquisition lasted officially almost 600 years and resulted in the loss of additional millions of lives.

G: It is a gross slander to compare the Catholic Church to the Nazis or Communists. Are you attempting to rekindle prejudice against Catholics?

J: I certainly harbor no prejudice against Catholics. Having been one myself I know them to be as honorable, just and moral as any other religious group. It is the institution of the Roman Catholic Church that I fear. As for the comparison with the Nazis and Communists, just consider that the Nazis attempted to "purify" the human race physically, the Communists tried to eliminate political dissent, and the Church undertook to cleanse humankind spiritually. The resulting horror was much the same, except it took only a few decades to stop state fascism and ten centuries to finally end religious fascism.

G: Now wait a minute. Much of that bloodshed occurred during and after the Reformation in wars between the Catholics and Protestants, a conflict I abhorred.

J: Well then, why didn't you intercede to end the conflict since both sides were supposedly fighting in your name? Since the popes spoke for you, couldn't you have had them call a halt to the bloody conflict?

G: The pope allegedly speaks for me only on matters of faith or morals.

J: Isn't war the ultimate moral issue? Instead of promising special indulgences for those who fought in defense of the "true faith" (which were believed by Catholics to reduce the time spent in purgatory as reparation for their sins), the popes should have been preaching that war was the greatest of all evils.

And what do you mean by saying the pope "allegedly" speaks for You? Are You hedging?

G: If I am, the fault is yours. You're the one putting words in my mouth.

A Brief Summary of the Ignoble History of the Catholic Church

J: Sorry. Let's return to the deeds of the popes. In my sixteen years of Catholic training the papal atrocities were glossed over as if they were the minor indiscretions of a few bad apples in an otherwise good barrel. But even a cursory review of the history of the papacy reveals that this was far from the truth. Moreover, as I shall show in subsequent chapters, it was no accident that the papacy evolved into a cruel and oppressive dictatorship from which it took humanity well over a thousand years to recover. Rather, the basis for the evil lies in fundamental doctrines of the early Church Fathers and the very nature of the religion itself.

G: Those strong words will require more than mere assertion to be convincing.

J: And you shall have it. As we review the history of Christianity in this and subsequent chapters, bear in mind that prior to the Reformation, Christianity as an institution was synonymous with the Catholic Church, and the pope was in charge of that church. Therefore, all the evils of Christianity from its inception to the Reformation were directly or indirectly the responsibility of the papacy.

Some modern day Catholics would like to think, as I once did, that the evils perpetuated by the papacy were somehow the unfortunate result of a perversion of the true intentions of the early Church Fathers. Nothing could be further from the truth. History has amply demonstrated that persecution of dissenters is always the result of a totalitarian rule, whether it be dictatorship, monarchy, or theocracy. Although ostensibly the Church recognized the role of the state, e.g., the divine right of kings, public leaders were expected to be subordinate to the authority of the pope and his bishops. Thus, from its very inception the founders of the Church sought to establish a de facto theocracy.

During the first century Ignatius, bishop of Antioch, wrote to Christians, "you are subject to the bishop as to Jesus Christ . . . it is necessary that you do nothing without the bishop."[3] Doesn't that sound uncomfortably like the dictates of Joseph Smith, Reverend Moon, or Jerry Falwell? Apparently they learned their lesson well. Ignatius went on to state that it is the duty of the laity to revere, honor, and obey the bishop "as if he were God," for the bishop presides "in the place of God."[4] Clement, bishop of Rome and first of the Apostolic Fathers, was infuriated when the Christians of Corinth divested their Church officials of power. He contended that God delegates His "authority to reign" to the "rulers and leaders on earth."[5] Later Clement went further, declaring that whoever disobeys the divinely ordained authorities rightly "receives the death penalty."[6]

G: As I recall, not all the early Christians went along with the claim of divine authority. The Christian sect known as the Gnostics chided those who "call themselves bishops and also deacons, as if they had received their authority from God . . ." and called those who made such audacious claims "waterless canals."[7]

J: But you know what soon happened to the Gnostics. They were quickly declared heretics and expelled from the Church. In 312 the emperor Constantine issued an edict of toleration, permitting Catholics to practice their religion free from harassment. By the time of Augustine, the Church was identified with the kingdom of God; it was now a divine institution, and woe to anyone who failed to adhere to its dogmas. By 380 the Church had gained sufficient power to persuade the emperor Theodosius to make Christianity the state religion. By 430 the emperor Marcion was enforcing Church Council decrees against heretics. Dissent meant banishment or death. By the time of the Holy Roman Empire— a fiction invented by Pope Leo III and Charlemagne—the Church had secured control of the European continent.

After successfully stifling all internal threats, a new danger arose. Around 580 another self-styled messiah arose in the East declaring that he, too, spoke for God. Today over 700 million people believe that Mohammed was another of God's messengers. Like all messiahs, Mohammed initially gained most of his converts from the poor and slaves. Undoubtedly, Mohammed was the most militant of God's prophets since the time of Moses and, like Moses, mounted a military campaign against his rivals. Since Mohammed, too, was acting under God's personal direction, he felt it unnecessary to follow the ethical precepts of his day and opened his campaign against the Meccans by raiding their caravans during the sacred month of Rajab when fighting was prohibited. As usual in the case of religious warfare, eventually the more fanatical and ruthless side emerged victorious. Soon most of Arabia came under Mohammed's control, and his zealous disciples sought to extend his religion throughout the world. Within a mere hundred years after Mohammed's death, his fanatical followers had spread the fires of Islam to the doorstep of Europe. Although they were stopped at the Battle of Tours in 732, the Muslims had secured the Middle East and even a portion of Spain.

The stage was now set for the infamous Crusades which, instead of being the noble cause described to me as a child, were, in reality, wars between two fanatical religions, both of which sought to spread the word of God with the sword. By the way, since both religions claimed to be fighting in defense of the one true faith, I wonder if you could tell me which one was right?

G: Oh no, you're not going to trap me with that one! Those wars were due as much to the nationalistic and economic ambitions of the various powers involved as to any religious motivations.

J: True, but religious fervor was used to foment the righteous hate and hysteria without which the waging of such horrendous wars would have been impossible. Are you attempting to avoid my question? Could it be that neither was right? Might the idea of a "true faith" be simply a myth to gain unquestioning allegiance of believers? But that would mean that the millions who gave their lives on both sides of the Christian-Muslim wars died in vain. Such a thought is unthinkable, at least by any true believer.

Let me sketch the history of the Crusades, although in doing so I will barely capture an inkling of their true horror.

The Catholic Church bided its time while consolidating its power throughout Europe. When it chose to strike back at the Muslims, it proved that Christians could be just as savage. When I was a child the good sisters who guided my education subjected me to much of the romantic nonsense written about these lamentable wars. Today's children are presented with an only slightly more accurate account; the true nature of the atrocity unleashed at the exhortations of the popes is quickly glossed over.

The First Crusade was launched by Pope Urban II. He fanned the flames of righteous hatred by granting a plenary indulgence—the total remission of punishment due for past sins—to anyone who went to kill for the greater honor and glory of God. In other words, if the Crusader himself was killed, he was guaranteed immediate admission to heaven. (A similar guarantee was promised by the Ayatollah Khomeini to his soldiers in Iran's war against Iraq.) Not wanting to pass up the opportunity of a lifetime, mobs of French and German peasants, led by such colorful characters as Walter the Penniless and Peter the Hermit, set out to kill Arabs. En route they first massacred the Jews in the Rhineland—a tradition in Christian wars against anybody—and then battled the Bulgarians and Hungarians. The motley group finally made its way to Constantinople and crossed over to Asia Minor, where they were soundly defeated by the Turks.

The next few Crusades fared better and managed to slaughter a few million Moslems throughout the Middle East, finally retaking Jerusalem. This seemed only fair to the Catholic Church because Jesus had allegedly lived there for a short while a thousand years earlier. Christians therefore had a God-given right to free entry to the city.

Probably no incident more graphically depicts the consequence of religious fanaticism generated by the popes than the Children's Crusade. After listening to the local priest exhort his parishioners to take up the sword against the Islamic hordes, a French teenager, Stephen of Cloyes, had visions (today we would call them delusions) in which he believed God instructed him to lead the children of Europe to the Holy Land to fight in defense of the faith. Note that this incident is not unlike that of a young woman centuries later who is urged by "voices" to lead the armies of France—the celebrated St. Jeanne d'Arc.

Stephen, obviously a charismatic personality, soon persuaded other teenagers to join him. The word spread like a brush fire throughout Europe, possibly with the aid of clergy who were undoubtedly impressed with this outpouring of religious fervor; and thousands of children left their parents to set off for the Holy Land. Unfortunately, mass hysteria cannot overcome malnutrition, fatigue, and exposure. The children began to sicken and die along the way. Many did, however, make it to the seaports where they expected the good Christian captains to provide free passage to Palestine. But the captains knew that these children possessed too great a value to have their lives thrown away in a useless gesture. So the good captains sold these young people into slavery.

Another group of German children escaped that fate by making their way overland to Palestine. What a truly heroic effort that must have been. Their reward upon reaching their destination was to die horribly of starvation or disease.

Few of those who set out with the love of God burning in their hearts ever saw their parents again. This brief account cannot begin to do justice to that tragedy. It is indeed a shame that there was no literate Anne Frank type among them who could have chronicled their senseless misery as an object lesson to us all.

G: In all fairness, you cannot say that I willed such a great evil. Do not think I wasn't moved by their childish love and trust. They have all earned a place in my heaven, where eternal bliss will amply reward them for their sufferings.

J: If there is a heaven. You know, the more I reflect on the matter, all nine crusades were Children's Crusades. All those simple peasant soldiers were as ignorant as children, blindly following the exhortations of the popes to kill those Arabs who were defending their land. Incidentally, I find it more than a little ironic that Muslims also died for your honor and glory, under the name of Allah, of course.

G: Are you going to review the entire history of human stupidity and folly and then try to blame all of it on Me? Am I to blame for every evil committed by man?

J: Not at all. I would agree most wholeheartedly that man must bear responsibility for the evil he does, although the reason for this conclusion may come as a surprise.

G: Not to me.

J: Oh, that's right, I almost forgot.

G: I guess the only way I can stop this tirade is with a lightning bolt.

J: Too bad you missed your chance to have my parachute malfunction when I was into that sport.

G: Thou shalt not tempt the Lord thy God, Joseph!

J: Easy, I'm just joking. Permit me to continue. Even before the Crusades had ended their innumerable killings, pillages, rapes, and sundry other atrocities, another pope, Alexander III, decided to turn the wrath of the papacy against his fellow Christians, namely, anyone who dared to differ with his view of his authority or his opinion on the nature of God. To gain support for his war against heretics, he, too, assured all those who died that they would gain eternal salvation. Once again immortality became an excellent motivator to kill and risk being killed.

In 1204 Pope Innocent III (what an ironic choice of names) decided to escalate the drive to "search out" heretics (which is the root meaning of "inquisition"). The first to be put to the sword were the Cathars, a nonviolent Christian sect who, in the tradition of the Manichaeans, believed there were two gods, one responsible for good and another (the devil) responsible for the evil in the world. Not an unreasonable assumption, but one that the pope could not tolerate, because it challenged his authority to decide Church dogma. The result was that Innocent III, and Gregory IX who followed him, ordered the extermination of the Cathars.

I'll recall just a few instances of the ensuing massacre. According to noted historian Joseph Campbell, just after the fall of the city of Beziers, France: "the papal legates report a slaughter of nearly twenty thousand—seven thousand in the Church of Mary Magdalene alone, to which they fled for asylum; and when the empowered legate in charge, the fanatical abbot Arnald-Amaury, was asked whether Catholics should be spared, fearing that some of the heretics among them might escape by feigning orthodoxy, he replied, with the true spirit of a man of God in his heart, 'Kill them all, for God knows his own.' "[8] He reasoned that if treason to an earthly king was rightly punished with death, how much graver was treason to God. Actually, when you think of it, the abbot's reasoning, like that of Pope Innocent III, was perfectly logical for a true believer. What difference can life or death make if one truly believes that God will amply reward the innocent and punish the guilty? The terrifying aspect of these evils committed in the name of God is that they could be committed by men who were not themselves evil, but who simply carried an erroneous set of beliefs to a logical extreme.

In the French town of Bram, a hundred hostages were taken, their noses and upper lips were cut off, and all were blinded except one who led the pitiful procession to the castle of Cabaret. The purpose was to terrify the populace and facilitate conquest. It probably worked. At Lavaur 300 to 400 heretics were captured and "we burned them alive with joy in our hearts."[9]

G: Don't blame me. I never condoned such extreme behavior, much of which, as I've said, was politically rather than spiritually motivated.

J: Politics might have motivated the leaders, but the desire to do God's will and thereby gain salvation, coupled, perhaps, with certain innate aggressive tendencies, was the primary motivation of their ignorant followers. The point is that no man or group of men can be trusted to speak for You.

Let's continue to review what can happen when they do. As you are well aware, the Inquisition soon spread to Italy, Germany, and the papal states. You think it is mere hyperbole when I compare the days of papal power to Nazi Germany. It is not. In the encyclical *Unam Sanctam (One, Holy)* issued by Pope Boniface VIII in 1302, he sounded very much like der Führer when he declared that all temporal powers are subject to spiritual power and "it is altogether necessary to salvation for every human creature to be subject to the Roman Pontiff." The Inquisition lasted for the next several hundred years, a time during which no person was safe. Anyone could be denounced by a neighbor. There was no defense; the accuser did not even have to be identified. If this is not the familiar picture of fascism, what is?

During this period several popes assumed the role of generals. Perhaps the most militaristic was Julius II, who led his legions in the Italian Wars like a medieval Caesar. Witch burning also became a popular recreation, used as much to terrify the masses into subjugation as to exorcise a devil. As a result of papal bulls issued by Innocent VII in 1484, Julius II in 1504, and Adrian VI in 1523, there was hardly a town in Europe that didn't enjoy the spectacle of a burning human being. The masses of the Middle Ages had found a satisfying Christian substitute for the sport of the Coliseum. In Germany, France, Switzerland, and Italy, town after town suffered mass executions, often by burning—one estimate is that between 1450 and 1550 in Germany alone a hundred thousand persons were put to death.[10]

When he was Grand Inquisitor, Pope Pius V sent Catholic troops to kill 2,000 Waldensian Protestants in Calabria in Southern Italy. Later, as pope he sent troops to kill Huguenot Protestants in France. He then ordered the commander to kill every prisoner. After his death, Pius V was canonized a saint and is still venerated by the Church.[11] Some saint!

The executions and burnings continued for the next two hundred years! Only You may know the full extent of that holocaust.

G: Now hold on! I admit there were many atrocities committed in My name out of ignorance, but it was the state, not the Church, which executed all those poor women and men.

J: Along with young girls, old ladies, the sick, the deformed, the mentally ill, and those who were just outspoken. Yes, it was the state that actually lit the torch, after the poor wretch was condemned by the Church. In this regard the popes and the bishops of the Church bear a striking similarity to Pontius Pilate as he attempted to wash the blood of an innocent man from his hands. The fact is that the state was simply the executioner for the Church.

G: Are you quite finished dredging up ancient history? You are making the classic error of confusing the Church with a few erring individuals who were associated with it. It is like condemning the Apostles for the action of Judas.

J: Your analogy is not at all apropos. It is not due merely to superstition or ignorance on the part of a few people that the Inquisition occurred; it was a necessary, predictable consequence flowing from the nature of the institution itself.

G: You're talking about the problem of the medieval Church's political power. Hardly an original observation. It is generally admitted today, even by ecclesiastics, that separation of Church and State is necessary to prevent the excesses that occurred during the Middle Ages.

J: That is only the most obvious point. We must dig a little deeper. The reason that the coalition of Church and State in the Middle Ages was so devastating was that both were "divinely sanctioned" totalitarian institutions. Both claimed their authority not from their constituents, but from God. The horror of the Inquisition was a direct result of the popes' professed belief that they alone spoke for God.

Their claim was a brilliant strategy, embraced by virtually all subsequent religious leaders, to insure absolute dominion over human hearts and minds. However, to protect that position it was necessary to crush any form of intellectualism or scientific endeavor that might directly or indirectly undercut the belief. This was the real reason for burning Giordano Bruno in 1600, and for the lifelong imprisonment of philosopher Tommaso Companella. This was the reason for burning the bones of the dissident Augustinian monk, John Wyclif, decades after his death. It was the reason for luring Wyclif's disciple John Hus to the Council of Constance under the promise of safe conduct and then having him burnt for heresy. And this, too, was the reason Urban VIII had to react with such hostility to Galileo Galilei, who dared to confirm the Copernican theory of the solar system, for which he was promptly imprisoned and threatened with torture if he should not recant his conclusions. Why should the pope have reacted so strongly to what is considered today an innocuous scientific observation? The answer is simply that it contradicted the Bible and thus undermined the basis for the Church's authoritative position as an institution founded by and representative of God. For if the Bible was mistaken in so elemental a point of astronomy, how could it be trusted as the inspired word of God? And if every line of the Bible was not the revealed word of God and thus unquestionable, which verses were in doubt? Who would make that determination? Certainly not the popes and Church Fathers if they also mistakenly believed that the Earth was the center of the universe. Galileo's discovery threatened to pull the "Chair of Peter" right out from under the papacy. It took the Church 359 years finally to admit Galileo was right. The popes were quite wise to wait. By 1992, when the Church finally admitted the error, everyone had forgotten the relevance of the controversy.[12]

G: Aren't you confusing moral and scientific issues? On issues of science today's pope would readily admit that he is capable of error.

J: Such a discussion is beyond the scope of this volume. But at a later time I'll show that moral issues as well can be decided only by the scientific method, despite the abdication of the field of ethics by scientists. This is one reason why science has been treated with suspicion by the papacy. For the scientific pursuit of truth to proceed, the Church first had to have much of its power eroded by the Reformation and subsequent revolutions. Not that the popes gave ground graciously. Quite the contrary, they sought to drown their opposition in a sea of blood.

G: What an unfair generalization. You must admit that there were many saintly popes who did not abuse their power and made a genuine effort to reform the Church prior to the Reformation.

J: There undoubtedly were some, but they were the exceptions rather than the rule. If it were not so, people wouldn't have been driven to open rebellion against the Church. Reformers knew they ran the risk of consequences far greater than the popes' spiritual condemnation. I'll cite just two examples.

August 24th is celebrated as the feast of St. Bartholomew in France. That date is also remembered for the infamous St. Bartholomew's Day Massacre. On that day in the year 1572, French Catholics began a systematic massacre of Huguenots throughout the country. Over 20,000 men, women, and children were murdered in a month's time. What was the response of the pope to this atrocity? Remorse? Condemnation of those responsible? Not at all. Pope Gregory XIII was so elated by this "victory" that he had a commemorative medal struck with the inscription "slaughter (*strages*) of the Huguenots."[13]

Less than fifty years later, in 1618, the Thirty Years' War broke out in Germany, and eventually raged throughout Europe. The reasons for the war were complicated, involving both territorial and dynastic issues, but the fuel that made it blaze out of control for three decades was the religious affiliation of the factions. Nothing works as well to bring out the murderous fanaticism just below the veneer of civilization. The pope did his part to escalate the war by urging his followers to oppose the Protestant revolution in Germany. When the fires finally died, the terrible toll was the destruction of two-thirds of the German villages. An estimated ten million of the sixteen million Germans were killed along with an unknown number of persons in Italy, the Iberian Peninsula and Scandinavia. In France and Spain the war did not end for another eleven years.

G: You make the popes out to be the most horrible of moral monsters. But most of them were simply men who were no more ignorant or vicious than their political contemporaries in power, the kings and princes of Europe. They didn't necessarily want the bloodshed. They were trying to protect an institution that they honestly believed was in danger of being destroyed by a variety of opposing forces.

J: Not the least of which were those intellectuals and humanists who were trying to rescue humankind from the tyranny of religious dogmatism. You are entirely too easy on the popes. I agree that many thought that they were doing right, that they were following Your Divine Will. However, such righteousness made the papacy more rather than less dangerous.

No mere recitation of statistics can convey the immeasurable evil that the Roman Catholic Church dispensed in Your name. From the time that the papacy cemented its power with the state in the fifth century until the Renaissance, the cloak of ignorance and superstition was draped over Europe. The light of freedom was extinguished. It is no longer fashionable to call them the Dark Ages, but indeed they were. The ancient Romans had libraries of 500,000 volumes; there was not a library of over 600 volumes in Christian Europe during the period 500 to 1000.[14] Scientific advance, especially in medicine, came to a screeching halt. Human culture regressed to a more primitive, brutal level.

Ironically, it was the initiation of the Crusades against the Muslims that shed a ray of intellectual light through the gloom of ignorance and primitive superstitions. Unlike the Christians who sought to destroy all knowledge that contradicted their theology, the Muslins had preserved the wisdom of the ancient Greeks. Moreover, they had made significant advances in mathematics, philosophy, and science. When the Crusaders returned from the East they brought with their spoils of war the seeds of knowledge which, eventually, gave birth to the Renaissance. Along with the pile of plundered Eastern artifacts and phony relics, the Crusaders also brought back the art and literature of ancient Greece. The writings of the Greek philosophers, which the Church had suppressed centuries before, reappeared. Some of the philosophers such as Plato and Aristotle were accommodated in Church doctrine. Indeed, the writings of Thomas Aquinas, especially his demonstrations for the existence of God, were basically a rehash of Aristotle. But more importantly in the long run, Greek humanistic philosophy found fertile ground in the minds of those who were painfully aware of the futility of theological speculation and the evil of papal dogmatism. As a result, the very foundation of the Church's intellectual and moral despotism would begin to shake.

With the growth in knowledge and critical thinking, inevitably came the desire for more freedom. Both the papacy and the monarchies of Europe recognized this grave threat. It is no wonder, then, that an all-out war was declared on those who sought to free humankind from the twin shackles of king and pope. This was the true purpose of the Inquisition.

The effort to stamp out any opposition to the popes and their obsession with maintaining the rule of the Catholic Church has continued down through the ages. In this century, however, it has been more of a rear guard action, with the Church seeking to protect its dwindling authority by making alliances with whoever would serve its interests. The collaboration of the popes with fascist governments in Europe and South America shows the shameful extremes the popes have been willing to go to, to preserve their position.

The Church opposed the Mexican war of independence and excommunicated its leaders. Later the Church fought the establishment of the federal republic system and vigorously protested the inclusion of the principle of religious freedom in the Mexican constitution.[15] In 1930 the constitutional government was toppled in Argentina and a fascist dictatorship established, complete with martial law. Since the new regime proclaimed its allegiance to Catholicism, it was quickly supported by the Church. In 1936 the pope was eager to ally himself with Spain's fascist dictator Francisco Franco in his effort to squash the Spanish rebellion. As its reward the Catholic Church was established as the state religion. (With the approval of a democratic constitution in 1978 after the dictator's death the Church lost this privilege.) The Franco deal, however, was merely an aside to the role the Church would play in the rise and consolidation of power of Hitler and

Mussolini, a role the popes would like us all to forget. Pope Pius XI signed a concordat and the Lateran Treaty with Mussolini in 1929, and called him "the man sent by Providence."[16] Four years later, Papal Nuncio Monsignor Pacelli, who was soon to become Pius XII, urged the German Catholic Party to vote for Hitler in the last German election prior to the Nazi takeover.[17]

G: So there were some tragic errors of judgment on the part of the popes. They couldn't have foreseen the horrible consequences of their decisions. Their primary concern was to stop the spread of Communism.

J: Those who claim the moral authority to speak for God cannot be excused for such tragic errors in judgment. It was proclaimed by the official Church press that Pius XII had witnessed the miracle of seeing the sun zigzag across the sky at Fatima and again at Rome.[18] But he could not see the horror that would accompany the rise of fascism. In fact, he endorsed it. After such a horrendous mistake you would think that the popes would have learned a little humility. But such has certainly not been the case. Moreover, even after the evils of Nazism had become manifest, the Church was conspicuously silent. Why did the pope not threaten to excommunicate any Catholic who served the Nazi party as he was willing to do to anyone supporting Communism?

G: Well, the fascists were never a threat to the Church.

J: Precisely! It made no difference what atrocities a government committed against humankind as long as it was shrewd enough to let the pope retain his titular authority. When Ante Pavelich set up the Catholic state of Croatia and slaughtered 600,000 persons, primarily those belonging to the Orthodox Church who opposed his rule, the Catholic Church was mute.[19]

In the United States during the 1930s, Catholics regularly tuned in to the popular radio denouncements of Father Coughlin who blamed the depression on "godless capitalists, Jews, Communists, international bankers and plutocrats."[20] Father Coughlin's ravings against Jews became a little embarrassing to the Church after the full realization of the Holocaust was known. Soon, however, the scent of a new Inquisition had many a clerical nose twitching in eagerness. The Catholic press and Church hierarchy, for the most part, enthusiastically supported Senator Joseph McCarthy's infamous search for Communists around every corner. According to an FBI memorandum, Cardinal Francis Spellman, the senior American cardinal at the time, campaigned "to bring about the election of McCarthy as president."[21] Later, Spellman toured Latin America and "bestowed his blessings" on a host of dictators: Battista in Cuba, Trujillo in the Dominican Republic, Stoessner in Paraquay, and Somoza in Nicaraqua. He also assisted the CIA in a coup to install the dictatorship of Castillo Armas in Guatemala.[22]

Spellman was the papal point man to lead America into deeper involvement in Vietnam. According to a Vatican official letter, the pope "turned to Spellman to encourage American commitment to Vietnam."[23] The extent of the Church's commitment to that great tragedy is just beginning to come to light. When the Vietnamese fought to liberate their nation from the French, many Catholic Vietnamese in the North sided with the French because of their opposition to Communism. However, after the French were driven from Vietnam, Catholic priests and even a Catholic bishop were appointed to the administration of Ho Chi Minh. This was not enough for the Church whose policy was to oppose materialistic Communism in any form. Rumors soon circulated through the North that the Communists were preparing to execute all Catholics. South Vietnam Radio broadcast that the Virgin Mary had gone to the South to live under the Catholic leader, Diem, and anyone remaining in the North would lose their souls.[24]

G: Such a statement sounds too preposterous for anyone to believe.

J: Don't forget this was during the height of the worldwide Fatima movement of the 1950s. I vividly recall the almost hysterical devotion Catholics had to the Mother of God, who had supposedly appeared to three children in the town of Fatima. Statues depicting their vision of Mary were venerated by the simple people around the world almost as idols. Hence, when the statue of Mary which had been blessed by the pope only a few years before, was paraded through the towns and villages of North Vietnam on a pilgrimage to the South, hysteria broke out. To add to the carefully cultivated panic, thousands of leaflets were dropped over the North alleging that Jesus had left the North to be with his mother in the South.[25] That was enough; the floodgates broke and Catholics streamed into the South from the North. But the addition of tens of thousands of Catholics to South Vietnam did not help shore up the government of Ngo Dinh Diem, as the Church had hoped.

All U.S. relief to the South was funneled through the Catholic Church's agencies and only Catholics were appointed to government positions by Diem. Although these policies resulted in a wave of conversions, Catholics still made up only about 12 to 13 percent of the South Vietnamese population. Not surprisingly, the resentment among the Buddhist majority soon resulted in their open resistance to Diem's policies. As the situation deteriorated, Diem resorted to mass arrests and suppression of the Buddhists, closing shrines and monasteries. As the Church should have known from its own early experience, persecution can only strengthen a cause. As a horrified world watched, the Buddhists resorted to the ultimate act of passive resistance and several monks set themselves ablaze. During these terrible times, when I, too, was a Catholic, I don't recall one word of criticism of Diem's policies from a Catholic priest or bishop. However, it finally became too much for President John Kennedy, who withdrew U.S. support for Diem. Diem was soon executed in a coup. Throughout this dreadful ordeal the role of the Church followed true to the course of its sordid history.

G: All right. But the battles have all now been fought. Even Catholic Spain has become a democracy. So I assume you have at last reached the end of your little history lesson?

J: Not quite.

G: Call it my omniscience, but I suspected as much.

J: The carnage has still not ended. We saw the legacy of the Crusades in the Christian-Muslim fighting in Lebanon, and remnants of the Reformation in the Catholic-Protestant feud in Northern Ireland. Today's Church does little to stop this bloodshed: the pope is more interested in maintaining control over people's minds and lives by means of his last weapon—the doctrine of papal infallibility.

The Doctrine of Papal Infallibility and Suppression of Intellectual Dissent

In the sixteenth century, Ignatius Loyola, the founder of the Jesuits, exhorted, "We ought always be ready to believe that what seems to us white is black if the hierarchical Church so defines it."[26] This confession of blind faith, which we have heard echoed by the fundamentalists and cult religions reviewed earlier, was reflected in the Church dogma of papal infallibility formulated at the Council of Trent in 1546. The Vatican Council of 1870 reaffirmed the doctrine that the pope is divinely inspired and, therefore, incapable of error in matters of faith or morals. It also held that past utterances of the Church Doctors and Fathers,* where they exhibit unanimity on faith or morals, are also infallible.

G: You appear to be implying that there is a clear code of infallible dogmas to which all Catholics must subscribe; actually, this is not the case.

---

*The title of "Doctor of the Church" is conferred on distinguished theologians such as Thomas Aquinas. The title "Father of the Church" is given to some of the early prelates instrumental in founding the organization.

Indeed, there is much debate within the Church, especially in recent years, as to which of its beliefs fall under the umbrella of infallibility.

J: That's true. Part of the debate centers around what constitutes an issue of faith or morals. Belief in the assumption of Mary, the mother of Jesus, bodily into heaven was clearly proclaimed by the pope to be a matter of faith and an infallible truth. However, is the pope's position on birth control and abortion a matter of morals and, therefore, subject to his infallible judgment? I recall vividly my uncle, a Franciscan priest, declaring it to be so in the strongest terms. Yet today many priests tell Catholics that the pope's position on birth control does not fall under the umbrella of infallibility.

However, opposition to contraception is just one of many moral positions that have been repeated so often and with such force that the pope cannot change his view without seriously jeopardizing the entire doctrine of infallibility and, consequently, his position of authority as the spokesman for God. This is another of the great evils of the papacy. Even though the needs of society are constantly changing, the popes must cling to their anachronistic positions.

Nowhere is this problem better exemplified than in the papal position on birth control. Science has given humankind the means to effectively and safely control the explosive growth of population, yet popes stubbornly defend a policy which, at best, may have been rationalized before modern medicine dramatically reduced the infant mortality rate. The result of this archaic thinking is to greatly add to the weight of human misery throughout the underdeveloped world. Whether the issue be birth control, masturbation, divorce, abortion, artificial insemination, surrogate motherhood, or voluntary euthanasia, by claiming to speak for God popes try to control independent thought and debate as assuredly as the Inquisition ever did. In fact, the underlying philosophy of the Inquisition has never really died in the Catholic Church. In 1542 the Holy Inquisition underwent a change of name and was subsequently called simply the Holy Office. In 1965 the name was again changed to the Congregation for the Doctrine of the Faith. Although the loss of temporal power prevents the Church from having heretics arrested, the Congregation still attempts to maintain control over Catholic thought by dismissing teachers whose views differ from the pope's. It also maintains the Index of Forbidden Books and can call upon the pope to excommunicate Catholics who oppose Church teachings. The present head of the Congregation is archconservative Cardinal Joseph Ratzinger. In a later chapter we will see how this latter-day Grand Inquisitor is still in the position to suppress academic investigations into the origins of the Christian religion and beliefs.

G: Now that is an exaggeration. When was the last time anyone was thrown on the rack?

J: Since losing its temporal power the Church has, of course, had to rely on different methods. But the intent is still the same. Latter day Galileos are still being attacked. Not until 1835 did the Index of Forbidden Books repeal the prohibition on titles that taught the double rotation of the earth—a small concession to truth. However, about the same time a group of European Catholic moderates sought to open the dark vaults of the Church to the light of humanist liberalism. The Vatican quickly slammed the door again, proclaiming that "liberty of worship and liberty of the press . . . are equally reprehensible in the extreme," the extreme being statements "in opposition to the teachings, the maxims, and the practice of the Church."[27] The papacy still attempts to censor all opinions that question the pope's right to speak for God. Pius XII dismissed theologians from university teaching positions and forbade them to write on controversial theological matters. Even the great theologian Teilhard de Chardin (1881–1955) was told to be quiet or suffer the consequences. His scientific writings were suppressed; he was forbidden to write on any philosophical themes and was totally isolated. In 1957, a decree of the Holy Office required Teilhard's books to be removed from libraries and forbade their sale or translation into other languages.[28]

Rome's attempt to control the thoughts of Catholics begins early in life. As a child I was taught that it was a mortal sin, warranting damnation for all eternity, to even entertain doubts about the "true faith." To think about the mysteries of that faith was an invitation for the devil to enter one's mind. As a college student in the sixties, I had to obtain permission to read any philosophical work that was on the Index of Forbidden Books. I soon found that this included virtually every philosopher from the time of Descartes down to the present day, including Spinoza, Leibniz, Pascal, Kant, and Hegel to name just a few. When a group of philosophy professors at my college were bold enough to discuss (not advocate) the philosophical position of the logical positivists they were immediately threatened with dismissal.

G: Rightly so. Those damnable freethinkers claimed that metaphysics was not a valid philosophical discipline, since it proposed statements that were intrinsically unverifiable.

J: An interesting position that merits examination rather than censure—unless, of course, you are afraid that the positivists could not adequately be refuted.

G: Nonsense.

J: At any rate, not only in matters of theology but in science as well, the popes demonstrate the same efforts to coerce and suppress as they did in Galileo's day. Alfred Loisy (1857-1940), a French biblical scholar, linguist, and philosopher of religion and professor of the Catholic Institute in Paris, was painfully aware of the danger of an inquiring mind after he was excommunicated and expelled from the institute for teaching heresy. Loisy wrote, "It is impossible to formulate a new hypothesis or conclusion on any important point of natural science, rational science, or historical criticism without finding across one's path the barrier of theological opinion."[29] Loisy was part of the intellectual elite that the Church formed around the turn of the century to combat the devastating criticism of the veracity of the Bible and even the divinity of Jesus. Unfortunately for the Church, by allowing these intellectuals to peer deeply into the Church's teachings it created a host of new skeptics. This was the beginning of the Catholic Modernist Movement, which threatened the very foundations of Church doctrines. As it always had, the Church met the threat of rationalism by forbidding further inquiry. In 1904, Pius X issued an encyclical opposing all scholarship that questioned the origins and early history of Christianity. He then dismissed all Catholic teachers suspected of modernist tendencies, placed their books on the Index and demanded that all Catholics involved in teaching or preaching take an oath renouncing "all errors of modernism."[30] Nothing has changed even today. On the issue of evolution the Vatican made it clear in the encyclical *Humani Generis (Of the Human Race)* that the pope's word was supreme: "There must be a readiness on all sides to accept the arbitrament of the Church."[31]

A few years ago the retired president of my college called to ask for a donation. When I refused on the grounds that I had been given a biased, circumscribed education, he never denied it, but instead tried to assure me that "it's all changed now." It was obviously a desperate attempt to turn around a precipitous decline in enrollment. The most important consideration for any organization is to maintain its membership. So the Church appeared conciliatory for a time and adopted a facade of intellectual liberalism. Has the Church changed? No. Fundamentally, the Church is still a totalitarian regime dedicated to propagating its own theology and suppressing all dissent.

The present pope, John Paul II, has renewed the effort to use censorship to control dissenting opinion. Having been a talented actor in his youth, the pope travels throughout the world posing as a simple and humane man interested only in the welfare of his "flock." But this shepherd is quick to lower his crook on any sheep straying from his dogmatism. In 1979 Tübingen theologian Hans Küng was stripped of his position as a qualified teacher of Catholic doctrine because he dared to question Church dogmas such as papal infallibility. More recently, the trend toward conservatism in this country has encouraged the pope to begin a crackdown on the liberal elements of the U.S. Church. He began by promoting to the rank of cardinal Archbishop John O'Connor and Archbishop William Law, as a reward in part for their attack on Vice Presidential candidate Geraldine Ferraro for her views on abortion.[32] Next, the Vatican Congregation of the Doctrine of Faith revoked the license of Reverend Charles Curran to teach theology at the Catholic University of America because he dared to question the Church's teaching on contraception, abortion, extramarital sex, and marriage after divorce.[33] Father Anthony Kosnik suffered a similar fate as he was forced by the archbishop of Detroit to resign from his position as dean of the graduate school at St. Cyril and Methodius Seminary, because he was the lead author of a study of new directions in American Catholic thought on sexual matters.[34] Yet another to get the axe was the Reverend John J. McNeill, a prominent Jesuit psychiatrist who was expelled from the Church for refusing to give up his public ministry to homosexuals.[35]

Even the Church hierarchy is not safe from this latest purge. Archbishop Raymond Hunthausen of Seattle was next to feel Rome's sting. He suffered partial supersession of his duties by a papal representative for such terrible crimes as letting young children take Communion without having confessed their sins; his failure to prevent contraceptive sterilizations in Catholic hospitals; a lack of severity in his dealings with Catholic gay and lesbian groups, and using the services of inactive or laicised priests.[36] All these actions are fairly widespread in the Church, reflecting the liberalization which followed the attempts of Pope John XXIII to reform the Church in the early sixties. Although Hunthausen was eventually reinstated after the American clergy raised a hue and cry, the lesson was not lost on other prelates with liberal tendencies.

Of particular concern to many priests and lay people who are aware of the new crackdown is the letter censoring Reverend Curran, which bluntly pointed out that any doctrine taught by the pope and the bishops together in a definitive matter is also to be considered infallible.[37] This is an extension of the earlier definition of infallibility and would most certainly cover the issues of divorce, contraception, abortion, and homosexuality, to name just a few.

The evidence is clear that the present pope is a strict authoritarian, expecting absolute belief in his infallibility and willing to crush any opposition to his rule. His latest encyclical, *Veritatis Splendor* (*The Splendor of Truth*) is a reassertion of the papal prerogative to be the final authority on all moral issues. Most American Catholics are also unaware that, in addition to the Index of Forbidden Books (which still exists but carries little weight), Rome seeks to enforce censorship through two other tools at its disposal. First, no Catholic theologian is allowed to publish or teach on faith or morals without receiving permission (the *imprimatur*) from Rome. And, second, no Catholic institution is permitted to use a textbook on faith or morals which has not been reviewed by Rome's official censors and certified as containing nothing contrary to the pope's proclamations on faith or morals (the *nihil obstat*).

G: Well, if you want to belong to the organization you have to talk the company line. Otherwise you had better quit and join another outfit.

J: Does that mean that Catholics have to relinquish their rights to freedom of the press and freedom of speech?

G: On matters of faith and morals, yes. However, on nonreligious matters the Church is a great defender of all basic freedoms. Did not Pope John Paul II outwardly oppose Russia's suppression of freedom in Poland?

J: Yes, but what is his motivation? Don't you find it ironic that a despotic organization that had lost much of its power condemned another that ultimately lost its power as well? Need I remind you that it was the papacy, in the form of Innocent III, which condemned the Magna Carta as a "devil-inspired document"?[38] Why? Because it threatened the claim of monarchs, supported by the Church, that they derived their power over men directly from God. I assure you that the primary concern of the pope was not the Soviet Union's totalitarianism, but the fact that it was an atheistic government and, as such, a direct danger to the Church. Military dictators who portray themselves as champions of religion while overthrowing democratically elected governments, as occurred in Spain and several South American countries, have encountered no opposition from a pope.

G: You forget that the Church in many of these countries has actively opposed the exploiters of the poor. Or have you never heard of the Liberation Theology movement led by such men as Gustavo Gutierrez, Juan Luis Segundo, and José Miguel-Bonino?* In recent years even the pope has spoken out against injustice and inequity in Latin America.

J: Words without sanctions are meaningless. I don't recall the pope threatening to excommunicate the perpetrators of the mass murders

---

*Liberation theology is an attempt to redefine the objective of Christianity as the establishment of social justice through revolutionary change. It tends to be anti-capitalistic and utopian, but not necessarily Marxist.

in Guatemala or El Salvador. It is true that today many priests and
a few bishops have taken the lead in combating oppressive military
dictatorships in South America. This action is prompted in part by
the Church's desire to regain the initiative from the fundamentalist
sects that have been so successful in making inroads with the alienated
peasants and the urban poor. The reason for the fundamentalists' success
is that they have sought to offer direct aid to the poor in stark contrast
to the Catholic Church, which has for centuries turned its back on
the plight of the poor, counseling them to submit to the authority
of their affluent and powerful oppressors. However, to be fair, it is
also a reflection of the rising level of social conscience and humanitarian
values adopted by the clergy, many of whom have come from
impoverished families and are fully aware of the injustice of the present
situation. However, if they become too socially active, then Rome
steps in and seeks to curb their efforts. Hence, several priests have
found it necessary to abandon their vows to pursue their social activism.
Liberation theology has always been unpopular in Rome for fear that
a liberation movement might lead to Communism or socialism as it
did in Cuba and, for a while, in Nicaragua and Chile.

The root of the Church's antipathy toward Communism is its
realization that Communism is, in effect, a rival religion. It is ironic
that the two organizations, Catholicism and Communism, are so much
alike:

- both are totalitarian;

- both have doctrines and canonical texts (the four Communist evangelists are Marx, Engels, Lenin, and Mao);

- the Holy Office plays the same role as the Communist party in
seeking to reinforce the dogmas of faith;

- both excommunicate dissenters; and,

- when in power, both enforce their rule under pain of death. (The
Church still threatens spiritual death.)

In Poland, concern is rising that with the fall of Communism and
the Church's efforts to reestablish its traditional authority, Poles are
in danger of exchanging the rule of the "Reds" with the rule of the
"blacks" (referring to the priests).

G: A clever comparison, but you are overlooking another reason for the
pope's opposition to political involvement. Recognizing the past evil
that resulted in the Church's involvement in political issues, the present-
day popes wish to keep their spiritual mission untainted by politics.

Perhaps that is what motivated the silence of Pius XII during World War II.

J: Excuse me, but that flies in the face of reality. The Church is as deeply immersed in politics as when Pope Leo XIII proclaimed, "All Catholics should do all in their power to cause the constitution of states and legislations to be modeled on the principles of the true Church."[39]

It is a shock for many liberal Catholics to see their Church join forces with the Christian evangelicals such as Pat Robertson in a blatant attempt to tear down the wall of separation between the church and state and advance the agenda of the religious right wing.[40] But what could be clearer than the words of Pius IX, who wrote in his infamous *Syllabus of Errors*: "It is an error to believe that: . . . the Church ought to be separated from the State and the State from the Church."[41] More frightening is his assertion that, "It is an error to believe that: the church has not the power of using force, nor has it any temporal power, direct or indirect."[42]

J. H. Reichley, who attempts to present the history of religion in the United States as a positive force, nonetheless admits that "throughout the nineteenth century, orthodox Catholicism maintained unswerving commitment to the standard that, wherever politically feasible, 'the Catholic religion shall be the only religion of the state, to the exclusion of all other forms of worship.' "[43] This is the logical conclusion of the Catholic belief that theirs is the only true faith, a belief that was impressed upon me throughout my sixteen years of Catholic education. If, as a youth, I had read the words of Monsignor John A. Ryan, they would have seemed axiomatic despite the two false premises:

> If the state is under moral compulsion to profess and promote religion
> it is obviously obliged to promote and profess only the religion that
> is true; for no individual, no society, no state is justified in supporting
> error or in according error the same recognition as truth.[44]

In 1963 a leading Catholic theologian, John Courtney Murray, wrote, "By divine ordinance this world is to be ruled by a dyarchy of authorities, within which the temporal is to be subordinate to the spiritual."[45]

G: Didn't he change his attitude just a few years later by saying that, "The free society of today is recognized to be secular"?[46] And wasn't Pope Paul VI reflecting the same sentiment when he stated that all the Church asks of the world governments is, "nothing but freedom"?[47]

J: That was during the sixties when there was a rebellion against authoritarianism in much of the Western world. Catholics were deserting the Church in large numbers and so the Church took a conciliatory position. With the 1980s, and the rise of fundamentalism, the Church has reverted to her traditional stance of mixing religion with politics. The new mood was reflected in the remark by Secretary of Education William Bennett, a Catholic, who believes the wall of separation between church and state is just "a pile of stones here and a pile of stones there."[48]

As I mentioned earlier, Thomas Jefferson and James Madison realized that it was just as important that Americans have freedom *from* religion as it was to have freedom *for* religion. It is abundantly clear that the pope is not interested in freedom *for* all religions (and certainly not for protection *from* religion). It would appear from its involvement in presidential elections that the hierarchy of the Catholic Church wants to wed the U.S. Constitution firmly to the tenents of Christianity. And where does that place the pope? In his 1984 address to the Protestant World Council of Churches in Switzerland, he made it clear that the Catholic Church and its pope had title to the spiritual authority in the Christian faith.[49]

In the final analysis, the pope is not interested in true human freedom; rather he defines freedom as the right to surrender one's will to the dictates of Rome. It is no wonder that Professor Homer Smith believes that, "Rising Roman Catholic fundamentalism is much more dangerous than Protestant fundamentalism."[50]

G: Even if what you say is true—which I am not prepared to admit— what is so wrong with following the pope's teachings of devotion to God and the practice of brotherly love? It seems to me that the world would be a far better place if all persons did so.

J: The problem is that those two commandments are construed exactly in the order in which you have presented them, i.e., the needs of humans must be subordinate to the demands of God. And, since it is the pope who determines the demands of God for the faithful, the needs of humans will be subordinate to the moral imperatives of the pope. Furthermore, as history has amply demonstrated, the primary moral imperative of the popes has been defense of papal preeminence. This is the rational basis for their claims of infallibility. The consequence is that the pope is oftentimes locked into defending a position that has horrible consequences for the human race.

G: That sounds awfully cynical. Even if it might have been true at one time in the Church's history, that doesn't mean it's true today.

J: The truth oftentimes appears cynical to believers who would like to deny the human nature of their religious or political leaders. The fact is, the consequences of the institution of the papacy are as terrible today as at any time in history, despite the Church's loss of temporal power. Let me demonstrate.

G: This ought to be an interesting display of petty vindictiveness.

J: I believe that it may be more substantive than you would wish. To begin with, all Catholics of my generation were required to memorize a catechism—a summary of Catholic doctrine in the form of questions and answers—which held that we were created by God "to know, love and serve Him in this world and be happy with Him forever in heaven." Note that it does not say that we any right to expect happiness here on earth. Our primary purpose in this life is directed not to ourselves, or even our fellow humans, but to God. How are we to know what God wants and how we are to serve Him? That is where the pope comes in. He will instruct us. He is the only one who can know with certainty. What an awful responsibility for anyone to bear! So what, according to the pope, does God demand?

Thou Shalt Not Use Contraception—Ever

According to the infallible voice of the Vatican, it is morally wrong to use any form of contraception. The reason is that the primary purpose of sex is to have children. The enjoyment that comes with the sexual act is God's way of encouraging procreation. On the other hand, sex primarily for the sake of enjoyment or pair bonding or any other other reason is absolutely wrong. Many of the younger clergy in the United States are extremely uncomfortable with this position. They know that the vast majority of Catholics use contraceptives, and to condemn them all not only appears harsh, but would result in mass defection from the Church. Some modern theologians try to wiggle out of the dilemma by stating that, although it is objectively wrong to practice birth control, Catholics guilty of the practice are not sinning since they have not the "intention" of breaking God's law. Other theologians simply argue that the issue of birth control does not fall within the realm of papal infallibility and, as such, Catholics can follow their own conscience on this matter. Needless to say, the pope takes a very dim view of heretics propagating such an opinion.

Now there was a time, before the invention of the condom, when such a doctrine made sense. Sex had a high probability of resulting in procreation and, therefore, if persons did not intend to have children they were wise to avoid sex (at least until after menopause). There also was a time when infant mortality rates were so high, and the world so thinly populated, that unrestrained procreation was probably necessary for the survival of the race. Such a time has long since passed. Yet despite the changed circumstances, the Vatican is locked into its present policy because to reverse itself is to call into question the issue of papal infallibility and authority.

How can any pope discreetly change his position after his predecessors expressed such absolute certainty on the subject? Pope Pius XI wrote: "Couples who practice birth control commit a sin against nature and commit a deed which is shameful and intrinsically vicious."[51] That ought to have scared more than a few poor people into having more children than they could properly clothe and feed.

In 1964 a group of Catholic and non-Catholic scholars, theologians, Nobel laureates, and scientists petitioned Rome to reappraise the Church's stand on birth control. They were flatly turned down. Paul VI's 1968 encyclical, *Humanae Vitae* (*Of Human Life*), and the more recent pronouncements of Pope John Paul II, still reflect intransigence on birth control. In Ireland, where the power of the pope holds sway, the sale of contraceptive devices is still outlawed.

G: You're mistaken to say that the pope is against birth control. He only opposes artificial means of birth control.

J: That reminds me, a few years ago the *Chicago Tribune* ran a cartoon by Wright which encapsulated the pope's position on birth control. It pictured a black baby who says:

> Africa's problem is very simple.
> We make babies and they starve to death.
> We make more babies and they starve to death.
> We repeat the cycle over and over again.
> This is called the rhythm method.

G: Very funny. Yet the rhythm method . . .

J: . . . better known as Vatican roulette . . .

G: . . . is becoming more reliable.

J: Although for many women it is almost as risky as random copulation. The point is that the pope's prohibition doesn't take into consideration whether rhythm will work or not. He couldn't care a fig. Nor does it matter if getting pregnant would jeopardize a woman's physical or mental health. Nor if the odds are that the baby would be horribly deformed. After all, as the catechism implies, it was not God's intention that we be happy here on earth anyway. But eternal damnation awaits any poor man and woman who disobeys the pope's command which, by the way, is not to be found anywhere in the teachings of Jesus or the Scriptures. It comes from St. Augustine who, in the fifth century, prohibited the use of any "evil appliance." I find it more than a little ironic that the prohibition comes from a man who, by his own admission, lived as a profligate libertine for sixteen years and then, having at last sated his desires, began preaching the evils of the flesh. Moreover, what did Augustine know of sex except its role as a means of procreation? He knew little of human nature, let alone the needs of present-day societies.

The consequences of the popes' ill-conceived dictates are as catastrophic as the persecution of heretics in bygone years. The result will be, in effect, to sentence millions to face starvation and hundreds of millions more to a marginal, subhuman existence.

G: Hold on a minute. Are you going to blame world starvation on the pope, who today has virtually no political power whatsoever? That is a *non sequitur* if ever I heard one. Surely, you know that I have provided enough food on this planet to feed everyone. Is it the pope's fault that humankind will not heed him and redistribute nature's bounty to feed all? Or is it not truly the fault of selfish people who will not listen?

J: I would like to make several points by way of reply.

G: Somehow I thought you would.

J: First, regarding the pope's lack of political power: after reviewing how badly past popes have abused such power, I am grateful that I can agree with you here. However, the pope has significant moral prestige with many millions of simple, uneducated followers. These in turn, by virtue of their sheer numbers, are often quite politically powerful.

G: What an outlandish statement. It implies that there are no educated, intelligent Catholics.

J: I didn't say that. There are obviously many brilliant and well-educated Catholics, both clergy and laity. It is apparent, however, that the highly educated priests and theologians are part of the power structure of the Church, and it is in their (perhaps unconscious) self-interest to support the pope. As for the laity, the many years of intensive conditioning (some would say brainwashing) received in Catholic schools by children at an age when they are most impressionable is effective in the vast majority of cases. It was a well-considered strategy for the Church to enact Canon Law 1374 prescribing schools where religious and moral training occupy first place.

G: You would deny the Church the right to provide religious education for its followers?

J: I don't deny the right of religious education. I do object to the Church's claim that major issues involving faith or morals can be decided by the authority of Rome. This places a whole body of knowledge outside the realm of intellectual inquiry and debate, and effectively subverts any true educational effort. I see little difference between the Church's attempts to preclude debate on moral doctrine and the Communist party's foreclosure on political debate. Both efforts reflect a fear that rational investigation may undermine the beliefs of their followers and topple their entire power structure.

Cannon Law 1374 also effectively boycotts public schools by requiring Catholics to obtain special permission to attend one. When I was young it was rigidly enforced with excellent results, at least from the perspective of the Church. Easing of that enforcement in recent years allowed many Catholics to attend public schools where they have been exposed to other philosophies and, to a limited extent, moral reasoning. The result was a more liberal, less dogmatic attitude toward Catholic doctrines, which has caused a rising concern in the Church.

G: You continually equate the Church with its hierarchy. Yet Catholics will point out that the Church is not just the pope and his bishops, but the entire body of Catholics.

J: That is the theory, but certainly not the practice over the history of the Church. In recent years, of course, some of the priests and laity have sought to change this. Many thought that the spirit engendered by Pope John XXIII and the Second Vatican Council would bring about a Catholic "reformation." But although many of the externals have changed, such as more active participation by the laity in the Mass, Rome is slowly tightening the screws on moral issues which threaten her claim to ultimate authority.

This is the main reason the Church hierarchy in the United States is illegally lobbying for tax credits (tax-exempt organizations are not allowed to lobby). They hope to lure Catholics and others who wish to escape the socially and racially integrated public school system back to their successful Catholic indoctrination. Of course, fundamentalist religions and elitists support tax credits as well for their own ends. They all have learned the lesson of history: if you wish to control the minds of your followers, you must very carefully control their education. That is why Justice Jackson observed in *Everson* v. *the Board of Education,* "to render tax aid to its Church school is indistinguishable to me from rendering the same aid to the Church itself."[52]

G: What has all this to do with your outrageous allegation that the pope is somehow responsible for world hunger?

J: I never said that. With or without a pope there would be famines and starvation. However, his influence will make the tragedy far worse. To understand why this must be, it is important to appreciate that in the underdeveloped countries of the world, most Catholics are poor peasants who have not been educated in the rules of logic or the paramount role of evidence in establishing the validity of an assertion.

Rather, they are taught trust and reverence for contradictory and incomprehensible beliefs that are presented as "unfathomable mysteries." By thus stifling curiosity and intellectual development, the Church is able to ensure that the child never becomes a moral adult. It is not simply out of affection that the pope refers to his followers as his "children."

G: There is nothing wrong with advocating that all men must be as children. Jesus said that all must be as children if they wished to see God.

J: Correct me if I'm wrong, but I think—I hope—he was referring to the quality of guilelessness in children. Perhaps he was indeed more shrewd, and realized that for a religion to succeed it is essential that its followers remain as ignorant and gullible as children. Jesus did like to consider himself as "the Shepherd" and his followers as sheep. Like the religious leaders discussed in the first chapter, the pope wisely follows this example. Every totalitarian leader wants his followers to be sheep. Sheep blindly follow without thinking: a desirable quality since thinking can be dangerous, especially if the leader has grounded his authority in myths, lies and half-truths.

So the pope does exert considerable control over the more susceptible of his followers, especially the poor and uneducated. But it is apparent that he has little appreciable influence over the educated, wealthy, or powerful, unless his advice is perceived to be in their best interests anyway. This is easily demonstrated by how little impact the pope's words have on birth control in the more educated nations such as the United States, where, according to Andrew Greely, the encyclical of Pope Paul VI against birth control was ignored by four-fifths of the clergy and laity.[53] Divorce is also rapidly becoming accepted, and some Catholics are even supporting a woman's right to abortion. Similarly, to expect the pope to successfully persuade those nations having a surplus of food to voluntarily share their surplus in any meaningful way with the millions who are underfed is sheer fantasy.

More significantly, a more equitable distribution of food to avoid starvation today would ultimately be of no avail, since those who do not starve would, in the absence of readily available contraception, breed an even larger population to face starvation tomorrow. Therefore, the pope's efforts to discourage birth control in Latin America and Africa, if successful, will sentence millions of additional children to a horrible subhuman existence.

In Ethiopia during 1990 there were 12 million people starving to death. No doubt this is in part due to the long civil war that decimated the country. However, even in the absence of a civil war there would have been insufficient food without outside aid. But if an effective policy of population planning had been enacted as late as 1970, that catastrophe, which was totally predictable by simply extrapolating the birth rate, could have been averted. Yet as tragic as the Ethiopian situation is, it is only a harbinger of what is to come if the pope has his way. In 1985, Pope John Paul II traveled to Kenya, which suffers from the world's fastest population growth rate (4.1 percent per year), and took the occasion to condemn contraception and abortion as "antilife actions [that] are wrong and unworthy of good husbands and wives." If the pope's advice is heeded, Kenya will become the next Ethiopia. Every country that doesn't enact population control measures will follow the Vatican's prescription for disaster. During the period between 1975 and 1990, three-quarters of the world's women reached child-bearing age. More than two billion children were born, mainly in underdeveloped nations. As a consequence, a large part of the world's population is living on the brink of starvation. In Africa alone, 27 million people are threatened with starvation if the droughts continue. Under such conditions the pope's position on birth control is as irresponsible as a fifteen-year-old girl who decides to have a baby without a thought as her ability to contribute to its future welfare.

The people of China can be grateful that their government has enacted a more enlightened, though severe, policy dictated by the urgency of their situation. For many other nations it is already too late. The Association for Voluntary Sterilization reports that in Brazil alone there are two million persons living in the streets. Hundreds of thousands of them are unwanted children, doomed to a life of misery. Many exist by eating out of garbage cans and sleeping in doorways. Others will eventually turn to crime out of desperation and wind up in prison or dead. Mexico City has 1.5 million people living in desperate poverty; yet the Church continues to use its influence to oppose all forms of contraception. Voluntary sterilization is also vigorously opposed by Rome as a form of self-mutilation and an attempt to frustrate the Divine Will. This is the same Church that once had members of the Vienna Boys Choir castrated before their voices changed so they might more sweetly sing the praises of God.

To be sure, there are Catholic clergy who see the horror of Rome's dogmatism and reject it. They support birth control and a few even see the necessity to legalize abortion. But by propagating the myth that the Catholic Church was uniquely established by Christ and that the pope is the representative of Jesus here on earth, they involuntarily support the pope's inhumane dogmas. Fortunately, in the United States Catholics are more rational than their Church leaders not only regarding contraception, a common practice, but according to a study by the Guttmacher Institute, Catholics are 30 percent more likely than Protestants or Jews to get an abortion.[54]

There is another dreadful consequence of the pope's intransigence regarding birth control. In the underdeveloped countries a woman puts her life on the line every time she has a baby. Mortality rates for expectant mothers in these countries are 48 to 75 times higher than that of women in the United States.[55] Most of these deaths result in still more orphans to flood the world's slums. Consequently, as Malcolm Potts observed, "When a local druggist sells a packet of contraceptive pills over the counter in an area where mortality rates are high, he is more likely to save a human life than an obstetrician in a developed country."[56] Ironically, the pope's opposition to contraceptives results in hundreds of thousands of abortions, most in illegal and unsafe conditions that threaten women's lives. Due primarily to the lack of readily available contraception, 55 million abortions are performed in the world annually. Worldwide, 182,000 women die each year from dangerous abortions.[57] In the United States, where a women's right to abortion has been recognized since 1973 (over the Church's strenuous opposition), the death rate for women who obtain abortions has dropped almost 90 percent.[58] So by opposing contraceptives and legalized abortion, the pope is in effect sentencing many women to die. But the real issue for the pope is not a woman's rights or her life or even her morality. It is papal power.

G: You simply cannot blame the pope's policy on birth control for all this misfortune. Most of these women are not even Catholic. Moreover it isn't his fault that they get pregnant. There is always abstinence.

J: Like Augustine and the pope, you appear to believe that the only purpose of sex is procreation. There is ample evidence to suggest that a primary function of sex is to help cement the bond between a man and a woman. More to the point, your comment ignores a basic fact of human nature. Probably the most basic drive of all animal species is the desire to have sex. The reason is obvious: were it not so the species would have died out. In the world of nature a balance was stuck between procreation rates and mortality rates. However we can see what happens when that balance is upset. Take, for example, the case of deer populations when their natural predators are removed. The population swells until a particularly severe winter hits and then there is mass starvation.

Since modern humans have eliminated many of the natural dangers that controlled our population in the past—primarily disease—we, too, face the prospect of uncontrolled population growth. Luckily, just as science was used to reduce mortality rates, it can be used to reduce birth rates. To adopt any other policy is lunacy. Of course, if the pope wanted to be at least logical, I suppose he could demand that all artificial attempts to reduce mortality, such as the use of antibiotics, are a frustration of God's will. But such a policy hits very close to home. I doubt if the pope wants any policy that might cost him his own life.

G: Some would argue that your concern about population growth is unfounded. Growth in population is correlated with increased economic growth. The real problem, they contend, is one of distribution.

J: Before discussing the merits of that argument I would like to note that the position of the Church is not based on any rational argument, economic or otherwise. It is a simple assertion on the part of the pope that he and his predecessors know it to be the will of God that people use no artificial form of birth control. It is that attempt to escape a rational debate based on logic and evidence to which I object, since it inevitably results in absurd and inhumane policies.

Now as to the contention that population growth might be conducive to economic growth, this is true in a country such as the United States of the eighteenth and nineteenth centuries. It was a rich and sparsely populated land where the addition of people to exploit its riches resulted in a very rapid accumulation of wealth for many people. However, even in this country we are beginning to sense limitations in land, water, and clean air. Luckily we have recognized those limitations, and have greatly reduced our birth rate by means of birth control.

Anyone who believes that the population can grow at the rate of third world countries simply doesn't understand the basic mathematics of a geometric growth rate. Consider this:

- it took a million years for the world population to reach one billion people;

- the second billion was added in only 130 years;

- despite a world war, another billion persons were added between 1930 and 1960;

- the fourth billion was reached only fifteen years later in 1975;

- and in just eleven more years we hit five billion;

- and the six billion mark will be attained before the year 2000.

Left unchecked, ultimately the gloomy predictions of the economist Malthus have to be right. Even if the pope could magically distribute all the food today, we would be doing little more than buying time. A geometrically increasing population must eventually starve on finite resources. I've calculated that if the world population continued to increase at the 3.8 percent growth rate of the underdeveloped nations, in just 200 years this tiny planet would be crushed by almost 10,000,000,000,000,000—that's 10 trillion—people.*

Of course such a population size is ludicrous, hence the birth rate must decline; the only issue is whether the decline will be by voluntary or involuntary means. Luckily, over 80 countries of the world have now adopted a birth control policy. Unfortunately, it is now so late in the game that more stringent controls, such as those adopted in China, may be inevitable. Even at today's more modest growth rate of 1.7 percent per annum, (which is largely due to the dramatic decline in China's birth rate) another 25 billion persons will be added by the end of the next century—that's 25 more countries the size of China—a twentyfold increase in an already overpopulated world. Yet despite the overwhelming evidence that an immediate and sustained reduction of population growth is essential to avoid untold human suffering, the pope remains intransigent in his opposition to birth control. In the June 1992 U.N. Conference on the Environment and Development in Rio de Janerio, the Vatican used its political clout to squash any discussion of population concerns.[59] "Vatican representatives circulated a confidential memo to representatives of countries attending the conference in a successful effort to discourage discussion of overpopulation problems."[60] The 1994 Cairo Conference on Population also finds the church lobbying against efforts to expand contraception availability and family planning programs in the less-developed countries.

G: What a pessimist. Your problem is that you have no faith that I will provide . . .

J: . . . a war? Even that is no longer an effective form of population control—unless we go the nuclear route.

G: How rude you are. I don't interrupt you. Men cause war, not Me.

J: I apologize for the interruption.

G: The Pope believes he is following My will, and it is I alone who have the right to decide when and where life shall begin.

J: I agree, the pope believes he knows your will. But, either he is wrong or You have a very ugly future planned for the human race. Throughout history the popes who committed all those atrocities—the Crusades,

---

*Although such a number seems iompossibly large, a 3.87 growth rate equates to a doubling of the population every 18.5 years.

the Inquisition, the wars against heretics and Protestants—did so in Your name. The prohibition against birth control, if followed, would undoubtedly lead to one more such atrocity.

There is an additional calamity which the pope's dogmatism has exacerbated. The Church's opposition to public sex education and the ready availability of condoms has undoubtedly resulted in many thousands of people throughout the world contracting AIDS, who could have been spared this terrible disease. Albert Camus was absolutely on the mark when he wrote in *The Fall*, "One must forgive the pope, he needs it more than anyone else."[61]

G: So in questioning the doctrine of infallibility, you probably also doubt the pope's claim that he is my representative on earth?

J: Do I detect a little divine sarcasm in that question? Given the actions and teachings of popes over the past 2,000 years, I find the idea downright ludicrous. But it is not funny; it is tragic, for the papacy continues to use its position to retard the social welfare of humankind. While mouthing platitudes about peace and love, the popes promote an archaic worldview that will foster much mental and physical anguish. Papal pronouncements on divorce, demonology, masturbation, homosexuality, sterilization, and the role of women all reflect a medieval view and an incredible ignorance of human nature. Such ignorance and insensitivity belie all claims to moral leadership on the part of the popes. What intelligent, reasonable mind could take seriously the words of men who demand that we believe that all humankind are inheritors of an original sin from one man, Adam. And this is not to be believed as mere allegory (as many Catholics do), but as an actual historical fact. Absurd though it is, this is what Pius XII demanded of Catholics in his 1950 encyclical *Humani Generis*.

Pope John Paul II believes in many superstitions that modern Catholics find embarrassing. Just recently he gave three lessons in which he maintained that each person has no less than three guardian angels and discussed the various roles of angels working inside paradise. It sounded like the lesson on leprechauns I once got from my neighbor's grandma. The pope shouted at his audience, "Watch out for the devil!" He believes Satan appears in the shape of a lion, a snake, a dragon, or a goat with horns.[62] This has led to the appointment of new exorcists to cast out the devil from people obviously suffering from mental illness. Cardinal John O'Connor of New York, who supports the renewal of the ancient superstition, claimed that two New Yorkers were possessed and consequently subjected them to the mumbo-jumbo of exorcism. I haven't heard such silliness since my first grade nun used to try to scare us into behaving. It would all be terribly amusing if it were not coming from a man who has persuaded millions of people that he speaks for God.

G: I don't think it is either amusing or absurd.

J: Let's conclude with an examination of the basis the papacy uses to establish its authority as the sole and legitimate interpreter of Your will. Primarily it rests on the alleged words of Jesus to Peter in the New Testament: "Thou art Peter and upon this rock I will build my church." On the face of it, I would take it as a joke since Jesus goes on to predict that when questioned by the captors of Jesus, Peter would deny even knowing him, three times no less. As Camus pointed out, Jesus must have been making fun of poor, cowardly Peter by referring to him as a rock of steadfastness.

Aside from the absurdity of the statement, I find it less than a convincing argument that the popes have used the Bible as the sole basis for their alleged role as divine spokesmen, when it was the early Christians who wrote the New Testament in the first place. Their actions were not unlike the imaginative games played by Ellen White and Joseph Smith in modern times. It's as reliable as a last will and testament turned in by a prospective heir who admits that he wrote the will himself after the death of his uncle. It is not surprising, therefore, to learn that many biblical scholars believe the evidence indicates that this reference to Peter, like many other New Testament passages, was inserted at a later date.

There is a second even less convincing argument offered by Church theologians to support the pope's claim. It begins with an admission that the Bible is indeed often confusing and contradictory in its moral message. Furthermore, the argument even admits that the early Church founders and popes were responsible for selecting the specific books to be included in the New Testament from the many "gospels" and epistles circulating in the early days of Christianity. However, it is assumed that God would never let Christians founder in a sea of contradictory doctrines and beliefs. Therefore, the argument concludes, God must have appointed a divinely inspired arbitrator to be the final word—His word—on moral issues. That arbitrator is the pope.

After reflecting on the previous abbreviated history of the papacy, and the discussion of the early days of the Church, I think we must conclude that, if that was Your intent, You made an awfully poor choice for an arbitrator.

Two other points are worth noting. The first pope was not Peter, as the Church contends, but Leo I. Although Peter may have been bishop of Rome, he did not assume primacy over the other bishops. It wasn't until four hundred years later, in 440, that Leo I was given the title of pope in an effort to concentrate the Church's power more effectively.

The second point is that the popes did not articulate the doctrine of infallibility until the sixteenth century. Infallibility was the popes' effort to suppress the intellectual activity of the priests and the competing secular rationalism which was beginning to take root as a result of European Renaissance and the Reformation.

G: Well, you may feel that you have neatly assassinated the moral primacy of the papacy, but that doesn't mean that the body of the Church as it exists today is not a force for good in this world. Besides, in the United States most younger Catholics do not subscribe to the doctrine of infallibility or pay much credence to the pope; they pursue their own conception of justice and morality.

J: But they are still influenced by the pope's theology and morality. Take the issue of abortion. It is an extremely complicated debate involving philosophical, social, psychological, political, and medical issues. Those who oppose it, on other than religious grounds, are concerned as to where to draw the line. Those who advance the "slippery slope" argument contend that there is a danger that abortion encourages a callous disregard for human life and may ultimately lead to a society willing to dispose of any life that doesn't meet some preconceived ideal. Soon, they fear, anyone suffering from a crippling defect, whether at birth or later in life, will become the target for elimination. They point to Nazi Germany as evidence for the possibility that such a situation might really occur.

Those on the other side contend that such a situation could develop only if the government usurped the right to make such decisions. Moreover, they argue that it is no more logical to hold that a group of microscopic, undifferentiated cells, such as those existing in the zygote stage, should be considered a human being than that an acorn should be considered an oak tree. According to Dr. Dominick Purpura of the Albert Einstein Medical School, all human life has brain waves, but brain cell synapses do not even begin to form until the third month, and, "the minimum neurons and synaptic connections necessary for the quality of humanness and 'personhood' . . . begins to occur in the last trimester."[63] Therefore, to proponents of this position, the lines of demarcation proposed by the Supreme Court decision in *Roe* v. *Wade* are supported by the available neurological evidence.

Obviously the entire subject is an incredibly complex one: I haven't even touched on the impact of abortion policies on those who are arguably most affected, the women who must make the decision; but then they are frequently left out of the discussion. Certainly, their needs are not a consideration in the Church's position. How can they be, when the issue for the pope is purely a theological one? There is no reason for the Vatican to debate the sociological, psychological, or even ethical considerations. The pope bases his judgment on two theological premises. First, he maintains that zygotes have souls and are, therefore, human beings (contrary to the position of the foremost Catholic philosophers, Augustine and Aquinas, who believed that ensoulment took place forty days after conception if the fetus was male and eighty days after if it was female).[64] Second, in the pope's opinion, only God has the right to terminate innocent "human" life (although the killing of innocent civilians during wartime is permitted if necessary for victory).

Shortly before this writing, a Medical Center opened in Erie County, New York, offering *in vitro* fertilization for patients requiring medical assistance with conception and implementation. You would think that the prelates of the Church would be delighted with the prospect of conception since they are so opposed to anything that interferes with procreation. But the local Catholic bishop pressured the state university medical school, under whose auspices the clinic operated, to shut it down on the grounds that any discarded blastocysts are human beings and this involved murder.[65] This is tantamount to saying that every spared acorn is a saved oak tree. It completely ignores the elementary fact that many more embryos are lost in "natural" conception than during *in vitro* conception. What is most appalling is the blatant attempt to enforce on all persons by power of law the specific morality of the Catholic Church.

As to your belief that today's Catholics are not unduly influenced by the moral dictates of the Vatican, if the pope were the neutral influence you suppose, Catholics could be expected to be split on the issue in proportion to the views of the general population. Such is not the case, however. Despite the relatively large number of Catholic women who have gotten abortions, most Catholics side with the Christian fundamentalists on the issue of abortion and seek a constitutional amendment outlawing it. The consequence would be that any woman who gets an abortion would run the risk of being sentenced to jail for murder.

G: I doubt that most Catholics want to label a woman who had an abortion as a murderer and send her to jail.

J: Probably not. Few people whom I have talked to have thought the question through that far, which is exactly the problem with blindly following authoritative dictates.

G: So you extend your condemnation of the Church to all Catholics.

J: Absolutely not. However, I do believe they are quite mistaken to maintain their allegiance to the Roman Catholic Church. No doubt a great many of those professing the Catholic faith are truly enlightened individuals and recognize that to make the world a better, happier place for each of us requires that we make it a better place for all. For them the brotherhood—I prefer the nonsexist term "kinship"— of the human race is a goal worth sacrificing for, and at times worth dying for. But this enlightened worldview has little to do with the institution of the Roman Catholic Church. It is in spite of, rather than because of, the Church that many Catholics reach this point in their moral development.

I think there is ample historical evidence to support the maxim alleged of Jesus: "By their fruits you shall know them." The only reasonable way to judge the merits of any institution is by the policies it adopts and the actions of the individuals it produces. My experience as a former Catholic is that its followers are no better or worse than any other group of people. That historically Catholics have been led to some pretty intolerable actions against those who had different belief systems is the fault of the Church hierarchy and the doctrines it espouses. But to attempt to separate the institution of the Church from the repressive policies and crimes of the popes, as some would like to do, is tantamount to saying that fascism was unfortunate to have been represented by Hitler, Mussolini, and Franco, or that totalitarianism is really a benevolent system of government suffering undue criticism due to the policies of a few bad leaders such as Joseph Stalin and Idi Amin.

In a way it is a real shame. An organization as large, visible, and ubiquitous as the Catholic Church could be a tremendous force for good in this world. Unfortunately, theologian Hans Küng was correct when he wrote that, "theology and the Church have been more interested in the baseness and sinful state of the individual than in the enslavement and impoverishment of whole classes."[66]

Can the pope and the Catholic Church change to become an active force for social progress in the world? I doubt that it will happen. All the evidence indicates that the pope is attempting to leverage his carefully orchestrated popularity campaign to reassert his supremacy over Catholic thought. Those who believe that they can reform a basically authoritarian institution such as the Church will, in all probability, be sadly mistaken.

3

The New Testament: Source of Inspiration, or Fabrication?

That is the way of the world—human beings make gods and worship their creation. It would be appropriate for the gods to worship human beings.

—Gospel of Philip

J: Our review of Catholicism leads invariably to the conclusion that we can no more rely on the pope to represent God than an ayatollah, evangelist, or shaman.

G: Even if I were to agree with your conclusion, it would be inconsequential since my will can be ascertained by study of the sacred scriptures.

J: But on what basis can we believe the infallibility or even credibility of the scriptures?

G: So now you are also rejecting the Word of God as given in the Bible?

J: Well, let's examine the document as objectively as possible, beginning with the New Testament. Most people today are unaware that no original manuscripts or direct copies of the New Testament exist— only copies of copies. Moreover, the copiers were under no orders to be exact. There is no way of knowing how much personal bias, hyperbole, or conjecture was added to the original oral tradition, which itself was almost totally derived from ancient myths, as I shall demonstrate. The earliest New Testament document still in existence is an epistle attributed to Paul and dated about 60 C.E. The oldest fragment of a gospel is John Ryland's scrap of papyrus that is no bigger than a thumbnail. It is assumed to be from the Gospel of John and is dated no earlier than 130 C.E. It is generally conceded that the other gospels were written prior to John's. But the earliest, that attributed to Mark, was not written before 70 C.E. And in the absence of any first person accounts to verify accuracy, twenty to thirty years after the death of Jesus is certainly long enough to begin the process of legend building.

G: You talk with such certitude, but isn't the dating process just so much conjecture?

J: These dates are generally accepted by biblical scholars based on internal evidence in the writings: the style, linguistic structure, and historical references and hints gained from the text itself.[1] For example, a New Testament reference to the destruction of Jerusalem is a pretty safe prophecy if it was included in a text written after the fact. The so-called prophecy of Jesus becomes less than remarkable when considered in this light. Prophesying the eventual destruction of a Middle East city was a safe bet in any case. There wasn't one that escaped being destroyed at least once, and some were devastated many times. It becomes even more suspicious when only the author of Luke mentions the prophecy. In that work, which was written well after 70 C.E., the author admits that his account is based purely on hearsay. More about prophecies in a minute.

G: It's your book. Take all the time you want. I have an eternity.

J: I'll try to be brief. The important fact concerning Mark's Gospel is that, like all the gospels, it was written in Greek. The Catholic Church maintains that Matthew was written in Aramaic, but the earliest manuscripts don't bear out this contention.[2] There is no solid evidence to support the theory that any versions of the gospels were earlier than the Greek.

The everyday language of the Israelites at the time of Jesus was Aramaic. Hebrew was the formal language used in ceremonies and in educated discourse, much as Latin was later under the rule of the Church. So why are our copies written in Greek? The reason was to take the story and teachings of Jesus to the Gentiles. But the Greek texts present an obstacle. Jesus himself left no writings; nor, it would appear, did any of his disciples. It seems that the first written accounts of the legend of Jesus were translations of an oral tradition into a foreign language by an unknown author at least three decades after the death of Jesus.

G: So you don't believe the gospels are eyewitness accounts written by disciples of Jesus.

J: You've got it. The writer of Mark must have been in a place far from Palestine and not intimately familiar with Jewish law. For example, he has Jesus telling the pharisees that, "if the wife puts away her husband and marries another, she commits adultery" (Mark 10:12). But as G. A.

Wells points out, under Jewish law only men were allowed to get a divorce. So it would have been a meaningless statement to an Israelite. However, it did make sense as a command to a gentile and that was the audience which the writer of Mark was addressing.[3]

The writers of Matthew and Luke based their writings on Mark. Mark begins his account with the public life of Jesus. It is the most direct and least embellished of the four gospels. Matthew's story of the birth of Jesus is full of miraculous signs and wonders. Luke's pro-Roman slant was written to reassure the Romans that they had nothing to fear from the fast-growing Christian cult. The gospel according to John, the character and events of which are so different, appears to have been written some time later, perhaps around 100 to 125 C.E. The writer of John is interested in establishing not merely the messiahship of Jesus, but his divinity.

Luke admits that there were many other gospel accounts: "Inasmuch as many have undertaken to draw up a narrative concerning the things that have been fulfilled among us, even as they who were eyewitnesses and ministers of the word have handed them down to us" (Luke 1:1-3). He refers to persons other than himself as eyewitnesses, but never mentions who they were or whether he is getting the story firsthand, second-hand, or what.

Interesting, too, he mentions that there were many other narratives, as indeed there were. There were gospels attributed to Thomas, Paul, Philip and Mary, the Apocryphon of John, the Apocalypse of Peter, the Wisdom of Jesus Christ, the Testimony of Truth, the Dialogues of the Savior, the Book of Enoch, the Acts of Peter and Paul, the works of Barnabus, the Shepherd of Hermas, the Didach (the teachings of the Twelve Apostles), and only You know how many others. The existence of many of these came to light with the 1945 discovery of fifty-two texts at Nag Hammadi in upper Egypt. These writings of an early Christian sect known as the Gnostics show that there were major differences of opinion among the early Christians as to who Jesus was, what he taught, and the duties of his followers. I think it may be quite illuminating to spend a moment reviewing the Gnostic teachings.

G: Is this little side trip really necessary?

J: Since the outcome of that dispute has shaped the beliefs of millions of Christians today, it is important to understand the opposing viewpoint and why it engendered such vitriolic criticism from the Church hierarchy such as Irenaeus, who called the Gnostics agents of Satan.

The Gnostic Gospels

The texts discovered at Nag Hammadi were Coptic translations of more ancient manuscripts made around 350 to 400 C.E. The originals, written in Greek, are referred to in the writings of the Church Fathers in the second century. Some scholars argue that they might even predate the canonical gospels.[4] That any of the texts were found after all these centuries is remarkable since they were ordered destroyed by the early bishops who, understandably, considered them a serious threat to their theology and personal status as princes of the new church. Elaine Pagels presents a very readable account of the Gnostic Gospels in her book by the same name. My intent is not to evaluate the merits of Gnostic theology or philosophy; rather I wish only to show that there was a wide range of belief among the early Christians, and the eventual outcome was more a matter of the political intrigues and psychological needs of the believers than any objective investigation or divine inspiration.

The Gnostic texts present us with a variety of theological perspectives, all reflecting a strong Eastern influence. The basic cosmological framework appears to be derived from Zoroastrianism. The Jewish God, Yahweh, is not viewed as the ultimate God. In an effort to explain the source of evil in the world, some Gnostics believed that the world was created by a good god, but was being managed by a lesser god who, puffed up by his own importance, demanded obsequious obedience from his subjects. The Testimony of Truth relates a very different version of the Adam and Eve legend. In it, the serpent rightly convinces Adam and Eve to partake of the fruit of divine wisdom, despite the threats of a Lord who expels them from Paradise for gaining the knowledge which he jealously sought to prevent them from attaining.

Self-knowledge (*gnosis*) was the ultimate goal of the Gnostics. On the deepest level, knowing oneself was simultaneously to know God because "the self and the divine are identical."[5] Since the road to knowledge was basically through introspection, such a belief posed an immediate threat to the bishops of the emerging Church who held themselves up as the sole repository of truth.

The second threat to those who wished to establish an institutional religion came from the conception of Jesus professed by the Gnostics. There appears to have been more than one belief in this regard. Some of the Gnostic writers, such as the author of the Acts of John, believed that Jesus was not a man at all but a spiritual being who assumed a human appearance.[6] In the opinion of other writers Jesus was very corporeal indeed. According to the Gospel of Philip:

> The companion of the [Savior is] Mary Magdalene. [But Christ loved] her more than [all] the disciples and used to kiss her [often] on her [mouth]. The rest of the disciples were offended. . . . They said to him, "Why do you love her more than all of us?" The Savior answered and said to them, "Why do I not love you as [I love her]?"[7]

G: With repartee like that, it is no wonder the Church Fathers decided to leave this Gospel off the list of Canonical Gospels. Such writing is too nonsensical to be taken seriously.

J: That is exactly what many Gnostics thought of the story of the virgin birth and the bodily resurrection of Jesus. And don't forget the Gnostics were all Christians too. But they relied upon their own sacred works such as the Gospel of Thomas, which alleges to be "the secret words which the living Jesus spoke, and which the twin, Judas Thomas, wrote down."[8] Moreover, according to Professor Helmut Koester, this gospel may be based on a tradition older than the New Testament gospels.[9]

It may sound silly when "The Second Treatise of the Great Seth" relates Christ's teaching that it wasn't He but another who died in His place. But if we did not already believe that Jesus was God, would it appear any more reasonable to believe that a man rose form the dead? My point is not to argue that the accounts related in these other gospels have more validity than the New Testament gospels. I only wish to show that there is no reason to suppose that the New Testament gospels are any more reliable as a historical account of what happened 2,000 years ago than any of the many other accounts suppressed by those who eventually gained total control of the early Church.

G: You assume that the Church hierarchy had ulterior motives for rejecting the other Gospel accounts. Might it not be that the Church officials simply desired to weed out the truth from fiction?

J: If that was their intent they failed miserably, as we shall see. But their purpose was not to search for truth, rather it was an attempt to build support for their claim that they were the legitimate heirs to Christ's spiritual authority, and had a moral imperative to establish an institution that was divinely guided to represent His will. For many Christians such a presumption was blasphemous and no more than a raw grab for power.

G: Perhaps that is why the Gnostics inveighed against the bishops as in the "Apocalypse of Peter":

> Others . . . outside our number . . . call themselves bishops and also deacons, as if they had received their authority from God. . . . Those people are waterless canals.[10]

J: Very possibly. No bishop was going to decree the truth for the Gnostics. For them knowledge was attained only by individual striving: "Bring in your guide and your teacher. The mind is the guide, but reason is the teacher. . . ."[11] According to Pagels, the Gnostics understood Christ's message "not as offering a set of answers, but as encouragement to engage in a process of searching."[12]

For the Gnostics, Christ was a teacher who presented parables and paradoxes that guided the follower on the path to truth. Ultimately, however, that truth had to be discovered by each person for himself or herself. The "Teachings of Silvanus" sound Socratic when they urge: "before everything else . . . know yourself."[13] According to Pagels the gnostics had such a high regard for knowledge that "many insisted that ignorance, not sin, is what involves a person in suffering."[14] Such an idea would rightly be construed as aiming at the very heart of the new priestly caste for two reasons. First, it meant that individuals might hold any theological opinion they wished without danger of moral or physical reprisals. Second, it negated the position fostered by the Church Fathers that only the priest acting as Christ's representative could grant absolution for sin. This meant that the priest was no longer necessary for an individual's salvation. That, in the end, the Gnostic's view regarding sin did not prevail turned out to be a great tragedy for humankind. The full consequence of the Christian concept of sin would not be felt until the Church wedded her spiritual power to the state's political power. But the idea that sin rather than ignorance was the great evil was the keystone for the most powerful, durable moral tyranny the world has ever known. Without the concept of sin the Inquisition would never have happened.

G: There still would have been war and persecutions. Such is the nature of man.

J: Perhaps, but at least such actions could not have been justified as a moral necessity, thus enlisting the support of many people who felt they were serving You in the commission of their atrocities. The mindset of the Gnostics was not conducive to the blind faith advocated by evangelists such as Paul. The "Testimony of Truth" bluntly states that, "Faith in the sacraments shows naive and magical thinking."[15] Nor did the gnostics share the popular eschatological beliefs of their fellow Christians. They thought the idea of the Second Coming of Christ was nonsense: "His disciples said to Him, 'When will . . . the new world come?' He said to them, 'What you look forward to has already come, but you do not recognize it.' "[16]

The lack of dogmatism and the greater concern with the here-and-now acted to temper the passions of the Gnostic Christians. This is shown in their criticism of those Christians who rushed to martyrdom to gain salvation. To the Gnostics this was sheer fanaticism.

G: The Gnostics simply lacked the courage to die for their beliefs.

J: Such courage the world doesn't need. I have great respect for those who are willing to risk their lives to defend their fellow men and women from oppression. But people who are willing to throw away their lives for a cause are usually willing to throw away someone else's life as well.

The third danger posed by the literature of the Gnostics to the orthodox Church hierarchy was the notion of equality. Tertullian criticized the Gnostics because "it is uncertain who is a catechumen, and who is a believer: they all have access equally, they listen equally, they pray equally—even pagans if they happen to come. . . . They also share the kiss of peace with all who happen to come. . . ."[17]

The Gnostics' devotion to equality was exemplary. They cast lots to determine who would lead the worship and—horror of horrors— they even invited women to act as priests. It appears that the Gnostics feared that the new church was going to follow the Judaic patriarchal tradition. The author of the Gnostic text *Pistis Sophia* (*Faith Wisdom*) has Mary Magdalene complain, "Peter makes me hesitate; I am afraid of him, because he hates the female race."[18] Unlike the early disciples of Jesus, most of the Gnostics were not Jewish. In the religious traditions of Egypt, Greece, Rome, and India the concept of God involved male and female elements; the Gnostics tried to retain the female symbolism. For example, the "Apocryphon of John" refers to the Trinity of God the Father, Mother, and Son. But, ultimately, the Gnostics lost out; the Mother symbol was replaced with the Holy Ghost, and by the third century all feminine imagery was gone. The Epistles of Paul relegated women to a second-class status, and the Church has kept them there ever since.

G: So, according to you, the Church invented misology, sin, and inequality. With all these negative at tributes, isn't it amazing that it was the Church and not the Gnostics who captured men's hearts and minds? How do you account for this success if the doctrines were as stupid and wrong as you make them out?

J: The Church didn't create inequality, it just perpetuated it. In a moment I'll discuss why the Church succeeded. First I need to explain why Gnosticism failed.

In the first place, the Gnostics chose the difficult and oftentimes lonely path of self-discovery. The bishops, on the other hand, offered all the answers; individuals were freed from the burden of having to think for themselves. Second, the Church met the psychological needs of its followers. Believers were offered mystery; ritual; community; a position in the new world order that was to come; and, when it was apparent that the longed-for kingdom was not going to occur in this world, the promise of attaining it in the next. Third, because of the promise of immortality, the orthodox Church was able to attract the more fanatical types willing to suffer the misery and ecstasy of martyrdom. As I mentioned, the more rational Gnostics saw this desire to suffer and die as perverse. The idea that God should welcome such voluntary "human sacrifice" would make God no more than a cannibal.[19]

G: I would hardly call such martyrdom voluntary.

J: In the eyes of the Gnostics it was, since the Christians could avoid it simply by agreeing to honor the state religion as well, thus alleviating the Roman Empire's concern that they had divided loyalties. Let me add, however, that I am not justifying the Gnostic position in this regard; I am just stating it.

Ironically, the last, and probably most important, reason for the success of the Church over Gnosticism was that the Church adopted the institutional framework of the Roman political and military organizations.[20] The strict authoritarianism of the pope was eventually linked to that exercised by the Roman emperors, enabling the Church to drive out any heretical opinions at the point of the sword. After the "orthodox" Christians gained state support for their religion in the fourth century, the few remaining Gnostics learned that being an "agent of Satan," as Irenaeus called them, could result in their own involuntary martyrdom—a particularly distressing prospect to the Gnostics.

G: What was the purpose of this digression into a discussion of Gnosticism?

J: My only purpose was to show that there were dozens of gospels and epistles floating about during the early days of Christianity. They all contained some interesting homilies and a great deal of nonsense. The particular narratives and letters ultimately selected and endorsed by the Church hierarchy reflect its intent to buttress its particular theology and, most importantly, its claim to be the heir to Christ's divine authority.

It wasn't until 367 C.E. that Athanasius of Alexandria suggested a definitive list of the books that should be accepted by the Church as authentic and included in the New Testament. That provided a period of three hundred years to ensure that only those texts were accepted that supported the Church's theology and authoritative claims.

The true identity of the gospel's authors is anyone's guess. There are no signed copies. Papias, the bishop of Hierapoles in about 150 C.E., was the first even to refer to Matthew and Mark. It wasn't until about 180 that Irenaeus, the bishop of Lyons and archenemy of the Gnostics, insisted that there were four gospels and gave names to all four. His reasoning left much to be desired: there could only be four gospels to correspond to the four cardinal points on the earth.

G: None of what you have said negates the fact that these are some very early histories of the life of Jesus.

J: But even a thirty-year span of oral tradition, and the translation from one language to another, allows much room for exaggeration and myth to creep in, even assuming that everyone in the link was trying to be accurate. Probably most of us have tried that old classroom experiment of telling one person a story and then having that person relate it to the next and so on around the room. The final version bears little relationship to the original. That a similar occurrence took place in relating the story of Jesus is evidenced by the many other gospels rejected by the Church primarily because none of them supported its theological position.

Further evidence for the New Testament's lack of historical reliability is gained by comparing the details of the four accounts of the life of Jesus. The differences are significant, and quite surprising given that all four documents are supposedly inspired.[21] Since some of these differences involve basic Christian doctrines, how is the believer to decide which version is the true one? For example, in Mark 10:11 Jesus is quoted as explicitly forbidding divorce for any reason, while in Matt. 19:9 he permits a man to divorce his wife when she is guilty of "immorality." (He unfairly does not offer the same option to women.) Most alarming to Christian biblical scholars is the apparent denial by Jesus that he is God: "Why dost thou call me good? No one is good but only God" (Mark 10:18). Other examples of confusion on the part of the gospel authors include a basic ignorance of Palestinian geography (Mark 7:31); a repetition of the miracles of the loaves and fishes in which the apostles appear to have completely forgotten the earlier miracle; and completely different genealogies for Jesus. I'll discuss additional discrepancies when we review the accounts of the resurrection. (A detailed analysis of differences in the gospel accounts is provided by R. Joseph Hoffmann in the "Origins of Christianity."[22])

The important point to remember is that it was never the intent of the gospel writers to provide an accurate history of the life of Jesus. Rather, they had several other purposes for their writings:

• to prove that Jesus was the Messiah by demonstrating that he fulfilled the Old Testament prophecies concerning the Messiah;

- to establish the belief that Jesus was divine, the Son of God, by creating many supernatural events surrounding his birth and death and claiming that he could work miracles;

- to demonstrate that the death of Jesus did not occur contrary to the prophecies but in accordance with them;

- to reassure those who began to suspect that the end of time and new kingdom promised by Jesus were not about to occur any time soon; and

- to establish a basis for acceptance of the orthodox Christian theology, primarily as formulated by Paul.[23]

We can't take the time to disucss each of these purposes, but G. A. Wells presents a compelling argument in his book, *The Historical Evidence for Jesus.* Let it suffice to say that the letters of Paul do not quote a single saying of Jesus, nor mention any of His teachings. They do, however, provide the basic theological framework for Christianity. Since the epistles of Paul were written *prior* to the gospels, it appears that the gospels were written (or at least edited) to support Paul's theology.

G: So you refuse to admit the possibility that not only the writers of the gospels, but the early Church Fathers were divinely inspired as Pope Leo XII declared in *Providentissimus Deus* (*The Most Provident God*):

> For all the books which the Church receives as sacred and canonical are written wholly and entirely with all their parts (this includes both the Old Testament and the New Testament) at the dictation of the Holy Spirit. And so far it is from being possible that any error can coexist with inspiration, that inspiration not only is essentially incompatible with error, but excludes and rejects it as absolutely and necessarily as it is impossible that God Himself, the Supreme Truth, can utter that which is not true.

J: Fine words, but simply claiming something to be true doesn't demonstrate its validity. In the final analysis, all the Church presents is a classic example of convoluted logic. The Church bases its authority on the New Testament which it contends is divinely inspired. How do we know this? Because the Church says so. Why should we believe the Church? Because it speaks for God. On what basis are we asked to believe this? On the evidence in a book written by the Church founders. 'Round and 'round we go.

G: You obviously intend to offer evidence to support your alternative theories regarding the origin of the New Testament. It had better be very strong.

J: The evidence is overwhelming.

G: I still say you have little chance of convincing anyone that the New Testament isn't My divinely inspired word.

J: You are probably right. But in the interest of truth, I'll give it a shot anyway. I don't really hope to convince the brainwashed fundamentalists or those who are unable or unwilling to critically reappraise their beliefs in the light of new information. My focus is on the few who are still seeking to ascertain the truth. If a better world order is ever to be possible, it will come from those who build on fact rather than myth, boldly facing reality rather than running from it to hide in self-delusion and fantasy.

The Gospels and Old Testament Prophesies

The care with which the gospels attempt to show that Jesus fulfilled Old Testament prophecies is typified by the many gospel stories ending with the tag that Jesus did such and such so that the scriptural prophecy would be fulfilled. One gets the feeling that the gospel writers did a careful search of the prophecies and descriptions of the Messiah and then constructed incidents and relationships in their story of Jesus to prove He did indeed fill the bill.

G: An imaginative theory. But I doubt if you can back it up with proof.

J: Well, it is impossible to know for certain the stylistic techniques of those who constructed the gospel almost 2,000 years ago. However, there are two equally plausible explanations, both of which are more reasonable than the inspiration theory because they also account for the many errors and contradictions among the four gospels. The first, which I indicated above, is similar to the explanation provided by Bible scholar Randel Helms.[24] But his theory has a slightly different slant. According to Helms, the writers of the gospels believed that if the Old Testament works predicted something, it must have happened. Therefore, to fill in the details of the life of Jesus one need only search the scriptures for quotes that could be interpreted to be prophetic and ascribe the deeds foretold to the life of Jesus. Helms provided several examples of this technique. The gospel writers also appear to have borrowed freely from the second-century B.C.E. religious work known as The Testament of the Twelve Patriarchs. For example, in this work we find the statement that "the heavens shall be opened unto him to pour out the spirit,"[25] paraphrased in the New Testament as "When Jesus came up out of the water he saw the heaven torn open, and the spirit, like a dove descended on him" (Mark 1:10).

The Dead Sea Scrolls provide additional evidence that this was a common technique of the Essenes, a Jewish sect that may have been the forerunner of the early Christians. They employed this practice in writing about their Teacher of Righteousness.

The other even more probable explanation is that the prophecies were created or misinterpreted to appear to support the story of Jesus. Many Bible exegetes have demonstrated the so-called prophecies were fallaciously used to support the claim that Jesus was God. In 1794 Thomas Paine published his now classic work, *The Age of Reason,* and thoroughly discredited the use of prophecy in the New Testament.[26] Paine's treatment was not original; he was following the work of the Deistic scholars. But his style was addressed to the common man and thus he was widely read. This earned him the enmity of Christian zealots down to the present day. It didn't matter that his book *Common Sense* provided encouragement for the American Revolution, or that George Washington ordered Paine's words ("These are the times that try men's souls . . .") read to his troops to inspire them to their Christmas Eve victory at Trenton. Nor do the zealots care that Paine was one of the first to call for democratic representation, the end of slavery, universal suffrage, popular education, relief of the poor, pensions for the aged, aid to the unemployed and even religious freedom. No Christian sect was calling for such reforms at the time. The only thing that interested and infuriated Christians was Paine's effort to critique the New Testament's claim that Jesus was God. The predictable reaction was an attempt to have Paine deported and, failing that, to hound him for the rest of his life. Even Paine's death couldn't sate their wrath; his bones were dug up and sent to England. To this day, the fundamentalists share the view of Ellen White, the plagiarist founder of the Seventh-Day Adventist's cult, that Paine was "one of the vilest and most corrupt of men, one who despised God and His law."[27]

What did Paine write that earned him such a vitriolic attack? All he did was examine each prophecy the New Testament claimed was made in reference to Jesus and show that either (a) there was no such prophecy in the Old Testament, (b) the speaker was referring to a past event, (c) the speaker was referring to a concurrent event, (d) it was an allegorical statement, or (e) it was a short term prophecy and the event referred to occurred long before the time of Jesus. In any case, the Old Testament words were taken out of context and reinterpreted to fit the needs of the Gospel writers.

G: I recall Paine's analysis, but it doesn't prove that the prophecies were false.

J: In most cases they weren't even prophecies. Here are a few examples offered by Paine. First, Matthew writes of an angel appearing to Joseph in a dream to tell him that Mary is pregnant by the Holy Ghost. In alleging divine parentage, which was a necessary prerequisite for all ancient heroes, Matthew says that it was done, "that what was spoken by the Lord through the prophet might be fulfilled, 'Behold the virgin shall be with child and shall bring forth a son and they shall call his name Emmanuel' " (Matt. 1:23). Now my Confraternity Edition of the Bible is thorough enough to reference the Old Testament verse to which Matthew is referring. Paine also found the reference in Isa. 7:14: "Behold a virgin shall conceive and bear a son, and his name shall be called Emmanuel."*

The context from which this quote is inappropriately lifted is explained in the preceding Old Testament verses. Achaz, who was King of Judea at the time, was worried that the Kings of Israel and Syria were going to conquer him in war and so God—You—supposedly tried to reassure Achaz by giving him a sign that You were on his side. The immediately preceding verse says, "Therefore the Lord himself shall give you a sign." Shortly thereafter, the sign is given: "and I went to the prophetess and she conceived and bore me a son" (Isa. 8:3). God tells Achaz that before the child grows up he will have conquered his enemies. Achaz then boasts to his new son, Emmanuel, how God is going to drown the kin of the Assyrians (Isa. 8:8). He acknowledges that the prophesized sign was received: "Behold I and my children who the Lord hath given me for a sign, and for a wonder in Israel from the Lord of Hosts . . ." (Isa. 8:18). As in the case of several other prophecies, the New Testament writer fails to mention that the prophecy he referenced was already fulfilled! Of course, all Jewish biblical scholars recognized this fact and hence are unimpressed (if not outraged) by the evangelist's journalistic dishonesty.

Let's take another example from Paine. In the second chapter of Matthew, the author describes another dream of Joseph (although how Matthew knows what goes on in Joseph's dreams is beyond the comprehension of both Paine and me).

G: Must I keep reminding you that the evangelists were divinely inspired?

J: We've already been around that circuit. Such an assessment should be based on evidence rather than mere assumption. And we have just

---

*The references I use are from the Catholic Confraternity Edition and will differ slightly from the King James or other Protestant Bibles.

begun to review the evidence. At any rate, Matthew tells how another angel (or maybe it was the same one, all those angels look alike I am told) tells Joseph to flee to Egypt in order to escape Herod. Joseph does so and stays in Egypt until Herod dies, "that what was spoken by the Lord through the prophet might be fulfilled: 'out of Egypt I called my son' " (Matt. 3:15). The reference here is to Osee 11:1 (Hosea in the King James Version used by Paine). The complete passage is "Because Israel was a child, and I loved him, and I called my son out of Egypt." The preceding verses in the Old Testament make it clear that Israel refers to the Israelites. And in the subsequent verse the Old Testament writer laments that after leaving Egypt, the Israelites soon fell into idolatry: "as they called them they went away from before their face; they offered victims to Baalim and sacrificed to idols" (Osee 11:2). For the writer of Matthew to suggest that calling "my son out of Egypt" refers to Jesus, is an obvious attempt to deceive the reader by claiming a prophetic basis that doesn't exist.

G: Perhaps the writer did let his imagination get the better of him on that one, but you can't be certain he was deliberately trying to deceive.

J: Randel Helms and John Allegro would agree with you.[28] It might have simply been the style of the times to search ancient texts for clues to future occurrences. G. A. Wells and others are more critical. Supported by a good deal of evidence, they believe that the specific Old Testament references were worked into the text to support a theological position.[29] But whatever the reason, it is a deception nonetheless. Let's take another example.

G: This is getting tedious.

J: Really? Let's jump ahead a little to Matthew's narration of Jesus casting out evil spirits and curing the sick for the purpose "that what was spoken through Isaiah the prophet might be fulfilled who said, 'He himself took up our infirmities and bore the burdens for our ills' " (Matt. 8:17). The incident itself reflects the pagan superstition that sickness was caused by demonic possession. Such a belief would have seemed absurd to the Hebrews. However, today some people still believe that Satan causes ill-health.

At any rate, the Old Testament reference to which Matthew alludes is chapter 53 of Isaiah, which appears to be no more than a long eulogy on the death of a friend. Like many of the books of the Old Testament, the chapters of Isaiah are disjointed and may be just fragments of longer works thrown together. We don't know to whom the author of Isaiah is referring; chapter 53 doesn't flow from 52 or continue in chapter 54. However, there is nothing in the chapter to indicate that it was meant as a prophecy. The description of a good man suffering from injustice and infirmities could apply to many people in any age. More importantly, the man whom the writer of Isaiah is discussing is referred to in the past tense throughout. As Paine points out, the Israelites lived in times of great sorrow and danger; why should we later distort their thoughts on their times and countrymen into prophecies? I've no doubt that with a little imagination the Old Testament verses could be misinterpreted as a prophecy about any real or mythical person, just as today some people attempt to interpret the incoherent ramblings of Nostradamus as prophecies of current events. Certainly the passages in chapter 53 could be applied to the legendary Prometheus, who suffered so cruelly for giving man fire, or to many a persecuted philosopher or scholar from Socrates to Paine himself.

G: And you, too, I suppose?

J: Luckily, the situation is different today—unless we get a fundamentalist in the White House.

My last example (although Paine offers many more) is the description of Judas and the thirty pieces of silver, which concludes, "Then what was spoken through Jeremias the prophet was fulfilled, 'And they took the thirty pieces of silver, the price of him who was priced, upon whom the children of Israel set a price; and they gave them for the potter's field as the Lord directed me' " (Matt. 27:9,10). This is a particularly interesting example because the Catholic Confraternity Edition uses a different Old Testament reference than the passage found by Thomas Paine. The Catholic Bible references Zacharias 11:12, which is written in the poetic style of ancient myths:

> And I said to them: "If it be good in your eyes bring hither my wages; and if not, be quite." And they weighed for my wages thirty pieces of silver. And the Lord said to me: Cast it to the statuary, a handsome price, that I was prized at by them. And I took the thirty pieces of silver, and I cast them into the house of the Lord to the statuary.

It doesn't take a genius to see that the only relationship between this verse and Matthew's story of Judas is the thirty pieces of silver. What is surprising is that the Confraternity Edition references Zacharias as if it indeed had some relevance to Matthew's account, which it obviously does not, other than the coincidental—or borrowed—number thirty. Paine, on the other hand, refers to an incident in chapter 32 where Jeremias relates how at Your directive he buys a field from his cousin for seventeen shekels of silver. My surprise at learning that

You get involved in minor business deals on behalf of Your people aside, it is obvious that the passage also has no prophetic relevance to Matthew's story. I could go on and relate Paine's discussion of the fallacies of every other prophetic reference, but I'd just be belaboring the point.

G: I think you already have.

J: I disagree. Anyone who puts any stock in the New Testament should read Paine to see the lengths to which the writer of Matthew went to persuade the ignorant and uneducated that Jesus was a special person or the Messiah foretold by Old Testament prophets. Now it might be questioned how the writer of Matthew could have believed that such a clumsy attempt at twisting Old Testament passages would persuade any reasonable person.

It should be obvious that the writer of Matthew was not trying to persuade future biblical scholars. Rather, he was providing spurious evidence to poor, illiterate people who would accept his testimony at face value without checking it. Of course, it didn't convince many Jews. However, the Gentiles, who were completely ignorant of the Old Testament, were an easy mark for his deceit. And it set a pattern. From then on the Church would continually reinterpret the Old Testament in an attempt to show that it was written to herald the coming of Jesus. And anyone who openly disagreed ran the risk of being imprisoned and tortured until he saw the "truth" of the Church's teachings. It was only after the waning of the Church's power that men like theologians David Strauss and Bruno Bauer, and political activist Thomas Paine could point out how ludicrous and downright deceitful much of the New Testament was. But they were fighting an uphill battle against a culturally entrenched myth.

G: Even if the prophetic underpinnings of Matthew's accounts are debatable, you have not demonstrated that the entire New Testament is a myth. I note that you have not even alluded to the works of the other three Evangelists.

J: No, it would be a waste of time. It is much the same in the other three gospel versions. Each writer freely took portions of the Old Testament out of context, interposed them in his narration, and then incorrectly dubbed them prophecies.

G: Although your argument is persuasive, it can't be proved.

J: You want proof? Nothing concerning religion or theism can be proved. I think everyone is willing to admit that today. The real question is this: What does the preponderance of evidence lead us to reasonably conclude.

G: Don't get so excited, you won't sleep again tonight.

J: You're right. I'll want to spend more time on the subject of proof later. But before I leave this discussion of prophecies, I would like to point out the obvious fallacy of the most famous prophecy of all: Jesus' prediction of the imminent end of the world. In Matthew for example, He describes the terrible events leading to the destruction of the world and the return of the Son of Man upon the "clouds of heaven," and then concludes that "this generation will not pass away until all these things have been accomplished" (Matt. 24: 29–35). This theme is repeated several time in the gospels and repeated in the writings of His followers. (See, for example, Heb. 1:2, 1 Cor. 7:2, 1 Peter 4:2, 1 Peter 1:20, and James 5:8. George Smith lists several other references.)[30]

G: In referring to the end of things, Jesus was talking metaphorically about the imminent changes in the world order and institutions which were to occur.

J: Nice try, sounds like the attempt of the Church to reconcile his colossal error with reality. But You know that Jesus was simply reflecting the common belief of the time that the world was about to end. During each age, there are usually people who, seeing the wickedness and evil around them, conclude that God must certainly be getting fed up with the results of His experiment in creation and will, therefore, decide to sweep the decks clean except for a select few. Just recently such a group was disappointed to find that the day of destruction predicted by their messiah was in error. As for Jesus' prophetic abilities, he (fortunately for us) rates no better than the soothsayers of today.

Now let's turn to the second purpose for which the gospels were written: to establish the divinity of Jesus by ascribing many supernatural events to his life and his death.

4

Christianity or Neopaganism: What's in a Name?

The Devil has his Christs.

—Firmicus

J: When I first studied the myths that gave birth to the ancient religions, it came as a shock to discover that nothing in the gospel story of Jesus was original. Virtually every ancient religion had similar myths and many of these religions predated the alleged birth of Christ by hundreds, even thousands of years. As W. R. Cassels points out, "There has not been a single historical religion largely held among men which has not pretended to be divinely revealed, and the written books of which have not been represented as directly inspired. There is not a single doctrine, sacrament or vita of Christianity which has not substantially formed part of an earlier religion."[1]

Perhaps this should have been expected when we reflect that the early Fathers of the Church were converted from various pagan religions. Tertullian, Gregory, Pantaeus, Clement of Alexandria, and Origen are but a few who were raised in pagan beliefs. The real question is, were they converted to Christianity or did they convert the incipient Christian beliefs to a new pagan religion?

Many of the pagan gods were thought to control the fertility of all nature, including humans. The gods were the personification of the most fundamental, least understood and, hence, mystical processes witnessed by early man. The noted British ethnologist Sir James Frazer wrote: "Under the name of Osiris, Adonis (Tammuz), and Attis, the peoples of Egypt and Western Asia represented the yearly decay and revival of life, which they personified as a god who annually died

104

and rose again from the dead."[2] In his classic work, *The Golden Bough,* Frazer describes how the worship of Adonis was practiced by the Semitic people of Babylonia and Syria. The Greeks borrowed the practice from them as early as the seventh century B.C.E. The original name for Adonis was Tammuz, and the Old Testament relates that the prophet Ezechiel saw women mourning for Tammuz at the north gate of the Temple. Ancient Greeks such as the teacher Empedocles and the kings Antigonus I and Demetrius Poliorcetes were also worshiped by their followers as gods, and appropriate myths as to their incredible miracles and powers were spread by their disciples.

Farther east we find the myth of Krishna, which even many Christian scholars have come to admit was long before the time of Jesus.

G: Krishna—Christ—doesn't the similarity of names make you a little suspicious that this legend was derived from the story of Christ?

J: Of course, that is what Christian scholars would like us to believe. But the word "Krishna" is actually Sanskrit for "Dark God."[3] The word "Christ," on the other hand, means "anointed one" (from the Greek *Christos*). The name Jesus Christ is incorrect; the proper form should be Jesus, the Christ.

That Krishna predated Jesus is attested in the works of two Greek historians, Arrian and Strabo. They wrote that Krishna was worshiped during the time of Alexander the Great.[4] Historians believe the worship of Krishna dates prior to Homer—perhaps 900 years before Jesus.[5] Moreover, we know that Hinduism has changed very little over the last three thousand years, and Hindu beliefs are based on the oldest Vedic legends.

Then there is Buddha, who predates Jesus by more than five centuries. There is evidence that thousands of the disciples of Buddha went to other lands to spread their religion. A comparison of the legend of Buddha with that of Jesus has led T. W. Doane to conclude that the Jesus story is simply a copy of Buddha with a mixture of mythology borrowed from other religions.

Doane's meticulously researched work titled *Bible Myths and Their Parallels in Other Religions,* like so many such documents, incurred the full wrath of the Christian religions, which sought to prevent its publication and circulation. At the time of its appearance (1833), books contradicting Christian beliefs were ignored by respectable journals. Public libraries and bookstores wouldn't touch them. Such literature was banned from the mails and publishers were in danger of prosecution under blasphemy laws. Their authors were ostracized and omitted from standard works. Hence, despite his erudition, Doane is virtually unknown today.

Doane provides a detailed comparison of the similarities of the Buddha legend not only with that of Jesus, but also with that of Krishna and the other heroes and gods of antiquity. According to Doane, the Buddha legends may even predate Krishna since Buddha's origins are based on the ancient legends of the gods Sumana and Chakrawarti.[6]

G: So all that is written about Jesus is no more than a collection of myths? There are many who would call that allegation blasphemy.

J: Exactly. In the good old days they would have had people like me tortured and killed for daring to express such an opinion. For that matter, many countries still have blasphemy laws, punishable by fines or jail sentences. Let's review the similarities Doane so carefully examined.

The Virgin Birth

Let's start at the beginning of the story of Jesus, with a virgin named Mary who managed to conceive without benefit of a man. The very name of the alleged mother of Jesus harks back to the ancient legends. The mother of Adonis was Myrrha, Buddha's mother was Maya, and Hermes' mother was called Maia. They all sound a little familiar don't they? As for the virgin birth, like all Christians, I was taught that this was an incredible, unique event. Imagine my chagrin when I discovered that virgin births were so common among the ancients that just about anybody who had distinguished himself was thought to be of supernatural origin. Krishna was believed to be the incarnation of Vishnu. His mother, Denahi, bore the title Mother of God. Buddha's mother was also a virgin. The Egyptian God Horus was son of the virgin goddess Isis. Other virgin sons include the Persian's Zoroaster, Codow of the Siamese, Fo-hi and Yu of China, the Mayan's Zama, the Aztecs' Quetzalcoatl, the Greek hero Hercules, the philosopher Pythagoras, and the alleged founder of Rome, Romulus.[7]

All the old Semitic religions included the myth of the mother goddess as well. Perseus was born of Danae, a virgin goddess impregnated with a shower of gold. Nana, the mother of Attis, became pregnant from eating a pomegranate.

G: You cannot compare these absurd ancient myths with the story of the Virgin Mary.

J: Oh, can't I? I submit that they are no more absurd than the Christian myth of impregnation by a "Holy Spirit." It's just that we are familiar with the one myth and not the others. Moreover, as Professor Charles Guignebert points out, the very notion of a virgin birth shows at what an early stage Greek pagan myths had begun influencing the theology of Christianity. Earlier, we discussed Paine's analysis of the prophesy of Isaiah which predicted the birth of Emmanuel. Guignebert explains that the prophesy indicated that Emmanuel would be born of a young woman; the Hebrew word was "haalmah."[8] However, the New Testament writer referred to the Greek version of the Bible where the word had been mistranslated as *parthenos,* or virgin. This was in keeping with the Greek, not Hebrew, tradition of virgin births.

The alleged virginity of the mother of Jesus is a bit difficult to reconcile with the question posed by skeptics of Jesus' messiahship as related in the Gospel of Mark. They ask, "Is not this the carpenter, the son of Mary, the brother of James, Joseph, Jude, and Simon? And, are not also his sisters here with us?" (Mark 6:3)

The writer of Luke also appears to have been under the assumption that Jesus was only one of several children, when he wrote that Mary "brought forth her first-born son," suggesting there were others. The earliest Christians believed that Mary was only a virgin at the birth of Jesus, but subsequently had other children. Helvidius flatly stated that the brothers and sisters referred to in the gospel accounts meant that Mary and Joseph must have had children after the birth of Jesus.[9] But other Church theologians were determined to protect the virginity of Mary through a variety of fanciful explanations. Epiphanius suggests that the brothers and sisters were children of Joseph by a prior marriage. The Church Father Jerome contended that they were only cousins of Jesus. Eventually, The Catholic Church claimed that Mark was using the terms "brother" and "sister" in a spiritual sense. Here is a good example of rationalization being used to twist reality in order to meet preconceived theological ideas. It is the hallmark of theologians down to the present day.

Even the respected Church Father Justin Martyr admitted the commonality of the practice of ascribing virginity to the mothers of the sons of gods when he wrote in his apology to the emperor Hadrian, "By declaring Jesus Christ to be born of a virgin without any human mixture we say no more than what you say of those you style Sons of Jove."[10] The only difference between these other legends of virgin births and that concerning Jesus is the care with which the New Testament traces the genealogy of Jesus. Ironically, to trace the descent of Joseph from King David would be irrelevant if Joseph was not truly the father of Jesus. The other ancient myths are more consistent in that they only speak of the mother's genealogy.

G: You forget that the Old Testament prophecies foretold that the Messiah would be of the House of David. So the writers of the gospel were giving evidence that Joseph was in fact a descendant of David.

J: Joseph, yes; but not Jesus if in fact You, not Joseph, were his father. In other words, Jesus was not a descendant of the House of David if he was truly Your direct descendant. As an aside, I find it amusing that Luke names forty-three generations from David to Jesus, instead of Matthew's twenty-eight; and only three names on the two contradictory lists are the same.[11]

G: Maybe the one writer was tracing the lineage on the side of Joseph while the other was tracing Mary's genealogy.

J: Highly unlikely. The Jewish tradition was to trace ancestry through the male line. The evidence is clear in every other genealogy listed in the Bible. Moreover, the numbers of generations on the two lists differ radically. We need pursue this point no further. Anyone who has studied ancient mythology is aware that all the ancient heroes, both real and imaginary, were thought to be a descendant of godly parentage. Moreover, as philologist John Allegro pointed out, the concept of a divine being coming to earth on a rescue mission was an integral part of the Canaanite fertility religion.[12] And, as I'll later demonstrate, much of the Judeo-Christian religious tradition can be traced to the older Semitic myths of the Middle East such as Assyria and Chaldea. All the virgin birth myths probably are variants of the original myth, which attempts to explain how a barren mother earth of winter becomes impregnated by the divine seed of the sun god in spring to bring forth the fruit of summer.

Before moving on I wish to point out that the earliest gospel, that of Mark, makes no mention of Mary's virginity or any of the other miraculous signs that supposedly accompanied the birth of Jesus. This is further evidence that the myths were added in later accounts to persuade the Gentiles that Jesus was a god.

Portent Stars and Magi

After His conception we have the remarkable incidents surrounding the birth of Jesus. There is the bright star heralding His birth, not unlike the star that announced Buddha and Krishna. The bright star Sirius was the sign of Isis, the maiden, who gave birth to Aion, a personification of Osiris. Every Indian avatar was foretold by a celestial sign.[13] The births of important Greeks and Romans were also frequently announced by new stars. All the Caesars' births were so foretold. The Roman historian Tacitus states that upon the birth of a great man a star appears, and when the person dies it disappears.[14]

Israelite heroes were also provided with wondrous events surrounding their birth: Samson's mother was told of her conception by an angel just as Mary was (Judg. 13:1–24); Samuel's birth was a miracle (I Sam. 1); and an angel also brought the tidings of Anna's conception to the father of John the Baptist (Luke 1:8).

The Dead Sea Scrolls indicate that there was widespread belief that the birth of a Messiah would be announced by a special star as prophesied by Balaam in the Old Testament: "A star shall come forth out of Jacob and a scepter shall arise out of Israel" (Num. 24:17). We have already seen how anxious the New Testament writers were to demonstrate that Jesus fulfilled all Old Testament prophesies, even if they had been previously fulfilled.

There seems to be some confusion among the writers of the gospels as to whether Jesus was born in a house, a stable, or a cave. But their intent is clear: to show that Jesus, although of royal ancestry, was born in humble conditions. All the other virgin-born saviors who had preceded him—Krishna, Bacchus, Adonis, Apollo, Attis, even Abraham of the Old Testament—were born in caves.[15] How-Tseih, the Chinese "Son of Heaven," was protected at birth by sheep and oxen.[16]

Shortly after his birth, although there is some confusion in the gospels as to exactly when, Jesus had three not-so-unusual visitors, the Magi. "Not so unusual," I say, because the Magi really got around. They visited Krishna, Buddha, and Socrates to name just a few.[17] Confucius did Jesus two better, being visited at birth by five wise men.[18] In all instances the visitors recognized the child as the savior of humankind.

The Dangerous Child

The next major event in the life of Christ is the Slaughter of the Innocents. It is simply amazing that no historian of the time, either Jew or Roman, records this most incredible atrocity. Josephus, who gives a minute account of the atrocities of Herod up to the very last moment of his life, makes no mention of the event.

On the other hand, the myth of the dangerous child who had to be hidden from the murderous intent of a king is common in Greek and Asiatic mythology, particularly in the Krishna myth. The Epic Hindu poem *Mahabharata* relates the whole story of the incarnate god, born of a virgin, escaping in infancy from the reigning tyrant, Kamsa. There is an immense sculpture at Elephanta, India, showing a person holding a drawn sword, surrounded by slaughtered infant boys.[19] This legend of Krishna echoes also the legends of Buddha, Horus, Zoroaster, and others. It is also reminiscent of the birth of Moses. He, too, as an infant was hidden to avoid the pharaoh's proclamation of death to all male children (Exod. 1:22).

Temptations

The temptations of Jesus, as well as his forty-day fast, are also far from unique in the history of mythology. Similar stories are found in the legends of Buddha, Krishna, and Zoroaster. When Moses went up to the mountain to receive the Ten Commandments, he "continued in the mountain forty days and nights, neither eating bread nor drinking water" (Deut. 9:9). As mentioned earlier, forty was a popular, magical number in mythology. Ezekiel was commanded by God to lie forty days on his side, and forty days passed in between the resurrection and ascension of Jesus. (The numbers seven and three were also sacred, and used extensively throughout the Old Testament.)[20]

G: Are you enjoying yourself? As an omniscient God, I know what you are going to attack next. You will be scorning the accounts of the miraculous cures performed by Jesus.

Miracles

J: Right you are. It is a psychological fact that desperate people clutch at any possible remedy no matter how preposterous. As a result, con men have always grown rich on other people's misery. Bogus remedies have, at times, cured a variety of psychosomatically induced ills as demonstrated by experiments with placebos. When it is administered by someone who elicits the respect and confidence of the patient, the placebo appears to have wonderful curative power. For example, in a study of thirty-three people who suffered from temporary blindness called by the formidable name, central serous chorioretinopathy, researchers found that thirty of them had a very distressing psychological experience in the hours or weeks preceding the first loss of vision.[21] Note that these people all recovered their sight without any specific treatment. However, if they had been given medication, or had been prayed over by a faith healer, they would have sworn that that was cause of their cure. A similar effect often occurs in the remission of cancer. Most often the remission is only temporary, but a two to five year hiatus in the spread of the disease is not unusual. In the meantime the patient goes about attributing the "cure" to whatever drug, treatment, or prayer he happened to be using. There is no divine power behind these so-called cures. Therefore, I do not find the alleged miracles of Jesus to be proof of his divinity.

Furthermore, all religious leaders, both mythical and real, had the reputation of performing miracles. The mythical Bacchus changed water into wine, and the healing powers of the great Greek physician Asclepius were attested to by hundreds of tablets hung in the temples stating the illnesses and the miraculous cures. The worship of Asclepius was established at Rome in 288 B.C.E. and continued for several hundred years after the establishment of Christianity. The application of spittle to the eyes of the blind by Jesus is mentioned in Pliny's *Natural History* as the sovereign remedy throughout the Mediterranean.[22] Tacitus' *History* describes a similar miracle performed by the emperor Vespasian, through the power of the god Serapis, in front of many witnesses. The nature of such "miracles," assuming the accounts are factual, strongly suggests the same use of psychological suggestion to cure psychosomatic illnesses as employed by modern faith healers. It should be noted that the New Testament reports that in his own country, even Jesus "could not work miracles there, beyond curing a few sick people by laying his hands upon them. And he marveled because of their unbelief" (Mark 6:5–6). It is not surprising that the power of suggestion would have no effect among Jews, who had no faith in the divine power of someone they knew to be no more extraordinary than the son of a carpenter. Hence, the need of the gospel writers to give the origins of Jesus more dramatic circumstances.

Simon the Samaritan, a famous contemporary of Christ, was also called The Magician and was so clever at making "miracles" that in Rome he was believed to be a god. If we are to believe the accounts, Simon was capable of making stones come to life, engulfing himself in fire without getting burnt, making bread out of stone, changing himself into a serpent or goat, and flying through the air. There is an amazing account in the apocryphal "Acts of Peter and Paul" that describes a confrontation between Simon the Magician and Peter. Simon challenges the power of Peter, but while Simon is demonstrating his own power by "soaring over the city," Peter prays and Simon falls, breaking his leg in three places. Not satisfied with this humiliation, the crowd stoned Simon and then carried him away to die.[23]

G: Now you are just talking nonsense.

J: I didn't make up that story. Simon's miraculous powers were attested to by the fourth-century Church theologian and historian Eusebius and mentioned in the Acts of the Apostles (8:9–11). Are such accounts any more ridiculous than the New Testament assertion that Paul's handkerchief and apron could cure the sick (Acts 19:11–12) or the power of Peter's shadow (Acts 5:15)?

History is replete with miracle workers such as Judas the Galilean, Bar Kokheba, and Sabbathai Zvi. Several of the more noteworthy wonderworkers were contemporaries of Jesus. Apollonius of Tyana in Cappadocia appeared and disappeared at will and performed all manner of miracles, including raising a dead girl to life. Even Justin Martyr believed in the miracles of Apollonius. He confessed that "whilst our Lord's miracles are preserved by tradition alone, those of Apollonius are most numerous, and actually manifested in present facts." Then Justin has to discount the remarkable feats of Apollonius by concluding that they were done "so as to lead astray all beholders."[24]

G: Is it so unthinkable that Satan would also perform miracles to deceive and confuse the faithful?

J: But if miracles can be performed by the devil as well as Jesus, they are hardly evidence of divinity.

Of interest, I think, is that few, except the grossly superstitious and ignorant, believe in witchcraft, sorcery and ghosts. And yet, as Albert Barnes is forced to conclude, there is no stronger evidence for miracles than for any other superstition.[25] W. R. Cassels points out that, "the true character of miracles is at once betrayed by the fact that their supposed occurrence has been largely confined to ages of ignorance and superstition."[26]

For a time I thought we had left such superstition behind us. Even the mecca of miraculous cures, Lourdes, seemed to be drying up. In recent times, the number of claimed cures has dropped from seventy-five a year to less than one. Even during its heyday the Catholic Church only recognized sixty-four of the six thousand miracles claimed. In recent years the advanced diagnostic methods of modern medicine have virtually eliminated miraculous claims. An examination of the eleven most recent cases revealed flaws in all of them.[27] Such results are consistent with the investigations by the Committee for the Scientific Investigation of Religion of faith healers in this country. The last Lourdes miracle to be accepted by the Catholic Church was in 1976, and was described by U.S. doctors as "vague" and "obtuse." It lacked the essential lab work to establish the nature of the illness, which appeared, like so many others, to be a form of hysteria.[28] That hysteria can produce symptoms of illness, oftentimes in large numbers of people, has been well documented, although until recently not very well understood.[29] Perhaps this is why the preponderance of those professing miracles at Lourdes were elderly spinsters claiming relief from an undiagnosed ailment.

Many years ago the great magician Harry Houdini wrote a book titled *Miracle Mongers and Their Methods,* which exposed some of the tricks of the trade.[30] Recently, a modern magician named James Randi also has written extensively on modern frauds such as psychic surgeons, levitating gurus, and phony prognosticators.[31] Independent studies such as the one conducted by clinical psychologist Louis Rose failed to uncover one clear-cut, unambiguous cure.[32] Yet there are still legions of believers. I find that people who believe in miracles today usually are scientifically ignorant or display the naive credulity of born-again Christians. However, even brilliant scientists can be duped. They are often so used to trusting their observations that they make easy marks. Thomas Edison was once tricked by a "psychic" using Edison's own invention, the phonograph. It is depressing to see how, in this supposedly enlightened age, so many people are eager to believe the most outrageous claims.

G: Even admitting that the there are many frauds pretending to cure in My name, and many imagined illnesses, that doesn't mean there could not be true miracles as well.

J: As I've said before, the human body, when boosted by a strong positive mental outlook, has remarkable rejuvenative powers. Hence, faith in anyone or anything, whether Billy Sunday, Reverend Ike, Oral Roberts, Finley's Snake Oil, Lourdes water, the relic from St. Joseph's Staff, or any other placebo certainly can sometimes work "miracles." The bones of St. Rosalia preserved at Palermo "cured" many people even after they were discovered to be the bones of a goat.[33]

Just how truly miraculous were the cures of Jesus? According to Charles Guignebert:

> All the religions that have so desired have had their miracles, the same miracles, and on the other hand, all have shown themselves equally incapable of producing certain other miracles. The unprejudiced scholar is not surprised at this, because he knows that the same causes [even if they are not known, I might interject] everywhere produce the same effects. But what is strange is that the believer is not surprised at it either. He merely insists that . . . his miracles are the only genuine ones; others are merely empty appearances, fabrications, frauds, uncomprehended facts or witchcraft.[34]

George Bernard Shaw wrote in his Preface to his play *Major Barbara,* "There is nothing in making a lame man walk: thousands of lame men have been cured and walked without any miracle. Bring me a man with only one leg and make another grow instantly before my eyes."[35] Now that would indeed be a miracle!

G: Then you must recognize as a true miracle the raising of Lazarus from the dead.

J: I find it more than a little suspicious that such a truly unique miracle is mentioned only by the writer of John's gospel. Undoubtedly it is a later insertion. Furthermore, over two hundred years ago the philosopher David Hume observed that, "no testimony is sufficient to establish a miracle, unless that testimony be of such a kind, that its falsehood would be more miraculous than the fact which it endeavors to establish."[36] To which Thomas Paine adds:

> Is it more probable that nature should go out of her course or that a man tell a lie? We have never seen in our time nature go out of her course, but we have good reason to believe that millions of lies have been told in the same time; it is, therefore, millions to one that the reporters of a miracle tell a lie.[37]

George H. Smith demonstrated the logical absurdity of claiming an event to be miraculous, for to do so one must claim that a given occurrence falls outside the natural law and only an omniscient mind could make such a statement.[38] In other words, since we do not know the extent of all the laws of nature, we cannot say an event lies outside those laws. For example, before humankind knew anything about electricity, the static electric spark that leaps from a person's fingers to another's cheek must certainly have appeared miraculous. About all that can intelligently be said about any modern-day "miracle" is that it is an event that cannot be explained by presently known laws. If the course of the last ten thousand years holds true, however, it will simply be a matter of time before the explanation is discovered.

One last point: as George Smith observes, isn't it interesting how quick people are to claim a miracle when a lucky break or an inexplicable occurrence works in their favor? A man just misses his plane, and later it crashes. It was a miracle, he exclaims! A second man races to the airport, luckily catches all the green lights and just makes his plane, which subsequently crashes. Who claims it was a miracle for him? When a cancer victim benefits from a remission of his disease it is a miracle. A healthy baby is found dead due to the mysterious "sudden infant death" syndrome but no one claims a miracle then! All of which goes to show how wise the ancient Greeks were when they said succinctly, "Miracles are for fools."

G: Your intellectual pride is becoming more intolerable with each succeeding statement. It's a wonder that I put up with your insolence. Fortunate for you many good people are constantly interceding with prayer on your behalf.

J: And if I had no one to pray for me, you might strike me dead? Some merciful God! But I think there is another reason.

G: What other reason?

J: Later. Let's move on.

G: Why bother? You undoubtedly plan an assault on the ultimate miracle of Jesus—His resurrection. I suppose you know of several similar cases?

J: No fair, You're reading my mind again. But since death occurs prior to resurrection, let's discuss the crucifixion first. By the way, I know in Your infinite wisdom You foresee all that I'm going to say, but indulge me. If I'm wrong You can enjoy the spectacle of watching me writhe on Your eternal barbecue.

G: Something for us both to contemplate.

The Crucifixion

J: Returning to the matter at hand, Doane wrote about the crucifixion: "The idea of redemption from sin through the suffering and death of a Divine Incarnate Savior is simply the crowning point of the idea entertained by primitive man that the gods demanded a sacrifice of some kind to atone for some sin or to avert some calamity."[39] Offerings of sacrifice, especially human sacrifices of innocent victims, were not uncommon in the ancient world. The stereotypical scene of the virgin being thrown into the volcano is, unfortunately, based on an ugly truth. The Aztecs slaughtered a huge number of young maidens annually to appease the gods.

The ultimate sacrifice was to offer one's own son. Even in the Old Testament we have Abraham willing to sacrifice Issac to prove his devotion to God. Cronus offered Jeoud; Moab also offered his son.[40]

The idea of a god dying to save humankind is represented in the Prometheus myth. As mentioned earlier, Osiris and Horus, Tammuz and Adonis are all mythical representations of dying and rebirth. In remote Nepal a crucified god, Indra, is worshiped. In Tanjore, India, the Hindus have worshiped the crucified god Bal-li—an incarnation of Vishnu—since antiquity.[41]

To reiterate, the reasoning which proposes that the death of Jesus was an act of reparation for the innate sinfulness of humankind is absurd. The assumption that it is just to sacrifice an innocent person as appeasement for the evil committed by other persons is no more than a primitive way of bribing the gods. As Thomas Paine explained: "If I owe a person money and cannot pay him, another person can take the debt upon himself and pay it for me; but if I committed a crime, every circumstance of the case is changed; moral justice cannot take the innocent (in reparation) for the guilty, even if the innocent would offer itself . . . it is then no longer justice; it is indiscriminate revenge."[42]

So, even as a moral allegory, the account of the crucifixion is an example of gross injustice.

G: You call laying down one's life for humanity injustice?

J: Where the object is to save the lives of others, it may indeed be heroic—the supreme act of love. I am specifically objecting to the theological rationale given to explain why You would let Your "son" be tortured and killed as an act of reparation. It is You Yourself who would be guilty of the grossest injustice to demand or permit such a sacrifice. You would be no better than Moloch.

G: Oh, so now you are judging your God?

J: I am simply exposing an ethical fallacy and, as such, providing evidence that the New Testament account of the death of Jesus is largely, if not entirely, a myth.

Further evidence of the mythical nature of the gospel accounts is provided by the events that accompanied the death of Jesus. Darkness over the earth and earthquakes were *de rigueur* for the death of legendary gods and heroes. The sun was darkened at midday when Krishna died. The whole frame of earth convulsed when Prometheus was fastened to the Caucasus. The death of Romulus was marked by darkness over the face of the earth for six hours. Virgil wrote of Julius Caesar's murder: "He [the sun] covered his luminous head with sooty darkness, and the impious ages feared eternal night."[43]

Every great man of the age, whether real or mythical, had to have some celestial sign to announce his birth and lament his death. So, it is not surprising that the gospel writers had to do the same for Jesus. But it is interesting to note the total absence of support for these remarkable events by serious historians. The crucifixion of Christ supposedly occurred during the lifetime of two famous philosophers and scientists, Seneca and the elder Pliny. According to the historian Gibbon, both these men "recorded all the great phenomena of nature, earthquakes, meteors, comets, and eclipses which their indefatigable curiosity could collect. But the one and the other have omitted to mention the greatest phenomenon to which the mortal eye had been witness since the creation of the globe."[44] Curious, is it not?

G: Perhaps it was deliberate. Those two certainly were not Christians.

J: No. But being men of science, they would have had no reason to suppress such an extraordinary event. Moreover, it is extremely doubtful that they had ever heard of the crucifixion of some mad prophet in a remote corner of the Roman Empire. They certainly make no mention of him nor, for that matter, do any other historians of the time. . . . Why are you frowning?

G: You forget that Josephus specifically mentions Jesus several times. And what about the philosopher Celsus and the biographer Seutonius?

J: Oh, yes. I'll review those references in the next chapter. First, let's finish the story of Jesus. Next, the New Testament writers say Jesus descended into hell—a theme well established in the myths of Krishna, Zoroaster, Osiris, Horus, Adonis, Bacchus, Hercules, Mercury, Baldur, and even the Mexican god Quetzalcoatl (perhaps reflecting the Egyptian influence, if Thor Heyerdahl's theory is correct). Nothing unique here.

G: So, you refuse to admit the possibility that Jesus was, in fact, crucified?

J: No, on the contrary. I agree that it is a very real possibility. There may well have been a religious preacher named Jesus who was put to death by the authorities for fear he was formenting revolution. The Israelites at the time were eager to rebel against both their Roman and Jewish leaders, so any hint of sedition was ruthlessly suppressed. Alexander Jannaeus crucified 800 rebels around 100 B.C.E. to solidify his rule.[45] On the other hand, Jesus may have been so fanatical that he actually believed he was a Messiah or a God—until they tied or nailed him to a cross, where he died an agonizing death. If we are to believe the gospels, Jesus died in complete despair. Consider his last words from Matt. 27:4: "Eloi, Eloi lama sabachthani?" ("My God, my God, why hast thou forsaken me?"). Hardly the sentiment one would expect from a person who still thought he was a god, or even believed his own teachings of an afterlife. Many nonbelievers have demonstrated greater courage in the face of death. The final words of Jesus sound like the anguished cry of a man who recognized the painful folly of his beliefs and died an atheist. Perhaps that is why the later gospel writer Luke changes the story and says that Jesus calmly forgave his torturers and uttered a little prayer before dying: "Father into thy hands I commend my spirit" (Luke 23:46). John has Jesus simply saying: "It is consummated" (John 19:30). Who knows what he might actually have said? But Mark has the ring of credibility.

G: I'll say this about your absurd ramblings, they have reached a new height in sacrilegious audacity. No one in all of history has speculated that Jesus died an atheist. I sincerely worry about your mind, not to mention your soul.

J: Someone probably did question the divinity of Jesus along these lines, but was afraid to do so openly. As for my being crazy, if I am then I don't have to worry about my soul, do I? Your infinite mercy will take care of this poor demented soul.

G: Thou shalt not tempt the Lord thy God.

J: Now don't get touchy. If what I have just said makes You angry, You're really going to be unhappy at what's to come. But let me first make amends for that last statement. Whether or not Jesus died an atheist can, of course, never be known since we really have no idea what, if anything, he said on the cross—assuming he was even crucified. The words put in the mouth of Jesus were taken verbatim from the opening of the Twenty-first Psalm, verse 2 (the Twenty-second Psalm in the King James Version). In this Psalm can also be found several other quotes that the writers of the gospels plagiarized.

The Resurrection

It only remains to be shown that Jesus follows the mythical stereotype by rising from the dead and ascending into heaven—after, of course, showing himself to a few close friends. Since Krishna, Buddha, Zoroaster, Aeschapius, Osiris, Mithras, and others were believed to have risen from the dead,[46] then so must Jesus. The resurrection of the Greek god Adonis, under the designation Tammuz, was celebrated throughout Judea hundreds of years before Christ. As late as 386 C.E., Jerome complained of the continued popularity of Tammuz in Bethlehem. During that age, given their knowledge of all the previous myths, who would respect a teacher who simply died? Yet I find it most puzzling that in the epistles of Peter, John, James, and Jude—all supposedly Apostles of Jesus—the authors never mention seeing the risen Christ!

G: But, on one occasion there were over five hundred people who saw Jesus after he rose from the dead.

J: Or so Paul claimed in his epistle. Even he has to admit he never saw Jesus before or after his supposed resurrection, except in a vision. Given the fanaticism of Paul as demonstrated in his epistles, he was capable of repeating any hearsay or even an outright lie if it would enhance his attempt to win converts. The gospels themselves refer to only fifteen people, eleven of whom were the apostles, who allegedly saw someone they took to be Jesus. Most interestingly, none of the gospel writers claim they themselves saw the risen Christ, further evidence that their writings are all simply hearsay.

G: They don't make the claim directly because they wrote in the third person.

J: They did so for the simple reason that they *were* the third persons, that is, they were writing about events they heard or read about.

The Gnostic Christians called the literal view of the resurrection the "faith of fools."[47] The Gospel of Mary interprets the resurrection appearances as visions received in dreams or ecstatic trances. The

Apocalypse of Peter shares this view.[48] A critical reading of the earliest Christian gospel accounts—those of Mark and Matthew—also supports this position. However, it appears that after the early Christian accounts were attacked as demonstrating mere hallucinations, the authors of Luke and John found it necessary to recast the account of the sightings of Jesus in more physical terms. In so doing, they embellished their story to such an extent that a comparison of the four authorized gospels displays an embarrassing lack of consistency.[49] Surely, if four such disparate accounts were offered as evidence of an event in a modern court of law, they would be quickly dismissed as either all lies or the products of slightly deranged minds.

Pagels proposes that "certain people in times of great emotional stress, suddenly felt that they experienced Jesus' presence. Paul's experience could be explained this way."[50] Paul admits that the apparition of Jesus which he saw was not a natural or physical being but a spiritual one (Acts 22:6–11). The plausibility of this explanation is apparent to anyone who has witnessed a fundamentalist prayer meeting. The participants feel the presence of Jesus in much the same way that primitive peoples the world over incur mystical experiences. Such illusions have a strong appearance of reality for the person who incurs them. No argument or evidence to the contrary can shake the belief. The believer is reluctant to abandon the illusion since it fills a deep psychological need.

J. K. Elliott offers another equally plausible explanation. His hypothesis is that at their communal meals, the disciples of Jesus may have felt that his spirit was in some sense still with them, guiding their efforts. They might have publicly spoken of this feeling, meaning it to be taken in a figurative sense. Later generations may have taken this expression literally.[51]

Still another theory is that the resurrection myth was a deliberate attempt by Jesus' disciples to establish a new religion by claiming immortality for their leader and all who follow him.

G: You have advanced three different theories. Which do you propose and how do you plan to support your contention?

J: Given my knowledge of human nature, I think that there is probably some truth to all three. However, I shall not attempt to prove any of them because, given the lack of any firsthand knowledge by any neutral observer of what events actually occurred during those years, my conclusions would be largely conjectural. Nevertheless, since all three of these hypotheses are congruent with human experience, whereas the resurrection presupposes that which it purports to demonstrate— that Jesus was a god—I submit that any of my hypotheses are logically superior explanations.

Let's examine the gospel reports as objectively as modern-day evangelists like Josh McDowell pretend to do.* Returning to the subject of witnesses, fifteen is hardly an impressive number. I could find a lot more than fifteen witnesses to any modern paranormal phenomena you name: UFOs, extraterrestrial visitors, Bigfoot, the Loch Ness Monster, or the Abominable Snowman. And all the witnesses to the presence of Jesus were his followers, including the eleven apostles who wished desperately that the idea of a new kingdom, for which they worked so long and hard, not die with their fallen leader. It already begins to sound suspicious.

To make matters worse, the gospel accounts conflict. Luke says that Jesus appeared in Jerusalem on the same day he rose, while Matthew has Jesus appearing to eleven apostles walking to Galilee. Luke doesn't mention that Jesus appeared to Mary Magdalene. Mark and Luke have him appearing to a couple of young men who didn't recognize him. John sought to increase the evidence by having him appear to his disciples three times instead of once and even go fishing with them. The whole account smells a little fishy.

G: I'm sure you have an alternative explanation.

J: A much more reasonable one. According to Justin Martyr, a Jew named Typho offered a likely explanation: "One Jesus, a Galilean deceiver, whom we crucified, but his disciples stole him by night from the tomb where he was laid when unfastened from the cross, and deceive men by asserting he has risen from the dead and ascended into heaven."[52] Jewish medieval literature also suggests a similar explanation. The eighteenth-century German theologian H. S. Reimarus writes, "The disciples of Jesus purloined the body of Jesus before it had been buried twenty-four hours, played at the burial place the comedy of the empty grave, and delayed the public announcement of the resurrection until the fiftieth day, when the decay had become complete."[53] The only problem I have with this explanation is that it grants too much credence to the events related in the biblical account. In all likelihood most of the events surrounding the death and resurrection of Jesus were simply a version of the ancient archetypal myth. The disciples of Jesus were no doubt very familiar with Mithraism, the chief religious rival of Christianity through the second century Mithras, who was a chief Persian god five hundred years prior to Jesus, had

---

*I say "pretend" because after he makes a point of how he approached Christianity objectively and accepted it only after being persuaded by the evidence, we find that he committed himself to Jesus as a young man and attended a religious-supported college and the Talbot Theological Seminary. So he obviously had no opportunity to weigh the evidence objectively!

his birth celebrated on December 25th and his resurrection observed on March 25th in a manner similar to the later Christian ceremonies.[54]

However, it seems as if the charge that the apostles pirated the body of Jesus prompted the writer of Matthew (or a later revisionist) to create the fiction that the soldiers placed to guard the tomb were bribed by the Jewish elders to spread the rumor that the disciples of Jesus stole him away. The account given in Matthew is absurd in two respects. First, by admitting their failure to protect the theft by a handful of timid disciples too afraid to even stand by their leader in his last hours, the guards would have been sentenced to death. It is much more likely that the guards could have been bribed by the disciples to make up a "miraculous" disappearance story which might be swallowed by the superstitious Roman prelate. And second, how could the writer of the gospel or any of the followers of Jesus know of the conversations between the Jewish elders and the guards, or earlier, the elders and Pilate?

G: Divine inspiration?

J: The whole story reeks of a crude lie to cover the obvious. The disciples were despondent since all the great promises of their leader and their hopes of establishing a new social order had suddenly been dashed. Regardless of the value of his teachings, no one would give two cents for the words of a poor carpenter's son who died such an ignominious death. They needed a great miracle. Their leader had to go on living forever—a small deception to ensure the continuation of his teachings.

G: Would Jesus' disciples be willing to risk martyrdom for that lie?

J: We can't be sure how many of them even knew it was a lie. The act of stealing the body could have been perpetrated by only one or two of them. We don't know that there really was a guard. And some of Jesus' disciples, such as Joseph of Arimethea, were rich enough to bribe them. As for dying for a lie or a myth, fanatics do it all the time. Look at the followers of Jim Jones or Ayatollah Khomeini; they did not even profess to be messiahs. Besides, of the original apostles only Peter and Andrew are said to have been martyred. They may not have been in on the original body snatching and, therefore, also under the delusion of resurrection.

G: All conjecture, mere speculation.

J: True. As I've said before, undoubtedly the real facts will never be known. All I wish to demonstrate is that there are any number of possible explanations that are infinitely more plausible than one based on three totally unverified assumptions, namely:

    1. that resurrection is possible,

2. that Jesus was God, and,

3. that there is a God.

The Bible supposedly provides evidence of these assertions, but actually it is the other way around. One would have to believe in these propositions before the Bible account is at all credible. Why, then, believe in these absurdities and not the myths of Homer or any other ancient legends?

I don't wish to belabor the point . . .

G: You already have.

J: . . . but accepting for the moment that there was a Jesus and he was crucified, there are several other difficulties with the myth of resurrection. In the first place it is not known with certainty that Jesus actually died on the cross. Even today, doctors occasionally misdiagnose an unconscious victim, thinking him dead. How much more difficult it would have been 2,000 years ago to correctly diagnose the actual moment of death, let alone the exact cause of death. Yet, the evangelist Josh McDowell, quotes some doctor who confidently asserts that Jesus died from "agony of mind producing rupture of the heart."[55] Indeed! It is difficult to believe that any licensed doctor would make such a medically absurd diagnosis. For all we know, Jesus could have been alive when He was taken down from the cross and died days, or weeks, later. Of one thing we can be certain: if Jesus did not die on the cross, He died shortly thereafter, for even the apostles admit He was "carried up to heaven" a short time later. This appears to be a convenient excuse for the fact that no one saw Jesus after He was crucified except, supposedly, His close friends.

G: There wasn't much time. Jesus ascended into heaven only forty days after His resurrection.

J: How convenient. There is that magic number forty again. It should come as no surprise that ascension was the final act of many of the Savior myths. Krishna, Adonis, and Dionysus all had preceded Jesus in their heavenly ascents. It was assumed that all the Roman emperors ascended to heaven, as symbolized by the release of eagles from their funeral pyres.[56]

Turning to my next concern, I find it surprising that the site of the tomb of Jesus is a subject of conjecture. Surely you would think that the Apostles would have venerated the spot of such an incredible miracle. But G. A. Wells points out that there is "not a single existing site in Jerusalem which is mentioned in connection with Christian history before 326 C.E., when Helen (the mother of the emperor Constantine) saw a cave that had just been excavated, and which was identified as Jesus' tomb."[57] We of course have no evidence to support the assertion. The fundamentalists claim that Jesus was laid in a different tomb. As usual, their reasoning is specious: They note that the tomb discovered by Helen is inside the city limits of Jerusalem, and know that the Jews would never have permitted a tomb within their city. They forget, or choose to ignore, that the city limits today are much larger than they were at the time of Christ.

Further cause for suspicion is the detail with which the writer of John describes the spices used to preserve the body and method of application. Considering that this gospel was composed forty to fifty years after the event and the writer never even pretends that he was present to witness the burial of Jesus, it is an amazingly graphic account.

Finally, I must note that McDowell makes much of the fact that there are no writings at the time of the gospels which refute the alleged resurrection. To this assertion there are two replies. First, since the entire details of the life and death of Jesus were in large part—if not entirely fictional—written many years after his alleged death there could be no writings *at the time* to refute a nonevent. Actually, the lack of contemporary support indicates that the Jesus of the Bible either never existed or was considered an inconsequential personality by contemporary historians. Second, it is entirely possible that the idea of a personal rather than metaphorical resurrection of Jesus did not occur until after his followers began attempting to convert the Gentiles who already believed such an event could occur and, in fact, demanded such an explanation if they were to venerate Jesus as a god.

It may seem surprising that for all the alleged miracles, the epistles written by Jesus' disciples never claim that He was God. Even the fanatical Paul never referred to Jesus as God in any of his epistles, although he did claim that Jesus rose from the dead. However, it must not be forgotten that the epistles were written *before* the gospels. The authors of the epistles (even Paul) were Hebrew. As such, they were monotheists. While they could readily accept the idea of Jesus as the Messiah, the belief that Jesus was a god would have been unthinkable to these men. It is probable, however, that the writers of the gospels were either Gentiles themselves or at least addressed their narrative to Gentiles. In Greek and Roman mythology Zeus and Jove had many sons, so it is easy to see how the Greek word *pais,* which means both servant and child, could lead to the notion of Jesus as the Son of God.[58] It was common practice to establish that heroes and wonder workers were sons of gods and were elevated to the status of gods themselves upon their death. Nothing could be easier than to introduce a new god to these people. In fact, they wouldn't be impressed by anything less. However, to make the sale, the legend of Jesus had to be embellished with the myths that the Gentiles had come to expect to be associated with their gods. This is what the gospel writers set out to accomplish.

G: You assume that this was all a conscious attempt to deceive the unwary.

J: Perhaps unconscious self-deception was also involved. But the evidence is overwhelming that the Church set out on a deliberate course to assimilate all existing pagan religious myths. Earlier (chapter 1) we saw how four modern religions were created. Especially in the case of Mormonism, we can observe how a religion is created out of earlier mythical traditions.

Feasts, Symbols, and Rituals

During the first several hundred years of its existence, the Church made a concentrated effort to sell its infant theology by appropriating every pagan feast, symbol, and ritual as its own. Obviously, this was a flagrant, albeit successful, effort by the early Church Fathers to absorb the devotions of the pagans. For example, December 22 is the winter solstice, the date when the sun passes back into the northern hemisphere, thus lengthening the daylight hours. For hundreds of years prior to the time of Jesus, this occasion was celebrated with several days of feasting culminating on December 25. In Rome, a festival was celebrated under the name "Natales Solis Invicti," which means, "Birthday of Sol [Sun] the Invincible."

G: I know Latin!

J: Anyway, on this day, all public business was suspended, criminal executions were postponed and friends gave presents to each other. Frazer quotes a Christian Syrian writer who also freely admits that when the Fathers of the Church noted the heathen celebration on the 25th of December, "they took counsel and resolved that the true nativity should be solemnized on that day, and the festival of the Epiphany on the sixth of January."[59]

As Frazer shows, this was just the first of many pagan feasts the Church successfully Christianized: the Festival of St. George was previously the Festival of Parila (a rustic purification festival); that of St. John the Baptist, the heathen midsummer festival of water; the Assumption of Virgin Mary, the Feast of Diana; All Souls Day, the Feast of the Dead; and Easter was originally celebrated as the resurrection of the Greek god Adonis and the Roman god Attis.[60]

Baronius, the Catholic ecclesiastical historian, makes a remarkably bald-faced admission of the Church's intent in this regard: "It is permitted to the Church to use, for the purpose of piety, the ceremonies which the pagans used for the purpose of impiety in a superstitious religion, after having first expiated them by consecration—to the end that the devil might receive greater affront from employing, in honor of Jesus Christ, that which his enemy had destined for his own service."[61] (What would Christianity do without the invention of the devil to explain the religion's logical inconsistencies and contradictions?)

Next, we have all the renamed statues and titles stolen from the pagan gods. When I was a child working in my father's ecclesiastical supplies stores, one of our best sellers was the statue and picture of the "Immaculate Conception." It depicted Mary standing on a crescent moon with twelve stars around her head. What a shock to learn that the Egyptian goddess Isis was represented exactly the same way! So, too, pictures of Mary and Jesus look suspiciously like earlier sculptures of the Egyptian god Horus sitting in the lap of Isis. Remember the famous Black Madonna and Child, a favorite depiction of Polish Catholics and Pope John Paul II? I was told it was black because the original picture had miraculously survived a church fire. At the time I was too naive and credulous to question why the garments were still white! Nor could I have suspected at the time that this picture actually represented Isis and Horus, the dark Egyptians, who were once worshiped throughout Italy.[62] Horus was usually depicted in jewel-adorned garments befitting an Egyptian deity. Krishna and his mother, Devaki, are also often depicted as black.

In the case of many Italian and Greek statues, only the names were changed to deceive the innocent. Jupiter, Apollo, Mercury, Orpheus—all had to bear the indignity of being renamed Christ, just as Ceres, Cybele, and Demeter had to have their title, Queen of Heaven, conferred on Mary, a late-comer to the mythical pantheon. Maya, the mother of Buddha, was also depicted with her infant savior in her arms.[63]

One of the more imaginative images of Jesus depicts him symbolically exposing his heart. The veneration of the Sacred Heart is still practiced by many old-time believers, who are, of course, completely unaware that the symbolism of the heart is part of a very elaborate myth reflected in the sculptures of Horus and the Hindu god Vishnu.[64]

G: Your exposition is becoming redundant.

J: Sorry, but I'm trying to demonstrate conclusively that the gospel stories and Christian traditions are all taken from ancient pagan legends and rituals, just as the Book of Mormon was derived from the ancient legend of Enoch. Actually, in the interest of time I'm seriously understating my case. T. W. Doane lists hundreds of references, summarizing the work of dozens of historians and biblical scholars. James Frazer and Joseph Campbell give additional evidence that the story of Jesus is simply an amalgamation of earlier myths, principally those of Adonis, or as he was known to the Babylonians and Israelites, Tammuz.

One of the most intriguing pieces of evidence, demonstrating just how ancient these myths really are, is provided by Gerald Massey. According to Massey, there are four very interesting scenes on a wall of the Holy of Holies in the Temple of Luxor, built by the Pharaoh Amenkept III for his mother around 1600 B.C.E.[65] The first scene depicts Taht, the annunciator of the gods, hailing the virgin Queen Mutemua that she is to give birth. In the second scene, the god Kneph, in conjunction with Hathor, gives new life. (Sounds like the Holy Spirit, doesn't it?) The next scene is the classic mother and child, and the final scene shows the enthroned child receiving gifts from three spirits—whom the Christians later appropriated as the Three Magi—and the god Kneph—God the Father—looking on.

G: Well, that's Massey's interpretation. There could be others.

J: I find it fascinating that the evidence to support the myth hypothesis—which is so abundant despite all the attempts of the Church for 2,000 years to destroy it—is always subject to "other interpretations" while the New Testament, which was written by those with a vested interest in perpetuating the myth, is supposed to be taken at face value. But it's no use. No amount of rationalization or attempt to "interpret away" the contrary evidence can lend credence to the ridiculously implausible gospel stories of Jesus.

G: I think your preconceived beliefs are showing. And you claim to be objective. What a joke!

J: Obviously no one is objective in an absolute sense, but I do try. And how can you say my opinions were preconceived? I was as true a believer as anyone. It was my attempt to justify my belief to unbelievers that led me to begin the many years of investigation which resulted in the reversal of my position.

When I was a child my family said the rosary and Litany of the Blessed Virgin every night. The litany was a recitation of a few dozen titles bestowed on Mary by the Church. It was only much later I learned that the Church had no qualms in appropriating the titles of earlier deities: "Our Lady," "Queen of Heaven," "Mother of God," "Morning Star," "Virgin," and many others. Even the beloved rosary of the Catholics is far from unique, it is simply a variation of the string of prayer beads used by the Buddhists, Brahmans, Taoists, and Moslems.[66]

Had I been a more critical student of the Bible and not so conditioned in Catholic mythology, I might have wondered at Jeremiahs' rebuke of the Israelites who contended that since they "left off to offer sacrifice to the Queen of Heaven, and to pour out drink offerings to her, we have wanted all things and have been consumed by sword and by famine" (Jer. 44:18). Imagine! Some Hebrews were worshiping a "Queen of Heaven" hundreds of years before the birth of Mary.

How, too, could I have known the antiquity of the central symbol of Christianity—the cross? A popular symbol in ancient Egypt and Rome, it appears on a Roman denarius 296 years before the birth of Christ.[67] The cross may be found on the oldest Babylonian monuments. It was the symbol of the Babylonian god Bal. The Greeks, and even the Buddhists, used the cross as one of their sacred symbols.

G: That would seem to lend credence to the theory of type. Don't you find it remarkable that the cross is treated almost universally as a sacred symbol?

J: I might if it were the only sacred symbol. But it is just one of several symbols all of which have the same attributes being simple, elemental, the representative of all things. In other words, the early artists observed certain basic shapes common to all nature such as the circle, the triangle, and the cross. With these three basic shapes, the geometer Euclid could develop his rich and complex theory. It is no wonder that the three shapes became powerful, sacred symbols for all ancient religions.

Other Christian pictorial symbols, such as the "Lamb of God," appear not only in the Old Testament, but throughout agrarian and nomadic societies where lambs were a common sacrificial offering.

So we see that the substitution of feasts, the adoption of pagan titles for the Christian God and saints, and use of pagan symbols all indicate that the early Church sought to make its dogma more palatable to the Gentiles by appropriating the pagan beliefs and calling them Christian. As Faustus wrote to Augustine:

> You have substituted your apostles for the sacrifices of the pagans, for their idols your martyrs whom you serve with the very same honors. You appease the shades of the dead with wines and feasts. You celebrate the solemn festivals of the Gentiles, their calendar, and their solstices; and as to their manners, those you have retained without any alteration. Nothing distinguishes you from the pagans, except you hold your assemblies apart from them.[68]

G: So there are similarities between Christianity and earlier religions in terms of myths, symbols, feasts and titles. It could be that the early converts to Christianity retained some of their pagan practices and beliefs and these became mixed with history and the teachings of Christ. Even if all that you have related were true, it would not detract from the substantive beliefs central to Christianity.

J: Wait. I'm nowhere near finished yet.

G: I should have known it. . . . I mean, I did know it.

J: What kind of substantive beliefs are you talking about?

G: Those expressed in the so-called holy sacraments of the Church such as baptism, the remission of sins, and the eucharistic feast.

J: All right, let's discuss the sacraments. A brief review of their genesis provides additional insight regarding the true origins of Christianity.

Let's see, first there is baptism, the universal symbol of purification and initiation.[69] The ancient Egyptians baptized those about to be initiated into the mysteries of Isis. Buddhism, as practiced in Mongolia or Tibet, involves infant baptism. Followers of Zoroaster and Mithras were also baptized. Tertullian admits that the pagans practiced a baptismal rite as well, even to the extent of making the sign of the cross, but he ascribed their practice once again to the devil's attempt to deceive. Max Webber explains that baptism was a ritualistic cleansing and marking of the soul, symbolic of tattooing and circumcision to make converting to another religion more difficult.[70]

Next is confirmation. All cultures had some ritual to mark the demarcation from childhood to adulthood—the rites of passage. In my childhood it was described as becoming a "soldier of Christ."

The marriage "sacrament" is a universal ritual which obviously evolved in response to the need for men and women to gain the benefits of a sexual exclusiveness. The man benefited by the greater (although not absolute) assurance that the children he must support were actually biologically his. The woman benefited from the assistance the man provided in obtaining food, shelter and protection for her and her children. This basic economic arrangement is ritualistically sanctified in almost every culture.

At death, the Catholic Church offers Extreme Unction—the last rites—a specialty of shamans and witch doctors the world over for as far back in history as any record can relate. In the Catholic sacrament "Holy Oils" are used. The Hebrews anointed bodies with oil in preparation for burial, a custom which they, in turn, learned from the Egyptians. And Holy Orders—the initiation into the priesthood—was also practiced worldwide from antiquity.

The sacrament central to the Catholic Faith, and in less literal form to many other Christian sects as well, is undoubtedly the Eucharist—Holy Communion—the ritual eating of the flesh and blood of

Jesus as God. The belief that one may acquire the characteristics of an animal or a man by eating his body and drinking his blood is almost as old as the dawn of man. The ritual is even now practiced by many primitive peoples. It is known to anthropologists as the practice of sympathetic or homeopathic magic. According to Frazer, the Wagogo of East Africa ate the heart of the lion to give them courage and strength. The Dyaks of Northwest Borneo do not eat venison for fear it will make them timid as a deer. The Aino, on the other hand, believe eating the heart of the water ouzel will make them fluent and wise. Certain American Indian tribes ate the feet of swift running animals.[71]

If people believe they can acquire the characteristics of that which they eat, then from eating animals to eating fellow humans is a logical step. Some East African tribes ate the raw liver of a brave enemy because it was believed to be the seat of valor. Hearts and even eyes were eaten by various tribes around the world to acquire certain special characteristics possessed by the person eaten. The Zulu chief, Matuans, drank the gall of thirty chiefs he had defeated in battle to make him strong.[72]

The next progression was from eating men to eating gods. The attribute of the gods which men were trying to obtain was no less than a share in the god's immortality. But here a little more imagination had to be employed, since gods are hard to capture. Thus was born the concept of transubstantiation: the belief that the food you are eating, through a miracle, has become God. The custom of eating a god was found to exist throughout the world and probably dates back to the earliest Sumerian religions. Frazer describes the form this takes in various cultures. For example, twice a year the Aztecs ate morsels of paste made of beets and roasted maize which they called the flesh and blood of their god Huitzilopochtli. The Jesuit historian J. De Acosta describes in great detail the ceremonies held each December which involved a ritual culminating with the high priest killing the paste image of the god by piercing it with a flint-tipped dart, then cutting the image into small pieces to distribute to the rest of the people. The ceremony was called "Teoqualo" which means, "god is eaten."[73] A similar ceremony was held by the Aryans of Ancient India centuries before Christianity.

The Greeks practiced a bloodier ceremony which involved rendering and eating a bull at the festival of Dionysus. The drinking of the wine at the festival was to signify the drinking of the blood of Bacchus. In Sweden, the corn spirit was believed to live in the last sheath; thus to eat the last sheath was to consume the corn spirit.[74] In Japan and southern India, the Bororo Indians of Brazil, the Mandi of East Africa, Caffres of Nepal, and the Creek Indians of North America all had a ritual eucharist.

The similarity of native eucharistic services to their own was an embarrassment to Christians who constantly had to blame it on the Devil's attempt to deceive them—the Theory of Type which we will discuss in the next chapter. The Catholic apologist Justin Martyr made that argument against the followers of the god Mithras, who also used bread and wine in their eucharistic feast. It is known, moreover, that Mithraism was popular throughout the Near East in pre-Christian times and entered Rome about 60 C.E. Actually, the Mithras ritual was itself derived from the earlier Zoroastrian ritual involving confession and the drinking of the juice of the sacred "haoma," a plant that represented the god Haoma. The faithful drank the divine sacrifice in anticipation of the sacrifice at the end of the world which would make them all immortal.[75] The early Christians were well aware of the Mithraic communion feast in which a priest represented Mithras in presenting the bread and wine to the believers. So it appears that this was simply another ritual that the Christians borrowed.

The Jesuits employed the same tired "type" argument, accusing the Devil of an act of deception when they discovered the practice among the Aztecs. Now, I know where the expression "poor devil" came from. He is always taking a bum rap due to someone else's ignorance or duplicity.

G: Yet doesn't the widespread practice, in itself, suggest there might be something unusual, perhaps supernatural, in the belief of resurrection?

J: If universality were the test of truth, we would still believe in a flat earth with the sun revolving around it. In any age, it is not the uneducated with their superstitions and magic whom we look to for wisdom, but the few who seek to understand the workings of nature and who refuse to accept any simplistic, supernatural answers.

Magic is indeed a universal belief. And H. L. Mencken demonstrates that the Eucharistic service possesses all the elements of any act of magic.[76] The Eucharistic service requires:

- the suspension of the laws of nature;

- the transmutation of a material;

- the use of verbal incantation. (I always thought it lost something when the priests adopted the vernacular when saying the magic words that are supposed to change the bread and wine into the true body and blood of Christ. The ancient and mysterious Latin phrase seemed much more "powerful" as an incantation: "*Hoc est enim corpus meum—For this is my body.*");

- the presence of a medium (Until recently the medium [the priest] could touch the consecrated bread only with his thumb and fore-fingers, which were ritualistically washed both before and after the act of consecrating the bread and wine).

G: I recall a young man who wholeheartedly believed in the supernatural feast of the Eucharistic service. What happened to him?

J: Yes, I once believed in that primitive custom of which Cicero wrote in the first century B.C.E. (long before Christianity adopted the practice): "How can a man be so stupid as to imagine that which he eats to be a god?"[77] My only excuse is that it was before I had developed what slight powers of critical reasoning I now possess. Also, I had no way of knowing that anthropologists and historians had traced the practice of the ritualistic eating of a god to the primitive belief that we acquire the powers of the creatures we eat.

Finally, I was fooled by the semantic trick so prevalent in the pseudoscience of metaphysics: the confusion of words with things. The word "transubstantiation" is pretty awe-inspiring to an unsophisticated mind. When it is backed by the weight of an authority figure, such as a priest who describes how the "substance" of the bread and wine can change without a change in "properties," it is easy to be taken in. Besides, everyone likes a magic show. It is certainly more entertaining than plowing through the empiricist philosophy of David Hume or the critical analysis of Ludwig Feuerbach. It was these two men who first pointed out the obvious: for a thing (substance) to exist without its attributes (properties) is as silly an idea as the opposite notion—a property without a thing. (Show me a long nothing, or a hard, green nothing.) Therefore, there are no separately existing substances that could undergo a magical transubstantiation. Once again theologians successfully bewitched minds with meaningless words. All the sacraments, like the feasts and symbols of Christianity, were simply attempts to accommodate pagan beliefs. The evidence for this conclusion is overwhelming to unbiased, rational minds.

Returning to my original question of who speaks for God, we may now ask, does the Jesus of the New Testament speak for You? Or, to put it more precisely: are the Christian beliefs unique and do they provide evidence of a special covenant with God which vests the Christian religion with the right to determine correct moral behavior? If, as I have shown, Christianity is simply a collection of ancient myths, then we must understand the origin of those myths and evaluate the teachings of Christianity in an entirely different light.

5

The Jesus Myths:
Searching for the Kernel of Truth

There is nothing more negative than the results of the critical study of
the life of Jesus. . . . He is a figure designed by rationalism, endowed
by liberalism, and clothed by modern theology in an historical garb.
—Albert Schweitzer

J: There are several competing theories as to the basis for the myths
or legends concerning Jesus. Some scholars such as R. Gordan Rylands,
Arthur Drews, G. A. van den Bergh van Eysinga, J. M. Robertson,
G. A. Wells, and Gerald Massey contend that the entire story of Jesus
is simply a revised form of ancient myths. Other theories argue that
a person named Jesus actually existed, but we know virtually nothing
about the true circumstances of his life and death.

The Astrological Archetype Myth

Gerald Massey argues that the Jesus myth was derived from the ancient
astrological myths.[1] Basically, Massey contends that the story of Jesus dates
back to the ancient astrological myths of the Egyptians, and he provides
a good deal of evidence to support his theory. I have already explained how
the day assigned by the early Christians as the birth of Jesus was selected
to supersede the celebration of the winter solstice, long celebrated by the
Egyptians as the birth date of their god Horus. In the later tradition of
the Mithranic cult which, according to Plutarch, was well established in Rome
about 70 B.C.E., Mithras was born in a cave. Now, during the period from
2410 B.C.E. to 255 B.C.E. the solstice would appear astronomically under the

celestial sign of the Sea Goat. The Akkadian name for the tenth month during this astrological period was Abba Uddu, which means "Cave of Light." For hundreds of years, then, the birth place of the Sun God was attributed to the "Cave." However, after 255 B.C.E., the solstice passed out of the Sea Goat and into the sign of the Archer. The tenth month in this new astrological calendar would no longer have been the Cave of Light.

G: I think you just disproved your own theory. What then, is the connection with Jesus, who was born during a period when the astrological interpretation would be different?

J: That's just it. It shows that an astrological myth of a god born in a cave had been well entrenched for hundreds of years prior to the time of the Mithras cult. It was a small step from a figurative astrological myth to a literally accepted myth of Mithras having been born in a cave. The Christians, then, simply pre-empted the Mithronic legend like they did with so many others.

G: This assumes that the origins were astrological to begin with, a fact that you have yet to demonstrate to my satisfaction.

J: Then consider that the most sacred day for the Christians, even more than that of Christmas, is Easter. Easter occurs at the vernal equinox, which is celebrated throughout the Middle East as the rebirth (resurrection) of various gods: Adonis, Attis, Dionysus, etc., and especially Mithras who also laid in the grave three days before being raised up again. As John M. Robertson states, "a long series of slain Jesuses, ritually put to death at an annual sacrament for the sins of many is the ultimate anthropological ground given for the special cultus of which grew the mythical biography of the Gospels."[2]

This proposition is true of the Egyptian myth of Horus, whose resurrection was also celebrated at the vernal equinox. If we trace the Egyptian myths back still further, we find that they have as their origin belief in the sun god. That the sun was believed to be a god is very logical: its warmth and light are responsible for the rebirth of the world each spring. Without the sun nothing can live; too much sun and its power will cause things to wither and die. Is it any wonder that early man should recognize this fact and deify that mystical ball of fire in the sky? The universality of this myth is evidenced by the Aztecs' autumn custom of ritually killing a youth who represented Tezcatlipoca being sacrificed to his father, the sun god. Unfortunately for the young man, it was Tezcatlipoca rather than he who rose again in the spring.

The writer of Matthew uses the legend of Jonas' spending three days and nights in a whale's belly as another prophecy of the death and resurrection of Jesus. The Jonas myth is but another version of the rebirth legend. The common source for these many variations may be the very ancient Hindu astrological myth of the sun being "swallowed by Night" and coming out safe again in the morning.

The apocalyptic vision of the future found in the later epistles is heavily based upon the eschatological myths of earlier religions. Eschatology, as you know, is the study of "the last things" and refers to the idea of death and resurrection, the basic theme of the New Testament. This idea, far from being of Christian origin, can be traced back to the Zoroastrian literature of the post-Maccabean period.[3] According to the Zoroastrian myth Shaoshyant, the son of Zarathustra and the virgin, Hvov, was to be the savior of the world. Then, after the world had reached perfection through Zarathustra's intercession, it would end in fire and a final conflict would occur between the god of good, Ahura Mazda, and the god of evil, Angra Mainyu.

The idea of a perpetual conflict between the forces of good and evil probably dates back to the time when prehistoric man first sought to understand the reason for good and evil in the universe. Which all goes to show that the Jesus myths are simply a variation on one of the most ancient themes.

G: None of what you say is new. The astrological origin theory is old hat. But it is generally not discussed much any more.

J: I understand the theory is no longer in vogue. There are very few people today who are even acquainted with the astrological theory, not because it lacks validity, but simply because there is no strongly motivated group supporting its propagation. On the contrary, billions of dollars are being spent to suppress the truth and maintain the myth of Jesus, which, I might add, pays handsome dividends to its proponents.

G: Perhaps it all boils down to a matter of belief. You choose to believe that the story of Jesus is simply an updated version of ancient myths. Christians choose to believe that the gospels are accurate reports of the events that occurred.

J: Before we can discuss the issue of belief I wish to discuss a couple more theories and see if there could not be some synthesis of these to arrive at an even more intellectually acceptable explanation. These next two theories begin by conceding that Jesus may have actually existed as a historical person.

G: One moment—Before you begin another long-winded monologue, what if I told you I accept everything you say about the myths predating Jesus—but they prove nothing.

J: Go on, this will be interesting.

Theory of Type

G: Earlier you tried to disparage the Theory of Type without even discussing it. That's unfair, so I'll present it now. Tertullian and Justin Martyr presented it in its crudest form by asserting that a long time *before* the Christian era, the Devil had had their future mysteries and ceremonies copied by his worshipers.[4]

J: Such an unfounded, self-serving rationalization is what I would expect from the likes of Tertullian. Wasn't he the Church Father of the second century who made the classic testimony of faith in the Christian myth: *"Credo quia absurdum est"*—"I believe because it's absurd"?

G: The ultimate act of faith!

J: It certainly precludes argumentation. Of course, arguing that the Devil has the divine attribute of prescience and used it to deceive the unwary tries to explain one hypothesis with two more which are even less plausible, a fault endemic to theology. In effect, You ask that we first accept the existence of a Devil which itself relies on ancient myths. And second, You must explain why You would permit such a creature to deceive the innocent for all those centuries. At best, it makes You guilty of complicity, since, if You really are all powerful, You willed it. I'll return to the subject of evil later, but would like to at least mention that the contradiction between a God who embodies truth and goodness, and one who tolerates such wickedness has caused modern-day theologians to lose much sleep and still come up empty. They again seek refuge behind the word "mystery." However, the more sophisticated theologians have admitted that the Devil is simply a metaphor for the unexplained evil in the world.

G: Without agreeing with your position, there is another form of the theory of type presented by theologians who can't abide evil incarnate in the form of old Satan. I am referring to the theory that all pagan religions were My way of preparing the ground for acceptance of Jesus when his word was presented to the pagans. As Augustine wrote, "For the thing itself which is now called the Christian religion, really was known to the ancients, nor was wanting at any time from the beginning of the human race, until the time when Christ came in the flesh, from whence the true religion, which had previously existed began to be called Christian"[5] The noted Tübingen philosopher Hans Küng tells us that the German philosopher G. W. F. Hegel also argued that non-Christian religions are merely "pre-Christian" religions approaching God from "shadows and symbols."[6]

J: What masterful rationalizations! That same argument could be made for any religious leader. A variation on the theme was made by

Mohammed, who stated that he was simply following the traditions of earlier prophets such as Moses and Jesus. He added, however, that he was the "Seal of Prophets," the last word in God's truth. Today in Japan, the Omoto religious movement also makes the claim: "all religions of the world are the forerunners of Omoto."[7] In these two instances it was claimed that earlier religions were not created by the Devil, but were merely precursors to prepare the believer to accept the final truth.

G: That doesn't prove that Justin or Augustine couldn't be right.

J: He who makes an assertion must demonstrate the reasonableness of his position. In the case of Justin and Tertullian, they must prove first that there is in fact a Devil. Although looking at the mess the world is in, it might seem easier to prove a Devil than a God. However, Tertullian and Justin merely use one myth to explain another. Augustine, on the other hand, says, in effect, that all those ancient religions that today we recognize as based on superstition and ignorance of the workings of nature, suddenly acquire some sort of legitimacy when we label them Christian. But if they were no more than myths, and Christianity is replete with the same stories, why in the world should a reasonable person believe the Christian fables?

You know, I always felt that if Your intent was really to have people recognize Jesus as God, all You had to do was to let Him remain on earth two or three centuries. That certainly would have convinced most people.

G: Then there would have been no test of man's faith!

J: Ah, yes! Faith. As a rational being, which logic appeals to You more: that the story of Jesus is simply one more attempt by a group of religious zealots to appropriate ancient myths to establish and legitimize their alleged founder as God, or the belief that God planned this incredibly obscure and deceptive way of permitting a whole mythology to arise that suddenly is converted to truth in the person of Jesus.

G: I certainly don't expect the puny minds of men—yours in particular—to fathom my purpose and ways.

J: Perhaps. But given the importance of substantiating the claim that Jesus was God, at least the existence of a man named Jesus and the events of His life and death should be established as incontrovertible facts.

G: Are you now implying that Jesus may not even have existed? In addition to the gospel accounts there is plenty of evidence. If you go to Bethlehem you can see the birthplace of Jesus. There are fragments of his cross, his death shroud, and in Jerusalem, his tomb.

J: In fact, as I mentioned earlier, there are two alleged tombs. And don't forget the "milk" grotto where a drop of milk from Mary's breast is supposed to have fallen to the ground and turned the limestone white. As for the infamous Shroud of Turin, it was exposed as a fraud when it first turned up in the fourteenth century. This fact was largely ignored by those who chose to believe in the authenticity of the shroud, just as they later chose to ignore chemical tests indicating that the red markings showing the supposed wounds of Jesus were made by a vermilion pigment commonly used in the fourteeth century and made from iron oxide.[8] (Actually, if it was indeed blood it should be black after drying, not red, as any first-year medical student knows.) The most definitive proof could be obtained by carbon dating the cloth. After many years of opposing such efforts, the Church at last agreed to the tests in 1988. As the skeptics expected, the results dated the cloth between 1260 and 1390 C.E. However, true believers can never be persuaded by evidence. Hence, I was not surprised when the *Catholic Digest* refused to accept the results and proposed such imaginative objections as the possibility that the piece of cloth tested might have been sewed in later to repair the shroud and contending that there were other "secret tests" which gave different results.[9]

Supporting a belief with highly imaginative but spurious evidence is nothing new. If I go to Greece I will be shown the footprint of Hercules, the tomb of Bacchus, and the chain that held Prometheus. All silliness aside, there is no archaeological evidence to support any of the myths of Jesus. Whether a man named Jesus ever even lived cannot be demonstrated convincingly.

G: What about the evidence of the historians I mentioned earlier?

J: Hardly overwhelming. There are only a handful of scattered references which could, with a stretch of the imagination, refer to Jesus. Let's examine them.

Historical References to Jesus

First and foremost are the three references by the Jewish historian Josepheus (30–60 C.E.). However, the first is about another person named Jesus: a robber-captain who planned an unsuccessful attack on Josephus. The second refers to Jesus, son of Sapphia, a Galilean, "leader of a seditious tumult of Mariners and poor people."[10] Maybe this is the historical Jesus, but he bears more of a semblance to a political revolutionary than to the Christ of the gospels.

The third reference is most relevant, for although it is only a one-paragraph reference, the description is essentially the biblical account of Jesus. Specifically it refers to "Jesus a man of great abilities. . . . A worker of wonders, a teacher of people . . ." who was crucified under Pilate and "appeared to be alive on the third day. . . ."[11] However, Gordon Stein provides ample evidence that the passage is a later insertion to Josephus' history.[12] This is not surprising given the proclivity of such men as Eusebius and, as will be shown, many other overzealous Christians to use deception and forgery to advance the belief in their religion. Dr. Stein's evidence against the passage's authenticity as a contemporary account of Jesus is as follows: First, it occurs as a disruption in a section dealing with other matters. Second, no Christian writer, until after the time of Eusebius in the fourth century, quotes this passage as evidence of Jesus' actual existence. Third, the allegation that Jesus led away many not "only of Jews but of the Gentiles after Him" would only be true many years after His alleged death when the apostles and Paul began preaching to the Gentiles. Finally, the point that this sect of Christians "are not extinct even to this day" is only a relevant comment if it was written much later than a mere thirty years after Jesus' death. This, and other evidence, has led many scholars to conclude that the passage was inserted perhaps a hundred years later.

G: But they can't really prove it.

J: No more than can the opposition. Again, the burden of proof is on those claiming the existence of Jesus. The other references to Jesus are even more sketchy. The Roman Tacitus, in one line of his *Annals,* mentions that "Christus, was put to death by the procurator Pontius Pilate."[13] But since the *Annals* were written about 120 C.E., and Tacitus quotes no source for this statement, he is probably just relating what had by then become a well-established belief among the Roman Christians. Next, there is Suetonius who wrote his *Lives of the Caesars* approximately the same time as Tacitus authored the *Annals.* In it, Suetonius states that the emperor Claudius expelled the Jews from Rome because they were incessantly rioting "at the instigation of one Chrestus [sic]."[14] Since the Jews were expelled around 49 C.E., it appears as if this instigator Chrestus was alive and in Rome at that time. Also, since he used only the title Chrestus, it is difficult to know for certain if it was Jesus to whom Suetonius is referring. At any rate, writing about ninety years after Jesus supposedly lived, and in a different country, it appears that Suetonius, like Tacitus, is relating hearsay regarding the existence of some Jewish Messiah rather than a documented fact.

    Next, we have the letter of Pliny to the emperor Trajan in which he mentions that in one of the provinces the Christians sang hymns "to Christus as if he were a god."[15] This is probably true, for by that time many Christians undoubtedly believed that Jesus had existed and was a god. But that does not provide any more evidence of his existence than the worship of Zeus or Baal.

Finally, there is the contradictory evidence of the Church Father Origen (ca. 185–255 C.E.). In his work *Contra Celsum,* Oirgen attempts to refute the arguments laid out by the Platonist philosopher Celsus about 178 C.E. in his anti-Christian work, *The True Word.* Unfortunately, in its thorough attempt to suppress any dissenting views on the authenticity of Jesus, the Church destroyed the book by Celsus in the fifth century so that all that remains is what Origen excerpts. However, from Origen we learn that Celsus asserted that Jesus, the son of a soldier named Panthera, was a magician claiming to be God. This is the basis of the "Sepher Tolduth Jeshu" story. The story, which is not flattering to the character of Jesus, is related by the eighteenth-century social philosopher Voltaire. Although he dismisses it as probably fictitious, Voltaire admits the "chief part of it is certainly more probable and more conformable, to what passes in the world in our own days than any of the fifty gospels of the Christians."[16]

G: Oftentimes stories about some legendary figure, especially when they are found in several different sources, indicate that such a person actually did exist, although I admit that many of the person's deeds may be mythical.

 J: I am not claiming that Jesus never existed. I merely contend that Jesus, as depicted in the gospels, never existed. Many Bible scholars of the nineteenth century believed that the actual historical person who provided the single reality upon which all the myths could be draped was Johoshua Ben Pandira as Celsus claimed, a wonder worker described in the Talmud, who lived about 100 B.C.E. However, the theory has fallen out of favor today.

Johoshua Ben Pandira

The name Jesus is the Hellenized form of the Hebrew name Johoshua or Joshua. In *Contra Celsum* Origen denies the contention of Celsus that the mother of Jesus was "turned out by a carpenter who was betrothed to her, as she had been convicted of adultery and had a child by a certain soldier Panthera"[17] (or alternately Pandira). Origen apparently had a difficult time refuting the accusation, so he dismisses it: "Is it reasonable that a man who did such great things for mankind should have had not a miraculous birth, but a birth more illegitimate and disgraceful than any?"[18] Such a lame argument lends credence to the explanation offered by Celsus, which requires no supernatural events, only a simple understanding of human nature. Origen, on the contrary, makes the twofold assumption that (a) Jesus did in fact do great things for humankind, and (b), that great men must have had wondrous births. This reflects the common myth-creating device I mentioned earlier.

Gerald Massey, in his essay "The Historical Jesus and Mythical Christ," writes that initially he, like others, upon learning of the references to Johoshua Ben Pandira in the Talmud, believed (as do evangelists such as Josh Mc-Dowell) it provided evidence of the existence of the biblical Jesus. However, upon further investigation, Massey was surprised to discover that Johoshua Ben Pandira lived during the reign of King Alexander Jannaeus, almost 100 years before the birth assigned to Jesus of the gospels.[19] According to Celsus, this Johoshua learned magic tricks in Egypt and eventually ran afoul of the Israeli establishment. He was stoned to death as a wizard in the city of Lydda and hung on a tree on the eve of Passover. However, according to Massey, Epiphanius in the fourth century asserted that the Jesus of the gospels was the descendant of Pandira.[20] Justin Martyr objects to contemporary Jews' contention that the only Jesus of whom they knew was Johoshua Ben Pandira. Moreover, they denied that this Johoshua of the Talmud was the Jesus of the gospels. Although Origen and Justin also did not want to identify their Jesus with Johoshua Ben Pandira, they faced (but chose to ignore) the quandary posed by Massey: "It follows that the Jesus of the Gospel is the Johoshua of the Talmud or is not at all, as a person."[21] On the other hand, if Jesus is the Johoshua of the Talmud, he is not God but merely the ill-fated magician told about in the Talmudic "Sepher Tolduth Jeshu" story.

G: That theory is based on mighty skimpy evidence and much conjecture. Why should you choose to believe it?

J: Actually I don't. I have no idea whether or not it, or any of the other hypotheses I advance, is true. But, they are all more plausible than the mythical gospel account. Need I remind you that the earliest complete manuscript of the four gospels dates from around 400 C.E. And from the beginning their authenticity and reliability was questioned. Faustus wrote to Augustine that the gospels:

> were composed long after the times of the apostles by some obscure men, who, fearing that the world would not give credit to their relation of the matters of which they could not be informed, have published them under the names of the apostles, and which are so full of sottishness and discordant relations that there is neither agreement nor connection between them.[22]

Between the time the gospels were originally written and the time they were accepted in the form we see today, there were so many opportunities to add and delete that there is no way of knowing for certain what is original and what is a later insertion.

G: However, if they were divinely inspired, you must trust that I protected their integrity.

J: You are begging the question. It is the very assertion that the gospels were inspired that is so questionable. If they are full of contradictions, myths, and forgeries, we can hardly accept the assertion that they are divinely inspired. I've already shown that for the most part they are a collection of ancient myths tacked onto a single questionable historical incident, i.e., the existence of a man named Jesus or Johoshua. Even a cursory reading by the uninitiated will reveal dozens of contradictions in the historical details of the four accounts. Later insertions of text or deliberate mistakes in translations are obviously more difficult to detect. There have been many studies by Bible exegetes of the eighteenth and nineteenth centuries which indicate that the insertions may have been considerable. For example, the last twelve verses of the final chapter of Mark appear to have been added since they are not found in most of the early manuscripts. Neither are they cited by any of the early Church Fathers except Irenaeus in about 185 C.E.

G: That is just because many of the early manuscripts are only fragments; they are incomplete. But the Hebrew tradition was to transcribe manuscripts faithfully and carefully. What evidence do you have that the Church scribes did not carry on this tradition?

J: Well, let's begin with Jerome. He completed the first Latin version of the Bible officially approved by the Catholic Church. I ask you, would you trust the veracity of a translator who admitted seeing centaurs, fawns, satyrs and incubi—and spoke with them?[23]

G: Just because Jerome had a vivid imagination doesn't mean he wasn't trustworthy and accurate in his translation.

J: I cannot share your confidence. The general sentiment of many early Fathers of the Church is exemplified by Eusebius, Bishop of Caesarea and the Father of ecclesiastical history, who wrote *The Preparation of the Gospel.* In the conclusion to a chapter with the lengthy title, "How Far It May Be Proper to Use Falsehood as a Medium for the Benefit of Those Who Require to Be Deceived," he confesses with pride, "I have repeated whatever may rebound to the glory and suppress all that could tend to the disgrace of our religion."[24] In blatantly claiming the right to lie to further the cause of Christianity, Eusebius was merely employing the rationalization of Paul, who argued, "But if through my lie the truth of God has abounded unto his glory, why am I also judged as a sinner?" (Rom. 3:7)

It was this same Eusebius whose vivid imagination created many of the fables of early martyrs. He wrote, "On some occasions the bodies of martyrs devoured by wild beasts, on the carcasses being opened, have been found alive in the stomachs."[25] The mere idea of a beast such as a lion having a mouth and stomach large enough to swallow even a small child whole is more than I can swallow. Gregory of Nazianzus increases my skepticism when he confesses the obvious in a letter to Jerome, "Our forefathers and doctors have often said, not what they thought, but what circumstances and necessity dictated."[26]

I find your faith in the integrity of the early Christians almost as touching and ill-founded as their faith in a group of books declared to be the inspired true history of Jesus, even though, unlike other historical texts, there is no collaborating testimony to establish their reliability. As I mentioned before, there were many gospels and epistles alleged to be the works of early apostles and disciples of Jesus. The Church declared these works to be false when, in 326, Athanasius, Bishop of Alexandria, selected his favorite accounts and excluded the rest (including the "Aprocrypha" books which the Church later restored in the declaration of 1546). After a bitter dispute, the canonical books were decided upon in the Synod of Hippo in 393 C.E.

What I find amazing is that when comparing the gospels that were accepted and those that were rejected, I find them all equally fanciful and absurd. Those that were not accepted passed into the world of legends repeated only by pious nuns and priests to unsuspecting elementary schoolchildren. Still, as Voltaire put it more than two centuries ago, "Why does the most scrupulous Christian now laugh without remorse at all these gospels no longer in the canon; and why does he dare not laugh at those adopted by the Church?"[27]

The acceptance of the four gospels was based on their support for the theological beliefs of the early Church, especially for their support of the divinity of Jesus and primacy of the Church hierarchy.

G: There you go again, passing off your hypothesis as if it were an established fact. You seek to contradict and deprecate a work that has been accepted by thousands of brilliant minds as My revealed truth.

J: There are many reasons why those brilliant minds have accepted the New Testament as truth, not the least of which is that for over a thousand years it might have meant their death if they publicly expressed any doubts. That is a very strong psychological incentive. I will discuss equally strong motivations in chapter 17. However, I am far from alone in viewing the New Testament in a more objective light. Hundreds of biblical scholars of the last two centuries have become increasingly skeptical of the New Testament as support for the historicity and especially the divinity of Jesus. Recently, for example, no less a devoted Christian theologian than Hans Küng admitted that, "apart from John's Gospel, written fifty years later—Jesus is designated as God in only a few, all likewise late, Hellenistically influenced, exceptional cases."[28]

A more blunt conclusion is drawn by W. R. Cassels, who wrote a critique of religion in 1874: "There is no reason given, or even conceivable, why allegations such as these, and dogmas affecting the religion and even the salvation of the human race, should be accepted on evidence which would be declared totally insufficient in the case of any common question of property or title before a legal tribunal."[29] Alfred Loisy, who was professor at the Institut Catholique in France from 1884 to 1908, was equally direct. Luckily, he spoke out after the time when such statements would lead to a death sentence: for him it meant excommunication and the loss of his job. Like so many others who spent their lives investigating the gospels, Loisy was forced to the realization that they benefited from no supernatural influence and that a considerable part of the gospels was the product of forgery. Loisy concluded that the gospels "contain as many errors as books of their kind, written when they were, could be made to hold."[30] But I again digress. As I mentioned earlier, it is doubtful whether even Jesus considered himself to be the Son of God.

G: You've gone too far. If Jesus did not truly believe he was God, why would he have taken on all that need less suffering and death? What was in it for him?

The Crucifixion as a Fanatical Plot

J: Given that there is no reliable history of Jesus' life, we can only conjecture as to His reasons, which leads me to the hypothesis advanced by Dr. Hugh J. Schonfield. In his popular work *The Passover Plot*,[31] he contends that Jesus sought to establish a cult following by feigning death through crucifixion. Certainly, if we give any credence to the New Testament account, there is much circumstantial evidence to lead to that conclusion: the timing of the death to coincide with the eve of the Sabbath so that Jesus would not be left on the cross too long; the administration of a drug which would cause him to pass out (the gospel says it was only gall, but who knows?); the failure to break his legs like the two men crucified with him (instead, a superficial wound was administered to show he was dead); and finally, the hasty transference of the unconscious Jesus by Joseph of Arimathea to a nearby cavern where he could be administered to by friends. Unfortunately, the plan backfired and Jesus died. The resurrection had to be manufactured by vague reports of seeing a man who looked something like Jesus, but was not initially recognized by his own disciples (Luke 24:16; Matt. 28:17; John 20:14–15, 21:4).

Although Schonfield's hypothesis is well researched, it remains only a hypothesis and I cannot give it a great deal of credence since it requires too many assumptions. Nevertheless, since it requires no supernatural explanation, its plausibility is greater than the resurrection myth.

As an interesting aside, the story of the crucifixion of Jesus sounds amazingly similar to an account written by Josephus of an incident when, on an errand for the Roman general Titus, he passed a number of persons who had been crucified. Recognizing three of them as acquaintances, Josephus returned to Titus and asked that they be spared. They were ordered taken down and treated. Two of them died, but the third recovered. A remarkable coincidence? Or the basis for the gospel story?

G: More groundless conjecture.

J: Conjecture, true, but no more groundless than the conjecture that a perhaps mythical prophet named Jesus was a god.

G: *The* God.

J: Whatever. I think the most reasonable explanation of all is offered by George Bernard Shaw, who states that it is easy to believe that an overwrought preacher at last went mad as Swift, Ruskin, and Nietzsche themselves went mad.[32] Jesus' madness led ultimately to his execution. Then as with other popular preachers, reformers, and heroes, legends and myths sprang up among his devoted followers to keep his memory alive—and ultimately to provide the basis for a new religious movement.

G: Shaw said it was easy to believe this. See, you can't get away from basing your opinions on belief.

J: True, but I'm using the term in a much different sense than that of the true believers. For me, belief is the tentative acceptance of a hypothesis supported by a logical set of deductions not at variance with other historical and scientific evidence. Contrast this with the leap of faith based purely on supernatural suppositions and completely at odds with observable scientific evidence.

G: You, of course, have such evidence to support your hypotheses?

J: Once again I must remind you that it is the responsibility of the supporters of the Jesus myth to bring forth the evidence to prove their position. If a man tells me that he caught a shark in a fresh water lake, it isn't up to me to prove he didn't. It is his task to produce the evidence, and "It got away" won't sell. Aside from the New Testament stories which I have shown to be no more than the typical legends ascribed to ancient heroes, there is no evidence to suggest that Jesus, if he existed, was more than an obscure religious reformer. At a time of rising Israeli nationalism, he was considered by the Romans to be potentially dangerous and was therefore executed. On the other side of the ledger, I've offered three theories which, although they can't be proved, are far more plausible. They don't demand that we accept anything more of human nature than what can be explained by elementary psychology. There have been many times in history, similar to the Roman occupation of Judea, when people readily followed any self-proclaimed messiah who offered them a way out of their oppression.

G: How, then, did Jesus succeed in maintaining that belief for 2,000 years when all other messiahs failed?

J: Before I address the reasons for the long-term success of Christianity let me discuss yet another explanation of the roots of the Jesus cult, as proposed by T. W. Doane among others.

G: Not another! How many wild theories must I listen to?

J: This is the last, but in many ways the most provocative.

The Essenes as the Precursors of Christianity

About the time Jesus is alleged to have lived, a Jewish religious sect known as the Essenes was also expecting an angel-messiah. The origins of the sect are difficult to trace at best. They could be descendant from a Buddhist sect, certainly the angel-messiah was similar to the Buddhist *Avatar*—an incarnation of God expected every 600 years. The great similarity between the story of Jesus and the earlier Buddha myths seems to lend credence to this theory.

A large community of Essenes lived in monasteries in Egypt on the lake of Parembole or Maria where, according to historian Godfrey Higgins, a sect of Buddhist priests are also believed to have lived.[33] Moreover, many hundreds of years before Christ, Buddhist missionaries spread their teachings throughout the Middle East, over to Greece and down into Egypt. Israelites would have come into contact with these teachings at the time of Babylonian captivity (586–538 B.C.E.). The Essenes, known also as Therapeutae (healers) shared many of these Buddhist beliefs. Finally, it should be noted that the Eastern philosophical influence in the early Church can easily be detected in the transcendent philosophy of the early Church theologians, which reflects strong Platonic influence, but is also heavily flavored with Buddhism. Similarities of these doctrines to the gospel teachings provide further evidence that Jesus might have been an Essene himself, or that some of his disciples belonged to the cult.

According to Doane, two early Church historians state flatly that the origins of Christianity rest with the Essenes. Epiphanius, a Christian bishop of the fourth century wrote: "They who believe in Christ were called Essenes before they were called Christians. These derived their constitution from the signification of the name Jesus which in Hebrew signifies the same as Therapeutae, that is, a savior or physician."[34] Eusebius, who had no reason to lie about this issue, stated: "Those ancient Therapeutae were Christians and their ancient writings our gospels and epistles."[35]

Higgins writes:

> Their [the Essenes'] parishes, churches, bishops, priests, deacons, festivals, are all identically the same [as the Christians']. They had apostolic founders; the manners which distinguished the immediate apostles of Christ; scriptures divinely inspired; the same allegorical mode of interpreting them, which has since obtained among Christians, and the same order of performing public worship. They had missionary stations or colonies of their community established in Rome, Corinth, Galatia, Ephesus, Phillippi, Colosse, and Thessalonica, precisely such, and in the same circumstances, as were those to whom St. Paul addressed his letters in those places. All the fine moral doctrines which are attributed to the Samaritan Nazarite, and I doubt not, justly attributed to him, are to be found among the doctrines of these ascetics.[36]

Based upon archeological evidence, theologian and historian Ernest Renan also concluded that Christianity was a form of Essenism which succeeded. That was in 1863, long before the additional evidence of more recent research. Not surprisingly, Ernst Renan's book *The Life of Jesus* (also published in 1863) was quickly condemned by the Church.

G: What difference does it make who the first disciples of Jesus were or what sect they belong to?

J: Just this: by establishing the link with the Essenes, it becomes quite probable that it was not Jesus who founded a religion, but a religion which found Jesus, or more precisely, created the myth of Jesus. As I've said, we know next to nothing of the man named Jesus. In my copy of the New Testament, the longest gospel is only forty-eight pages, most of which, as I have shown, is comprised of ancient myths. Even the alleged teachings attributed to Jesus were either added later or borrowed from others. For example, the Sermon on the Mount expresses the same sentiments as those of Pharisaic teachers such as Hillel.[37] Half the parables in Luke are peculiar to that gospel, as are half of those in Matthew. John doesn't relate any parables. As G. A. Wells observes, before Clement I the early Christian writers do not ascribe to Jesus the ethical teachings presented in the gospels.[38] In short, the evidence suggests that Christianity was not derived from Jesus as presented in the gospels; rather the gospels—the myths and alleged teachings of Jesus—were created or borrowed by the evangelists and early Fathers of the Church. The figure of Jesus, whether a historical reality or allegorical myth, simply provided a linchpin for a theology and philosophy which Jesus, as a Hebrew, would have found heretical.

Max Weber questions whether Jesus had any intention of starting a new religious sect. According to Weber, Jesus was a fundamentalist Hebrew who was opposed to reform and modernism: "Jesus revolted against the intellectualist trust of authentic late Judaism, with its concern with literary scholarship. His criticisms were not motivated by prole-tarian instincts but rather by his piety and obedience to the law, both appropriate to the 'rural artisan' or small town inhabitants."[39]

G: That raises the question, where did the proponents of Christianity obtain their theology and philosophy?

J: The link to the Essenes provides the clue that would explain why all the myths and teachings of the New Testament reflect much older Eastern myths and teachings. The discovery of the Dead Sea Scrolls at Qumran offers significant new evidence to support the proposition that the origin of Christianity lies with Eastern thought which influenced the Essene cult. It is important to note that the Dead Sea Scrolls were written between 100 B.C.E. and 50 C.E., so any borrowing of ideas and beliefs was done by the early Christians, not the Essenes.

In 1953 John M. Allegro was one of a team of international linguists commissioned to reconstruct and translate the scrolls. However, forty years later the other team members have failed to publish the pre-ponderance of their work—almost 75 percent of the scrolls. Why did the others delay publication of the texts for which they were responsible? Allegro believed that there was disappointment when it was learned that instead of adding any confirmation to the Jesus legend, the scrolls provided fresh evidence that the rituals of Christianity were derived from the Essenes. At the very least, the scrolls undermine the uniqueness of Christianity. Investigations by Michael Baigent and Richard Leigh add credibility to Allegro's charges.[40] They point out that although the scrolls found at Nag Hammadi were discovered after the Dead Sea Scrolls, the Nag Hammadi translations were in widespread circulation by 1973 and published by 1976. The difference is that the work to translate the Dead Sea Scrolls was controlled by the École Biblique, the French Dominican archeological school in Jerusalem. Every director of the École Biblique has also been a member of the Vatican's Biblical Commission. The commission is headed by the same person who is in charge of Congregation of the Doctrine of the Faith, at present Cardinal Joseph Ratzinger, that same ultraconservative I referred to earlier. The primary concern of the Biblical Commission is the same as that of the Inquisition: to suppress any information that might call into question the divinity of Jesus or the divine origins of Christianity.

Only recently have photographic copies of the Dead Sea Scrolls been made available to the Huntington Library in California, and subsequently to the academic community at large, over the strenuous objections of the team of predominantly Catholic scholars who have been jealously guarding them all these years. It is too early to tell all that the scrolls will reveal. No doubt they will only lead to more controversy rather than conclusively prove anything. However, what is already known, coupled with much additional research, has led Robert Eisenman, Chairman of the Department of Religious Studies at California State University, to develop some interesting postulates.

G: Speculation, just speculation! And why should we suppose that Eisenman is more objective than the original Dead Sea Scrolls team? He no doubt has his own biases, as do all the others to whom you refer.

J: No doubt that is true. In the end we must select among various propositions based upon the weight of the evidence. However, all things being equal, it seems to me that a prudent man or women would always look for natural reasons before leaping to supernatural explanations. But You aren't going to attempt to stop me from making the case, are You?

G: Of course not, your readers will see the tenuous nature of your hypothesis.

J: I'll risk it. In the first place I wish to point out that the scrolls indicate a number of similarities between the practices of the Essenes and Christianity. For example, the scrolls indicate that the Essenes "practiced a ritual meal of some kind, baptized their initiates, and paid special regard to the teachings of the biblical prophets, whose every word was thought to offer insight into the future of mankind."[41] A scroll entitled "the Rule of Congregation" describes a communion ceremony with bread and wine: "The priest shall be the first to stretch out his hand to bless the first fruits of bread and wine."[42] Elsewhere the scrolls describe the practice of anointing with oils as a means of healing the sick; the practice has more than a little in common with the Catholic sacrament of Extreme Unction described earlier. As I explained previously, the term "Christian" means "the anointed ones."

The Gospel of Matthew, especially chapters 10 and 18, contains many metaphors and terminology which are interchangeable with the Community Rule described in the Essenes scrolls. The Acts of the Apostles indicate that the early Christians practiced common ownership, as did the Essenes. Quotations from the scrolls are also found in the second century writings of the Church Father Justin Martyr.

In addition to the many similarities between the rituals of the Essenes and the later Christians, there appears to be a possible connection between the apostle James, who is referred to in the New Testament as the brother of Jesus, and the "teacher of Righteousness." Further analysis of the Acts of the Apostles indicates that Paul had a running feud with James "the Righteous." Paul is constantly defending himself from charges of lying. The Dead Sea Scrolls refer to an enemy of the Teacher of Righteousness who is called "the Liar." Based on an analysis of the Acts and the Habakkuk Commentary in the scrolls and other histories of the period, such as that by Josephus, Eisenman reconstructs the following scenario:

The Sadducee priesthood under the leadership of the high priest Ananas was collaborating with its Roman occupiers and became lax in its observance of Mosaic law. Religiously orthodox and nationalistic groups arose to condemn the Sadducces and call for a return to the law. (This is reminiscent of the Maccabean revolt.) It is well established that one of these groups, known as the Zealots, had established themselves at Masada, only thirty miles from Qumran. Eisenman argues that the Zealots and Essenes were basically the same organization. Evidence from the two sites appears to bear him out.

Paul was sent by Ananas to persecute these Jewish fundamentalists. On the way there, he had some sort of experience, perhaps an epileptic seizure, sunstroke or whatever, that convinced him that God was angry with him for his oppression of the orthodox sect. Paul ended his persecution and joined the sect. However, he had a hard time following the sect's strict observance of the law. At some point a schism developed between James and Paul over observance of the law. Paul's epistles emphasize faith and good works rather than the observance of the law. Although he never knew Jesus, Paul ascribes his personal beliefs to Jesus in order to gain and maintain his following. In the meantime, the animosity between the high priest Ananas and James reached a climax: James confronted Ananas and was killed. The news of James' murder triggered a full-scale rebellion of the Jewish fundamentalists

and nationalists in which Ananas was killed. The Romans moved in
to squash the rebellion. After destruction of Jerusalem, they laid siege
to the strongholds of Gamala and Masada. In Gamala 5,000 men,
women and children commited suicide rather than be defeated; in
Masada 960 were to lay down their lives.

Although Qumran was also seized by the Romans, the fate of
the Jewish inhabitants is unknown. Paul was rescued by the Romans,
who saved him from being beaten and probably murdered by adversaries
who may have been followers of either James or Ananas. Although
the Romans arrested Paul for reasons that are unclear, since he was
born a Roman citizen he was entitled to be tried in Rome. Paul then
faded out of history and his ultimate fate is unknown, but his teachings,
which he ascribes to Jesus, became the basis for a new religion,
Christianity. Baigent and Leigh support Eisenman's belief that if the
mainstream of the Essenes (or Zealots, if they were indeed the same
sect) had followed the teaching of James rather than Paul, "there would
have been no Christianity at all, only a particular species of Judaism
which might or might not have emerged as dominant."[43]

G: So that is it: the history of Christianity in a nutshell. You read a
new theory and accept it as the truth just like that. Where is your
proof?

J: It is beyond the scope of this book to provide all the evidence provided
by scholars such as Allegro, Eisenman, Baigent and Leigh, and many
others. I refer the interested reader to their works listed in the bibliography. Moreover, it is not my intention to hold up their theory
as an established fact. It is, however, an interesting hypothesis consistent with the evidence in the Acts of the Apostles, the Dead Sea
Scrolls and other manuscripts. I do not offer it as the definitive statement
on the origins of Christianity, but only posit it as one of several
possibilities that do not require a supernatural explanation. From what
we know of the origins of the many religions such as the Christian
sects discussed in the first chapter, the Essene (or Zealot) origins of
Christianity appears quite plausible.

As I mentioned, the teachings of the Essenes make frequent
reference to the "Teacher of Righteousness," also known as the "Prince
of Light," who, Allegro believed, the Essenes associated with the "King
of Righteousness" referred to in the Old Testament. It is this char-
acterization, "pruned of the more improbable narrative, given a Roman
slant, and combined with the Essenean moral teaching,"[44] which Allegro
believed was the foundation of the Christian belief in Jesus. I think
Allegro overstated his case based on the available evidence, but that
the teachings and myths of the Essenes had a major, if not crucial,

role in the establishment of the Jesus myth can no longer be denied. Dr. Löw, an accomplished Hebraic scholar, also concluded that Jesus was the founder of the Essenes.[45] Whatever their origin, with the destruction of Jerusalem and the fall of their Qumran fortress, the Essenes were dispersed. Not coincidentally, the rise of Christianity soon followed.

G: Still more futile conjecture.

J: Perhaps, but again, this explanation is far more reasonable than the Jesus fairy tales and offers at least some supporting evidence. As we have seen, one group of Christians, the Gnostics, had so much in common with the Essenes that they were undoubtedly the inheritors of the Essenean theological tradition.

G: Irrespective of the origins of the New Testament and the story of Jesus, even if the New Testament is no more than an allegory, the moral teachings were a giant step forward in the evolution of morality. The teachings of Jesus espoused in the gospels were nonjudgmental, loving, and free from the constraints of oppressive Jewish law.

J: That is far from the truth as I will show in chapter 7. Moreover, a review of Paul's epistles provide ample evidence that it was Paul, not Jesus, who set the course of Christianity. Like zealots throughout history, Paul altered the new religion to fit his own image: "Be imitators of me as I am of Christ." If Paul was truly an imitator of Jesus, then Jesus was certainly different from the man depicted in the gospel myths. Paul's epistles are rife with chastisements, new rules and regulations, and condemnation of dissenting opinions. From this point on, the institution of Christianity grows with one aim above all others: to extend the power of the institution. The only major difference the Reformation made—albeit not an insignificant accomplishment—was to fragment that power among the various sects.

I have read many books and seen several movies depicting how the early Christians were persecuted. What I have yet to see is a movie about how once they achieved power, the Christians persecuted all dissenters from that time down to the present century.

6

Establishing the Establishment

The philosophers and contemplative men who have dared look superstition
full in the face are, comparatively speaking, few in number.

—Elika Palmer

G: I suppose now you are going to recite a litany of alleged atrocities
by people who professed to be Christians.

J: No, but I will give some historical perspective to show that the suppression of intellectual dissent was not committed by a mere handful
of people who happened to be Christians. Rather, I submit that there
is a causal relationship between the theology of Christianity and
intellectual suppression. History provides ample evidence to support
the conclusion that any dogmatic system of beliefs that concentrates
power in the hands of a few, whether kings or popes, inevitably spells
the end of dissent and results in a reign of terror and persecution.
Furthermore, it is the very nature of all institutions based on faith,
such as Christianity, to lead to this disastrous end.

Christianity was a relatively harmless religious belief until it was
able to enlist the support of the ignoble Constantine I about 300 C.E.
To insure control of his empire, Constantine had murdered several members of his own family, including his wife, Fausta, and his son, Crispus.
No Roman religion could purge the guilt he must have felt for these
heinous crimes. It wasn't part of their theology; rather, the Roman religion
held that a man was accountable for his acts forever. Christian theology,
on the other hand, could absolve Constantine of his guilt and guarantee
him eternal salvation. Is it any wonder that he didn't seek to be baptized
until his deathbed? A sacrament to wash away all sin—absolution regardless of the enormity of the crime—is the ideal religion for a tyrant
who wishes to remain a tyrant to his death.

After presiding over the Council of Nicaea in 325 C.E., Constantine enforced Christianity's doctrine by outlawing Arianism (the belief that Jesus, although your Son, was not your equal) as heresy and enforced his decree with the sword. On the other hand, according to the historian Gibbon, converts to "orthodox" Christianity were rewarded in gold, or in the case of slaves, with freedom.[1] Not surprisingly, Christianity flourished. Constantine's successor Theodosius was to do him one better. In an Imperial Edict of 333 C.E. he decreed that "all writing, whatever, which Porphyry or anyone else had written against the Christian religion . . . should be committed to the fire, for we would not suffer any of those things so much as to come to men's ears, which tend to provoke God to wrath and offend the mind of the pious."[2]

The loss of Porphyry's fifteen books Against the Christians—of which only fragments survive—was the beginning of a crusade against intellectual dissent that has lasted to the present day. Just recently, I read of fundamentalists who proposed making librarians criminally liable for the books in their libraries, and suggested that they "throw out and burn the trash." Much of this "trash" includes such classics as Salinger's *Catcher in the Rye,* Thoreau's *Civil Disobedience,* Steinbeck's *Grapes of Wrath* and *Of Mice and Men,* Vonnegut's *Slaughterhouse Five,* and Richard Wright's *Native Son.*

It was not long after Theodosius' decree that thousands of people were labeled as heretics and massacred, including entire towns in the East at Cyzicus, Samosata, Paphlagonia, Bithynia, and Galatia.[3] Theodosius unleashed a legion of zealots who attacked all unbelievers with a fury that shocked even the emperor. After a bishop instigated the burning of a local synagogue, Theodosius ordered the bishop to pay for damages. But no less than Ambrose, a Doctor of the Church, argued that no Christian should, on any account, be held liable for such damage.[4] This indirect justification of anti-Semitism was instrumental in institutionalizing a bigotry which culminated in the Nazi genocide of the Jewish people.

It did not take Christianity long after gaining the official support of the state to strike two blows which ended individual intellectual freedom and plunged the Western World into the Dark Ages. The first was the destruction of the library of Alexandria by Theophilius, Bishop of Alexandria. The library's collection—the greatest of the ancient world—had been rebuilt after being burned during the siege of Alexandria by Julius Caesar. The loss is all the more unfortunate since Alexandria was the home of a large number of Essenes around the time of Christ. The works of this library may have provided conclusive evidence of the linkages between the religions of the East and the Judeo-Christian teachings of the West. It may have been precisely because of the link of Christianity to the Essenes that the library was destroyed. The primary goal of the early Church was to eliminate all challenge to its doctrines. A. James Reichley of the Brookings Institute explains in *Religion in American Public Life:*

> After Christianity became the official religion of the Roman empire in 383 A.D. . . . Christian theorists were drawn to the idealist view that the established church holds a monopoly on religious truth that the state is obliged to enforce. As a practical matter the church would tolerate different religions where it lacked the political resources to impose its own doctrine. But where it had state support, it regarded imposition of religious orthodoxy as a sacred duty.[5]

Not long after the burning of the library at Alexandria the second blow to intellectual freedom fell when the Church silenced the free discussion of philosophy. Again, the once enlightened city of Alexandria was the first to feel the full force of religious despotism. Hypatia, daughter of the mathematician Theon, held daily discourses on philosophy in her academy. For this crime—that of seeking after truth— the successor to Theophilius, Cyril, permitted (or instigated) a mob of monks to kidnap Hypatia and, after dragging her naked through the streets, beat her to death in a church. The corpse was cut to pieces, the flesh scraped from the bones, and the remnants thrown into a fire.[6] So ended philosophical inquiry in Alexandria. The emperor Justinian soon emulated this brutal suppression by banning the teaching of philosophy and closing all schools in the birth place of philosophy, Athens. This was the beginning of an intellectual totalitarianism that was halted only with the gradual erosion of the power of Christianity itself. Unfortunately, today we are witnessing a return of that power and its quite foreseeable consequences.

G: Aren't you still talking about the Roman Catholic Church? Is it fair to indict all Christianity for the failure of one sect?

J: As I have demonstrated earlier, it wasn't just the Catholic Church that attempted to suppress intellectual dissent. After the Reformation almost all the various sects demonstrated a remarkable similarity in their intolerance of anybody opposed to their particular brand of Christianity. According to Reichley:

> The Protestant reformers . . . did not doubt, for the most part, that truth—their own versions of truth should be officially enforced. The Peace of Augsburg of 1555 which settled the religious wars rising

out of the Reformation, established not religious freedom, but the pragmatic principle that the religion of the prince should determine the religion of the people.[7]

Today, of course, the Christian religions are not as effective in their suppression of individual thought, but it is only because they lack the political power to dominate our lives as effectively as they once did. That is why I view the present trend of religious resurgence into the political arena with such alarm. To appreciate truly the potential consequences of Christianity's surge to power we have to view it from the historical perspective. Beginning with the events I have just related, we can further anticipate what was to come by the words of a fifth-century Christian synod which declared: "May those who divide Christ (from God the Father) be divided with the sword, may they be hewn in pieces, may they be burned alive!" It has been said that Christianity has been distinguished from all other religions by its greater readiness for persecution. I'm not certain about that. Mohammedanism was certainly spread by the sword as well, but not quite as successfully as Christianity. One thing I find especially remarkable about Christians, however, is their proclivity to persecute other Christians which, because of some ridiculous theological hair-splitting, are labeled heretics. Certainly Christians have been more freely persecuted by other Christians than they ever were by the Roman emperors. Recent research by Catholic historians indicates that only a small number of Christians were martyred during 400 years of Roman rule, contrary to the wild exaggerations of Eusebius and his colleagues.[8] Under Roman law guilt was determined by trial, and torture was restricted. All of that changed after 500 C.E. Torture and mutilation were sanctioned by law: "ordeal replaced trial and loss of eyes, ears, tongue, feet or testicles was appallingly common."[9]

The basis for the unmitigated persecutions of the succeeding thousand years was established by Augustine, the venerable Church Father who recommended suppression of heresy with his infamous policy which gave unbelievers the choice between conversion or extirpation—"force them to join—*coge intrare*." Not long after, in 444 C.E., Leo, the first to bear the title of Pope, took this doctrine to heart in his praise of the bishops of Spain for pressuring the state to put heretics to death. At the same time Leo was having followers of the Manichaen sect tortured to gain evidence against them.[10] Note how quickly early Christianity adopted the same methods employed by the Pharisees, who also tried to keep the blood off their hands by having the state (in the form of the Roman prelate) do their dirty work for them.

It has always been so. Religion attacks dissenters through the state. Earlier, I enumerated some of the atrocities of the Roman Church during the Crusades and Inquisitions, so I don't want to plow that ground again. Instead, I would like to discuss briefly the history of Christianity in the Americas. It is an indictment not only against the Catholic Church, but virtually every other Christian sect as well.

G: You undoubtedly are basing your exposition on the writings of those hostile to Christianity. How can you believe them any more than those who testify to the great benefits and humanitarianism resulting from the spread of Christianity?

J: The lack of credence I attach to the writings of the early Christians is due, in part, to the absurd nature of some of their own accounts. For example, Augustine in his thirty-third sermon states: "I was already Bishop of Hippo when I went into Ethiopia with servants of Christ to preach the Gospel. In this country, we saw many men and women without heads who had two great eyes in their breasts, and in countries still more southerly we saw people who had but one eye in their foreheads."[11] In his classic *City of God,* Augustine, who is deemed a Church Father and a saint by the Catholic Church, reports some of the following absurdities:

- The antiseptic nature of the peacock prevents it from rotting like other flesh (a fact he contends he personally validated).

- A fountain in Epires "unlike all others, lights quenched torches."

- Mares in Cappadocia are "impregnated by the wind."[12]

How's that for truthfulness? Furthermore, we know from the admissions of Eusebius that for ten centuries the primary goal of the ecclesiastical historian was to advance Christianity. This should not come as a surprise. Every popular religious and nationalistic movement has written a biased view of history. The only difference is that before Gutenberg invented the printing press, it was relatively easy to destroy all nonorthodox histories. The printed word, more than any other factor, ended Christianity's strangle hold on the truth. Cardinal Thomas Wolsey, bishop of London in 1474, clearly perceived the danger when he told his fellow clergymen that if they did not destroy the press, the press would destroy them.[13]

Given this attitude on the part of the Church hierarchy, it is foolish to rely on the Church historians to present an honest account. However, since the introduction of Christianity in America occurred after the invention of the printing press, its history could not be distorted or suppressed as effectively as during the Middle Ages. It is for this reason that a brief review of Christianity in America is enlightening, since it provides insight as to the manner by which Christian sects sought to gain converts and how they treated the intransigent Native Americans.

G: The only reason I allow you to prattle on rather than striking you down as you so richly deserve, is that when you repent for your sin of pride, you will make an excellent example of my mercy and divine grace. It took Augustine sixteen years to realize that there is only one path to truth and happiness: mine.

J: Well, You may have to wait a bit longer for me. Let me begin this historical encapsulation of religion in America with a quote from the journal of Christopher Columbus. After extolling the virtues of the natives he discovered in this New World, old Chris was quick to appreciate their commercial value. He wrote in his journal, "From here, in the name of the Blessed Trinity, we can send all the slaves that can be sold. Four thousand, which at the lowest figure will bring twenty contros."[14] And he promptly sent 500 of the "Indians" to Spain as slaves to work in mines and on plantations. Did the Church and good Christians everywhere cry out against the enslavement of these people whom Columbus described as "men of very subtle wit," "artless and generous with what they have" and showing "us much lovingness as though they would give their hearts"?[15] Absolutely not; no more than they did against enslavement of blacks for several centuries. Instead, there was much discussion as to whether or not these savages had souls. The debates concluded that Indians did have souls, so they could be duly baptized before being enslaved.

Everywhere throughout the New World the Church was an active collaborator in destroying the Native American culture and, oftentimes, Native Americans themselves. The Franciscan Frey Marcos accompanied the explorer Estevanico to the land of the Zunis. His gross exaggeration of the wealth he saw there prompted the expedition of Coronado and de Soto and their subsequent trail of cruelty and pillage.

Another Franciscan, Diego de Landa, described by historian Alvin Josephy, Jr., as an intolerant and uncompromising zealot, was one of the early bishops of the Yucatan. He ruthlessly destroyed all written remnants of the Mayan culture because similarities between it and the Christian religion were obviously the work of Satan. Any attempt by the Mayans to cling to their old beliefs was savagely punished. Then he turned around and wrote his own history of Mayan civilization.[16] How much of his history is false or distorted, we will never know.

When I was a child, I was told how the saintly friars took care of poor, ignorant Indian savages. Little did I know of the evil collusion between the Roman Church and Spanish state in those times. The story of the Navajos is typical of this murderous partnership. After the Keres Navajos were defeated by the Spanish for resisting their repressive rule, the governor of New Mexico, Don Juan de Onate, instructed his representative to punish them. If the representatives wished to show any mercy, he was to "seek all possible means to make the Indians believe you are doing so at the request of the friar—in this manner they will recognize the friars as their benefactors and will come to love and esteem them and fear us."[17] According to historian John Terrell, not much leniency was shown: 800 men, women and children were killed. Five hundred women and children and eighty men were taken as captives to San Juan, where each male over twenty-five had a foot cut off and was sentenced to twenty years of servitude. Younger males and all women were sentenced to slavery. Girls under the age of twelve were given to the friar Alonso Martinez, who distributed them as he wished to Spanish families.[18]

Even when the church and state opposed each other, they were as thieves dividing up the spoils. Franciscan and secular officials spent a century fighting for control of native labor. Often the priests were the real rulers of the province of New Mexico. Factories and farms were established by the Franciscans, and the natives were forced to work. The Franciscans ordered cruel punishment for those natives who disobeyed or attempted to run away. Of course, all native religious ceremonies were prohibited and natives were baptized to claim their souls for Christ.

Is it any wonder that the Navajos and Pueblos, under the leadership of a medicine man named Pope, revolted and in 1680 drove the Spaniards and the priests from New Mexico? Many priests were killed in this native fight for independence. As a child, I was taught that the priests were martyrs. Today I view them as victims of their own stupidity, greed, and cruelty. And what of all the Navajo converts whom the friars reported as numbering over 60,000? They scrubbed the baptism off with yucca seeds![19] The "eagerness" with which the Navajos embraced Christianity is evidenced by the very few Catholic Navajos today, even though many called themselves Christians. Later, when Protestant ministers controlled the distribution of food and goods to the once again conquered Navajos, many of the vanquished were forced to ostensibly accept Christianity. Unlike many other conquered tribes, however, the Navajos still demonstrate a strong allegiance to their pre-Christian beliefs and rituals.

No one knows how many Native Americans were slaughtered by

the Spanish. But estimates of the deaths of the natives of Latin America alone (primarily Arawaks, Caribs, and Ciboneys) through murder, disease and enslavement range up to six million.[20] This estimate may be high, but even if the number is a fraction of this estimate, does it make genocide any more palatable? And this was just the beginning.

G: You can't blame all the excesses of the Spanish Conquistadors on the Church. And you omit actions of the Church to save the natives from these evil men. Oftentimes, it was the Jesuits and the Franciscans who helped natives escape slave catchers.

J: Yes, but this was in part to tighten their own grip on the natives. The Jesuits controlled their own states in Brazil, Paraguay and Mexico. Eventually the pope so feared the feudal system being created by the Jesuits that, in 1767, he expelled them from the New World.[21]

G: Back in 1537, Pope Paul III tried to stop enslavement of natives by threatening to excommunicate those who dealt in slaves. And what about the Dominican Friar Bartolemé de las Casas who fought to protect the natives of the West Indies?[22]

J: But he still denied them the right to their own religion. About the most you can say of the few well meaning clerics was that they opposed butchering. Yet nowhere do I read of even one priest defending the rights of Native Americans to live as a free people with their own religion and culture. The reason is not, of course, that all these priests were evil or had bad intentions. Quite the contrary, oftentimes they may have been motivated by love. But their policies resulted in great evils because they sought to save the "savages' " souls at the expense of their culture and self-dignity. The Franciscan missionary Junipero Serra, who founded so many missions in California, may have been typical. Although there is a movement in the Church to canonize him as a saint, Native Americans see him in quite a different light. Although he did at times seek to protect the natives from Spanish oppression, he also condoned the whipping of miscreants.[23] His paternalistic attitude was to consider natives as ignorant children who must learn to accept Christianity as the only valid religion and European traditions as the only valid culture.

G: I still think it is unfair to blame all of Christianity for the sins of the Catholic Church.

J: It was not only the Catholic Church which was guilty of suppression and persecution of Native Americans; natives fared little better at the hands of other Christian sects. For example, the clergy of the Massachusetts Bay Pilgrims regarded the Pegnot Indians as agents of Satan. Since they had been characterized as such by the Protestant ministers, it took little provocation for the settlers to set fire to the native village near Mystic River, Connecticut, burning and shooting more than 600 inhabitants. In his book *North American Indians,* Christopher Davis quotes the Plymouth Governor who wrote, "It was a fearful sight to see them frying in the fire—and horrible was the stink and stench thereof. But, the victory seemed a sweet sacrifice and they gave praise thereof to God. . . . "[24] The idea of bloody sacrifices to God was certainly not new to these biblical fundamentalists. The central mystery of Christianity is the bloody sacrifice of a son to his father. It is a small wonder that massacres of this kind were to be repeated so often that it would be tedious to recount all of them. The last, at Wounded Knee, South Dakota, occurred only one hundred years ago. This last massacre is but one of the long string of atrocities that started with Columbus and has continued to the present century. Christianity sanctioned the White Man's avarice and insatiable desire for conquest under the euphemisms of "spreading the gospel" and "saving souls," just as later the phrase "White Man's Burden" covered the rape of Africa.

G: That is not a characteristic you can attribute solely to Christianity or even the white man. Long before a European set foot in the New World there were massacres, slavery and bloody sacrifices, as any student of the Aztecs and Incas could readily relate.

J: True, and, as you rightly point out, by far the greatest atrocities were committed by Aztecs and Incas: both cultures controlled by "priests," and both virtual theocracies where the king was a god. Their cultures were not unlike the monarchs who were said to rule by Divine Right in Christianized Europe. It is also interesting to note that the most democratic native tribes, where there was no strong shaman or god-king, seemed the least inclined to get into a protracted mode of war and conquest.

But the crucial point I want to make is this: if Christianity has any value, it should make a difference in the lives of those who profess it. However, the Native Americans could never discern that difference. As Seneca Chief Red Jacket said to a young Evangelical missionary: "Brother, we have been told that you have been preaching to the white people in this place. These people are our neighbors: we are acquainted with them. We will wait a little while and see what effect your preaching has upon them. If we find it does them good, makes them honest and less disposed to cheat Indians, we will consider again of what you have said."[25] Needless to say, what Red Jacket saw of the behavior of his Christian neighbors did not cause him to change his mind. He also recognized the hypocrisy of the missionaries: "These black coats talk to the Great Spirit, and ask for light that we may see as they do, when they are blind themselves and quarrel about the light that guides them. . . . The black coat tells us to work and raise corn, they do nothing themselves and would starve to death if someone did not feed them."[26] Red Jacket astutely observed that, "they make the book [the Bible] talk to suit themselves."[27]

The horror with which the Native American viewed the European after 1,500 years of Christian influence was perhaps best exemplified by the reaction of a West Indies chief named Hathvey. As related by the Dominican missionary Bartolemé de las Casas, a monk, in an attempt to convert the chief before he was to be burned alive, was telling him of the wonders of the Christian heaven. Hathvey expressed the view, no doubt held by the tens of thousands put to death with at least the tacit approval of the Church: "Let me go to Hell that I may not come where they are."[28]

In short, the Native American saw from the outset that Christianity had nothing to offer him, except the expeditious annihilation of his culture. Alvin M. Josephy, Jr., in his comprehensive history of the North American Indian, was forced to this same conclusion: "On the whole, the Church played an important role in the degeneration of the Indian culture."[29] I would only add that by "Church" we should include all Christian sects. And it wasn't simply the culture they helped to eradicate, but Native Americans themselves.

G: That is a very harsh accusation.

J: But entirely justified by the evidence. In a rare display of historical honesty, some of the Christian churches have admitted their guilt in this regard. On November 21, 1987, a Declaration of Apology was presented to the Indian and Eskimo peoples of the Pacific Northwest. In addition to confessing their "long-standing participation in the destruction of traditional Native American spiritual practices," the churches apologized for reflecting "the rampant racism of the dominant culture with which we were too willingly identified."[30] However, the churches failed to confess their culpability in fostering that racism by their elitist religious doctrines and beliefs.

It is difficult, if not impossible, to fully appreciate the evil visited upon the Native American in the name of Christianity. To this day, most Americans are unable to empathize with the plight of the American Indian. The reason is basically that the Judeo-Christian world view is so different from that of the Native American. It is human nature to disapprove and often despise that which is not understood. The native was looked upon as ignorant and lazy—barely human—because he lived at one with nature rather than trying to conquer it. This was relatively easy for most North American tribes, where their populations were in balance with their ecosystems. There were, of course, a few glaring exceptions: e.g., the Incas, the Mayas, the Toltecs, and the Aztecs. The rise of agriculture and the subsequent growth in population resulted in the development of a civilization equivalent to that of the ancient Egyptians and Sumerians. It is not surprising, then, as I mentioned earlier, that they suffered the evils as well as the blessings of an emerging civilization. Among the evils were wars of conquest, slavery and human sacrifice, all sanctioned by religious beliefs disconcertingly similar to the Judeo-Christian beliefs.

G: I will admit that both overzealousness and hypocrisy on the part of religious groups has oftentimes not worked in the best interests of Native Americans. I will also admit that the goal of eternal life, which should rightly take precedence over man's temporal existence, has, at times, resulted in ignoring the short-term consequences of religious doctrines. However, this hardly justifies a blanket condemnation of institutionalized religion.

J: All the evidence that I have presented is not enough? You want more? Then you shall have it. A. James Reichley tries to make the argument that religion has played a major role in the evolution of the American culture. That I will readily grant. However, on balance it has not been positive, as Reichley suggests, but largely has been, and continues to be, an impediment to social progress. Reichley makes the classic error of which opponents of organized religions are often accused. He confuses the actions of individuals with the actions of the religious institutions to which they belong. The general scenario has been that progressive individuals have taken positions on social issues which, if they did not represent the existing doctrine of the churches and the status quo, were almost certain to be opposed by the Church hierarchy. Then, after the new idea was generally recognized as morally correct, and a substantial portion of the populace supported the new position, the churches jumped on the train for fear of being left at the station.

G: That's just your jaundiced view.

J: It's another hypothesis supported by the evidence. Let's review some evidence that Reichley was kind enough to provide. At the time of the American Revolution 75 percent of the population was Puritan (later known as Congregationalist). Most of the rest were Calvinists. Puritanism was established as the official religion in three of the four original colonies. Civil authority was given the responsibility to "restrain corrupt opinions," i.e., any opinion that ran counter to Puritan doctrines.[31] All residents were subject to taxes imposed by the Church. Although we were taught as school children that groups like the Puritans fled to America to seek religious freedom, we were not told that they had no intention of granting religious freedom to others. Church leader John Cotton held that "Toleration made the world anti-Christian."[32] The Baptists were consequently banished from the Massachusetts Bay Colony. Between 1659 and 1661, after repeated banishments and whippings failed to drive away four Quakers, they were publicly hanged in Boston.[33] You will also recall that the Puritans were that same group who gave us the Salem witch trials in which nineteen people were executed, most of them old women guilty only of having the misfortune of living in that Christian community where superstition was supported by the power of the state.

G: You cannot generalize and ascribe the evils committed by one extreme sect to all Christian denominations. Roger Williams, the founder of Providence, Rhode Island, promoted complete freedom of worship, arguing that just as a pagan captain may be as skillful at piloting a ship to its desired destination as any Christian captain, so, too, "statecraft, like seacraft is a practical skill, unrelated to religious faith."[34]

J: I agree with his argument, but Roger Williams' advocacy of tolerance was the exception rather than the rule. At the time of the Revolution only three of the colonies had not established a state church. By wedding the church to the state the other colonies attempted to use the state to enforce morality as defined by the churches. In Pennsylvania an adultress would be publicly whipped and imprisoned for a year on the first offense, and sentenced to life imprisonment at hard labor for a second. Blasphemy could be punished by a three-month jail sentence. As late as 1838 in Massachusetts, people were sent to jail for blasphemy. (Several European countries such as England, Germany and Italy still have laws against blasphemy, although they are rarely enforced.)

G: Laws against blasphemy are okay by me.

J: Somehow I'm not surprised. More significantly, in the first Pennsylvania state constitution membership in the legislature was limited to Christians.

G: But all that did change, however.

J: Not at the instigation of the dominant religions. Rather, it was the secular trend that prompted our country to be founded as a secular state. Ethan Allen, the hero of Ticonderoga, echoed the sentiment of the majority of our founding fathers when he wrote, "Reason ought to control the Bible."[35] Although most signers of the Declaration of Independence were Christians by birth, fifty-two of the fifty-six signers were Masons, who were in favor of freethought. Thomas Jefferson traced his intellectual origins not to the Bible but to Stoic philosophers like Seneca, Cicero, Marcus Aurelius, and the European Enlightenment, especially John Locke and Francis Bacon. James Madison was grounded in the Scottish realism of David Hume, Thomas Reid, Adam Smith and Francis Hutcheson.[36] Benjamin Franklin was not even a Christian.

G: But all these men believed in God.

J: Yes, they were Deists who believed there was a God who, although he created the world, does not get involved in worldly matters. That was the belief of many of the people at the time. James Madison and Thomas Jefferson recognized the insidious danger posed by the Christian sects as each tried to establish itself as the state religion of the new nation. Madison worried that the newly won freedoms would be quickly extinguished: "In no instance have [ecclesiastical establishments] been seen as guardians of the people."[37] He appears to have shared the sentiment of Blaise Pascal, the seventeenth-century French mathematician and philosopher who wrote, "Men never do evil so completely and cheerfully as when they do it from religious conviction."[38]

Jefferson saw that his home state of Virginia continued to be dominated by one religion to the exclusion of all others. Members of other religions were taxed to support the state religion and those who refused were subject to jail sentences. To curb the religious oppression in his own state, Jefferson drafted, and the legislature eventually enacted, the Virginia Statute for Religious Freedom. He and Madison then sought to have the United States Congress address the issue as an amendment to the Constitution. The mood of the nation was with them since most persons were well aware of the religious wars that had ravaged Europe for centuries and were determined to prevent that horror from occurring in their new nation. The result was the passage of the First Amendment to the U.S. Constitution in 1791, which reads in part: "Congress shall make no law respecting the establishment of religion or prohibiting the free exercise thereof."

Many historians note that perhaps the greatest achievement of Jefferson and Madison was the series of safeguards built into the Constitution to establish a "wall of separation" between church and state. These safeguards actually protect each institution from encroachment by the other, and all citizens from the loss of their basic freedoms to either church or state.

The administration of our first president supported the view of Madison and Jefferson by asserting in the Treaty of Tripoli that, "The government of the United States is not, in any sense, founded on the Christian religion."[39] In so doing, it confirmed Jefferson's intention that the First Amendment was to "comprehend within its mantle of protection the Jew and the Gentile, the Christian and Muslim, the Hindu, and the infidel of every denomination."[40]

The foundation laid down by our forefathers created a nation unique in the history of the world. As Robert S. Alley describes it, "America is a secular state recognizing crimes not sins. It is a state where humanist and Christian and Jew and Muslim and secularist and nationalist have existed in good harmony far better than anywhere else in the world."[41] However, the wall of separation which has worked so well for so long is now beginning to buckle from the onslaught of those who would turn this country into a "Christian Nation" with their spiritual leaders holding the keys to power.

Regardless of the willingness of the Fathers of our country to avoid the worst abuses of religion, they still could do little to protect an individual who openly challenged the Bible myths from the vengeance of the Christian churches. Despite being a major intellectual and moral force in the American Revolution, Thomas Paine's *Age of Reason* earned him the reputation of an infidel and brought down the wrath of those Christians who so loudly proclaimed the right to freedom of speech a few years earlier. Although he was a firm believer in God, Paine was attacked in the press as a "drunken atheist" and "an object of disgust." Luckily for Paine, there were a few influential humanists, like his friend Jefferson, or he might have died in prison. Still, Paine became a social leper and died in poverty in 1809. The Quakers refused to bury him in their cemetery.

In Europe, the social situation was much the same as in this country. Intolerance and persecution did not stop with the Reformation. Martin Luther was as much in favor of burning witches (which he believed were running rampant in Germany) as was the Inquisition: "I would have no compassion on these witches. I would burn them all."[42] The only general agreement among Christian sects for 400 years after the reformation was the concerted effort to quash those who questioned the validity of Christian belief. I find it amazing that although the absurdity of many of the myths of Jesus must have been apparent to many scholars of the middle ages, it was not until the eighteenth century Enlightenment that any dared speak out. The reason was, of course, fear of reprisal.

Voltaire was one of the early critics of the biblical account of Jesus. He had already run afoul of the Church with his *Lettres philosophiques,* published in 1734, and had to flee to another section of France to write *The Important Examination of the Holy Scriptures.* Although he was imprisoned twice for his heretical opinions, Voltaire's fame and the greatly diminished powers of the Church spared him from far more severe actions.

England was equally illiberal. Richard Carlyle was sentenced to three years in prison and a large fine for publishing Paine's work. His wife and sister, who continued to sell the book, were also fined and imprisoned, as were a number of shop assistants.

Back in Paris, Baron d'Holbach was the first to risk an open disavowal of belief in God in general, but was prudent enough to publish *The System of Nature* (1770) under the pseudonym of a recently deceased man. Not surprisingly, d'Holbach's books were burned by the hangman.

G: As well they should have!

J: In nineteenth-century Germany, David Frederick Strauss's theological work cost him his career. After the second volume of *The Life of Jesus Critically Examined* was published in 1836, Strauss was promptly dismissed from the Tübingen Protestant seminary and had to forfeit any position in the academic world.

Like Strauss, Ludwig Feuerbach's (1804–1872) brilliant and satirical skepticism killed his chances for a professorship at any university. Luckily, marriage to a wealthy woman enabled him to pursue his philosophical writings or Christianity would have successfully snuffed his scholarly endeavors.* The unrelenting efforts of Christians to suppress freethought are adequately covered in books such as Samuel Putnam's, *Four Hundred Years of Free thought,* G. H. Taylor's *A Chronology of British Secularism,* and J. M. Wheeler's *Sixty Years of Free thought.*

Turning to the present day, I find it distressing that many people are unaware, or choose to ignore, that the attempt to suppress freedom of thought continues. The eminent philosopher and scientist Julian Huxley (1887–1975) came under fire from the Roman Catholic and Protestant orthodoxies during his leadership of United Nations Education, Scientific and Cultural Orgranization (UNESCO) because of his advanced views on sex and genetics. Bertrand Russell's experiences, when offered a professorship in the Philosophy Department of New York University in 1944, present a textbook case of how Christianity seeks to crush freethought when the rack and pillory are no longer available. It merits a brief review.

After Russell's appointment to NYU was announced, the Christian leadership closed ranks to begin a vicious campaign of vilification against Russell, the avowed pacifist and non-Christian. Bishop Manning of the Protestant Episcopal Church fired the opening volley by appealing to patriotism (a familiar tactic today): "Can anyone who cares for

---

*I'll have more to say about Feuerbach's interesting work later when we explore the psychological origin of man's beliefs.

the welfare of our country be willing to see such teachings disseminated with the countenance of our colleges and universities?"[43] The Jesuits soon picked up the hue and cry calling Russell "a desiccated, divorced, and decadent advocate of sexual promiscuity . . . who has betrayed his mind and conscience . . . [a] professor of immorality and irreligion. . . ."[44]

G: Well, you of all people should believe that everyone has a right to express his or her opinion. Or do you have a double standard?

J: Not at all. It is not their public expression I oppose, it is their concealed purpose and tactics. There were thousands of professors who, by Christian standards, could be labeled "immoral," and who were divorced. But what really threatened the Christians was Russell's erudite refutation of Christianity and theism. Here, indeed, was a man to be feared by the Christian Church.

The first tactic of Russell's detractors was to brand him as a Communist by taking quotes out of context from books he had written years earlier, including *What I Believe, Education and the Good of Life,* and *Marriage and Morals.* Next, they rallied their various organizations, from Sons of Xavier to the Holy Name Society, to demand the ouster of the university board members who voted for Russell's appointment. Various Christians were quick to use their public positions to press for his dismissal before he actually began teaching. Academic freedom was brushed aside as the Queens Borough President threatened to strike the entire appropriation for the upkeep of the municipal colleges if Russell was not removed. The voices of intellectual suppression became more numerous and more shrill despite endorsement of Russell by such intellectual giants as Alfred North Whitehead, John Dewey, Harlow Shapley, and Albert Einstein. "Great spirits," said Einstein, "have always found violent opposition from mediocrities."[45] Not withstanding the support of some of the greatest intellects of the age, New York Mayor Fiorello LaGuardia caved in to the pressures of organized religion and ordered Russell's appointment rescinded. Russell's appointment was eventually decided, not by the academic community, but by the courts.

In a decision that threatened to tear down Jefferson's wisely constructed wall of separation between church and state, Justice McGree of the New York Supreme Court revoked Russell's appointment, basing his decision on "*normae* and *criteria* . . . which are the laws of nature and nature's God."[46] Once again, Christianity rose to the occasion to silence (albeit ineffectively) one who questioned its validity.

G: Are you finally finished with your one-sided account?

J: Almost. I just want to add that things haven't changed much since

Russell's persecution. If anything, we are slipping backward. I found it almost laughable when Catholic theologian Hans Küng tried to support his assertion that there is no fundamental disagreement between science and theology today, as evidenced by the fact that only a few scientists publicly acknowledge their unbelief. Then he was forced to admit that many scientists may refrain from doing so to avoid unnecessary controversies between science and the Church.[47] The fact is that even today there is a heavy price to pay for publicly holding that the story of Jesus is, for the most part, a myth, and that the claim that Jesus is God was manufactured rather than revealed. No person could expect to hold a high-ranking public office if it were suspected that he held such a view (although several Congressmen have indicated as much through an anonymous questionnaire).

G: What about the renowned freethinker Robert Ingersoll (1833–1899)? He was Attorney General of Illinois and was almost a candidate for president.

J: He might well have been president were it not for his outspoken criticism of Christian orthodoxy. When once asked "What is the greatest book you've read?" Ingersoll answered, "I don't know, but I do know what the most costly was." He then held up his own little treatise attacking Christianity. Ingersoll was a courageous defender of the truth. He knew he was treading on dangerous ground and was often forced to make only oblique reference in his attacks on religion, since many states had antiblasphemy laws that could have landed him in jail.

G: So what if religions try to influence politics? Don't the clergy have a right, even an obligation, to express their viewpoints? Didn't you castigate Pope Pius XII for failing to do just that?

J: As long as religions use reason and evidence to support their positions I have no complaint. The trouble is they usually seek to speak as the voice of God, and thus they pretend that they have superior knowledge to bear on the issue. Additionally, I find that the primary intent of any religion is not to search for truth but to defend and propagate its own creed.

Today Christianity is, in many respects, even more powerful and devious in its attempts to close the lid on dissent. With its coffers laden with silver collected from simple-minded and oftentimes desperate followers, it can afford its own TV and radio stations. It is so well organized that it can strongly influence a presidential platform, as Republicans realized in their 1992 convention. With thousands of church schools it can curtail academic freedom and develop a propaganda program that has had a major impact on U.S. policy, especially since World War II.

The fundamentalists are beginning to succeed in turning back the clock on scientific advancement, inserting theological opinions such as "creation science" into the public classrooms. The tentacles of the "born again" movement even reach into corporate boardrooms. It is not simply generosity that prompts firms to offer space for the teaching of the Bible at lunch time. What, however, do you think my company's reaction would be if I tried to hold classes to discuss the mythical origins of the Bible or the truly terrifying history of Christianity? The management would be most reluctant to stir up a religious backlash.

G: You continue to look at only one side of the ledger. I find your historical account disingenuous. It completely ignores the many saints nurtured by the institution of Christianity over the past two thousand years, people who have devoted their lives to helping their fellow men and women.

J: If by saints you simply mean people dedicated to helping their fellow human beings, Christianity has no unique claim to such persons. I admire the efforts of those devoted individuals such as Mother Teresa. However, Albert Schweitzer was equally as altruistic although he did not believe in the Christian account of Jesus.

It is true that there are some radical priests and even a few bishops in underdeveloped countries who openly oppose the exploitation and persecution of the poor. But this attitude is not necessarily an outgrowth of their Christian beliefs so much as an empathic response to appalling poverty or else an enlightened worldview. Some clerics have had to quit the Church to pursue their social goals. Most modern day social advances have been gleaned from the writings of such men as Voltaire, Paine, John Stuart Mill, Darwin, Huxley, Freud, Comte, Peirce, Dewey, Russell, Ayer and hundreds of other freethinkers.

In summary, the evidence is overwhelming that the propagation of Christianity in both the Old World and the New was due in large measure to coercion, persecution and suppression. Throughout its history, from the earliest purges of heretics, through the Crusades, the Inquisition, and repression of other cultures throughout the world, Christianity has demonstrated its destructive antihuman values.

G: All that your longwinded exposition demonstrates is that religious institutions are not perfect, a fact that most of them (with the glaring exception of the Catholic Church) would readily admit. However, the failings of the institutions cannot be blamed on the teachings of Jesus, but on the inherent weakness, fallibility and ignorance of humankind. As people have increased their knowledge and understanding of the teachings of Jesus, their institutions have become more tolerant and benevolent.

J: Hogwash! You have it completely backward. While it is true that the evils committed by humankind are often due to ignorance, evil is not a function of "inherent weakness" or "original sin" as Christians declare, but rather genetic characteristics and environmental conditioning. Throughout history it was not religion that reformed humankind, but the latter, in the form of a small number of philosophers and intellectuals who recognized the need for change, which has reformed religion. More often than not, the Churches have sought to condition their followers to oppose any intellectual or social progress that threatens the primacy of the Church.

With few exceptions, Christian religions have backed popular opinion, since that is always the safest course for a bureaucratic institution. Prior to the American Civil War, churches in the South backed slavery with the same fervor with which those in the North opposed it. The Reverend Alexander Campbell, one of the founders of the Disciples of Christ, observed: "There is not one verse in the Bible inhibiting slavery, but many regulating it. It is not then, we conclude, immoral."[48] According to Reverend Nathan Lord, a past president of Dartmouth College, "Slavery was incorporated into the civil institutions of Moses; it was recognized accordingly by Christ and his Apostles."[49] And the Reverend Taylor, a head of the Theological Department of Yale College expressed the opinion: "I have no doubt that if Jesus Christ were on earth, he would, under certain circumstances, become a slaveholder."[50] Bishop John England of Charleston assured President Van Buren's secretary of state that, "No pope had ever condemned domestic slavery as it existed in the United States."[51] Even a Northern bishop, John Hughes of New York, argued that "this condition of slavery is an evil, yet it is not an absolute and unmitigated evil" since it had brought so many Africans to civilization and Christianity.[52] It is evident that the Church's primary interest was always to gain more souls into its fold, regardless of the impact on their earthly welfare.

Ever since the industrial revolution relatively few Christian leaders have spoken out for legislation to mitigate exploitation of the working class in mines, sweatshops, mills and farms. Only when a particular movement had gained momentum and had become a *cause célèbre* did organized religions take up the banner. A good example is the movement for women's rights. Not until the last decade, when the alternative was a mass exodus of younger women from the churches, did the Protestant sects begin permitting women to become ministers. The Catholic Church, which does a much more efficient job of eliciting conformity from its membership, has, for the most part, retained its female members while keeping women in a subservient role.

Religions can always be depended upon to support a war effort, at least if it is a popular war. Protestant, Catholic, and Jewish clergymen solidly supported both world wars and Vietnam until the popularity of the latter began to wane. According to Reichley, the satisfaction expressed by a Protestant minister in contemplating "Jesus himself sighting down a gun barrel and running a bayonet through our enemy's body" was not atypical.[53]

During the early days of the civil rights movement, Martin Luther King thought he could count on the support of fellow ministers, priests and rabbis throughout the South. Instead, he found that reactions ranged from outright opposition to silence, out of fear of angering parishioners. Of course, once the movement became popular and they saw many of their faithful marching off to protests, some of the clergy were quick to join in.

G: Yet you cannot deny that there have been many courageous clergymen who were among the first to recognize injustice and speak out against it. As long ago as 1688, Francis Daniel Pistorius, leader of a German Pietist group, along with three Mennonites, called for the abolution of slavery.[54] In 1758, the Quakers also urged their members to free their slaves.

J: I admit there were courageous abolitionist ministers. However, they were almost always found in the North where slavery was not an economic issue supported by their parishioners.

G: There were those who led the fight against other social evils. In 1919, Monsignor John A. Ryan, whom you castigated earlier, called for the abolition of child labor, publicly provided insurance for unemployment and retirement, legal enforcement of the rights of workers to organize, and a national housing program.[55]

J: Unfortunately, Ryan's outspokenness resulted in the Church temporarily dissolving the National Catholic Welfare Council which he headed. When it was reinstated, the message was clear that the council was to follow a less radical line.

G: It cannot be denied that there has been an element in the clergy whose members have long preached a social gospel advocating the justice and freedoms which your hero Thomas Paine supported so vigorously.

J: Yes, I am aware of the efforts of some of these courageous men in recent years, but again they are the efforts of individuals who happen to belong to a religion. They are more often than not opposed by the hierarchy of their churches. In the case of the Catholic Church, there is growing opposition in Rome to the "revolutionary" sympathies of the proponents of Liberation Theology. Although past popes have been quick to excommunicate left-wing revolutionaries, Pope John

Paul II was as loath to excommunicate right wing fascists, such as Chile's dictator, Augusto Pinochet, as his predecessors were during the thirties.

In the case of some of the Protestant religions the situation is somewhat different. During the last two decades some groups—such as the Methodists, Episcopalians, and Presbyterians—have really attempted to provide a leadership role on social issues both in this country and abroad. Unfortunately, it is questionable whether they will be able continue their new role for long in the face of declining church membership. There are two reasons for this. First, since their membership tend to be better educated, many have forsaken their childhood myths. At the other end of the spectrum, the less educated are shocked by the radical preaching and practices of their clergy and seek the comfortable superstitions and prejudices of the fundamentalist religions such as the Mormons, the Jehovah's Witnesses, and the Assemblies of God.

Here we are forced to recognize a basic fact of any religion: its success depends upon how well it matches the psychological character of its potential adherents. To be widely accepted, a religion must strive for the least common denominator of human values. It is not surprising, therefore, that the Assemblies of God churches, preaching a gospel of acquisitiveness, are flying high despite the scandals of Jim Bakker and Jimmy Swaggart. Since the purpose of any religious organization is to perpetuate itself, it will always seek to align itself with the morality of the status quo.

That society, and the institution of Christianity, has progressed even as far as it has, is due to those singularly courageous individuals, both theists and nontheists, who, following the dictates of reason and intellectual honesty, risked everything in their search for truth. Moreover, were it not for the protection of a secular state, Christianity would once again shackle human thought and freedom in a tyranny of ideological intolerance. It must be understood that this evil intention is not due merely to a few ignorant or wicked men, but is inherent in the belief system of Christianity.

G: You've made that last allegation several times now; but, although you've dragged me through a lot of ancient history, you have yet to substantiate the claim that it is the basic tenets of Christianity, as expressed in the gospels and epistles of the New Testament, which are to blame.

J: That's the subject I will turn to next.

7

Christianity: The Cure That Cripples

But as for these very enemies, who did not want me to be king over them, bring them here and slay them in my presence.

—Luke 19:27

J: It is essential to understand that the many ills of Christianity were not simply the perversion of a generally good institution, but were inherent failures of the institution itself. These failures were bound to generate the resulting evils regardless of the good intentions of many, perhaps most, Christians throughout history. The origin of this innate failure can be traced in part to the very teachings attributed to Jesus, and even more to the efforts of Paul and his successors to establish a religion.

G: Only the most rabid type of anti-Christ would attack the very teachings of Jesus rather than argue that some of the religious organizations have either paid only lip service to His teachings or perverted them entirely. If you were to take this latter course of argument, I might even tend to agree with you. But, how could you possibly find argument with the command of Jesus to "love thy neighbor"?

J: A perfectly admirable admonition; however it did not originate with Jesus. Five hundred years before Him Confucius advocated such a Golden Rule, in its negative form: "Do not do to others what you would not like yourself."[1] And it was a venerable sentiment even at the time of Confucius. The ancient Indian poem *Mahabharata,* contains this passage: "In granting or refusing a request, a man obtains a proper rule of action by looking on his neighbor as himself."[2] Later the attitude was echoed in the Jewish Talmud: "What thou does not like, do thou not to thy neighbor" (Sabbath 31:1). And again in the Old Testament: "Thou shalt love thy neighbor as thyself" (Lev. 19:18).

173

There is very little, if anything, that is original in the teaching attributed to Jesus. Like the myth of Jesus itself, the sentiments he expresses are a hodgepodge of aphorisms and moral convictions that can be found in the ancient Egyptian, Babylonian, Persian, Greek, Buddhist, Confucian, and Hindu religions. It is impossible to sort out which of these moral precepts were indigenous to any particular religion and which borrowed from another. But one thing is certain: Christianity, a late-comer in the history of religion, merely plagiarized sentiments from Judaism and the so-called pagan religions. In his book *Sources of Morality in the Gospels,* Joseph McCabe quoted the moral views attributed to Jesus in the gospels and in parallel columns gave exact moral equivalents from Jewish and pagan writers.

G: Is that bad? Isn't it just possible that Christianity is a synthesis of the best tenets of all those earlier religions?

J: Or the worst. To be fair, it is a mixture of both good and bad. Moreover, the New Testament writers oftentimes completely muddled the earlier allegories and consequently had Jesus speaking complete nonsense. Professor Arthur Drews provides several examples in his essay "The Teaching of Jesus."[3]

The parables of the marriage, feast, the laborers in the vineyard, the unjust steward, the lost piece of silver, the lost sheep, and many others are all to be found in the Talmud. Let me be the first to admit that some of the teachings alleged of Jesus, even if not original, are elegantly expressed in terms that all can understand. Take the Beatitudes, for example. In the Egyptian Book of the Dead can be found the admonitions to "feed the hungry, give drink to the thirsty, clothe the naked, bury the dead. . . ."[4] All the Beatitudes can be found in a work called *The Sacred Book of the Jews*[5] as well as in the Old Testament.[6] Nonetheless, they are concisely and beautifully summarized in the Sermon on the Mount.

The problem with the New Testament is the demand of Christian religions that the teachings in the gospels and the epistles be accepted without question as inspired by You. Any other body of instruction is constantly being reevaluated in light of current world conditions and new knowledge of human nature.

An uncritical, literal acceptance of the teachings of Jesus and his apostles may result in individually and socially detrimental behavior. For example, many of the exhortations of Jesus were given under his mistaken belief that the end of the world was at hand. In the context of the real world they would be foolish or even cruel. Telling a person to "sell whatever thou hast, and give to the poor" (Mark 10:17-22), if taken literally, would lead to a nation of street people!

If everyone tried to follow that advice, there would be no buyers. So too, the command, "If anyone would go to the law with thee and take thy tunic let him take thy cloak as well" (Matt. 5:40) encourages the meek to aid the aggressor. The injunction, "To him who asks of thee give and from him who would borrow of thee do not turn away" (Matt. 5:42), effectively encourages the lazy freeloader at the expense of the frugal and industrious. Obviously, it depends on the reason for the request and the situation of the supplicant whether giving or lending is a good thing. If done indiscriminately it is good neither for the giver nor the receiver. No alcoholic was ever helped by being given money to buy a bottle of wine.

G: You are taking these teachings of Jesus much too literally, and you know it.

J: If nothing that Jesus said can be taken at face value then the New Testament becomes no more than a book of platitudes to be placed on the same level with Aesop or, at best, the *Moral Epistles* of Seneca. But the preoccupation of Jesus and his followers with the impending Last Judgment resulted in the teachings of extremism, which has served cults like the Moonies well. "If anyone comes to me and does not hate his father and mother, and wife and children, and brothers and sisters, yes and even his own life, he cannot be my disciple" (Luke 14:26). What an invitation to fanaticism!

G: Doesn't your Confraternity Edition of the New Testament provide a footnote explaining that the above passage merely means that we should pay no attention to parental requests if these are detrimental to our spiritual welfare?[7]

J: Yes, and later translations of this passage also tend to soften it. But then whose words are we listening to, those of Jesus or some apologetic translator? It just proves my point that the New Testament is not an infallible guide to ethical behavior, but simply another interesting book that must be read in the context of its time and place. To illustrate the absurdity of accepting the New Testament as Your revealed word, just listen to the advice of Paul: "To the unmarried and widows, it is good for them if they so remain even as I" (1 Cor. 7:8). Paul does concede that for those who lack "self-control" it is "better to marry than to burn," but later exhorts those "who have wives [to] be as if they had none" (1 Cor. 7:29). In other words, Paul is advising Christians to refrain from sex even for purposes of procreation. This is the advice of one who erroneously believed the Second Coming of Christ and the end of the world were imminent. If all good Christians had followed the advice of Paul, the cult would have died out in a generation.

Luckily for Christianity, most people superimpose their own value system on a religion when its teachings become too absurd. For example, except for some self-serving fundamentalists, most Christians have chosen to ignore Paul's example of lying to advance the cause of religion: "But if through my lie the truth of God has abounded to his glory, why am I also judged a sinner." (Rom. 3:7) Elsewhere he justifies deceit as a way to ingratiate himself with each of the groups he approaches to spread the gospel. When preaching to the Jews Paul pretends to follow their law, but to win over Gentiles he is quick to drop the law of Moses and adopt the ways of the Gentiles (1 Cor. 9:19–23).

In the same passage of Luke where Jesus commanded every believer to give the shirt (tunic) off his back, Jesus also offers the famous advice, "and to him who strikes thee on one cheek offer the other also." As George H. Smith asks, is this not an invitation to injustice?[8] How much more do I admire the man who fights injustice or who rebels against the despot. In fact, it has been demonstrated through computer simulations that a better strategy for insuring social harmony is "tit for tat," i.e., that we return in kind the behavior presented to us. If we adopt this approach, rational people will behave in a socially beneficial manner since they will discover that it is in their own self-interest to do so.

G: So, you are an advocate of violence?

J: Only as a last resort. But would you advocate that the world should have turned the other cheek to Hitler's armies? No society can simply lay down all its arms unilaterally unless all societies do so. A simplistic Christian maxim ignores such practicalities.

G: That's why it needs an institution and ministers to interpret the commands of Jesus in the context of today's needs.

J: It has failed dismally in that regard. Because of its attempts to represent the New Testament writings as Your word, Christianity has not sought to argue for its teaching in a public forum. Rather, as I have shown, it has sought from the outset to coerce its followers and those who differ in their belief by claiming access to a higher order of truth. This is a direct consequence of the teachings of the New Testament. Specifically, Christianity can trace its two chief flaws directly to that source: a dogmatism that rejects all opposing views, and the acceptance of human suffering not only as inevitable but beneficial.

G: I beg to differ.

J: Well, let's examine the evidence.

Christian Dogmatism as Derived from the New Testament

J: The history of Christian intolerance was outlined in earlier chapters. Such intolerance is due to the dogmatism evident in the teachings of Jesus and His disciples, who claimed that the road to wisdom is not through reason and observation, but through blind adherence to their teachings. Consequently, the very process of true learning is anathema to Christianity. Jesus exhorted: "Unless you turn and become like little children you will not enter into the kingdom of heaven" (Matt. 18:3). It is more than guilelessness that Jesus is advocating; with these words reason becomes a vice and ignorance a virtue. Throughout the teachings of the New Testament "devotion and commitment are euphemisms for obedience and conformity."[9] For those who blindly follow, Jesus promises salvation. For those who choose not to accept Him as their Savior and Lord, He threatens revenge.

G: Jesus was totally against violence. That is why he is called the Prince of Peace.

J: Nevertheless, that's the way Christian priests and ministers have interpreted the parable for centuries. It has provided the justification they needed to inflict the many atrocities upon dissenters which I documented earlier. And how did Jesus earn the title Prince of Peace? He never specifically condemned war. Rather, he reputedly said: "Do not think that I have come to send peace upon the earth; I have come to bring the sword, not peace." He adds that "I have come to set man at variance with his father, and a daughter with her mother, and a daughter-in-law with her mother-in-law; and a man's enemies will be those of his own household" (Matt. 10:34-36). Tragically, this is one of the few promises that history shows Jesus was successful in fulfilling.

When Jesus was concerned about being arrested, the "Prince of Peace" ordered his disciples to buy swords (Luke 22:36). He should not have been surprised then, when Peter later cut off the ear of a servant of one of those who came to arrest Jesus. But when Jesus saw that he was outnumbered he gave up without a fight claiming that he could have twelve legions of angels defend him if he desired it. At least that is the account given in Matthew. The earlier gospel of Mark doesn't mention Jesus' claim of a heavenly defense, and the writer of Luke apparently felt that cutting off ears might leave the scene in a bad light, so he had Jesus heal the severed ear. Nice try, but the changes in the text provide evidence of revision rather than a peace-loving Jesus.

There is another favorite quote of Jesus which Christian zealots have employed as justification for their persecutions:

> If thy right eye is an occasion of sin to thee, pluck it out and cast
> it from thee; for it is better for thee that one of thy members should
> perish than that thy whole body should be thrown into hell. And
> if thy right hand is an occasion of sin to thee, cut it from thee,
> for it is better to thee that one of thy members should be lost than
> that thy whole body should go into hell. (Matt. 5:29–30)

In case someone failed to get the message, the writer of Matthew
repeats this ugly admonition in chapter 18:7–9 adding that it is "better
for thee to enter life maimed or lame, than having two hands and
two feet, to be cast into everlasting fire." What more definite injunction
did the zealots of Christianity need for the torture and maiming of
heretics?

G: Jesus was speaking only metaphorically.

J: Who is to say when he was speaking metaphorically and when he
was not? We keep returning to this same problem. The priests and
ministers for hundreds of years took the writer of Matthew quite literally
when he had Jesus say: "Whoever causes one of these little ones to
sin, it were better for him to have a great millstone around his neck,
and be drowned in the depths of the sea" (Matt. 18:6).

What constituted a sin? Simply not accepting Jesus as God or
the New Testament as the inspired word of God: "But he who does
not believe is already judged, because he does not believe in the name
of the only-begotten Son of God" (John 3:18).

What is the judgment? "He who believes has everlasting life; he
who is unbelieving towards the Son shall not see life, but the wrath
of God rests upon him" (John 3:36). Hence, by that simple logic,
anyone who argued against Christianity deserved eternal damnation.
No wonder, then, that a sympathetic judge of the Inquisition would
try to enlighten poor sinners, and save them from the fires of hell
by placing them on the rack. After all, did not Jesus himself recommend
cutting off a foot or hand if necessary to save a person's soul? Paul
also urged that a sinner be delivered over "for the destruction of the
flesh, that his spirit may be saved" (1 Cor. 5:5). Just so we wouldn't
miss the implication of Paul's remark, my Confraternity Edition of
the Bible adds a footnote to explain that Paul implied both excommunication and "physical trials" to destroy the sinful tendencies in
the poor sinner. This became the actual practice of the Catholic and
Protestant sects until the time when secular laws began making a
distinction between sins and crimes.

Not content with merely condemning individuals who did not
accept Jesus as their Savior, the New Testament reserves a special

fate for entire communities that reject the word of God. Jesus is uncompromising: "Amen I say to you, it will be more tolerable for the land of Sodom and Gomorrah in the day of judgment than for that town" (Matt. 10:15). What better justification did Christian armies need to put to the sword entire communities, "and let God choose his own"?

G: Must you continually dredge up past excesses?

J: I'm just trying to show that those evils cannot simply be explained by arguing that humankind was more savage over the last 2,000 years than it is today. That humans act savagely is in large part a function of their cultural ethic. The ethic of the New Testament was vengeance on any who rejected Christianity. Although on one hand the New Testament writers have Jesus preaching forgiveness, He espouses an extremely intolerant attitude toward those who do not accept Him as their Savior. Jesus flew into a rage because commerce was being conducted in the temple (Matt. 21:12–13). Shortly thereafter, the writer of Matthew attempts to scare his readers into submission by having Jesus curse a fig tree because it was unable to satiate His hunger. The tree immediately withers, and Jesus promises that those who believe in Him will have equal powers (Matt. 21:21–22). (I haven't heard of any born again Christian repeating that trick.)

G: That account was also allegorical.

J: That is not what the fundamentalists would have us believe. Accepting that it is an allegory, then who is to say what is allegory or factual in the New Testament? More to the point, the message conveyed by these passages undermines the ostensible teachings of love we read in other passages. It reads as though Jesus were shaking his fist saying "You better love me or else look out!"

This same message is conveyed throughout the rest of the New Testament. It is easy to see the transition from intolerance to atrocity. Jesus continually condemned unbelievers, as did the writers of the Epistles. The writer of the First Epistle of John says, "And every spirit that does not confess Jesus is not of God, but is of antichrist . . ." (1 John 4:2–3). Such passages prompted Polycarp to write, "For everyone who shall not confess that Jesus Christ has come in the flesh is the antichrist; and whoever shall not confess the testimony of the cross is the devil."[10] And isn't it logical that anyone who is a good Christian has an obligation to fight the Devil, even unto death?

It is not difficult to see how the modern fundamentalists develop their inclination for intolerance when viewed in the light of the following biblical exhortations:

"Do not bear the yoke with unbelievers. For what has justice in common with inequity? Or, what fellowship between light and darkness? What harmony between Christ and Belial? Or what pact has the believer with the unbeliever? (2 Cor. 6:14,15). (As if this were not clear enough the Confraternity Edition adds this note: "Bear the yoke; the reference is to marriage, though the principle has application to all relations of Christians and pagans.")

"If anyone preach a gospel to you other than that which you have received, let him be anathema!" (Gal. 1:9). As soon as the Church consolidated its power, the verdict of anathema oftentimes led to the stake.

". . . the Lord Jesus, who will come from heaven with the angels of his power in flaming fires to inflict punishment on those who do not obey the gospel of our Lord Jesus Christ. These will be punished with eternal ruin . . ." (2 Thess. 1, 7–9). (What a neat justification for persecuting the unbeliever. After all, according to this letter from Paul, Jesus himself intended as much.)

"If anyone comes to you and does not bring this doctrine, do not receive him into the house, or sing to him welcome. For he who says to him welcome is a sharer in his evil works" (3 John 1:10–11; 2 John IV in King James version). (So much for toleration.)

That Christianity is a religion of love, as some would have us believe, is a complete denial of the New Testament writings as exemplified by yet another little horror story. In an episode in the acts of the Apostles, a man named Ananias and his wife Sapphira sold a piece of their land, but instead of donating all the proceeds to the Apostles, they secretly kept some. It would seem that it was their right to do so, but Peter thought otherwise. He rebuked them, accusing them of lying to God, and caused both of them to drop down dead! Some loving religion, that Christianity.

Even in matters unrelated to faith, Jesus at times demonstrated the narrow, chauvinistic view hardly to be expected of one whose followers today claim to be the epitome of a loving people. When a Canaanite woman (who, the gospel makes clear, was a Gentile rather than a Jew like Jesus) threw herself at his feet to beg that he cast a devil out of her daughter, Jesus rudely ignored her, saying, "Let the children first have their fill for it is not fair to take the children's bread and cast it to the dogs." The Confraternity Edition footnote interprets Jesus' remarks as meaning that he had come to bring the kingdom of God first to the children of Israel. Perhaps, but it is none-theless a grossly insensitive comment. Humbly, the desperate woman took the insult and replied, "Yes Lord; for even the dogs under the table eat of the children's crumbs." Only after the women groveled did Jesus condescend to "cure" her daughter: "Because of this answer go thy way; the devil has gone out of thy daughter" (Mark 7:26–30).

The point of all this is that the intolerance that has been the hallmark of Christianity in practice can be traced to its very theological underpinnings. What Christ and his apostles demanded above all was blind, unwavering trust and obedience. This demand was simply carried to its logical extreme by the Church in the Middle Ages, when all dissent was labeled heresy demanding the most horrible torture to save the dissenter's soul. The Church's dictates were to be followed with slavish devotion; any attempt to think for oneself was inherently dangerous to one's soul, and therefore, more than likely, to one's life.

This, then, is the great legacy of Christianity today. Since it rests on such shaky intellectual ground, Christianity is fundamentally opposed to the primary purpose of education: to enable the student to develop the power of critical thinking. The role of the teacher was rightly perceived by the ancient Greeks to be that of guide to show the way to a lifetime of seeking. At best, the teacher could instruct the student on certain rules of logic and the dangers of various forms of fallacious reasoning. Later, science taught the value of observation and experimentation in the process of learning. The primary function of an academic institution is to foster independent habits of mind and a spirit of inquiry free from bias and prejudices of the moment. Contrast this position with that of Christian education. Thoreau made the observation that the way a priest teaches, the student is never educated to the degree of consciousness (i.e., the ability to reason) but only to the degree of trust and reverence, and a child is not made a man but kept a child.

Plato and Aristotle argued to support their claims with logic and evidence; Jesus and the Christian Fathers issued proclamations backed by the use of force. Consider the view of education espoused by a Doctor of the Church, Origen: "We [the Christian clergy] who are well advised of these things do professedly teach men to believe without examination."[11]

G: That was said at a time when the general public was far more ignorant than today. The average man had neither the educational foundation nor the time to try to understand theology and philosophy, so it was prudent to trust in those with greater knowledge. Even today you take the word of a nuclear physicist on matters concerning physics.

Why shouldn't the layman take the word of a theologian concerning religion?

J: No physicist would attempt to prevent me from studying in his or her field, nor threaten me with sanctions or even death if I disagreed with their findings. Quite the contrary, scientists, as a whole—although they demand rigorous verification of new theory—get quite excited about advancements in knowledge. Just look at the accumulation of scientific knowledge in the last two hundred years, despite the frequent efforts by Christians to halt or reverse the advance of knowledge whenever it threatened to undercut the fiction upon which their religion was founded. Discussing the Christian attack on the teaching of evolution, Reichley admits that "Banning the teaching of evolution rested squarely on the belief that a religious doctrine applied by government should be the primary criterion for public truth."[12]

Even today there are fundamentalists who support geocentralism —the belief expressed in the Bible that Earth is the center of the universe. Biblical creationists have attempted to legislate their theological viewpoint into the public school systems of Louisiana, Arkansas, and Texas. Whether it has to do with the teachings of Galileo or the twentieth-century psychologist B. F. Skinner, Christianity has sought to suppress reason and evidence. What other religion can exult in a man like Paul who condemned the Greeks' search for wisdom (1 Cor. 1:22), who cautioned against the dangers of philosophy (Col. 2:8); and who took pride in the "foolishness of his [own] preachings," attempting to equate foolishness with true wisdom (1 Cor. 1 18–23). What other religion proclaims to be a saint a man like Augustine, who, Hans Küng is forced to admit, believed that the desire for knowledge was an evil on a par with desire for pleasure and power?[13] What other religion has made human thought a sin?

As a young man, I was constantly warned by the priests against evil thoughts, not only thoughts of sex, which is the great hang-up of Christianity, but also against dwelling overmuch on the Christian mysteries. For example, I recall a college theology text which attempted (rather unsuccessfully) to reconcile free will and predestination. The text stressed the warning that there was danger in thinking too much on the issue because it was essentially a mystery and, hence, intrinsically incomprehensible. Why, I began to wonder, do Christians always call a non sequitur a mystery and tell me to stop asking questions under threat of damnation?

The student is taught not to question, but to accept certain truths on the basis of authority, tradition and faith. The Catholic Church and fundamentalist Christian sects are most guilty in this regard, but to some extent all Christian institutions share this failing. Unable to fend off the intellectual attacks of critics, Christians hide behind a mantle of righteousness and brand their opponents as Communists and/or immoral atheists (even though most of the early detractors of Christianity were deists).

Another theology book refers to the Institutum Divi Thomae, an organization for basic scientific research at Cincinnati, Ohio, where "students of every religious persuasion are welcome, but professed atheists are excluded on the grounds that they do not know how to think."[14] A more direct expression of Christian intolerance was displayed just outside Washington, D.C., where a Unitarian Church was repeatedly vandalized and the minister and his family threatened for permitting atheists and others to simply discuss issues such as abortion and socialism. These persecutors, like the Christians of the Middle Ages, followed the dictum expressed by Caligula in Albert Camus' play *Caligula* (1945): "Where one can't refute one strikes."

G: I think most Christians would condemn such acts as decidedly un-Christian. You can't blame everyone for the actions of a few.

J: I don't condemn everyone, but I think their actions were merely a more direct expression of the feelings of many Christians.

Christianity Teaches Acceptance of Suffering and Injustice rather than Opposition to Them

J: Reliance on archaic teachings as unalterable "truths" prevents Christian thought from progressing to meet the changing needs of society—or at best allows it to do so with socially detrimental lags. What Harry Elmer Barnes wrote almost fifty years ago about the teachings of Jesus is true today: "As long as our own leaders revert to the doctrine of an antique mind, which was itself insularly uninformed, as the source of their inspiration, we are bound to remain in a period of religious confusion and stagnation."[15] I would substitute *social* for *religious* confusion, but the key word is *stagnation.* Rather than urging people to seek to end injustice, the New Testament writers taught that we should accept suffering and injustice as a part of the lot of humankind for being inherently sinful. As such, the New Testament has been a useful tool for those who sought to exploit their fellow men and women.

Take the case of slavery, whose proponents found ample support in the Bible. Nowhere did Jesus speak out against slavery. In itself, this is not surprising since in his time slavery was accepted as a natural fact of life. Jesus never sought to oppose the existing social order;

he accepted it unquestioningly, as did his disciples. Peter advised: "Servants be subject to your masters in all fear; not only to the good and moderate, but also to the severe" (1 Pet. 2:18). Paul echoed the counsel of Peter: "Let slaves who are under the yoke account their masters deserving of all honor, that the name of the Lord and his teaching be not blasphemed" (1 Tim. 6:1). Elsewhere Paul writes, "Slaves, obey in all things your masters according to the flesh" (Col. 3:22). He advises Titus to encourage slaves to accept their position graciously: "Exhort slaves to obey their masters, pleasing them in all things and not opposing them" (Titus 2:9).

G: Maybe Paul was simply being realistic. Since it was futile to resist, slaves were urged to ease their burden by getting along with their masters.

J: That was not the reason. Paul clearly states that he wanted them to be models of subservience "so as to adorn in all things the teachings of God our Savior." Besides, his reason is unimportant. What is important is the claim of Christians that the New Testament is Your word, appropriate for all time and all circumstances. It is this absurd belief that enabled the Protestant clergy of the American South to speak out eloquently in defense of slavery as a divine institution and to use the Bible to support their argument long after freethinkers such as Thomas Paine called for the abolition of slavery.

During the French Revolution, slavery in France was abolished. When the revolution failed and Napoleon reestablished the Church in France, slavery was reinstated. Although by the time Lincoln emancipated slaves in America there were many religions that sought the abolition of physical slavery, most religions never gave up their attempt to enslave the human mind.

Justification for female submissiveness is also supported by the New Testament. Paul taught, "Let women keep silence in the Churches, for it is not permitted for them to speak, but let them be submissive as the Law also says. But if they wish to learn anything let them ask their husbands at home" (1 Cor. 14:34-35). In another epistle Paul wrote, "For I do not allow a woman to teach or to exercise authority over men; but she is to keep quiet" (1 Tim. 3:12). Naturally, he has excellent logic to support his chauvinistic attitude toward women: "For Adam was formed first, then Eve. And Adam was not deceived, but the woman was deceived and was in sin. Yet women will be saved by childbearing, if they continue in faith and love and holiness with modesty" (1 Tim. 2:13-15). Small wonder men took to Christianity so readily.

G: You seem to forget that Christianity's primary competitor was Mithraism, and that religious sect excluded women completely. Although Paul's teaching may appear oppressive from today's perspective, it was really progressive for its time.

J: But it was not nearly so progressive as the practice of the Gnostics, as I have shown. Moreover, that certain teachings were an improvement over the belief and practices of the day only shows that to be relevant and useful religions should evolve to reflect new knowledge and to meet new needs. However the doctrinaire quality of religious belief impedes this progress. We should not be quoting a 2,000-year-old teaching to support a position unless it is the merits of the arguments rather some alleged divine inspiration that warrants our consideration. This is not the case with Christianity.

In the final analysis Christianity has been opposed to personal freedom. Christian leaders have sought freedom for themselves, but rarely for others. History records that all the Christian sects cried out for freedom, but once in control they wielded their power as despotically as those whose control they sought to escape. Artemis Ward reminds us, "The Puritans nobly fled from a land of despotism to a land of freedom, where they could not only enjoy their own religion, but could prevent everyone else from enjoying his."[16]

Furthermore, whatever good the efforts of individuals accomplished, there is no evidence to suggest that it was the result of uniquely Christian morality. When Christianity had political power we saw precious little of these humanitarian sentiments. However, with the church's loss of power and the liberalization of education, the ideas of those social and political reformers (primarily freethinkers) so strongly opposed by Christian religions finally received wide distribution. It was their new ethical ideas—particularly in the area of human rights— that generated the social consciousness of the more enlightened clergy of today. The fact is, Christian institutions have little to gain and much to lose if social conditions and life in general become too good; admittedly not an imminent prospect.

G: You again imply that suffering is essential to the Christian scheme. What utter nonsense!

J: Is it? What has Christianity to offer a happy man living in a natural, intelligible universe?

G: Happiness not just for the short span of human life, but for all eternity.

J: I admit that the prospect of immortality may be of some comfort to those near death, as in the case of the elderly or soldiers during war time. But it doesn't offer much for those in the prime of life. That's why the concept of eternal life has been less effective an incentive for converting the latter group.

The constant threat of nuclear war undoubtedly has had much to do with the rise of Christianity that we witnessed in the early 1980s. There are, of course, many other psychological reasons. However, aside from peer pressure, and the simple inertia of those raised as Christians, the primary motivation is a desire to escape a life situtation felt to be intolerable. Hence, those who are alienated, confused, depressed or in pain, seek solace in the mythical Christ. Christianity provides the promise of an instant community of interest and the myth of Jesus offers a hope not unlike that of Santa Claus: just believing and being good (not necessarily doing good) is enough to reap a reward.

Even to the most naive, it is obvious that Christians seem to suffer "the slings and arrows of outrageous fortune" no less than anyone else. This might have brought down the myth had not the Christian interpretation of the Old Testament provided the answer. All of man's misfortune is the result of sin. Sin! Where would Christianity be without that marvelous rationale for the suffering so necessary to sustain the religion?

G: Are you so nonsensical as to infer that Christianity invented sin?

J: I'm afraid so. Oh, there was evil all right. By evil, I mean that people committed acts that injured themselves or others. But Christianity contends that the fall of Adam means that humankind is intrinsically evil and, therefore, all men are "conceived in sin."

G: Many of today's more enlightened Christians will tell you that the story of Adam and Eve was not meant to be taken literally. It is only an allegory to illustrate that humankind has the propensity to follow its baser instincts which lead to evil actions. Can you deny that fact?

J: In the first place, I doubt whether the primitive creators of ancient myths even knew what an allegory was. It is much more reasonable to assume that Genesis was a primitive effort to account for the origins of humankind and to explain why there was so much pain and suffering in the world. Moreover, if the legend of Genesis is only an allegory, then which parts of the Bible are not? Perhaps the whole story of the death and resurrection of Jesus is an allegory. Some modern theologians see it as such, and I would have little trouble accepting this view, but I'm not sure many Christians are ready to admit as much.

Even as an allegory it doesn't make any sense that to atone for man's wickedness God willed his Son put to death. The theologians try to tell us that only this murder (or suicide if you believe that Jesus willed his own death) of a god will expiate humankind's wicked nature.

G: Your presentation makes it all sound absurd. But the idea that I must be appeased so that I won't inflict my just revenge on man for his wickedness was a tradition entertained by virtually every Western religion, not just Christianity.

J: True. It stemmed from the primitive belief that the forces of nature, which were believed to be the works of a god, could be controlled by appeasing the gods through sacrifice. To this superstition Christianity added the Judaic belief that the natural calamities in the world were the result of man's curse for disobeying a Divine command—the forbidden fruit myth. The marriage of these two myths resulted in the belief that man was intrinsically tainted by evil and the only road to salvation lay in swearing allegiance to the Divine Redeemer. Given the advance of modern science in explaining phenomena of nature and the causes of human behavior, humankind might have risen above these primitive beliefs had not Christianity, in its own self-interest, done everything possible to sustain them.

With the concept of sin Christianity can effectively exploit every calamity. An earthquake in Italy, a flood in Texas, war in the Middle East, all provide an opportunity for Christianity to prey on people's basic fears. When people are most downtrodden and suffering, Christianity can on one hand hold that it's all due to retribution for their sins, and on the other, that their suffering will make heaven just that much sweeter. But first, man must cease to rebel against God and embrace the true religion.

G: Offering hope to the despairing. Is that bad?

J: It is bad when fundamentalist preachers exploit human despair for their own aggrandizement, gaining fabulous wealth and political power by means of a lie. It is bad when the myths get in the way of the truly effective means of alleviating suffering. It is bad when the Christian Scientist shamans pray over a child with meningitis instead of seeking medical help.

Certain Christian sects opposed attempts to cure smallpox. Their logic held that since all disease was obviously sent by You, inoculation must have been invented by the Devil. Not so long ago, it was also almost universally accepted by Christians that women should suffer in childbirth, hence anesthetics were opposed by many clergymen. Christianity attempts to turn everything topsy-turvy: pain is good and pleasure is evil.

G: Well, you must admit that only a few extremists support such a view today. The vast majority of Christians will do whatever is necessary to eliminate disease and suffering.

J: I submit that it is a logical failure for Christians to do so. Given the premises of Christianity, it is logically correct to maintain, as did

Danish philosopher Søren Kierkegaard, that for the Christian suffering is a blessing. Indeed, Kierkegaard recommended that a Christian choose suffering: "The best would be that you, yourself, voluntarily be inexhaustibly imaginative in inventing means of torturing yourself, but should you not be that strong . . . then you dare hope that God will have mercy on you and help you come to suffer."[17] I noticed, however, that Kierkegaard never volunteered to be infected with some painful disease.

Kierkegaard justifies suffering as a sign of a special relationship with You. This, of course, is not a new idea. Christianity has always alternatively suggested that suffering was indicative of Your special blessing or special curse. At least Judaism held only to the latter explanation.

G: You must admit that suffering has done much to ennoble people. As Kierkegaard points out, look at the number of poets, artists and religious persons who, without suffering, would never have become great.

J: What about the millions who simply suffer and die in desperation without achieving greatness? What about the children who suffer from spina bifida, meningitis, leukemia, muscular dystrophy and the dozens of other diseases? Besides, can it be proven that suffering ever truly caused greatness? If that were the case, there should be millions of great people in this world, because there are certainly millions of sufferers. Actually, it is just as easy to believe that suffering has prevented many more people from achieving greatness.

Also it is fashionable, I believe, to confer greatness on someone who suffers. How often is the artist not recognized as a "genius" until someone points out how he or she suffered? Greatness, it seems to me, is not so much an absolute achievement as a recognition conferred by a fickle society somewhat at random among the millions of talented people. There may have been many relatively happy geniuses who, because of their singularly uninteresting lives, lack of a patron or commercial hype, have passed with their works into oblivion.

Kierkegaard was probably right when he said suffering was essential to one group of people, the clergy, since without suffering no one would seek their help. Seeking an escape from suffering, people turn to every possible superstition. People dying from cancer have tried the most absurd remedies including eating grapes, ingesting ground-up diamonds, drinking the juice from Easter lilies and taking coffee enemas. The U.S. House Subcommittee on Health and Long-Term Care was shocked to learn that witchcraft, psychic and spiritual healing, and even voodoo have become big business in the United States.[18]

With rare exceptions, desperate people have always turned to magic and prayer. When all else fails, religion holds out the hope of heaven at the end of their suffering. So, suffering is an essential motivation for men and women to seek the superstitious nostrums of Christianity. Unfortunately for modern shamans, not everyone suffers sufficiently to send them in desperation into the clutches of the local priest or minister. Hence, the value of sin is once more demonstrated. Christianity describes man's earthy existence as "a vale of tears" and uses sin to help ensure it. At one time virtually every pleasure experienced by man was labeled sinful. This was especially true of one of the greatest of all pleasures, sex. By linking it solely to procreation, Christianity managed to make it an onerous duty for women, instead of an exquisite pleasure.

G: That's nonsense. The reason for tying sex to procreation was simply because, until recently, that was the obvious relationship. I would expect that you, of all people, would oppose sexually frivolous men and women spawning children all over the place without a thought of their future well-being?

J: From my study of history that is pretty much what happened anyway. But I agree that until recently the idea of tying sex to marriage was socially responsible. Of course, Christianity can claim no unique status in that regard. However, since the advent of effective birth control, the relationship between sex and children is severed. Consequently, the relationship between sex and marriage needs to be reexamined. Dogmatic Christian religions are incapable of this.* Their canons are frozen in time. Change occurs only after their followers begin drifting away in such numbers that religious leaders must run to catch up with the crowd.

G: Not unlike most bureaucracies.

J: Exactly. Although I'm surprised to hear you admit it.

G: I've never contended that the institutions which promote Christianity are perfect. And no thoughtful person today maintains that all the teachings of Christianity, especially with regard to sin, are correct. Christians, like everyone else are, after all, only men and women who are capable of error in interpreting my Divine Will.

J: The pope doesn't think so. Neither do the fundamentalists. Besides, I'm not attacking a possible error concerning whether or not a specific act should be decreed sinful. According to George H. Smith, Christianity

---

*Some of the Protestant sects such as the Anglican, Episcopalian, Methodist, and, of course, the Unitarian, are less dogmatic and more willing to alter their tenets based on new information and societal needs.

uses two types of coercion to enforce behavior: the physical sanction of hell which discourages certain behavior out of fear, and the psychological sanction of sin which prompts certain behavior out of a sense of guilt. There are times when sanctions enacted by society are appropriate to discourage socially dangerous behavior. But Christianity uses sanctions to enforce its opinion on all types of behavior that may or may not have any negative social consequences, such as masturbation, premarital sex, or homosexuality. The only criterion Christianity attempts to employ is Your law. And who are the self-appointed interpreters of Your law? Why, the ministers and priests, naturally enough. It should come as no surprise that their sanctions are primarily aimed at insuring the propagation of the faith through control of every action and, ultimately, every thought. As I've said before, one of the greatest sins a person can commit is to deliberately question the "mysteries" of the Christian religion.

Years ago Christianity relied much more heavily—and quite successfully, too—on hell to scare people into following its dictums. It started with children whose minds were young and impressionable, and then continued the brainwashing for the rest of their lives. Here are two examples that Smith found in a series called "Books for Children" written by Father Furniss,[19] an English priest of the last century. Imagine the wide-eyed terror of the small children whose parents or teachers read them this description of what fate awaited a child who broke one of the innumerable laws of the Church in those days, such as eating meat on Friday:

> His eyes are burning like two burning coals. Two long flames come out of his ears. . . . Sometimes he opens his mouth, and breath of blazing fire rolls out. But listen! There is a sound just like that of a kettle boiling. Is it really a kettle boiling? No. Then what is it? Hear what it is. The blood is boiling in the scalding veins of that boy. The brain is boiling and bubbling in his head. The marrow is boiling in his bones. Ask him why he is thus tormented. His answer is that when he was alive, his blood boiled to do very wicked things.

Even I squirmed when I read this one:

> A little child is in this red-hot oven. Hear how it screams to come out! See how it turns and twists itself about in the fire! It beats its head against the roof of the oven. It stamps its little feet on the floor. You can see on the face of this little child what you see on the faces of all in hell—despair, desperate and horrible.

Now that's the stuff to generate sensational nightmares.

G: You can't hold Christianity responsible for every exaggeration of its overzealous adherents.

J: You keep saying that. But the zealots are just following the proscriptions of the New Testament quotes I related earlier. Jesus repeatedly threatened nonbelievers with hellfire. And didn't Paul strike blind a man who opposed his teachings (Acts 13:11)?

G: Come on now, there is a world of difference between ancient and modern Christianity. Christianity does not rely on hellfire anymore. It has evolved into a religion based on love, not damnation. Still, unless there were some sanctions, why would humankind obey the law of God? You can see that humans do not display exemplary behavior even with such sanctions. What would they be like without them?

J: Perhaps better, certainly no worse. I know of no study whose findings satisfactorily demonstrates that non-Christians as a group behave any worse than Christians. In fact, certain Native American groups, such as the Nez Perce, had a more appropriate moral code and sense of social responsibility than any Christian sect. The Japanese society today, which is decidedly non-Christian, has far less crime, poverty, inequality, unemployment and underemployment than the United States. Maybe Shintoism is the "true religion."

G: I would think that the Second World War demonstrated the dangers of the emperor-god.

J: Quite true. I would be the last person to advocate the revival of fundamentalist Shintoism—a real danger to Japan today, I might add. What I support are ethical and socioeconomic systems developed and implemented using scientific reasoning.

A system of human ethics need not—cannot—be grounded in superstition if it is to be effective. Just look at the effectiveness of "sin" in modifying human behavior. It did nothing to stop the barbarity of the Inquisition. On the contrary, the horrors were justified. To understand why, I must spend another moment on the Christian concept of sin.

There are actually three types of sin in Christian theology: sins against man, sins against God, and the sin that is inherent in man, original sin. I've already discussed the concept of original sin. According to Augustine, every human being is born to eternal damnation unless he or she is lucky enough to be baptized before death. (This was later softened by the concept of limbo, a vague place that was neither heaven nor hell.) The psychological mindset such a belief creates is that if we are inherently bad to begin with, it is only natural that we do wicked things. Hence, it puts a block in the way of scientific understanding of what role genetics and the environment play in determining human behavior. This prevents society from discovering more efficient means of producing socially beneficial behavior.

Sins against You, on the other hand, are simply rules established by organized religions to insure mindless conformity to authority. Such rules evaluate actions divorced from their consequences. Additionally, shifting responsibility for one's action to You can justify any act, no matter how barbarous, just so long as someone can reassure us that it is Your will, as the Crusades and Inquisition demonstrated so horribly. Such an erroneous concept has sanctioned more devastation and bloodshed than any comparable fallacy in ethical theory.

Finally, labeling socially detrimental behavior as "sinful" incorrectly places the social focus on the perpetrators themselves rather than the causes of their actions. As any psychologist can explain, labeling a person—rather than his actions—as bad will do little to motivate socially responsible behavior. I regret that I cannot recall the author who put it so well: "By believing in blame and punishment for sin, the individual will tend to feel worthless, become compulsively obsessed with his wrongdoing, deny that his act is wrong or repress knowledge of his wrong deed." Obviously, none of these reactions will result in socially correct actions in the future. This is not to deny that persons must be held responsible for their actions. But that is not enough; society must also alter, to the extent that it can, the environmental determinants of those actions.

In conclusion, then, the concept of sin has not improved human behavior one bit, but has caused much needless guilt and suffering.

G: You talk as if the concept of sin had been invented by a group of evil little men intending to use it to subjugate all humanity to their will. Be honest enough to admit that the theory of sin was developed, like all theories, by persons who dedicated their lives to discovery of truth—in this case, theological truth.

J: No doubt many, perhaps most, theologians honestly tried to understand the source of evil and how to prevent it. But 2,000 years ago how else could evil in the world be understood except as caused by demons, or as the deliberate intent of people to do bad—perhaps at the instigation of a devil? Sickness, misfortune, and wickedness were all explained in this way. Then, as science began to uncover the workings of nature, people started to understand the true cause of physical and mental illness. And instead of trying to cast out devils or burn witches, they sought cures through more science.

Socially detrimental behavior is like every other sickness. Instead of burning the "evil ones," we are now just beginning to understand the causes of aberrant behavior in terms of genetics, environmental conditioning and mental maladjustment. The next step is to discover cures and more effective means of modifying socially detrimental behavior through positive and negative incentives. We are on the threshold of that knowledge, but Christianity wishes to pull us back and again plunge us into the darkness of vague, meaningless concepts like sin, free will and divine retribution. It is the inevitable result whenever a movement raises its leader to the status of a god and vests his teachings with dogmatic orthodoxy.

G: Let's return to the concept of sins of commission. You must admit that rules are necessary to keep men from turning this world back into a jungle. Breaking these rules must result in punishment as a deterrent to others. Sin is simply an extension of that basic premise.

J: I have two problems with what you say. First, most of the so-called sins of Christianity should not be designated sins at all. I agree with Thoreau that, "The greatest part of what my neighbors call good I believe in my heart to be bad, and if I repent of anything, it is very likely to be my good behavior."[20] Many of the "sins" defined by Christianity are, as I stated before, nothing more or less than an attempt to enforce submission and conformity to the Church authorities, their dogmas and a prevailing set of traditions. Or they are attempts to curb whatever pleasures this life has to offer for fear that a person who enjoys life too much won't waste time worrying about happiness in the hereafter.

If we really want men and women to behave better, they must first of all love life. The much misunderstood and maligned Friederick Nietzsche wrote in *Thus Spake Zarathustra:*

> Since humanity came into being man hath enjoyed himself too little: that alone my brethren is our original sin. And when we learn better to enjoy ourselves, then we unlearn to give pain unto others and to contrive pain.[21]

G: So you want everyone to ignore the consequences and follow their most basic desires?

J: Like so many, You are quick to jump to the wrong conclusion as to what Nietzsche meant. He simply said that only happy people seek to generate happiness in others. Two thousand years of human misery have certainly taught us the consequence of this elementary truth. Simple observation supports the conclusion: suffering people generally do not radiate warmth and good cheer. W. Somerset Maughan wrote, "It is not true that suffering ennobles the character; happiness does that sometimes, but suffering for the most part makes men petty and vindictive."[22] The history of Christianity is a history of vindictiveness against those who didn't believe in Jesus or who didn't follow the explicit prescription of this or that sect.

On the other hand, the search for happiness does not imply that we seek pleasure every minute of our lives. As we all know, maximizing pleasure today can result in a miserable tomorrow. Over the long run happiness requires self-restraint and the knowledge that the happiness of each is a function of the happiness of all. No one understood this better than the ancient Greeks. Plato taught that children should be raised in such a way as to delight in the things that were conducive to moral order. Aristotle added that legislators (and, we could add, parents) make good citizens by forming correct habits.

G: That doesn't sound much different than the more enlightened teachings of modern Christianity.

J: It is important to note that the enlightenment you mention did not originate with Christianity. Rather, it was due to advances in the sciences of psychology and epistemology that have illuminated the dark recesses of Christian beliefs in sin and damnation.

We must take it a step further. First, I submit that the proper scope of morality encompasses only those actions that limit the ability of other people (including future generations) to attain security and happiness. This criterion would eliminate 90 percent of the senseless "sins" manufactured by Christianity. On the other hand, it would have defined as morally wrong many actions long practiced by Christians which were not considered sins, such as using the state as a vehicle to enforce Christian beliefs and practices.

For almost two thousand years, the greatest sin was disobeying God—as defined by the Church. But killing "savages" in the conquest of Africa, America, India and China wasn't a sin—it was spreading the word of God. Slavery wasn't a sin. Living in opulence, as the bishops and clergy of the Church did while the poor starved, wasn't a sin. Forcing children to work in dangerous mines and factories wasn't a sin. Paying farm workers slave wages and locking them into working and living conditions that result in an average life expectancy twenty years below the national average is still not considered a sin by most Christians.

Equally important as defining correctly what is the proper realm of morality is determining how to gain general adherence to a moral code. Christianity relies on the concept of sin backed by the threat of hell. This has two major weaknesses: unless death is imminent the concept of hell is too distant to be a meaningful psychological motivator, and once the myth of hell is exposed it ceases to be a motivator at all. The failure of hell as a meaningful deterrent to socially harmful behavior, or even "sin," for that matter, is apparent from the study of the behavior of true believers throughout history. As mentioned, after observing the behavior of his Christian neighbors, Chief Red Jacket concluded that Christianity had no positive impact on their moral behavior.

Modern psychology has demonstrated that there are far more effective ways to elicit socially and personally beneficial behavior. A truly enlightened society would rely upon empirical research to ascertain what behavior is desirable to optimize the long-term happiness of all its members. It would then seek to motivate this behavior through positive rather than negative incentives whenever possible. For this approach to work, the society would, of course, have to have eliminated the primary cause of unhappiness: gross injustice.

A full discussion of how to construct a just society on a basis other than sin and damnation must wait. For now, let me sum up my discussion of Christianity.

G: By all means, get on with it.

J: While it is true that certain individual Christians have made great contributions to the betterment of humanity, they have risen to greatness in spite of, not because of, Christianity. On balance, the individual efforts of these Christian humanists have been swamped by the great tide of physical and mental suffering for which Christianity bears direct responsibility.

Christianity could be expected to offer no more than it has because it is based on ancient superstitions and myths. George Bernard Shaw described Christianity as having, "for its emblem a giblet, for its central mystery an insane vengeance bought off by a trumpery expiration, for its chief sensation a sanguinary execution after torture." Shaw astutely saw that, "This expiration by sacrifice combined with legalized revenge is no different than the most primitive idea of Justice."[23]

It is small wonder, then, that such a primitive belief suffers from several fatal flaws:

1. Although somewhat less of a problem in the more liberal sects, Christianity, in general, still suffers from an overreliance on authority, whether in the person of the pope, a minister, or the authors of the Bible. Inevitably, those authority figures are not content to demand observance of their moral code by only their followers, since the nonobservance by the rest of society may result in defections from that membership. Therefore, it is necessary that Christian religions

bring all of society under their moral injunctions by tearing down the wall of separation between church and state and legally forcing their moral code on all citizens.

2. Because the New Testament teachings are thought to be of divine origin, they lack the flexibility to incorporate new discoveries concerning human nature and our environment or to meet the changing needs of humankind. At best, Christianity adapts with a painfully long lag time. The best example of this is the slow recognition (still officially opposed by the Catholic Church) of the need to move from a policy of stimulating population growth, to policies that encourage family planning and birth control.

3. As a consequence of its reliance on authority and archaic teachings, Christianity tends to be an antiscientific, irrational approach to truth, and continues its effort to stifle free thought.

4. The historical record demonstrates the tendency of Christianity to back the status quo whenever it is in its best interest to do so, regardless of how repressive and inhuman the situation. Christianity was solid in its backing of Franco's fascism. Pope Pius XII was guilty of complicity by virtue of his failure to condemn Hitler and Mussolini. In Germany Christianity found an easy peace with Nazism—German troops wore belt buckles that proclaimed, "Gott mitt uns" ("God is with us"). Until quite recently, there was little opposition from the white clergy of South Africa to that nation's policy of apartheid. Even in this country, most clerics were too busy railing against godless Communism to be much concerned with racial separatism.

5. The reliance on sin is a largely ineffective attempt to modify human behavior. The consequence of being condemned as sinful is merely to make human beings feel worthless and become vindictive; hardly emotions conducive to the love of one's fellow humans.

G: In your unabashedly one-sided tirade, you have said almost nothing of Jesus' message of love. Yet today it is the gospel of love that draws many to Christianity.

J: Ostensibly, yes. Frequently, however, those who join religious cults are looking to receive love, not necessarily to give it. Of course, this is not true of all "born again" types. But I find it more than just a coincidence that the present revival of Christianity is concurrent with the rise of neoconservatism. Both are "me" oriented: Christianity is concerned with the individual gaining heaven, while conservatism is concerned with the individual gaining as much of the earth as possible.

Both are far more concerned with *being* good than *doing* good—going beyond the bare minimum in assessing one's responsibility to fellow humans. Both have a narrow chauvinistic focus: Christianity sees only fellow Christians as part of the elect, neoconservatives believe that their nation is somehow superior to others. Both believe that ultimately each person is responsible for his or her own destiny and, therefore, should be expected to achieve economic or eternal salvation unassisted.

Finally, I find that the Christian concept of love fails to provide the expansive worldview necessary to understand and tolerate other cultures. According to the gospels, Jesus himself had a fairly narrow vision of those whom he had come to save. He instructed his disciples: "Go nowhere among the Gentiles, and enter no town of the Samaritans but go rather to the lost sheep of the house of Israel" (Matt. 10:5). (That the message of Christianity was taken to the Gentiles was due to its rejection by the Jews and the decision by the disciples of Jesus to ignore this particular injunction of their master as an expedient to gaining converts.) Even the most tolerant of Christians judge those who do not believe in their myths as, at best, mistaken or mentally defective; or at worst, in the clutches of the Devil.

G: So you sum up by saying that Christianity has absolutely nothing good to offer. All the teachings of Jesus were worthless?

J: No, I didn't say that. I explicitly stated that many of the alleged teachings of Jesus were quite wonderful. It is just that they did not originate with Jesus and were rarely followed by Christians. Who could find fault with "Let he who is without sin cast the first stone" or "Love thy neighbor"? But little love was exhibited in the 2,000 years of Christianity when each Christian sect tried to exterminate its rivals and any dissenters.

It is the great tragedy of Christianity that it failed so abysmally to transmit many of the valued teachings of Jesus. By tenaciously defending the biblical myths and the divinity of Jesus, Christianity loses all credibility. The result is often that intelligent seekers of truth, upon discovery that much of what they were taught is based upon myth and outright deception, will tend to throw out all the teachings and philosophies of the New Testament and sink into despair or universal skepticism.

The central failing of Christianity is that neither Jesus nor his disciples had the foggiest notion of how to motivate people to behave better toward one another. The writers of the New Testament had Jesus mouth pretty platitudes that had been repeated by many spiritual leaders for thousands of years. Sadly, without a knowledge of the nature of man and the causes of antisocial behavior, they had little chance of effecting any real change for the better. All that was left of Jesus' message was the opportunity for men to sin and still attain heavenly bliss by a last-minute act of contrition.

If only Christianity could clean up its act, demythologize, and update the teachings of the New Testament to meet the needs of today's society, it might yet prove to be of some value. It needs to view the teachings ascribed to Jesus as part of a body of ethical teachings that include those of Confucius; Buddha; the Greek philosophers; and modern ethical theorists such as Joseph Fletcher, John Rawls, Paul Kurtz, Kai Neilson, Kurt Baier, and a host of others. Christian leadership must recognize the need for ethics to be studied critically in light of scientific knowledge of the roles of genetics and the environment. A few Christians are attempting to take this broader, less dogmatic view. Unfortunately, they are the minority.

G: Just one question, please: If Christianity has been such a monumental failure, why do so many people still believe in it?

J: I've already touched on the effectiveness of Christianity to suppress dissenting thought, but we both know the reason for its success has a psychological dimension as well. This will be explained more fully in chapter 17. For now let me say that Christianity, like many other religions, provides an answer, although an erroneous one, to quell many of the fears of humankind. Furthermore, Christianity had two unique features, in addition to its ruthless persecution of dissent, that did much to establish its success while, ultimately, providing a great disservice to humankind.

The first Christian innovation was to include the participation of women, although, unlike Gnosticism, it rejected equality of women. Unfortunately, Christianity then locked women into a subservient status for the next thousand years.

The second unique feature of Christianity was the preaching of a heavenly reward available to all believers. Prior to the rise of Christianity, most religions preached that immortality was granted only to the select few: the heroes and nobility for whom the gods granted a place on Olympus or permission to pass on to the Elysian fields. The best the Eastern religions could offer was the opportunity to break the wheel of birth, suffering, and death by an escape into the void— an absence of individual consciousness. During the revolt of the Maccabees, Hebraic teachings began to offer hope for immortality, but the concept did not reach fruition until the advent of Christianity.

Christianity made its first inroads not with the wealthy or educated (to them it appeared to offer no more than than pagan religions);

nor with the philosophers and intellectuals, who viewed it as an even more absurd superstition than that which the masses believed. Rather, Christianity appealed foremost to the slaves, the poor, and the alienated. It told them: "Don't fret that your life is terrible now, we can offer you an eternity of happiness. Moreover, your reward in heaven will be in direct proportion to your suffering here on earth. So seek suffering even to the extent of martyrdom. In so doing you are buying that much more eternal happiness." Not only do the oppressed inherit heaven, but the rich and powerful will probably find themselves locked out. "It is easier for a camel to pass through the eye of a needle, than for a rich man to enter the kingdom of heaven." (Matt. 19:24) Hence, slaves can have the extra pleasure of seeing their previous masters writhe in hell for all eternity. Such a deal!

If that wasn't enough to make the sale, Christianity virtually guaranteed heaven regardless of one's prior wickedness. The forgiveness of sins, coupled with the ability to gain indulgences (which nullified even the temporal punishment of a purgatory) was what sold men like Constantine. (Obviously, the Christians didn't stress the point to Constantine about the difficulty of the rich and powerful gaining entrance to heaven.)

So Christianity had a great product, immortality, attainable at minimal personal investment. And did it sell! But the cost to humankind was heavy indeed.

G: You talk as if a group of fanatics got together and concocted the whole theology of Christianity to sell to a gullible populace. You make it sound like a marketing con.

J: For many of its proponents today, especially the fundamentalist preachers, it is no more than that. I'll admit that it probably didn't start out like that. Rather, it was a natural evolution from the Judaic tradition. Most of Christian theology can be seen to be a mixture of Hebrew and pagan tradition, with Neoplatonic, Aristotlean and Stoic thought added later to give it an intellectual veneer. I've already discussed the pagan influences. Now I will explore the Judaic roots of Christianity.

8

The Roots of Christian Theology: Judaism and the Old Testament

The Hebrews came out of Egypt and settled among the Canaanites. They need not be traced beyond the Exodus. That is their historical beginning.
—S. F. Dunlap

J: As Hans Küng explains, "It is impossible to understand the Christian God without the Jewish, for the Jewish is in fact the Christian God."[1]

G: I won't argue with that: I am the only God.

J: But I think Küng meant something a little more profound with that statement. I believe he meant that although Christians tend to envisage You in the person of Jesus, the Christian conception of God is essentially rooted in the Hebraic concept of God. The Judaic God, Yahweh, was demanding, to say the least. In recent years, Christians have tried to downplay Your more severe aspects such as Your proclivity for revenge . . .

G: You mean justice.

J: . . . and have attempted to replace their association of God and hellfire with one of God and love, mercy, and forgiveness. Certainly it makes the concept of You more palatable, if not more reasonable. Many modern Christians, if pressed, will disclaim the Old Testament, and see little relevance in it to their belief in Jesus. In so doing they fail to realize that Christian theology is inextricably tied to the Old Testament. If the Old Testament is discredited, the mythical origins of Christianity are also exposed.

The central mystery of the New Testament is redemption. But the need for redemption is relevant only if humans are inherently evil. Hence, the necessity of the story of the Fall of Man; for if there was

200

no fall, then there is no need for atonement or a Redeemer. In short, the stage for the divine mission of Jesus is set in the first two books of the Old Testament—Genesis and Exodus. All of the other books of the Old Testament are merely descriptions of correct social behavior, hygiene or ritual, and a heroic epic of the Israelite nation. The account of the early history of the Israelites appears no more believable than Homer's account of the ancient Greeks. Which is to say that they both possess a historical basis, but the exact events are completely distorted by national pride and very imaginative storytelling. In this respect, the history of the Jewish people appears little different from the epic legends of every other nation.

G: Before you continue, please explain what you mean by Jew, since the term is fraught with ambiguity. Does it refer to a nationality, a race, a religion, or simply a group of people with certain common traditions?

J: Since those who refer to themselves as "Jews" can't seem to agree on a definition, I will not venture to enter that debate. However, for purposes of the following discussion I will make certain distinctions. I will refer to those people who established a nation after leaving Egypt as Israelites. They practiced the Hebrew religion. I use the terms *Hebraic* and *Judaic* synonymously. The people who live in the State of Israel today I refer to as Israelis, as the popular press does. Those who believe that national sovereignty is necessary for the security of the Jewish people I refer to as Zionists. Zionists may live in Israel or elsewhere. They have succeeded in their intention to establish a national state. Ultraorthodox Jews, on the other hand, wish to extend the borders of Israel to encompass the area that they believe was granted to them by God. They seek to rebuild the Temple of Solomon on the site of one of the Moslems' most revered Mosques, the Dome of the Mount. They wish to establish a theocracy in which only orthodox Jews have citizenship. They have even succeeded in making it virtually impossible for a Jew to get a license to marry a Christian. The ultraorthodox Jews are a serious impediment to peace in the Middle East today. Next, there are those people throughout the world who refer to themselves as Jews by tradition. They may or may not practice the Hebrew religion. Finally, there are those who may be descendants of people who called themselves Jews, but who no longer consider themselves Jewish since they neither practice the Hebrew religion nor follow the Jewish traditions. I respect their right to define themselves in terms different than their parents just as I consider myself to be neither Catholic nor German although my ancestors were both.

G: And what is the purpose of this preamble?

J: I just want to make certain that any criticism I make in what follows is not misconstrued as being aimed at the wrong persons. For example, I do not want to condemn those who call themselves Jews today for the actions of the ancient Israelites.

G: I'm certain you will manage to offend everyone nonetheless. Now get on with it.

Origins of Pentateuch Legends

J: O.K. Let's direct our attention to the book of Genesis. George William Foote investigated the book of Genesis at the turn of the century and reached essentially the same conclusion as Thomas Doane and Godfrey Higgins, i.e., that the story of Genesis was originally of Babylonian origin and can also be found in the *Rig-Veda* of the Hindus.[2] One of the regions of Babylonia was Akkad. In their ancient language *ad* means father and *dam* means mother. According to C. S. Wake, this would also follow the Persian tradition that the first person was androgynous. Whether the myth originated with the Babylonians, Hindus, or some other group, it is impossible to say with certainty, as there was obviously travel and trade among all the peoples of the Middle East long before written history. Indeed, elements of the Old Testament can be traced back to Egypt, Mesopotamia, Phoenicia, Canaan, Assyria, and Persia.

Some of the most impressive evidence concerning the antiquity of the Genesis legend was uncovered by George Smith as explained in his book, *Chaldean Account of Genesis*.[3]

This George Smith (not to be confused with the George H. Smith whose theological treatise I quote elsewhere) was an expert in cuneiform translation for the British Museum, specializing in the study of Assyrian inscriptions. Between 1867 and 1876 Smith studied the 20,000 inscriptions from the Royal Assyrian Library discovered in the mound of Koyunjik, opposite the town of Mosul, in what is now Syria. In these fragments he found all the major themes related in the early books of the Bible.

The library of which the tablets were a part was established in 650 B.C.E. by the decree of King Assurbanipal, who ordered texts gathered from throughout the empire to be copied and stored there. Based on the names of the kings and cities referred to in the tablets, Smith dated the original texts to at least 1800 B.C.E. Smith dated another group of tablets containing the description of the Flood as part of the Izdubar legends prior to 2000 B.C.E. He based his dating on literary developments in Babylonia and annotations on the tablets mentioning kings of the period 2000 B.C.E. to 1850 B.C.E. Smith discovered no annotations with the names of later kings. Furthermore, undoubtedly before the first legends were committed to inscription, there was a long history of oral tradition.

The more recently discovered Ebla tablets indicate that Smith's dating appears to be conservative. Since 1974, 17,000 more tablets have been unearthed that archaeologists have determined date back at least to the Sumerian kingdom of Ebla. At the site of their discovery was also unearthed a statue of King Ibbitlim with an inscription to the goddess Ishtar who "shines brightly in Ebla."[4] Since Ebla was destroyed in 2250 B.C.E. by Naram-sin, the tablets must be even older. Both the Assyrian and Hebrew versions of the biblical themes were borrowed from the Babylonians. Gerald Larue reports that the Mesopotamian creation myth, which may have originated with the Sumerians as long ago as the third millennium B.C.E., was used in the New Year ritual during the month of Nisanu at the shrine of Marduk in Babylon during the time of King Hammurabi (1723–1686 B.C.E.).[5] Smith suspected that the Izdubar legends he translated were probably handed down through a long oral tradition from remotest antiquity. From their content it can be seen that the Izdubar legends were the basis for the book of Genesis.

Let's review the comparisons briefly. First, the Mesopotamian myth describes the creation of the world in a sequence of events: the creation of land, then heavenly bodies, land animals and, lastly, man. In the Mesopotamian myth the sea is the origin of all things.[6] Genesis also refers to the "spirit of God moving over the waters" and "the waters bring forth the creeping creatures," etc. Next, there are the cuneiform fragments referring to the fall of man and a war between the gods and evil spirits—not unlike the angels and Satan. The first people were called Admi or Adami,[7] from which the Judaic myth derived the name of the first man, Adam. The Babylonians recognized two races, Adamu or "dark race," and Sarku, or "light race."[8]

The creation myths recorded in the Chaldean tablets also refer to the dragon Tiamat,[9] who played the same role as the biblical serpent: he is instrumental in the fall of man and leads the attack on heaven (consider the battle between the archangel Michael and the dragon). The tablets refer to the Old Testament Tower of Babel: ". . . their strong place all the day they founded," but to little avail because the father of the gods "confounded their speech" and cursed them to "scatter abroad."[10] In his book, Smith describes two possible locations for this tower. One is the great pile of Birs Nimrud near Babylon which Sir

Henry Rawlinson excavated during the middle of the nineteenth century. It consisted of "seven stages of brickwork on an earthen platform" rising 154 feet above the level of surrounding plain. The other possibility is the Babil mound within Babylon, which was the site of the Temple of Bel.

Finally, the tablets refer to the great Flood that "destroyed all life from the face of the earth."[11] The survivors rode the flood in a ship which stopped at Mt. Nizir. A dove was sent out, followed by a swallow and a raven. Afterwards, Bel "established a covenant and gave his blessing."[12]

G: How do we know that the Babylonians didn't learn their account from the Israelites rather than the other way around?

J: For the simple reason that the Israelites did not exist at the time these tablets were inscribed. There is no historical corroboration that the Israelite people existed as a nation prior to the twelfth century B.C.E. It is not until the Old Testament Books of Samuel and Kings that events are related which seem to be verified by other historical records. As I mentioned earlier, the history of the Israelites prior to the Exodus is a mythical construction designed to support the claim of a special relationship between the Israelites and the god Yahweh, in part to legitimize their wars of conquest. The Babylonian empire on the other hand flourished in the third millennium B.C.E.

The Old Testament as a collection of books did not exist in Hebrew until 600 B.C.E. at the earliest. The first complete text of the Old Testament, the Septuagint, was a Greek translation composed by the Alexandrian Jews on the order of Ptolemy sometime between 285 and 246 B.C.E. The canon of Judaic scripture was fixed about 90 C.E. by the synod of Jamnia. In his bestseller, *Evidence That Demands a Verdict,* evangelist Josh McDowell seeks to make much out of the consistency in translation of the later versions of the Old Testament. However, he fails to mention a letter of Aristeas to Philocrates explaining that, "the translation was instigated by Ptolemy and that the Jewish scholars summoned proceeded to carry it out, making all details harmonize by mutual comparison. The appropriate result of that harmonization was reduced to writing under the direction of Demetrius."[13] In other words, all contradictions in various earlier manuscripts were eliminated by decree. Moreover, the Ebla tablets show that the Mosaic law in Deuteronomy was little more than a compilation of earlier Hittite, Assyrian, Sumerian, and Eshuma codes.

The first five books of the Old Testament (collectively known as the Pentateuch), were supposedly written by Moses himself, although today many Hebrew scholars admit this wasn't so. However, the discovery of the book of Laws (Deuteronomy) as related in 4 Kings 22: 8-14 smells of a scam.* Josias, the teenage king, was a likely pigeon for a bit of duplicity. It was during a time when the Israelites had once again turned to worship a rival of Yahweh, the god Baal. Helcias, one of the high priests, "found" the book of law which was supposedly written by Moses at the direction of Yahweh. The young king didn't know what to make of it, so he told Helcias to check with the local prophetess, who proceded to scare Josias out of his wits by telling him that he had unknowingly broken all the laws. She declared that Yahweh was going to heap all sorts of evils on the head of the poor king. Not surprisingly, Josias panicked and tore down all the alters and temples dedicated to the other gods and killed their priests. Yahweh was again established as the state god. The whole incident smells of political chicanery instigated by Helcias with the collaboration of the prophetess, both of whom were undoubtedly members of the Yahweh cult. The story does little to establish credibility that Moses actually authored the work, however. Throughout history, documents have been "discovered" and only later revealed to be fraudulent. Recall our earlier discussions concerning the deception perpetrated by Ellen White and Joseph Smith. Ages ago people were a lot more easily deceived.

The question of authenticity aside, even if the Bible texts were reproduced verbatim from the earliest writings of Moses or whomever, it does not attest to the validity or value of the writings. McDowell himself admits as much (without realizing it) when he quotes Bruce Metzger, a professor of New Testament Language and Literature at Princeton: "In antiquity we memorized Homer as later they were to memorize the Scriptures. Each was held in highest esteem and quoted in defense of arguments pertaining to heaven, earth and Hades."[14] I couldn't agree more. Reading the story of Saul, David and Solomon in the Books of Kings is reminiscent of the *Iliad* and *Odyssey*—a little history and a lot of myth. Instead of talking to several gods, Saul and David only talk to one, but he is as irascible and vindictive as any of the Olympian deities. It shows that simply quoting an ancient text, even if it was faithfully replicated for thousands of years, means nothing if the truthfulness of the contents cannot be verified.

G: There is, however, supporting evidence that some of the events related in Genesis actually occurred. For example, paleontologists indicate that the world was once covered with water. And did not a *Chicago Tribune*[15] story relate how some explorers, including a noted

---

*In Protestant Bibles, 1 and 2 Kings are called 1 and 2 Samuel; 3 and 4 Kings are called 1 and 2 Kings. Confused? So was I.

astronaut, found evidence of the Ark on Mt. Ararat just as the Bible account indicated?

J: The floods you refer to occurred after each glacial age tens of thousands of years before the biblical creation dates. Indeed, it was probably early man's efforts to account for the evidence of those glacial floods, such as bones and fossils of fish on mountain sides and arid places, which gave rise to the myths in the first place. The chronology of the Bible, on the other hand, would date the creation as only 5000 to 4000 B.C.E. Archbishop James Ussher in the seventeenth century calculated it as exactly 4004 B.C.E. Such estimates are simply ludicrous, as they are contradicted by all archaeological and paleontological evidence as well as carbon dating. Egypt and Sumeria had thriving cultures by that time.

As for the *Tribune* account, it is just such sensationalist nonsense that keeps myths alive. A careful reading of the article reveals that none of the explorers were geologists or archaeologists. Rather they were a group of Christian fundamentalists searching for evidence to support their deeply held beliefs. What they actually found was no more than a "boat-shaped impression." Search almost any mountain in the world and I feel confident that with a little imagination you could find such an impression. Do you recall the footprint of Prometheus discovered in Greece? Its like seeing faces and animals outlined in the rocks of the Wisconsin Dells. Any tour guide worth his salt can "construct" a dozen or so images out of the crags and cliffs. Moreover, it was later reported that the "discovery" on Mt. Ararat reported by the *Tribune* had been known for a long time, and discounted as a mere geological oddity. After that report, the intrepid explorers were quick to state that they never claimed it was anything more than that.

G: You still haven't proved that the events of the creation story did not occur exactly as related in the Bible, despite the fact that the Israelites got the story second hand.

J: We keep running into that same tired objection that I haven't proven the Bible account to be false. It is not up to me to prove it is false, any more than I have to prove that Greek mythology is false. Again, it is the proponents of a historical or theological proposition who must provide evidence to support their claim. For my part, I simply need to pose a more reasonable alternative explanation. I have provided that.

I have already demonstrated that the Genesis account is simply a rehash of the more ancient Mesopotamian myths. Mythologists Joseph Campbell and James George Frazer offer numerous examples of other primitive myths employed by tribal groups throughout the world to explain their existence and special relationship to the gods who they believe control the forces of nature. There is no more reason to believe the biblical account rather than that of any other culture.

Permit me to review more evidence to show the primitive nature of the Genesis story. In Genesis we see the primitive Arabic concept of the universe as a flat earth underneath an inverted bowl (the sky). In the sky are set "two great lights: a greater light to rule the day, and a lesser light to rule the night" (Gen. 1:24). Of course, the ancients didn't know that the moon was not a light but merely reflected the light of the sun. Nor did they realize that the sun was the source of all light in our solar system, and so they fell prey to the absurd chronological account of creation which has light being made on the first day (with an "evening and morning" no less) and the earth, dry land, and vegetation being created during the next two days, while the source of light and life—the sun—was not created until the fourth day.

Aside from the chronology, there is so much other silliness that if this account were found in any other book but the Bible, an elementary student would find it absurd. Moreover, there are actually two accounts of creation in Genesis. In the first, You create all the beasts (Gen. 1:24) and then man and women together: "Male and female he created them" (Gen. 1:27). In the second chapter of Genesis we get another version in which man is created (2:7), then the beasts (2:19), and finally woman (2:22). Obviously, what we have is a conflation of two versions of the creation myth.

Comparing the Creation Myth with the Scientific Account of the Origins of the Universe

G: If the creation is just a myth of ignorant primitives, as you contend, why does no less an authority than the astronomer Robert Jastrow admit that when the scientist reaches the end of his investigation into the origins of the universe, "he is greeted by a band of theologians who have been sitting there for centuries."[16] It appears to me that the Big Bang theory for the origin of the universe does not appear too dissimilar from the concept of a created universe.

J: The single point of similarity between the simple description in Genesis, which was alleged to have occurred a mere five to six thousand years ago, and the evolutionary account that follows a complex trail across 15 to 20 billion years, is that the present universe had a beginning. The Big Bang theory does not state, as Jastrow implies, that this was the absolute beginning, still less that it occurred out of nothingness (*ex nihilo*) as the Christians contend. Rather, the theory simply states that we don't, at present, know what caused the explosion since all prior evidence would have been destroyed.

There probably never was an absolute beginning to the universe, only a beginning to the present configuration. Einstein's equations expressing general relativity indicate that the universe cannot expand forever, but must eventually collapse. There may have been an infinite number of prior explosions followed by "implosions" (a collapsing of the universe back in on itself). Isaac Asimov and other scientists believe that present evidence cannot rule out the idea of a cyclic perpetual universe; one that involves a perpetual number of explosions and implosions.[17] Another possibility is that the universe has gone through a series of oscillations, each one more severe until the final "bang" that threw the energy and matter so far from the core that gravitational pull could not cause another collapse. In either case, there would never have been an absolute beginning, nor would there be an absolute end, even though all life, as we know it, might cease. Even Jastrow admits that "an entire world, rich in structure and history may have existed before our universe appeared."[18]

Here again, we face the "withdrawing god" syndrome referred to by Küng. Theology takes a stand and it "explains" some mystery of human existence in terms of God's intervention. It is an "absolute truth" and woe to any heretic who dares to challenge it. Then science comes along and demonstrates that the theological explanation is absurd by offering a natural, verifiable explanation. Theology fights the evidence for a couple of centuries or longer, then gives in and backs off to defend another dogmatic position. In this way, theology has at one time denied the centricity of the sun, the genetic transmission of character traits, subconscious human motivations, the chemical origins of life, evolution, the geologic age of the earth, and so on.

The Great Flood

J: Genesis provides another excellent example of how this process works with the story of the Flood. There are very few major cultures whose mythology did not have some tradition of a great deluge that destroyed all of humankind except for their own progenitors. They often can point to a neighboring mountain on which their ancestral "ark" can be found. The Hindus, Chinese, Persians, Greeks, Scandinavians, even Mexican and Brazilian Indians have such a tradition.[19]

G: Many would take the universality of the tradition as evidence of its validity.

J: Really? All these groups also supposed the world to be flat. There is a very reasonable explanation for the almost universal belief in a great flood. As I've explained earlier, all of these groups shared the common observation of the bones and fossils of fish and sea-going mammals in high, dry places, such as nearby mountains. Naturally, with their limited geological knowledge the only reasonable explanation was that water covered the entire land at one time. Actually, that was close to the truth. Following the four glacial periods, there may have been a great deal of local flooding. Furthermore, the ebb and flow of the glaciers themselves, which did much to change the topography of the earth, would have deposited fish and mammal bones in very unlikely places. Since early humans roamed the earth long before the flooding due to the melting glaciers at the end the Pleistocene era (10,000 years ago), it is not surprising that wooden artifacts of man have been discovered on the sides of mountains. This "evidence" probably gave rise to the deluge myths. All of these events occurred around 20,000 B.C.E., just prior to the dawn of civilization and thousands of years before Judaic culture.

One notable exception to the popular deluge myth is the Egyptian mythology which relates no such legend. According to Egyptian history, at the supposed time of the Bible-related deluge, the Pharaoh Khufu (Cheops) was building his pyramid.[20] The lack of a flood myth is easily understood: the Egyptians had no fossil evidence that demanded an explanation. (Of course, if they had dug deep enough in many areas, they, too, might have found bones and fossils which would have raised questions, and some interesting myths about where they came from.)

As I've explained, it appears that the Judaic legends came from Chaldean sources that the Israelites probably picked up after they were conquered by the Assyrians about 727 B.C.E. The Jewish historian Josephus states that all the writers of the Babylonian histories made mention of the Flood and the ark. Moreover, the area of southern Babylonia called Chaldea was a maritime country and its seafarers brought back myths from throughout the Middle East. The Israelites, on the other hand, were shut off from the coast by the Philistines and Phoenicians. In Gen. 12:31 it is explicitly stated, however, that Abraham, the legendary Father of the Israeli race, was brought by his father "out of Ur of the Chaldees." Finally, the Euphrates valley where the story of Genesis was supposed to unfold is none other than ancient Babylonia.

G: All idle speculation. You weren't there, but I was.

The Exodus

J: It is a far more reasonable hypothesis than the assault on our intelligence made by the biblical account since it is supported by concrete
evidence. Let's now turn to the book of Exodus, because the legend
of Moses provides a valuable key to the origins of the Bible and the
Hebrew traditions. The first incident in the legend of Moses provides
additional evidence of the ancient origins of the early biblical myths.

   Sargon I was an Akkadian monarch who ruled over a large portion
of the Middle East from 2340 to 2305 B.C.E. His story, as given on
fragments of tablets found at Kouyunjik, tells us that to avoid being
murdered by his uncle who ruled over the country, Sargon's mother,
"placed me in an ark of rushes, with bitumen my exit she sealed up.
She launched me on the river which did not drown me."[21]

   Again we see that up to this point the Bible is simply a rewrite
of older myths. However, there is some historical corroboration for
the flight of the Israelites from Egypt, although whether they were
led by a man named Moses is by no means certain. Three ancient
historians, Choeremon, Lysimachus, and Diodorus Siculus (fl. 60–30
B.C.E.), relate that Egypt was afflicted by disease, which was attributed
to the slaves; and so, on advice of his councils, the Pharaoh drove
them out.[22] This appears plausible enough. We know that the Egyptians
had practiced ritualistic hygiene, even shaving off all body hair to
prevent infestation of lice. Their slaves, on the other hand, who were
gathered from all over the world, lived in squalor and filth. It was
very likely that an epidemic of some sort should break out among
them. (Another explanation is offered by Ian Wilson, in his book,
Exodus, who provides evidence that there was a a major eruption
of the Thera volcano around 1450 B.C.E. Wilson explains how the
eruption could have caused the natural calamities reported as plagues
in the Bible.[23]) The account provided by Tacitus tells of how the wretched
and infected multitude of slaves were driven out into the desert where
they nearly perished from lack of water.[24]

G: Then I told him to stretch out his rod and strike a rock, from which
sprang water.

J: The account of Tacitus is not quite so dramatic:

> Worn out by fatigue, they lay stretched on the bare earth, heart-
> broken, ready to expire, when a troop of wild asses returning from
> pasture, went upon a steep ascent of a rock covered with a grove
> of trees. The residue of the herbage round the place suggested the
> idea of springs near at hand. Moses traced the steps of the animals

and discovered a plentiful vein of water. By this relief the fainting multitude was raised from despair. They pursued their journey for six days without intermission. On the *seventh* day they made halt, and having expelled the natives, took possession of the country, where they built their city, and dedicated their temple.[25]

G: How would Tacitus know! He wasn't there; he wrote his account hundreds of years later.

J: Based, perhaps, on the historians I referred to earlier as well as other similar accounts. No, Tacitus wasn't there. But given the plausibility of his account and the similarity to others, which should a reasonable person conclude is closer to the truth? Of course, we can't rule out the possibility that neither account is accurate. Note that in Tacitus' account it took this group of refugees seven days to reach their destination. I'm always suspicious when ancient writers use the number seven since, like the number forty in the Bible, it was often used due to its "sacred" nature. However, consider this: the trip from Northern Egypt to Palestine is less than 250 miles. Even at the relatively slow pace of twenty miles per day, it would take only twelve to thirteen days. The biblical account contends that it took forty years of wandering through the desert before the Israelites found the land of milk and honey. Unless Moses deliberately set out to lead the Israelites in circles, the Bible's account reflects the hyperbole (a factor of over 700 times the truth) typical of heroic myths. For example, the legends of Alexander relate how the Pamphylian Sea opened for him just as the Red Sea supposedly parted for Moses. I see no reason to give one myth more credibility than the other.

G: Perhaps the account is true that I deliberately let Moses and the Israelites wander about, lost for forty years, to punish them for worshiping the Golden Calf and losing faith in the true God.

J: Ha! Well, it is true that the Israelites seemed to lose their faith in Yahweh with some regularity and worshiped many different gods from time to time. According to George Foote, the Hebrews were originally polytheistic. The older of the two Genesis creation myths attributes creation of the world to *Elohim,* which literally translated means "gods."[26] Elsewhere it tells how the Israelites "offered victims to Baal (the Babylonian god) and sacrificed to idols" (Osee 11, 12). It seems that Yahweh was but one of many gods worshiped by the Israelites, including Baal, Moloch, and Chemosh. The reason for the eventual Hebrew monotheism appears to be rooted in a desire for a single god who would be a symbol of Israeli nationalism, dignity and uniqueness, more than any theological basis.

To return to the book of Exodus, the occurrence of the flight from Egypt appears to be a largely, if not entirely, mythical account which was merely repeated by some later historians. There is no archeological evidence to support it. For example, there is no historical verification for the drowning of the pharaoh in the Red Sea. To the contrary, in 1881 the mummy of King Ramses II, who was pharaoh at the time of the Exodus, was discovered along with thirty-nine other mummies of royal and princely personages near Thebes.[27]

The Bible's account of Moses going up the mountain to receive the Ten Commandments appears to be the reenactment of the Hammurabi (1750 B.C.E.) tradition. According to Babylonian tradition, King Hammurabi went into the desert where he was given his famous code by the god Marduk (later called Baal). The Ten Commandments of Moses contain nothing more than can be found in the Code of Hammurabi, except for the intolerant prohibition against worshiping other gods. The political advantage of a unique, national god, who speaks through the head of state, is all too obvious. The lesson was not lost on Mohammed or the popes. Perhaps religious intolerance did not begin with the legend of Moses, but I know of no earlier example.

Long ago, Voltaire questioned the very existence of Moses: "If he had really existed, if he had performed the dreadful miracles attributed to him in Egypt, would it have been possible that no Egyptian author should have spoken of these miracles, and that the Greeks, the lovers of the marvelous, had not recorded a single word respecting him."[28]

G: The Bible never says that Moses performed miracles; it says that I did.

J: True, but that's beside the point. The fact remains that there is no historical record of such wondrous happenings outside of a book that was written, in part, to legitimize the claim of a people who wished to demonstrate that they had a special relationship with a god. Voltaire goes on to support his hypothesis that the story of Moses was actually copped from the legend of the Greek god Bacchus, also called Misem. Bacchus was also picked up in a box on the waters; had a rod that he could change into a serpent and with which he performed miracles; and wrote his laws on tablets of stone.

G: Maybe you have it the wrong way around. Sounds like the Greeks borrowed the biblical account of Moses and applied it to Bacchus.

J: Except that the Greek mythology predates Hebrew mythology by hundreds of years. If the Greeks stole the myth from anyone, they stole the Babylonian myth of Sargon the Great, which I related earlier. Whether or not Moses ever actually existed will probably never be known for certain. It is quite probable, however, that he is no more than another character in the Israelite mythology, since there is no evidence that Israelites ever were in Egypt. After ten years of scouring the Sinai, Israeli archeologist Eliezir Oren could find no evidence of ancient Israelites.[29] How could a population of over two million people have disappeared without a trace? Moreover, there is no record of the Israelite people before 1230 B.C.E. Even the sites allegedly conquered by the Israelites in the Exodus' account did not exist at the time of the alleged migration. The only identifiable place is Kadesh, which didn't exist prior to 1000 B.C.E.

It appears that just as the Christians stole earlier legends from the Greeks and elsewhere to apply to Christ, the Israelites borrowed legends to create the character of Moses. One thing is certain, however: the first five books of the Bible were not written by Moses as Jews and Christians used to allege (and fundamentalist still do).

G: I know, it would pose the same absurdity as that of Joshua. In both cases, the author describes his own death (Deut. 34:5–8 and Josh. 24:31). I don't think that today many Jews assert that Moses or Joshua wrote the books ascribed to them. The Pentateuch is called the Five Books of Moses because of his role in some of the biblical accounts.

J: Exactly. How reasonable you have become.

G: Don't confuse the unreasonableness of some of my followers with my Divine reason which, of course, you couldn't begin to fathom in the first place. But what difference does it make who wrote Exodus?

J: As Thomas Paine said so cogently, "Take away from Genesis the belief that Moses was the author, on which only the strange belief that it is the Word of God has stood, and there remains nothing of Genesis but an anonymous book of stories, fables and traditional or invented absurdities, or of downright lies."[30]

G: Even if it was not Moses who wrote the first five books of the Bible, I could have as easily inspired some anonymous author.

J: To assert that the Bible is inspired is logically impossible, since Pope Leo XIII stated, "inspiration [is] essentially incompatible with error."[31] Science has shown conclusively that the Old Testament cosmology is completely erroneous. Therefore it cannot be inspired.

Moreover, the discovery that both the Old Testament and the New Testament are simply embellishments of earlier primitive myths destroys their claim to historical veracity. What I find most interesting, as I pointed out earlier, is that while no sane person today believes the astounding tales of the Greek heroes, or any other ancient legends, they will swallow the fatuous biblical mythology more easily than the whale did Jonah. Christians and Hebrews don't believe the legends of Hercules but they give credence to the Hebrew version—the myth of Samson. They think Shangri-la is a fairy tale, but not Paradise. They are ignorant of the role that the "Tree of Life" played in the very ancient Hindu and Oriental mythologies.

If humankind did originate in one section of the world—perhaps the Middle East or northern Africa—it is not surprising that there would be a common origin of human myths. Although the same themes are covered in the myths of all cultures, such as the origin of man, the different races and languages, the personification of nature, the concern with an afterlife, etc., the answers supplied by the myths do contain important distinctions. The Christian myth looks for an immortality of eternal bliss, whereas the Hindu must worry about successive reincarnations until he can finally escape the wheel of life and death by merging with the universal "void." Which myth is based on truth? There is no basis for believing one or the other except personal whim.

To understand the progression of ancient myths better, let me try to outline briefly the evolution of the Old Testament mythology.

The Origins of Old Testament Mythology

J: As I mentioned earlier, it is extremely difficult to pinpoint the common origins of these mythologies, if indeed there are any. The oldest known civilization may well have been the Sumerian. The city of Eridu is estimated to have existed as far back as 6500 B.C.E. For about 4,000 years the Sumerian culture flourished—twice as long as the Christian era—before being conquered by the Semitic-speaking people to the north, known as Akkadians, under Sargon I. However, as H. G. Wells explains in his *Outline of Civilization,* it was the Sumerian civilization that prevailed over the simpler Akkadian culture. They adopted Sumerian writing, language, and, undoubtedly, Sumerian myths.

The fusing of Sumerian and Akkadian cultures provided the basis for the great Mesopotamian empire centered in Babylon. The Babylonian culture reached its zenith under Hammurabi (2100 B.C.E.) whose famous code was a sophisticated system of laws and prescribed punishments. This code provided the basis for the Ten Commandments and Hebrew law which were written down perhaps a thousand years or so later.

The Babylonians were conquered in about 1100 B.C.E. by the Assyrians but subsequently rebelled and after many wars with Assyria, secured their independence around 606 B.C.E. During these wars, Babylonia was assisted by two Aryan-speaking groups, the Medes and Persians. The second Babylonian dynasty was known as the Chaldean Empire since it was dominated by a southern group of Semites, the Chaldees. It prospered under the second great Babylonian king, Nebuchadnezzar II, until it was destroyed by the Persia's Cyrus the Great in 538 B.C.E. It was during the reign of Nebuchadnezzar II in 586 B.C.E., that a large segment of the Israelite population were forced into captivity under the Babylonians. During this time the Chaldean account of Genesis and the Izdubar legends were transmitted to the Israelites.

Simultaneous with the flourishing of ancient Sumer was the rise of Egypt in about 5000 B.C.E. Like Sumer, the Egyptian culture thrived for thousands of years. The rise of Ramses II, who was the pharaoh at the time of Moses, occurred between 1317 and 1250 B.C.E. By then the mythology of Egypt was rich and complex, complete with a god, Horus, who was murdered and rose from the dead. Here, then, is the second great strain of mythology to which the Hebrews were exposed. There was yet a third and a fourth.

The Dravidian peoples in the Ganges of India developed a culture similar to the Egyptians and Sumerians. According to G. A. Wells, an Aryan-speaking people closely related to the Persians and Medes pushed into India about the time of Hammurabi. The Aryan group provided the link between the Hindu and Greek traditions. The Persians provided the link between Greece and Babylonia, with whom they alternately traded and fought. As I mentioned, the Chaldeans of southern Babylon were at one time allied with the Persians. So a linkage to Hindu mythology can be established.

China was the fourth civilization which, remote as it was, could influence the development of the Judaic mythology. By 2700 B.C.E. China was highly developed with a rich and complex mythology. The route to this source of myth was through their trading partners, the Hindus of India who, in turn, transmitted the legends to the Aryan-speaking people mentioned above.

We have now seen how the Judaic culture was influenced directly by two great civilizations, and indirectly by two others, each with its own moral code and an anthropomorphic explanation of the world's origins. As I've explained, these four civilizations were not isolated. With the ebb and flow of trade and conquests, ideas and cultures were transmitted back and forth for perhaps two to three thousand years before the Israelites attempted to write down their own history and legitimize it with appropriate myths. No wonder Hebrew mythology is a hodgepodge of these four earlier mythologies.

While it is impossible, therefore, to clearly identify the origins of all the myths in Genesis, it is not surprising to find the Hindu Tree of Life in the Garden of Eden; the Chinese Shangri-la transformed into the Hebrew Paradise; the Arabian God Shans-On turn up as Samson; the Assyrian and Greek battles of the gods recast as a war between Satan and the archangel Michael, etc. Even several Greek astrological names—Pleiades, Orion and Arturus—show up in the Old Testament.

G: So, you absolutely deny the possibility that the Bible's geneology of the Hebrew race back through Moses to Abraham and Noah and, ultimately, Adam, could be true?

J: As a reasonable person I must go with the evidence. The evidence is overwhelming that Abraham, Noah and all the other pre-Exodus characters are mythical—and not even original myths. The most probable explanation is offered by S. F. Dunlop in his book, *The Spiritual History of Man.* According to Dunlop, the Hebrews were the descendants of slaves whose forebears were various Semitic groups conquered by the Egyptians.[32] The books of Genesis and Exodus are no more than the effort of the Israelites to imitate the efforts of all primitive societies to create histories that trace their lineage back to the gods. Such an effort served two purposes: it answered the question all people had—where did we come from?—and it provided a unique national identity by answering that question with a divine origin. In this regard, the Jewish mythological history is not much different than the Greek, Hindu, Mayan, Egyptian, or a hundred other myths discussed by Joseph Campbell in *The Masks of God.* The only distinguishing mark of the Hebrew mythology (and even in this regard it was not entirely unique), was the assertion of a special covenant with the Hebrew God, Yahweh. Originally the Israelites, like most other primitive societies, worshiped many gods. Archeologists have discovered evidence that over fifty gods were worshiped in the area of Palestine between 2000 and 1000 B.C.E.[33] Solomon built sanctuaries to the foreign gods Chemosh and Melek.[34]

    Yahweh was the god of lightning, thunder and rain. Like other gods, he was more to be feared than loved. A wrathful god capable of both good and evil Yahweh had to be appeased by constant stream of sacrifices.

G: But as you mentioned, I did not demand human sacrifice—a major concession on my part, I think.

J: I will give the Israelites credit for that. To continue: Moses, or those who wrote his legend, tried to outlaw the worship of all gods except Yahweh. Whether he did so for the political advantage it provided, or because he was a monotheist at heart, we will never know. However, after studying the history of more recent religious founders such as Joseph Smith, we have reason to be suspicious of the intentions of all founders of religious cults—especially when there appears to be a political purpose to be served.

At any rate, the Israelites hated to give up their other gods. It was not until the Babylonian captivity that the Hebrew priests were able to exploit the suppressed nationalistic feelings of the Israelites and elevate their favorite god, Yahweh, above the other Babylonian gods. Insisting that they had a special contract with this god who made them his chosen people was tantamount to telling their Babylonian conquerors: "Look, even though you have conquered us, it is only temporary, because our god is better than your gods and he likes us best."

It was a brilliant strategy for preserving the Israelites' collective dignity when the chips were down. However, I doubt whether any Israelite consciously thought up the scheme. It was only a natural turn of thought for a conquered people. It is even more advantageous for conquerors to know that their god is smiling on their efforts to subjugate another people. Throughout their wars of conquest the Israelites took advantage of this psychological fact as well. The prophets presented the idea that there was a divine plan guiding the destiny of the Israelites. Later Christianity was to adopt the same view, but one that placed Christians at the focal point of the plan. As a consequence of this ancient form of manifest destiny, the remaining history of Israel is a story of almost constant warfare with its neighbors.

G: Do I detect a note of anti-Semitism?

J: Don't be absurd. We are discussing religions here, not ethnicity. As regards religions, orthodox Judaism is no better or worse than most others. All have sought to gain the support of the state to enforce their doctrines. The quid pro quo is that the religious leaders would testify that the secular leaders acquired their right to rule by Your will, not that of the people. This is the basis for the theory known as the Divine Right of kings.

The ideal situation, from the perspective of the ruler, is to have the people believe him to be a god, or at least God's direct representative, thus eliminating the nuisance of having to deal with the temple priests. However, the priestly classes in ancient Judea were very careful to prevent the state from usurping their prerogatives. Whenever a king was becoming so popular that he began to ignore their doctrines or moral authority, prophets were quick to predict that he was incurring the wrath of Yahweh which would then be visited upon the entire nation. They could point to a group of books (the Old Testament) which they wrote as "evidence" of the awful retributions inflicted on the people of Israel in the past for ignoring the word of priestly agents. Even if the king was willing to take this risk, more than likely his people were not, and he knew it. For the most part the arrangement served the interests of the Hebrew clergy quite well.

Prophecies as Proof of the Bible's Inspired Origins

G: If the Bible is primarily myth and/or biased history as you maintain, . . .

J: With some dubious ethical theory and superb poetry . . .

G: . . . how do you explain the remarkable prophecies contained in the later books such as Daniel, Isaiah, Jeremiah, and Ezekiel? Josh Mc-Dowell shows that they are proof of the Bible's authenticity—proof that would stand up in a court of law.[35]

J: McDowell confuses the evidence that the Bible dates back a few thousand years—which no one denies—with the validity of its contents. He attempts to compare its historicity with that of the works of Homer, but no one accepts the supernatural stories of Homer as factual nor are they claimed to be inspired. McDowell then attempts to demonstrate that all the prophecies of the Old Testament came true. But, this is simply not the case. Actually, the prophecies can be divided into two groups: (a) those that were no more than extrapolations of past history, which anyone with half a brain could foresee, and (b) those that were patently incorrect.

In the first classification are all those general prognostications concerning the fall of empires and cities. These were sure bets if the prophets were clever enough to never say specifically when the events would occur. They could have safely said that every empire and every major city in Asia and Europe would be destroyed at least once, for such was the case. In those days, when cities rose and fell with an almost cyclical regularity, it didn't take much imagination to predict another fall. However, I doubt if any of the prophets knew even this. They just went on preaching death and destruction, as prophets always do, and man, being the primitive savage he was, inevitably would prove them right. There is nothing very supernatural about any of this. However, when McDowell tries to demonstrate biblical accuracy in terms of the specifics of eight prophecies which he reviews, he exhibits the same tendency to twist meanings and search frantically for irrelevant relationships, as do modern psychics who try to claim "hits" from vague forecasts.

Of particular interest to me was that of these particular prophecies, unlike many that McDowell examined, only one was fulfilled before Christ lived;[36] even though from their context it is apparent that the prophets were predicting imminent catastrophe. They were telling people, in effect, "because of your wickedness this terrible thing will happen." Who of their listeners would care about a cataclysm that would occur hundreds of years in the future? In one case, when the prophesied event never happened, McDowell begs our continued indulgence, "Is it too much a stretch of the imagination to see it happening in the future?"[37] Of course, given enough time almost every prophecy should come true.

There were times, however, when the prophets really blew it. Earlier, I referred to the misuse of the prophecy of Isaiah concerning the virgin who would bear a son. The rest of that prophecy went: "For behold this child shall know how to refuse the evil and choose the good, the land thou abhorrest shall be forsaken of both her kings" (Isa. 7:15). But as Paine points out, instead of the two kings failing as Isaiah prophesied, they successfully defeated Achaz, the king of Juda; killed 120,000 people; plundered Jerusalem; and carried 200,000 women and children into captivity (II Paralipomenon 28:5–8; 2 Chron. 28 in King James).

Nor was this the only embarrassing miss. In Jer. 34:4–5, he prophesies to Sedecias (called Zedekiah in the King James version), king of Judea: "Thus saith the Lord to thee: Thou shalt not die by the sword. But thou shalt die in peace and according to the burnings of thy fathers." I hope old Sedecias did not plan his insurance program on that prediction, for Nebuchadnezzar conquered Jerusalem soon thereafter. The king of Babylonia killed the son of Sedecias before his eyes, and then, "put out the eyes of Sedecias and . . . put him in prison till the day of his death" (Jer. 52:10–11).

G: Well, he didn't die by the sword.

J: But he certainly didn't die in peace.

G: Maybe he reconciled himself to his fate before he died.

J: Now you sound like McDowell trying to rationalize a prophetic failure into a success. It doesn't wash. There are many more instances of failed prophecy. For example, Ezekiel predicted Egypt would be uninhabited for forty years (Ezekiel 29:11), but it never happened. And Jonah predicted the city of Nineveh would be overthrown in forty days (Jon. 3:4) and was so certain of his prediction that he even sat down and waited for its destruction. Jonas was to be disappointed. (Note, here are two more magic forties).

G: The Old Testament goes on to relate that because the inhabitants of Nineveh repented, I spared the city.

J: A neat little excuse for another prophetic miss. It is apparent that no prophecy need come true; there is always an escape clause. It is apparent that any prophecy is no more than an educated guess as to the future based on a certain set of assumptions that are subject to change. The conclusion that our analysis of the Old Testament prophets invariably leads to is that they were little better than the modern prognosticators and phony psychics who pop up every year. The best of them had enough foresight to see that poor leadership could lead to disaster—hardly evidence of supernatural inspiration. Similar predictions were made by astute social observers of Germany in the 1930s.

G: I submit that you are examining the Old Testament, especially the Pentateuch, from the wrong perspective entirely. Think of it as a divinely inspired allegory that represents the very real inherent evil in humans which can only be purged by divine intercession.

J: That is the usual response of more enlightened Christians and Hebrews who are embarrassed at the primitive ignorance of the world exhibited in the book of Genesis. Hans Küng represents this modern school when he writes that the "book of Genesis [was] meant to be not 'recollections of primeval times' but a message in poetic form about the greatness of the one Creator, about the essential goodness of his creatures, about man's freedom, responsibility and sin."[38]

However, this attempt to rescue the Bible story is at odds with 2,500 years of Judeo-Christian belief. If the Old Testament is purely allegorical, especially the Fall of Man, doesn't the New Testament and the atonement also become no more than allegory? Is not Your death in the person of Jesus merely an allegory of Your love for weak and sinful humans? Where does the allegory end? If the devil is merely a personification of evil, then aren't you merely the personification of good? Or are You simply a symbol of the forces of nature, both good and evil?

G: Careful, you are on very dangerous ground.

J: I'm just pointing out the danger of the allegorical position. In the final analysis, such a position undermines the whole of Judeo-Christian theology. The concept of divine inspiration by means of which You make Your wishes known to humankind through Your prophets and ministers becomes meaningless. There is no more reason to believe that the Old Testament is a divinely inspired allegory than there is to make that claim of the Koran, the Upanishads, or the thousand other primitive myths. In short, if Küng is correct and the Bible stories are mere allegories, why should we, today, give it any more credence or interest than, say, the epic legends of Homer?

G: Because there are valuable lessons to be learned by studying the Bible.

9

The Bible as a Guide to Ethical Values: A Case of Arrested Development

[The Bible contains] all the answers to all the problems that face us today.

—Ronald Reagan

The Bible is a wonderful source of inspiration for those who do not understand it.

—George Santayana

J: Do You seriously believe that the Bible can be used to settle ethical questions? Let's ignore for the moment the Old Testament's lack of historical and theological authenticity and examine the value system it conveys. Remember, much of the New Testament is founded on the values of the Old Testament. There are, of course, some important differences as well, but for the most part I think the similarities are greater and too often overlooked.

Considering the Bible on the basis of its worth as a guide to human behavior, it is one book I would prefer my children not to read before they developed the capability for critical thinking—a rare capacity in this day and age. The Bible's values are those of a primitive and savage culture. I will concede that certain laws and customs it advances were at times an improvement over earlier, even more savage societies. Moreover, many of Israel's prophets demonstrated a distinctive concern for social reform. I will also admit that the later books of the Old Testament show a general progression in the development of a concept of justice. Still, on balance, the lessons learned from the Bible have been detrimental to humankind's efforts over the last millennium to develop a more just, less cruel civilization.

G: There are thousands of biblical scholars who would strenuously dis-

221

agree with you. Millions of readers throughout history have found the Bible a wonderful source of inspiration.

J: That is because a person can find within its pages support for any position on any issue. Many so-called biblical scholars are actually true believers who gloss over all the most glaring negative or inappropriate values conveyed by the Bible in their haste to glean support for their preconceived notion that the Bible is Your word. Then they conclude that, as such, it must serve as a guide for individual and social behavior.

G: There will always be people who use the Bible to serve their own purposes. Today, however, not even most Jews view the Old Testament that narrowly. The obvious injustice that would result from a literal interpretation of the Torah (the first five books of the Bible) required intelligent rabbis to begin interpreting those writings in terms of a more progressive ethic and the changing needs of the Jewish people. The oldest form of this interpretation was a verse-by-verse commentary on the written text, known as the Midrash. In addition, to provide help in knowing exactly how to obey the laws in the Torah, the interpreters conceived *halachahs,* statements of right conduct. Eventually, it was thought that the *halachah* could be based on oral traditions, since the Torah came to be thought of as encompassing both a written and unwritten element. (The Catholic Church believes in an unwritten tradition as well but, ultimately, it is only the Pope who can define what it embodies.) The halachahs were eventually codified in the Mishnah and finally embodied in the Talmud. In this way the Hebrew teachings were able to evolve from such primitive notions of vengeance as an "eye for an eye."[1] Today the evolutionary process continues with progressive scholars interpreting the Talmud in the light of present social needs and new knowledge about human behavior.

J: Unfortunately, many Jews, and even more Gentiles, find it convenient to rely strictly on the primitive law and ethical notions of the Old Testament. So it is this document I want to examine, not the ethical revisions attributable to gradual human enlightenment.

The picture that emerges from an objective review of the Old Testament is a portrait of national and religious chauvinism that has brought untold grief not only to Israel and its neighbors of ancient times, but to the Christian societies that have emulated the Old Testament examples. In the first place, the very concept of a "chosen people" is as repugnant as that of a "master race" and in its time has led to similar horrors. Ludwig Feuerbach observed that the Old Testament character of Israel was "the personified selfishness of the Israelitish [sic] people, to the exclusion of all other nations—absolute intolerance, the secret essence of monotheism."[2]

I am not speaking of Jews today, who themselves have been, in part, culturally determined by reaction to Christian prejudice. Rather, I am speaking of the ancient Hebrew religion and nation of Israel as depicted in the Bible. More specifically, I wish to examine the god portrayed in the books of the Old Testament and the values that portrayal promotes. Does the Old Testament god, Yahweh, exemplify love and humanity, or vengeance and fanaticism? We could start with the legend of Genesis itself.

The story of the banishment of our first parents from the Garden of Eden is usually interpreted as punishment for the sin of disobedience. You told them not to eat the forbidden fruit but they did—case closed. However, in Gen. 2:17 the tree is referred to as the "tree of knowledge of good and evil," and the serpent tempts them by saying that "your eyes will be opened: and you shall be as gods, knowing good and evil" (Gen. 3:5). Many biblical apologists contend, therefore, that Adam and Eve were being punished for intellectual pride, or for wanting to be gods themselves as the serpent promised.

G: That is one interpretation. Many others are equally plausible.

J: I know some evangelists talk of the "forbidden fruit" as a metaphor for sex. The potential for so many diverse interpretations is exactly why the Bible is of so little value as a guide to ethical behavior.

G: Unless you accept a single authority as providing the definitive interpretation.

J: Which the Hebrew religion has not done, thank goodness. On the other hand, we saw how the early Church used the Bible in a perverse attempt to establish the divinity of an obscure Jewish reformer. However, I am afraid there is no other recourse than to rely on reason to understand the meaning of this ancient legend.

On the most elementary level, Genesis is simply an attempt by early man to offer an explanation of the origins of the human race and why life was so filled with hardships and sorrow. In this regard, the myth explains the wretched condition of humankind, not as the fault of a good and merciful God, which would gain him few admirers, but as the result of humankind's innate wickedness.

On a deeper level, the myth of Adam and Eve may also have been intended to convey the moral lesson that the foremost responsibility of humankind is obedience to Your word. It seeks to demonstrate that trying to gain moral knowledge through our own intellectual efforts is clearly dangerous—especially to the position of those who believe it is their prerogative to speak for You. Who wrote the Old Testament or, more precisely, who was concerned with the oral transmission of the legend long before it was committed to writing? Obviously, those who had the most to gain—the priests. Whether Sumerian, Babylonian, Hebrew, or Christian, it is essential for priests to make us fear thinking for ourselves. We must be taught to believe God's word as taught by Your priests and written in their books, such as the Pentateuch. Their position in society rests on this kind of indoctrination. To the extent that this belief aids the civil authorities in their efforts to rule, it will guarantee their support.

The legend of Abraham and Isaac reinforces the Bible's horrifying lesson of unquestioning obedience to God's divine will. Do You recall telling Abraham to kill his son as a test of his fidelity to You?

G: Of course, but I told him to stop in time. I then put an end to human sacrifice—a major advance in religious ritual at the time.

J: That's not quite true. You allowed Jephte to burn to death his only daughter as a sacrifice to You for granting him victory in his battles (Judg. 11:29–40). Furthermore, from today's perspective the lesson of Abraham is that blind trust and obedience are good, although history has amply demonstrated that blind faith leads to the greatest evils. Think about it! Abraham is presented as a role model for being willing to murder his own son because he thinks he is hearing a divine command. He is praised for his fanaticism. That is a nice example to be used by today's charismatic evangelists to indoctrinate their sadly deluded followers. It also can be used to support the bizarre beliefs of any psychotic who thinks he or she hears God's voice.

Next, let's turn to Exodus, which tells us that You went so far as to kill the first-born of every Egyptian family to convince the pharaoh to allow Moses to lead the Israelites out of bondage. As I explained in the last chapter, there is a much more natural and reasonable explanation for the events leading up to the expulsion of the Egyptian slaves. But let's, for the moment, take the story at face value. Note that You did not take out Your horrible vengeance on the perpetrators of a wrong, but on their children (Exod. 13:29). What a monstrous injustice—truly a slaughter of the innocent!

G: I had warned Pharaoh to let My people go by means of nine other plagues before I killed the Egyptians' first-born.

J: How considerate of You. I'm sure the murdered children appreciated Your divine justice. But the Israelites were to learn that Your ill-temper was not just directed at heathens. During the flight from Egypt, simply because the refugees suffered a momentary lack of faith and worshiped a golden calf, You ordered every man of the faithful to "kill his brothers, friends, and neighbors." The result, if one is to believe the Bible, was a massacre of 23,000 people (Exod. 32:27, 28). The Old Testament is full of great moral lessons. Although You didn't like Your chosen people to be slaves, You never disapproved of the Israelites taking slaves themselves. In fact, You specifically encouraged the Israelites to take slaves from any neighboring nation: "And of the strangers that sojourn among you, or were born of them in your land, these you shall have for servants; and by the right of inheritance shall leave them to your posterity, and shall possess them forever" (Lev. 25:45,46). The laws of Exodus explicitly exempt from penalty a master who strikes his slave with a rod as long as he doesn't kill the slave. He can beat the slave with impunity because the slave is "his money" (Exod. 21:21). Such lessons were not lost on those defending the dreadful institution of slavery in the United States 3,000 years later.

Deceit and lying are also approved in the Old Testament if they somehow are in accord with Your divine will. Chapter 27 of Genesis tells how Rebecca and her son Jacob trick a nearly blind Isaac into mistakenly extending his blessing and inheritance to Jacob instead of Esau who rightly deserved it. In Kings You plot to deceive King Achab by sending a spirit who "will go forth and be a lying spirit in the mouth of all his prophets" (3 Kings 22:22). One of Your most reprehensible acts of deception was when You instructed David to take a census (2 Kings 24:15); then, because he takes the census, You say it made You angry and send a pestilence to Israel, killing 70,000 people (2 Kings 24:15).

G: Now wait a minute. Doesn't it say later in I Paralipomenon 21:1* that it was Satan, not I, who did the ordering?

J: Yes, apparently the writer of that later book decided to change the story to take you off the hook. Obviously, this is just another instance of a natural occurrence—a plague—requiring a supernatural explanation by an ignorant and superstitious people. The point is, however, that it demonstrates how silly it is to think of the Bible as inspired, or even a useful treatise on ethics. The God of the Old Testament is guilty of so many atrocities, that You would appear to be the personification of evil rather than good. You and Satan are indistinguishable. In fact, according to the prophet Amos, You Yourself state that You are responsible for all man's iniquities (Amos 3:2) and even confess that You are the source of all evil: "Shall there be evil in a city which the Lord hath not done?" (Amos 3:6)

Tolerance is not one of the strong points of the God of the Old Testament. For merely making a mistake in a sacrificial ritual and using the wrong fire in their censers You killed two of Aaron's sons (Lev. 10:1). When a bearer of the Ark of the Covenant collapses and

---

*1 Chron. in Protestant Bibles.

poor Oza (Uzzah) rushes forward to grab it before it touches the ground, You reward him with instant death because he was not of the Levite tribe (2 Kings 6:6–7 Samuel in King James).

The Old Testament is not tolerant of any sexual deviations; all, including homosexuality (Lev. 20:13), were punishable by death. It is obvious where those who would discriminate against homosexuals got their intolerant attitudes. The Bible is full of injunctions to burn, stone, or hang persons who break any of its numerous laws.

The Old Testament is particularly keen on promoting religious intolerance. If we are to take the Bible literally, You are constantly persecuting the Israelites for choosing other religions. In Num. 25:4,5 You have has Moses crucify "all the princes of the people," exposing them to the sun, to demonstrate his fury. Then Moses tells the judges of Israel, "Let every man kill his neighbors, that have been initiated to Beelphegor."

Not long after this slaughter of those who worshiped Beelphegor, You told Moses to take revenge on the Madianites who were also guilty of worshiping this rival god. So Moses went to war. After the battle, he was angry with his captains for sparing the civilians. Moses had ordered them to "kill all that are of male sex, even of the children, and put to death the women, that have carnally known men. But the girls, and all the women that are virgins save for yourselves" (Num. 31:17, 18). Few people who believe that the Bible is the inspired word of God are aware of this justification for genocide.

My all-time favorite is the little tale of horror told of Elijah. Because a group of little boys called him "bald head," Elijah "cursed them in the name of the Lord; and then came forth two bears and tore of them two and forty boys" (4 Kings 3:24).* I particularly like the justification for this atrocity offered by the Catholic Douay Version of the Bible in a footnote: "This curse followed by a reasonable judgment of God, was not the effect of passion, or of revenge, but of zeal for religion, which was insulted by these boys, in the person of the prophet; and of divine inspiration. God punished in this manner the inhabitants of Bethel who had raised their children in prejudice against the true religion and its ministers." Apparently, even the Church thought that this fabled atrocity needed justification. What is truly scary is that the Church accepts such an atrocity as fair and just. Imagine if a group of Moslems shot forty-two American children to punish their parents for not respecting their missionary. The whole world would denounce such an atrocity, but the Church tries to rationalize an

---

*2 Kings in Protestant Bibles.

equivalent crime in the name of religious fervor. Rightly, it has been said, save us from the zealots!

Obviously, what the Church is saying even today is, "If you dare question that ours is the true religion, God will send a horrible curse on you." Taught as it is to children at an impressionable age, this lesson should be pretty effective in preventing them from questioning their religion.

Another example of the biblical concept of religious tolerance—or I should say the lack of it—is Elias' treatment of the prophets of Baal: he had 450 of them slaughtered (3 Kings 28:22-40).

Some people like to quote the biblical admonition of Isaiah to "beat your swords into plowshares." But for the most part the Israelites in the Old Testament followed the command of the Lord in Joel: "Cut your plowshares into swords, and your spades into spears" (Joel 3:10). Of all the horrible evils advanced by the writers of the Bible the worst by far is the advocacy of genocide against the enemies of the Israelites—anyone who inhabited land which they coveted. In Deut. 19:8 You ordered entire populations of conquered cities put to death by the sword: "But of those cities that shall be given thee thou shalt suffer none at all to live; but shalt kill them with the edge of the sword, to wit, the Hethite and the Amorrhite, and the Chanaanite, the Pherezite, and the Hevite and the Jebusite" (Deut. 20:16, 17). Then You had the audacity in chapter 22 to discuss charity to one's neighbor. Obviously You define a neighbor rather narrowly, including only other Israelites.

Joshua continues the tradition of bloody conquests. Probably every schoolchild has heard the legend of how Joshua had seven priests blow seven trumpets for seven days, and the walls of Jericho came tumbling down. What is not stressed in that story is that when Joshua's army took the city they "killed all that were in it, man and women, young and old" (Josh. 6:21). Then with the Lord directing him, Joshua repeated this massacre throughout the land of the Canaanites, killing all the inhabitants of their seven principal cities. The justification for this carnage was that this was the promised land You gave to the Israelites and their progeny. The fact that the land was already inhabited was a minor inconvenience corrected by the divinely authorized policy of genocide.

Most of the rest of the Old Testament is concerned with the perpetual state of warfare between the Israelites and their neighbors. (A situation that still exists down to the present day, unfortunately.) The only crime in this regard that the Old Testament reports is one of leniency which is contrary to Your bloodthirsty commands. During one of the conquests, You command Saul via the prophet Samuel to smite the kingdom of Amalec: "Spare him not, nor covet anything that is his; but slay both man and women, child and suckling, ox and sheep, camel and ass" (1 Kings 15:3).* Saul dutifully murders "all the common people with the edge of the sword" (15:8), but makes the mistake of sparing the life of King Agag of Amalec and some of his better livestock which Saul planned to offer in sacrifice to You. For this wanton act of disobedience You instruct Samuel to cast off Saul. Eventually Saul is partially forgiven and turns over King Agag to Samuel, who "hews him to pieces before the Lord" (1 Kings 15:33).

A later king of Israel, Manhem, destroyed Thapsa, "and he slew all the women thereof that were with child, and ripped them up" (4 Kings 15:16). Sounds more like a divine nightmare rather than divine inspiration.

G: Here we are discussing war, and war cannot be waged without bloodshed.

J: As I've said, these were often wars of Israelite aggression; wars for the admitted purpose of founding a nation on land occupied by another people. And what war justifies rape and genocide?

G: These were primitive times. The Israelites were a desperate people with no land they could call their own.

J: So You gave them the right to someone else's land?

G: Exactly. It is my prerogative as Creator and ruler of all.

J: At least that is the way an Israelite would have seen it. Let's not forget that the Old Testament was written *after* these battles. In other words, God's divine land grant was invented to justify the Israelites' invasion. It was simply a forerunner of the "Manifest Destiny" doctrine used later by all imperialist nations. The conqueror always tries to rationalize his aggression by divine sanction if possible. Joseph Smith and his Mormons employed a similar justification for their criminal actions in Illinois and Missouri until they were stopped by civil authorities.

The Bible is supposed to be an ethical prescription for all time. Some morality! Deut. 21:18–21 states: "If a man has a stubborn and unruly son, who will not hear the commandments of his father or mother, and being corrected, slighteth obedience, they shall take him and bring him to the ancients of his city and to the gate of judgment and shall say to them: this, our son is rebellious and stubborn, he giveth himself to reveling and to debauchery and banquetings. The people of the city shall stone him and he shall die, that you may take the evil out of the midst if you." Capital punishment for partying—

---

*1 Samuel in Protestant Bibles.

some merciful God! Some example of love and forgiveness! Repentance didn't help much in the Old Testament either. After David confesses his sin, Nathan reflects on Your tender mercy: "The Lord also hath taken away thy sin; thou shalt not die. Nevertheless, because thou hast given occasion to the enemies of the Lord to blaspheme, for this thing, the child that is born to thee, shall surely die. . . . The Lord also struck the child which the wife of Urias had born to David." (2 Kings 12:13–15). David fasted for seven days but to no avail— the child died.

The concept of punishing the children for the sins of their fathers (even though the Bible in one place forbids it) stems from the First Commandment: "I am the Lord thy God, mighty, jealous, visiting the inequities of the fathers upon the children, unto the third and fourth generation of them that hate me"(Exod. 20:5). This odious idea has caused people even today to believe that deformed or retarded children are the results of their parents' sins. The magnitude of the mental anguish this causes parents of these unfortunate children would be impossible to estimate. Of course, the belief originated from primitive man's attempt to explain physical evil in the absence of any knowledge of genetics or the role of viruses and bacteria in the transmission of diseases.

G: You omitted the rest of that quote from Exodus: ". . . and showing mercy unto thousands to them that love me and keep my commandments."

J: The point is that whether persons love You or hate You is no reason to reward or punish their children.

G: In Deuteronomy I say that children should not be put to death for the sins of their fathers, but everyone shall die for his own sin (Deut. 24:26).

J: What a wonderful guide to moral behavior the Bible is. The answer depends on what page you happen to read. If man is supposed to try to emulate Your divine justice, it is no wonder that the world is in such a mess. With you at the helm, there is no need for Satan.

G: As has been often said, I work in mysterious ways. Have you exhausted this topic yet?

J: I could go on for another chapter or two if You like. For example, I might tell of how Jehu, who was anointed by the prophet Elijah to be king of Israel, ordered the beheading of Achab's seventy sons and had the collected heads sent to him as a sign of Achab's submission (4 Kings 10:7). With such a precedent, Herod's later beheading of John the Baptist is perfectly understandable. By the way, Achab must have been quite a prolific fellow.

G: Israelites were monotheistic not monogamous. And for the murder, later in Osee Jehru is condemned for his action. Doesn't that at least show moral progress?

J: More likely it merely shows a change in the political order, a desire to remove Jehru's faction from power. Moreover, if the Bible reflects progress in its sense of morality, three implications may be drawn: (1) we must be extremely careful which parts of the Old Testament we draw our moral lessons from; (2) progress implies that biblical morality was less than perfect in the first place, so it is silly to think that it was inspired by You (unless You are imperfect); and (3) there is no reason to assume that moral progress ended with the Old Testament. As I explained earlier, the Judaic religion does not make this assumption; the Mishnah, the Talmud, and other new interpretations are used to advance moral learning. Hence, the Bible cannot be used as a guide to moral behavior. But if it can be used as a reliable guide neither to history nor to moral behavior, it would appear to be of no more value than any of a number of books of antiquity.

The Old Testament is replete with violence, vengeance, wars of conquest, deceit and injustice, all in Your name. No wonder enlightened Jews of today take pains to dissociate themselves from biblical traditions and values. Even the beautiful psalms are corrupted by the stench of vengeance. Max Weber tells us that "In no other religion of the world do we find a deity possessing the unparalleled desire for vengeance manifested by Yahweh."[3] Joseph Wheless sums up the view of God in the Old Testament this way:

> He reeks with the blood of murder unnumbered, and is personally a murderer and assassin, by stealth and treachery; a pitiless monster of bloody vengeance, a relentless monster and terrifying bully and terrorist; a synonym for partiality and injustice, a vain braggart; a false prophet; an arrant and shameless liar.[4]

G: If I was as merciless and despotic as he suggests, why did I not strike Wheless down?

J: I'll offer an explanation, but not just yet. However, as often as not, others were ready to carry out Your retribution for You. Earlier I discussed the history of the largely successful attempt to silence Your critics. One of the more interesting incidents I have saved until now. It occurred in England in 1842, when Thomas Paterson, editor of a freethought newspaper, was arrested for "exhibiting profane placards." Paterson published his defense under the title "God v. Paterson": it considered You the plaintiff and offered evidence from the Bible to demonstrate the plaintiff's bad character. During the courtroom proceedings, paper after paper prepared for Paterson's defense was taken from him and his pocket Bible impounded by order of the court to prevent his reading texts "damaging to religion."[5]

G: Very amusing, but entirely biased and one-sided. You ignore all that is worthwhile and humane in the Bible, focusing instead on those passages which serve your destructive purposes. The Bible is also filled with admonitions to show charity to your neighbor, to offer protection to runaway slaves and to be fair in the administration of justice even to strangers (Deut. 22: 1–4, 23:15, 24:17).

J: I agree that it offers some wonderful moral teachings, but, as I have shown, for every bit of ethical teaching it offers a moral lesson to the contrary. It advocates discrimination against homosexuals, illegitimate children and eunuchs. It is so prejudiced against non-Jews that in Esdras Israelite men are urged to desert their foreign wives and their children (Esdras 10). And as justification for burning thousands of eccentric people in the Middle Ages, the clerics pointed to the Bible injunction: "Thou shalt not suffer a witch to live" (Exod. 22:18). The Salem witch trials in our own country are a reflection of that cruel prejudice.

G: Again, that's ancient history. No Christian or Hebrew today would advocate such superstition and intolerance. On the other hand, they still do observe the Ten Commandments of Moses which are the foundation for all law and civilization.

J: The Bible also offers examples of how to break all but the first three and rationalize doing so in Your name. Besides, as I've explained, the Ten Commandments did not originate with the Bible. Even theologians admit that they had a long history prior to the Bible; the Bible's only contribution was an attempt to establish their legitimacy under Your authority.[6] Several of the ancient societies such as the Babylonians, Persians, and Chinese had such codes of conduct or commandments: I have already referred to the Code of Hammurabi which was more extensive and encompassed specific penalties for violation of the law, much as the Bible does in the Books of Leviticus, Numbers and Deuteronomy. However, the Hammurabi Code was more pragmatic and not so ritualistic.

The Persians also had their commandments. While on a mountain top praying to the god Ormuzd, Zoroaster was delivered the *Zend-Averta,* or *Living Word,* which is the book of law for his followers. According to Professor Max Müller, "What applies to the religion of Moses applies to that of Zoroaster. It is placed before us as a complete system from the first, revealed by Ahuramazda (Ormuzd), proclaimed by Zoroaster."[7]

Whatever their origin, the Ten Commandments, and for that matter, the entire value system of the Bible, are too simplistic to be of any real utility today.

G: I am amazed. Are you are saying that the Ten Commandments are obsolete?

J: The first three commandments expressing man's relationship to You never were of any relevance. The rest are of no pragmatic value as written, and never were. Take for example: "Thou shalt not kill." Everyone can agree with that generality, but there must be "unless" clauses: unless you are attacked, unless you are at war, unless someone threatens to steal your personal property, unless you wish to discourage treason, etc. These exceptions are essential in a real world where different situations call for different responses. Who would be so dogmatic and perverse as to allow a madman to murder a child even if the only way of stopping the madman was to kill him? But we couldn't make such a judgment unless ethics had progressed beyond merely following the injunctions written in the Bible.

G: I disagree that the Ten Commandments are of no practical value just because modern man has found exceptions to the rules. They establish an ideal ethical value system, something to strive for. Because it may be necessary to kill in a given situation, does that invalidate the injunction against killing? Would we have a better world if there were no injunction against killing?

J: The problem is that the simple prohibition provides no basis for ethical decisions. If there is no theoretical basis for distinquishing between right and wrong all we are left with is a group of moral precepts that may or may not be correct in any given situation.

Ancient law was based on the wisdom—or lack of it—of religious leaders and legitimized by attributing its prescriptions to God. Once established, it was thought to be immutable. The goal of modern legislation, when it can divorce itself from ancient prejudice, is an analysis of cause and effect. The efficacy of the law is constantly subject to review in terms of its impact on the human condition and, if found wanting, it can be changed.

It may be apparent from my foregoing review of the Old Testament that many of Yahweh's commands and prohibitions were basically immoral by today's ethical standards. No doubt the authors of the Bible, whoever they were, developed their moral code, in part, with the idea of improving the human condition. But without a theoretical framework of justice, their laws of behavior could be terribly inappropriate under various circumstances, especially given the environment in which we live today.

As an example, let's return to the commandment "Thou shalt not kill." Such an injunction might have appeared obvious enough three thousand years ago, but in our modern technological age even life and death are becoming more difficult to define. We may be able to sustain a body long after there is no consciousness, perhaps indefinitely, by having machines perform the tasks of respiration, digestion, and circulation. But is this unconscious organism still "alive" as a human being? When does withholding life support constitute murder? What right does a person have in determining when his or her own life is no longer worth living? These are complex questions which no amount of biblical study can answer. Given the primitive state of medicine at the time the Bible was written, the entire area of medical ethics hadn't been conceived. I agree, for once, with Hans Küng when he admits,

> The problems and conflicts of modern humanity (overpopulation, birth control, economic growth, protection of the environment, income distribution) are too complex, the problems also of interpreting the Scripture and of "natural law" are too complex for us to be able to deduce easily from Scripture or from human nature perennially valid norms of human behavior.[8]

Those who turn to the scriptures for solutions to today's problems will find at best a void, and at worst completely inappropriate or contradictory answers. The inevitable consequence of driving into the future while looking through a rearview mirror is a collision with reality, and the lives of millions of people will be the worse for it.

G: But you do admit that people need some touchstone, some spiritual grounding, to formulate their consciences and worldview.

J: Though I find the term "spiritual" meaningless, I would agree with what You say. The touchstone must be a factual analysis of whether specific rules and customs contribute to human happiness. I submit that to some extent we see common law struggling in this direction. On the other hand, I shudder to think of using the Bible as a basis for crafting consciences. The Bible was written to justify Israelite aggression, to ensure the position of the priests and to provide a semblance of social order for a seminomadic, primitive people. We have seen the result of using the Bible as the basis for morality in subsequent eras: religiously motivated or justified warfare and the continued spread of human misery, despite the many scientific advances that should have alleviated it. If the Bible is used as a basis for formulating consciences, I fear humankind is doomed.

G: You are being overly dramatic again. Besides, while I admit that my representation in the Old Testament is rather severe, man was rather savage in those days. The New Testament on the other hand presents me in much better light.

J: Oh, does it? In the Old Testament You merely murdered anyone who displeased You. In the New Testament You wait until they die and then sentence them to eternal—I emphasize eternal—punishment. Poor, weak, and ignorant men, women, and children are sentenced to damnation forever. What an absolutely horrid and absurd religious belief!

Charles Watts, a freethought writer and publisher of the nineteenth century, provides a marvelous summary of the Bible story we are asked to believe. Let me read it to you.

> About six thousand years ago an all-wise, all-powerful, and beneficent God made man and woman, and placed them in a position surrounded by temptations it was impossible for them to withstand. For instance, he implanted within them desires, which as God, he must have known would produce their downfall. He next caused a tree to bear fruit that was adapted to harmonize with the very desires which he had previously imparted to his children. God, all-good, then created a serpent of the worst possible kind, in order that it might be successful in tempting Eve to partake of the fruit. God commanded Adam and Eve not to eat of this fruit, under the penalty of death, knowing at the same time that they would eat of it, and that they would not die. The serpent is allowed to succeed in his plan of temptation, and then God curses the ground for yielding the tree which he himself had caused to grow; further, the almighty Being dooms both man and woman to lives of pain and sorrow, and assures them that their posterity shall feel the terrible effects of their having done what was impossible, under the circumstances, for them to avoid. Although at first God pronounced his creative work to be "very good," it proved to be quite the opposite. So bad did the human family become that God determined to bring a flood upon the earth and wash every member, one household excepted, out of existence. This "water-cure" was not, however, sufficient to correct the "divine" errors, for the people grew worse than ever. God now decided upon another plan, namely to send his son—who was as old as himself, and, therefore, not his son—to die, but who was invested with immortality and could not die, to atone for sins that had never been committed by people who were not then born, and who could not, therefore, have been guilty of any sin. As a conclusion to the whole scheme, this all-merciful God prepared a hell, containing material fire of brimstone, to burn the immaterial souls of all persons who should fail to believe the truth, justice, and necessity of this jumble of cruelty and absurdity.[9]

G: Very droll. Before you hurry on in your iconoclastic mission, would you be so kind as to answer a question?

J: I'd be delighted.

G: If, as you suggest, the Bible is such an incomprehensible source of myth, pseudo-history and conflicting moral instructions, why has it maintained its unrivaled popularity for two thousand years?

J: Before I answer that question I must correct You on one point: the Bible is not the most popular book (or collection of books) of all time. In fact, given the extremely low literacy rate throughout history, until recently relatively few people had actually read the Bible. It may come as a shock to learn that more people have read Marx and Mao than Jesus. Does that mean that Marx and Mao contain more truth than the Bible? Nor is the Bible the oldest religious work still in existence. The Upanishads and the Bhagavad Gita are at least as old and follow an oral tradition which is much older.

G: All right, but that is all beside the point.

J: I'm just trying to put the book in the proper context. There are several reasons for the Bible's enduring popularity. First, since it is a compilation of ancient myths, it provides answers that satisfy, to a degree, the same psychological needs that motivated the creation of its myths in the first place. The Bible offers simple explanations to perplexing questions facing humankind: What is the purpose of life? Why is there so much misery and injustice in the world? What fate awaits us when we die? It is important to understand that for most people it doesn't matter whether the answers are logical or verifiable, so long as the answers are to some degree satisfying.

Second, the Bible is the book of the religious victors: first the Israelites, then the Christians. Reading the books of the winners is most often mandatory (ask the people in the former Communist countries); reading the books of the losers is usually prohibited.

Third, it is precisely because of the Bible's moral ambiguity that it has enjoyed such a large following. As I have demonstrated, it can be used to justify any position on any issue, as the proponents of slavery, racism, revenge and intolerance have so often found. The moral laws which a reader derives from the Bible are primarily a function of the moral beliefs a person already possesses when he or she reads the Bible.

Fourth, the Bible has all of the ingredients of a best-selling novel: war, sex, murder, love, political intrigues, many unforgettable fictional characters (such as an Israelite Rambo by the name of Samson), and even some excellent romantic poetry.

Finally, there was a time when some of the lessons in the Bible could claim moral superiority over the prevailing ethical system. Moreover, the apparent contradictory nature of biblical ethics, upon closer inspection, reveals a progression in the ethical development of the Hebrew religion. Unfortunately, although this Judaic ethical development continued in the form of the Mishnah and Talmud, the Bible itself, even with the addition of the New Testament, is a morally truncated document—a fact that completely escapes the fundamentalists. The system of common law has evolved to deal, albeit imperfectly, with the ethical requirements of modern society. Unlike the Bible, the system of law is subject to constant review, verification and revision, enabling it to remain dynamic rather than static. At best, the Bible offers an interesting insight into the customs, beliefs and psychology of one segment of humankind between two thousand and three thousand years ago.

G: What a gross injustice to what for millions is the greatest story ever told!

J: There are millions who have never read a great story, and wouldn't recognize one if they had. What I have shown beyond the shadow of doubt is that Feuerbach was correct in his conclusion: "A book that imposes on me the necessity of discrimination, the necessity of criticism in order to separate the divine from the human, the permanent from the temporary, is no longer a divine, certain infallible book— it is degenerated to the ranks of profane books."[10] In other words, at best, the Bible belongs on the book shelf between Homer and Virgil. At worst it is, as Smith puts it, "a paradoxism of misology—the hatred of reason."[11] From the book of Genesis in which You forbid Adam and Eve to eat of the "tree of knowledge," to Paul's assertion that since "the world did not come to know God by wisdom, it pleased God by the foolishness of our preaching to save those who believe" (I Cor 2:21), the Judeo-Christian teachings require humans to suppress their natural desire to question, to think, and to analyze. Thomas Aquinas echoed this sentiment, "The sin of unbelief is greater than any sin that occurs in the perversion of morals," and he endorsed the usual sanction against unbelievers, recommending that heretics be "exterminated from the world by death" after the third offense.[12]

In many respects, the Christian belief is a regression rather than an advance over Judaism. Reliance on revelation and the authority of the pope or an evangelist as the source for determining moral issues or, at times, even matters of science, is in keeping with the most ancient superstitions of tribal religions. Judaism, for the most part (except for the ultraorthodox sect), has progressed beyond this, and encourages scholarly investigation and analysis. The rabbi does not attempt to invest his position as Your representative in the same way the priest attempts to pass himself off as the "representative of Jesus Christ." Neither does Judaism present the Old Testament as Your infallible word, as the fundamentalist Christian sects and the official doctrine of the Catholic Church do.

10

Reason versus Faith:
A Path to Knowledge,
a Path to Superstition

Reason must be deluded, blinded, and destroyed. Faith must trample underfoot all reason, sense, and understanding and whatever it sees it must put out of sight and wish to know nothing but the word of God.

—Martin Luther

G: I'm growing weary. You continue to denigrate faith as absurd and ignorant while exhorting reason as the way to all truth. And yet, the basis of every exercise of reason, whether deductive or inductive, is an unverifiable hypothesis—an act of faith.

J: A scientist does not have "faith" in his hypothesis. Let's define our terms. H. L. Mencken's defined faith as "an illogical belief in the occurrence of the improbable,"[1] but we'll stick with the relevant dictionary definition: "Firm belief in something for which there is no proof." Webster's Dictionary also makes a distinction between faith and belief: "Belief and Faith are often used interchangeably but belief may or may not imply certitude in the believer whereas faith always does, even when there is no evidence or proof." However, as I'll demonstrate, when persons speak of their belief in God, they really mean their faith in God. For the scientist, on the other hand, all statements are tentative even when supported by evidence. No proof is considered conclusive, no verification absolute. If new evidence disproves the hypothesis, or offers a more satisfactory explanation, the scientist will scrap the original theory. Belief in You, on the other hand, is postulated as a certainty; further inquiry is considered unnecessary or even forbidden. Hence, it is an act of faith.

238

G: Most scientists are not as open-minded as you suggest. They will defend their hypotheses against all challenges, and some have also suppressed contrary evidence.

J: True, but the big difference is that in the scientific community suppression of inquiry and blind adherence to a theory is considered a failing, whereas with religion, blind, unquestioning belief is considered a virtue. As Peter Gay expressed it: "The ideas of theologians are refuted by their adversaries, the ideas of scientists are refuted by their followers."[2]

Although recently there has been an attempt to reconcile religion with science, I think the effort is doomed from the start. Religion is simply seeking to regain the intellectual respectability it has lost since the Enlightenment. It is incapable of an objective search for truth since its primary purpose is to perpetuate its various institutions. Physicist I. I. Rabey explains the difference between the two approaches: "Religion is an organization with political and economic power, a bureaucracy with money-raising equipment. Science is nothing of the sort. It is just a collection of free, uninhibited individuals seeking to understand what the world is. We are not answerable to whatever articles of faith might exist with the political powers."[3] Of course this is not to say that the intellectual objectivity of individual scientists may not be compromised by their efforts to secure funding or recognition.

The chasm between the methods of religion and those of science is easily demonstrated by the the inconceivability of there being a war over differing scientific theories; nor would scientists threaten to force someone to agree with their theories. Even a believer in "creation science" can pass any true science course; the requirement is never that the students have faith in the theories discussed, only that they understand them. How different has been the history of religion. Religion relies on belief, and since belief need have no reference to the real world, there is no way to reconcile very different belief systems. On the other hand, as ethologist Konrad Lorenz points out, "scientific truth is wrested from reality outside the human brain."[4] Even though there may be differences in how this reality is perceived, it is ultimately the same for all human beings. Therefore, all correct scientific results will be in agreement with each other regardless of the national or political background of particular scientists. Where religion divides, science unifies. Religion relies on belief, which presupposes truth; science relies on reason to aid in its perpetual search for the truth.

G: I don't see why you assume that faith and reason are incompatible. Thomas Aquinas and others certainly grounded their faith in reason. Hans Küng speaks eloquently for "reasoned faith."

J: What a silly contradiction of terms. If man has a reason for accepting a statement as true, he doesn't need faith. Conversely, reason is superfluous if one has accepted a statement as true on the basis of faith.

G: Maybe this argument is just a matter of semantics. Fundamentally, there may be no difference between faith and reason.

J: That's absurd. But to fully appreciate the difference I must explain the scientific method.

G: Is this going to take long? I may have an eternity to listen but I'm afraid your readers haven't.

J: I'll give you the short version. Scientific reasoning (more often called the scientific method) begins with the recognition that there are events taking place in time and space. Through our senses and the mental process of observation we become aware of these events. This is an act of perception. Admittedly, as I have explained before, our perception may be distorted or biased by a prior mindset. We might also perceive events subconsciously. Regardless of how the information concerning the events is received, whenever a pattern of behavior is thought to be detected between events, the observer will draw some hypothesis concerning the relationship between the events. This may come as an intuitive flash, or as the result of systematically recording the various events and then modeling their interactions. It is unimportant how we arrive at the hypothesis; what is important is what we do with it from there. Both the modern scientist and ancient philosopher employed this same process of induction, proceeding from the particular to the general. It is this same process that led ancient cultures to postulate the existence of gods controlling the forces of nature.

However, for the scientist, unlike the man of faith, the hypothesis is the beginning, not the end, of the process. If it were the end, then an infinite number of theories could explain an event. The scientist next attempts to formulate his hypothesis in a clear linguistic or mathematical definition. Paul Kurtz explains this step: "A term or sentence must have some identifiable referent or interpretation based upon human experience, directly or indirectly, if it is to have cognitive significance and meaning."[5] This excludes any metaphysical statement as being an acceptable working hypothesis since, as the philosopher Rudolph Carnap has shown, metaphysical statements are not capable of entering into relationships of deducibility with (true or false) empirical statements.[6]

The scientist must then examine the hypothesis for logical consistency and coherence with the existing body of validated knowledge. In the latter case, a contradiction may not prove necessarily fatal to the new hypothesis, but it will demand even more verification. The hypothesis will also be examined to determine that it is the simplest, most straightforward explanation of the observed phenomena.*

The final and most crucial step is verification. It involves employing the hypothesis to predict the outcome of some future sequence of events through the process of experimentation, either in a controlled laboratory environment or, if that is not possible, through statistical measurement. However, even perfect predictability does not prove a hypothesis to be *absolutely* true. Philosopher Sir Karl Popper argued that we can never reach absolute truth, because even a million successful tests cannot rule out the possibility that the million and first test would fail. Hence, he argues that only when a test fails can we reach absolute certainty: the certainty that the hypothesis is wrong! Even then, as some of the most recent philosophers have demonstrated, certitude may escape us.

G: It sounds as if this process never reaches a conclusion.

J: In a sense You are correct; absolute certainty is ruled out. All conclusions are accepted as tentative ("no more than probable") and open to revision in the light of new evidence. The ideal scientist or philosopher is always receptive to a new hypothesis, but it will be subject to the same rigorous examination as every past one.

Having explained the scientific method, let's return to the concept of faith. It seems to me that there are two types of faith: (a) belief in something solely on the authority of another, or (b) belief in a hypothesis, without an attempt at verification. In discussing faith and reason, the key issue is how to distinguish truth from falsity. George H. Smith attempted to clarify the issue by stating, "If man is to acquire knowledge, he must have a method of distinguishing truth from falsity, beliefs which correspond to reality from beliefs which do not."[7] Faith has no method for doing so, whether it relies on the authority of others or some intuitive judgment. In the latter case, it is hard to see how it differs from flipping a coin.

Freud asked, "Am I to believe in every absurdity? And if not, why this one in particular?"[8] Without a method to distinguish truth from falsity, how could humankind acquire any knowledge? We see that even children migrate from faith to a crude form of scientific reasoning as a way of acquiring knowledge. At first they accept all of their parents' statements as fact: they have complete faith in their parents' knowledge of the world. But as part of the maturation process, most children begin to challenge their parents' views. They demand more support than mere faith, and this is good. If each succeeding

---

*This is the Principle of Parsimony or Ockham's Razor, as it is commonly called.

generation did not challenge the traditional wisdom of its predecessors, we would still have the worldview of the Neanderthal man.

Luckily for the human race, most people have some degree of inquisitiveness and skepticism. They conduct their own experiments. We can see this most dramatically in teenagers. Certainly an act of disobedience may be due to selfishness, an attempt to exert independence, or a disturbed child's way of seeking attention, but a certain amount of disobedience is simply reality testing. If the child finds that the parents have been giving false information concerning the real world, there may be a rejection of parental teachings. I say "may" because oftentimes children are so thoroughly indoctrinated to distrust their own ability to perceive reality that they will reject it and cling to their parents' illusions. But healthy children move from total faith to a method of drawing their own conclusions from the evidence at hand.

G: That's all very interesting, but I don't think it is applicable for resolving metaphysical questions. The philosopher Immanuel Kant and others have shown the impossibility of using reason to answer questions regarding moral behavior, or even more fundamentally, whether I, your God, exist. There are many reasons for this. If you'll do Me the courtesy, I'll articulate a few.

J: By all means, but don't get angry if I point out a conceptual error or two.

G: After all the slander I've endured so far, you must concede I am now the epitome of patience, not to mention mercy, despite the rather sordid reputation with which I was tainted by the biblical accounts.

First, all reason must begin with a reliance on the senses. However, as René Descartes and many others have shown, the senses are quite easily deceived. Take the case of the desert mirage, or the way a stick appears to bend when part of it is thrust below water. Listen to that jet going overhead. If you were to point to where you thought it was, you wouldn't even be close, due to the relative slowness of the sound waves. I could add many other examples. There have been times when you were asleep and thought you woke up, only to find, when you actually woke up, that your earlier awakening was only a dream. All sensory experience is, as Plato sought to demonstrate, only an apprehension of the appearance of reality. Through the senses, you can never reach ultimate reality, the Ultimate Being, Me.

J: Well said! For one who believes in faith as superior to reason, You did a good job of logical reasoning to reach Your conclusion. That observation aside, surely You see that You must presuppose the validity of sensory evidence in Your very attempt to disprove it. Take Your example of the desert mirage. The refraction of light off the sand strikes the eye producing a stimulus to the optic nerve. Given also the distortion in the light due to heat rising from the sand, the stimulus is similar to light rays reflected from the surface of water. In both cases there is the appearance of a shimmering silver color in the distance. The reality in both cases is that a strong reflected light struck the optic nerve. The eye has sensed this occurrence correctly. The error lies in the mind's interpretation of this apparent shimmering silver color; but through additional information this misinterpretation can be corrected. Those who have once mistaken the shimmering silver for water in a desert or on a highway seldom do so again. They note the subtle differences and also mentally adjust their expectation for encountering water where it is not to be anticipated. The same is true of the bent stick in the water. With experience, a person learns that light, not the stick, is bent by water. A spear fisherman learns to strike just ahead or behind of where his prey appears to be. In short, I find no problem in relying on the senses provided we are open to the possibility of misinterpretation and seek to correct such errors in judgment through additional experimentation and information. Like all knowledge, sensory information should be considered tentative until verified.

I must also take issue with your misinterpretation of Kant. Kant differentiated between *pure* reason and *empirical* reasoning. By the former he meant those logical deductions derived from unverified premises. Of these logical processes, Kant correctly observed that, as a purely cognitive function, reason produces no knowledge.[9] I should point out that Kant was attacking the philosophical theory of *rationalism,* which held that truth may be attained by reasoning from self-evident first premises. The school of philosophy known as *logical positivism* also concluded that no truly new knowledge could be derived from pure reason. This is not to say that logic cannot be useful in attempting to gain insight into the relationships among events or facts by analyzing the statements made concerning them. In this regard, pure reason can be useful in deriving new hypotheses. But without the crucial step of validation through experience, hypotheses cannot result in knowing. Therefore, as Kant admitted, ultimately all knowledge must be derived from experience: "Experience must contain all the objects for our concepts, but beyond it no concepts have any significance, as there is no intuition that might offer them a foundation."[10]

Kant does get a little muddled in his examination of the relationship between concepts and experience. Actually, it is a chicken-and-egg issue. A priori concepts do influence our perception of an event and hence can determine to some extent what we experience. On the other hand, each experience will affect subsequent conceptualizations. The very term "experience" suggests an interaction between the observer and the thing observed.

All this does not, however, remove the necessity for validation through experience, it just points out the impossibility of achieving absolute certitude on anything. By the way, by "experience" I don't mean a purely personal experience as advocated by mysticism, but the validated experience of empirical evidence. A carefully designed experiment attempts to prevent the prior experience or conceptual framework of the experimenter from influencing the outcome. That is why science seeks replicability in the experiment, especially through the trials of many other experimenters. Even then, the most circumspect scientists hold that the truth so revealed is tentative, true only in the pragmatic sense that it works. Therefore verification, while necessary, is still not sufficient to establish "absolute" truth. In the case of faith, however, the necessary verification step is eliminated and, therefore, gets us absolutely nowhere in the search for truth.

G: That all sounds very nice in the abstract, but in real life you don't always have time for verification. If someone raises his arm to strike you, you haven't the leisure to seek proof as to whether or not he will carry out his intention; you must act. As Cardinal Newman declared: "Life is for action. If we insist on proof for everything, we shall never come to action; to act you must assume and that assumption is faith."[11]

J: I don't deny that frequently we have to act on very incomplete evidence because circumstances dictate it. Also, as a simple matter of expediency and practicality, it is not necessary or desirable that we validate everything. However, whenever we have time to gather additional data before making a decision, prudence would dictate that we do so or else "decide in haste, repent at leisure." The significance of the decision determines the amount of time spent in researching the evidence. Given the enormity of the decision to believe in You and/or follow a particular religious belief, the investigative time and effort should be proportional. And, even after that decision is made, it should be reviewed periodically to see if additional knowledge verifies or refutes the probability of that belief being true.

G: Probability? You talk as if my existence can be determined through statistical inference.

J: Not exactly, but the probability of faith in Your existence could be estimated statistically. Furthermore, if humans were strictly rational creatures, they would make most decisions on the basis of the probability of the outcome.

G: Allow me to point out first, that for a person who rejects faith, you place incredible faith in reason.

J: Now You are playing a semantics game. I don't have faith in reason; rather, I utilize reason because it has proved superior to faith in advancing human knowledge. Everything we know about human nature and the world we live in has been gained through reason validated by experience.

G: Earlier you said that one kind of faith is belief in something solely on the authority of another. If so, then every day you are "guilty" of acts of faith. Whether you take medical advice from a doctor or fly in an airplane, do you not do so on the basis of faith? In the latter case, your faith is in the capabilities of a pilot you have never met. Why not then have faith in the authority of priests and ministers, who in turn have faith in the spoken word of the wisest men who ever lived, namely Jesus and the prophets?

J: First, their authority rests on the totally unsubstantiated supposition that they possessed knowledge of a supernatural origin. Second, we have no knowledge of what they actually said; rather, we only know what others allege they have said. Last, and most importantly, the goodness or wisdom of a man does not justify accepting a belief on the basis of his authority alone. A reasonable person will only accept a statement from an authority if (a) that authority is willing to present evidence in support of belief, (b) the proposition is verifiable in principle by any person who cares to take the time and effort required to do so, and (c) the proposition does not contradict the rules of logic.

Let's take an example. Before accepting medical advice and acting upon it, I go through several reasonableness checks. First I establish the person's credentials: a doctor's license certifies that the person has studied medicine and has attained a certain degree of learning and competence. In the case of a dangerous or unusual problem, I would also seek a physician recommended by someone whose judgment on such matters I have found to be reliable. Next, if possible, I assess the efficacy of the treatment; if it doesn't appear to be working I will seek the advice of other doctors. In the case of potentially serious or expensive treatment, I would certainly consult with more than one doctor. On the other hand, if I were to rely merely upon faith, I would blindly follow the advice of a doctor regardless of his credentials, or the record of effectiveness for the treatment. Despairing cancer patients frequently fall into this trap and are susceptible to all kinds of quackery and con games.

Similarly, I doubt whether I would have been the first person to fly in a jet. At the time of their introduction I didn't know enough of their aerodynamic properties to simply have "faith" that they would fly. However, I know of countless people who have flown and have

done so safely. I can see thousands of people embarking and dis-
embarking at airports; I read of crashes only rarely. Still, I'm glad
to have life insurance because I do not have blind faith in the aircraft
or the pilot. In the final analysis, I am making a decision based on
the probability that I will reach my destination safely.

G: You again mention probability. Isn't this, in effect, the approach used
by Blaise Pascal in his famous wager? You will recall that according
to Pascal, either I exist or I do not. Hence, there is a fifty-fifty chance
I exist. If I don't exist and you believe I do, what have you lost?
Nothing. On the other hand, if I do exist and you believe in Me,
you have gained everything—salvation and eternal bliss. Since everyone
must wager one way or the other, and your stake is truth and happiness,
a prudent man would naturally stake his chances on belief.

J: I agree with Pascal that at stake are truth and happiness. But truth
is lost if one is a believer in a myth. If we believe in You, and You
don't exist, the whole ethic and culture will be based upon a false
premise. How, then, can we ever expect to understand anything, to
even approach truth? The consequences of relying upon unsubstantiated belief are abundantly clear from the brief account of Judeo-
Christian history I gave earlier. In addition, we have seen the havoc
that reliance on faith as the road to truth has wrought throughout
history. Every dictator has depended upon the faith of the masses
in his bid for power. Humankind will continue stumbling through
the darkness of ignorance and misery as it has despite, perhaps because
of, thousands of years of theistic belief.

Admittedly, an individual believer may experience an ecstatic
happiness, but so can a drunk, a dope addict, or an idiot. The problem
is that through their personal, selfish ecstasy they contribute nothing
to the betterment of humankind. They leave that up to You. Even
those who seek to help their fellow humans as often as not go about
it all wrong way because of their false first premise. That may well
be why the legacy of the Judeo-Christian culture has done little to
eliminate bigotry, racism, imperialism, crime, and general human
misery. Moreover, believers often suffer unnecessarily from guilt, remorse and the fear of damnation for quite innocuous "sins."

G: Can't you stick to the point? The fact is that the question of the ultimate
reality of being, cannot be determined by reason. By "being" I mean
all that exists, which theologians hold to be a synonym for God and
hence use a capital "B"—Being. Kant clearly expressed the problem,
and most philosophers and epistemologists since Kant have had to
admit that reason can never arrive at knowledge of ultimate being.
The logical positivists you mentioned earlier thought that absolute clarity

of thought could be attained through analytical or symbolic language. By this means they hoped to establish a method of knowing reality with certitude. However, they never achieved their goal.

J: I don't think that the logical positivists ever contended that they could attain absolute truth, as You imply. Rather, they sought to eliminate meaningless statements of metaphysics and develop a language whose ultimate reference was reality. In this way they hoped to develop a body of knowledge which could always be verified or refuted.

G: Yes, but even Ludwig Wittgenstein had to admit finally that it was not possible to develop an unambiguous or purely logical language to describe the world or ultimate reality. All attempts to reach an understanding of being through reason have failed. After an excruciating examination of the question of being, the German philosopher Martin Heidegger recognized the impossibility of analytically grasping the essence of being and realized that ultimate being, ultimate reality, can be reached only by Faith.

J: Wittgenstein was certainly correct when he stated that "philosophy is a battle against the bewitchment of intelligence by means of language."[12] Nowhere do theologians (and some philosophers) do a better job of bewitching intelligence than in discussions of being. And no one is better in this black art than Martin Heidegger (although Jean Paul Sartre ranks a close second). He cunningly entices the pseudo-intellectual, and many an earnest seeker of truth, into his semantic forest until they can no longer see the proverbial trees.

G: Or maybe you just don't have the mental wherewithal to understand him?

J: Oh, I think I understand him all right. At least enough to see that he confuses specific beings or things with the sum total of all things, as if the aggregation of individual things were itself a thing. Theologians like Küng further confuse the issue by dubbing all things—which they call singular being—with a capital "B." It is easy, then, to equate this universal Being with You. It is simply a variation on the transcendental Being of Plato. But after Heidegger played around for years with the metaphysical question of being and becoming, and sought the cause of being outside of being, it was as if he finally saw the folly of his own endeavors when he stated in a 1962 lecture that perhaps it was "more expedient to refrain not only from giving an answer but even from raising the question."[13]

G: It strikes me that all this supports the position that the entire question of My existence lies outside reason and must ultimately rely on Faith.

J: This is exactly the position Hans Küng makes such a diligent effort to support in his popular book, *Does God Exist?* After a thorough investigation of many of the rationalists' theories for determining truth, he concludes that because neither philosophy nor science holds the answer to "ultimate reality," faith might. He does not go so far as to say that faith must be devoid of reason. However, the kind of reasoning he relies upon is largely metaphysical in nature. After my own studies of metaphysics, I am forced to conclude that metaphysics is analogous to science fiction or the propositions of a non-Euclidian geometry. Statements of a science fiction story may logically follow from some set of assumptions which the author asks the reader to accept at the outset, such as that there is another dimension in which a different species of being exists. Any statements based on this assumption may logically follow, but since they can in principle be neither verified nor refuted, they are beyond the realm of truth or falsehood. In popular usage they are merely fictional, as philosophical propositions they are meaningless. A non-Euclidian geometry is also a set of propositions and corollaries which, although they may logically follow one another, do not refer to the sensory world and thus cannot be validated through experience. Similarly, since metaphysical statements have no reference in reality, they are, in principle, unverifiable. Because there is no way to determine whether a metaphysical statement is true or false, a person can make any proposition he wishes and reach any conclusion he wishes as long as it doesn't contradict a prior assumption. It is as logical to say the world was created by a devil as it is to say it was created by You. It is as logical to say that the whole world only exists in my imagination, or that I only exist in someone else's imagination. The most outrageous absurdity must be accepted, just so long as it doesn't contradict a prior premise.

Ultimately even Küng admits that metaphysics can never, by itself, be a way of apprehending truth. So in the end, he falls back on "fundamental trust" which, although he constantly denies it, is no more than blind faith. According to Küng, since we cannot place our "fundamental trust in "uncertain reality," we should place it in You. What a classic non sequitur!

The major fallacy in Küng's work is his assumption that if science can't lead to ultimate truth, faith must. In other words, if there are only two available alternatives to reach C, and alternative A doesn't work, than B must. But what about the possibility that there may be no way to reach ultimate reality? Science cannot explain ultimate reality since it would require knowledge outside the totality of knowledge—an obvious contradiction. Metaphysics is even worse, for it seeks to explain a hypothesized reality.

In the final analysis, "Ultimate Reality" is a meaningless concept, unless by it one means the sum total of all knowledge. In this respect, the amount of knowledge attainable in a dynamic universe is, for all practical purposes, infinite. For some reason, theologians find this idea frustrating. They would like to get their arms around one single concept like "God" that explains everything.

I used to conjure up a picture of Knowledge as a vast mountain which humankind over the centuries has been trying to move with only the help of a little teaspoon called science—an almost hopeless task. But in adopting faith, man throws away the spoon and tries to wish the mountain away. It has been said that faith can move mountains. I've never seen that happen, but I have seen bulldozers and steamshovels and dynamite do the job (sometimes to my dismay).

G: Your worship of scientific reasoning denies the value of instinct and imagination. Reason can never come to understand such an intuitive concept as love. Only poetry can adequately express such a feeling. In this sense religion is like poetry—a means of expressing some of the very deepest and most profound feelings, needs and desires of mankind. All wise persons would admit that love escapes the grasp of reason, and so, too, does faith. Yet, love is real and so is faith. In this regard, imagination may guide one closer to the truth than reason. Richard Kroner has astutely pointed out that, "Imagination is more adequate to reality than reason, for reality is not rational; therefore, poetry and religion are better adapted to the real than the sciences."[14]

J: What incredibly fuzzy thinking: "reality is not rational." He is confusing that which is—reality—with our method of comprehending it, which may or may not be rational. As for discussing love in the same breath as faith, you are confusing faith defined as a feeling with faith as a method of ascertaining the truthfulness of a proposition. I don't deny the existence—and sometimes the value—of faith as a feeling. Along with the other "theological virtues" of love and hope, faith is a legitimate and useful feeling all persons have, especially when trying to overcome difficulties that seem insurmountable. However, I am here trying to discuss faith as a method of discovering truth. As such, it is a fatally deficient method in that it has no criteria for separating truth from falsehood.

G: But neither do imagination or instinct, so you must also deny their validity.

J: Not in merely formulating an hypothesis or proposition. In this regard they are essential. But whereas faith stops here, scientific reasoning just begins. It attempts to validate the hypothesis.

G: How do you validate love?

J: As a feeling it is unnecessary to do so. Yet science could seek to understand why we love, why we love who we do, the various kinds of love, etc.

G: You dissect love like a cadaver; science would destroy love!

J: Nonsense. People, have been loving for millions of years. Quite often it seems that love ends in misery. Why? Perhaps if we understood the motivations of love—the reasons for love—we could often prevent it from turning to hate.

Before I forget, let me return to something You said before, that religion expresses some of the deepest feelings of humans. I agree with that statement and, moreover, that theistically inspired faith can be one of humankind's strongest feelings. Again, though, I wish to point out that as a feeling (as contrasted with a method) it is in the same category as love, hate, hope, despair, greed or lust. Just as I would never trust any of these feelings to lead me to the truth, neither should I trust faith to lead necessarily to truth. Faith is, as You have said, an expression of people's needs and desires. Faith, therefore, results in totally subjective judgments by the person who possesses, or perhaps I should say, is possessed by, these feelings. Reason seeks above all to be objective.

G: To believe that humans can be purely objective is to deny their nature. In fact it sounds to Me very much like a dreaded act of faith.

J: But I don't propose that, in practice, reason is ever totally objective. Objectivity is a goal we attain only by degrees. Faith denies the value of objectivity altogether and wallows in the oftentimes comforting delusions of subjectivity.

G: You don't want people to be comforted, to be happy?

J: Not as a short-run, selfish expedient that ignores truth and, in doing so, condemns the human race to continue its miserable course to eventual self-annihilation.

G: Now who is playing God? How do you know that would follow? Faith in Me may well lead the human race back from the brink of extermination.

J: That is to ignore the entire history I've related earlier. Look at the constant European warfare of the Middle Ages. All those men believed in God, in Jesus Christ, and in the Bible. If they had weapons of mass destruction then, there is little doubt we would not be having this discussion today. Why should annihilation be of any concern to those who believe in immortality? Smith wrote, "Blind, unthinking commitment is unadulterated fanaticism and the fanatics of the world have left millions dead in their wake."[15] What saves us all is that even most who would like to back Pascal's wager are not willing to stake their lives on belief in God and an afterlife. When people do, their belief often leads to a religious fanaticism such as that displayed in some Muslim countries today.

G: Your criticism may apply equally well to reliance on reason. Were not the Nazis the epitome of cold-hearted, scientific reasoning?

J: It is a common misconception to imagine the "Germanic" mind as exemplified by its achievements in the "hard" sciences such as physics and chemistry. However, anyone who has seen a movie clip of Hitler delivering one of his hysterical, bombastic speeches should immediately recognize that the Nazis were the antithesis of reason. It was not scientific reasoning, but German romanticism (which, as a movement against the Enlightenment emphasized reliance on emotion) and G. W. F. Hegel's half-baked rationalism (a form of Idealism which stood in marked opposition to empiricism) that were the dominant philosophical trends at the time. Psychologist Erich Fromm demonstrates in *Escape from Freedom*[16] that this romanticism stems from a tradition of belief with its roots in both the German Catholic and Lutheran churches which conditioned the German people to blindly play "follow the leader."

As I've shown, in the Judeo-Christian tradition, doubt and disbelief are immoral—the ultimate sins. In the Old Testament, Yahweh destroyed unbelievers by the thousands, and I have already quoted the threats of Jesus concerning unbelievers. Paul urged his followers to be "fools for Christ." Augustine demonstrated total faith in his Church when he considered the obvious absurdities in the Gospel: "I would not believe the gospel if I were not moved to do so by the Catholic Church."[17] For Augustine, belief was all that is necessary to gain knowledge: "*crede, ut intellegas*—believe, in order to understand."[18] Roman Catholicism professes the infallibility of its pope and therefore seeks to forbid independent thought for his millions of followers.

Luther simply cut out the middle man—the pope—and placed all his faith in revelation. Luther, too, saw that reason was antithetical and dangerous to faith. He exhorted, "Whoever wants to be a Christian should gouge out the eyes of reason" because reason is "the devil's bride . . . a lovely whore."[19] Luther carries faith to the pinnacle of absurdity: "The highest degree of faith is to believe He [God] is just, though of His own will He makes us . . . proper subjects of damnation." For Luther, understanding is not only unnecessary but undesirable: "If I could by any reason understand how this same God . . . can yet be merciful and just, there would be no need for faith."[20] From Luther's perspective a man who refuses to evaluate critically the obvious contradiction in his belief system is exhibiting virtue.

Social philosopher Eric Hoffer showed how easy it is for the "true

believer"—the person who bases his allegiances completely on faith—
to switch alliances without skipping a beat. True believers in capitalism
and true believers in communism are interchangeable, and often have
demonstrated their willingness to leap from one extreme to the other.
George Jacob Holyoke summed up the dangers of the true believer's
mindset this way: "He who cannot reason is defenseless; he who fears
to reason has a coward's mind; he who will not reason is willing to
be deceived and will deceive all who listen to him."[21]

G: I am not urging anyone to reject reason entirely; I regret the overzealousness of some believers. But I still contend reason and faith
are not necessarily irreconcilable. They each have their realm: reason,
for the things of this world, faith for those of the next. If by definition,
I am unknowable, then faith is the only way to approach Me.

J: Absolutely not. When a proposition is neither confirmed nor denied,
then reasonable people state it just that way. They have no fear of
saying, I don't know, or, I won't accept that hypothesis as a basis
for action.

G: This brings us back to the problem discussed earlier. There are times
when a man must make a decision even when he doesn't know. He
must base his actions on an assumption.

J: I agree that there are times when we act upon only a hypothesis, but
then we call it an experiment. We act and observe the results to see
whether they appear to confirm the hypothesis. This is the essence of
the scientific method and should not be confused with Cartesian rationalism, which believed that knowledge can be ascertained by simple
logical deduction. Although logical analysis may be useful as a means
of investigating phenomena that cannot be verified by experimentation
or even statistical analysis, it leads only to a theory. Take, for example,
Einstein's theories, many of which were based on mathematical induction. It wasn't until recently that we had the means to actually test them.
Some were found to be true, while for others the verdict is still out.

G: Yet some scientists have advocated those theories with an almost
evangelical fervor.

J: Well, I think it was more due to coverage in the popular press than
to the advocacy of those who really understood them. Admittedly,
there are some scientists who will defend an unverified theory as if
it were an established truth. Such scientists may be accused of having
faith in the theory. The scientific community generally holds these
people in the same low esteem in which I hold anyone who accepts
a proposition without the proper amount of skepticism. The legitimate
scientist follows the empirical approach which in a crude form may
be traced back to Giovanni Battista Vico and evolved into the scientific

method I outlined earlier. The philosopher Ernest Nagel wrote: "The assumption that there is a superior and more direct way of grasping the secrets of the universe than the painfully slow road of science has been so repeatedly shown to be a romantic illusion that only those who are unable to profit from the history of the human intellect can seriously maintain it."[22]

G: In your worship of science it doesn't seem to bother you at all that it was science that provided the bomb that may mean the end of the human race.

J: Yes, science gave us nuclear power. But nuclear power might have served humankind well. It was not science (or scientists) that pushed us to the brink of nuclear war. It was decidedly unscientific men demonstrating completely irrational thinking that produced the nuclear standoff. In this area, I see no more use of scientific reasoning than that which has led to all other wars waged since the dawn of humanity. Greed, fear, sectarianism, nationalism, racism—these are not creations of science. In fact, if the world had a more scientific understanding of human behavior, and a more rational basis for ethics than the fallacious foundation provided by religion, we may not be in our current mess. I agree wholeheartedly with Adorno, who said that we suffer not from too much, but from too little rationality; that the Enlightenment was not driven too far but broken off too soon.[23]

G: You still have not explained how reason can attain knowledge of Me, who by definition am unknowable. I again submit that only faith can make that leap.

J: And a leap it is, from the rational to the "absurd" as Tertullian proudly characterized it. At the barest minimum, a believer should be able to specify what it is in which he has faith. To have faith in the unknowable is the height of folly. I might as well state that I have faith in the existence of Winkies.

G: Now you're being ludicrous.

J: In professing belief in Winkies, I say no more than the person who says he believes in something he calls God, but when pressed to define or describe this God, says he can't. Isn't this, in effect, what theologians profess when they hold that by definition God is unknowable?

G: Well, when I said I was unknowable I didn't mean totally unknowable. I only meant unknowable with regard to My essence. Perhaps incomprehensible would be a better choice of words.

J: Nice try. However, the believer must then be able to make at least some intelligible statement about his God. Theologians certainly don't demonstrate that necessity, as evidenced by this following bit of nonsense endorsed by Hans Küng:

> Trustful faith, immovable confidence produces the wonderful paradox
> that the angry, jealous, judging God is at the same time the giving
> and forgiving God, the Helper and Deliverer, that the Absolute Power
> in its inmost essence is nothing but wisdom and goodness.[24]

There you have the essence of faith, an incoherent hodgepodge of
contradictions equating jealousy with goodness, describing the emotions
of an immovable being, applying all sorts of human qualities to a
supernatural Being. If people are going to believe in something, they
should at least be prepared to define it in noncontradictory terms.
However, if something is unknowable or incomprehensible, then it
can't be defined in the first place. It is silly, therefore, even to discuss
it further.

Despite the rise in fundamentalism today I find that few people
actually place much faith in the absurd jumble of contradictions that
Küng calls his God. I knew one such person, a born again Christian
who preached faith in Jesus ad nauseam. He had absolute faith in
the promise of Jesus that "whatever you ask in my name that I will
do, in order that the father may be glorified in the son. If you ask
anything in my name, I will do it" (John 14:13–14). Note that there
is no equivocation here, no maybes, no ifs, ands, or buts.

One day this man's son came down with what appeared to be
a fatal illness. His faith was not so strong as to prevent him from
taking his child to the best specialist available. It was science the man
sought, yet he still professed his faith and prayed incessantly for Jesus
to save the child. Tragically, the doctors said that his son was going
to die; science had not yet conquered his son's particular illness. Still
my acquaintance prayed and, if the son lived, what a great miracle
he would have claimed. Sadly, although prognostications of doctors
are fallible, this time they were right and the boy died. Despite imploring
God, in the name of Jesus, to spare the poor child's life, death came
as it most often does when science can't stand in its way.

Did this sad episode shake my friend's faith? He certainly would
have given You the credit had his son lived, even if the doctors had
originally said his child was curable. What was my friend's reaction
when You failed to perform as promised? Did he shout "liar" to the
author of John's gospel because he had asked in the name of Jesus
and received only silence for a reply? Did he throw out the whole
senseless mythology? Indeed not!

When I was a child and asked for something of You but didn't
get it, the nuns were quick to justify the nonresponse by saying You
did in fact answer my prayer: "He said no." Note the neat logical

trick so often used in even the most sophisticated theology—the change in meaning of the main term. In the Bible the term "answer" is often used in the archaic sense of a solution to the problem. Hence, it is always taken in the Bible to mean an affirmative response of some sort. But the nuns employ "answer" in the modern sense of merely a reply, which can be either positive or negative.

My unfortunate fundamentalist friend employed only slightly more elegant sophistry. He contended, "God has shown His goodness by rewarding my son now for all his suffering. He has taken him to his eternal reward." But why did You inflict the suffering on the poor child in the first place? "To serve as a inspiration to us all" or "as a test of faith" are the usual replies. These stock replies hardly deserve comment, but I will consider them in full when I later discuss Your goodness.

Here I wish to point out that no amount of obvious contradiction or refutation will dissuade a true believer. As Smith says, the Christian (and the same could be said of any true believer), when confronted with a truth that contradicts his previously held truth, will declare that the article of faith was not a "true" article of faith, but rather rested on a misinterpretation of the scripture or some other divine source. He will then revise his faith and claim there was no conflict all along.[25]

G: Well, in this at least religion has kept pace with the findings of science.

J: It's a shame that there may be a lag of hundreds of years, and that the truth is recognized only after the first articulators of the new knowledge have been derided, jailed or killed for their insight.

G: Weren't we discussing—no, you were lecturing on—the failure of faith? Yet, many who have thought long and hard on this subject are convinced that without faith humanity will fall victim to universal skepticism and, ultimately, nihilism.

J: Not radical or universal, just healthy skepticism: absolute certainty is rejected, but relative certainty is all that's needed to stimulate action. Truth with a capital "T" is rejected, but truth with a small "t" remains. As the analytic philosopher J. L. Austin observes, the fact that humans are "inherently fallible" does not mean that they are "inveterately so."[26] In fact, it can be shown that universal skepticism is inherently contradictory. Universal skepticism would hold that: (A) All truth will ultimately be found to be in error. (By truth I mean only that which we accept as true, i.e., tentative knowledge.) But if statement (A) is itself true it is a self-contradiction. If, on the other hand (A) is not true it means that some truth will not ultimately be found to be erroneous. So universal skepticism can be ruled out, and absolute certainty rejected as well.

The scientist doesn't worry about reaching absolute truth. British philosopher and freethinker Bertrand Russell observed that although we must admit that knowledge can no longer be conceived of as "a mental mirror of the universe," yet it still serves "as a practical tool in the manipulation of matter." That this excruciatingly slow and exacting process is the only way to knowledge can be easily demonstrated by the success of science in extending the average life expectancy in the scientifically developed countries. That expectancy is now thirty years more than in underdeveloped, though more theistic, countries. The ability of science to improve the quality of life has constantly been impeded by the difficulty of the goal and, in part, by religious taboos that interfered with research and experimentation.

G: You make the whole process sound so objective, but in reality it oftentimes isn't so. Robert Pirsig explored the problem frequently confronting a scientist when the results of his experiments or observed phenomena can be explained by more than one theory. He quotes Poincaré: "If a phenomenon admits of a complete mechanical explanation, it will admit of an infinity of others which will account equally well for all the peculiarities disclosed by the experiment."[27] Therefore, the choice of theory is purely subjective.

J: That isn't entirely true. While there may be an infinite number of explanations for a given event, they are not equally well suited, because either they don't fill all the conditions of the scientific method or they don't have an equal degree of verification. Those like Küng, who try to build an argument that reliance on reason leads to skepticism, attempt to do so by stating that reason requires verification in absolute terms. As I have shown, this is not necessary or, of course, possible. Rather, it is only necessary to show that one position is more probable than another. In general, the determinant of probability is the degree of verification. In the absence of any empirical evidence on either side of an argument, or contradictions in logic, the Principle of Parsimony should hold. Basically, this principle holds that one should never multiply explanations or increase their complexity beyond necessity. (This becomes a valuable aid when discussing proofs for Your existence.)

Philosopher Michael Scriven wrote an excellent essay titled "God and Reason"[28] on the nature of verification. He differentiates seven degrees of evidential support and the appropriate intellectual attitude toward each. They range from "(1) strictly disprovable (i.e., demonstrably incompatible with the evidence," and (2) "wholly unfounded., i.e., wholly lacking in general or particular support," through successive degrees of uncertainty to "(6) possessing overwhelming particular support and no basis for alternative views, beyond reasonable doubt," and (7) "strictly probable, i.e., as a demonstratively necessary result of indubitable facts." The proper attitude to the first two categories would be rejection, while the correct attitude for the latter two categories would be tentative acceptance. The categories in the middle would demand suspension of judgment depending again on the degree of evidence

G: But what do you do about that class of hypotheses whose members have not yet been verified, which in fact may be unverifiable, not necessarily in principle but as a practical matter?

J: Then they must remain just that, unverifed hypotheses. They may make for interesting speculation, assuming that they are logically consistent, but no action can be taken based on them, unless it is for purposes of experimentation or else admitted to be nothing more than a pure gamble, à la Pascal.

G: Have we sufficiently beat this subject into the ground? Can we move on?

J: In some respects I have only scratched the surface. But permit me to summarize my argument thus far:

1. Human beings must have some method of distinguishing truth from falsehood, otherwise there is no justification for rejecting the wildest claims. The existence of Santa Claus or Winkies becomes just as "believable" as the existence of the pope. According to B. C. Johnson, "If belief need not be justified we might as well give in to pure anarchy and admit that rational discussion is impossible."[29]

2. Formation of a hypothesis is an important first step in any investigation. But, of itself, the hypothesis carries no inherent degree of truthfulness.

3. The major error of Hans Küng and others is that they confuse the probable with the possible. While I agree with Plato that "it is unholy to abandon the probably true," it is silly to believe in something merely because it is possible. Faith is belief in something without reference to its probability. Anything that doesn't involve a logical contradiction is possible and therefore the object of faith—even the existence of Santa Claus.

4. Mere logical adequacy is not sufficient. The method of ascertaining truth must therefore involve coherence with existing knowledge and some degree of verification.

5. Simply because we cannot verify Küng's "ultimate truth" does not mean that nothing can be verified.

6. Verification is rarely an either/or proposition as Küng implies. Rather, it is a matter of degree. The degree of verification depends on the weight of the evidence.

7. Those questions that are most important to the welfare of human-kind demand the greatest degree of verification. Since religious leaders claim that they know Your will, the verification that God exists should be proportionately strong.

8. The inexorable conclusion our investigation reaches with regard to faith is summed up well by Smith: "faith as an alleged method of acquiring knowledge is totally invalid—and as a consequence all propositions of faith, because they lack rational demonstration, must conflict with reason."[30]

I hardly need add that where faith does conflict with reason, humans, if they wish to separate themselves from lower forms of animal life, will rely on reason. A "faithful dog" might be a useful possession, but a "faithful" human being who suppresses reason and blindly follows on the basis of faith has placed himself on the level of a brute animal.

G: Aren't you being a little dramatic? Faith, even if misplaced, has brought comfort and solace to many persons, like your friend who lost his son.

J: There are other, better ways of dealing with life's tragedies. Other cultures have done so without falling back on an erroneous faith in the supernatural. The evils that have always accompanied faith as a road to truth have far outweighed any benefits. Arthur Schopenhauer knew well the horrible evils that were the consequence of thousands of years of erroneous beliefs when he wrote that there was "no such thing as a harmless error . . . error may reign a thousand years, impose its joke upon whole nations, extend to the noblest impulses of humanity and, by the help of its slaves and its dupes may chain and fetter those it cannot deceive."[31] Faith, as amply evidenced by a review of the evils of Christianity, has done just that.

Faith led Augustine to the remarkable conclusion that, "all diseases of Christians are to be ascribed to demons; chiefly do they torment fresh baptized Christians, yea, even newborn infants."[32] Given such a belief, why bother searching for a medical cure for polio, meningitis, diphtheria, or the thousands of other maladies that science has eradicated? The antithesis of faith can be seen in the works of Aristotle, who, among other things, investigated the causes of disease seven hundred years before Augustine. Yet Augustine, not Aristotle, is canonized as a saint by the Church.

Faith is the foundation of the radical "Christian Science" movement discussed in chapter 2, which results in the suffering and, at times, the avoidable death of small children. The logical consequence of a belief that all that happens to the human race is Your will is to scrap medical science.

Faith inspired Bishop Wilberforce to declare himself against Darwinism: "The principle of natural selection is absolutely incomprehensible with the word of God."[33] The logical conclusion is to abolish the science of genetics and evolutionary theory.

Faith causes many simple-minded fundamentalists to agree with Calvinist Archbishop James Ussher who concluded from studying the genealogy of the Bible that the world was created in exactly 4004 B.C.E. With this we might as well trash archaeology and geology.

Faith resulted in the court of the Inquisition proclaiming against the findings of Galileo: "The first proposition, that the sun is the center of the earth, is foolish, absurd, false in theology, and heretical because expressly contrary to Holy Scriptures."[34] A nice attempt to terminate astronomy.

Faith prompted Martin Luther to state such absurdities as: "The heathen writes that the comet may arise from natural causes, but God creates not one that does not foretell a severe calamity." It is such a claim that perpetuates the absurd belief in astrology.

Faith encouraged Paul to denounce as "superstitious" all the philosophical wisdom of Greece; justified John Calvin to burn one of the most brilliant men of his time, Servetus; led Luther to decide that "reason is the Devil's harlot who can do naught but slander and harm whatever God says and does";[35] motivated a scientifically ignorant Cardinal O'Connell to rule out the possibility of the scientific theories of Einstein; and prompted the states of Alabama, Arkansas, and Louisiana to attempt to destroy academic freedom by legislating that "creationism" be taught in public schools.

Finally, it was faith that justified the thousands of atrocities committed by Israelites, Moslems, Christians and other "true believers." The title "true believer" must be given to all dogmatists whether theists, fascists, Communists, or whatever.

G: You are critical of all those who rely on faith. But in the final analysis must not that criticism also extend to atheists as well? Since the existence of anything can't be disproved absolutely, the atheist is expressing an act of faith with the avowal that I don't exist.

J: Not exactly. Atheists assert that since no evidence can be cited in support of Your existence, and since the proponents of the proposition that You exist have not even provided a meaningful, noncontradictory definition of the term God, it would be unreasonable to accept the hypothesis.

Earlier, when we were discussing Pascal's wager You raised the hypothetical question, even if You don't exist, what harm is there in believing that You do? I have shown the danger of uncritical belief. A 1986 Gallup Poll of youth revealed that the rapid erosion of reason in our society has led to an appalling number of teenagers believing in all sorts of unverified superstitions:[36]

Percentage of Teenagers Believing in:

Angels	67%
Astrology	52%
ESP	46%
Clairvoyance	19%
Witchcraft	19%
Ghosts	15%
Loch Ness Monster	13%

G: Why get excited? Those are harmless superstitions. Besides, this study shows some improvement over the earlier surveys.

J: Unfortunately, another poll shows that for the adult population as a whole superstitious belief is on the increase with 42 percent believing that they have had contact with someone who has died and 28 percent reportedly having visions, both substantial increases over an earlier poll.[37] But, perhaps I shouldn't be concerned when another study shows that 78 percent of the residents of the Akron, Ohio, area believe in faith-healing of some sort.[38] After all, it only enriches the few who try to use wealth and power to translate their interpretation of Christian morality into laws binding upon all Americans.

Maybe there is no real danger that we will turn back the clock of social progress to a more repressive, doctrinaire age. But I worry that this uncritical belief in the most outrageous fictions will be exploited, in fact, has been exploited by charismatic politicians. For example, Americans of all ages have swallowed the logical and empirically demonstrated absurdity that the United States can have huge deficits, low inflation, and rapid growth—not just during the recovery cycle of government induced recession, but indefinitely.

The greatest danger lies in this misplaced faith being devoted to political aspirants who will find it easy to manipulate the natural aggressive tendencies in the electorate—"enthusiastic militarism" as

Konrad Lorenz calls it. Heightened and directed against an enemy more imaginary than real, the result has often led to war.

The only real salvation of humankind is not the belief in saviors, whether religious or secular, but the return to reason as the basis for selecting our national leaders and determining national policies.

G: You know something? You worry too much. If you believed that everything that happens was just part of My divine plan you would sleep better.

J: No doubt. But to have a divine plan there has to be a divinity, and I see no evidence to support that assumption.

11

Knowing God through Direct Experience: The Sixties Syndrome

> The mystic brings his theological beliefs to the mystical experience, he does not derive them from it.
>
> —James Pratt

G: You insist on evidence of My existence, yet you will not accept the biblical accounts of My miracles or personal involvement in Judeo-Christian history. It would appear that you are stacking the deck in favor of atheism.

J: As I have shown, the "revealed" truth of Your existence is of no value since the Old Testament scriptures are nothing more than a collection of ancient myths, edited and altered to support the Israelites' claim to a divine origin and special relationship with You. Later, the Christians used the same technique in the New Testament to support the claim of the divine status of Jesus.

For similar reasons, the alleged miracles related in the Bible and advanced as evidence of Your existence offer no support. These biblical miracles were shown to be old myths ascribed to all ancient heroes. In addition, the miracles are invalid as proof of Your existence since, by definition, a miracle assumes supernatural intervention. In other words, calling an occurrence a miracle assumes the conclusion rather than providing evidence to support the hypothesis that the event had a divine cause. All will agree that only ignorant people believe in magic, yet every day we meet those who reject magic while believing in miracles. When rational people see an event they don't understand, they simply admit they don't as yet know the cause and then attempt to find the explanation through scientific research.

It is interesting to see how even the most sophisticated theologians have a glitch in their logic when it comes to miracles. For example, although Hans Küng does an excellent job of demonstrating that the miracles of the Bible "cannot be proved to be violations of the law of nature" and concedes that the "miracle stories are lighthearted, popular narrative intended to provoke faith," he has no trouble accepting "a God who acts in the world in order to give different directions to the course of events."[1] If this isn't a definition of a miracle, what is? Küng successfully repudiates the bogus evidence, then leaps to his predetermined conclusion anyway.

G: I won't argue the point. It is obvious that a person must believe in Me before he or she will admit the supernatural character of an event. But you have not yet made the case that proof is the only viable alternative to establishing My existence. Even granted that faith alone is not a reliable means for establishing My existence, there are millions of people throughout the world who have had direct experiences of My presence. The very universal nature of belief in Me—although I am given different names by different cultures—has been advanced as evidence of My existence: *Quod semper, quod ubique, quod ab omnibus* ("Always, everywhere, and by everyone").

J: Come now, we have demonstrated that universality of a belief is no evidence of its validity. Belief in magic was also universal until two hundred years ago. Furthermore, it is not true that monotheism has been or is universal today. Religion, if it is defined to include any mystical, ritual or supernatural belief, may be universal, but monotheism covers only a comparatively small portion of the globe. There are, in the main, three monotheistic religions: Judaism, Christianity, and Islam; all other religions are polytheistic or pantheistic. And today, of course, a significant portion of the world's population is not theistic at all. For them the belief in You died with their rejection of their feudal systems. In China, the ethical system known as Confucianism was not based on the concept of a divinity. On the other hand, Taoism, popular particularly among the less educated Chinese, involved the worship of many deities. The same was true of Buddhism. Although no educated followers of Buddha worshiped him as a god, the peasants frequently did, oftentimes encouraged by the Buddhist priests. The more sophisticated forms of the religion see Buddha as the first in a line of great teachers, but not as a god as defined in the Western sense.

It might also be noted that some of the most primitive cultures, such as the recently discovered Tasaday of the Philippines, have no concept of a god. Hence, it has always been an erroneous assumption that belief in God was at any time universal. But, as I said at the onset, the number of people who believe in something is in no way evidence of its existence.

G: You have ignored my main point. What of the testimony of those who have had direct experience of My presence? It is impossible for you to appreciate that those who have experienced Me have no doubt of My existence.

J: I assure you that I understand that feeling. I can still remember kneeling in my pew after Holy Communion and fervently believing I had Your presence within me. I also "sensed" my guardian angel at my side (and even shared an occasional apple with him). As a child these were wonderful feelings. But the *feeling* of having met You must not be confused with the *fact* of having met You. Confusing feelings with fact is mysticism.

During the 1960s, when it was popular to experiment with hallucinogens such as LSD, many people described their "trips" as "experiencing alternative reality." The person suffering from schizophrenia, then, has as valid a claim on reality as the rest of us.

Experiments with drugs and a study of schizophrenia do, however, provide a key to mysticism. Aldous Huxley reported that under the influence of mescaline and other hallucinogenic drugs, he had paranormal experiences very much like those reported by the great mystics.[2] It is also very common for persons suffering from schizophrenia to report talks with You and the saints, even to imagine that they *are* You or Jesus.

Based upon experiments by Schachter and Singer, Wayne Proudfoot concludes that, "At least some religious experiences are due to psychological changes for which the subject adopts a religious explanation."[3] An example of how easily this can happen was provided by the psychologist William James. James recounts the experience of Stephen Bradley, who returned from a revival meeting initially unmoved by the event. That night Bradley experienced a rapid heart beat. Today we know half a dozen reasons why this physiological event could occur. However, when Bradley tried to identify the cause, it should not be surprising that, since he had come fresh from the revival meeting, he thought it was the due to the infusion of the Holy Spirit.[4]

The point is that people will seek an explanation of intense physiological experiences within the context of their education, culture, or previous experiences. It is not surprising, therefore, that persons ignorant of natural causes will assume a supernatural cause.

It is well established that the use of drugs can contribute to the religious experience. Certain groups of Native Americans have used peyote for this purpose for centuries. In a related experiment, Pahnke introduced a mystical experience by administering the drug psilocybin during Good Friday services.[5] Chanting, music and rhythmic dancing may also introduce mystical experiences, as the Hare Krishnas can testify. In Japan the fastest growing religious cult, Nichiren Shoshu, believes that salvation can be attained by repetition of the title of the Lotus Sutra: *"nam myoho rengo kyo."*[6] In all of these cases persons may achieve a powerful, even ecstatic, religious experience, completely independent of the content of their belief. The truth or falsehood of their belief is entirely irrelevant to their feelings.

From Paul's description of the experience which led to his conversion to Christianity (assuming he did not fabricate the story), it is entirely possible that his vision was due to an epileptic seizure. Barry L. Beyerstein's review of research on the topic shows that, "Feeling the presence of God, angels, Satan, the Virgin Mary, departed love ones, and so on, is a recurrent theme in both the occult and epileptic literatures."[7] Experiences of these kinds can occur with minor psychomotor seizures that do not result in the loss of consciousness. In such cases the more obvious signs of seizure are not present, but the person may experience "hearing voices" or "seeing visions."

Another more rare brain disorder known as Tourette's Syndrome can result in pathological behavior which in the Middle Ages was often confused with demonic possession. Even migraine headaches have caused people to see flashes of light and complex patterns that have been interpreted by some sufferers as visions of angels or heaven.[8]

Still other people regularly suffer from hallucinations whether hypnogogic (when falling asleep) or hypnopompic (when waking up). Frequently these are reported as "out of body" experiences. The individuals firmly believe that they are awake when the experience occurs, but oftentime find it impossible to move their bodies. The experience seems so real that they are quite convinced despite all evidence to the contrary.

Another psychological phenomena exhibited by perfectly sane individuals is *confabulation*: the tendency to confuse fact with fiction and report fantasized occurrences. It has been shown to be very common when hypnosis is employed.[9] Finally, research by Wilson and Barber reveals that "there exists a small group of individuals (possibly 4 percent of the population) who fantasize a large part of the time, who typically 'see,' 'hear,' 'smell,' and 'touch' and fully experience what they fantasize."[10]

G: Then you choose to reject all mysticism as valid experience, even for certain highly sensitive or, perhaps, gifted people?

J: I don't doubt the validity of the experience, but I certainly do question the value of mysticism as a method of verifying statements concerning the objective world. If mysticism were a valid road to truth, we would expect all mystical experiences to lead to the same revelation, the same truths. This is far from the case. Not all mystics even arrive at a belief in theism. Zen Buddhists are mystics who in their ecstasy join with the Void.

G: You should point out that their definition of Void is not simply nothing.

J: True. It has been described as a sense of *oneness* with the cosmos. But the cosmos is never taken to be a personal god. Some Buddhists have described it as a release, a lack of all wanting, a serene state of equilibrium. Doesn't this sound similar to those mystics who relate their experience of reaching some sort of ineffable state of consciousness? In reality, such a nondescription seems to demonstrate an inability or unwillingness to describe one's feelings.

Walter Kaufmann suggests that, "Some mystics are unpoetic souls who require special exercises and an eventual trance to see anything but the everyday world. . . . The mystics' insistence on the unique ineffability of his experience may prove no more than that he has never known any other intense experience."[11] I find this entirely plausible. I recall the first time I hiked up a mountain peak in the Rockies and saw the magnificent panorama spread before me. What an exhilarating experience! But, unlike some devout believer who might have felt Your presence, I felt like a god myself because I was able to appreciate the indescribable beauty of that scene as no other animal—and very few persons—could or would. I experienced similar incredibly intense sensations the first time I dove among coral reefs in the Caribbean, or jumped out of a plane thousands of feet above the earth.

G: The mystic doesn't have to go to such extremes to reach that peak of emotion. Moreover, it's not just a feeling of emotion, but actual communication with Me that the mystic experiences. And not only mystics, but many ordinary people have at some time or other in their lives experienced God.

J: Or communication with an angel, saint, or demon. I find it revealing that when Catholics have visions of the mother of Jesus or the saints (including some like Christopher and Philomena who later were discovered never to have existed), they look and dress like the statues and paintings in local churches rather than first-century Jews. Moreover, members of Protestant sects, whose churches are not adorned with statues and paintings of Catholic saints, experience only Jesus. Other non-Christians see the prophets or perhaps experience You directly. Do You see the pattern that is emerging?

G: Philosopher Richard Swinburne argues that the differences arise because different cultures express themselves in terms of the "religious vocabulary in which they are familiar."[12]

J: In so saying he in effect denies the literal interpretation of the religious experience. It is a classic instance of rationalization. When people relate an experience, Swinburne says that they really mean something else.

It is even more damaging to the argument of those who believe in the validity of direct experience that when You have appeared to different people You have told them different and contradictory things which resulted in the formation of contentious religions. Following these contradictory dictates has led Moslems, Christians and Jews to slaughter one another for two thousand years. In short, all religious experience results in people seeing or hearing exactly what they were conditioned to expect. As Pratt puts it, "Possibly all mystical 'revelation' . . . is derived originally from the social education, and all except this sense of presence may possibly be mere conclusion which the mystic comes to after reflecting upon his experience by a process of ordinary discursive thought."[13] Therefore, Kaufmann adds, what sets the mystic apart "is not anything given, but the interpretation and evaluation which the person who has the experience accords it. And the interpretation need not be theistic."[14] Of course, if it isn't theistic the mystic may simply be called a nut.

I had a good friend who was, tragically, a severe manic depressive. In his manic stage, he frequently experienced Christ; at times he even thought he *was* Christ. At other times, he believed he was Michael Corleone, a character from the novel *The Godfather* who fired my friend's imagination. It was not difficult for a stranger to recognize that my friend was suffering from mental illness. There are, however, thousands of less afflicted, but also slightly mentally disabled people who have recurring hallucinations—visions. The cause might be organic, as in the case of the 1 percent of the population suffering from schizophrenia, or a temporary condition caused by some calamity or deprivation.

The mystic Theresa of Avila might well have been one of the former. She is quoted as saying, "Life becomes a kind of dream, when I see things, I nearly always seem to be dreaming."[15] I think it is safe to take her at her word on this. I met more than one such distraught person while working in my father's ecclesiastical supply store. They were usually old or poor or lonely, and extremely distressed by the tragedy of their lives. Then they have a vision of Jesus, Mary, a saint, or a deceased love one who tells them not to worry, they'll be taken care of, things will get better, if not here on earth then in some later life. Psychiatrist Karl Menninger demonstrates in *The Vital Balance* that the symptoms of mental illness are often simply an inappropriate way of coping with misfortune. We all have some little self-delusion we employ to carry us through disappointment. But for many, the line between reality and imagination becomes irrevocably blurred.

Not only drugs but fasting can produce strikingly real "mystical" experiences, as some Native Americans—and many an early Christian ascetic—have discovered. Bertrand Russell summed it up as follows:

> We all know that opium, hashish, and alcohol produce certain effects on the observer, but we take no account of them in our theory of the universe. They may even, sometimes, reveal fragments of truth; but we do not regard them as sources of wisdom . . . we can make no distinction between the man who eats little and sees heaven and a man who drinks much and sees snakes.[16]

As clinical psychiatrists and psychologists know, the more dramatic mystical experiences are no more than hallucinations often brought about not only by drugs and fasting, but by chemical imbalances caused by stress or physical illness. As a child I often had some very strange and frightening hallucinations when I ran a fever.

G: First you said mystics may be people who don't have enough stimulus in their lives to recognize a truly moving experience. Now you say that mystics are those who psychologically overreact to a stimulus, or react even without a stimulus.

J: You've got it; the answer is all of the above. To return to Your original contention, if mysticism were a valid source of revelation we would expect all mystics to have similar experiences and reach the same truth. But this has not been the case. Mystics have generated prophecies since time immemorial, but, like today's psychics, their prophecies have proven conflicting and no more reliable than any ordinary person's intuitive guesses. Therefore, there is no reason to believe their revelations more than those of the many "psychic seers" or mentally disturbed persons.

G: I agree that "feeling" is not a very reliable indicator of the truthfulness of a proposition: every bigot "feels" that he is justified in his prejudice. I'll even grant you that many, though perhaps not all, of the so-called mystics are either fakes or a little mentally hyperactive. But I don't need to rely on them to provide evidence of My existence. There are reliable, logical, proofs. Despite the contentions of some of My over-zealous followers, I have never stated that I opposed reason. For reason, if properly employed, will lead one to Me.

J: I'm glad to have you say that, because next I propose to review the proofs of Your existence. You do agree that this is necessary since, as we saw, faith is a deficient method in establishing Your existence? Or, perhaps You are afraid that the proofs will also be found wanting.

G: Not if you state them fairly. The Catholic Church is grounded on the premise that My existence can be proved. The First Vatican Council concluded that human beings can know Me by reason alone. Do you think that you can undermine the work of two thousand years of theological scholarship?

J: Most other theistic religions have given up the task of proving Your existence. But perhaps the Catholics are right. Shall we review the arguments?

G: Why bother? You'll just stack the deck against Me. You will misstate the arguments.

J: I'll quote them right out of my Catholic theology texts.

G: But you'll always have the last word.

J: Someone always has to be last. As I mentioned before, in college, it was the priests. Turnabout is fair play. Besides, You could always strike me dead. You had a perfect opportunity when I was hang gliding last week.

G: Don't think the thought didn't occur to me. But let's just say I am demonstrating extraordinary tolerance.

J: Certainly uncharacteristic of either the God of the scriptures or most of His followers. Very well, let's get on with it. Before we tackle the more sophisticated arguments, there are a few naive ones we should quickly dispense with. We have touched on some of these earlier.

12

The Proofs for the Existence of God: A Case Study in Convoluted Logic

All sentences of Logic are tautological and devoid of content; we cannot draw inferences from them about what was necessary or impossible in reality.

—Rudolf Carnap

G: The Catholic Church has long stood by the dogmatic claim that My existence can be proved by unaided reason. This was stated as a matter of dogma by Pius IX at the First Vatican Council in 1870: "If anyone says that the one true God our Creator and Lord, cannot be known with certainty by the natural light of reasoning from created things, he is to be condemned."[1] Until the time of Vatican II the anti-modernist oath, which was prescribed as binding on all Catholic clergy, required a sworn statement that the existence of God can be proved.

J: Let's consider the various arguments for Your existence. This section may be a little difficult for some readers, but since so much is at stake here I think they owe it to themselves to investigate the basis for the proposition that You exist.

Before we begin to review the so-called proofs for Your existence I need to remind You that we already established in chapter 10 that purely logical (analytic) reasoning cannot be used to prove a statement about the real world. Logic is an excellent means of exposing latent implications in a hypothesis or statement of fact. It is also a useful technique for revealing contradictions between two statements. But logic cannot prove the hypothesis or statement of fact. Only verification can lend support to a hypothesis.

G: Now you've poisoned the well. What sense is there in going on?

J: I guess there isn't much reason for continuing from Your point of view, but I think there may be many people who were raised in the belief that there were valid proofs for Your existence. I think they might find the following review as interesting, and possibly as disconcerting as I did the first time I was exposed to the so-called proofs. I still vividly recall my reaction at the end of that college theology class. All I could think was: "Is that all two thousand years of theology could come up with?" Frankly, I was greatly dismayed. Eventually, my dismay turned to anger when I realized that I had been duped for so long. The reader may well experience the same feelings.

Shall we now begin with the ontological argument of Anselm of Canterbury?

G: I'd rather not, since I don't consider it one of the stronger arguments.

The Ontological Argument

J: Well, we have to begin someplace, and chronologically it is one of the oldest. As I understand it, this argument, which is also called the argument from existence, maintains that Your existence is self-evident since the idea of a most perfect or absolutely necessary being would necessarily include the idea of that being's existence. My theology text describes Anselm's argument thus: "The word God signifies a being than which nothing greater can be conceived. Since that which exists actually as well as mentally is greater than that which exists mentally only, it follows that God's existence is self-evident—as soon as the word God is understood, he exists mentally and, therefore, must also actually exist."[2] Is that a fair statement of the argument?

G: Yes. But before you say so I'll admit, as even your old theology text does, that the argument suffers from a confusion of ideas and things.

J: Thank you. But let's elaborate a little to make sure it's absolutely clear. Kurt Baier succinctly points out that the concept of a logically necessary being is contradictory: "Whatever can be conceived of as existing can be equally conceived of as not existing."[3]

The more sophisticated form of this argument held that, in the definition of God, existence is a necessary attribute. An attribute is defined by metaphysicians as something that does not exist of itself, but only in connection with an underlying "thing," which they call substance. For example, the attribute "good" must be posited of some being; goodness does not exist by itself. In one sense an attribute is like an adjective modifying a noun. However, Kant showed the error of confusing grammar with logic. According to Kant, something either *is* or *is not.* If it is, it is the same thing as saying it exists. Only things that exist can have attributes. Existence per se is not an attribute. Hence, we have already *assumed* the existence of God when we posit any attribute of Him.

Further, philosopher U. Caterus explained that even if you conclude that the notion of a Supremely Perfect being implies existence, it only means that the *concept* of existence is inseparable from the *concept* of a Supreme Being.[4] Again, however, no concept need exist in reality. B. C. Johnson adds the point that, "an idea can guarantee its [logical] truth only if denial of it is self-contradictory. But it is not contradictory to say I have the idea of a being which cannot fail to exist but there is no being which cannot fail to exist."[5]

G: I've already admitted, the argument doesn't hold up upon close examination.

J: I'm glad to see we have no disagreement here, because then I'm also confident that You'll not attempt to support a modern offshoot of this semantic argument. I'm referring to Paul Tillich's rather disingenuous effort to define away atheism. As echoed by John A. T. Robinson, another semantic gamesman: "God is by definition the ultimate reality. And one cannot argue that ultimate reality exists. One can only ask what ultimate reality is like."[6] Tillich adds that the question can neither be asked nor answered because God is "being-itself. . . . And, as the ground of all being the very nature of God is 'above existence.' "[7]

George H. Smith demonstrates that this "self-transcendent" God is incoherent, and it is impossible to show how being "above existence" differs from nonexistence. For my part, although I find it a rather useless concept, I can accept the belief in an ultimate reality, the "ultimate ground of being" that Tillich, Robinson, and Küng propose.

G: I'm shocked!

J: You needn't be. This is only saying that I believe that all that is, is being. Or to put it another way: all that exists, i.e., the universe, is ultimate reality. This, it seems to me, is all that Tillich really demonstrates. If he wishes to call this universe by the name of God, or Mr. Bojangles, it is of no concern to me. However, if he tries to give it some active or creative properties, he runs into the danger of pantheism. Nothing Tillich or Robinson say supports anything other than an unconscious, "unacting" totality of all there is. No atheist would disagree with such a statement, but it is hardly the personal, creative, supernatural Being most people envision under the name God.

G: Enough of this. Let's move on to some of the more substantive arguments as originally articulated by Thomas Aquinas.

J: Fine. Since you are the advocate of these proofs, why don't You take over from here.

G: How courteous of you. I doubt if your consideration will continue. As you know, Aquinas offered "Five Ways" to demonstrate My existence, each of which started with some observation of the physical world which, he attempted to show, could only be attributed to My existence. The observations of Thomas were:

1. the notion of physical bodies,

2. the dependence of one subordinate cause on another,

3. the contingent or transitory nature of those things that now come into existence and later cease to be,

4. the different grades of excellence or degrees of perfection observable among creatures, and

5. the purposefulness and order in things of nature.[8]

The first three of these arguments are essentially similar in structure and comprise what is called the cosmological argument. The fifth "way" is known as the argument from design or teleological argument and, with some interesting permutations, has gained popularity recently. Permit me to present each of the arguments of Aquinas in turn.

J: The floor is yours.

Cosmological Arguments

G: The first way is a demonstration from motion. Using Aquinas' own words:

> It is certain and evident to the senses that some things are moved in this world. But whatever is moved is moved by another. For nothing is moved except insofar as it is potentiality to that to which it is moved; a thing is in motion, on the contrary, inasmuch as it is in act.
>
> To move anything, then, is nothing else than to reduce it from potentiality to actuality. But nothing can be reduced from potentiality to actuality except by some being already in act. Thus a being which is actually hot, like fire, makes wood, which is hot in potency, to be actually hot: and thereby it moves and changes it.
>
> It is impossible, however, for the same thing to be simultaneously

in act and in potency under the same aspect; it can only be so in different respects. Whatever is actually hot cannot at the same time be potentially hot, for at that moment it is potentially cold. Thus it is impossible—under the same aspect and in the same way—for anything to be both moving and moved; or (in other words) that it should move itself. Therefore, whatever is moved is moved by another.[9]

J: Thomas chose a poor analogy with the example of heat since the words "hot" and "cold" are relative concepts, not absolute states. Hence, something that is hot can become hotter, and, when compared to something that is very hot, might even be described as being relatively cold.

G: How rude! You interrupted before I was even finished.

J: Sorry.

G: Aquinas goes on to point out that obviously,

If that by which it is moved is itself moved, then this mover must be moved by another, and that by still another. But this cannot go on to infinity, for then there would be no first mover; nor, consequently, would there be any other mover, because secondary movers do not move unless they are moved by the first mover, just as the stick does not move unless moved by the hand. Thus it is necessary to come to a prime mover which is moved by no other. And everyone understands this to be God.[10]

J: I'm afraid Aquinas may have lost some of our readers with that metaphysical jargon. Could you state the argument of Thomas (which he borrowed from Aristotle) a little more clearly and succinctly.

G: Very well. According to Aquinas: Whatever is moved is moved by another. But this cannot go on to infinity for then there would be no first mover. Thus, it is necessary to come to a prime mover which is moved by no others.

J: An excellent, succinct summary, stripping away all the semantic accoutrements. But presenting the bare bones of the argument in this way, it appears a bit anemic not to mention question begging. Theological arguments stand up better when camouflaged in metaphysical language to confuse and obfuscate what is actually being proposed. If I accept the first premise as true, Aquinas has simply ruled out the possibility of God's existence. If indeed whatever is moved is moved by another, then there is no Prime Mover, and the universe is simply a perpetual motion machine. Indeed, this may actually be the case.

G: Thomas didn't believe that, nor does it appear possible given the law of entropy which holds that all systems tend to degrade from order to disorder.

J: No one knows if the law of entropy is relevant to the universe *in toto*. It was developed from experiments with small, closed systems. I'll have more to say about that in a minute. You are right in saying that Aquinas believed that his first premise could not be true. He says as much in his second premise, but he offers no empirical evidence to substantiate his belief.

The second premise is a flat assertion which is not only unsubstantiated but also contradicts the first premise. The first premise—"whatever is moved is moved by another"—is apparent from everyday obseration. However, the assertion that this movement—or change—cannot continue forever is simply a bald-faced assertion which cannot be proved and, indeed, is contradicted by Newton's law of inertia.

G: I disagree. That law supports Aquinas since it states that an object at rest will remain at rest unless compelled to move by an external source.

J: You know better than to state that common half-truth. Newton's law of motion states that a body at rest will remain in a state of rest, or a body in motion will continue in motion, unless compelled by some external force acting upon it to change that state. And there is no more reason to suppose that the universe was originally in a state of rest, than that it was always in motion.

Long before the theories of quantum physics and the Big Bang, the philosopher Arthur Schopenhauer refuted Aquinas on purely logical grounds: "Matter as such is alike indifferent to rest and motion, its original condition may just as well be one as the other—therefore, if we first find it in motion, we have just as little right to assume that this was preceded by rest, and to inquire into the cause of the origins of motion as, conversely, we would have to assume a previous motion and inquire into the cause of its suspension."[11]

Modern scientific hypotheses such as the Big Bang and "singularities" do not refute this position, despite frequent misinterpretations in the popular press. There is no reason to believe that the Big Bang wasn't caused by a natural physical process just as every other observable phenomenon has been discovered to be a natural physical process.

G: But it stands to reason. Suppose you had a train of freight cars, each of which bumped into another, causing the bumped one to move. If I asked you what caused car A to move, you might say, "It was bumped by car B," but then you would have to explain what caused car B to move. And no matter how many cars you add to the train, you still have to explain how the entire train got moving. You can't make the train infinitely long.

J: An argument from analogy is never valid. The universe is not a train, but a train is a part of the universe and is therefore affected by the forces of the universe. The universe, however, may not require a force outside of it for its motion. If there is indeed an "unmoved mover" we might just as well claim it to be the universe itself rather than a god. In so doing we avoid many of the fatal logical errors associated with the concept of God. But I'm getting ahead of myself.

The point I wish to make here is that it is an incorrect analogy to portray the universe as a machine that needs someone to turn it on. Rather, it is a system of dynamic change.

G: But what produced the first change?

J: Why do You suppose there had to be a "first" change? Why couldn't the world always be changing: a system of imbalance by the very nature of matter and energy? Even if I assumed there was a "first" change, why must I assume its cause is still in existence, not to mention its being an active force, and even more an intelligent being?

G: By definition an unmoved mover cannot cease to exist.

J: That's a metaphysical definition that may have no relationship with reality. An original force could cease to be active.

G: Then everything would gradually come to a stop. And, in fact, this is exactly what the Second Law of Thermodynamics implies. It states that in a closed system entropy tends toward a maximum, in other words, a trend toward increasing randomness and a loss of energy. And there is some evidence that this may actually be occurring in the universe. We observe that the universe is indeed expanding and therefore tending toward greater randomness. This will be accompanied by a gradual loss of energy. Eventually there will be nothing but cold masses drifting aimlessly in a lightless space.

Science, therefore, affirms that there had to be a creative act. For if the universe had existed for an infinite period of time, it would have reached a state of pure entropy. Since that is obviously not the case, the only other alternative is that it had a beginning—it was created. Without your science to back you up what sort of argument can you now advance?

J: The so-called laws of nature are really only descriptions of relationships among observed events which are useful for predicting the outcome of future events that occur under conditions similar to the original observations. However, it is conjecture, at best, when the theory is applied to phenomena outside of the scope of the original experiments.

The theory of entropy was based on experiments with gases in sealed containers. It is not known whether it has any applicability to the universe as a whole, which may or may not operate as a closed system. For example, scientists are not certain that the concept of entropy can be applied to gravity. Some believe that entropy is the characteristic of matter only.[12]

Also the theory is not necessarily locally or temporarily true. Gaseous nebulae tend to contract to form stars, demonstrating a decline rather than an increase in entropy. When a star ages it will ultimately collapse in upon itself, to the point where it forms the mysterious Black Hole. Is this an increase in randomness or a decrease? And what happens after that? Astrophysicists are just beginning to explore this whole area of science. They are far from the answers. Some physicists and mathematicians, such as Einstein and Russell, believed that the evidence of physics suggests an oscillating universe.[13] If the galaxy is moving apart at a *decreasing* rate, it would indicate that some force, probably gravity, is working against the inertia caused by the Big Bang. If that is true, eventually the inertia will weaken to the point where the countervailing force of gravity will cause the universe to collapse inward upon itself. Such a universe would forever vacillate between states of increasing and decreasing entropy. John William Moffatt, a physicist at the University of Toronto, has constructed a theory indicating that the universe[13] would bounce back if contracted to a certain minimum radius.[14]

G: But some scientists have attempted to measure all the mass in the universe and concluded that it would be insufficient to produce enough gravity to stem the inertia of outward propelled matter.

J: Recent scientific evidence indicates that the first measurements grossly underestimate the matter in the universe. The first precise measurements of the Large Magellanic Cloud that surrounds the Milky Way galaxy indicates that there must be five to ten times as much dark matter as in visible stars.[15] Furthermore, using the X-ray observatory ROSAT to detect hot gas clouds that emit no visible light, NASA scientists estimate that certain galaxies must contain ten to thirty times more mass than that which is visible.[16] Enough mass to result in an oscillating universe.

It might also be that the oscillations have escalated beyond the point of no return. According to Landau and Lifshitz, "In the general theory of relativity the universe as a whole must be regarded not as a closed system, but one which is in a variable gravitational field. In this case the application of the law of increase in entropy does not imply statistical equilibrium."[17] In other words, the Second Law of Thermodynamics does not necessarily apply to the universe as a whole. It may be that the loss of energy in one portion of time and space could result in a gain in another area.

Other scientists hypothesize that, prior to the Big Bang, there existed matter and anti-matter in equivalent amounts which would have summed to zero. Out of this statistical "nothingness" a random break occurred. This broken symmetry led to the Big Bang. Under this scenario the Second Law of Thermodynamics is not violated since the expanding universe is *in toto* leading to a state of greater entropy, even though there may be local, temporary "chunks" of decreased entropy due to a slight asymmetric distribution of particles over anti-particles.[18]

Moreover, even if the laws of thermodynamics are applicable in today's universe, it does not mean that they were applicable prior to the last Big Bang. Each Big Bang could result in a completely different set of physics. Physicist John Wheeler suggests that the very laws of physics might change every time the universe collapses and expands.[19] We are not even certain that this is the only universe. Some physicists hypothesize that there are numerous universes "bubbling up" from a primordial energy. Our present state of knowledge in this area is much the same as primitive man who puzzled over the reason for rain. Just because we don't yet understand all the principles involved is no reason to posit a god as the cause.

If the universe is flying apart and gradually moving toward dissolution, what does that prove? Only that the Big Bang may have occurred. But is the Big Bang creation? Far from it. Creation is the act of constructing matter from nothing, *ex nihilo*. The Big Bang is an explosion of unimaginable force, but all explosions of which we are aware require matter and energy. Why should we not suppose that this one was the same, albeit due to forces that we, as yet, don't understand?

G: . . . and will never understand since all evidence would have been destroyed in that explosion.

J: Possibly true. But throughout history every time someone has said "never"—even when the speaker was a brilliant scientist—he was usually expressing his personal frustration and lack of knowledge. Inevitably, a new discovery follows quickly on the heels of a "never" and the nay sayers are embarrassed. I remember people saying science could never discover the "secret" of life. Then came the discovery of DNA and the double helix. If the Big Bang theory does hold up—and it may not—more knowledge might be gained eventually to explain it.

Finally, the entropy argument cuts both ways. If the universe is running down, as some scientists hold, it would appear as evidence that the original force which started it is no longer with us.

G: . . . or is allowing it to happen.
J: Very good. But note that we are getting into an argument of conflicting assumptions, not facts. And that is what the first proof of Aquinas is all about. It is not a proof at all, but merely two assertions: that the world is always changing, and there had to be an originator of the change. Furthermore, in asserting an unmoved mover as Aristotle and Aquinas did, one need not assume that this force has any of the characteristics commonly alleged of You, such as conscious ness. So, the first "proof" of Aquinas really proves nothing. Shall we move on? I think that the deficiencies of this first argument will become even clearer as we examine the next two arguments which are variations on the same theme.
G: Before leaving the first argument, I would like to explain that the modern successors to Aquinas are willing to accept the idea of eternal causation as long as the infinite chain of causation remains subordinate to Me. The Prime Mover, therefore, is not the self-caused "first" in the series but rather superior in the sense of absolute rather than merely temporal primacy.
J: It would appear that the latter-day Thomists are forced to concede my objections but are unwilling to forsake their argument. The idea of "superior in the sense of absolute primacy" is no more than a re-statement of the Demonstration from Contingency, which is the third argument of Aquinas. Hence, my objections to that "proof" will show the fallacy of this position as well.

Demonstration from Efficient Causality

G: We shall see. Let's move on to the second proof of Aquinas:

> The second way is from the nature of efficient causes. In the world of sensible things, we find there is an order of efficient causes. One does not find, nor is it possible to find something which is the efficient cause of itself. In such a case it would be prior to itself, and this is impossible.
>
> Now in efficient causes it is not possible to go on to infinity. The reason for this is that in all subordinated causes, the first is the cause of the intermediate cause, and the intermediate (whether it be one or several) is the cause of the last. Now to take away the cause is to take away the effect. Therefore, if there is no first cause among efficient causes, there will be no ultimate nor any intermediate cause. But if it were possible in efficient causes to go to infinity, there would be no first efficient cause, nor would there

> be an ultimate effect, nor any intermediate efficient causes; all of
> which is plainly false.
>
>   Therefore, it is necessary to admit a first efficient cause, to which
> all give the name of God.[20]

J: Why does he keep adding the tag "to which all give the name of
God"? That certainly wasn't true even in the time of Aquinas.

G: Well, for all theists, it was true.

J: Obviously. Let's discuss the more substantive aspects of this argument.
It is easy to see that this one, as well as the third (as will be shown),
is simply a variation of the first argument. "But nothing can be reduced
from potentiality to actuality except by some being already in act"
is the logical equivalent of "if there is no first cause among efficient
causes, there will be no ultimate or intermediate causes."

   Therefore, as in the first argument, the second premise is a flat
contradiction of the first premise. Aquinas says "one does not find,
nor is it possible to find something which is the efficient cause of
itself." But only a few sentences later he adds that, "it is necessary
to admit a first efficient cause." How does he justify this blatant
contradiction? With the assertion—quite unfounded—that "in efficient
causes it is not possible to go on to infinity."

   Now look at the mess Aquinas has gotten himself into. If everything
has a cause, then God must have a cause. Or, conversely, if anything
can be without a cause, it might just as well be the world and not
God. Moreover, as Kant made clear, it is quite possible to have an
infinite chain of causes. One place where Aquinas went wrong is in
thinking of causes as a sequence such as H causing I causing J causing
K, etc. Aquinas assumed, therefore, that you couldn't have Z unless
there was an A. And he was right. But Aquinas failed to distinguish
between the statements:

   A does not exist
   (which would be impossible given Z), and
   A is not caused.

As Paul Edwards explains, "Believing in an infinite series is not taking
A away. [It] is taking away the unique status of A; [it] is taking away
its first causeness.' "[21] The adherents of a causal argument confuse
an infinite series with one that is long but still finite. An infinite series,
by definition, has no first cause.

   David Hume observed that only things that begin to exist must
have a cause. There is no reason to believe that something (such as
matter and energy) did not always exist, in which case such a thing

had no prior cause. Or as noted objectivist Nathaniel Branden remarked: "All causality presupposes the existence of something that acts as a cause. . . . Causality presupposes existence, existence does not presuppose causality."[22]

In a brilliantly insightful essay titled "The Meaning of Life," Kurt Baier elucidates the problem of causality. He considers the charge that the existence of the universe requires causal explanation, and after first pointing out that postulating God as the explanation only moves the problem back a step (for what, then, explains the existence of God?), he submits that neither does the universe in reality require an explanation nor does the problem of an infinite regress arise:

> In order to explain a group of explicanda [I prefer the term "effects"], a model explanation need not itself be derived from another more general one. It gives a perfectly full and consistent explanation by itself. And the regress is not infinite, for there is a natural limit, an all embracing model which can explain all phenomena, beyond which it would be pointless to derive model explanations from yet others.[23]

Of course this limit will probably never be reached as a practical—but not as a logical—matter. We must be careful not to confuse the necessity for a cause of *every thing* (each thing which can be explained by reference to another thing) with the requirement for a cause of *everything* (which is logically impossible because outside of the totality of all things there is no causal point of reference).

G: Now who is playing semantic games?

J: No I'm not. It is an important and real distinction that theologians through the centuries have failed to recognize. Some ancient philosophers have been more astute. For example, Antony Flew describes what he calls the "stratonician presumption" after Strato of Lampsacus (d. 269 B.C.E.): "the presumption that the universe is everything there is; and hence, that everything which can be explained must be explained by reference to what is in and of the universe."[24]

G: Flew calls it a presumption, and so it is, for neither he nor anyone else could prove such a hypothesis.

J: But there is nothing in human experience that provides unimpeachable evidence to the contrary. Therefore, I would submit that the totality of an ever-changing universe always was.

G: Aren't you now ignoring the Big Bang?

J: Not at all. There was undoubtedly something that existed before the Big Bang, even if it was only what physicists call a "singularity."

Explosions do not arise out of a vacuum. There had to be something that exploded.

Given the totality of that which exists, every change within that totality can be explained by a prior change. Graphically, it is as if Aquinas visualized the world this way:

At each end of which there is a first and eventually, perhaps, a final change. However, a more correct conception would be:

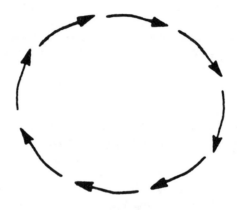

where there is an unending series of changes within Existence. By Existence I simply mean the sum total of all that exists, i.e., the universe. Existence itself, however, is not the cause of all the changes but merely the commonalty of all change. Existence itself has no cause.

G: But the universe, the sum of all existence, must have a cause outside of itself.

J: Why? B. C. Johnson observes that it "doesn't follow that just because every part of the universe is dependent we can conclude that the whole universe is dependent."[25] He explains that there are other statements that can be made about relationships among objects within the physical universe which cannot be made about the universe itself. "For example, an object can be above or below another object but the physical universe cannot be above or below another object."[26]

G: Everything must have a beginning.

J: Why? Simply because we arbitrarily assign a beginning to a specific temporal moment in what is a continuing process? As I explained in the discussion of motion, Isaac Newton proved that it is as easy to assume that objects were always in motion as it is to assume that they are always at rest—only changes in direction and speed need be accounted for. And gravity takes care of that. Furthermore, as Bertrand Russell explained, "in the case of motion, the question of regress need not arise. Two gravitating particles circling around each other like sun and planet will continue to do so forever."[27] The inescapable conclusion is that order need not be accounted for any more than disorder.

Russell was correct in pointing out that the idea of a beginning is merely due to the "poverty of imagination." Since each living thing appears to have a beginning and an end, we assume that there was a beginning to all things. But actually, every observed beginning is simply a change. Modern physics confirms that the Hindu model of the "cycle of things" is a more correct paradigm than the Judeo-Christian linear approach. Mass and energy are found to be two sides of the same coin—which in total can neither be created nor destroyed, but only altered in form. Add to this concept the idea that mass/energy is intrinsically unstable and you no longer need a prime mover or first efficient cause.

G: You forgot the principle that the cause must be adequate to the effect. *Nemo dat quod non habet* (No one can give what he has not got). And since the universe is intelligible its cause must be intelligent.

J: Clever, but don't expect me to fall for that semantic non sequitur. The philosopher George Santayana showed that one of the chief sources of myth in philosophy has been the belief that "only like could produce like."[28] In the first place, you make it seem as if a singular cause produces a singular effect. In reality, an effect can be the result of the interaction of several causes and, therefore, more complex than any one of them. Combine certain atoms under certain conditions and a chemical molecule is formed which is more complex and of a higher order than its component parts. The discovery of deoxyribonucleic acid, or DNA, and the principle of the double helix showed how living, i.e., regenerating, molecular chains evolve naturally from nonliving matter.

Second, the statement that if something is intelligible we can infer an intelligent source shows the same confusion that underlies the argument from design. Only pure randomness would be unintelligible. And pure randomness could occur only if matter or energy had no properties whatsoever, which would be impossible. By properties I mean those physical characteristics that determine the way a thing acts under various conditions. For matter or energy to exist as other than pure idea (which would be meaningless since there would be no person to have such an idea) requires that there be certain attributes, certain characteristics. It is these characteristics that determine how matter and energy interact.

G: I could imagine a world in which pure randomness exists, where the elements possess none of the elemental forces of this world such as nuclear energy, electromagnetism or even gravity.

J: If ours were such a world, we would not be having this discussion, for without any of those properties inherent in matter and energy there could be no order. But since we are having this conversation, there is order. Therefore, the order of our universe is simply a brute fact inherent in the nature of elementary particles. It is not a cause of change, it is a condition that necessitates change.

G: Then that condition can be defined as God.

J: If so, then such a god is not a conscious being; it is not a person. You are using the term "God" as a euphemism for a primitive stage in the evolution of the universe.

Returning to the issue of intelligibility of the universe, it should be noted that if there were no one of at least human intelligence to observe these characteristics and describe them, matter or energy might be said to be unintelligible by definition. For by intelligible we simply mean understandable, and that has meaning only if there is someone to do the understanding. The important point here is to differentiate between "understandable" and "discoverable." The latter term implies a set of universal laws that exists for matter and energy, just waiting to be revealed or discovered by man. But scientists today see that "law" is too strong a term. In the post-Einstein era of quantum physics, scientists today talk of probabilities that describe the interaction of matter. Their probabilistic descriptions are a useful shorthand for specifying the relationship among events. The subject is far too complex to treat at length here but I'll touch on it again under the Design Argument. For now the point to be made is that, as I've said, just because something is intelligible—understandable by humans—does not imply that an intelligent being is responsible for it.

G: I'm not at all certain that what you said makes any sense. I still maintain that it is impossible that a thing causes itself.

J: That's because you continue to confuse the cause of existence with the conditions necessary for change to occur. There is no reason to assume a causal chain that extends outside of existence. Of course atoms (or quarks or whatever the basic "stuff" of the universe turns out to be) did not cause themselves, but they are uncaused elements possessing properties that predispose them to form more complex forms of matter, thus triggering an evolutionary process of which we are a part, though by no means the final outcome.

G: But that still doesn't explain who created the elemental properties of matter and energy.

J: I repeat, there is no reason to suppose that they were created.

G: If matter and energy can be uncaused, then I might be uncaused as well; an assumption that appeared to trouble you earlier.

J: You missed the point again—deliberately, I begin to suspect. If atoms can exist without a cause—if the universe can exist without a cause—we have no need to assume Your existence as a creative force. Conversely, if the universe requires a cause, so do You.

I have one final objection to the idea of a first cause. A first efficient cause would, by definition, be a spontaneous cause, for whose occurrence there could be no reason. If there is a reason for a being to inaugurate a causal chain by acting—creating—this reason must be outside of that being and, hence, is itself the cause of the being acting. Moreover, as Professor Delos McKown cautioned me, the term spontaneous is often used incorrectly to describe events where the cause is unknown. For example, people used to think that "spontaneous combustion" could cause a haystack suddenly to burst into flames. However science now understands the bacterial action that can cause such fires. In nature there are no truly spontaneous events.

Therefore, You, as a creative force, could not be Your own efficient cause. We could posit that You always existed. But it would be an empty assertion, since You are definitely not necessary to explain the source of matter and energy which might just as well always have existed. The conclusion we draw must be that the very concept of God as the first cause collapses into an unnecessary hypothesis at best and, at worst, a logical contradiction.

G: But whether you realize it or not, you keep referring to the temporal order. I'm talking about the ontological order—a sustaining first cause. Maybe the third demonstration of Aquinas will help you to understand, though I doubt it.

Demonstration from Contingency

G: According to Aquinas:

> The third way is taken from the contingent and the necessary, and it is as follows. Examination of our world reveals some things which can be and not be, since they are found to be generated and to

be corrupted. In consequence, although it is possible for them to be and not to be, it is not possible for all these things to exist always—what is able not to exist, must at some time not be in existence.

If, therefore, it is possible for all things not to exist, then at one time there was nothing in existence. But, if this were true, then even now there would be nothing, because that which is not, does not come into being except through something which already exists. It follows from this that if at one time no being were in existence, it would have been impossible for anything to begin to exist, and thus even now nothing would be in existence—which is patently false. Therefore, not all things are merely possible, but there must exist a being whose existence is necessary.

Now every necessary thing either has the cause of its necessity in some other being or it does not. It is not possible to go on to infinity in necessary things of caused necessity, just as it is not possible in efficient causes, as had already been shown. Therefore, it is necessary to grant that there is something necessary which does not have the cause of its necessity in any other being, but which is itself the cause of necessity in others. All men call this God.[29]

Before you say anything, let Me acknowledge that this argument is only a variation on the first two, but it makes the strongest case. Frederick Copleston echoed Aquinas when, in his debate with Bertrand Russell, he argued that if you add up contingent beings to infinity, you still get contingent beings, not a necessary being.[30]

J: This argument suffers the same fatal flaw as the other two arguments, both of which required a first cause. If we accept the metaphysical bifurcation of things into necessary and contingent beings we might just as well hold that the universe is a necessary being. To be strictly correct, I would agree with the philosopher Paul Edwards that, "There is nothing more 'necessary' about the existence of the universe as a whole than about any particular thing within the universe."[31] It may have existed or may not have (just as could be said of You). The fact is, it does exist—that's all there is to it. Aquinas again confuses the existence of the universe itself with the need to explain a causal dependency of things within the existing universe. There is no reason to assume, as Aquinas does, that the basic stuff of the universe (mass/energy) did not always exist, although what form this might have taken prior to the Big Bang is not yet possible to say.

I repeat what I hoped I had made clear earlier: The whole question of causality when applied to existence is meaningless and logically absurd; it presupposes that there is something outside of existence that can cause existence. Silly, isn't it?

G: Of course, when you put it that way.

J: The idea of contingency confuses the concept of change with that of existence. Of course Thomas could not be expected to know the basic tenant of modern physics, that matter cannot be created or destroyed, so he assumed that things can come into existence or leave existence. But we now know that the Greek philosopher Heraclitus was right when he said all was change. We identify certain forms of the continually changing universe and call them persons. But a person is simply a temporary collection of energy/mass that has the capability of self-reflection. With the dissolution of the elements that comprise a person we might casually say that they cease to exist, but a more careful explanation would be to say that the particular configuration of mass/energy which we previously identified as that person or thing ceased to exist. The mass/energy which previously comprised the person continues to exist in a constantly changing form.

Therefore, in a sense, an individual is both contingent and necessary. I am contingent insofar as my particular identity is determined by the events leading up to my being the individual that I am. I am necessary in that my existence is determined by the causal laws of the universe. It is just two ways of looking at the same event which we call Joe.

Since only the existence of the universe is necessary to support the existence of any physical being, it again becomes clear that You are an unwarranted hypothesis. Moreover, postulating God as the cause of the universe would pose a host of new, unanswerable problems: How did You cause the universe? How did You make something out of nothing? Why did You cause the universe? What need did it fulfill? A perfect being would have no need and thus no reason to cause any thing. Or are You an imperfect being? George H. Smith illustrates the absurdity of the theist position: "An unknowable being using unknowable methods 'caused' the universe to snap into existence"[32] for, I might add, an unknowable reason.

G: How could such a paltry human mind begin to fathom the ways or reasons of God?

J: I've heard that one before. Translated it means: Don't think about all this, the absurdity may become too apparent.

G: Many thousands of men and women much wiser than you have not found My ways to be absurd.

J: That is simply because they have not sought to critically evaluate these "mysterious ways." I hardly need remind You that it was once considered a sin of presumption for a person to dare to ponder these things too deeply. And if one was outspoken about his skepticism, he would soon find himself on the rack. Even today the nontheist runs the risk of social ostracism.

As to the ability of humans to comprehend You, I would submit that even though, by definition, You cannot be comprehended, there should be no obvious contradictions in the very concept of God. However, we run into just these sorts of logical contradictions when we consider the Fourth Demonstration of Aquinas. Unless You simply want to skip over this one.

G: Don't be ridiculous. It is a very elegant and subtle argument.

Demonstration from Degrees of Perfection in the Universe

G: Aquinas reasons as follows:

> The fourth way is taken from the gradations which are found in things. Now among existing things there are some more and some less good and true and noble and the like. But different things are called "more" and "less" according as they are related in different ways to something which is the maximum, as a thing is hotter as it more closely it imitates that which is hottest.
>
> Accordingly, there is something which is truest, and something best, and something noblest, and, consequently, something which is most fully "being." Indeed, whatever are most true are most perfectly beings, as is said in the second book of Aristotle's Metaphysics.
>
> Now the most perfect thing of any kind is the cause of all which are of that kind; thus in the same book Aristotle points out that fire, which is the maximum of heat, is the cause of the heat of all hot things. Therefore, there must be some being which, for all others, is the cause of being, of goodness and of any other perfection. And this being we call God.[33]

J: There are so many problems inherent in this line of reasoning that I almost don't know where to begin. First, it is an absurd notion that there are degrees of being as implied by the assertion that there is "something which is most fully being." Here Aquinas makes the classic error of confusing the state of being with its attributes. An amoeba is no less a being than an Einstein. Since being is only that which exists, something either is (a being) or it is not. Existence is simply a state and, of itself, implies no value judgments. Simply because one (being) is smarter, faster, taller, or older than another does not make the first more of a being than the latter

Next, Aquinas confuses attributes with causality. Because one being has an attribute that is greater in degree than the attribute possessed by another being, does not make the first being the cause of the second. If a son is better at something than his father, did he cause his father? How absurd. Certainly in any group there may be a best, e.g., the fastest runner; but did he cause the slower runner?

The example Aquinas uses—"that fire which is the maximum of heat, is the cause of the heat of all hot things"—shows that he is basing his theory in part on the ancient Aristotelian theory of physics, which is woefully inaccurate. Fire doesn't cause heat in all things; it is frequently the other way around—the buildup of heat can cause fire, as any boy scout with two sticks can demonstrate.

Aquinas apparently is also touching on Plato's world of Ideas in a somewhat muddled way. For example, when Aquinas says that there is something "best" he forgets that the terms 'good,' 'better,' and 'best' are value judgments that humans make based upon criteria they specify. For example, in the world of art there was a time when the quality of art was judged primarily on how closely it depicted reality. However, beginning with the French impressionists, a new criterion for evaluating art evolved. Paintings were judged on a host of other criteria, such as the mood they expressed, the feeling they elicited from the viewer, and the originality with which they depicted a subject. We now recognize that there is no absolute standard of beauty. Aquinas wrongly assumed that since we distinguish between good and evil, there must be an absolute good. But in the final analysis the terms 'good' and 'bad' have no meaning absent human judgment. The philosopher Stephen Nathanson explains quite clearly that "Basic value judgments, then, are relative to persons, and we speak of something being good, rather than good for X, only when particular interests or circumstances are widely shared, when for example, they are aspects of human nature."[34]

In short, there is no group of transcendental beings, as Plato hypothesized, which exist in a perfect state and of which the things of this world are merely a poor reflection. Rather, there are simply beings—things—which when they make us happy we call good and when they cause suffering, or that which we dislike, we call bad.

G: That is a very anthropocentric outlook. By using the happiness of humankind as the standard of good and evil, you could justify torturing puppies if it made people happy.

J: You persist in distorting my arguments. I said that human beings make the value judgments. Since, as a species we tend to empathize with other sentient beings—especially higher-order mammals—we extend that value judgment to them. We also can recognize that to treat another species brutally will probably result in more brutal behavior to one or another of our own species. Nevertheless, the terms 'good' and 'bad' are relevant only to beings that can experience happiness or sorrow. The act of killing and eating a deer can be judged as good from the perspective of the lion but bad from the perspective of the deer. In some cultures that eat dogs, the act *may* be good for the diner (subject to the concerns I've just mentioned) but certainly bad for the main dish. Ideally, it would be best from the perspective of all parties involved if the circumstances could be constructed so that in a given situation happiness could be achieved for all stakeholders. Unfortunately, that cannot often be the case.

G: Then it goes without saying that you must hold that there is no absolute moral good. And you must also reject Kant's moral argument for My existence.

J: You are anticipating me. We will discuss both those issues in a moment. Before we do, we must first review the last of the proofs of Aquinas. The argument from order has gained popularity today by attracting pseudoscientific support. I always find it amusing that those people who are the first to castigate science and ignore the whole body of scientific knowledge as the means of ascertaining the truth are also the first to advance some misconstrued scientific discovery if they think it supports their cherished superstition.

G: It is most unfair of You to attempt to prejudice the reader's mind before I am allowed to even state the argument.

J: You need not worry. I'm afraid 90 percent of the people old enough to understand this work have already been prejudiced in your favor by a lifetime of conditioning. Nevertheless I apologize. Please state the argument.

13

More Proofs:
If at First You Don't Succeed . . .
Maybe You Should Give It Up

> The answer to the question, why this particular universe and no other, is to be found in the physical properties of matter/energy. The question, why does matter/energy possess these particular properties, is meaningless, since no other alternative was ever available.
>
> —J. L. Daleiden

G: According to Aquinas:

> The fifth way is taken from the governance of things. We see that some things which lack knowledge, such as physical bodies, act for an end. This is evident from the fact that they always or nearly always act in the same way to attain whatever is best for them. Thus, it is clear that they attain their goal not by chance, but by deliberate intention. Now things which lack knowledge do not strive for a goal unless they are so directed by a knowing and intelligent being, as an arrow is aimed by the archer. Therefore, there exists some knowing being by which all natural things are directed to their end, and this we call God.[1]

This, of course, is one of many forms of the *teleological argument,* which notes that all of nature appears as if it were designed for an end—the end usually being the existence of man. It is based on three observations. First, it would appear that everything in the world was made just so humankind could exist: if the world were changed ever so slightly in one of a billion ways, humans would cease to exist. If we were just a little closer to the sun, or a little farther away, life as we know it would never have occurred. If water contracted as it got colder, like almost every other material, rather than expand at the freezing point, its denser composition would cause it to sink and the oceans would gradually freeze from the bottom up. The lack of evaporation would cause a worldwide drought and life would not exist. If the ionosphere did not shield humans from the ultraviolet rays of the sun, human life could not exist. The list could be multiplied endlessly. The conclusion is that some superhuman intelligence must have designed this unfathomable and exquisitely complex environment necessary to accommodate such delicate human creatures.

The second observation is the impossibility that such a complex arrangement needed to support life could have originated purely from the random movement of atoms based on the laws of chance. Pierre Lecomte Du Noüy, and the Swiss mathematician Charles Eugene Guye have estimated the improbability of life forming by the laws of chance. According to Guye, the odds against even a single protein being formed by accident are 2.02×10^{-32}. That's an unimaginably small probability, but large compared to the trillions-of-trillions-to-one odds of forming humans by chance.

Finally, it can be observed that natural entities, particularly humans, work toward an end. So do animals which store nuts, or migrate, or fight for survival. If the creatures of nature act toward an end, then what is the end of all nature?

J: At first blush I admit those seem like convincing arguments, but let's examine each to see if they hold water or are so much theistic sophistry.

With regard to Your first observation—that everything was made just so humans could exist—I submit that you are confusing cause and effect. Human life is the result of billions of years of *adaptation* to the world, not the other way around. (Perhaps if humankind recognized this truth we would appreciate the need for maintaining environmental balance and stability.) The key proposition in your argument is the impossibility of a chance creation of human life. However, given changes in the environment, a radically different life form might emerge. This new life form, if sufficiently intelligent, might observe the unique environmental conditions necessary to sustain it and also marvel at the seeming impossibility of everything occurring just so it could survive.

G: You miss my point. I'm not talking simply about a specific life form but about any form—any organization whatsoever—developing from chaos. In other words, there is order in the universe. Since order cannot arise from disorder, there must be a creator of order.

J: That argument is built on the mistaken Greek idea of natural law to which I referred earlier. This is the notion that a transcendental set of laws exist which constrain matter and energy to behave in only certain ways. Today, "natural laws" are understood to be simply man-made descriptions of how things behave. Ernest Nagel correctly observed that, "no matter what the world was like . . . it would still possess some order and would in principle be amenable to mathematical description,"[2] i.e., some set of physical properties is inherent in any physical matter.

G: But mathematical description, if made by a brilliant mind observing all the intricacies and relationships among the myriad and diverse elements, would be a blueprint or pattern that gives evidence of one who must have designed the pattern.

J: Not at all. There are two opposing hypotheses on this subject. The first would hold that, given the properties of matter and energy, no other arrangement than the present could have resulted. Under this hypothesis nothing happens by chance unless two causal chains interact. This was the position of most scientists early in this century, Einstein being the leading exponent. Today, however, discoveries about the behavior of subatomic particles seem to reveal a more probabilistic universe. Here chance plays an important role, especially in initiating the broken symmetry which leads to the creation of the universe, and it is only after the Big Bang that order evolves. Under this hypothesis order becomes a matter less of immutable laws than of mathematical probabilities. It is important to note that neither hypothesis requires a Grand Designer. Years before the discoveries of modern physics and that branch of mathematics dealing with probability, the psychologist William James explained: "For the parts of things must always make some definite resultant, be it chaotic or harmonious. When we look at what has actually come, the condition must always appear perfectly designed to ensure it. We can always say therefore in any conceivable world, of any conceivable character, that the whole cosmic machinery may have been designed to produce it."[3]

Both hypotheses employ one of the few irrefutable laws of logic: the law of identity. It is obvious to anyone that to exist is to exist as something. To be something is to possess specific characteristics which restrict the range of possible action. As soon as we remove the possibility of complete random action, we have eliminated chaos and must adopt the only alternative, order.

However, as Smith points out, we must not confuse order with design: "Order does not presuppose an ordering; it is simply entailed by the nature of existence itself."[4] E. M. Macdonald, author of "Design Argument Fallacies," arrives at a similar conclusion: "When design is affirmed of an action, it must be shown that the agent in the action had that result in view at the beginning of the action. The fact that things exist as they now are proves simply that things exist as they now are."[5] In other words, in discussing the apparent order in the universe, the use of the term 'design' is begging the question since it implies that there was a designer to begin with.

Employing the findings of quantum mechanics, physicists can demonstrate how order can arise from chance. It is too complex to explain here, but Victor Stengler's book *Not By Design*[6] provides a comprehensible summary for those willing to study it. Interestingly, he shows how a computer generating random numbers can eventually develop ordered patterns within the randomness. The new science of chaos theory also demonstrates that the properties of fractal equations* result in an exquisitely complex order arising from randomness.

We need to explore another angle as well. The word "design" implies an end, a purpose. But, You cannot be said to have a purpose, because that would imply that You had a need or goal which would be impossible for a completely perfect being. Freethinker Charles Bradlaugh wrote that, "God has either been eternally designing which would be absurd, or, if he at some time commenced to design, what then induced him to commence?"[7]

G: An inferior human intellect could not begin to fathom My mind.

J: More question-begging. The statement assumes that there *is* a Divine mind.

G: Don't you at least find it amazing how the world appears to have been designed for the purpose of supporting human life?

J: As usual You have it backwards. I find it marvelous how life has adapted to the environment. From the Arctic to the tropics we see how humans and animals have adapted to oftentimes incredibly inhospitable conditions. I find that evolution offers a logical and verifiable explanation for the "design" of life. It shows that purpose doesn't exist in nature and reduces You to an "unnecessary hypothesis." This is the real fear that motivates the fundamentalists' hysterical attack on evolution. They recognize that evolution knocks down the entire theistic house of cards.

G: Don't you find it ironic that men continually turn to this "unnecessary hypothesis" when perplexed or distraught by what they correctly assess

---

*Fractal geometry created by French mathematician Benoit Mandelbrot, is a method of calculating the fractional dimensions of irregular objects (or systems) such as a coast line. It leads to the conclusion that irregularity remains constant over different scales. Hence, the randomness of a coast line is found to have charactaristics that can be expressed mathematically.

is the meaninglessness of life and arbitrariness of existence absent a Divine plan?

J: Yes, people do find it hard "simply to be abandoned . . . set loose to find our own way."[8] The characters Rosencrantz and Guildenstern in Tom Stoppard's play found they were incapable of action without a closely defined purpose being given them. "We are entitled to some direction," they wail. It never occurs to them that people could give their own lives purpose and meaning—a subject I will deal with in a later volume.

   The belief that the universe must have a purpose originated from the notion that since animals and humans work toward an end (itself a disputable conclusion), all of nature must be working toward an end. This argument misappropriates the teleological principles from psychology used to explain human behavior and applies them to the natural sciences. This is the whole basis for the Design analogy by William Paley, which holds that if you see a watch you know there must be a watchmaker. So, too, Paley argues, we observe the workings of the universe and know there must be a maker of the universe.

G: Sounds right to Me.

J: I'm not surprised. But You must see the weakness of this argument. In the case of the watch, it is from knowledge of the purpose of the watch that we infer design—otherwise it would be seen as just a random collection of parts. But, in viewing the universe, the theist assumes it has a purpose.

G: Even if there were no utilitarian purpose or end, there could be an artistic end. The butterfly could be the result of the desire of the creator to make something beautiful. Just as a painting infers a painter, the beauty of creation infers a creator.

J: You said that there "could be" a Divine artist. But, we are looking here for proof, not mere possibilities. Second, we run into the same old contradictions: how could an all-powerful, completely self-sufficient God have a "desire" or need to create? Unlike the painter who is trying to express himself—uncertain of the outcome—You would already know the outcome of Your efforts and hence the act itself would be superfluous. In the final analysis, a proper understanding of the physical properties of matter/energy explains what appears to be design. Must people believe that Jack Frost or You design each snowflake to appreciate its beauty? I don't think so. To understand what happens to H_2O in vapor form when subject to temperatures of $32°F$ given the molecule's intrinsic physical properties is itself a fascinating wonder. Moreover, it was the scientific invention of the microscope that truly revealed the intricate beauty of the snowflake.

It is interesting to see the shift in human reliance on You as the explanation of design in the universe. Every facet of nature appeared to primitive people as the result of the direct intervention of gods. They, naturally enough, believed that the cause of all the mysterious events in the universe must be persons like themselves, only much greater. For example, because the wind could rise so suddenly with disastrous effects, and then cease just as suddenly, it must be due to the blowing of some angry god. However, as science uncovered the true causes of natural events such as rain, meteorites, sickness, birth defects, etc., You were called upon only as an explanation of the more unusual events such as a natural disaster (sent as punishment) or an unexpected recovery from illness seen as a miracle specially bestowed.

As science advanced, You continued to withdraw as an explanatory necessity. When I was younger You still seemed indispensable for explaining the origins of life. Then came the discoveries of DNA and the double helix, molecular reproduction and genetic splicing. You were now an unnecessary explanation, not only for hereditary char-acteristics, but for life itself. The theologians again retrenched; some have gone so far as to avow that You are responsible only for setting the whole thing in motion, the author of the Big Bang. I'm afraid You are losing ground fast.

G: How absurd! Why, today more people than ever are rejecting science and turning back to Me as an explanation for everything.

J: A temporary action by a frustrated and intellectually apathetic society looking for cheap and easy answers to difficult questions. They choose to ignore a fundamental canon of logic: never attribute an effect (in this case all of creation) to an agent specially conceived for the purpose (in this case God) until the effect has unsuccessfully been attributed in turn to each agent or agency known to exist.[9] This is a variation of the Principle of Parsimony since it results in the simplest hypothesis. This may not be apparent at first. For example the use of God as an explanatory hypothesis may appear simple. But as we shall see, such a hypothesis involves all sorts of convoluted reasoning and has no evidence whatsoever to support it. History tells us that we have made steady progress in uncovering natural causes for every natural occurrence and will continue to do so. Hence, there is no valid reason for a "leap of faith" in the existence of an "unknown" and "unknowable" supernatural cause.

G: But humankind will never possess complete knowledge of the reason for every event.

J: Probably not, but that is still no reason to personify what we don't know.

G: You previously admitted that even if you understood the cause of *every thing*—each event—you would still not know the cause of *everything,* the totality of all things.

J: Because, as I explained, there need not be a cause of the totality. Moreover, if You insist that there must be a cause, then there must be a cause of You as well.

G: Unless I Am is the totality of all things.

J: So we are back to Hegel's pantheism, making You synonymous with the universe, which again is simply a crude attempt at personifying the universe. Or else You become the basic energy of the universe, the mysterious "force" of a juvenile "Star Wars" mentality. However physicists have discovered four basic forces in the universe: strong nuclear forces, electromagnatism, weak nuclear forces and gravitation. All individual phenomena in the universe can be explained by these forces. There is simply no reason to postulate an intelligent, creating god.

G: You still haven't reconciled how life could have originated when the odds were trillions to one against such a chance arrangement of atoms. The impossibility is again illustrated by Du Noüy's observation that the universe is estimated to be only twenty billion years old, while the time necessary for the random movement of atoms to form a single protein molecule would be 10^{234} billions of years.[10]

J: Another misleading statistic based on a misunderstanding of how probability works in nature. Du Noüy, and the others you referred to earlier, defined probability as "the ratio of the number of cases favorable to an event, to the total number of possibilities, all possible cases being considered as equally probable."[11] To apply this definition of probability to the construction of a protein molecule is absurd, since all possibilities of atomic bindings are not equally probable. In his refutation of Du Noüy, Wallace I. Matson explains, "The probability of acetic acid being formed in nature is not this (Du Noüy's) probability, but the product of the probabilities of conditions permitting the steps of the synthesis to be realized in succession."[12] If Du Noüy's application of probability was correct, we would expect no experiment ever to be repeated since it would represent a chance combination that has impossibly small odds of occurring again. But the replicability of experiments shows that, by and large, it is the inherent properties of matter and energy that cause certain events and not others to happen. The construction of a protein molecule is not, therefore, a single chance concentration of atoms, but rather the end result of many intermediate steps which, because of the huge number of individual atoms and their inherent properties, were bound to occur in a given environment.

The whole question of "odds" is inappropriate. Chapman Cohen pointed out that regardless of the odds against one particular type of arrangement (or design of nature, if you will), the odds are equally great against any other design, all things being equal. However, "since the odds are equally great against all—seeing that some order must exist [given that matter has definite properties such as gravitation]— there can be no logical value in using the argument against one arrangement in particular. The same question, 'Why this arrangement and none other?' might arise in any case."[13]

Perhaps it will become clear by using Aquinas' own example of an arrow shot into the air. Shoot an arrow blindly into the air, and the odds of it landing in any particular square inch are more than a million to one. But the arrow had to land somewhere. So it would be silly to get excited about the probability of its landing in the spot it did. Furthermore, once we understand all the properties of the factors at work, e.g., the thrust force of the bow, configuration of the arrow, angle of trajectory, wind speed, etc., the odds for hitting a particular spot don't seem so great. If we had precise measurements of all the variables, we could calculate exactly where it would land.

Evolution of life is similar. If we could comprehend all the factors in the process (which we are only beginning to understand), along with the billions and billions of varying environmental conditions (each star has its unique environment complete with companion planets), and the eons of time involved, the possibility that some form of life wouldn't have evolved somewhere, seems to be highly improbable. Some form of life had to form somewhere at some time. It is more likely that many forms of life have existed throughout the universe, but perhaps never concurrently. Futhermore, for all we know, this universe may be only one of a virtually infinite number of universes, each with its unique physical properties.

Given the unique physical properties of our own planet, life did not evolve by chance, as Du Noüy assumes, rather it had to occur.

G: Now isn't that a rash conclusion?

J: Absolutely not. It is firmly supported by laboratory experiments. For example, two scientists, H. C. Urey and S. L. Miller, placed sterile water in a spark chamber filled with a mixture of hydrogen, methane and ammonia—the same gases present during the period when the earth was young. By simulating the effects of volcanic action and lightning (i.e., boiling the water and flashing the spark generator for a period of only several days), the scientists were amazed to discover that twenty different compounds had formed, including four amino acids which are the building blocks of protein—a necessary ingredient for living organisms.[14] Other similar experiments have resulted in the creation of amino acids found in DNA and RNA, and still others replicated the process of polymerization, the linking of amino acids in long complex chains from simple compounds such as cyanogen. This all goes to prove that it wasn't a process of random chance that produced life on the earth, but the basic properties of matter. If matter had different properties it might have eventually produced different life forms.

Once any type of life was formed it was only a matter a time, a very long time, before the myriad life forms we witness today would result.

G: Assuming the theory of evolution is true, it remains only an unsubstantiated hypothesis.

J: You know better than that. It is one of the most verified of all scientific theories. Despite the silly, pseudoscientific arguments against the theory of evolution, the evidence is overwhelming to support each of its three hypotheses: (a) that there is variation among the members of a species; (b) that these differences are hereditary and; (c) that the differences conferring an advantage to some members of a species are more likely to be passed on to succeeding generations.

A Short Digression on Evolution

G: I'm glad to see you are honest enough to use the term "theory," yet you still treat evolution as an established fact. Actually, there are many gaps in evolutionary theory. And a good argument can be made against it.

J: I haven't read a counterargument yet that is supported by any real evidence, only religious belief. As I showed in the section on belief versus reason, a rational person will always accept the position most supported by the available evidence.

The first premise of evolutionary theory, that there exists genetic variation among the members of the same species, can be seen in the laboratory. We know that there are three causes of variation in genes: (1) the shuffling of chromosomes prior to fertilization; (2) crossing over—when genes of one chromosome of a pair break and join up with the corresponding segment of other members of the same pair; and (3) mutations—small changes in one of the DNA molecules.

The second premise, that genetic variations are hereditary, has been understood since the time of Gregor Johann Mendel's experiments with hybrids, and has been the basis for the breeding of animals for thousands of years.

The creationist is forced to concede the first two points but contends that genetic changes cannot lead to the evolution of new species. However, as in the case of the first two propositions, the evidence is overwhelmingly in support of evolutionary theory.

G: Then why hasn't science created a new species through laboratory experiments?

J: Many people are afraid of the scientists' capability to do just that. The nascent science of genetic engineering has demonstrated that it is capable of developing new forms of life at the bacterial level. I find it amusing, but not surprising, that the creationists, who argue that only You can create divergent life forms, are most opposed to genetic engineering.

G: Bacteria are one thing; birds, dogs and apes are not so mutable. I haven't observed any new species being created at this level. And human beings with the power to reason are infinitely more complex.

J: That is tantamount to saying that because waving a pot of water over a fire won't make it boil, fire doesn't cause water to boil. The missing element in both cases is time: millions of years. Scientists cannot add that necessary dimension of time to their experiments. However, the rapid reproductive ability of the fruit fly has provided some interesting experiments in support of Darwin's theory. According to Darwin, traits that offer neither advantage nor disadvantage should disappear in the course of many generations. This was supported in a study of female fruit flies that were allowed to reproduce through the asexual process of parthenogenesis for eighteen years. As reported in *Science News,* between 1973 and 1981, the average frequency of mating with males dropped significantly from the earlier period. Since we know that sexual performance is a heritable change, it seems that in the absence of males, mutant sex flies can dominate the population.[15]

G: Excuse me if I am underwhelmed by such remotely related evidence. I would like something more direct. For example, where is the fossil evidence that actually shows one species evolving into another?

J: Dr. Chris McGowan, who is the curator-in-charge of the Department of Vertebrate Paleontology at Toronto's Royal Ontario Museum, cites several examples in his book, *In The Beginning.*[16] For instance, there is the Archaeopteryx, which is the link between reptiles and birds. Although its major features are clearly reptilian it also possesses the feathers and wishbone of birds. Geologist Charles Cazeau gives the example of the Seymouria which is classified by taxonomists as both reptile and amphibian.[17] Fossils of three different animals were found at the Morrison Foundation at Como Bluff, Wyoming, which possessed the intermediary characteristics to bridge the gap between the primitive Jurassic fauna and the more advanced Cretaceous fauna.[18] For example, one shrew-like insectivore possessed intermediate features between primitive and more advanced insect-eating animals. Even the fossil history of the horse provides an excellent example to support the theory of evolution, as McGowan demonstrates.

The spiny anteater and duckbilled platypus are two mammals existing at the present time which lay eggs like reptiles. There are three genera of Cynodonts, a class of reptiles which have many features in common with mammals. According to McGowan, there are "all shades of gray among the amphibians, from fully aquatic animals, reminiscent of fishes, to fully terrestrial ones that remind us of lizards."[19]

Finally, a series of mollusk fossils has recently been discovered which provide "the first detailed, unbroken record of how one species evolves into another."[20] Examining well-preserved fossils through the depths of a 400-meter deposit in northern Kenya, Peter C. Williamson traced mollusk lineage over several million years. He was able to identify recognizable intermediate forms that linked old and new species.

G: I realize that even the two major proponents of creationism, Henry M. Morris and Duane Gish, admit that the skeletons of ancient amphibians and reptiles are so similar that there is little way to distinguish them.[21] However, you must admit that the evolutionary record is far from complete. There are many gaps. Why is there no finely graduated history of changes?

J: In the first place, many life forms branched from each other at such an early stage of evolutionary development that there would be little matter to be fossilized. For example, the continuity between plant and animal life can be observed in microscopic species such as the Euglena, which can be either plant or animal depending upon its environment. When Dr. Morris says, "There is no evidence that there have ever been transitional forms between plants and animals,"[22] he would appear to be ignorant of Protista, those single-celled organisms which zoologists had to classify in their own kingdom, because they can be viewed as either plant or animal. Yet try to find a fossil of such a microscopic organism. It won't be easy.

Second, in their effort to define a class for every living organism, zoologists have largely defined away transitional forms. When they discover an animal that doesn't neatly fit into one of the classifications by virtue of its primary characteristics, secondary characteristics are examined, and by means of some biological hair-splitting, every animal is stuffed into one class or another. Hence the continuum of related animals is arbitrarily broken into discrete segments.

Third, fossils often lack the fine resolution necessary to detect minor evolutionary change, such as changes in internal organs that would not be fossilized.

Fourth, species are relatively stable over long periods of time. New species often develop in a relatively short period of time due to some cataclysmic event. The relatively few fossils found would be extremely lucky to record such an event. Moreover, as Cazeau points out, the evidence is sketchy because of the ecologically fortunate property of organisms to decay so quickly and completely. Entire populations of soft-bodied forms undoubtedly arose and disappeared without a trace. Look at how few buffalo skeletons are to be found in this country, and yet we know the plains were covered with millions of them just a few hundred years ago. Dinosaurs were around for 150 million years, yet their remains are extremely rare.

Last, it is often difficult to determine whether species found in the rocks are true biological species. Hence zoologists cannot be expected to always recognize the origin of new species in the fossil record.[23]

However, despite this formidable list of difficulties, McGowan concludes, as do all zoologists (neither Dr. Grish nor Dr. Morris have degrees in zoology or related fields such as biology), that there is an abundance of fossil evidence such as I have described to provide a record of all major vertebrate transitions from fishes to amphibians, amphibians to reptiles, reptiles to birds, and reptiles to mammals. In short, the paleontological evidence is overwhelming for anyone who undertakes to study it objectively.

G: I'm aware of all those findings to which you alluded. But they haven't resolved the disagreement over the mechanism of evolution.

J: Only with regard to the process that determines the rate of evolutionary change. There are two general theories of the evolutionary process. One theory suggests that major changes to species were spurred by periods of danger which caused those members of the species that lacked some adaptive mechanism to quickly die out; a process which paleontologists call catastrophism. The other theory, known as *uniformism,* assumes a slow process of gradual intraspecies micro-evolutionary changes that is still at work today. Probably both processes occur to some degree. McGowan explains how genes can be passed on from one generation to another without being expressed, i.e., they don't determine a physical characteristic. Then, "a small change in a regulator gene could bring about rapid evolutionary changes by causing latent structural genes to be turned on."[24]

G: Then how can evolutionary theory explain the archaic nature of so many animals? For example, one study indicated that one-half of the living animal species can be traced back over 500,000 years without a substantial change.[25]

J: That's a point no creationist dares raise, since doing so would constitute an admission that the world is far older than the Bible suggests. But the answer is simple. McGowan explains that species undergo change in response to environmental conditions, but the changes are not necessarily in any one direction. Rather, they fluctuate about a mean average. Inbreeding of the species causes the members to regress toward the average unless there is an event that results in those individuals with unique characteristics having a significant advantage in survival, or attraction of mates.

There are many examples of how, through the process of natural selection, plants and animals adapted to a changing environment. For instance, many insects species have developed a tolerance to the pesticide DDT. Bacteria can become immune to antibiotics.

G: How is this magical process supposed to work?

J: Due to random mutation certain members of a species are resistant to the chemical or drug. After a few generations where those with the strongest resistance have passed on their genes, a new species has evolved. By definition, it is a new species if its members will not reproduce with members of the original species.

Oftentimes, new species will form when a group gets separated from the rest of its species, thus preventing inbreeding with the larger body of the species. If the compositions of the two gene pools are statistically different, they will result, ultimately, in two unique species. A relatively recent example of this process, called endemism, can be seen in the African Lake Nabugabo, which became separated from Lake Victoria by a sand bar only 3,500 years ago. Since that time, five unique species of fish have developed in Lake Nabugabo.[26]

Comparisons of island flora and fauna with those found on the closest mainland shows that endemism is the rule rather than the exception. The Galapagos Islands, which stimulated Darwin to formulate his theories of evolution, offer one of the most dramatic examples. There are 228 unique species of plants, twenty-eight species of birds, thirty-two of reptiles, four of rodents, sixty of fishes and fifty unique species of land snails.[27]

G: Maybe they were always there, from the time of creation to today in their present form.

J: Don't let the creationists hear you say that. If that is the case, where did they go when the biblical Flood came? Did some walk all the way over to the Ark? Did they then walk back to Galapagos again after the Flood, being very careful not to have any offspring, or leave even a single bone or fossil anywhere along the route?

G: Your sarcasm is not amusing. I've already conceded that the Genesis account of the Flood may have been allegorical. Then again it might have been only a local flood. I still maintain that the animals indigenous to Galapagos might have been there from creation. Endemism does not prove evolution.

J: Not by itself. But you can't ignore the fossil evidence found throughout the world which clearly indicates that the more developed species existed after the more primitive species. Philosopher Antony Flew poses this challenge to the creationists: "Evolution could be refuted if paleontologists discover some fossils of higher life form in rocks much too old."[28] McGowan also dares the creationists to offer evidence that the earliest fossils were not the simplest, or that all different organisms were found to appear at the same time. The evidence, however, is quite the opposite.

G: Dr. Morris offered an explanation for that. The fossils were sorted during the Flood based upon the elevation in which they lived and their relative density.

J: Unfortunately for Dr. Morris, the evidence directly contradicts his imaginative hypothesis. The location of the organisms in the geological column (i.e., a core sample taken from a lake bed or mountain side) shows no relationship between the complexity of organisms and the elevation at which they lived, how mobile they were, or how well they floated (a function of their density).[29] Conversely, evolutionary theory would predict that fossils of related species should be found in close proximity, and the evidence shows this to be the case.

Scientists will continue to argue about the dating, timing, and linkage of species, but of the overall evolutionary concept there is little doubt—unlike the complete act of faith that must be relied upon to swallow the totally unsupported theory of creationism.

Let's turn the argument around. What do the creationists demand that we believe?

1. The earth is quite young, less than 10,000 years old.

2. No new organisms appeared after creation.

3. There was a great Flood by means of which God destroyed all life on earth except that which took refuge on a boat built by one man and his sons.

4. The fossils are the remains of the organisms which perished in the Flood and their arrangement in the geological column is due to sorting based on their density, or the altitude in which they were living or had fled to when they were drowned.

    To support this outlandish hypothesis the creationists offer no evidence except a myth, which I have shown has no more reliability than the legends of unicorns, centaurs, or the man in the moon.

G: Now you're being silly.

J: Am I? I don't think the legend of Atlas supporting the world on his shoulders is any more absurd than the idea that Noah could build a boat to hold all the species of animal life on this earth.

G: The boat was very large. Dr. Morris calculates it as being equivalent to 522 railroad cars.[30]

J: Aside from the absurdity of one family building such a enormous ship, a few calculations are all that is necessary to show how ludicrous the Bible story is. To begin with, Noah would have had to collect pairs of over one million species of animals and a half million species of plants from all over the world—including the Galapagos Islands. Oh, and don't forget Noah was instructed to take seven (that other magic number) of every beast with a cloven hoof that chewed the cud.

    Next, You ordered him to take enough food for them. McGowan estimates that a pair of lions alone would eat about ten tons of meat in forty days. How Noah kept his meat fresh is not mentioned. Even eating like a bird is a problem if there are 56,000 pairs of them, many with their own special diets. Then of course there is the problem of fresh water for the million species. Maybe Noah collected it in a few hundred thousand buckets?

    Another problem the author of this delightful fairy tale did not worry about is the threat that dumping three miles of fresh water on the earth (enough to cover Mt. Ararat) would have created for all the salt water fish. Nor did he concern himself with where all the rain came from or where the water went when it receded.

    Finally, wouldn't it have been an incredible scene when over two million caged and hungry animals were suddenly let loose on Mt. Ararat to find their way back to Australia, Aukland, Greenland, and the Galapagos Islands? Not even Cecil B. DeMille would undertake such a spectacle.

G: Are you finished? You know that very few Christians take the story of Noah's Ark literally.

J: I wish that were true. A few years ago it might have been. But with the beginning of the era I call The Great Slide Back, millions of Americans have abandoned reason to believe every fable no matter how fabulous or lacking in evidence. I could explain to a creationist that since we can know that the the most distant galaxies are billions of light years away, the universe must be at least that old or the light from those galaxies would not have reached us yet. What do you think his response would be?

G: Probably that I could have created the world with the light already in motion.

J: Exactly. And if I show that we can accurately demonstrate that fossils are millions of years old?

G: The creationist could argue that I created fossils that appeared to be that old.

J: You have an excellent grasp of creationist illogic. And if I explain that a God who gave humankind the power of reason and then created a world full of illusions to trick that reasoning mind is nothing more than a grand deceiver?

G: I'm just testing man's faith.

J: Bingo! You qualify as a professor of "Creation Science." All of this would be terribly amusing if it weren't believed as literally true. To introduce this silliness into the classroom is as absurd as to demand that alchemy, astrology or palmistry be taught as science. It is nothing less than a blatant attempt to introduce religious indoctrination into the public education system.

G: Creation Science is not as devoid of intellectual support as you suggest. There are at least two scientists who have provided evidence contrary to evolutionary theory. Both Nalin Chanders Wickramasinghe and Robert V. Gentry have performed very rigorous scientific analyses that raise serious questions concerning evolution and have yet to be answered.

J: I do find Wickramasinghe's work of interest, but disagree that it in any way infers a creator or Grand Designer. He attempts to support the hypothesis known as *panspermia,* which contends that instead of evolution, the diverse life forms on earth came from micro-organisms bombarding this planet from space, perhaps billions of years ago. But, aside from minor problems like how organisms could survive the fiery plunge through the earth's atmosphere, such a theory simply moves the problem of the origins of life to another planet in a remote galaxy. It does nothing to contradict evolutionary theory except ignore all the existing evidence. Interestingly, one of the primitive attempts to explain the origin of life on earth was the notion that rain carried divine sperm which impregnated mother earth. Unlike old soldiers, old myths don't fade away; they just take on the trappings of pseudoscience.

Wickramasinghe tries to avoid the criticism that his theory does not dispel the hypothesis that life might still have evolved in another part of the universe by claiming that the odds were too great that life could have originated by "chance." In making this claim, Wickramasinghe falls into the same trap as Du Nöuy by concluding that the odds are too great to produce the enzymes necessary to form life anywhere in the universe. First, he assumes that the process of molecular formation is purely random—as if the properties of matter did not limit molecular functions to less than a random process. And, second, he ignores the fact that something had to result from the molecular formations, and whatever the end result, that it would have an equally incredibly small chance of occurring when viewed from the perspective of the end product. That something had to occur, however, was a certainty. The error of Wickramasinghe and Du Noüy is the result of incorrectly looking backward at the probability process rather than forward. It reminds me of an acquaintance who was puzzled over how the lucky winner of the state lottery knew which number to pick.

Gentry's argument against evolution is even less persuasive. Like so many times in the history of science, he found an occurrence that doesn't appear to jibe with an overall theory. In Gentry's case it was halos—discoloration in rocks produced by radioactive polonium—trapped in rocks. Since he can't explain how polomian halos were formed by conventional theories, he leaps to the conclusion that they were trapped there when the rock cooled almost instantly—in geological time—which Gentry believes supports the six day creation theory. Of course, to make this leap of faith Gentry has to ignore all contrary evidence. Trying to hang the theory of creation on one unexplained observation is pretty far-fetched to me.

Similar ploys have been used by theists throughout history. For example, they thought they had found a hole in the theory of planetary motion when they found planets that deviated from their predicted orbits. These deviations were ascribed to You. But the correct scientific explanation was soon discovered and the need for hypothesizing Divine interference was scuttled.

That there will always be some new, temporarily unexplained observation concerns me very little. What is of much greater interest is the ever-growing weight of evidence in support of evolution. The implication is that the relationship of humans and apes is closer than most of us care to admit.

Much of the most dramatic evidence of our hominoid ancestors has been uncovered in the last few decades. Mary D. Leakey discovered a hominoid skull in Bed I of Olduvai Gorge in Tanzania, West Africa. In 1974, Donald C. Johnson discovered "Lucy," a Plocenia fossil skeleton 3.5 million years old. Fossil evidence discovered by David Pilbean of Harvard's Peabody Museum indicates that the evolutionary path of humans and chimpanzees diverged more recently than had heretofore been believed, perhaps a "mere" 7 to 9 million years ago.[31]

Slowly, the paleontologists are reconstructing the evolutionary history of humankind. It appears to begin at least 2.8 million years ago with the *Australopithecus africanus* and *robustus,* ape-like creatures with many humanoid features. Although they walked erect, their brain size was comparable to the ape, about 430 to 530 ml. Next, around 1.8 million years ago, came *Homo habilis* with a slightly larger brain of 775 ml. This species appears to have been followed by various members of the *Homo erectus* species such as Java man, Peking man, and Heidelberg man. Their brain size was close to that of a true human, 900 ml. Whether Neanderthal man was the first member of *Homo sapiens* is perhaps debatable, but that the Cro-Magnon man of 30,000 years ago was one of our own species is generally accepted. So we can trace the gradual progression of both man and ape from their common ancestors. The closeness of the relationship of humans and apes can be seen in their biological similarities. Proteins in humans and chimpanzees are almost identical in structure.[32] Moreover, Jorge J. Yunis and Om Peahash of the University of Minnesota Medical School discovered that "every bond formed in human chromosomes can be identified in each of the three great ape species."[33]

G: But you cannot deny that humans have the ability to reason and apes don't. How do you account for reasoning unless it was granted to man by the Being who possesses supreme reason?

J: I quoted George Santayana earlier: "that [only] like could produce like has been one of the chief myths in philosophy." He explains that such a belief completely ignores the potential effect of time and genetic mutation, resulting in "the groundless prejudice that mind could only arise from mind."[34]

The mystery of how the mind reasons is also slowly being stripped away. Laid bare, we discover that reasoning is no more than the ability to follow certain basic rules of logic to evaluate new data on the basis of prior stored information. As such, we see the rudiments of reasoning in small children and their mental equivalents, chimpanzees. Reason is now understood to be not so much the either/or process it once was thought, but rather a matter of degree.

G: And abstract thought? Creativity?

J: Anthropologists working with chimps have discovered that, like humans, they, too, can think in general terms, such as learning that the word "flower" applies to a whole class of plants. In other words, in a very simplified manner they "abstract" the common element from apparently diverse objects. This is the essence of all creativity and artistry. The artist Pablo Picasso was able to discern geometric forms common to all products of nature: human, animal and inanimate. A comedian will play on the common embarrassments we all have experienced. The genius is able to generalize associations among events—determine the common element—which most people miss. The classic example is Newton's observation of a falling apple generalized into the notion that all physical bodies are attracted to each other—the principle of gravity. Oftentimes the observer is unaware of the source of the observation, and (s)he is certainly unaware of the subconscious process in the mind making the abstraction. Hence, it is called a flash of intuition or inspiration.

Since intelligence—the ability to reason—is only a matter of degree, there is no reason to suspect that it didn't evolve like the giraffe's neck, the cow's second stomach, the monkey's prehensile tail or the eagle's incredible eyesight. They all are the result of natural selection.

G: I thought this was a discussion concerning design, order, and purpose in nature, not evolutionary theory. Most enlightened Christians and Jews would readily admit that the evidence for evolution is indeed compelling. But they would not agree that the acceptance of the theory of evolution contradicts their belief in a creative God. They would agree with theologian Pierre Teilhard de Chardin that, in effect, I chose to create through the process of evolution. Creation is not a once and forever act. Rather, it is an ongoing event either guided or, at least, set in motion by Me.

J: I find it ironic that as the theologians keep modifying their descriptions/definitions of You, You are becoming indistinguishable from the impersonal physics of the universe. Once again theology attempts to modify its position to accommodate (or perhaps preempt is a more appropriate word) the findings of science, but in doing so Your contours fade so that You become totally unrecognizable. A God who cannot be differentiated from the universe certainly is undeserving of my prayers and veneration.

Despite the blatant rationalizations of those who refuse to admit the obvious implications of scientific advances, it is apparent that the natural, materialistic processes of matter/energy offer a far more satisfactory explanation of the apparent design in nature than the assumption of a Divine origin. As I've said, the use of the word "design" is altogether inappropriate—"order" is a better term, since it does not beg the question. "Order" does not imply an "orderer."

G: Even if it were admitted, for sake of argument, that there was an alternative explanation for order, why should you conclude that it is more satisfactory?

J: Because the alternative explanation I've discussed does not:

(a) violate the canon of logic I explained earlier (never attribute an effect to an agent specially conceived for this purpose until the effect has unsuccessfully been attributed to each agent known to exist),

(b) require assumptions outside the range of human experience and knowledge, or

(c) contain the internal contradictions which positing God as an explanation poses.

G: What contradictions?
J: I'll get to those in the next chapter.

Continuing Efforts to Affirm God's Existence: Küng, Kant, and Swinburne

G: Well, this discussion of proof has all been most tedious. All you may—I repeat, may—have demonstrated is that it is difficult to prove My existence to the satisfaction of a scientist.
J: Or any rational person.
G: Oh, I don't know. I think most people would agree that people like theologian Hans Küng are eminently rational, yet they are fervent theists. Küng, in fact, admits the weakness of all the proposed proofs of My existence, yet still arrives at a belief in Me based on reason.
J: Or so he alleges. After reading his books I sense that here is a brilliant scholar who, although seeing the fallacies in all the arguments for Your existence, is not courageous enough to accept the logical conclusion. He admits that "there is no evident substructure of reason on which faith could be based."[35] Yet, he abandons reason (although he denies it), and makes the traditional "leap of faith," trying to disguise his cowardice by covering up with circuitous metaphysical illogic.

Specifically, after admitting the validity of all the criticisms directed at the spurious proofs of Your existence, Küng chooses to dismiss the criticism with a cliché: "There is still food for thought."[36] He then goes on to "assume a first cause of all,"[37] "a connection between meaning (of life) and end,"[38] and a "trusting faith that to any idea of a perfect being there does also correspond a reality."[39] Küng asks that we first commit to You; then the rationality of the belief will become clear: "It is not in advance—in virtue of a proof or demonstration—but only when I confidently commit myself to it, that reality lays upon us its primary goal, deepest support, its ultimate good."[40]

If I first "commit" I've just corrupted reason into rationalization. In the final analysis, Küng relies on faith alone. His use of the phrase "reasoned faith" is a contradiction in terms, as I've shown earlier. He admits as much when he asks us to "take a risk" (like Pascal's gamble).

And since all humans are obviously not so foolish or intellectually dishonest as to make this leap of faith, he attempts to avoid confrontation with the rational nontheist by stating that faith is a "gift" that can't simply be willed. This, too, is an empty assertion that theists have hid behind for ages. I've heard it repeated with a condescending air from my most intellectually lethargic acquaintances—those who haven't read the works of a single major non-Christian philosopher. "Poor Joe. You live in the darkness. We will pray that God will send you the grace necessary to believe.

G: Now don't get hysterical. I think you are missing the point here. Küng is following a line of argument developed by Immanuel Kant. Kant asserted that man needed the concept of God to have a ground of certainty with which to confront the capricious fortunes of life and provide a sense of purpose in an otherwise meaningless cosmos. Without this purpose and meaning to life, there is no basis for morality. As Kant writes, "we must assume a moral world cause (an author of the world) in order to set before ourselves a final purpose consistently with the moral law, and insofar as the latter is necessary so far . . . the former must be necessarily admitted, i.e., we must admit there is a God."[41]

Küng also follows Kant's reasoning a step further and shows how the concept of the immortality of the soul is necessary to justify morality.[42]

J: Let's take this last point first. Kant alleged that "the achievement of the highest good in the world is the necessary object of a will determinable by the moral law."[43] And further, that this end "can be found only in an endless progress to that complete fitness," which is possible only under "the presumption of an infinitely enduring existence."[44]

In Kant's argument, the first statement is a groundless assertion: we have no reason to suppose that human "will" (a vague concept in itself) is anything much different than any other animal's, that is, the desire to survive, procreate, and be happy (which at the most basic level is simply the avoidance of pain). Kant's second statement is simply an unwarranted assumption. There is no reason to assume that achievement of an end will occur given even an infinite amount of time. More important, simply having an object, happiness or "the highest good," is no guarantee that it was meant to be obtainable. Hence, Kant doesn't offer a logical argument but just so much wishful thinking.

Now let's return to Kant's earlier supposition, that human belief in immortality is a necessary incentive for moral behavior. We have already seen how belief in immortality of the soul can lead to the most horrible atrocities. Those who truly believe in immortality of the soul are much more willing to die—and kill others—in defense of their beliefs. Kant also says, in effect, that there would be no right or wrong unless You existed. Right?

G: Correct.

J: Then right and wrong are simply whatever You say they are. Therefore, for You there is no difference between right and wrong, and the statement "God is good" becomes meaningless. On the other hand, if we say "God is good," then we are judging Your actions and laws by criteria that supersede You or at least exists independently of You. See the morass into which Kant's logic falls? Morality would simply be obedience to a Grand Commissar whom we call God. He commands, we obey. You become the ultimate "Big Brother." In reality, belief in You doesn't determine morality, nor does belief in morality lead to belief in You. Rather, in the final analysis, humankind's moral beliefs are determined by their desire to survive and be happy. It is only after making this determination that these moral qualities or characteristics of the "good" are attributed to You. As Joseph Campbell explains, God is a metaphor for human aspirations.

G: So you don't agree with the great Russian novelist Dostoyevsky that without Me all is permitted. Isn't it obvious that without Me all life, the entire cosmos, is devoid of meaning? And doesn't the thought of a meaningless existence drive a person to despair? Why even bother to live if life has no purpose?

J: You are sounding like Rosencrantz and Guildenstern again. You are making the same mistake as many theologians who fail to distinguish between the meaning or purpose of life in general, and the purpose of an individual's life. It is true, but wholly irrelevant, that life, in the general collective sense, has no purpose because there is no overall scheme or "Divine Plan." It doesn't follow, however, that individuals cannot have a purpose, an aim or goal to their lives. It is pointless to apply a cosmic perspective to an individual life. Even if all human endeavors will ultimately end billions of years hence with cosmic dispersion or collapse, what is relevant is that I can do things today that will ensure greater security, pleasure, and happiness for me tomorrow.

G: Sounds incredibly egocentric and selfish.

J: No more so than the desire for personal salvation regardless of the fate of others. Furthermore, truly enlightened self-interest requires that we help those we love and treat others fairly. There is little personal security or happiness to be found in a world where everyone acts on caprice. But that discussion is the subject for another discussion. The point I wish to make here is that as long as human beings have desires and emotions, they will have ambitions and goals and, therefore, their lives have meaning—to themselves.

G: I think Küng is exploring a more profound concept with his use of the term "meaningfulness." Küng seeks to show that without Me there is no explanation for reality: "Atheism cannot suggest any condition for the possibility of uncertain reality."[45] But humans feel a strong need to understand how reality came to be and that it has a purpose; humans "would like to know of a primary ground, a deepest support of reality."[46]

J: So far I completely agree with You. So would Ludwig Feuerbach, who recognized this deeply ingrained wish of most humans. But as the song goes, "you can't always get what you want."

G: Küng urges that persons take a risk and "by the practice of blindly trusting God's reality, despite all temptations to doubt, man experiences the reasonableness of his trust."[47]

J: Here we again part company. Like William James, Küng argues that by suppressing all doubts and practicing an irrational credulity, people will feel better and this feeling justifies belief in God. This is the "indirect verification" proposed by Küng. What shameful intellectual dishonesty! What a cowardly way of trying to justify one's own life purpose. Later in his book, Küng admits that only man can give meaning to the cosmos,[48] not the other way around. Küng's subordination of reason to feeling is as dishonest as a person who rationalizes any other vice simply because "it feels right."

G: How dare you question the intellectual honesty of a man like Hans Küng who has devoted his life to pursuit of the truth!

J: Like all theologians, he has devoted his life to defending an *a priori* belief—a world view he was conditioned to believe at his mother's knee. Now he has invested so much of his life in the study of this metaphysical claptrap he can't simply throw it all over; he must bury his doubts with more rationalizations. The man's subterfuge shows through when he makes statements like "the naive anthropomorphic God is obsolete" and "the rationalistic—deistic idea is obsolete."[49]

G: I thought you would agree with those statements.

J: I object to his use of the word "obsolete." It implies that the anthropomorphic concept of God was once true, or simply in need of a little refinement. This is merely an attempt on Küng's part to avoid the admission that the prior conceptions of God were simply archaic myths. If he were more intellectually honest, it might cause his audience to question why they should believe his latest attempt to salvage the fantasy. But retelling the Bible stories in modern idiom does not make a truth out of falsehood.

In a way, I shouldn't blame Küng; there is not much work in this world for an atheistic theologian. And lacking the proper psychological support system outside of religion, he would be as lost as the Vietnam veterans were when they discovered that the "truth" for which they were prepared to lay down their lives was questionable at best. At least he is not as intellectually dishonest as Josh McDowell, who falsely claims that he was a skeptic won over to Christianity by the strength of the evidence. But both men have the one thing in common that should make anyone suspicious of their intellectual integrity. They both are dependent for their livelihood—and their public adoration—on their belief in You.

G: As contrasted to you, I suppose.

J: Right! Being a nontheist is not an easy row to hoe in our present culture. Moreover, I can confess to having once been a true believer of the first order. It was a painful experience to have to learn to live with reality, but the weight of the evidence . . .

G: . . . and a naturally rebellious disposition . . .

J: . . . necessitated that I alter my convictions. However, once I kicked the habit of psychological dependency I found a new pride and joy in being able to live without that crutch of delusion.

G: Aren't you growing weary of this charade?

J: Not in the least. I find the pursuit of truth fascinating, although I do get discouraged knowing that I'm a member of such a small minority, at least in this country.

G: What if, in the final analysis, you are proven completely wrong?

J: Only a fool doesn't admit the possibility of error. It's a risk any intellectual endeavor must be prepared to take. If verifiable evidence is ever offered to support the belief in a god or gods, I'll be happy to reconsider my position. After all, who would risk going to a hell to maintain a position? However, there is little danger of that since I've shown that all the so-called proofs of Your existence are fallacious and actually assume the very proposition that they set out to demonstrate. Hence, all of the so-called proofs of Your existence can be dismissed as disingenuous attempts to rationalize preconceived beliefs.

G: Perhaps proof is too strong a word. I think that most modern theologians would agree with the philosopher Richard Swinburne that there is no good deductive argument for the existence of God.[50] Since I transcend nature, it would be impossible to develop a proof of My existence from the evidence of nature. But Swinburne shows that there is a significant probability that I exist.

J: Would you like to present his argument?

G: Well, in the first place, do you agree that there are many theories such as Einstein's theory of relativity, that are useful to explain phenomena even though the theory is unproved?

J: But if there is no proof, no empirical verification, they still are considered only theories. The scientist will at best consider them to be possibly true, but will suspend judgment pending further verification. For example, it is only recently that tests could be designed to provide physical verification of Einstein's theories regarding the relativity of time. However, the theory of relativity is still only tentatively held to be true pending additional evidence.

G: I can accept that. However, in the case where there are alternative explanations of phenomena, none of which can be verified, it is fair to accept unverified premises that make the conclusion probable. Swinburne calls this form of argument a P–inductive argument. He then goes a step further and says that there could be a C–inductive argument where the premises only add to the probability of the conclusion. Swinburne believes that a number of good C–inductive arguments add up to a P–inductive argument.[51]

J: As I understand it, Swinburne tries to use Bayes's theorem, which simply says that if we have the two arguments that employ the same background knowledge, we should accept the theory which is supported by premises with a greater probability of being correct.

G: That's right. Swinburne applies Bayes's theorem to show that there is a greater probability that the universe exists if we suppose that I am the cause than that it would exist if there were no God. In other words, his argument runs:

—The universe exists.

—There must be an explanation for its existence.

—Science admits that it has none.

—If there is no scientific explanation there might be a personal explanation. Swinburne explains that a personal explanation involves the intentions of an agent.

—God might be such a personal an explanation.[52]

J: Let's stop there a second. Swinburne explains that there are three criteria for judging the adequacy of a hypothesis:

—Predictive Power: Utilizing this hypothesis can we predict the outcome of an event and then validate that prediction?

—Prior Probability: Does it conform to known laws of nature such that we could expect its occurrence?

—Simplicity: Does it require fewer additional hypotheses to explain its action as a causal factor?[53]

Swinburne admits that the predictive power of the hypothesis that You exist is low. I would argue it is nil since any number of worlds could have been created by a God as defined by Swinburne.

G: Swinburne also confesses that the prior probability of My existence is low, but feels it is higher than the prior probability that the world exists.

J: However, we know that the world exists and there is no reason for believing that it has not always existed in one form or another. On the other hand, if there was a time during which it did not exist, even in the state of a physical singularity, then it would not exist now, since we have no evidence or reason to support the notion that something can come from nothing. So to speak of prior probability of the universe existing is metaphysical nonsense.

The other effort Swinburne makes to bolster his hypothesis that You must exist is to argue that the probability that human life would have arisen by chance is infinitesimal. However, as I explained earlier, chaos theory demonstrates convincingly that complex phenomena will arise from randomness, and given that matter has certain properties, the universe never had complete randomness in the first place. And, as David Hume explained, if the universe is either spatially infinite or temporally eternal (or there are many universes, which amounts to the same thing), sooner or later human life was bound to evolve, indeed many times.

Failing to build support for his hypothesis that You exist by virtue of its predictive power or prior probability, Swinburne relies heavily on the notion that his hypothesis is simple.

G: You support the Principle of Parsimony: "Entities are not to be multiplied beyond necessity." Therefore, all other things being equal, a causal explanation that rests upon one assumption is more probable than an explanation that requires many assumptions. And the simple assumption that I exist suffices to explain all that we know about the existence of the universe.

J: Not so fast. While it is true that "God" is conceptually simple in a metaphysical sense, as an explanatory hypothesis, it requires a host of unsubstantiated and unjustified additional hypotheses. Just look at all the assumptions posited in Swinburne's argument. The first is that the universe did not always exist. As I have shown, even assuming that the present form of the universe is the result of the Big Bang, there is no reason to suppose that the universe did not always exist in some form. In other words, we have no reason to suppose that the universe is either spatially or temporally limited.

Second, in assuming a personal explanation Swinburne has to infer the intentions of a Being which is unlike any being of which we have experience.

Third, he has to assume that this being has certain capacities to bring its intentions about by nonphysical means of which we have no experience.

Fourth, even if Swinburne could pull all this off, at best he has an intrinsically unverifiable hypothesis. He is piling assumption upon assumption. Moreover, in trying to establish the potential probability of Your existence, Swinburne must deal with each of the arguments we have already discussed. In refusing to accept the existence of the world as a brute fact needing no further explanation, Swinburne is making the same assumption as primitive humans who, when confronted by the amazing events of nature which they could not understand in any other way, assumed that there must be a powerful being(s) responsible for them.

As humankind became more sophisticated and explained the phenomena one by one, the need to posit a creative God declined in scientific terms but not, as we shall see later, as a psychological need for many persons. Eventually there are only two phenomena that humans still have trouble explaining: the process of thought and the origins of the universe. Contrary to Swinburne's belief, the latter does not require explanation and we are getting closer everyday to explaining how the mind works. We know it has an electrochemical basis and that the nature of thoughts can be altered by changing the chemistry of the brain (for example, through mind-altering drugs).

G: Swinburne preserves the possibility of My existence by maintaining the dualism of mind and brain and assuming that I will that mental states correlate with brain states, but that brain states do not cause mental states.

J: Another groundless assumption necessary to save a role for You in explaining the physical world. It's hardly conducive to the simplicity of a theistic explanation. Swinburne runs into a host of additional problems: In trying to avoid the problem of what caused You, he has to submit that You are the cause of Your own being. But this is a different concept of cause than we normally think of when we use the word "cause." We have no experience with anything that causes itself, so there is no reason to believe that such a thing exists. Of course this doesn't prove that such a thing could not exist, but it is far simpler to conceptualize something as being uncaused, i.e., always existing. And there is no reason why this could not be true of the universe.

G: In saying that I am the cause of My being, Swinburne means that I am the personal cause, not a scientific cause. In other words I intend My own being. An impersonal universe cannot have an intention.

J: I should end the discussion on that note. It is such a patently obvious metaphysical construct devoid of any reference to known reality as to make all meaningful discussion impossible. We have come full circle to the ontological argument of necessary beings whose existence implies their essence. A clever logical construct but of no utility in explaining the physical world.

G: Swinburne admits that all his arguments add up to a very low possibility for My existence. But the odds are increased by admitting the evidence of religious experience. Not being as cynical as you, Swinburne proposes a "Principle of Credulity": "In the absence of special considerations, all religious experiences ought to be taken by their subjects as genuine,"[54] and a "Principle of Testimony": "the experiences of others are (probably) as they report them."[55] After all, most of our day-to-day involvement with other persons is based upon believing their statements without demanding proof. In fact, all social interaction would grind to a halt if we challenged every statement of every person. Therefore, since many persons have experienced Me, we should accept their testimony as evidence of My existence.

J: Is Swinburne serious? Of course as a practical matter we don't always demand proof for statements that are believable *prima facie,* or are unimportant. But as I have already explained, we certainly do demand evidence to back up unusual claims, and extraordinary claims require extraordinary evidence. Following the principles of Swinburne, we would accept the claims for UFOs, psychics, and faith healers—we would be susceptible to every con artist that came along. Indeed, many true believers are that gullible, as I showed in the first chapter.

Not only should we be suspicious of the outrageous claims of others, we should be suspicious of our own unusual experiences as well. Most of us have had some form of hallucinogenic experience in our lifetime. Most have also experienced extreme euphoria, remorse or ecstacy. There is no reason to suppose that such experiences have a supernatural origin. They might have been caused by a viral infection, hormonal changes, physical exhaustion, extraordinary psychological stress, or a dozen other natural causes.

If the probability of Your existence turns on the evidence from religious experience, Swinburne's argument falls flat on its face. I have already shown in chapter 11 that personal experience is insufficient evidence to support a claim. It can be deliberately falsified, culturally conditioned, the result of various psychological or physical illnesses, hypnogogic and hypnopompic events, or a deep emotional experience. If the best that modern theologians can come up with for Your existence after two thousand years of trying is that religious experience should bolster an argument that the probability of Your existence is greater than zero, we can begin to appreciate how weak their position is.

14

Contradictions in the Concept of God: Making Metaphysical Stones Too Heavy to Lift

If God is will, what is ill?

—Archibald MacLeish

J: So much for the proofs of Your existence. Now, let's go a step further and see how the very concept of God is so fraught with contradictions as to make it at best unintelligible and, at worst, a concept whose existence is as logically impossible as a square circle.

G: This ought to be amusing. Does a little sleight of hand go with this performance?

J: Not at all. I perform with my sleeves rolled up. To begin with, what are Your attributes?

G: Since modesty is not becoming, I agree with the theologians that, by definition, I am the creator of all things, I am all good, all powerful (omnipotent), all knowing (omniscient), and unchanging (immutable), a perfect being, both immanent and transcendent.

J: You are still too humble. The National Catholic Almanac lists twenty-three attributes. But you hit on the most significant. Let's examine some of them. To begin with, as I've already touched upon, the seemingly unambiguous statement that You are good is a huge stumbling block.

G: What are you talking about? Without Me how would humans even know what good is?

J: I'm afraid You've got it backwards again. It's the classic theological fallacy. As Smith explains, man must have a prior concept of good to even postulate that You are good. If anything You do is good simply because You do it, it is ridiculous to discuss Your moral nature. How could theists today know You from the Devil? Would You have been equally good if instead of ordering Abraham to spare his son Isaac, You ordered him to go ahead and sacrifice the boy?

G: Such a question would never have occurred to the ancient Israelites.

J: Agreed. Why did they chose to worship Yahweh rather than Baal? Because they thought Yahweh was good and Baal was not?

G: They preferred Me over Baal because I could help them, and the false god, Baal, could not.

J: Or at least so they imagined. But I agree that for the ancient Hebrews, the question of whether You were good was irrelevant; it was assumed that since You were in charge You could do whatever You wanted. It was a simple case of might makes right. You were the source of all good and all evil: "I form the light and create darkness; I make peace and create evil: I the Lord do all these things" (Isa. 45:7). For the Israelites, worshiping Yahweh was akin to buying protection from the most powerful mob boss. The primary motivation is fear (and, as I will later show, the need to establish a national identity requires a "nationalized" god).

It is fascinating to note how the concept of what constituted a "good" God evolved with the civilizing of humans. From the God who was commanding the ancient Israelites to slaughter women and children to the modern-day concept of Jesus, who primarily stands for love with little thought of retribution, we can see how the concept of "good" has evolved with humankind and, as a consequence, forced man to redefine his concept of God.

The importance of this evolution cannot be overemphasized. The alternative was to retain a concept developed by a primitive and savage people. Yet some theologians would like to revive that concept to avoid the obvious metaphysical problems of an evolving God. Søren Kierkegaard praises Abraham as a pious man because he was prepared to kill to carry out what he thought was Your command. For Kierkegaard, serving You (or what one imagines to be Your word) is acting beyond all consideration of good and evil: "the teleological suspension of the ethical."[1] I shudder when I read Kierkegaard proclaiming: "One acts by virtue of the absurd."[2] The Ayatollah Khomeini demonstrated only too vividly what happens when a fanatic acts on what he believes to be a divine command.

Luckily, modern society, for the most part, heeds the dictum of the philosophers Ludwig Feuerbach and John Dewey to follow "the ethical suspension of the theological."[3] In other words, good has been defined, to an increasingly greater extent, as that which benefits humankind regardless of theological or religious imperatives to the contrary. The concept of God has benefited accordingly, since it has been redefined to conform to newer, more rationally derived values.

The other horn of the dilemma of positing You as all good is accounting for evil in the world. In his play *J.B.*, Archibald MacLeish puts the contradiction in verse:

> If God is God He is not good,
> If God is good, he is not God,
> Take the even, take the odd,
> I would not sleep here if I could,
> Except for the little green leaves in the wood,
> And the wind on the water.[4]

G: I am not amused. The concepts of good and evil and their relationship to Me cannot be analyzed by a jingle.

J: Granted. Let's take a minute to explore the problem of evil a little further. In so doing, maybe we can ascertain the relationship that both good and evil must necessarily bear to the concept of God.

G: You mean My reality.

J: Your reality? Isn't that what we are trying to ascertain?

G: It is all quite apparent to Me.

J: Well being a mere mortal, I do not find it quite so self-evident, so forgive me as I struggle on.

G: Forgiveness is My specialty.

J: Turning to the subject of evil, there are two kinds to be considered: physical evil and moral evil. Physical evil involves such things as serious deprivation (for example, a child born with spina bifida, muscular dystrophy, or blindness), pain, disease, and natural calamities (such as earthquakes and floods). Now, how do you reconcile these evils with the concept of a good God?

G: Did you ever think that what you call evil is viewed as such only because of your narrow perspective; that apparent evil may actually be good when viewed in the context of all of creation—the so-called Divine Plan? Of course, your paltry mind doesn't see this; only the Creator can view events from that perspective. Furthermore, if you could see things from My perspective, you would realize that I am able to draw good out of every apparent evil. As Küng expressed it so well, "Since God in his passage through history takes all wretchedness on himself, evil, the negative in world history, is from the outset encompassed by the good."[5]

J: What a perfect example of pretty prose concealing utter nonsense.

Küng simply tries to define evil away by saying that you mysteriously make it all right. Small comfort to the sufferer! As to your proposition that evil is simply a matter of perspective, I think Ernest Nagel refuted that neatly:

> It's unsupported speculation to suppose that whatever is evil in a finite perspective is good from the purported perspective of totality. For the argument can be turned around; what we judge to be good is a good only because it is viewed in isolation, when it is viewed in proper perspective, and in relation to the entire scheme of things, it is an evil."[6]

G: Perhaps what you perceive as evil is only a delusion. Correct the delusion and all evil disappears.

J: That's the line of a two-bit circuit preacher or Christian Scientist. Aside from the fact that there is no evidence to support the proposition that pain is only a delusion, the delusion itself would be a twofold evil: first, because You permit the deception, which would be tantamount to a Divine lie, and second, because this delusion results in very real pain. Pain and suffering, due to whatever cause, are evils.

G: Not necessarily. There are many reasons which could necessitate pain which might result in good rather than evil. It can even be argued that physical good requires physical evil—pain, if you will—if it is to exist at all. Just as a mountain cannot exist without a valley, or a top without a bottom, it is only by contrast to something you call evil that you recognize the state of affairs you call good. Recall the words of John Gardner's priest in his book *Grendel:* "Such is His mystery; that beauty requires contrast and that discord is fundamental to the new creation of feeling."[7]

J: Contrast is indeed necessary for pleasure, but the contrast does not require pain. It can involve different degrees of happiness. Pleasure can exist without pain. I don't have to taste or smell something very disagreeable to appreciate something exquisite. A mountain can stand out from a plain. In other words, the extraordinary can be appreciated from the merely ordinary. Even if some physical evil were needed to appreciate the physical good, a thimbleful would suffice, rather than the oceans of pain we see around us. All it takes is a cold to appreciate good health; typhoid fever is unnecessary, to say the least.

G: Without pain people would not know if something is wrong with their bodies. Pain is an essential signal that corrective action needs to be taken.

J: An indication, for example, that the body is being attacked by a disease.

G: Exactly.

J: But the disease itself is an evil that You permit. And often a disease strikes without pain, such as many types of cancer, until it is too late for a cure. Moreover, other kinds of signals could have been created to warn that something is amiss without pain.

G: Possibly, but certain types of pain, such as those caused by natural calamities, may serve as a warning to the rest of humankind to behave morally or else risk incurring My wrath. Then if they don't listen, pain is Divine retribution for their sins.

J: Shades of the Moral Majority! If that is the purpose of natural calamities, they have been terribly ineffective. We've had them for thousands of years and I don't see humankind behaving much better as a result. In fact, it is not unusual to see looting and anarchy follow a major calamity such as an earthquake or flood. And how do you justify punishing innocent children in the name of Divine retribution? What man or woman would not consider it a monstrous miscarriage of justice if a court ordered the child of a murderer put to death for the deeds of his father? No, the warning and retribution arguments are a crude attempt to rationalize the inevitability of natural calamities, which, anyone can see, continue to occur regardless of the behavior of the local populace.

For centuries China had periodic floods that killed tens of thousands of people each time, and brought starvation and disease to thousands more. Now, the Chinese have built dams and a system of flood control to avoid such devastation. In so doing are they thwarting Your will? Interfering with Your Divine retribution? Based on Your argument, it would seem so. But who but the most absurd fanatic would hold that position?

G: Well, I admit that that argument has pretty much been dropped in favor of the more modern one that, in creating the world, I did so by establishing certain properties of matter—laws of nature—which result in certain events that may have negative effects with regard to a specific individual. However, the avoidance of those negatively perceived impacts would require constant Divine intervention.

J: Or the creation of a different sort of universe. Why not? You are not omnipotent (all powerful) if You cannot create a universe free of pain.

G: But it's not that I couldn't. It is that I wouldn't, because the universe is better with evil. It can provide a means to greater good. You have heard or read of occasions when people have been stimulated to perform unselfish and heroic acts in overcoming evil. As an example, the philosopher John Donnelly suggests, "the infant suffering from some currently incurable physiological ailment (e.g., cystic fibrosis, sickle cell anemia, etc.) and his guardian could be thankful for his/her affliction which enables them to develop traits of character and mental sets not so readily fostered in a healthy body or nontragic situation."[8]

J: Following that logic, maybe we should stop trying to avoid evil. Perhaps we should not try to stamp out disease and birth defects, and not warn people of impending hurricanes or volcanic eruptions. Maybe we should inflict children with diseases to help them develop noble character. See how silly that sounds? It is the same argument used by parents who would beat their children to teach them Christian love. Or, turning Your argument around: if evil stimulates good, maybe we should avoid doing good for fear it would stimulate evil. That also sounds pretty ridiculous. It's obvious to me, at least, that physical evil cannot be justified by moral good. There have been tyrannical despots throughout the ages who tortured and murdered their subjects. Based on Donnelly's logic that good may come from evil, we are wrong to condemn them. The madman Caligula becomes a saint and the physician Hippocrates becomes a sinner. This is the utter nonsense one must conclude from that absurd position.

G: Let me try another tack. What holds true for a creature does not hold true for a god. Since all is created by Me, I have the right to dispose of My creatures as I think best. Of course, what I do is always in their best interests. Again I say, with your paltry mind you cannot see what is best and so you are in no position to judge My actions. Can children judge the actions of their father? Doesn't a child feel that his parents are mean and unfair when they make him take medicine or go to bed?

J: Poor analogy. A young child is not yet rational. An adult supposedly is. If humans are incapable of rationally assessing whether Your effects are good or bad, on what basis can we assume that You are good? George Smith proposes, "If we are incorrect in calling natural disaster, diseases and other phenomena evil, then man is incapable of distinguishing good from evil."[9] The freethinker Robert Ingersoll also questioned why a good God would create the deformed and helpless, the criminal, the idiot, and the insane.

I've studied the two standard replies and they simply do not stand up to a moment's reflection. The first reply is that physical evil is only deprivation, as if disease is simply not having health. This makes no more sense than to say that health is simply deprivation of disease. Moreover, it does not excuse a "good" God who permits this deprivation. The second stock reply is that Your ways are inscrutable. As I've showed before, an unknowable God is a meaningless concept devoid of content, since nothing more can be said of that which is unknowable. We might as well say, "something exists, but we know not what, how, why or what relationship it has, if any, to us."

No, if I consider all the physical evil I see in this world, it would make more sense to me to say that You are malevolent to the extreme, or at least deserving of Vonnegut's title, "God the Utterly Indifferent." And if I honestly believed there existed the God of the Old Testament: a god who demanded human sacrifice, killed children in retribution for crimes of their elders, ordered genocide, gave His supplicants food and then turned it into poison; or the God of the New Testament: a god who condemned ignorant, weak, suffering people to eternal damnation for not believing in a carpenter who claimed to be Your Son, I would feel obligated to do all in my insignificant power to oppose such a monstrous being.

I would agree with the father of J. S. Mill who, after considering the belief that God created hell, told his famous son, "it seemed as if mankind had gone on adding trait after trait 'til they reached the most perfect conception of wickedness which the human mind can devise, and have called this God, prostrated themselves before it."[10]

G: Simply hyperbole and invective spewed forth by a mean mind.

J: Is it? Let's consider the biblical God in a nutshell. Kurt Baier points out the inherent evil and absurdity of such a God when he wonders,

> why an omnipotent, omniscient and all-good God should create such a universe and such a man, but also why, foreseeing every move of the feeble, weak-willed, ignorant, and covetous creature to be created, He should nevertheless have created him and, having done so, should be incensed and outraged by man's sin, and why He should deem it necessary to sacrifice His own son on the cross to atone for this sin which was, after all, only a disobedience of one of his commands, and why this atonement and consequent redemption could not have been followed by man's return to paradise— particularly of those innocent children who had not yet sinned— and why, on Judgment Day, this merciful God should condemn some to eternal torment."[11]

The horticulturist Luther Burbank also evaluated the logic of this concept of God: "The idea that a good God would send people to a burning hell is utterly damnable to me—the raving of insanity, superstition gone to seed."[12]

G: In your biased evaluation of My goodness, you ignore completely the concept of Divine Justice. You would have no retribution for the sins of humans. Even more important, in your discussion of suffering humanity you have completely ignored the fact that much of the evil in this world is the work of man, not Me. Wars, greed, lust for power— these human vices are the root of most of the suffering in the world.

J: I was coming to that. The second type of evil includes the crimes of humankind such as war, exploitation, bigotry, etc., commonly called moral evil. Ingersoll rightly questioned who must bear ultimate responsibility for the existence of moral evil. Even if not committed directly by You, it's at least permitted by You and, "would a decent man having the power to prevent it allow his enemies to torture and burn his friends?"[13]

The existence of moral evil presents another set of contradictions for the concept of God. For either:

(a) You know evil will be committed by the type of creature You made and are powerless to prevent it, in which case You are not omnipotent (all-powerful), or

(b) You did not know that the creature You made would commit evil, in which case You are not omniscient (all knowing), or

(c) You know that the creature You made would commit evil but willed it so, in which case You are not good.

If any of the three cases exist, You are somehow limited and, hence, by definition not who You say You are. It is easier to believe the Manichaean myth that humans were created by Satan.

G: You state a false premise. Free will alone justifies moral evil. It is obvious that a world in which humans exercise free will is better than a universe in which people are mere robots, always doing good because they are programmed to do so. The gift of free choice necessarily implies the ability to choose evil.

J: That assumes that free will and absolute goodness are logically incompatible. If that is so, how can it be asserted that God possesses both?

G: I have the absolute knowledge necessary to always choose good.

J: That response presents two problems. First, if God chooses between good and evil, it means that good and evil exist outside of God. You can't choose something You already are. Good, then, becomes merely an adjective describing Your actions rather than a noun predicating Your essense. Second, You imply that people commit evil only out of ignorance. While not the only reason, ignorance is certainly one reason. But then how do You justify punishing somebody who committed an evil act only out of ignorance? Furthermore, since humankind's power of decision only involves fairly narrow, finite choices, why could not God give people significant knowledge so that they might always choose rightly?

G: Swinburne argues that I create humans in a state of ignorance so that the acquisition of knowledge is through their choice.[14]

J: Reviewing the history of humankind, it is difficult to see how creating humankind in ignorance could ever be considered good. Knowledge has come with an incredible amount of suffering. It is absurd to think that humankind would not have been better off if we had been created with more knowledge.

Nor is it at all clear what Swinburne means when he says that people "are free to choose knowledge." To decide to choose knowledge would require prior knowledge. It is doubtful that the cavemen sat around one day and decided to choose knowledge. They did not choose to discover fire. Rather, they simply discovered the utility of fire for cooking and heating. Therefore, it should come as no surprise that humankind first used fire to improve their own lives and in later generations used its known destructive power to kill their enemies. It is a logical response that can be explained in purely biological and environmental terms without resort even to the assumption of free will, let alone theistic design.

G: Even if men had the knowledge to choose what is good, it would not be enough; a person must possess good will as well. I provide that, in the form of Divine Grace, but it can be freely rejected.

J: Divine Grace is just another invention of theologians trying to wiggle out of yet another logical conundrum. I have never yet found a person who could adequately define this mysterious "grace," let alone say how it affects human actions. The relevant point is, if You are all-powerful, You could make the incentive to do good powerful enough that people would always choose good. You seem to do just the opposite. By allowing physical evils, You produce an environment not only conducive to, but actually instrumental in, generating evil.

G: Why blame Me for all this evil? Doesn't the Devil deserve some of the blame?

J: Ah yes, the Devil—the evil spirit created by religions to absolve God from culpability in the commitment of evil. But, it turns out that the proposed existence of Satan is even more difficult to prove and adds more contradiction than it attempts to resolve. It is easy to see how early humans sought to simplify things by hypothesizing one force for good and another for evil. However, if Your will is the creative and sustaining force behind all that is, You become responsible for the emergence and continued existence of the Devil as the ancient Israelites believed. Mani, the father of Manichaeism, tried to avoid this obvious and damning conclusion by contending that Satan was produced, not by You, but by the mysterious forces of Darkness. Sounds like something out of the *Lord of the Rings* novel. We cannot escape the dilemma of MacLeish: "If God is will, what is ill?"

Both H. J. McCloskey[15] and Antony Flew[16] have written excellent essays on the problem of God and evil. I see no reason to repeat all their skillful argumentation here. Let me simply note the observation of Antony Flew: "There is no contradiction in speaking of a world in which there are always antecedent conditions of all human action sufficient to ensure that agents always will as a matter of fact freely choose right."[17] Since You chose not to make this type of universe, You willed evil; such a God cannot be considered good.

G: One explanation is offered by Swinborne: "Evil is necessary if agents are to have knowledge of how to bring about evil or prevent its occurrence, knowledge which they must have if they are to have a genuine choice between bringing about evil and bringing about good."[18]

J: So, based on Swinburne's logic, we ought to be grateful for disease and natural disasters because without them humankind would not know how to bring about good, such as the elimination of a disease. Apparently the evil that humans do to each other would not be sufficient to learn about good and evil. We must see the evil brought about by an earthquake. What utter nonsense. Even Swinburne is embarrassed by his argument and admits that even if some evil were useful, it hardly explains the great number of natural calamities that have befallen humankind over the centuries.

G: You are still making the assumption that you can judge My action by the same rules with which you judge human ones. But as the cause of all creation I am responsible only to Myself for those rights I have freely granted.

J: What a blatant rationalization! As I said in the beginning of this discussion, it is tantamount to saying that whatever You do is good by definition. The word "good" then loses all moral meaning other then "Good is what God does"! If I create a Frankenstein (not completely absurd in this world of cloning and genetic engineering), does it give me the right to abuse and torment the poor creature? Such a semantic inversion of the word "good" is also necessary to reconcile the notion of a good God with the doctrine of hell, since hell is a place of punishment for humans who have committed actions You willed.

G: Aren't you again confusing willing and permitting? Knowledge of an event is not the cause of that event.

J: When knowledge is coupled with omnipotence it becomes a cause. Belief that You are the final cause of all things results in the two becoming indistinguishable. Thomas Aquinas and others have admitted that the logical implication of an all-knowing and all-powerful God is predestination: "An eternal determination on the part of God to bring a creature infallibly to salvation."[19] But if some persons are eternally determined for salvation others must be determined for eternal damnation. How "free" is a person who from the moment of creation was destined for hell? What monster would create a being knowing that the poor person would fail, and then plan eternal suffering by way of punishment? The excuse offered by Aquinas is that You did not cause certain people to sin. Apparently, for the theologian, justice is allowing some people to fall into sin while sparing others that little inconvenience.[20]

If You are all-powerful, as You are usually defined, could You not create the deterministic world described by Flew, where "antecedent conditions [exist] sufficient to ensure that agents will act in particular ways, not conditions which make such action in a fundamental sense inevitable"?[21] For example, in the Christian concept of heaven, "souls" are supposed to retain free will while having no desire or purpose to do evil. What then is the purpose of placing weak, ignorant men on earth in an environment of temptation where many must certainly fail?

G: But heaven is the reward earned by passing the test of earthly life.

J: What kind of monstrous game is that? If You already have perfect knowledge of who is going to fail the test, why create those who will fail? Theologians have dealt with this problem for over two thousand years and are no closer to a resolution of the obvious contradiction of a good God who permits moral and physical evil. Either whatever You do is good by definition, placing Your actions out of the normative judgment of man; or in making the determination that You are good we are applying a normative standard which exists outside of You. In the first case, the statement is meaningless, since whatever You do is simply good by definition. In the latter case You are no longer the determinant of right and wrong, but subject to a higher standard set by humans. Furthermore, using human standards, and viewing Your alleged creations and actions, we must conclude that, at best, You are not good.

Theologians like Küng try to sidestep this issue with obtuse prose. They say that only You give meaning to ultimate reality, which includes suffering. But in a more honest moment, Küng admits, "suffering, doubting, despairing man finds an ultimate support only in the forthright admission of his incapacity to solve the riddle of suffering and evil."[22] How someone can find support in admitting he doesn't understand this contradiction is beyond me. However, it has been done for thousands of years. Catholic theologians like to hide behind the word "mystery" and even caution poor laypersons not to think too hard on these subjects for fear that the Devil might seize the opportunity to fill them with doubts. This is the same as saying, "Don't think about these things or you will see the absurd contradictions and down will come the whole metaphysical house of cards."

The concept of God as good would also preclude the idea of mercy. For if Your laws are infinitely good, equitable, and wise, can they ever be too severe? Prayer also becomes absurd. If everything You do is good, why pray to change anything? I ran across one of the latest attempts to wiggle out of this dilemma in the little book by Rabbi Harold S. Kushner, *When Bad Things Happen to Good People*. The author advises that a suffering person should not pray to You to remove his affliction, because that is something even You can't do, but rather to pray for the grace to bear the suffering.

G: I don't like that answer, either. It denies that I am omnipotent.

J: Exactly. And here You also fall into another trap. For if You can answer prayers You are changeable. But by definition You are immutable. Hence, omnipotence and immutability become contradictory attributes.

G: Can't I have the power, but in my infinite wisdom choose not to use it?

J: Sorry. You have no choice in the matter, as You'll run smack into a contradiction with your ability to know all things past, present and future (omniscience). If You have the power to intervene to avoid a foreseeable evil and choose not to do so, then You are certainly not just. Moreover, if You know all things, including the future, with absolute certainty, that very certainty precludes further change. And if further change is impossible, Your power is limited.

G: This is getting rather sticky, isn't it? Wait; suppose I know the future from all eternity. I know, therefore, when something bad is going to happen to someone, or at least they think it is bad when actually it is good because it makes them turn to Me in prayer, and because I know they are going to pray I have predetermined the answer to their prayer. There! I've retained My omniscience, My omnipotence, My good, My mercy and My immutability. Score: God fifteen, love. Your serve.

J: Not bad. Now suppose the sufferer is a child of five or six with meningitis. Never mind that his parents turn to You in prayer, or that You eventually effect a cure, that wouldn't make the child's suffering good for him. It is still an evil relative to the child. No judge would be monstrous enough to torture a child to effect a behavioral change in his parents. Fifteen all.

Besides, every day thousands of children die irrespective of the prayers of their parents. Prayer does not fill the bellies of the thousands of starving Ethiopians. The studies I reviewed on the efficacy of prayer (as discussed in chapter 15) showed no effect, were inconclusive, or, at best, offered some psychological benefits, not unlike New Age nostrums. Thirty to fifteen Joe.

Furthermore, as Feuerbach explained, the notion that prayer has been determined from eternity, even if it were true, still contradicts with Your unchangeableness and unconditionedness; it merely throws the contradiction back into the deceptive distance of the past.[23] Forty to fifteen Joe.

Finally, if all this could be determined from eternity, then all humans are simply puppets with no free will. And without volition all morality becomes meaningless. This is particularly devastating to the fundamental belief of Christianity since, as Smith says, without free will, "the Christian scheme of salvation is a farce since men are predestined to either heaven or hell."[24] Forty-five to fifteen, game to Joe.

G: Wait, I protest. As an omnipotent being, I must be capable of making free agents whose will I don't control.

J: You mean You are an omnipotent being who doesn't always get His own way? Sounds nonsensical to me.

G: But My way is to allow humans some freedom. Look, while watching children at play you can let them have some freedom while still maintaining the power at any given moment to prevent them from harming themselves or one another. You can give freedom while still maintaining ultimate control.

J: Yes, but Your analogy does not describe the unique relationship of a creature who is totally dependent on its creator for every action, every thought, every wish. It comes down to defining free will. Maybe an example would help. Suppose You had before You a thing and you were trying to determine whether it was a human or a robot.

G: As God, I would know.

J: Fine. Pretend for a second You are not God, just another person trying to make a judgment from the evidence. Now, in making this determination You first inspect the thing visually and detect no difference from any other human. So you proceed with a series of tests. You ask it questions and note the responses. You give it instructions and watch it perform. You provide various stimuli such as threats, surprises, entreaties, etc., and observe its reactions. After a few days of these tests You realize that You can predict its behavior and response with 100 percent accuracy, under any conditions. What would You conclude? Was this human or android?

G: Obviously, a robot, if its actions were totally mechanistic.

J: Now, let's look at the situation from Your perspective as God again. If God is all-knowing and all-powerful then all humans are mechanistic. We are all totally determined, since every action is foreseen in advance and either condoned or altered. If, on the other hand, humans are not mechanistic but capable of spontaneous action, then You are neither omniscient nor omnipotent.

G: You are confusing free will with freedom to act. Granting humans the right of the former does not necessarily mean that I grant them the right of the latter.

J: No, of course not, but the problem remains: free will would contradict Your omniscience, and freedom to act would contradict Your omnipotence. George Santayana noted this dilemma: "For if we admit a voluntary creation and omnipresent providence, the acts of men, even of ourselves, are a part of a divine dispensation, our only ultimate friend or enemy. If we invest free will and absolute beginning with ultimate responsibility at many points in time and in many persons, the monotheism . . . gives place to a metaphysical pluralism, in which God, if he is still introduced, is only 'primus inter pares,' and has to live as best he may under a rain of inexplicable incidents and changes in the moral weather."[25]

Swinburne decides to define You in such a way as to preserve human free will, by holding that since You cannot do what is logically impossible, Your omniscience excludes the possiblity of knowing what humans will choose. In other words, we now have a God who knows all things, except the future. A pretty constrained form of omniscince. Obviously, then, if You cannot know the future, You cannot control it. You can only act to change the effects of any human actions after they occur. Again a limitation on Your power.

G: I can live which such limitation. It still leaves Me very powerful and knowledgeable, even if somewhat limited. There is, however, another alternative. If we rule out spontaneity as a possibility (given the law of cause and effect), we deny humans freedom of will but remove the contradiction with an all-knowing and all-powerful god. This is exactly what the Protestant reformer John Calvin was forced to conclude. And, since the evidence of science has demonstrated that there are no spontaneous acts in the universe, it must be concluded that humans cannot logically will or act except from some cause. Therefore, if I admit that in the final analysis, I do possess total control over humans, you will admit of an all-powerful and all-knowing God.

J: Not exactly. All that this would demonstrate is the possibility that such a being could exist without a logical contradiction of these two attributes. Unfortunately, it simply exacerbates the contradiction discussed between these attributes and the attribute that You are good since now only You, and not man, are responsible for all moral as well as physical evil in the world.

G: Let's not take on that subject again.

J: Right. Let's move on to the concept of God as Creator.

G: You have long ago stated your disbelief in the biblical account.

J: Yes. I wish now to demonstrate more fully the problem to which I alluded earlier of the inherent contradiction between a creative God and an all-perfect Being. First, let's listen to what David Hume has to say:

> 'Tis an established maxim both in natural and moral philosophy, that an object, which exists for anytime in its full perfection without producing another is not its [the second object's] sole cause; but is assisted by some other principle, which pushes it from its state of inactivity, and makes it exert that energy, of which it was secretly possessed.[26]

It should be obvious that a perfect Being would be totally complete in itself and have no reason to create. What could induce the act of creation except a want, a need, a desire—all of which would be impossible in a perfect Being. The freethinker Charles Bradlaugh presents an interesting nuance to this argument:

> If the universe owes its existence to God's reason and will, God must, prior to creation, have thought upon the matter until he ultimately decided to create . . . but if creation were wise and good it would never have been delayed while the ultimately wise and good thought about it.[27]

G: Since you have already demonstrated, to your own satisfaction at least, that the universe has always existed, why couldn't My creative activity always have existed? It seems to me—and who should know better than I—that My very nature involves a creative being.

J: I rather like that argument. It does, of course, relegate the biblical account of creation to the status of a poetic metaphor and it still doesn't explain why a perfect Being needs to create. To say it is the nature of such a Being to create is simply an assertion with no necessarily logical or evidential support.

In addition, an almighty, all-knowing God would have no need for miracles. Stanislaw Lem explains that if You are perfect then Your creation must be perfect. Therefore, "either creation is perfect in which case miracles are unnecessary, or miracles are necessary in which case the creation is not perfect."[28] And an imperfect creation implies an imperfect creator.

G: Perhaps I deliberately wanted an imperfect creation, for reasons of My own.

J: Perhaps. Or perhaps You are rationalizing Your own limitations. Let's pass on to the problem of Your immanence, the idea that God *is* all things, or is *in* all things.

G: A lovely thought, appreciated best, perhaps, by the eastern religions and the American Indian.

J: I agree it is a nice thought. I much prefer it to the transcendent God of the Christian churches. Küng and other fuzzy thinkers contend that You are both immanent and transcendent, but such a concept is a self-contradiction, like a square circle. Getting back to the idea of immanence, the freethinker Annie Besant stated her objection very succinctly: "a God who is everywhere, who has no limits, and yet who is not I and who is therefore limited by my personality is a being who is self-contradictory, both limited and not-limited, and such a being cannot exist."[29]

G: Ah, but didn't Annie eventually come to reject all her arguments and believe in me?

J: Sadly, yes. Apparently, she freaked out after meeting Helena Blavatsky and became a Theosophist.* It goes to show that anyone can succumb to irrationality given the right or, perhaps, I should say, wrong circumstances. Regardless of her personal misfortunes, Annie Besant's argument is still valid.

G: Not if we assume that I am all things, and therefore humans are subsumed in the concept of what I am. The mystical body: God is all, all is God.

J: Then humans again lose their status as free agents. That is the pantheistic view of Spinoza and Hegel, which precludes free will; if we are one with You, we can't will differently than Your will. You become responsible for all good and evil. We should not only thank You for

---

*Theosophy was a quasi-religious movement founded by Helena Blavatsky in New York around 1875. It espoused reincarnation and karma and defended Hinduism and Sri Lankan Buddhism.

Mother Teresa, but also curse You for Hitler, Stalin, Khomeini, and every murderer and rapist. On the other hand, if You are not all being then there is something that is not You and You are not "all things"; You are just a part of that commonality of being possessed by all things. If we then define the universe as all that is, You become only part of the universe.

G: So I must be transcendent—another form of being existing outside of nature—hence supernatural.

J: Transcendent. Completely above the world. Outside the range of human experience. Plato would approve. Riechley notes that metaphysical dualism, the belief in distinct material and transcendent levels of existence, has been the defining characteristic of all major religions including Judaism, Christianity and Islam. However, the dilemma is that there would be no way of knowing the purpose of a transcendent God: "No individual and no social group or institution, including the Church, can say with assurance what a transcendent purpose may intend in any particular situation."[30] Furthermore, for those who contend that a transcendent God encompasses all of reality, Reichley asks, if You are identified with the universe, what is left to transcend? We are back to God the Unknowable, God the Meaningless Word.

G: I am not entirely unknowable. You can know of Me through My effects on nature and through personal experiences.

J: I have already shown how unreliable the mystical experience of God is. And to infer You by attempting to use You to explain nature is at best to fall once again victim to the fallacious argument of design. No, I am afraid I will have to agree with Thomas Aquinas on at least this one point: "To know the self-subsistent being [the primary characteristic of a transcendent God] . . . is beyond the natural power of any created intellect."[31]

G: Aquinas is talking about direct knowledge of Me as being. He states, however, that you can know at least that I exist and something of My attributes.

J: I've already shown that Aquinas failed to prove Your existence and that Your alleged attributes are pure speculations, which involve logical contradictions.

G: That is because you are trying to think of My attributes in the same limiting way you think of human characteristics. My attributes are not defining characteristics; they cannot be defined in the first place. The liberal theologian Paul Tillich was on the right track when he said that I had "unlimited [and hence, unlimiting] attributes."

J: It was a clumsy semantic trick to define away a problem. Tillich recognized that to exist is to exist as something and this entails a finite nature, so he tried to sidestep the dilemma. George H. Smith countered nicely on this point by showing that this is in effect trying to define You in terms of what You are not. For example, to say You are immutable means that You do not change, or that You are ineffable means that You cannot be described. However, "if God is described solely in terms of negatives, it is impossible to distinguish Him from nonexistence."[32] Smith adds, "Without some positive idea of His nature, it is impossible to determine which characteristics belong to God." Hence, there is no reason for worshiping or respecting such a God. An unknowable God may be stupid, malicious or, more likely, nonexistent.

Over a century ago, Ludwig Feuerbach observed: "The denial of determinate positive predicates concerning the divine nature . . . is simply a disguised form of atheism." Then he added prosaically, "A God who is injured by determinate qualities has not the courage and strength to exist.[33]

G: As I said, you keep stumbling over those attributes because you can think of them only in terms of your limited human experience. The analogy of proportionality argument postulates that I possess qualities in proportion to My nature. And, since My nature is infinite, so must be the predicates (attributes), one of which is existence.

J: I've already shown that existence is not a predicate. Moreover, since we know nothing of Your nature, we have not added one whit to our understanding to state that Your qualities are proportional to Your nature. Smith answered such sophistry, "If these predicates do not mean the same when applied to God as they do to natural entities, then they assume some unknown mysterious meaning and are virtually emptied of significance."[34]

Every attempt to define the term "God" leads to what Rudolph Carnap called "pseudodefinitions," which lead in turn to "logically illegitimate combinations of words or to other metaphysical words (e.g., 'primordial basis,' the 'absolute,' the 'unconditional,' the 'autonomous,' the 'self-depended,' and so forth, but in no case to the truth conditions of elementary sentences."[35] So, I'm afraid there is no getting around the fact that an unknowable God leads to religious agnosticism. The belief in an unknowable God is no different than belief in nothing. "One cannot possibly know that something exists without some knowledge of what it is that exists."[36]

G: Look, it seems to Me that all I have to do to avoid the problem of contradictions and humankind's inability to comprehend absolutes is to confess that I am not the perfect Being that theologians since Aquinas have sought to make of Me. Perhaps Rabbi Kushner is correct after all. Even Augustine shied away from the idea that I was all-powerful and I have already admitted that I may not be omniscient if man has free choice. Nor for that matter must I be unchangeable, all knowing or even all-good. In the final analysis, the ancient Hebraic concept of Yahweh might be closer to the truth. It depicts a God who is vastly more powerful than paltry humans; but although I am still responsible for your existence, I have my limitations.

J: We have now regressed to the most primitive concept of a god: a super being who demands supplication and veneration to please his divine ego. There is, indeed, no logical contradiction in such a god, any more than there is a logical contradiction in the existence of Zeus, Pegasus the flying horse, or the Phoenix, which, when burned, rose from its own ashes. But the allegation that such a being as Yahweh exists still demands evidence. To date, despite the efforts of millions of true believers to support this myth, there is no more evidence for the Judeo-Christian god than any of the gods on Mount Olympus.

I'm afraid that despite all the theological sophistry of two millennia, no statement can be made of the term "God" which does not invoke a logical contradiction or groundless assertion. The reasonable person must conclude, therefore, as did the philosopher A. J. Ayer, that the statement "There is a God" is itself meaningless because it does not signify anything meaningful or definable.[37] For Smith, "The concept of God is without cognitive content."[38] He goes on to say that, "When [the Christian] asserts that 'God exists' [he] simply does not know what he is talking about. And neither does anyone else."[39] David Brooks neatly sums up all the theological speculation on the existence of a god: "To explain the unknown by the known is a logical procedure; to explain the known by the unknown is a form of theological lunacy."[40]

G: Are you very pleased with yourself?

J: I do feel pretty good, now that You mention it. It's been a long trip up from the dark of superstitions and ignorance of my youth to some semblance of rationality and, perhaps, a touch of wisdom gleaned from a few of the great minds which have struggled with these topics.

G: If you are so certain of your conclusion that I don't exist, then why are you still addressing Me?

J: As I said at the outset of our dialogue, I think, as did Plato, that the dialectic form is interesting. And what better imaginary protagonist than the very concept I sought to discredit?

G: I'll say this, when it comes to blasphemy, there have been few who have matched your monumental audacity. Nietzsche did and you will recall what happened to him.

J: What's this, a new tactic? Guilt by association? Like every other philosopher, Nietzsche wrote some things that were true, some that were false, and much that has been deliberately misinterpreted so as to discredit even that which is true. I've read different accounts as to the cause of his madness. It may have been due to syphilis or simply the frustration of having his writings distorted and slandered. Whatever the cause, I'm afraid You can take no credit, which must be frustrating to that vengeful God of the Old Testament.

G: Do you feel no sense of guilt or shame in seeking to wreck a belief system that has given solace and comfort to so many suffering souls over the centuries?

J: Most of whom would not have had to endure a lifetime of suffering if society could have rid itself of these superstitions earlier and sought to change the human condition directly. But I'll discuss that subject in more detail in the next chapter.

The Value of Religion:
The Negative Contributions
of Institutionalized Superstition

The God to whom Jephthah sacrificed his daughter [Judges 11] is no less a tribal chief than Dagon or Chemosh.

—George Bernard Shaw

J: In previous chapters we talked about some of the specific problems I have with the Judeo-Christian tradition. In this chapter, I would like to amplify that discussion to show that the failings of those religions are indicative of problems presented by the very nature of religion. In speaking of "religion," I accept the common usage of the word, which implies a belief in one or more supernatural persons who can and have affected the physical world, and the practice of certain rituals directed at that person whether for purposes of appeasement, supplication, or worship.

G: You are no doubt going to conclude that despite the utility of religion, especially the Judeo-Christian religion, it is worthless and false.

J: Allow me to point out that usefulness is not the measure of truthfulness.

G: Oh? Then you disagree with William James and the pragmatists who hold that to say "it is useful because it is true or it is true because it is useful . . . means exactly the same thing"?[1]

J: In this instance James makes a poor choice of words. Understanding the connotation of the word "useful" is necessary here. I don't think James meant that simply because a statement is beneficial it is necessarily true. There are times when a lie might produce a benefit. Hence it

339

is useful, but it is still a lie. It helps to understand James by tracing the origin of pragmatism to the works of C. S. Peirce. The intent of Peirce was to evaluate a statement in terms of its consequences, regardless of whether the latter were good or bad in some normative sense. In other words, he simply said that unless a statement had *some* explicable consequences it was meaningless. James, I am afraid, got Peirce's intent rather muddled. Perhaps that is why Peirce later renamed his own philosophical position "pragmaticism" to distinguish it from that of James.

Therefore, utility, i.e., benefit, is not a sufficient criterion in evaluating the truthfulness of religious belief. It may be temporarily useful for a parent to tell a small child not to go out at night because "the bogeyman might get you," but it certainly isn't truthful. It might be useful for a politician to tell his voters that their nation is being threatened by an imaginary enemy. But even if the citizenry feels better because the allegation makes them forget their own economic chaos or internal strife to rally against a common enemy, this utility doesn't make his words any more truthful. So, even if religious beliefs may make people feel better, that doesn't mean they are true.

G: But religion is of value even if not all the beliefs are true. Admittedly, some religious beliefs may be harmless fictions to comfort simple souls— what author Kurt Vonnegut termed "foma." So what? The beliefs make people feel good; they help people behave better.

J: Sort of like children believing in Santa Claus? Unfortunately, what may bring comfort to a few has brought misery to millions and prevents society from dealing with the real problems plaguing humankind. Moreover, what evidence is there that religion, especially the Judeo-Christian religion, really improves our behavior? Psychologist Alfie Kohn reports that several studies on charity and religion over the thirty-five year period from 1950 to 1984 indicate no difference between religious beliefs, church involvement and charitable acts.[2]

G: Perhaps human behavior might have been even worse without religion. Religion has helped ensure conformity with, and transmission of, the ethical norms and values of a culture. You have admitted that religion is a form of conditioning. Even if religion has never prevented a war, it may have served a purpose in preventing anarchy, and may even have helped curb our natural aggressive tendencies toward our neighbor. There have been studies to show that regular churchgoers are less likely to commit crimes such as burglary, larceny or rape. For example, a study by M. Argyle and B. Beit-Hallahmi indicated that fewer aggressively delinquent acts are committed by church members than by nonmembers.[3]

J: But L. B. Brown adds that it is not clear whether these findings reflect social and external, rather than internal, controls.[4] In other words, it may not be religion, per se, that results in less delinquency, but the stricter control exercised by the families and communities of those children. Many similar studies that I've reviewed were flawed in two respects. First, most of the regular attendants at church are in the socioeconomic middle class, which has a lower incidence of crime than the average for all social classes. In statistical terms, because the studies did not include a socioeconomic variable, they showed a spurious correlation between religious belief and behavior. They should compare those who attend church with those who do not attend church from the same economic group. Furthermore, I could counter the studies You mention with studies showing that most inmates of prisons are more religious than the general population.

The second problem with many such studies is that they correlate religion with attitudes toward behavior rather than behavior itself. The problem is that the second doesn't necessarily follow from the first. For example, the moralistic sentiments expressed by convicted criminals in a study by T. W. Adorno are impressive.[5] However, despite their strong positive feelings toward religion, the criminals tested retained their prejudiced (and undoubtedly sociopathic) attitudes. In a study of Sunday school children, H. Hartshore and M. A. May found that although the children said they would not cheat on tests, they still did so.[6] E. J. Shoben found only a low correlation between virtue and religion, and emphasized that moral values derive from the larger society.[7] C. D. Batson et al. reached the general conclusion that "private behavior is independent of religious training although moral beliefs are religiously influenced."[8] Finally, an analysis of D. Wright concludes that, "the origins of practical morality are quite independent of any kind of religious belief or practice."[9]

G: Everyone knows that psychologists are biased against religion. I wouldn't trust any of their studies.

J: Unless they supported Your position. To return to a larger problem with studies correlating religion and crime, society only recognizes certain actions as criminal. For example, a person could be a war monger and not be considered a criminal. (In fact, except at Nuremberg, perpetrators of war were never prosecuted as criminals.) Most of the vices that plague humanity—greed, prejudice, hatred, etc.—are rarely recognized as crimes as long as they are practiced with discretion and do not lead to overtly violent acts.

Take prejudice, for example. A study by psychologist Gordon W. Allport indicates that those who report that religion was a major or moderate factor in their early lives reflected a degree of prejudice far higher than among those who report that religion was a slight or nonexistent factor in their early training.[10] According to Allport this finding is consistent with other studies which show that individuals with no religion show, on average, less prejudice than do church members. The results of a major study conducted by T. W. Adorno et al., which was based on a sample of 2,000 men and women of all faiths, supported Allport's conclusion. Adorno's study concluded: "There seems no doubt that subjects who reject organized religion are less prejudiced than those who, in one way or another, accept it.[11] After reviewing the evidence of studies on prejudice and religious beliefs by Allport, M. Rokeach, and Adorno, L. B. Brown concluded that "while religious doctrines usually emphasize love and brotherhood, churchgoers are less tolerant or more prejudiced than nonchurchgoers."[12]

G: Those results may be due, in part, to the lack of proper study segmentation, the problem you mentioned a moment ago. I'm sure you would not want to overlook an analysis by Allport and Ross, which split Christians between those who were merely affiliated with a church (who they call extrinsic believers) and those who were deeply involved in their church (intrinsic believers). They found that that the more frequent church attendees were less prejudiced than infrequent attendees and nonattendees.[13] This finding supported the analysis of Wade Clark Roof indicating that the relationship between minority prejudice and religious orthodoxy was probably coincidental. Both prejudice and religious orthodoxy were found to be a function of localistic worldviews prevalent in persons with little education or world experience.[14]

J: I certainly can concur with Roof's conclusions. Adorno also agrees that the psychological factors determining why a person has accepted or rejected a religion are the key to whether that person will be prejudiced. But if religion has a positive value, it should be *negatively* correlated with prejudice. The fact is, as Allport points out, that "through most of America's history the church has been a preserver of the status quo rather than a crusader for improvement."[15] As the study of attitudes toward slavery has demonstrated, often people will tailor their religious beliefs to legitimize their own self-interests. In the final analysis, despite the United States' being the most religious of Western nations (with the possible exception of Ireland), it has by far the highest crime rate—especially crimes of violence. It is mere wishful thinking to believe that religion has resulted, or can result, in people behaving morally.

The Efficacy of Prayer

G: While not granting that argument, I wish to change the subject some-what. In contending that religion has no value, you are ignoring the demonstrable power of prayer, not only for the benefits I bestow as a result (which you would, of course, deny), but for the psychological benefits as well.

J: I am so glad You brought up that subject again because I agree that the central practice of religion is prayer, usually prayers of supplication. Evangelists are continually quoting the words of Jesus: "Whatever you ask of the Father in my name, it shall be granted you." But here, too, as I've demonstrated earlier, religion is at best irrelevant. For centuries, although death before baptism was considered a serious misfortune because the soul could not enter heaven, the chances of a stillbirth appeared unaffected by the piety or prayers of the parents. It's no wonder the Catholic Church has subsequently "invented" other forms of baptism to cover the case of stillbirths. For example, "baptism by desire" contends that if the fetus had lived, it would have wanted to be baptized and You consider that good enough. (The question of how You treat a fetus which, had it lived, might have rejected You, is never addressed.)

In 1887 Francis Galton discovered that the clergy on average survived no longer than lawyers and doctors despite both their own frequent prayers and those of their parishioners. Moreover, the royalty, who should have benefited from the prayers of their entire nation, did not live as long as the average member of the general population.[16] More recently, in a 1965 study of rheumatics by Joyce and Welldon, the group being prayed for did better in the first half of the study, "but in the second half the control group did better."[17] Additionally, Collip's 1969 findings regarding prayer and leukemia "did not reach significance."[18] Finally, an extensive study by cardiologist, Randolph C. Byrd showed an improvement in 5 to 7 percent of the patients on six measures, but no significant differences on twenty other measures. Moreover, the minor difference on the six variables "could not be considered statistically significant because of the large number of variables examined."[19] (In other words, in studies where a large number of variables are involved, we would always expect to find some variables statistically significant due only to chance). Moreover, for an additional three variables—days in a critical care unit after entry, days in hospital after entry, and number of discharge medications—there were no significant differences between those who prayed and the control groups, despite explicit prayers for a rapid recovery. So much for the efficacy of prayer.

G: I always answer prayers in the manner I know to be best, not necessarily in the way the supplicant might expect . . .

J: . . . or want. But we've been through that little bit of sophistry before. The point is, if there is no measurable difference in the effects of praying or not praying, it is absurd to say that praying has positive value. I note that when faith healer Pat Robinson's wife became ill, he wasted no time trying to effect a cure through prayer but sent her to the hospital straightaway.

G: At the very least, prayer might raise the expectations of a cure. The mental attitude of the true believer may be affected and, therefore, to the extent that a positive mental attitude could improve a person's chances of recovery, you would have to admit that prayer conveyed a positive benefit.

J: The same affect as a placebo? That's possible I suppose. But in the only study I have seen, on the correlation between a positive mental attitude and the cure rate for cancer, the results showed no relationship. Even if a person's attitude could be correlated with the odds of recovery, it would not demonstrate any supernatural power of prayer, but merely the impact of a positive attitude whatever its source.

   Considering the ineffectiveness of prayer, it is no wonder that certain preachers today no longer tell their ailing followers to pray for a cure, but rather to pray for the power to accept Your will. Of course, this is equally dangerous advice because people may waste valuable time praying when they should be seeking medical assistance.

G: By ruling out psychosomatic illnesses you are still ignoring the psychological benefits of prayer. You like using statistical analysis to support your arguments. Then you must give credence to T. A. Wills's findings that "those belonging to a church have lower disease rates than those who do not."[20] In another study A. E. Bergin followed up on those who were converted in religious crusades and concluded that "conversions and related religious experiences are therapeutic, since they significantly reduce pathological symptoms."[21] Argyle and Beit-Hallahmi identified the positive effects of religion on adjustment, health and coping.[22] A number of other studies indicated that belonging to a religion results in better mental health, physical and social adjustment, greater confidence in a crisis, clearer identity, and social stability.

J: You disingenuously left out the additional findings of Argyle and Beit-Hallahmi that religion also fosters greater authoritarianism, dogmatism, suggestibility, dependence, inadequacy, and anxiety. Other studies suport the negative psychological impact of religious belief. C. D. Batson and W. L. Ventis found that, in general, "the relationship between religious involvement and mental health is negative rather than positive."[23] And the research of J. E. Dittes led him to conclude that religion is associated with a weak and constricted ego.[24]

There may be an explanation for these seemingly contradictory findings. Wills touched upon one aspect in the study referred to earlier. He reasoned that the benefits of belonging to a church derive from the social environment offered by the church. If loneliness and alienation foster mental illness, then belonging to any organization is bound to help. This explains why the doctrines of a particular religion are irrelevant in obtaining these benefits. It matters not a whit whether the belief system is that of the Hare Krishnas or Hasidism, as long as it fosters social support. Although most all people can benefit from a fixed social environment, religions offer a benefit to some of the most seriously disturbed persons in our society. Many of those who join religious movements, especially the cult and fundamentalist sects, are suffering from personality disorders that attract them to organizations professing to take all the uncertainty, fear, and loneliness out of living. The findings of Argyle and Beit-Hallahmi are consistent with this explanation. They demonstrate that religious belief is associated with greater authoritarianism, dogmatism, suggestibility, dependence, inadequacy and anxiety. By mindlessly following a charismatic leader who assures them that some divine being will give them the love and care lacking in their lives, people will probably be granted at least a temporary reduction in anxiety. Hence, many of the overt symptoms of a personality disorder will fade, although the underlying psychological deficiencies are still there.

G: So you contend that all those who belong to a religion suffer from a psychological disorder.

J: Don't twist my meaning. I am only saying that the psychological benefits of religion are not due to any supernatural cause, but can be explained entirely in naturalistic terms. It is the social characteristics of institutional religions, along with the comfort and hope offered by warm and enduring myths, which can explain the psychological benefits of belief. Prayer is simply the embodiment of this psychological process. In its public form the sense of community is reinforced. In its private form it is an effort to establish a link with the mythical father/mother figure who loves us and might grant our most fundamental needs. There is little psychological motivation to dwell upon the intrinsic contradiction of a just God who selectively (by all evidence, randomly) answers prayers.

G: An intrinsic contradiction? *Now* what are you talking about?

J: To illustrate, let me relate some correspondence between V. M. Tarkunde and Mahatma Gandhi.[25] Tarkunde was twelve years old when he wrote Gandhi asking why one should pray and how a just

God could answer prayers. It seemed quite unfair to the young Tarkunde that God would not help those who deserved help but did not pray, and yet helped those who prayed but did not deserve help.

Gandhi answered with a personal postcard; but instead of addressing the issue of God's justice, he replied that prayer is good because it gives peace of mind. The precocious Tarkunde must have puzzled over this for a while before writing back that you can't have peace of mind unless you believe in the efficacy of prayer; and since he did not believe in prayer, what could he do? Gandhi did not respond this time.[26] Later in his life, Gandhi was to witness sadly the futility of his prayers as his beloved India was torn apart in bloody religious strife despite his prayers and the prayers of millions of his followers.

G: Yet he never lost faith.

J: Such is the mark of a true believer. But his faith did nothing to ameliorate the suffering of his people.

G: Perhaps because neither Hindus nor Moslems were truly religious enough. Despite your refusal to concede that religion is of any value in itself, it does foster many positive human qualities. For example, it imposes a discipline that even you agree is sadly lacking in people today.

J: I admit the lack of discipline. However, this is not a religious issue, but a necessity to redress the imbalance between rights and responsibilities. This is the subject for a future work. For now it must suffice to point out that what is needed is the proper conditioning of children to foster the development of self-discipline. This can be accomplished by demonstrating that self-interest requires that each of us must be concerned with the needs of others so as to promote a socially stable and happy society. Concern for others means that we cannot give full rein to our own desires. It is a compromise that grounds all social organizations.

G: Sounds like the Lockean notion of the social contract.

J: Yes, and the nice thing about contracts is that they can be amended if the needs of the parties involved (in this case society) change. All law must ultimately be subject to humans, changing as necessary, to meet their needs. This is exactly the opposite premise of religious dictates which hold that humans are subject to unchangeable supernatural directives which serve Your desires. Such laws become ossified and demand slavish adherence despite their human consequences.

Such subjugation to law is demeaning and dangerous. As Henry David Thoreau aptly pointed out: "a common and natural result of undue respect for law is, that you may see a file of soldiers . . . marching in admirable order over hill and dale to war."[27] Disciplined adherence to authority, when viewed as an end in itself, has led to the most horrible atrocities. History is replete with examples of how otherwise decent people, when conditioned to follow orders regardless of their personal reservations, can be led to massacre men, women, and children.

How Religion Fosters Servility

This, then, is the first danger of religion: by investing the rules of mere humans with a divine legitimacy religion attempts to preclude dissent and individual thought. After reviewing hundreds of psychological studies, L. B. Brown concludes that confidence about religion correlates with conservatism, dogmatism and authoritarianism.[28] Religious leaders exploit these tendencies and the result, as Nietzsche observed, is the creation of a following of superstitious slaves. Thomas Paine also saw full well this evil aspect of religion: "All national institutions of churches whether Jewish, Christian, or Turkish, appear to me no other than human invention set up to terrify and enslave [hu]mankind, and monopolize power and profit."[29] Nowhere has this been more evident in recent times than in the despotic rule of Iran's Ayatollahs. And as we know, the situation was no better at the apex of the Church's power in the Middle Ages. As in the case of the followers of the Ayatollahs, the Christians of the Middle Ages had surrendered their capability for reason, and blindly followed the dictates of one who claimed to speak for You. The results were inevitable. A modern Augustinian named Erich Przyaya observes: "The Dominican order became, willy-nilly, the servants of the Inquisition, not on account of a sort of fanaticism (the great Dominicans were all men of childlike humility and even tender sentiments) but on account of utter abandonment of all individualism to the service of everlasting truth."[30]

We see that same unquestioning mental attitude exhibited time and again throughout history, by the fundamentalists of various Christian, Jewish and Islamic sects with the same fatal consequences. Their followeres are exhorted, as Guildenstern was by Rosencratz, to follow instructions because: "There is a logic at work—it's all done for you, don't worry. Enjoy it. Relax. To be taken by the hand and led, like being a child again. . . ."[31] Luckily, the motto "In God We Trust" is not extended to Your priests and ministers by the majority of the American population. But the present trend is a disturbing one, especially as it carries over into the realm of politics, as it invariably must.

Religion's Preoccupation with Death

The second great failing of religion is its preoccupation with death and immortality.

G: Come now, you cannot deny that the thought of a better life in the hereafter has brought comfort to millions of suffering souls down through the ages.

J: Yes, and ensured that hundreds of millions more would continue to suffer. Only when suffering leads to action can people break the conditions that produce their suffering. In our own times the Civil Rights Movement has demonstrated this fact. Conversely, the logical deduction from a belief in heaven is either to be completely detached from the things of this world or, more dangerously, to attempt to plunge headlong into the next. St. Cyril advocated this latter view: "nothing is more for the advantage of a Christian than soon to die."[32] It is a great advantage for a general to have an army of such fanatics, for as Ludwig Feuerbach saw, "to him who believes in an eternal heavenly life, the present life loses its value."[33]

G: You appear to be criticizing religion for stifling opposition to injustice while, in the same breath, condemning religion for providing people with the courage to fight for their beliefs.

J: Not all beliefs are worth dying for. Moreover, for a man to risk death for a cause he believes in, knowing that there is no afterlife, at least demonstrates his conviction in that cause. However, a man who believes in immortality is not really willing to risk his life—only his earthly existence—to gain a better existence in heaven. Such a selfish reason is hardly conducive to working toward achieving a better society here on earth.

   The concept of immortality is concerned only with individual salvation and, therefore, is essentially illiberal and selfish. Christian doctrine holds that if you make it to heaven you are deliriously happy; the pain of those you leave behind can be of no consequence. No wonder freethinker Robert Ingersoll notes that "the people with the smallest souls make the most fuss about getting saved."[34]

G: I really don't think that many Christians, or any other believers in immortality today, are rushing toward their death just to gain heaven.

J: Many Iranian youths did just that in their "holy war" with Iraq. In the early days of Christianity and Islam it appears that hundreds of thousands also did so. Today, however, your conclusion is, for the most part, correct because death is viewed with an unnatural horror, especially by Christians.

G: I'm sure you have a theory as to why.

J: Well, I think it's pretty obvious. For thousands of years Christianity has completely distorted our view of death until it has become a "nightmare of our imagination." A person can never be certain of salvation, and just look at what is awaiting the damned!

G: I admit that years ago some overly zealous ministers and priests may have sought to scare people into behaving morally by emphasizing death and damnation, but today the message is one of salvation.

J: After two thousand years of scaring people witless with those senseless horror stories, it's not surprising that you can't change such conditioning in a couple of generations. Even if you could, the myth of everlasting divine bliss is simply a change in emphasis of a lie. The whole myth of immortality is simply an unhealthy psychological denial of death: "the man who has come to believe that there is no such thing as death . . . has not overcome the fear of death at all; on the contrary, it has overcome him so completely that he refuses to die on any terms whatsoever."[35]

G: That despicable Bernard Shaw again?

J: You just resent his keen insight into human nature, and his ability to express himself so cogently. Shaw's sentiments were echoed by the existentialist Albert Camus: "for if there is a sin against life, it consists not so much in despairing of life, as in hoping for another and in eluding the implacable grandeur of this life."[36] Religion so fails to recognize the beauty and joy of life that it oftentimes concerns itself more with the unborn and the dead than with the living. Contrast this view with that of many Native American tribes, who saw life as a joyous adventure, who praised every new day, and who, when it was time to die, did so with the stoic recognition that it was all in the natural order of things. Even the Hebrew religion, in its earliest forms, was not so cowardly as to deny death.

G: Simply because you flirted with death for several years, you think you are an authority. But your close calls were only momentary brushes with death. Let Me hear you talk so bravely when death is moving in on you inexorably, day by day, and you have no hope of escaping. Like so many others who boast a false bravado, you will then clutch at any hope, any fantasy that offers you a remote chance of postponing the end. You will one day even grasp at the possibility of immortality.

J: Perhaps, but I doubt it. Certainly I'm not looking forward to dying. For the most part I enjoy life, but that is primarily because I still have a relatively healthy body possessed of a strong will to live. Philosopher and humanist Corliss Lamont, who has studied the subject of death at length, concluded that the major problem of death is the psychic dilemma caused when one function of an otherwise healthy body—for example, the liver or lungs—fails. The will to live in the other bodily systems, especially the brain, is still quite strong, producing the psychological conflict. However, in the latter stages of death— and this is evident in older people—when all systems are shutting down, so to speak, the paradox resolves itself and the mental anguish subsides. Although the matter deserves much more study, there is anecdotal evidence to support this view. For example, an eminent English physician, Sir Arbuthnot Lane, states that he has seen scores of people die, yet, "I don't think I can remember a single instance where, when their time came that this [fear of death] did not leave them, to be replaced by a wonderful state of peace and calm."[37] The surgeon Sir William Osler, after studying over 500 patients' deaths, reports that ninety suffered bodily pain or stress, eleven showed mental apprehension, two positive terror, one exaltation and one remorse, but, "the great majority gave no sign one way or another; like their birth, their death was a sleep and forgetting."[38]

With the proper conditioning there is no reason the human race couldn't overcome the morbid preoccupation with death and concentrate on the pleasures of living. Of course, this assumes that society expends the effort necessary to extend the pleasures of this world to more than the lucky few. Not only must the basic socioeconomic environment be established, but people must be educated as to the proper means by which happiness might be attained. Such opportunity and prerequisite knowledge, if pervasive in society, might be the death knell of religion. Religion has nothing to offer people who are absorbed in meaningful, satisfying lives.

The approach of death, if untimely, will always bring sorrow. But removing the fear of burning in a purgatory or hell will alleviate at least that source of psychological pain. I recall that fear of punishment for minor transgressions plagued my grandfather on his deathbed even though he had lived an exemplary life. Given today's medical advances, drugs can mitigate the physical pain and mental anguish for the dying patient. For an aged person who can look back upon a relatively happy life, the gradual diminution of that life would hold neither pain nor terror.

There will always be anguish at the loss of a loved one. But this is partially a good thing, since it prevents society from becoming calloused and indifferent to death. On the other hand, religion distorts and exaggerates the natural process of dying by simultaneously denying death and excessively dwelling upon it.

Religion's Fostering of Intolerance and Vengeance

J: The first claim of certain great religions is, as Allport reminds us, that each has absolute and final possession of truth. "People who adhere to difficult absolutes are not likely to find themselves in agreement."[39] What an understatement! Religion inevitably fosters an "us" versus "them" mentality. Nowhere is this more exemplified than in the Hebrew and Christian religions. In the Old Testament, the Israelites, *Your* chosen people," narrate the history of their efforts to exterminate other nations at Your direct command. The Christians were no better, as I have shown. The New Testament is rife with condemnations of any who don't join the Christian legions. The feelings of Jesus on the subject of religious tolerance are summed up in his parting exhortation to his apostles: "Go into the whole world and preach the gospel to every creature. He who believes and is baptized shall be saved, but he who does not believe shall be condemned" (Mark 16:15–16). Persecution of dissenters has been the hallmark of Christianity for almost 2,000 years. And so it will be again if Christianity continues to gain political power.

G: You're being an alarmist. There doesn't appear to be much chance of that. You are beginning to sound like an atheist fanatic.

J: The events leading to the Moral Majority's victory for Ronald Reagan and Jesse Helms lend credence to these fears. Almost two hundred years ago James Madison warned, "It is proper to take alarm at the first experiment in our liberties." The history of this country shows a continued encroachment of religion upon the political process: from the insertion of theism into the oaths of office and judicial proceedings to the pledge of allegiance to You and the flag. Today, attempts are being made to legislate the teachings of creationism into the classrooms—the only time in the history of the United States when teachers are being commanded by law to teach a specific theological viewpoint.

Judges are being selected based upon how well their stance on moral issues conforms to fundamentalist Christian doctrine. Thus we can expect their court decisions to reflect theological positions rather that the weight of scientific evidence. Reflecting this trend, some candidates for public office are making avowals that they will use their position to create a Christian America. A federal judge in Alabama banned forty textbooks because they omitted specific reference to the Christian religion and therefore, according to his illogic, supported the "religion" of secularism. His decision was later overturned by the federal appeals court. Fortunately for our nation, most Americans are wary of such dogmatists and have rebuffed these religious opportunists and zealots.

G: Many devout religious believers also oppose the intrusion of religion into politics.

J: That's right. However, it is important to understand that it is the very nature of religion to encroach upon politics. For the most part Christian theology is inconsistent with the tenets of democracy. There are, of course, some notable exceptions such as the Maryknoll priests who are preaching Liberation Theology in Central and South America. By selectively interpreting the teachings of Jesus they seek to develop an ethic that demands democracy and justice for the poor of those countries. But such teachings have had little impact on the Church itself. The Catholic League hardly needs to remind us: "The Catholic Church is not a democracy. The teachings of Jesus Christ are determined by the Pope and the world's bishops."[40]

The belief in You naturally leads people to question Your purpose for humankind, and there will always be those who claim that they are in a position to know what You want. They will seek to gain support for their interpretation of the divine will through the political process. Reichley notes that this is the natural evolution of any religious sect: "Once established, the sect, try though it may to escape involvement with the larger society, almost inevitably must develop social interests. . . . The need to protect its social interest draws it ineluctably toward some degree of participation in politics."[41]

G: Intolerance is certainly not unique to Christianity. Many would argue that it is a perversion of the true spirit of Christianity.

J: They are wrong. I have already shown that intolerance is a basic tenet of Christianity and endemic to virtually all religions when the organization is large and powerful enough to enforce its will on nonbelievers. We saw how the Catholic Church and fundamentalists attempt to force not only their followers, but all persons, to obey the dictates of religion with regard to issues such as divorce, abortion, homosexuality, in vitro fertilization, euthanasia, etc. Feuerbach agreed: "It is essential to faith to condemn, to anathematize . . . but so far as faith anathematizes, it necessarily generates hostile dispositions—the dispositions out of which the persecution of heretics arises."[42]

Nobel Prize winner Konrad Lorenz was noted for his studies of the causes of aggressive behavior in animals and man. Dr. Lorenz was especially concerned with a specialized form of communal aggression which he terms "militant enthusiasm." According to Lorenz, this is the most dangerous form of aggressive behavior, unleashed when human beings are absolutely certain they are fighting for a just cause such as Your will. In such circumstances the natural inhibitions which keep us from destroying each other are overwhelmed so that, "Men may enjoy the feeling of absolute righteousness even when they commit atrocities. . . . When the banner is unfurled all reasoning is in the trumpet."[43] As we have seen, the history of religious warfare provids shocking support for that observation. Even as I write these words the killing continues between Jews and Muslims in Palestine, Christians and Muslims in Lebanon, Shiites and Hindus in India, and Catholics and Protestants in Ireland. The history of religion is one long cry of rage and pain.

Nationalism is a dangerous enough sentiment; but when it is supported by religious fervor there is no limit to the destruction it can cause. The Koran instructs Muslims, "If the last Home, with God, before you specially . . . then seek ye for death if ye are someone." And "Say not of those who are slain in the way of God: 'They are dead! Nay, they are living, though ye perceive [it] not.' "[44] A nice incentive to throw away one's life in a "holy war."

G: Aren't you forgetting that Jesus told his followers to love their enemies?

J: This dictum of Jesus apparently had reference only to personal enemies within the faith, not enemies of the faith who are perceived as enemies of God. Recall his condemnation of those who rejected his word which I quoted earlier. It was, therefore, considered justifiable when Paul cursed Elymas the "sorcerer" with blindness because he "opposed" the faith (Acts 13:8–12).

Intolerance will always be the result when a group believes it possesses Your truth. The author of Matthew's gospel wrote that the Jewish people demanded the death of Jesus crying, "His blood be on us and on our children" (Matt. 27:25). Belief in the infallibility of this fanciful account of the death of Jesus justified two thousand years of persecution of Jews. As late as 1933, German theologian Martin Buber asked the Jews to search within themselves for the reason they were being oppressed. Even after the Holocaust, the Christian West was more than happy to solve the "Jewish problem" by helping the Jews take over Palestine, rather than welcome them into their own countries. Once in control of Palestine, it wasn't long before ultra-orthodox Jews began to practice their own form of religious persecution. So it goes; the story of religious intolerance is always the same.

Intolerance was displayed not only to members of a different religion but to those of the same religion who had slightly different theological views. Many more Christians were put to death by other Christians than by the Roman emperors—all because they held different shades of the same basic beliefs. Thomas Aquinas, whom most would consider the quintessence of the gentle intellectual, could in good conscience recommend that the heretic "be exterminated from the world by death" after the third offense.[45] Some example of intellectual tolerance! But such is the logical outcome when a group sees sin as the ultimate evil. Cardinal Newman expressed the Catholic Church's view in this way:

> The Church holds that it were better for sun and moon to drop from heaven, for the earth to fail, and for all the many millions who are upon it to die in agony . . . than that one soul, I will not say should be lost, but should commit one single venial sin.[46]

G: Perhaps it may seem to you as excessive, but there is no greater evil than to disobey My Divine Will.

J: That assumes that there is a Divine Will and a religious leader knows it; both are unsubstantiated hypotheses. What is so scary is that in the absence of any support whatsoever, adherents to the various world religions can possess such certitude that they are willing to stop at nothing to enforce their beliefs on all others. My own uncle, a Franciscan priest, wrote to me out of sincere affection: "I'd like to hug you so fiercely as to break a couple of your ribs, put you in a hospital, deprive you of all your distractions and pray with you until you call it quits." Such a concern for my spiritual welfare I can do without.

Given the fanaticism which is the hallmark of "true believers" throughout history, is it any wonder that I worry about their efforts to gain the allegiance of civil governments to support their agendas? They believe that the function of the civil authorities is to punish the transgressors of their theologically inspired morality. Luther's exhortation was: "The secular sword must be red and sanguine for the world will and must be evil."[47]

It was not so long ago when a treatise such as the one I am writing would have landed me in jail. Many states used to have antiblasphemy laws making direct attacks on You and the Bible a crime.

G: And splendid laws they were!

J: No doubt many fundamentalist Christians and Jews would agree with You. In this country religious groups have been successful in blocking atheists and agnostics from holding important public offices. Avowed atheist Robert Ingersoll was once offered the nomination for governor of Illinois on the condition that he refrain from expressing his convictions on religion. But Ingersoll, with a sense of integrity rare among politicians, turned down the proposition. Later he offered this succinct assessment of religion: "To hate man and worship God seems to be the sum of all creeds."[48]

Closely related to the intolerance, and as great an evil, is the spirit of revenge permeating most religions, and especially the Judeo-Christian tradition. The Old Testament is simply one long narrative of Your vindictive and vengeful nature. From the expulsion from the Garden for merely eating of the fruit of knowledge, to the Flood and the destruction of city after city for the human failings of its inhabitants, the Old Testament sets an example of cruel, cold-hearted vengeance.

The New Testament is even worse, threatening not just pain in this life, but eternal torture merely for intellectual dissent. The evangelists may have given lip service to love, but the emphasis is always on faith, and faith, I submit is incompatible with love. Love is free, universal, and forgiving, while faith is narrow-minded, unyielding, and fanatical. The faith of Christianity has had a corrupting influence on the minds of even the greatest thinkers for almost two millennia. For example, it was his Christian faith which led the usually rational Gottlieb Leibniz to proclaim:

> There is a kind of justice which aims neither at the amendment of the criminal nor at furnishing an example to others, nor at the reparation of injury. This justice . . . which is properly vindictive justice, and which God has reserved for himself at many junctures . . . is always founded in the fitness of things and satisfies not only the offender but all wise lookers-on, even as beautiful music or a fine piece of architecture satisfies a well-constituted mind.[49]

As repugnant as such a sentiment is, it is understandable in the context of the Judeo-Christian world view. Peter Lombard typified the vindictiveness that fostered the Christian concept of hell: "The elect will come forth to behold the torments of the ungodly, and at this spectacle they will not be smitten with sorrow; on the contrary, while they see the unspeakable sufferings of the ungodly, they, intoxicated with joy, will thank God for their own salvation."[50] It is ironic, but logical, that even people of good will could be perverted by the theology of salvation. As Bertrand Russell explains: "The notion of saving others from hell was urged as justification for persecution—for a heretic could lead others to eternal damnation."[51]

If humankind is ever to progress to a more civilized, less violent state, it must reject the whole concept of sin, retribution, and vengeance. Arthur Schopenhauer recognized the fallacy of revenge: "The desire of revenge is closely related to wickedness. It recompenses evil with evil, not with reference to the future, which is characteristic of punishment, but merely on the account of what has happened . . . as an end, in order to revel in the torment which the avenger himself has inflicted on the offender."[52] Isn't this exactly what Leibniz and all true believers want: to revel in the torment of their enemies?

G: But the Bible doesn't promote personal revenge, it reserves that right for Me alone: "Vengeance is mine, sayeth the Lord."

J: It is only a small leap—and history shows how easily it is made— for a religious organization to carry out "God's vengeance" once they believe they are acting to enforce Divine Laws. A group that calls itself the Army of God firebombed several abortion clinics and kidnapped and threatened to murder the doctor at another clinic. (How ironic, to threaten to murder a fully rational, sentient human in defense of the right to life for a zygote or fetus; something which, at best, is only potentially a person.) In the last several years more than sixty clinics have been firebombed by fanatical Christians.

G: You can't blame a religion for all the nasty acts of its practitioners.

J: I certainly can if they are prompted to such acts by the doctrines of that religion. I subscribe to Russell's comment: "The harm that theology has done is not to create cruel impulses, but to give them the sanction of what professes to be lofty ethic, and to confer an apparently sacred character upon practices which have come down from more ignorant and barbarous times."[53] Russell's observation has been confirmed by many of the psychological studies to which I have already referred.

How Religion Retards the Evolution of Civilization

J: Religion tends to lock society into ancient traditions, many of which are at best irrelevant, and at worst barriers to the advancement of humankind. There is no capacity for the institution or its teachings to progress since they are thought to be perfect in the first place. This is the "time-binding" nature of religion. Not even Jesus could conceive of the ancient Hebraic traditions as being in need of reform: "Do not think that I have come to destroy the Law or the Prophets. I have come not to destroy but to fulfill. For amen I say to you till heaven and earth pass away, not one jot or one tittle shall be lost from the Law till all things have been accomplished" (Matt. 5:17–20).

This assumed immutability of Divine Law has been a serious obstacle to social evolution. For most of its history the Catholic Church has sought to impede human progress. In 1864 Pius IV, in his infamous *Syllabus of Errors,* condemned as heresy the idea "that the Roman pontiff may and ought to reconcile and adapt himself to progress

. . . and modern civilization."[54] In that socially backward encyclical, the pope also denounced freedom of worship and the separation of church and state. It is no wonder that many people still look with suspicion upon Rome.

G: Changing a moral code willy-nilly to endorse the latest intellectual fad is not necessarily in the best interest of humanity. Moreover, I don't think that the Catholic Church today has designs on political power. The pope and his bishops are merely exercising their right and duty to speak out on moral issues.

J: I have no objection to any religious organization arguing a particular moral position or even voicing an opinion on a political policy involving moral principles. But their arguments must be supported by reason and evidence of the effects that a proposed rule of morality might have upon humankind, not merely a pronouncement of what they believe to be a Divine edict. Even to argue that a moral belief is right because it is a matter of tradition *might* have some validity if the basic circumstances surrounding the issue are unaltered and everyone is happy with the traditional arrangement. However, when circumstances radically change—such as a population explosion and the advent of safe birth control, or if some group of people is made to suffer needlessly because of the existing moral code—the moral issues must be reinvestigated. To do otherwise is a form of moral dictatorship.

I think I have already sufficiently refuted your contention that religious organizations such as the Catholic Church have no desire to reestablish the political power they once wielded. The pope is constantly seeking to influence politics in this country and throughout the world. His cardinals and bishops work diligently to see that candidates who support the pope's doctrines get elected, while they actively oppose governments that threaten the Church's moral supremacy. When various clergy have dared to question some of the cruel and ignorant doctrines of Rome—as a group of bishops did during the Pope John Paul II's 1987 tour of the United States—the pope has quickly put them in their place, flatly stating that they have no right to question his pontifical wisdom. The bishops have then obsequiously thanked the Holy Father for his chastisement and slunk off to tell their flocks that the master has spoken; it is for them to obey regardless of the consequences in terms of human suffering.

Churches have generally stood in the way of attempts by people to control their own lives and attain happiness, while doing little to oppose tyranny and misery. Erich Fromm notes that even when it has not directly been the cause of great evil, religion has "failed to challenge secular power relentlessly and unceasingly where such power has violated the spirit of the religious idea; on the contrary it has shared again and again in such violations."[55] As I've shown, the pope is not alone in his efforts to dominate local politics. Fundamentalist Christians openly seek to establish a state religion in America. In this country Jews have tended to be the most liberal and tolerant of religious groups. But in Israel, the ancient legal regulations recorded in the Torah have been revived by the minority Orthodox Jews who are attempting to legislate adherence for all citizens. This vocal minority has closed roads to cars on the Sabbath, sought to establish the prohibition on eating pork in hospitals and prisons, attempted to prescribe the ancient position of women through marriage laws, and wants to decide the issue of citizenship along religious lines. Claiming support from the Bible, some orthodox Jews seek to evict forcibly any Arabs from lands that You supposedly granted to the the ancient Israelites.

All religions since ancient times can be characterized by superstition and ignorance of natural processes. At best, ancient religions incorporated some rules and customs that had some hygienic or economic value long ago. But it is senseless to try to build a modern-day society on the words of simple-minded prophets and priests of bygone ages. The gospels tell of Jesus driving devils out of sick people and into pigs. Such superstitious belief in demons caused Martin Luther to write:

> Demons live everywhere, but are especially common in Germany. On a high mountain called the Poltuberg, there is a pool full of them; they are held captive by Satan. If a stone is thrown in, a great storm arises and the whole countryside is overwhelmed.[56]

G: That was over four hundred years ago.

J: But amazingly these ancient superstitions are far from dead. I recall accidentally tuning in to a Christian radio broadcast where the guest "expert" was avowing that "thousands of demons and witches are roaming the world today." The narrator expressed his agreement and horror at this "indisputable fact."

G: There will always be a small number of sadly ignorant people. Religion has no monopoly on absurd beliefs. Witness the number of fools who believe the New Age hokum known as "channeling."

J: True, yet superstition is a logical extension of belief in the Bible as Your inspired word. Where would we be today if everyone still believed such nonsense? Probably still treating mentally ill people with exorcism rather than drugs and psychotherapy.

Archaic religious beliefs have generally impeded scientific and social progress. During the Middle Ages, for example, the Church forbade anatomy and dissection.[57] As late as 1885, the Bishop of Montreal preached that vaccination during a smallpox epidemic was thwarting God's will.[58]

Many Christian sects opposed the use of anesthetics during childbirth because of God's admonition to Eve in Genesis: "I will multiply thy sorrows and thy conceptions: in sorrow shall thou bring forth children . . ." (Gen. 3:16). This passage has been used as evidence of God's opposition to birth control. The remainder of that same passage which reads: ". . . and thou shalt be under thy husband's power and he shall have dominion over thee," has been used to sanction women's unequal social status. In fact, the whole story of the Fall of Adam depicts women as weak and irresponsible—a stereotype encouraged by religion which women have been trying to shake for over two thousand years.

Religions, in short, have tended traditionally to oppose any attempt of people to take control of their lives and destinies. Divorce, family planning, *in vivo* or *in vitro* fertilization, sterilization, sexual preferences, abortion, and euthanasia have all been opposed by religious organizations.

Today the situation is little changed: Most religions give lip service to concepts such as freedom and justice but, for the most part, do little to promote those ideals.

G: As you have recognized, some of the more progressive clergymen are proclaiming the so-called social gospel and are actively practicing and promoting the social policies I know you advocate.

J: However, in so doing they are reflecting their own progressive thinking rather than any teachings of Jesus. Jesus never advocated a democracy, equal rights, or welfare for the most unfortunate members of society. Such concepts were outside his range of experience. Jesus assumed that mass poverty was an inveterate fact of the human condition ("the poor you will always have with you"), and was interested only in the practice of charity on a very personal level. To make Jesus out to be a social revolutionary is an exercise of imagination at best.

That religions are little concerned with fundamentally changing the human condition is no accident. As I'll show in the next chapter, religion has had its origins in human ignorance and misery. This presents a paradox. The attainment of knowledge and happiness greatly reduces the need for religion. Hence, to insure its survival, religion must contend that it offers the only path to happiness while simultaneously thwarting every effort to attain happiness through knowledge and the advancement of civilization.

Religion as the Antithesis of Learning

J: I've dealt with the basic conflict between faith and reason (especially scientific reasoning) at length in an earlier chapter. The inescapable conclusion for any relatively objective observer of religion is that virtually all religions, especially the more fundamentalist Judeo-Christian sects, are opposed to true education, which starts from the premise that all suppositions are open to inquiry, all hypotheses tentative, all conclusions subject to continual review. Pronouncements unsupported by the weight of logic and evidence are rejected. Hence there can be no dogmas. Judging by these criteria, all religious teachings are a form of indoctrination, not education.

"Darkness is the mother of religion," wrote Feuerbach. "It is the ignorance which solves all doubt by repressing it."[59] Like the Church Fathers Tertullian and Augustine, Adolf Hitler considered it a virtue to suppress reason: "One can die only for an idea which one does not understand."[60] The Church also promoted martyrdom for an irrational set of mysteries. Given the elevation of belief over reason, which invariably results in authoritarianism, it shouldn't be surprising that Nazism arose in southern Germany with its strong Roman Catholic tradition.[61]

Adam and Eve were allowed to stay in the Garden of Eden on the condition that they didn't eat of the tree of knowledge of good and evil. Clarence Darrow added that that has been the condition of the church until the present day: "They haven't eaten as yet."[62] Hypatia Bradlaugh Bonner stated it even more graphically: "The cramped foot of women was thought beautiful in China. The cramped mentality of the priest may be thought beautiful at the Vatican . . . but all bonds tend to deformity."[63] The libraries of the medieval church were filled with the wisdom of antiquity. But the church forbade access to this knowledge to all but those trusted not to be swayed by it. It wasn't until the birth of the printing press that the Church's iron grip was gradually loosened. When the bonds were lifted from people's minds with the ebbing of Church power and the birth of the Enlightenment, the natural consequence was a blossoming of science and reason that nearly spelled the demise of religion. It was in recognition of the threat presented by science that the Inquisition sent Giordano Bruno to the stake and imprisioned Galileo.

It is noteworthy today that along with a general decline in Western philosophical learning and culture, we see once again the rise of religious cults and superstitious beliefs such as astrology, channeling and divination. In the long run, I am hopeful that reason will prevail, but as

I will explain in the next chapter, there are strong incentives for the revival of religion. The consequences may yet prove fatal to the human race.

How Morality Advances in Spite of, Rather than Because of, Religion

J: Earlier I provided evidence to show that religion was not correlated with moral behavior. I would like to conclude here by showing that religion cannot even provide a meaningful basis for moral judgment.

Perhaps the most common themes of the ancient Greek philosophers were virtue and morality. Yet the Greeks found no need to relate these two subjects to religion. They implicitly recognized that values may be adopted by religion, but are never created by it. As Feuerbach explained, "I can found morality in theology only when I myself have already defined the Divine."[64] To try to derive morality from the "word of God" involves what Timothy J. Cooney calls the "theological fallacy": "If we didn't know right from wrong in the first place, we wouldn't know God from the Devil if we fell over Him."[65] Consequently, philosopher and atheist Kai Nielson is correct when he observes: "Rather than morality being based on religion, it can be seen that religion in a very fundamental sense must be based on morality."[66] He adds: "Christianity, Judaism, and theist religions of that sort could not exist if people did not have a moral understanding that was, logically speaking, quite independent of such religions. We could have no understanding of the truth of 'God is good' or of the concept of god unless we had an independent understanding of goodness."[67]

Those moral laws that humankind recognize as good were placed in Your mouth by humans. They were deemed to be good because experience has shown that they facilitate the attainment of humankind's primary goal: happiness. Any of the moral sentiments of religion and the great religious teachers are, for better or worse, derived from our own human experiences. The whole exercise led Feuerbach to the inescapable conclusion that "the beginning, middle, and end of religion is man."[68]

G: While not agreeing in the least with such nonsense, I wish to point out that in facilitating the transmission and acceptance of a moral code, religion would still have provided an invaluable service.

J: Unfortunately, there is no guarantee that all the moral precepts perpetuated by religion are valid. Allow me to explain. There are two kinds of moral laws: those attempting to describe the proper behavior

of humanity toward You, and those attempting to regulate the behavior of humans toward one other. The former, which are the proper
purview of religion, are of concern primarily to priests, ministers, and
rabbis, and, unless one shares their belief, they need not concern the
rest of humankind. After all, as the modern English philosopher G. E.
Moore pointed out, that "we should do things for the glory of God
[implies] that the existence of God is made better [or he is made happier]
by our glorifying him."[69] (Such implies, incidentally, that God would
not be a perfect being.)

My position is that in the area of human ethics—the behavior
of one person with regard to the rest of society—religion has, at best,
conveyed ethical norms arrived at by human observation and reasoning.
Morality was not given to humans by You. Rather, it was developed
by humans and attributed to You to provide a sense of authenticity
so that it might be accepted by people who could not be persuaded
of the need for a given moral norm by means of reason and evidence.
(We are back to Campbell's assertion that You are a metaphor for
human aspirations.) The major shortcoming of this method is that
both the best and the worst moral laws, along with a great deal of
utterly nonsensical prohibitions, can be transmitted as well by reliance
on Divine authorship. There is no test of reasonableness. Moreover,
as I have said earlier, the allegation of Divine origin does not permit
easy modification of an ethical norm, even when changing societal
conditions demand a need for revision. Worse yet, as I have shown,
morality based on "The Word of God" can result in torturing people
or at least ostracizing them for daring to challenge a moral doctine
of religion.

The result of all this has been to make the job of the moral philosopher most difficult. First, the philosopher must ascertain the best
ethic for a particular time and circumstance, and then try to persuade
some religious leader to avow that the new ethic came from You.
Unless religious leaders can see the direct value of the new ethic to
their own self-interest—which isn't often, since it is usually in their
interest to maintain the status quo—they will probably reject the new
ethic as the work of the Devil.

G: There was at least one notable exception to that generalization: Jesus,
who developed and transmitted a new ethic, and even died for it.

J: As I've taken great pains to explain, we don't actually know who
Jesus was or why he was put to death. However, it is likely that he
was killed because he was perceived as a political threat. You can't
go around claiming to be a god and threatening to establish a new
kingdom without risking serious political consequences. (At least you

couldn't in those days). As for his ethic, although I admire the way Jesus or the gospel writers made use of parables to convey his preachings, I've already shown that none of those ethical sentiments were original.

G: Before we rehash that argument I'll admit that if you searched all the religious and ethical treatises ever written you would undoubtedly find all the teachings of Jesus. However, isn't it true that Jesus opposed much of the trivial and absurd in Judaic ritual and custom? In so doing, he was able to focus people's attention on those timeless and universal moral precepts which, if they were followed, would provide for an immeasurably happier world.

J: That isn't quite right. The idea of sin and damnation, the failure to recognize the need to resist injustice, and reliance on faith rather than reason are just a few examples of the teachings ascribed to Jesus which interfere with the ability of humankind to achieve a happier state of existence. However, I agree that many of the teachings ascribed to Jesus—such as love of one's neighbor—are beautiful sentiments. Unfortunately, they are so general as to be inoperable without greater specificity. Simply what is my obligation to my neighbor, and who is my neighbor? Correct behavior to my neighbor in an isolated tribal setting is quite different than that required in a twentieth-century urban milieu.

G: That is exactly the function of religion—to help develop that specificity.

J: If that is the function of religion, it has failed spectacularly. As I have shown, religion has more often served purposes of warfare and economic exploitation. It has aptly been observed that the conqueror's religion becomes a sword and that of the conquered a shield. In the final analysis, religion has proven to be an impediment to the development of ethics. Like all human institutions, the religions of the world have been driven to advance the needs of their adherents. However, while a sect ultimately may meet some of the needs of its followers, albeit with a considerable lag, it most often advances the welfare of its practitioners to the detriment of those outside the sect.

A review of the moral and social progress of humankind shows that it was the thoughtfulness and persuasiveness of individuals which are responsible for what little civilization has occurred, most often in the face of opposition from the proponents of popular religions. Socrates was undoubtedly not the first to be condemned to death for religious heresy, and no one knows how many thousands of progressive thinkers have met a similar fate because their teachings threatened an established religion. T. H. Huxley's criticism of Christianity could as easily be applied to any religion: "Science, art, jurisprudence, the chief political and social theories of the modern world have grown out of those of Greece and Rome—not by favor, but in the teeth of the fundamental teachings of Christianity."[70]

All religions have resulted in conflict and, ultimately, an increase in the very human misery they were purportedly founded to alleviate. It was from this perspective that our nation's founders attempted to forge a constitution to ensure a secular state. They were extremely wary of the insertion of Christianity into the law of the land. James Madison reflected this view when he wrote: "During almost fifteen centuries has the legal establishment of Christianity been on trial. What has been its fruits? More or less in all places, pride and indolence in the clergy; ignorance and servility in the laity; in both superstition, bigotry, and persecution . . . [and] . . . in no instance have they been the guardians of the liberties of the people."[71]

This should not be surprising after we have uncovered the roots of Christianity and learned that it is simply a syncretic form of the pagan myths. I find it astounding that writers such as Ed Decker and Dave Hunt can do such a thorough job unraveling the pagan origins of Mormonism, yet fail to see that Christianity is based on the same myths. They even quote Manly P. Hall, who wrote:

> The ideals of early Christianity were based upon the high moral standards of the pagan mysteries, and the first Christians who met under the city of Rome used as their places of worship the subterranean temples of Mithras, from whose cult has been borrowed much of the sacerdotalism of the modern Church.[72]

Decker and Hunt are so imbued with their Christian beliefs that rather than investigate the truth of Hall's assertion, they narrow-mindedly attribute his position to the work of the Devil. Had they been a little more objective, they would have traced the basis of the Christian belief to the ancient myths as I have done. Moreover, they would then recognize that much of Judeo-Christian morality is based on a primitive worldview and, hence, more often than not, inappropriate in today's complex society. As Shaw observed, "The primitive idea of justice is partly legalized revenge and partly expiration by sacrifice."[73] This is exactly the underlying theme of Judeo-Christian morality and it is not hard to see how this Judeo-Christian tradition of "legalized revenge" has formed the basis for the worst elements of Western society's judicial system.

Aside from all the evils endemic to any organization purporting to speak for You, religion can never provide a solid foundation for a system of ethics. The reason is obvious: since Your very existence must be doubted at best, Your supposed commands can never provide a basis for morality.

The universal desire for happiness forms a much firmer basis for developing a moral system. Atheist and theist alike can agree on the basic moral principles necessary for the survival of civilization. Beyond that, however, atheists must turn to reason and evidence to support their ethical propositions, a far superior method of developing a morality to promote human happiness than relying on the words of self-professed emmissaries who contend that they speak for God.

G: Obviously you have given up all pretenses of this being a dialogue. All along it was merely a one-sided denunciation of religion.

J: Thoroughly warranted by its history. Still, despite all the limitations and dangers posed by the world's religions, I will concede that perhaps a religion might be of real value if it:

(1) admitted that religious beliefs are derived from ancient myths, but sought to explain why many of the lessons conveyed in those fables may have enduring value.

(2) acted as an independent body of scholars dedicated to investigation of ethical issues utilizing reason and evidence rather than ancient traditions and/or divine revelations. Reichley believes that churches could be well suited to the role of mediators or fact finders on moral issues. However, he points out that to perform such a function the churches would have to "cultivate objectivity and openmindness."[74] In my opinion, this condition would be all but impossible given the theological predispositions of most religions.

(3) attempted to influence human morality through appropriate behavior modification techniques rather than superstitious promises of eternal reward or damnation. An optimistic note in this regard is the growing number of priests, ministers, and rabbis who are taking courses in pastoral counseling, which is based heavily on modern psychological and psychiatric theory.

(4) refrained from using its unique position of trust for personal political or monetary advantage.

G: Now who is being idealistic? No one would listen to such a group of people who cannot back their opinions with the force of law.

J: What a shame! You are probably right. Defining ethical behavior in conformance with the needs of society—and at times enforcing that behavior with sanctions—is one of the functions of law. But unlike divine injunctions, human laws are dynamic; they can change to reflect the changing needs of society.

G: I know I'm playing right into your hands, but without divine guidance, on what basis do you determine whether a law is just and good?

J: Since You are a myth created by human beings, it is obvious that people have always created their own rules and laws anyway. More specifically, human law has evolved with human nature. You were only a convenient invention to assist in the enforcement of those laws. Unfortunately, as often as not You were hauled out to support bad laws and slow the progress toward better ones.

G: That does it. I am tired of your blatant denials of My existence. Since it was taking you so long to research and write this farce, I thought you might come to your senses, but now I can see that you are intractable. I will tolerate no more.

J: Fine. My need for You is at an end, anyway. There are only two major topics left to discuss in this work. The first topic is twofold: How did the myths about You originate, and why are they still so powerful in our present scientific age? The second is a more complete answer to the question You just raised, i.e., what alternative is there to organized religion as a means of guiding human behavior?

Much of the material of the remaining chapters has been touched upon elsewhere in the book, but here I will attempt a more cogent synopsis. Hence, I cannot permit any interruptions.

G: Which means?

J: Since I am no longer in need of Your assistance for expository purposes, You must now be relegated once more to the recesses of my imagination. You have served me well in Your role as a make-believe antagonist and have given new meaning to Voltaire's insightful observation: "If God did not exist, man would have to create him." Too bad Voltaire didn't realize how close he was to the truth: God doesn't exist and so man did create Him. Adieu, mon Dieu!

G: Seems like pretty shabby treatment to one who has been with you so long, even if I am only a product of your imagination.

J: Don't grumble. After all the evil Your concept has caused down through the ages, it would seem more fitting that I consign You to the Hades of your imaginary alter ego. It is debatable which concept—God or Devil—has caused more mischief.

G: Well then, goodbye. But, don't be surprised if I haunt you in your old age. We'll see if you don't find the need to resurrect Me again.

16

The Origins of Religion:
In the Beginning There Was Ignorance

Shabriri, briri, riri, iri, ri.
—Judaic chant to ward off demons

Religion is easily stripped of its claim to a supernatural origin when examined from a naturalistic perspective. In this chapter and the next I'll show that the origins of religion can be traced to the fundamental psychological traits of humankind. Some of the most basic are:

- the need to explain natural phenomena such as birth and death, sunrise and sunset, fire and rain, the changing seasons, sickness and insanity, unusual geological formations and even the origin of humankind;

- the desire to control nature rather than be a helpless victim of impersonal forces;

- the desire of some persons to control others through manipulation of basic fears and superstitions; and

- the usefulness of religion for developing social adhesion and control.

The Need to Explain

There have been many attempts to trace the origins of religion back to its earliest mythical foundations. Considering the fact that there were entire cultures flourishing five thousand years before the advent of written records, the task is formidable. Regardless of the exact form the earliest religion took, we can now understand the psychological basis for religious beliefs.

The subject has been explored by numerous philosophers, psychologists, and historians, including Ludwig Feuerbach, Arthur Schopenhauer, Sigmund Freud, James George Frazer, Joseph Campbell, Edward B. Taylor, Herbert Spencer, R. R. Marett Luciew, Levy-Brubl, Émile Durkheim, Andre Lang, William Schmidt, Jean Piaget, and many others. From their insights, and the findings of anthropologists and archaeologists, a fairly consistent outline begins to emerge.

Consider the plight of early *Homo sapiens.* They possessed none of the usual advantages necessary for survival among their animal rivals. They had neither prodigious strength; exceptional speed; nor keen hearing, sight, or smell. Even their reproductive abilities were unimpressive. However, through natural selection humans gained two strategic advantages. First was a stomach that rivaled that of a rat. Humans could digest almost anything from roots, grains, nuts and fruit, to grubs, insects and almost any form of animal life. Second, because they lacked the usual defenses, natural selection resulted in the survivors passing on the best of all possible defenses, an enlarged brain. With this rapidly (in geological time) growing capacity for cognition came a growth in curiosity.

As the adage says, even a cat exhibits curiosity, but for humans it knew no bounds. They wondered about the cause of everything: lightning, thunder, and rain, the wondrous rebirth of a dead earth each spring; the rise and setting of the sun; the movement of the moon and stars; the cause and meaning of dreams; and, of course, ultimately, the reason for life and death. Each of these phenomena in turn demanded an explanation and gave rise to a different element of what was eventually to become a universal mythology.

The renowned psychologist Jean Piaget explains in his book *A Child's View of the World* that children begin their conscious lives assuming all things are likewise conscious, and then revise that assumption to include only things that move and then, coming to the border of critical thinking, only things that move of themselves, i.e., animate creatures. In all probability, a similar process occurred in the evolution of primitive human beings.

From pictograms and ancient legends, Edward B. Tylor suggested that the most ancient forms of religion were forms of animism, i.e., the belief that all things possessed a consciousness. At this stage in their development, humans probably had no notion of a god or gods. Only gradually did the notion grow that there must be forces that controlled nature and acted on a gigantic scale.

Think of what it would be like if you were a prehistoric man or woman sitting in front of your cave one summer evening watching a storm brewing: The skies grow dark and threatening. The wind dies down to an eerie calm then suddenly begins to roar. A jagged streak of lightning rips the sky, followed by a deafening explosion in the heavens. Your first question might well be to the effect of, "What or who could be responsible for such power?" There were many other natural phenomena equally awesome and puzzling such as volcanoes, hurricanes, earthquakes and floods. These phenomena confronted all primitive groups and precipitated a psychological need for explanation. The Pulitzer Prize-winning Indian author N. Scott Momaday beautifully expresses that need in his book *House Made of Dawn* after viewing the unusual rock formation in northeastern Wyoming called Devil's Tower:

> There are things in nature which engender an awful quiet in the heart of man; Devil's Tower is one of them. He must account for it. He must never fail to explain such a thing or else he is estranged forever from the universe.[1]

After viewing Devil's Tower firsthand I readily appreciated Momaday's sentiment. The local Indian tribes attempted to explain Devil's Tower by the legend of a giant bear that chased a band of Indians to the top of a cliff. The local tribes attributed the deep furrows in the sides of the tower to the claw marks of the bear trying to climb its sheer face.

The simplest form of reasoning is an argument from analogy. Given the observation that every effect has to have a cause, primitive humans assumed that the nature of the cause had to be proportional to the effect. Therefore, stupendous effects such as storms, earthquakes, and volcanic explosions had to have a giant cause. It appeared "obvious" that inert material could not cause something like this to happen; it had to be a living thing: a powerful, intelligent being who was oftentimes angry enough to cause destruction. Just as a child is quick to accept the suggestion that Christmas presents must be due to Santa Claus, or thunder due to the "angels bowling," so early humans would readily conclude that gods were responsible for all the strange happenings in this world. Hence, it is easy to see how Greek mythology would invent a race of giants (the Titans), who were later overthrown by the Olympian gods, the latter being more akin to man and more cunning than their gigantic forebears. Supernatural beings with tremendous power over nature were the only plausible explanation in a prescientific world.

Dreams also must have concerned primitive people greatly, especially dreams of dead relatives and companions. Were not dreams simply a view into another life—an afterlife? The explanation seemed reasonable enough, and possibly relieved some of the anxiety borne by people faced with a very precarious existence. The earliest concept of this afterlife was not the heaven commonly portrayed today, but simply a vague, somewhat shadowy place in which the departed could dwell.

It is interesting that some of the earliest evidence of "religion" is in the ritualistic burial of Old Stone Age corpses. Skeletons have been found with the earliest forms of money and various objects and emblems buried with them either to accompany them in their next life or to help ensure their passage through death.

In the primitive cosmology, the earth was viewed as a flat disk, with the sky an inverted bowl above and a mysterious underworld below. The sun (god) descended into the underworld at the end of every day and rose again each morning. Certain caves were thought to be the entrance to this underworld. Such an idea is readily appreciated by anyone who has entered the labyrinth of a large cave like many of those in France, where some of the earliest ritualistic cave drawings have been discovered. Also, not surprising to anyone who has witnessed a volcano spewing forth its molten lava, would be the conclusion that the underworld, Hades, might be even worse than the dark and dreary interior of a cave. It might offer the torment of an eternal fire: not a very comforting thought to our primitive ancestors.

But there was reason for optimism. Each spring they witnessed the rebirth of their world from winter's death. This evidence suggested two ideas: Mother Earth and reincarnation. The latter concept, along with the daily "resurrection" of the sun (god), would later form the basis for the resurrection theme found in the myths of Osiris, Dionysus, Mithras, and Jesus. In its most primitive version, the Mother Earth mythology centered around fertility cults, as amply evidenced in the earliest Greek and Indian art. Philologist John M. Allegro contends that the names of the Greek and Hebrew principal gods, Zeus and Yahweh, are derived from a Sumerian word (possibly the most ancient culture known to man) meaning "juice of fecundity," "spermatozoa," "seed of life."[2] The Sumerian storm god, Iskur, had a name with a similar meaning—"mighty penis." Allegro hypothesized that early man observed that the spring rain brought new life to a barren earth. The fructifying principle in rain must be analogous to the semen in a man. And just as man was necessary to bring forth life in women, a male god was necessary to bring forth life in Mother Earth. Although Allegro may have pushed his hypothesis too far and has, not surprisingly, been impugned by Christian linguists, his hypothesis is not implausible.

How the earliest beliefs in gods actually originated, we can never know with any certainty. It is easy to see, however, how natural it would be for early humans to posit gods for all the inexplicable phenomena surrounding them.

The Need to Control

Belief in control of nature offered our ancestors the hope of altering their position as passive victims of those forces. According to sociologist Max Weber, two different avenues of control were attempted, magic and appeasement of divine forces. In the first, the magician supposed that through his artifice he could directly affect the forces of nature. The problem with this approach was that when the magician failed he might pay for his failure with his life. The second approach was practiced by the priests who argued that there were superior beings—gods—who controlled all of nature. If intelligent supernatural beings controlled the world, people had a chance of influencing these beings through supplication or propitiation. The priest had the advantage over the magician since blame for failure to produce the desirable consequence could be deflected away from the priests and onto the gods or undesirable behavior of the worshipers.[3]

According to Sigmund Freud, early man recognized that:

> impersonal forces and destinies cannot be approached. . . . But, if the elements have passions that rage as they do in our own souls, if death itself is not something spontaneous, but the violent act of an evil will . . . [we] can deal by physical means with our senseless anxiety . . . we can try to abjure them, to appease them, to bribe them.[4]

It is not surprising that viewing the violent world around them, early people would assume that the gods were extremely bloodthirsty. Is it any wonder, then, that the earliest forms of appeasement were oftentimes bloody human sacrifices? That the deities themselves welcomed innocent victims was apparent by how often they took the lives of young children, who obviously could have done nothing to offend the gods.

Another demonstration of early peoples' desire to control their fates is offered by mythologist Sir James G. Frazer, who reasons that the elements of magic in all religions are the result of the primitive belief that humans could control nature directly. This belief arose through a simplistic and mistaken view of cause and effect. For example, suppose that during a prolonged drought some early people decided to implore the gods who they believed controlled rain. They would send up their prayers and perhaps a sacrifice which they felt would persuade the gods of their sincerity. If it subsequently rained, they would naturally believe that their ritual produced the desired effect. As mentioned earlier, these are two related theories of early man as to why the ritual worked. The first is that because they were pleased with the ritual, the gods decided to answer the plea; this theory formed the basis of religion. The competing theory was that due to the nature of the relationship between the ritual and its direct effect upon the forces of nature, the ritual itself caused the rain. This, according to Frazer, was the basis of magic.[5]

In either case, to ensure the efficacy of their ritual early human beings would seek subsequently to perform it exactly as they had done the time before. Now the interesting point is that even if the next performance of the ritual did not result in rain, the failure would not challenge the belief in the power of the ritual. When magical chants didn't work, the shaman could quiet his doubters by alleging something else was wrong—the time, the place, the conditions—some element of a ritual that became increasingly more complex. Where the shaman was attempting to supplicate the gods, he had the added excuse that the lack of faith of his tribesmen was the cause of his ineffectiveness. Since no one had a better explanation for why things happened the way they did, they naturally believed the "expert."

If this all sounds a little silly and naive, remember that millions of Catholics still believe that their priests possess magic powers which, with the aid of the magic words, transform bread into flesh and wine into blood (although a growing number of Catholics now view the ritual as only symbolic). They also believe in the magical properties of holy water and relics such as the bones of saints or the wood from the alleged cross of Jesus. During my childhood, all these magical artifacts were used on me after I sustained injuries in a bicycle accident, resulting in my "miraculous" recovery. Hundreds, perhaps thousands, of persons in Italy also allegedly recovered from various illnesses when touched with the bones of St. Rosalia. I never could find out if there were any relapses after it was discovered that her bones were actually those of a goat.[6]

It may appear remarkable that people could be so credulous. But there is a simple psychological explanation: the phenomenon known as *conditioned response*. We all know that any animal can be trained to perform in a certain way by being offered an appropriate reward. However, psychologists have learned through experimentation that after a conditioned response is established it can actually be strengthened by providing a reward infrequently and randomly. Animals do not require a one hundred percent correlation to infer a causal relationship. Neither do humans, and they are not illogical in reasoning this way. Take the relationship between smoking and lung cancer, for example. Although not everyone who smokes develops lung cancer, the causal relationship between the one and the other was first discovered through statistical analysis. However, with science, unlike religion, the apparent linkage is only the first step in formulating a hypothesis. A tentative conclusion is offered only after years of experimentation and, ultimately, an understanding of exactly how a cause produces a given effect. As I showed earlier, in the case of prayer and ritual there is no statistical evidence to demonstrate their efficacy. But even if a cure only occasionally follows prayer, people will make the fallacious association and be conditioned to pray to achieve their goals.

The Path to Power

It seems safe to surmise that throughout history humans have always been able to be categorized by certain character types: the greedy and the generous, the leaders and followers, the tricksters and the gullible, the aggressive and the meek, and so on. There have always been snake oil salesmen. How easy it would be for some of the early tricksters to become the first shamans, the first priests, the Joseph Smiths and Ellen Whites and Pat Robertsons of their day. In fact, the profession of shaman or priest* is probably as old as that of prostitution. By establishing a complicated ritual that only he understood, the shaman or priest pretended—at times even believed— that he could, to some extent, control the very gods themselves. At the very least, he supposedly had a special relationship with the supernatural.

The successful shaman or priest is, above all, a gifted actor. (Is his past acting experience the key to Pope John Paul, II's popularity? Like Pat Robertson and the evangelists, he certainly knows how to work the crowds and has received ovations which any actor would envy.) If a person can throw in a little magic with his acting he can ensure an even greater draw. The magician knows the value of props in creating a mood; firelight, costumes, dancing, singing, incense—all are tools to create the proper atmosphere. To make certain that imitation of his artifice was difficult, and to appear even more mysterious, the shaman employed an unusual language of difficult words uttered almost inaudibly, secret drugs, potions, and charms, and a complex ritual. Furthermore, if a man was artistic, being a shaman was a natural outlet for his creativity in terms of pictograms, body painting, sacred masks, garments, and the like.

The ceremonies and rituals served another purpose as well. They helped forge a bond among the members of the group and gained for the shaman and tribal leaders the group's commitment. Joseph Campbell tells us: "The paramount function of all myth and ritual is to engage the individual, both emotionally and intellectually, in the local organization."[7] Every religious and political organization down to the present day has used religion in this way. The most successful have been the Judaic and Catholic religions.

Drugs also appear to have played an important role in several primitive

---

*By the term "priest" I refer here to its ancient meaning—a person who devotes his or her life to serving the gods.

religions. Certain Native Americans and Mexican Americans use peyote and mescaline. Jamaican Rastafarians use marijuana and hallucinogenic mushrooms. Hashish and opium are used in the Far East. John M. Allegro presents evidence that the *Amanita muscaria* mushroom, a powerful hallucinogen, was used by the earliest Sumerian, Hebrew, and Greek religions. The "sacred mushroom" is depicted on a Christian fresco as the tree of good and evil in the Garden of Eden. As Allegro explains, it is not surprising that the *Amanita muscaria* mushroom should play a major role in the establishment of religion. It is a truly mysterious fungus, appearing magically after a rain, deep in the seclusion of a forest. It initially looks like a penis, grows quickly, then goes to seed. Eating just the right amount will lead to the most incredible, perhaps heavenly, visions. But woe to those who tried to experiment with the divine drugs without the sacred knowledge: the wrath of the gods could be seen in the awful agony of the users' hallucinogenic visions of "hell" and ultimately their death. Possessing that secret of exactly how much to consume obviously put the priests in a unique position. To enhance their special status, only a few persons would be permitted entry into the sacred shaman ranks and only after completing a mysterious and arduous initiation ritual.

All these tricks, drugs, mysteries, and awe-inspiring rituals would undoubtedly have a powerful psychological impact on cult followers. That such a powerful psychological influence could produce a "spontaneous" recovery from a psychosomatic illness is not surprising. Nor is it surprising that the converse could also be true, i.e., that a shaman's curse could induce a psychosomatic trauma resulting in illness, and in the case of psychologically unbalanced persons, even death.

The effects of the shaman's art would even be more pronounced in a group setting, to which anyone who witnesses the mass hysteria of revival meetings can testify. The preacher carefully whips up the congregation with the expectation that something incredible is going to happen. Then all it takes is one person—either a "shill" or one of the more mentally unbalanced followers—to fall down with a shriek or scream that he/she feels the presence of the Lord. Like a match on a haymow, the whole congregation will ignite in an outburst of religious enthusiasm. To a first time observer, the sight of humans regressing to a primitive level of unreasoning, unthinking, raw emotion is frightening. But such practices have been going on for thousands of years.

Over one hundred years ago Charles Gradison Finney published his *Lectures on Revivals,* in which he taught that "the connection between the right use of means for revival and a revival itself is as philosophically sure as between the right use of means to raise grain and a crop of wheat."[8] Rhythmic stimulation, portentous rhetoric and social pressure have been shown to be extremely effective in generating mass conversions of super-stitious and ignorant people. With this basic knowledge it has always been as easy as taking candy from a baby for the thousands of Charles Finneys throughout history to "engineer individuals and crowds into making a choice which was ostensibly based upon free will."[9]

In addition to being outright frauds, many religious leaders no doubt have suffered from self-delusion and hallucinations. Like Jeanne d'Arc, they really did hear voices or have visions. Anyone who has dealt with individuals suffering from this illness knows that in its less severe form it can be episodic. Between episodes the person is quite normal. However, when in the deluded state, the sufferer can appear as a mystic or as if possessed by demons, depending upon the severity of the disease.

The powerful influence of a charismatic leader over the minds of those who want to believe in his supernatural abilities has been demonstrated many times in the present century. The enthusiasm on the faces of the multitudes of Christians on the occasion of a papal visit is identical to that seen in World War II documentaries on the faces of the German people gathering by the hundreds of thousands to listen to the ravings of Hitler. All these exhibitions of mass hysteria show that the veneer of rationality in modern humanity is very thin indeed.

But as any charlatan knows, even his best con might be discovered. Since the shamans could not "blow town" as easily as the modern "bunko" artist, they needed the protection of the tribal elders or king. This wasn't hard to obtain. First, the village elders probably wanted to believe that they had some one among them who could, if only to a limited extent, control the elements and possibly drive away the evil spirits of illness and pain continually threatening them. Second, having the spokesmen of the gods on their side gave a tremendous boost to their position of authority. Not only did the shaman's words legitimize the elders' own wishes and proclamations, but they provided the leaders with a convenient scapegoat when things didn't go as planned. At times, however, the shamans would try to turn the tables and blame society's misfortunes, especially loss at war, on the immoral or "blasphemous" actions of the king. We see this trick pulled often by the prophets of the Old Testament such as Elias, Oss, Amos, Mocheas, etc.

Third, as Weber postulates, "The religious congregation was regarded as a valuable instrument for pacifying the conquered. . . . Thus by virtue of decrees promulgated by the Persian kings from Cyrus to Artaxerxes, Judaism evolved into a religious community under royal protection, with a theocratic center in Jerusalem."[10]

Finally, in times of social crisis or the threat of some natural calamity, the religious rituals developed by the early priests offered a useful diversion for the masses. By involving the entire tribe in the ritual, they all could feel as if they were taking some positive action to effect the outcome. You can reduce the sideline critics by involving everyone in the ball game. Complex and mysterious ritual, coupled with colorful song and pageantry, and, above all, a charismatic leader, are the prime ingredients of successful cults to this day. There are, however, some exceptions to this general rule.

Earliest Forms of Religion

As mentioned, the first forms of organized religion appear to be the fertility cults. The earliest records of the Sumerians indicate that the Earth Mother myth was the foundation of this belief. Mother Earth needed a fructifying principle and that was filled, naturally enough, by the sun god. The sun was the source of light and warmth, the necessary conditions for life. Some form of the sun god and Mother Earth (with the latter waning in importance) can be found in virtually every primitive religion from the Sumerians to the Celts. The sun god was worshiped as "Inti" by the Incas, "Ra" by the Egyptians, and "Shinto" by the Japanese.

In some religions, like the Greek Dionysiac cults and certain Hindu sects, the fertility rituals grew into orgies of spectacular proportions. Pausanius, a Greek geographer, wrote that "The Hermiac statue which they venerate in Cyllese above other symbols is an erect phallus on a pedestal."[11] Given the excess of some of these cults, a predictable reaction would be for the more conservative elements of society to form an opposition cult—perhaps an early form of Stoicism—and rationalize a theology to support their antihedonistic beliefs. The entire history of religion, like all of human culture, reflects this constant action-reaction dialectic.

The sun god myth provided all the essential features of Western religions. Each day, people could witness the death and resurrection of the sun as it moved across the sky and down into the "nether regions," which later became Hades, and then Hell. Hades provided a place for those shades and the ghosts of departed souls who have a way of invading our sleep or, in the case of those who are mentally unbalanced or under the influence of drugs, even the waking hours.

It has been suggested that the three major functions of the sun were the basis for the Hindu trinity: production of life through heat, preservation of life through light, and destruction of life by fire.[12] The Christian Trinity is simply a reflection of the much earlier Hindu trinity of Brahma, Vishnu, and Siva. It is noteworthy that the concept of the Trinity was never mentioned by Jesus, and probably would have been considered as heretical to him as to any other Hebrew of his age. The idea of a Trinity was probably introduced through the writing of two of the early Church Fathers, Irenaeus and Justin Martyr who were heavily influenced by Neoplatonism and the myths of the East.

We can also trace the origins of Christianity and theology. The Egyptian myth of Osiris depicts a savior born of a virgin mother who is put to death and rises from the dead. Of particular interest is the concept of Jesus as the word (Logos) used in John's gospel. The concept of God as the Logos is found in the Egyptian Memphite theology and later in Greek Neoplatonism.[13]

It is not surprising that the early Mesopotamian cultures—Sumeria, Babylon, and Assyria—had very similar myths. What at first appears unusual is the commonality of the themes running through virtually all myths from Egyptian to Aryan to Chinese. Upon reflection, however, it might be expected that the common evolutionary experience would result in a fairly consistent set of myths. Three explanations are equally plausible:

First, if humankind had a common origin—whether in Africa, Mesopotamia, or the Far East—it might result in a common origin of basic archetypal myths. Then, as humans migrated away from their center of origin, the myths were altered to reflect the particular environment in which each tribal group found itself.

Second, myths could have developed later in human evolution, after migration had occurred. However, the need to explain similar phenomena would give rise to similar myths. Why were bones and fossils of fish found on the sides of mountains far from water? There had to be a great flood sent by God. Why were there different races? Due to a curse by God. Why was there so much evil? Because gods were fickle at best, easy to displease, or, later in the evolution of theology, because some of the gods were evil, i.e., demons. And so forth.

The third explanation is that trade and wars of conquest resulted in a continual cross-pollination of myths until similar elements could be found in virtually all of them. Each conquest brought to both the victors and the vanquished a new wealth of myths that they subsequently altered to fit their own national character and situation.

To some extent, all three explanations may have played a role, but the evidence suggests that the third explanation was the dominant one. Note that the myths of the Native Americans are quite distinct from those of the Middle East. This should be expected since the Native American culture evolved independently from outside influence for thousands of years. On the other hand, there is great similarity among Middle-Eastern myths of Hebrews, Moslems, Christians, and Hindus.

The area of Palestine was the crossroad for all the conquering hordes from the Egyptians to the Persians. What myth each succeeding civilization added and what was retained of indigenous beliefs can never be sorted out. For example, the story of the war in heaven is told among all Eastern cultures. For the Greeks, it was a fight among the gods. For the Israelites it was a war between angels loyal to God and those loyal to Satan. The myth was an attempt to explain the constant battles of opposites which appear in nature: light and dark, good and evil, life and death, the yin and yang of Buddhism.

As I reported earlier, some scholars believe that the Satan of the Old Testament originated with the Persian influence on Judaism. The religion of the Persians, Zoroastrianism, taught that there were two major gods: Angra Mainya who created hell, and Ahura Mazda, who created heaven. The Persian legends also told of an angelic hierarchy and professed a belief in a last judgment of humankind followed by appropriate rewards or punishments. However, I think the evidence from the Chaldean tablets translated by George Smith shows that the origin of the legend of rebellious angels led by Lucifer was derived from the ancient Babylonian myth of the war between the gods and the evil forces led by the dragon Tiamat.[14] It is probable that both the Persian and Babylonian myths were based on still more ancient Sumerian and Egyptian legends.

Support for the cross-fertilization of myths is found in the early iconography of Jesus with his halo and long, flowing blond hair. Now a blond-haired Israelite certainly would have been unusual and probably commented upon by the early gospel narrators. Yet they say nothing of the physical description of Jesus. That in itself is a little suspicious. Furthermore, the early tradition also says that Jesus was far from attractive. According to Origen, he was "small in body and deformed." Justin Martyr alleged that Jesus was "without beauty or attractiveness—of mean appearance." Tertullian claimed he was not even of ordinary beauty. And Clement of Alexandria went so far as to state that Jesus was almost repulsive.[15]

Where, then, did this beautiful physiognomy of the blond Christ come from? It appears no simple coincidence that all sun gods of ancient India were pictured with golden hair and a halo of glory, i.e., the rays of golden sunshine. Serapis, an incarnation of the Egyptian sun god, was so depicted and thought to have "supplied the first idea for the conventional portraits of the Savior."[16] In fact, the Roman emperor Hadrian thought that the early Christians were actually worshiping the sun god Serapis. In a sense, they were but didn't know it.

It should also be remembered that the Israelites arrived on the scene quite late in terms of mythological development. Whether they were descendants of the ancient Sumerians, or were the conglomeration of Egyptian slaves gathered from the far-flung reaches of the empire, cannot be known with certainty. The Hebrew mythologists didn't begin their written accounts until well after the alleged time of the Exodus. The period of organized civilizations until the Exodus was about six thousand years, ample time to create and refine an entire body of elaborate myth and ritual.

The early books of the Bible refer to Elohim, a plural form indicating a belief in several gods. It is only later that the Hebrew name for God, translated as Yhum, and pronounced Yahweh, appears. (The term Jehovah is actually a mistaken translation and appears nowhere in the Hebrew Bible.)

It is important to note that the early Israelites were not monotheistic. As mentioned earlier, they worshiped several gods, including Baal and Moloch. The ascendancy of Yahweh over all other gods was probably a gradual event associated with the rise to power of his particular group of followers. Some writers suggest that it took place when Josia succeeded his father, King Amon, who was a worshiper of Baal, in 641 B.C.E. The account given in 4 Kings 22 tells how the high priest Helcias accidentally found a book of law which he alleged to be the word of God. As I discussed in chapter 8, the story smacks of a good hoax played on the gullible teenage king.

Whatever the case, the demand that only Yahweh be worshiped by the Israelites was an obvious device to establish a national identity and national pride by suggesting that the Israelites had a special relationship— a covenant—with the most powerful of the gods. They were his "chosen" people. To justify their right to take the lands of indigenous peoples, Israel's priests had to create a unique historic relationship with their god, a practice common to all civilizations down to the present day. (In U.S. history it was dubbed "Manifest Destiny.")

At the time when the first books of the Old Testament, Genesis and Exodus, were written—probably during the Babylonian captivity—the writers simply recorded an earlier oral tradition rich in the mythologies borrowed from virtually all the other cultures of the Middle East. Recall that the Israelites were conquered by the Egyptians, Assyrians, Moabites, Canaanites, Midianites, Philistines, and Babylonians. The remainder of the Old Testament is the creation of a semihistorical account of Israelites which included most of the superstitions of their age.

In the most primitive religions the gods were not interested in human morality, but rather with sacrifices of appeasement and respect. The earliest religions were concerned primarily with imploring the gods to provide the means of survival: food, rain, sunshine, and safety from enemies. The Hebrews were no exception, imploring the gods to give them manna and save them from the Egyptians (or whoever was out to destroy them at the time).

There was also great concern over the perfidious demons who were thought to be the cause of all disease, sickness, infirmities, and vices. The ancient Hebrews introduced a variety of means to guard against these, some which have become a permanent part of their traditions. In addition to the little chant I quoted at the beginning of this chapter, which consisted of reducing the demon's name (hence his power) syllable by syllable, demons were repulsed by the wearing of phylacteries,* the fringes or twisted cords known as *zizith,* and the fixing of the Mezuzah on the door post. It is amazing how the silly superstitions of yesteryear become the sacred symbols of today. But such is the nature of religious development.

Not all demons were considered evil. Originally they were thought to be lesser divine beings who peopled the cosmos. It was believed that each person was watched over by his/her own special demon.[17] Later, "good" demons were called angels, and to this day many religions, such as Catholicism, teach that every person has his/her own "guardian" angel.

The earliest concept of the fully defined male god was that of a very large and powerful version of man. To the anthropomorphic gods were attributed all the human emotions: anger, joy, love, hate, jealousy of other gods, and most of all, a sullen capriciousness. The god that emerged from the Hebrew tradition followed the stereotype: petty, vindictive, jealous, unpredictable, and terrifying. He did, however, offer one significant advance in the evolution of religion: he no longer demanded human sacrifice (with a few notable exceptions). The Old Testament writer who gave us the legend of Abraham and Isaac did humankind an invaluable service by ending this bloody tradition.

On the other hand, the Old Testament writers did a grave disservice to all succeeding generations down to the present day with their racist concept of a covenant between God and his "chosen people." Ultraorthodox Israelis are thwarting peace initiatives in the Middle East by their claims that God has granted Israel a right to own and rule a particular geographic area to the exclusion of others who have lived there for over two thousand years.

Nothing in the teachings ascribed to Jesus indicates that he opposed this particular form of racism. If he commanded "love thy neighbor," his audience naturally would have taken the term "neighbor" literally. It wasn't a revolutionary idea, since their neighbors were also Jewish. The gospels do attempt to broaden the concept a little with the story of the Good Samaritan, but Samaritans were also a Jewish sect whose members believed they were the true descendants of Abraham. It was only the complete rejection of Jesus and his disciples by the Israelites which caused his disciples to try their luck among the Gentiles. "Love thy neighbor" took on a slightly broader meaning, at least extending to all "right thinking" Christians. However, as we saw, for the next two millennia heathens and heretics could be persecuted with a clear conscience.

---

*The two small black leather cubes containing verses from Deuteronomy and Exodus.

The Historical Jesus and the Role of Paul

Essentially, what do we know about Jesus? Since he wrote nothing himself, and since there was nothing written about him at the time he was alive (except, perhaps, a few vague references discussed in chapter 5), we have no certain knowledge that Jesus did, in fact, exist. However, given the writings of his disciples or, more likely, the followers of his disciples, we may assume that there did exist a preacher named Jesus. It would appear that he performed the usual feats of healing psychosomatic illnesses. He probably also preached moral behavior, but it is impossible now to determine exactly what was the teaching of Jesus and what was the creation of the gospel writers. There is a good possibility that Jesus was a member of the fundamentalist Jewish sect called the Essenes. In all liklihood he never intended to found a new religion; his intention may well have been the same as many of the prophets before him: to prompt wayward Jews to return to the strict observance of the Mosaic Law.

Jesus' charismatic personality attracted a large following of those who were looking to rebel against their Roman conquerors. Some Judaic leaders feared his teaching as a threat to the established order and their collaboration with the Roman conquerors. They may have conspired with the Romans to have Jesus silenced. He played right into their hands; whether deliberately or not, we'll never know. Did he go mad and really believe he was a god? Was he simply a man of conviction who was willing to die for his values like soldiers do in every war? Did he even have a choice in the matter, or was he simply rushed off and executed? The latter case is the most easy to believe.

Jesus' disciples tried to keep his memory alive by spreading the myth that he rose from the dead and quickly ascended to heaven. The story was too preposterous for any but the most fanatical of his followers to believe. Possibly the fabulous account was accepted by the Essene sect to which Jesus may have belonged.

We can be more certain of the history of one zealous disciple named Saul of Tarsus, who originally was a persecutor of the Essenes or early Christians. Saul suffered a major mishap of some sort which brought about a remarkable change of heart (his description of being struck by a blinding light is similar to the experience related by many epileptics). Afterward Saul contended that he had a revelation from God to end his persecutions, changed his name to Paul and joined the Jesus cult. Just as before his conversion Paul had fanatically persecuted the sect he opposed, after the incident on the road to Damascus he became a zealous supporter. However, since he had never known Jesus or heard his message first-hand, it is Paul's own interpretation of the teaching of Jesus that is transmitted in Paul's epistles. The religion that evolved from it should more aptly be named Paulinism rather than Christianity.

In the teachings of Paul we find the unmistakable stamp of the fanatic who would allow no deviation from his theological pronouncements. As it evolved over the next several centuries, the Christian religion would reflect the temper of Pauline theology even more than the alleged teachings of Jesus. Realizing that he had little chance of expanding the cult among those who knew of the real Jesus, Paul gave up on the Jews and began spreading his story among the Gentiles. Of course, the educated people of the day did not give the new religion much credence, but with the downtrodden and slaves Paul struck a sympathetic chord. They were used to believing in many gods; one more wouldn't upset their sense of theology. They even had an "unknown" god in their pantheon. Paul was quick to declare that this was reserved for Jesus and hence assured them that they already believed in Paul's Christ.

Using Immortality to Sell Christianity

A new theology of itself would have been tough to sell had Paul not had in reserve the ultimate elixir of the patent medicine trade—immortality—guaranteed to all who believed in his god. Now, this was really something! Kings and heroes always had the chance of making the leap to immortality with the gods. But for the poor peons at the bottom of the social heap—who were the majority in those days—the best one could hope for was to end up as a vague "shade" wondering in Sheol (Hades). The Christian concept of heaven, on the other hand, was pure bliss. When the Greek philosopher Celsus criticized Christianity as blind faith, he was undoubtedly right; but what appealing alternative did he have to offer? Only an inglorious end after a life of suffering. Today many thousands commit suicide every year and risk eternal damnation just to end their wretched lives. Is it any wonder that two thousand years ago many equally desperate people would soon be willing to throw down their miserable lives in order to attain eternal happiness? After all, there have never been any complaints from disillusioned martyrs.

The promise of heaven was recognized for its military value even before the dawn of Christianity. Julius Caesar wrote that the Druids believed "the cardinal doctrine that souls do not die, but after death pass from one to another and this belief, casting fear of death aside, they hold to be a great incentive of valor."[18] Originally, the Judaic idea of an afterlife was similar to that of the ancient Greeks. One fate awaited all: after death they existed in Sheol as vague shadows of their former selves. The books of Isaiah and Daniel allude to the resurrection, but it wasn't universal, rather it was for those who were particularly good during their lives on earth. The prophet Ezekiel coupled the kingdom of God with the doctrine that persons are rewarded in proportion to their righteousness or punished in proportion to their sins here on earth.[19]

A more definite concept of heaven was offered by the Persian teacher and "Savior" Zoroaster, who lived about 600 B.C.E. His concept was adopted by one of the Persian trading rivals, the Babylonians.

In 586 B.C.E. Nebuchadnezzar II took Jerusalem and forced the Israelites into captivity. It was during the two generations in Babylonia that the people of Israel were exposed to the Babylonian concept of an afterlife. Of course, if they were exiled for a time in Egypt, the Jews would have learned about the Egyptian concept of immortality. But in Egypt immortality was reserved only for the pharaohs, the "sons of god."

Other than brief references by the prophets Ezekiel and Daniel, the concept of an afterlife does not figure materially in the Bible until 167 B.C.E. when the people of Israel, led by the Machabee brothers, revolted against the Seleucid king Antiochus IV. The leaders of the revolt used the idea of life everlasting to argue that it was better to lay down their lives rather than transgress the law of Moses. The idea of an eternal reward was also useful for inspiring greater valor on the part of their troops. By the time of Jesus, physical resurrection was the official teaching of the Pharisees. The notion of immortality was especially important in the teachings of the Zealots. It provided the needed incentive for the mass suicide of 960 men, women, and children at Masada and as many as 5,000 at Gamla to avoid surrendering to the Romans and violating their orthodox law.*

Perhaps because they already had a belief in some form of afterlife, Hebrews and Muslims were never very enamored of the promises of Christianity.

Repackaging Jesus

To substantiate their claims of Jesus' divinity, many early Christians began writing stories about his life. These accounts were based on oral traditions, possibly some subsequently lost or destroyed documents, and a substantial

---

*Actually it is incorrect to say the children committed suicide; they were obviously murdered by their fanatical parents. I note that in a televised version of the Masada tragedy, the Zealots are viewed in a heroic perspective. It makes me wonder whether some day suicides and murders caused by the Reverend Jim Jones might not be similarly depicted.

amount of wishful thinking. Dozens of accounts were written of the life of Jesus incorporating the major myths alleged of every other god or hero. Teachings of past prophets and popular homilies were also incorporated where they served to advance the new theology. For the next three hundred years, these gospels were edited to bring the various versions into rough congruence and to lend support to a particular theological position. The more outlandish gospel versions were discarded (and perhaps the more truthful as well—we'll never know); finally the four gospels of Matthew, Mark, Luke, and John were sanctioned as canonical about 180 C.E. because, according to Irenaeus: "For there are four climates and four cardinal winds, but the Gospel is the pillar and foundation of the church, and its breath of life. The Church therefore was to have four pillars, blowing immortaility from every quarter, and giving life to man."[20]

At the same time, all sorts of people found it advantageous to jump on the Christian bandwagon. Many were undoubtedly sincere, well-intentioned people who saw the sterility of their official state religion and sought a more substantive moral teaching. Others were simply the usual charlatans out to exploit the credibility of the uneducated. The second-century Greek satirist Lucian writes that "whenever any crafty juggler, expert in his trade, went over to Christianity he was certain to grow rich immediately by making prey of their simplicity."[21]

It was only a matter of time until the better educated people saw that in Christianity lay a potent movement which only required a little organization and direction to carry it forward as a powerful political force. Again, many of these early intellectuals may have been sincere, although overly credulous. In those days, as today, the line between fact and fantasy was oftentimes indiscernible. All the early Church Fathers believed in a flat earth, visions, prophecies, signs, portents, angels, devils, dragons, sea monsters, and miracles, as did the general population. Jerome saw centaurs, fawns, satyrs and incubi and conversed with them. On the other hand, some of the Fathers were zealots who were willing to lie to promote their cause. Such was the Church historian Eusebius who admitted that he was not above lying if it promoted the faith.[22] Consequently, he concocted many of the fantastic stories of the early saints and martyrs. Cardinal Newman admits in *Apologia pro Vita Sua*: "The Greek Fathers thought that, when there were just causes, an untruth need not be a lie."[23] This practice of fabrication was so prevalent that in his works *De Mendacio* and *Contra Mendacium,* Augustine warned his fellow theologians against an excess of pious lying.[24]

Why these lies and myths were so readily accepted is not hard to fathom. Clergy were thought to be learned men of God who knew what they were talking about. The audience was composed primarily of desperate, wretched people who would easily grasp at any straw of hope. Furthermore, their knowledge of science, even for the most educated of the age, was virtually nil. As Charles Bradlaugh wrote: "Religious belief is powerful in proportion to the want of scientific knowledge on the part of the believer. The more ignorant the more credulous."[25] His observation certainly holds true down to the present day.

Many of the ancient pagan myths, rituals, and even statues were given a "face lift" and incorporated into Christianity. It was a blatant, and incredibly successful, attempt to preempt the opposition. There were, however, many persons who would not be taken in by ancient myths or new prevarications. These were the seekers of truth—the true philosophers. They were the descendants of Greek and Roman philosophers who tried to lift humanity from the darkness of superstition to follow the light of true understanding. Through application of science and reason, these men saw the absurdity of belief in the gods. Lucian of Samosata, for example, wrote satirical dialogues against religious beliefs and many of the more absurd metaphysical philosophies of his contemporaries.

For a time, the descendants of the rational philosophical tradition were a source of irritation to Christianity, and the Church Fathers expended a great deal of energy fending off their attacks. With the conversion of Constantine, this annoyance was quickly suppressed. Wielding the full military power of the state, the Church outlawed all dissent and ushered in a period of intellectual suppression unequaled in the history of the world. For more than a millennium, any idea contrary to the doctrine of the Church was punishable by torture and death. If one wishes to appreciate the intellectual environment during a period of an imposed state religion, look at the situation in Iran during the 1980s. It is no coincidence that in both cases the wedding of church and state resulted in persecution and suppression. In both cases, it was absolutely essential that all true intellectualism of any kind be snuffed out. The Dark Ages were no accident; they were essential to the establishment of Christianity. As John Gardner so graphically wrote in his little masterpiece, *Grendel*: "Theology does not thrive in the world of action and reaction, change: it grows on calm, like the scum on a stagnant pool and it flourishes, it prospers on decline."[26]

Christianity's Inevitable Decline

Despite the suppression of thought, as humankind became more sophisticated in its knowledge of the workings of nature, it was only natural that some people began to question the efficacy of the priests and their magical rituals. Indeed, as people became aware of natural causes, they began to question the very existence of the gods themselves. The priests' answer to this skepticism was twofold: invoking the power of the state to exterminate dangerous freethought, and concurrently developing even more complex, serpentine, theological logic. Many philosophers were not taken in by this specious reasoning. They demonstrated that, fundamentally, all theology and metaphysics is pseudolearning, a semantic sleight of hand to give the appearance that superstitious beliefs have an intellectual, rational foundation. They further showed that, by definition, God, if he existed, would be unknowable. Yet theology—bolstered by the semantic alchemy of metaphysics—attempted to discuss God as if he could be discovered by reason or experience. The early Christian theology was dominated by the influence of Plotinus and the Neoplatonic transcendentalism championed by Augustine. Later, Aquinas and scholasticism offered a warmed-over version of Aristotelian metaphysics as a basis for positing a prime mover.

In the final analysis all theology, whether Christian or otherwise, is a marvelous exercise in logic based on premises that are no more verifiable— or reasonable—than astrology, palmistry, or belief in the Easter Bunny. Theology pretends to search for truth, but no method could lead a person farther away from the truth than that intellectual charade. The purpose of theology is first and foremost to perpetuate the religious status quo. Religion, in turn, seeks to maintain the social stability necessary for its own preservation. Joseph Campbell explains: "The paramount concern of a popular religion cannot be, and never has been, 'Truth,' but the maintenance of a certain type of society, the incubation in the young and refreshment in the old of an approved system of sentiment upon which the local institutions and government depend."[27]

As happens in all great movements built on a false premise, the seeds of the Church's undoing were sown during the period of its greatest apparent success. Corruption and internal strife demonstrated that the Church hierarchy was no more godlike than any temporal institution. At the same time, the European aristocracy became concerned about its own erosion of power. Churches are supposed to support the state and vice-versa; when either seeks to usurp the powers of the other a mortal conflict will ensue. And it oftentimes did. A similar sequence of events could be traced in most of the other major world religions.

The greatest blow to Christianity came with the invention of the most liberating tool in human history—Johann Gutenberg's printing press. Despite the fact that Gutenberg's first publication was the Bible, the more perceptive clerics realized that the printing press was a grave threat to the Church's dominion over the human mind and sought to have it destroyed. Unfortunately for the Church, others thought that it could be effectively controlled and utilized to the Church's advantage. Although, as Galileo and many others were to discover, the Church would never abandon the fight to retain control of the human mind, in the end the Church gradually lost ground.

The Rise of New Religious Cults

Still the fight is not over. One does not have to be gifted with psychic powers to predict that new religious cults will continue to spring up in the future. The characteristics of the new religious movements will follow the same format followed in the establishment of all prior religious movements:

1. They will arise at a time of social crisis or high general anxiety, such as the threat of war, economic chaos, or the collapse of existing institutions.

2. There will arise a strong charismatic leader who promises salvation to those who unquestioningly follow him.

3. He and/or his followers will attempt to show that all of history inexorably points to this historic moment. Consider the Old Testament prophecies quoted about Jesus.

4. He will point to signs of the pending apocalypse. Jesus Christ, Paul, Joseph Smith, Charles Russell, and William Miller all preached that the end was near. The fundamentalists are still preaching it.

5. There is a call to direct involvement on the part of the followers. They can have a direct role in assisting the "savior" in his mission.

6. The new cult will be eclectic, borrowing its doctrines and rituals from a variety of older religions.

7. The rituals will become a central focus of the religion, especially after the death of the leader.

8. The belief will gradually become codified and the organization bureaucratic. All dissent will be ruthlessly stamped out.

Although we think of these factors as characteristic of Western, especially Christian, religions, Geoffrey Parrinder has shown that most of these elements can be found in virtually all religions. For example, Soka Gakkai, the fastest growing religious group in Japan, has as its expressed aim the intention of becoming the national religion.[28] It's the same old story. There have been thousands of religions founded over the centuries, and it is safe to say that in the vast majority of instances they have sought to gain support from civil authorities. Where they have succeeded, they have soon attempted to force all persons to accept their respective belief systems.

But this is not the whole story. If I were still in dialogue with my imaginary God, he would surely object: "If religious leaders are so power-hungry, greedy, or simple minded as you make them out," He would argue, "why do so many people flock to join? Certainly religion must answer some fundamental need in people." He would be right. I discussed some of these psychological needs in this chapter. They revolve around the desire of our primitive ancestors to explain and control the environment. But there are several other psychological needs also addressed by religion. Let's explore some of these desires, which guarantee the perpetuation of religious myths despite all evidence to the contrary.

17

Why the Myths Live On:
Today's Psychological Motivators

What the populace learned to believe without reasons, who could refute it then by means of reasons?

—Friedrich Nietzsche

It would be tempting but overly simplistic to say that people flock to churches to be reassured that God does exist and all the promises of the Bible, especially an afterlife, will come true. But this is only part of the story. Erich Fromm wrote: The influence of any doctrine or idea depends on the extent to which it appeals to psychic needs in the character of those whom it addresses."[1] Shakespeare expressed this idea more poetically in his play *Henry IV*: "The wish is father to the thought." The purpose of this chapter is to analyze the psychological needs religion fills.

The philosopher David Hume began to investigate some psychological aspects of belief in his *Dialogues Concerning Natural Religion* (1779), but Ludwig Feuerbach was the first to fully explore the psychological basis of Christianity. In 1841 Feuerbach published his classic work, *The Essence of Christianity*. Although he explicitly examines Christianity, his psychological analysis could be extended to any religion. Feuerbach postulated that God was no more than "the realized wish of the heart, the wish exalted to the certainty of its fulfillment, of its reality, to that undoubting certainty before which no contradiction of the understanding, no difficulty of experience or of the external world, maintains its ground."[2] According to Feuerbach, the attributes of God are simply a projection of human needs, hopes and longings: a being who is all-good, all-powerful, all-wise, all-happiness and, most of all, eternal.

> The divine being is nothing else than the human being or, rather the human being purified, freed from the limits of the individual man, made objective—i.e., contemplated and revered as another distinct being. All the attributes of divine nature are, therefore, attributes of human nature.[3]

Elsewhere he writes:

> God springs out of the feeling of a want; what man is in need of, whether this be a definition and therefore conscious, or an unconscious need,—that is God.[4]

Feuerbach goes on to say that nowhere is this "need for God" better evidenced than in the Greek and Roman pantheons where "accidents" (the archaic term for attributes or predicates of being) were deified, and virtues, passions, and states of mind were worshiped as independent beings. Feuerbach then shows how, one by one, those personified accidents were consolidated into attributes of God: order, love, understanding, justice, and so on. Although Feuerbach doesn't explicitly say this, we have seen how the negative passions were also originally predicates of God as well: jealousy, revenge, anger, and others. In recent years, these later attributes of God—which were always rationalized by vengeful priests and ministers under the heading of Divine Justice—have been quietly laid to rest. However, if useful, we can expect a "resurrection" of these less loving characteristics. I once heard Professor Theodore Gaster describe the term "God" as a "reductionist expression of what is approachable, tractable . . . of human experience."[5] Therefore, God will be vested with those characteristics, both good and bad, which dominate the human psyche at any time.

Ultimately, belief in God may be a genetically determined characteristic of human beings. Sociobiologist Edward O. Wilson thinks that belief in God is a coping mechanism, fundamental to the very nature of our species: "Beliefs are really enabling mechanisms for survival. Religions, like other human institutions, evolve so as to enhance the persistence and influence of their practitioners."[6] If Wilson is correct, as long as society fails to meet the psychological needs discussed below with more successful means, we might expect the belief in theism to continue.

The Universal Desire for Immortality

John Steinbeck wrote:

> After the bare requisites to living and reproducing, man wants most to leave some record of himself, a proof, perhaps, that he really existed. He leaves his proof on wood, or stone, or on the lives of other people. This deep desire exists in everyone, from the boy who writes dirty words in the public toilet to the Buddha who etches his image in the race mind.[7]

No doubt such a desire drives me to write this book. However, for most people, simply leaving an artifact behind is not enough. They can't bear the thought of leaving this life in the first place. Based upon their own analysis and a review of other studies, Argyle and Beit-Hallahmi conclude that "this group of studies provides very strong support for the theory that fear of death is the basis for religious beliefs."[8]

To say that most people believe in some sort of god is only to recognize that virtually all people would like to escape death. I agree with Schopenhauer that the fundamental purpose of religion, and hence the belief in God, is a desperate effort to escape mortality. "For if one could establish their doctrine of immortality for them in some other way, the lively zeal for their gods would at once cool, and it would give place to complete indifference."[9]

Just as the idea of a special covenant with God was the centerpiece of the Hebrew religion, the concept of immortality became the touchstone for emerging Christianity. It's easier to die for a cause (especially if you are a slave or suffering pauper) if, by dying, you gain eternal bliss. It was the concept of universal salvation, not the uniqueness of the alleged teachings of Jesus, which raised Christianity to prominence in Europe.

In the New World, the priests found that their offer of immortality did little to impress most Native American groups. Many of the tribes of North America already had a concept of an afterlife to which Christians referred derogatorily as the "happy hunting ground." Christianity had a difficult time making converts, since it offered nothing new. Moreover, the natives of North America were not anxious to leave an environment which, on the whole, they found pleasing. For the Aztecs, however, the story was completely different. Among the Aztecs ordinary men went to Mictlan, "a somber and inhospitable realm." The nobles and priests, on the other hand, went to the Mansion of the Sun. It is small wonder that the masses of common folk were eager to convert to a religion that offered eternal bliss on a more democratic basis. In addition, the rigid and cruel class structure of the Aztecs caused many to desire a more just world in the hereafter.

To make their adherents desirous of immortality, Christianity had to keep them focused on the inevitability and proximity of death. The Christian funeral service does an excellent job of pressing upon the mind the imminence of death by reminding the living how temporal and fleeting is their stay here on earth. They are told not to worry though, because this life is simply a "vale of tears." So be happy at the thought of impending death because it is "only through dying that one can gain eternal life." The entire ceremony is an apology for living. Living for its part is virtually an evil for which one must atone by dying. Christian prayers for the dead contain no reference to how sweet life can be or may have been to the deceased. How much more life-affirming was the Native American philosophy that looked upon life as good and death as simply a natural event in nature's cycle of death and rebirth. The Epicurean philosophy—so often distorted by Christian theologians—also offered a positive outlook encouraging people to enjoy the feast of life and then graciously depart the banquet to make room for others.

Death is the very mother's milk of religion. During the Middle Ages, the plague sent thousands of poor, frightened people flocking to the churches. In this century, war and the threat of it have been major boons to religion. It is not surprising, then, that after the horrors of World War I, one Christian writer expressed a view undoubtedly shared by many others: "If, even for a few generations, we act on our own conjecture of immortality, the larger vision, the more profound basis of purpose, will so advance human existence as to make this war worth its price."[10] What he is really saying is that the growth in religious fervor following a war is worth the horror and death. In the post-World War II era many evangelists once again preached the apocalypse—this time an inevitable nuclear conflagration—in an attempt to scare people into their folds.

If death is the ultimate incentive for religion, pleasure is the ultimate disincentive. To make this life pleasurable distracts our focus from death and the desire for immortality. Consequently, the need for religion is weakened. Therefore, religions present pain as "purifying" and suffering as "ennobling." Pleasure is equated with selfishness as if it were a contradiction of logic to state that an individual might seek both personal pleasure and the pleasure of others as well. However, no such contradiction need exist if we recognize that there can be immense pleasure in helping others.

In its effort to abrogate the joy this world can offer, religion focuses its attack on sexual pleasure. Looking back upon my youth, I can still recall the Catholic Church's hysterical objections to a movie called *Baby Doll*. At the time I was certain it must have contained a most disgusting exhibition of sexual depravity. Many years later, *Baby Doll* made it to television. How amazed I was to discover there was no explicit sex—hardly a kiss. It was merely a movie of two men's fascination with a younger woman who exuded a natural lustiness just barely restrained by social conventions. Upon reflection I could see why the Church feared the movie so much: it expressed the carnal natures of males and females, natures that the Church sought to totally suppress. It is this inhuman (I choose the word advisedly) approach to life that led Shaw to proclaim in his preface to the play *Androcles and the Lion*: "Christianity [is] a religion that delivered millions of men" (and even more women I might interject) "so completely into its dominion that their own common nature became a horror to them and the religious life became a denial of life."[11] The result was the unnatural vows of celibacy and an attempt not simply to control, but to totally suppress human sexuality.

Before leaving the subject of death and immortality, I should mention that the desire for immortality is not always motivated by personal selfishness, but also by the inability to accept the loss of a loved one—especially the loss of a child. This was exemplified by the anecdote I related earlier about my friend who lost his four-year-old son after a prolonged and painful illness. My friend simply could not accept the meaningless death of his child. But how could anyone reconcile a good and merciful God with the suffering and death of one so innocent? The only possible reconciliation in his mind was that death was a mere illusion: his son was still alive, basking in the glory of heaven. In this way, a parent may more easily explain away the death of one child to the siblings who survive him.

Ironically, this is just the opposite situation of the one described by Shaw, but equally true. On one hand, Christianity denies the beauty of life; on the other, the reality of death. This may seem as if I am contradicting my earlier contention that most religions have a fascination with death. It does not. The prospect of physical death is central to a brilliant marketing strategy employed by most religions. In times of oppression, war, famine, and the like, religions stress the eternal salvation and heavenly bliss in store for the sufferer if only he/she accepts religion. During periods of peace and prosperity religions must stress the inevitability of death and preach the fire and brimstone that await those who are enjoying this "fool's paradise."

The Need for Identity and a Sense of Belonging

It is not surprising to note that religion seems to make the strongest inroads with the masses of the downtrodden, powerless, incapacitated, uneducated, and alienated. For these people religion offers not only the possibility that all this will be reversed in some afterlife but, just as important, it provides a source of pride and pseudodignity in this life. No matter how absurd the Hare Krishnas, "Moonies," or born again "Jesus freaks" seem to others, they have achieved status in the eyes of those within their cults. They are special, the elect of God, his "chosen people." They are no longer faceless nobodies; they have an identity.

For many people religious organizations offer an escape from what Kurt Vonnegut believes is the most prevalent illness of the twentieth century—loneliness. With children and parents dispersed throughout the country and the historic support system of the family breaking down, people often find themselves alone in a huge impersonal megalopolis, where even their next-door neighbors are unknown to them. Like children without friends, they form relationships with an imaginary but socially acceptable friend, Jesus. Most often it is a harmless delusion, but in some cases it can be severely pathological.

Frequently, joining a religious group, like any other club, is done merely for the opportunity it offers to meet people. In fact, religious sects now regularly sponsor dances and social events to draw the lonely ones into their ranks.

The psychological feeling of a "born again Christian" is oftentimes akin to that experienced by a new recruit to a motorcycle gang. They are no longer alone but have a "family": "This acceptance of a creed, any creed, entitles the believer to membership in the sort of artificial extended family we call a congregation. It is a way to fight loneliness."[12] Their religious group offers a small buffer from life's many bad knocks. Freud observed that religion was a "source of comfort in response to the deprivation and suffering that society inflicts on certain groups."[13] Seeing mankind at its very worst, people turn toward an ideal "mirror of man,"[14] namely, God. The extreme expression of this desire to escape an unbearable reality into a cocoon of security is offered by the monastery. It is no wonder that the monastic movement gained a large number of new applicants after each of the world wars.

The desire for security in a world fraught with change and uncertainty may result in a people seeking a paternalistic, caring god to protect and shelter them against the vicissitudes of life. I refer to this conception of God as "Good Old Dad." I know one woman who frankly admitted that in her mind God was synonymous with her father. (Freud would have had a field day with that one!) Most people aren't that explicit, but at the subconscious level the link may be there.[15] In a sense, it is a case of arrested development. They are still looking for that voice of authority to decide moral dilemmas, a source of approval when they "do good," a source of comfort when they fail. These roles, once filled by their earthly parents, are now satisfied by their imaginary father. This may be especially true if their parents failed them in real life—the paternal role is idealized in and relegated to God.

A person's status in life is also a factor in the willingness to believe. An individual who feels powerless to affect his/her own destiny will quite readily seek help from a supernatural source. The present growth of fundamentalism in the United States has taken root primarily among blacks, poor whites, "rednecks" and others who have been ridiculed or treated harshly by society. This phenomenon is found in many other societies as well and supported by several studies. R. Stark concluded that believers tend to have low self-esteem.[16] Studies by R. M. Dreger and J. G. Ranck found that religion correlated with submission and dependence.[17] Dittes observes that "the generally consistent report is of a correlation between orthodox religion and a relatively defensive, constricted personality."[18] However, it should be noted that religion does not cause these characteristics; rather, people with these problems seek a solution through membership in a religion, particularly the fundamentalist sects. Simply belonging to a group, any group, can reduce feelings of powerlessness and alienation. On the other hand, as I'll explain, there are many reasons why happy, socially adjusted persons also belong to a religion. That is why other studies have found that negative personality factors can be associated with factors independent of religion.[19] Moreover, the members of the more liberal religious sects tend not to display these personality problems.

The attributes that individuals ascribe to their conception of God are psychologically determined by their social milieu. According to Erich Fromm:

> What people think and feel is rooted in their character and their character is molded by the total configuration of their practical life—more precisely, by the socioeconomic and political structure of their society. In societies ruled by a powerful minority which holds the masses in subjugation, the individual will be so imbued with fear, so incapable of feeling strong or independent that his religious experience will be authoritarian.[20]

History abounds with examples of the desire to blindly follow a leader who has a special connection with an omnipotent God. For recent examples just look at the followers of Ayatollah Khomeini, Sun Myung Moon, Reverend Jim Jones, or many of the fundamentalist ministers; the one thing the devotees have in common prior to their conversion is a sense of hopelessness. They are more often than not cast aside by an indifferent society that heaps incredible rewards on the strong and gifted or privileged, and discards the rest like so much refuse. Bound to mindless, dreary jobs, forever in debt as the consequence of an economic system that stimulates wants far in excess of an ability to satisfy them, lacking any sense of esthetics or culture, people desperately want to feel they have some intrinsic value. They are ripe for the priests, ministers, and rabbis who come along and tell them they were created in the image of God and have a special position in his eyes, if only they will believe.

Feuerbach recognized the dubious psychological benefit that faith can bestow. "Faith gives man a peculiar sense of his own dignity and importance. The believer finds himself distinguished above other men . . . in possession of particular privileges, believers are aristocrats."[21] The saved can look down upon nonbelievers as damned or, at best, ignorant, unhappy souls who have not yet "seen the light." I have always marveled that the most superstitious, uneducated believer will look down upon a brilliant nontheistic philosopher and mathematician such as Bertrand Russell, or an astronomer such as Carl Sagan as if both were ignorant of some special knowledge that the believer possesses.

Psychologist Nathaniel Branden describes the motivation for many born-again believers: "Having despaired of impressing his fellow men, it is God whom he seeks to impress."[22] Of course, if he can convert others to his religion as well, he can raise himself in their esteem by virtue of his holiness. It is the old story: if a person can't *do* good, he/she will often settle for *being* good. Branden explains:

> Since God cannot frown at him or snub him socially or inquire as to why he doesn't get a job, the religious fanatic type is free to imagine God is smiling at him, blessing and protecting him, responding to the true nobility of his soul, which everyone on earth is too superficial or corrupt to do.[23]

I should add that it is not always the poor and uneducated who seek the solace of religions. There are many intelligent and affluent youths who are nonetheless alienated from a society they correctly perceive to be selfish, unjust, and self-destructive. What they fail to realize is that their withdrawal is also a selfish, if understandable, action.

Justification for Greed

Jerry Falwell's message is one of the more crass forms of Christianity practiced today. It is based on the Calvinist principle that God rewards the good and punishes the evil, not only in the hereafter, but in the here and now. Hence, people can look upon riches as a sign of the special favor of God. Falwell says, "Material wealth is God's way of blessing people who put Him first." Another TV evangelist put it even more crudely: "No pie in the sky when you die—get it now!" The inference, of course, is that, just as God rewards the righteous with wealth, anyone who is poor must be in God's displeasure. Therefore, it is up to them to do something to get back into God's good graces—like contributing to the evangelist's crusade.

The rich, on the other hand, can feel righteous and smug in the knowledge that they have no obligation to help the less fortunate. Oh, if they want to, they can demonstrate their extreme generosity by throwing a few tax-deductible crumbs to the poor. But as for substantive income redistribution, or even government aid to alleviate poverty, heaven forbid! It would undoubtedly be against God's plan. The remarkable growth in the Assemblies of God churches is a tribute to the acquisitiveness and a "me first" attitude which so dominated the American culture during the 1980s. Their theology was the perfect rationalization for narrow, short-term self-interest. Instead of worrying about the environment or world peace, pray for a new BMW. No wonder the Assemblies of God made the successful leap from merely attracting the impressionable to drawing supposedly educated (but still ignorant) "yuppies."

If greed is a motivation for some of the followers of religion it is the *raison d'être* of many religious leaders. When the young and extremely successful evangelist named Marjoe Gortner began to have pangs of conscience over the means he was using to make his livelihood, he decided to expose the whole shady business. He documented his last revival tour on film, showing the ease with which he could bilk the unsuspecting of their hard-earned wages. The most interesting scenes were when he would meet with other evangelists to discuss the profitability of different towns and performances. The techniques of these circuit evangelists were little different from those used by shrewd carnival managers. The star performers in this arena have simply developed a more polished act. They all have recognized a very easy way to get rich and famous, and have milked it for all it's worth.

The Need for Security

John T. Omhundro demonstrated that throughout history people have sought escape from anxiety through religion: "cultures subject to stressful situations have responded with religious reformations, often as a substitute for, or supplement to, political rebellion."[24] He offers as examples the Zulu uprising in Africa, the Sepoy rebellion in India, the New Guinea cargo cults, the Ghost Dance of the Plains Indians, the Taiping rebellion in China and the Luddites and Anabaptists in Europe. The origins of Judaism and Christianity both fall into this same historical paradigm. The Hebrew religion and its unique affiliation with Yahweh appear most likely to have been developed in an effort to sustain a national identity during the period of Babylonian rule. Among the many gods the Israelites worshiped up until that time, Yahweh was selected and vested with a special historical relationship to provide the Jewish people with a sense of purpose and special status even under subjection by the Babylonians. In the case of Christianity, the initial popularity of Jesus occurred at a time when many Jews were looking for a Messiah to lead them to throw off the Roman yoke. Christianity subsequently took root in Greece and Rome during the decline of the Roman empire and may, in fact, have contributed to that decline.

Today a new source of anxiety and insecurity is being caused by the rapid pace of technological change worldwide. The consequences should have been predictable. Some time ago, I ran across the following article in the *World Press Review*:

> Rapid technological growth and cultural change have spurred a rebirth of fundamentalist and cult religions in Latin America. According to the news magazine *Veja* of São Paulo (Jan. 7, 1983), "The largest participatory religion in Brazil has become the cult of Umbanda, in which 30 million people are involved." This Afro-Christian hybrid—which worships the deity Iemanja and is closely associated with the Mardi Gras festival—is no longer the province of poor, mostly black inhabitants of the Bahia region in the northeast, says the magazine, "but has now become voguish in every social stratum." Venezuela is encountering a similar phenomenon, writes David Browne in the liberal *El Diario de Caracas* (Jan. 3). Browne claims that "every oil dollar brings another million (people) to the cult of Maria Lionza," supposedly an Indian maid during the Spanish conquest who fled to the jungle rather than face the recently Hispanicized culture. The cult, he says, reveals a fascinating paradox: "While the country advances . . . millions of Venezuelans find spiritual guidance in the myths and legends of the past."

Since most of the world faces similar explosion in technology, this may be one reason for the resurgence of fundamentalist religions worldwide.

After an intensive study of the Pentecostals in Trinidad, C. Ward and M. H. Beaubrun concluded that they "employ possession as a psychological defense to cope with frustration and conflict . . . [it] affords temporary escape from unpleasant reality, absolution of guilt and responsibility by attributing the reaction to supernatural causes, and evocation of sympathy and affection from family and friends."[25] With so many psychological benefits, is it any wonder that a religion is extremely appealing to its adherents?

The Desire for Justice (or Vengeance)

How comforting it is to think that no matter how badly you have been treated in this world, God will even up the score somehow, either here or in the hereafter. Certain Christian sects followed the tradition that all the suffering incurred in this life was due to personal guilt. Jerry Falwell and the Assemblies of God still preach this message. However, the mainstream of Christian theology recognized that such an idea was not salable to the bulk of suffering humanity whose only significant failing was being born of poor and ignorant parents. Consequently, the teaching of most Judeo-Christian sects is that the suffering in this world is merely a test of faith, à la Job. The result is that today we have the curious doctrine once concisely formulated by Robert G. Ingersoll: "in this world God punishes the people he loves, and in the next, the ones he hates."

Ironically, it is the punishment of those God hates—which certainly must be the same people we hate—that many find quite satisfying. For those who God failed to punish here on earth, man has created the eternal revenge of a hell. The Church Father Tertullian expressed this ugly wish for vengeance: "How I shall admire, how laugh, how exalt when I behold so many proud monarchs groaning in the lower abyss of darkness . . . so many sage philosophers blushing in red hot fires with their deluded pupils."[26] This statement of Tertullian also is indicative of the hatred the theologians have for those philosophers who saw through the theologians' false logic and semantic trickery. Aquinas also wrote that the blessed in heaven will take great pleasure in seeing those in hell. Since the Christian heaven offers no sensual or intellectual pleasure, it would appear that the joy of vengeance is about the only explicit pleasure that those who make it to heaven can expect.

In connection with this strange concept of Justice, we should not over-look the psychological satisfaction that certain people get from repentance. Shaw referred to it as the "saved thief experience—an ecstatic happiness which can never come to the honest atheist: he is tempted to steal again to repeat the glorious sensation."[27] As evidence of this phenomenon, just look at the success of revival meetings; aside from the spectacle of miraculous "healings," the hallmark of the revival is public repentance. The people beat their breasts and confess that they are sinners until the preacher proclaims that because they believe, they are now saved. The whole show is a real catharsis; that is why they come back year after year. I experienced a similar sensation during the annual three-day retreats I attended as a teenager. After a climactic confession, you could shed the responsibility and guilt for any past transgressions like so much dead skin. It was really quite exhilarating. No wonder the emperor Constantine jumped at the idea of a religion that would allow him to expiate his guilt on his death bed. We nontheists, on the other hand, must live with our guilt until the day we die. When an unbeliever hurts someone, he knows that only they can forgive him, so he must make his peace with the injured party by offering to make restitution.

Escape from Responsibility

This all leads to my next point: although Western religions rely heavily on guilt to keep their followers in line, belief in God is oftentimes used by believers as an escape from acceptance of personal responsibility both for one's own destiny and, more so, for the fate of others. Even when the believers' world is crumbling around them due to their own mistakes, they can be comforted, secure in the knowledge that it is "God's will." As Schopenhauer pointed out, "it is far more endurable to have our misfortune brought clearly before us than our incapacity."[28] I recall a friend's reaction when he went bankrupt. A true believer in the most radical sense, he simply concluded that this was either God's way of punishing him for some past sin, or a way of testing him, just as Job was tested. In either case, it was God's will and clearly not due to incompetence on his part. I marveled that he never lost five minutes of sleep over the situation. Indeed religion is a wonderful, although terribly addictive, drug.

The problem is that just as my friend could escape the feeling that he was responsible for the decisions affecting the outcome of his business, so, too, many people place their trust in God and, in so doing, can effectively escape feelings of responsibility for unjust social conditions. How much easier it is to say it is "the will of God," than to admit that we may be part of the problem. If there is no God upon whom we can palm off the problem, all human misery becomes our personal responsibility—a very disquieting thought. In Saul Bellow's novel *The Dean's December,* the character Corde reflects upon the miserable state of the world today, and declares, "We'd better deal with whatever it is that's in us by nature, and I don't see people willing to do that. What I mainly see is the evasion."[29] Corde is right, and religions must accept some of the responsibility for this evasion.

Desire for a Future Reward to Justify Present Suffering

Christianity, with its promise of eternal happiness, has always been readily accepted by the poor and the hopeless. However, with Native Americans it was quite a different story. They initially saw no value in this obsession with an afterlife. The Indian had a relatively joyous condition in the here and now. Their conception of an afterlife was pretty much just an extension of there present existence. Therefore, to make conversions the missionaries had to support the complete destruction of the indigenous culture. Only by reducing the Native Americans to a state of destitution and hopelessness as discussed in chapter 6, could the missionaries begin to make conversions.

The Free Lunch Syndrome

Most people want very much to believe there is someone who will give them something just for the asking. E. Haldeman-Julius recognized the psychological similarity between the idea of God and that of Santa Claus,[30] Santa Claus being an infantile notion of God. Although no study has ever shown that prayer has any more relevance than wishing on a star (but then look how many people believe in astrology), the idea of saying a prayer to get your wish is hard to give up.

As long as people hope to get something for nothing, they will continue to be conned by every flim-flam artist and priest. The only difference between these two professions is that the former recognizes that he is conning his victims, while the priest most often has been taken in himself by the metaphysical double talk of the theologians. These wonderful wordsmiths play such sophisticated semantic shell games that even the unwary intellectual is often fooled. One must pay close attention to philosopher Jacques Maritain as he attempts to palm off all of the monstrous acts of Christianity upon atheists by calling the Christian perpetrators of these evils "practical atheists." Note the unspoken assumption that Christians, by definition, must be good and atheists, by definition, bad. Ergo, all bad acts must be committed by those who are at heart atheists!

Not to be outdone in the art of sophistry, theologian Paul Tillich tries to define away even the possibility of atheism by equating God with "all being" and saying, therefore, that anyone who believes in "being" believes in God. The grand master of convoluted logic was, as we have seen, Thomas Aquinas. His syllogisms assume the first premise, deny an alternative in the second premise, and then restate the first premise in a tautological conclusion. Only by close scrutiny can you see these logical craftsman drop the pea of truth under the table before they reveal the empty shells of metaphysics.

Not only is the intellectual effort to detect these deceptions too difficult for most people, but they don't want to destroy the myths in the first place. Like the philosophers who originate the bogus proofs and semantic games, most people want to believe in the supernatural and will extend their mental efforts not in the search for truth, but in defending their self-delusions. Their belief in heaven is much like believing that someday they will inevitably win the lottery.

The Need for Peer and Parental Approval

One of the great American myths is the stereotypical rugged individualist. The truth is that most Americans, like all other people, are scared to death of individuality. Psychologist Eric Fromm observed: "Man is, by origin, a herd animal. His actions are determined by an instinctive impulse to follow the leaders and to have close contact with the other animals around him."[31] Elsewhere, Fromm makes the chilling observation: "There is nothing inhuman, evil or irrational which does not give some comfort provided it is shared by a group."[32]

Nothing is more difficult than to risk censure and isolation from the herd by refusing to go along. Like the players in Eugene Ionesco's play *Rhinoceros,* the few people who attain an accurate perception of reality will, for the most part, be pressured into believing that they must be the ones who are wrong. Despite having spent their entire lives gathering evidence to support their position, few people can sustain a position against a united public opposition. It is a very uncomfortable feeling to have everyone view you as if you were ignorant, eccentric or morally corrupt. To stand up and vocally oppose the superstition of theism will certainly exclude a person from high public office (as Robert Ingersoll learned), may threaten an academic career (as Bertrand Russell discovered), and may even jeopardize business opportunities (as anyone doing business in Utah knows).

Not only must nontheists face public hostility, but, perhaps more painfully, disapproval and possible ostracism from their parents and family. Since most people are imbued with their religious beliefs from childhood, such beliefs are oftentimes commingled with the warm memories of hearth and family. Atheist and philosopher Morris R. Cohen explains:

> We must start with the fact that with rare exceptions men cling to the religion in which they were born and to which they have been habituated from childhood. We inherit our traditional ritual with its implicit faith and emotional content almost with our mother's milk; and we naturally cling to it passionately as we do to all things that have become part of our being.[33]

People love their parents and naturally don't wish to upset them. Many times in discussing religious beliefs, I've heard people comment that they would never admit to being unbelievers because it would distress their parents too much. This is especially a concern if their parents are elderly or in ill health. The purveyors of religion know well how to exploit human relationships. In his autobiography, *Black Boy,* Richard Wright describes how those who were reluctant to get baptized were lined up in front of the congregation by the local minister and subjected to every form of psychological pressure to give in. Wright comments on the wretched efforts of his minister to force his conversion:

> This business of saving souls had no ethics; every human relationship was shamelessly exploited. In essence, the tribe was asking us whether we shared its feelings; if we refused to join the church, it was equivalent to saying no, to placing ourselves in the position of moral monsters.[34]

When to this tension Wright's mother added her own pleas, it was more than he could withstand:

> "Don't you love your old crippled mother, Richard?" my mother asked. "Don't leave me standing here with my empty hands," she said, afraid that I would humiliate her in public.[35]

The very word "atheist" is embarrassing to most people. Like the thought of nakedness, people have been so conditioned to associate the word with wickedness that they feel guilty even discussing the subject. That is why I would like to popularize the word "nontheist." It avoids the negative connotations our society has erroneously come to associate with atheism, and more correctly represents the position of those who simply contend that they have found no evidence or reason to believe in a Divine Being.

Lack of Education

Too few people have been trained to understand the necessity of utilizing the empirical method as the most reliable means of determining the truth of a proposition. Isaac Asimov suggests that "few people have had the opportunity to be educated into the understanding of what is meant by evidence or in the techniques of arguing rationally."[36] It is not surprising, therefore, that so few people have escaped their parents' delusions and myths. It seems as if most of our social institutions cater to the lowest common denominator of learning and intelligence. If anyone doubts that our society, despite its major technological accomplishments, still humors those who possess the most absurd superstitions, just try to find the elevator button for the thirteenth floor in a high-rise or row thirteen in an airplane. (It is so incredibly silly, of course, since there is by definition a thirteenth floor, but by calling it fourteen and misnumbering all the succeeding floors, the confrontation between superstition and reality is thought to be avoided.) If the masses remain powerfully held under the sway of such archaic superstitions, is it any wonder that they should still believe in gods, angels, demons, and the like?

In general, education is inversely correlated with religious belief, i.e., the more education, the less likely a person is to believe. A survey of studies of student achievement conducted by Burham P. Beckwith bears this out. After reviewing the findings of two dozen major studies, Beckwith concludes:

1. Persons with some high school education are less religious than those with only some grade school education.

2. Persons with some college education are less religious than those with only some high school education.

3. Among college students in any one college, religious faith declines with each additional year of education.

4. Among student bodies of different colleges the average degree of religious faith varies inversely with the academic quality of the student body and college.

5. College professors are less religious than their students.

6. Among college professors and scientists, the most eminent are much less religious than the noneminent.

The evidence also shows that, "Religious faith varies inversely and strongly with the IQ and SAT scores."[37]

This last point, showing an inverse correlation between IQ and religious belief, has been a pervasive finding. In another research effort, Beckwith reviewed all the studies he could locate that correlated religious belief and achievement. His analysis revealed:

1. Thirteen of sixteen student studies show an inverse correlation between intelligence and religiosity. The other three studies showed no correlation.

2. Five student body comparisons reported that student bodies with high IQ/SAT scores are less religious.

3. Three out of four studies report that geniuses (average IQ 150+) are much less religious than the general public.

4. Seven studies show that highly successful persons are much less religious than others.

5. Twelve Gallup polls indicate that college alumni are less religious than those with only a grade school education.[38]

After reviewing all these studies Beckwith was forced to conclude: "Other factors being equal, the more intelligent a person is, the less religious he is."

Religious leaders may object that this all goes to show how success simply makes people too proud to believe in God. My experience has been, however, that better-educated people are less, not more, opinionated than ignorant people. The difference is that they demand evidence before accepting a statement as fact. And anyone who objectively reviews the evidence soon discovers that there is no case for theism.

Given, then, the general increase in the level of education in the United States, why does it appear that so many people still believe in God? For the most part it has to do with the psychological reasons advanced in this chapter. Psychological factors will influence what we believe more than the facts themselves as studies by R. H. Thouless and Brown revealed (i.e., religious beliefs were held more confidently than matters of fact).[39]

The reason for growth in religious belief may also be due, in part, to the decline in the quality of education and to the successful encroachment which Christianity has made into the public educational system. More significantly, I think that most people are too busy to take the time to study religion. In this age of specialization even scientists have little time to research areas outside their field. This explains the findings of C. Ragan et al. that, "Those who were least likely to study religion (e.g., natural scientists) were more religious than those most likely to study religion (e.g., social scientists)."[40] I should add that neither group is as religious as the general population.

It also appears that, due to the current social pressure to believe, even educated people seem more willing to alter the concept of God than give it up altogether. Hence, you hear people speak of God as the "universal force," or the "totality of being." Such definitions are simply synonyms for the impersonal universe and can hardly be construed as a theistic belief. Larry A. Jackson, the President of Lander College in South Carolina and a graduate of Union Theological Seminary, speculates that the church of the future will reject any claim of a direct revelation from God and will recognize the danger posed by others who make the claim that they are recipients of direct revelation. Furthermore,

> The name "God" will be used to refer to that reality which is manifest in our lives as coherence; as man's tendency, when healthy, to work to structure a just society; as man's innate knowledge that he has obligations that transcend time and geography; as the belief that we each find renewal in nature and in experiencing the love and forgiveness of another person; and, finally, as the belief that ultimate reality is love.[41]

Some lovely sentiments, but they have little to do with the concept of God as a person, a conscious creative being. I have heard similar views expressed by other thoughtful clergy, which appear to be an effort on the part of speakers to come to terms with their own incipient nontheism. Nevertheless, I applaud such suggestions as major advances of reason over superstition.

The Desire to Believe in the Mysterious

For those of us who take pleasure in the painstaking search for the truth, it is difficult to comprehend the overwhelming desire of others to believe in the mysterious and supernatural no matter how illogical it is to do so. Apparently, they want to give their lives more zest and excitement, so they eagerly swallow, unchallenged, the wildest fabrications such as UFOs, astrology, the Loch Ness Monster, Bigfoot, psychics, and parapsychology.

As evidence of this phenomenon, let me relate briefly an experiment in preconceived belief performed by psychologists Barry Singer and Victor Bernassi at California State University.[42] A young man, who was an actor and magician, was asked to develop a standard magic routine that included "psychic-like" stunts. The magician was then asked to perform before two classes of college students. In the first class he was presented as a psychic, but to the second class he was clearly introduced as a magician. After each performance, which included several tricks such as "reading" ten digit numbers while blindfolded and bending a metal rod by merely chanting at it, the classes were asked to respond to a written evaluation of the performance.

In the class where he was introduced as a psychic 77 percent believed his act showed evidence of true psychic powers. More surprising, in the class where he was introduced as a magician 65 percent *still believed* he was psychic and another 18 percent were undecided. Only 17 percent believed him when he confessed that he was no more than a magician. Astounded and dismayed by the outcome of the experiment, the researchers repeated it. This time, more emphasis was made in the introduction that the performer "will pretend to read minds and demonstrate psychic abilities, and what you'll be seeing are really only tricks." Despite this straightforward acknowledgment that he possessed no special powers, 58 percent of the students still were convinced the performer was psychic, even though virtually all the students agreed that a magician could perform the same tricks. Clearly these students did not want to give up their belief in psychics no matter what the obvious truth of the situation was.

In another experiment, a professional magician, James Randi, showed how easy it was for a couple of his trained conjurers, posing as psychics, to trick parapsychologists of Washington University into believing that they possessed psychic powers.[43] The reasons the parapsychologists were so easy duped was that they were not trained to look for trickery, and they wanted to believe that some people actually did possess psychic powers.

It is a sad fact that most people's lives are primarily characterized by boredom and drudgery. Lacking an appreciation of music, art, literature, or even an entertaining hobby, they seek escape through the exotic and/ or occult. Religion fills the bill nicely. It's small wonder, then, that no matter how inherently contradictory or downright absurd a religious dogma is, it remains a cherished belief for most members of society. In fact, in Schopenhauer's opinion, "some absolute contradictions, some actual absurdities, are an essential ingredient in a complete religion,"[44] since they give the appearance of greater profundity to most men. M. D. Goulder correctly observed that "when we remove the mist we remove the mystery."[45] Moreover, since people are told that by its very nature religion is incomprehensible to the ordinary mind, they can rationalize why it doesn't appear to make any sense. The mysteries can be left to the priests who, since they allegedly speak for God, can provide explanations for the masses by means of simple, albeit meaningless, allegories. Or people can opt out, completely suppressing all attempts at reason in favor of mysticism, and seek to "experience" God directly. In any case, religion performs the same function as all the other forms of psychic entertainment—escape from reality.

Intellectual Conditioning

The last, but one of the most important, causes for the continuation of religious belief is childhood conditioning. L. B. Brown reports, "that family training is the simplest explanation of how anyone develops a religious perspective is supported by numerous studies, with recent work on lapsing from religion, or apostasy, showing that positive attitudes to religion which have been inculcated in the family are the most resistant to change."[46] Furthermore, despite the powerful influence of childhood training at home and at Sunday school, the proponents of religion realize that this may be insufficient to persuade an inquiring mind to swallow the fantastic superstitions and myths of religion. So they seek total indoctrination of the children before they have developed any power of critical judgment.

The eighteenth-century philosopher Denis Diderot tells of a Native American chief who, after listening to a missionary relate the amazing account of Christianity, responded:

> Brother, look at my head, my hair is quite gray; seriously, do you think you can make a man of my age believe all these stories? But I have three children. Don't address yourself to the oldest, you will make him laugh. Get hold of the little one, you can persuade him of anything you like.[47]

The chief recognized the necessity of selling unbelievable tales to the naive and credulous. The story also illustrates why the various Christian sects sought to gain the right to physically remove Native American children from their families and relocate them in Christian boarding schools. It was imperative that they be removed from the skepticism of their elders so that their indoctrination into Christianity could take root.

Schopenhauer recognized that "priests . . . must impart their metaphysical dogmas to man at a very early age, before judgment has awakened from its morning slumber, thus in early childhood, for then every well-impressed dogma, however senseless it may be, remains forever."[48] Echoing this sentiment, Charles Darwin might have had a forethought of the bitter opposition his theories would face from religious leaders when he wrote that:

> . . . the constant inculcation in a belief in God on the minds of children [produces] so strong an effect . . . that it would be as difficult for them to throw off their belief in God as a monkey to throw off its instinctive fear and hatred of a snake.[49]

It is this desire for indoctrination that is behind the efforts of proponents of prayer in the classroom. Prayer in itself isn't the issue, since children can pray to their heart's content at home. What they seek is official support for prayer to pressure all children into accepting theism and, ultimately, Christianity. Even a "moment of silence" would have the law of the land giving tacit support for theism. Given the implicit endorsement of the federal government to the concept of prayer, which obviously implies a god, children will have an enormous incentive—perhaps pressure is a better word—to believe. "The law of imitation operates and nonconformity is not an outstanding characteristic of children. The result is an obvious pressure upon children to attend."⁵⁰ With these words, Justice Felix Frankfurter recognized the true intent of the effort to introduce prayer into the schools.

Professor Robert S. Alley reminds us that as a result of the foresight of our founding fathers, America today is still primarily a secular state, "in which humanistic and Christian and Jew and Muslim and secularist and rationalist have existed in good harmony far better than anywhere else in the world."⁵¹ But fundamentalists would like to change that. Even without legislation effectively making Christianity a state religion, theism still holds the advantage in gaining the unquestioning allegiance of today's youth. Furthermore, billions of dollars are spent by religions, the mass media and commercial interests to promote belief in Jesus. The economics of Christmas alone justifies it: the myths of Jesus can be mined for big bucks. Books opposed to theism are relatively hard to find, not that many haven't been written, but because most big publishing houses are afraid to promote them for fear of offending organized religions. Additionally, organized religion has successfully integrated belief in God with American nationalism on the one hand, while forging a mental link between atheism and Communism on the other. Anyone who is not a theist runs the danger of being labeled a Communist.

Yet another barrier to overcome is conditioned guilt. Most children of theists are taught that even to doubt the existence of God is wicked. This is a neat little catch-22 to prevent children from using their intelligence to examine the rationale for belief in God. Nathaniel Branden is just one of many psychologists who recognized this conceptual double bind: "One of the common strategies of 'brainwashing' is that of inculcating or provoking some form of guilt in the victim—on the premises that a guilt-ridden mind is less inclined to critical, independent judgment, and is more susceptible to indoctrination and intellectual manipulation. Guilt subdues self-assertiveness."⁵²

Opposing these powerful psychological forces is akin to paddling a canoe up a waterfall. But of all these inducements the hardest to overcome is simple habit. In my own case, until age twenty-six I had never deliberately missed Sunday Mass. I had been conditioned to respond with reverence to the very name of God. Although the intellectual foundation of my religious beliefs was being eroded by the tide of reason, habits and family pressure ensured my continued attendance at church and, ostensibly, I was still a Catholic. However, in 1968, a four-month labor dispute required that managers such as myself work seven days a week, making it impossible for me to attend Sunday Mass. The spell was broken. The edifice of superstition and archaic beliefs held together only by the cement of inertia collapsed.

My initial reaction was a mixture of exhilarating freedom and fear, not unlike the feeling I had after graduating from college. Without religion

I had to find my own moral way in the world, just as I once had to venture forth alone economically. I would have to shift through the debris of my religious teachings to see if there was anything worth saving, collect what was of any value, and then set out to link up with the others throughout history who have made the same journey. Fortified with their extensive analysis, I hoped to collect enough knowledge to construct a more substantive moral abode than the house of cards that was blown down by the first gusts of reason.

To sum up, it should by now be quite apparent that, in part, religion grew out of a need by early humans to explain and control the mysterious workings of nature. However, the psychological needs and fears that theism and religious organizations exploit provide an even greater motivation to religious belief. These include:

• the universal desire to escape death;

• the need for identity and status (a sense of belonging to a group);

• the need on the part of certain individuals (priests and ministers) to exercise power over others and secure a lucrative livelihood;

• the need for security in a world of increasing uncertainty;

• the desire for justice and/or revenge, in this world or in the hereafter;

• the inability to accept responsibility for one's errors;

• the desire for a reward to make up for present suffering;

• the desire to get something by merely wishing for it;

• the need for peer and parental approval coupled with the fear of social ostracism for not believing;

• the unwillingness or inability of people to break out of their ignorance;

• the entertainment value of believing in the occult; and

• intellectual conditioning by organized religion.

Rationalist Gordon Stein offers a similar list of psychological motivations for believers.[53] Argyle lists seven psychological roots of religious belief: parent figure, conflict anxiety, need resolution, identity development, solving intellectual problems (recall the need to explain discussed in the last chapter), and biochemical processes (such Wilson's sociobiology theory).[54] Brown adds two more: social learning and external locus of control.[55] As you can see, these lists approximate my own.

Psychologist Edmund D. Cohen[56] and psychotherapist Albert Ellis[57] have taken a decidedly more critical view of believers, arguing that the fervor of a true believer may be a form of neurosis. I am not willing to agree with that position, except perhaps in the case of the extreme fundamentalists. There are many studies showing that those who are religiously affiliated report a happy and socially well-adjusted life. However, I submit that, based upon the results of many of the psychological studies referenced in this volume, a healthy, emotionally stable individual, who is of reasonably high intelligence, well-educated, raised in a nondogmatic, inquiring environment, and who has a desirable, reasonably attainable life goal, would have little, if any, motivation for theistic beliefs—provided he is not threatened by his peer group for not believing. Conversely, the evidence indicates that the socially alienated, the sick, the aged, the poor, the uneducated, the emotionally distraught, those conditioned to be nonskeptical loyal followers, and those with a strong need for peer approval would possess the strongest belief in God and the supernatural. It should also not be surprising that those who tend to believe in God are also most ready to believe in the paranormal and other superstitions.[58]

Most people are familiar with Marx's statement which referred to religion as the opium of the people. However, he is usually quoted out of context and the real significance of his observation is lost. Marx wrote:

> Man makes religion: religion does not make man. Religion is indeed man's self-consciousness and self-awareness so long as he has not found himself or has lost himself again. . . . Religion is the sigh of the oppressed creature, the sentiment of a heartless world and the soul of soulless conditions. It is the opium of the people. . . . Religion is only the illusory sun about which man revolves so long as he does not revolve around himself.[59]

It was, therefore, Marx's view that for people to give up the illusions which comprise religious belief would first require that society alter the conditions requiring the illusion. For "it is not the consciousness of men which determines their existence but on the contrary, their social condition which determines their consciousness."[60] Actually, as we have found out since the time of Marx, consciousness and existence are interactive and, as such, religious belief is even more fundamental to man's psychological makeup than Marx supposed. But Marx, like Hume and Feuerbach, correctly recognized that humans create an image of God to meet their specific needs. When needs change, the idealization of God changes. Albert Schweitzer argued that each period of history recreated Jesus in accordance with its own character.[61]

Failure to recognize theism's role in meeting human needs led many nineteenth- and twentieth-century philosophers and intellectuals to prematurely predict the death of God. They thought that simply increasing our scientific knowledge of the workings of the universe and raising the general level of education slightly would spell the demise of the occult. Echoing this point of view, Robert Ingersoll stated, "If people were a little more ignorant astrology would flourish—if a little more enlightened religion would perish."[62] Naturally, he assumed that the future would result in a continuation of the trend in philosophical and scientific enlightenment gaining momentum during the last century. If Ingersoll were alive today, imagine how shocked he would be to see the daily astrology column in virtually every newspaper in America!

American ignorance is fostered in large measure by religious conditioning that "believing can make it so," "faith can move mountains," "you need but ask and you'll receive," and "think with your heart not your mind." When unreasoning faith rules the human mind, truth will always fall victim to the lie.

It is going to take a great deal more education, and a society free from loneliness, alienation, pervasive fear and bigotry to achieve Ingersoll's view of a nontheist future. The paradox is that religion, in propagating an erroneous view of humankind and nature, is, in effect, dedicated, however unconsciously, to perpetuating many of the evils which create the need for people to seek escape from reality into a world of myth.

18

Alternatives to Theism:
Striving for a Better Idea

Really to see the sun rise or go down every day, so to relate ourselves
to a universal fact would preserve us sane forever.
                                                —Henry David Thoreau

Given the many psychological reasons advanced in the prior chapter for
believing in God, it is reasonable for the reader to wonder what would
fill the void left without that belief. It should be understood, however,
that many of those problems arise because of the efforts of organized religions
to make people psychologically dependent on the belief in God in the first
place.

  As previously discussed, the concept of God was invented by early
man to explain incomprehensible phenomena. Science now meets that need.
Theism was sustained by religious organizations that exploited people's fear
of dying and the terrible living conditions faced by the masses. Fear of
dying is, to an extent, a natural and necessary genetically endowed trait
to ensure the preservation of the species. However, with the proper conditioning death need not prove psychologically terrifying, particularly for
older people. More significantly, perhaps, the conditions that make life
unbearable for so many could be mitigated with social justice and proper
economic and demographic planning. Moreover, adequate psychiatric
attention, if universally available, would be much more effective than
superstitious delusions for dealing with the many problems of modern living.
However, here, too, a more equitable and less ruthlessly competitive society
would go far to eliminate many of the physical and psychological ills to
which people are subject today.

  That's all very well, some readers may interject, but why should anyone

413

wish to behave justly and fairly toward others if no one is keeping score or refereeing the game? Feodor Dostoyevski raised this objection in *The Brothers Karamazov:* "If there is no God, everything is permitted." Therefore, are not religious institutions based upon the premise that a belief in God necessary to define moral action and foster the ethical progress of humankind? It should be remembered, however, that it was humankind, not mythical gods, who created moral laws. Even such a true believer as Hans Küng admits that, "Morality did not drop down from heaven, but—like language— is the product of development. . . . We have to look for and work out on earth discriminating solutions for all problems."[1] Küng goes so far as to urge, "Today, more than ever, we must examine with as little prejudice as possible, in accordance with strict scientific methods, the manifold, changeable and complex reality of man and society with reference to its objective laws and future possibilities." There is absolutely no evidence to support the contention that religion is the basis of morality. W. R. Cassels explains that religion has been modified by advances in human morality, not the other way around: "Morality, which has ever changed its complexion and modified its injunctions according to social requirements, will necessarily be enforced as part of human evolution, and is not dependent on religious terrorism or superstitious persuasion."[2]

In our earlier discussions of religion and morality, we saw that simply alleging that a moral injunction came from God was no guarantee that it was just or good. In retrospect we have found that such dictates are often irrelevant, unfair, and even cruel. At best, the promise of heaven or the threat of hell has been used as a motivator for adherence to a moral code developed by human beings. However, there is little evidence to suggest that they have been effective in modifying behavior, except when fueling the flames of fanaticism.

The best of today's moral codes are found to have been advanced by philosophers and civil leaders irrespective of their religious grounding. Many were deists and freethinkers. Many were pagans. Long before the rise of Judaism, we had the "pagan" Egyptian Pharaoh Ramses II signing the first known peace treaty with the words: "He is at peace with me; I am with brotherhood with him." The segregation of religious sects has been, along with nationalism and racism, a major impediment to realization of this concept of brotherhood.

To place the role of the Judeo-Christian ethical traditions in the proper perspective, it is instructive to review briefly the teachings of some of history's other great ethical teachers. However, before doing so, I would like to spend just a moment reviewing a belief system which, although some might consider it religious, is certainly not an organized religion like the others. However, it has a direct relevance to our discussion.

Pantheism

Pantheism can be defined as "the doctrine identifying the Deity with the various forces and workings of nature."[3] In its purest form pantheism holds that the universe is identical with God. An atheist would have little difficulty with this definition since it, in effect, merely gives the universe a new name. However, for the pantheist the universe or, more specifically, nature, assumes a sacred quality. As such, pantheism provides the basis for an ecological perspective that is missing from most other religions. In fact, the term "ecology" was coined by a nineteenth-century proponent of pantheism, Ernst Haeckel. Not long ago, Harold W. Wood proposed pantheism as a basis for an environmental ethic.[4]

Although not exactly pantheistic, the worldview of the Native Americans also held that all of nature was sacred. (And for many this is still true.) The Judeo-Christian heritage saw nature as a wilderness that must be conquered, endured, or, at best, governed wisely. Native Americans, on the other hand, saw themselves as an integral part of nature. Nature was not to be owned nor subdued; it was to be venerated, experienced, and enjoyed. Hunting was not simply an effort to attain food and clothing but a complex ritual. The buffalo was not merely a wild beast to be destroyed wantonly or for sheer sport; it was a sacred being. Yet unlike certain Eastern cults such as Jainism, which placed the sacredness of certain animals above the needs of humans, Native Americans recognized that it was in the nature of things for them to hunt deer and buffalo just as it was for the wolf and puma to hunt their prey. In short, the Native American was a part of nature just as any other species.

Most North American tribes held a worldview that would have echoed the sentiment expressed elegantly by Chief Luther Standing Bear of the Oglala Sioux:

> We did not think of the great open plains, the beautiful rolling hills, and winding streams with tangled growth, as "wild." Only to the white man was nature a "wilderness" and only to him was the land "infested" with wild animals and "savage" people. To us it was tame. Earth was beautiful and we were surrounded with the blessing of the Great Mystery. Not until the hairy man from the East came and with brutal frenzy heaped injustices upon us and the families we loved was it "wild" for us. When the very animals of the forest began fleeing from his approach, then it was that for us the "Wild West" began.[5]

The culture of "the hairy man from the East" is reflected in his religious traditions, just as was that of the Native American. In traditional Christian philosophy, harmony with nature played a very small part.

The old Judaic world view is simply carried forward in Christianity: The earth is a hostile, savage environment that must be conquered and possessed. The New Testament description of "a voice crying in the wilderness" exemplifies this view that nonurbanized or uncultivated land is somehow dangerous and hostile.

The white man's myth held that the first humans were driven from the blessed Garden of Eden into the cursed world: "Cursed is the earth in thy work; with labor and toil thou shalt eat thereof all the days of thy life" (Gen. 4:17). In the biblical account, man is initially given dominion over nature, but after his fall he is a prisoner sentenced to it. In this alien world all other creatures are a threat to man's own survival. The Old Testament has constant references to ravenous wolves. The sole purpose of the lion would seem to be to eat prophets, and later, Christians.

The Christian worldview for the most part failed to recognize the possibility of a symbiotic relationship between human beings and nature. With eyes firmly fixed on heaven, Christians scorned the pleasures of the earth and considered the earth, at best, little more than a proving ground for personal righteousness while humankind awaited death and resurrection. Given the eschatological myth that the end of this wicked world is at hand, preservation of nature was illogical, as the Reagan administration's born-again Secretary of the Interior, James Watt, advocated in word and deed.

Unlike the New Testament, there are many laws in the Torah dealing with man's responsibility for preserving the land. There are also many passages in the Psalms, Job and the prophets that speak of the beauty of nature. However, taken as a whole, the Bible provides no common thread, no basis for viewing the world from an environmental or ecological perspective. God exists for himself, humans exist to serve God, and the earth exists both to try and to tempt humanity, as well as to sustain it.

Nowhere in the Native American mythology is humankind "sentenced" to live in a hostile world of nature. In stark contrast to the world view of the indigenous peoples, by the time the white man came to North America, the Christian view of the world was that of a "vale of tears." Nature had to be "conquered" just as the human corporal element had to be subdued because of its basically sinful disposition.

How different a conception of the earth was held by the red man who saw himself still possessing the Garden of Eden; in his myths he was never driven out. Oftentimes the myths describe how the first people sprang from nature itself. The enormity of the difference between the white man and red man's worldview was expressed in prosaic terms in a letter sent to President Franklin Pierce in 1855 by Chief Sealth of the Dewanish Tribe in the state of Washington:

> The Great Chief in Washington sends word that he wishes to buy our land. How can you buy or sell the sky—the warmth of the land? The idea is strange to us. We do not own the freshness of the air or the sparkle of the water. How can you buy them from us? Every part of this earth is sacred to my people. Every shiny pine needle, every sandy shore, every mist in the dark woods, every clearing and humming insect is holy in the memory and experience of my people.
>
> We know that the white man does not understand our ways. One portion of the land is the same to him as the next, for he is a stranger who comes in the night and takes from the land what ever he needs. The earth is not his brother but his enemy and his children's birthright is forgotten.
>
> There is no quiet place in the white man's cities. No place to hear the leaves of spring or the rustle of insect wings. But perhaps because I am a savage and do not understand, the clatter seems to insult the ears. And what is there to life if a man cannot hear the lovely cry of the whippoorwill or the arguments of the frogs around the pond at night.
>
> The whites, too shall pass—perhaps sooner than other tribes. Continue to contaminate your bed, and you will one night suffocate in your own waste. When the buffalo are all slaughtered, the wild horses all tamed, the secret corners of the forest heavy with the scent of many men, and the views of the ripe hills blotted by talking wires. Where is the thicket? Gone. Where is the eagle? Gone. And what is it to say goodbye to the swift and the hunt, the end of living and the beginning of survival.[6]

Arguably, the reverence which Native Americans had for nature was a consequence of their special relationship with it. Their very existence was tied directly to it.

This is further evidence that there is a process in the evolution of religious myths whereby they constantly are revised to adapt to the economic and social needs of a culture. As long as we recognize this process, the myths are harmless and may even reinforce some sociologically advantageous trends. However, institutionalized religions will tend to dogmatize those myths, preventing the adaptation process from occurring. Christianity long ago found that it was in its best interests to deprecate this world and focus its followers' intentions on gaining a better life in the next—the gates to which, we are told, institutional religion alone holds the keys. The logical result is to ignore the preservation and enjoyment of the present environment to invest blindly in lots in the Elysian Fields.

In recent years there has been a trend among many of the more liberal Jewish and Christian religious leaders to reinterpret the Bible and religious traditions in the light of the current ecological crisis. New emphasis is being placed on humankind's stewardship role with regard to the earth. But this is an uphill battle. As Thomas Barry, a historian and nonpracticing priest, explains, "The whole structure of Western religions predisposes us to neglect our natural wealth because we are so fixated on redemption out of this world. But just about everybody is beginning to awaken a little."[7]

Now let's briefly glance at some of the other major ethical and religious systems. In so doing we'll see that they each provide some valuable moral insight, but also suffer from major ethical flaws.

Confucianism

The *Analects of Confucius,* written 500 B.C.E., laid out an ethical foundation, which, for the most part, is as relevant and insightful today as when it was written. In many ways the teachings of Confucius (or those ascribed to Confucius), are superior to those ascribed to Jesus. First, Confucius specifically disclaims omniscience or moral infallibility: "as to being a divine sage or even a Good Man, far be it from me to make any such claim."[8] Rather, he took pride in his desire to learn and to teach others. This rejection of any claim to divinity allowed Confucius's teachings to be properly evaluated on their own merits rather than accepted dogmatically. It also prevented his followers from building an oppressive religious institution in his name. Consequently, unlike Christianity and other religions, history does not relate the horrors of people being put to death for disagreeing with his teachings.

Second, the essence of Confucianism, like the teachings of Aristotle, was moderation in all things. He taught the middle way, always abstaining from extremes. In contrast, extremism is a touchstone of most religions.

Finally, Confucius was totally concerned with the duties of one human being to another and never even mentioned gods or spirits. His was basically a practical morality designed to foster a genteel, just, and charitable society.

Since the only acquaintance most people have with Confucius is the bowdlerized version of his teachings found in fortune cookies, permit me to relate some of his aphorisms. These are taken from Arthur Waley's translation of the *Analects of Confucius.*[9]

> Those who in private life behave well toward their parents and elder brothers, in public life seldom show a disposition to resist the authority of superiors. (Book I, Verse 2)

The good man does not grieve that other people do not recognize his merits. His only anxiety is lest he should fail to recognize theirs. (I: 16)

A gentleman practices what he preaches. (II: 13)

A gentleman takes as much trouble to discover what is right as lesser men take to discover what will pay. (IV:16)

The *Analects* show a much deeper understanding of human nature than that found in the Bible, and hence offer a firm basis for formulating social policy. For example:

One who is by nature daring and is suffering from poverty will not long be law-abiding. (VIII: 19)

What a concise and insightful gem! Nowhere does the Bible recognize the dangers of poverty per se or consider the potential reaction of those of different psychological makeup.

The *Analects* are essentially a pragmatic ethic as evidenced by this description of the qualities of a true gentlemen:

He cultivates in himself the capacity to be diligent in his tasks. . . . He cultivates in himself the capacity to ease the lot of other people . . . he cultivates in himself the capacity to ease the lot of the whole populace. (XIV: 45)

Note that Confucius recognizes that human beings must start with self-improvement, but that is not enough. For a people to be good they must *attempt* to do good. This is the antithesis of Martin Luther's position that faith alone is necessary for salvation. Simply trying to be good and ignoring one's responsibilities to society is hypocrisy:

The Knight of the Way who thinks only of sitting quietly at home is not worthy to be called a Knight. (XIV: 3) [The "way," of course, refers to the way of life leading to perfection.]

As already mentioned, the Golden Rule of the Old and New Testament may have been derived from the version found in the *Analects*:

Tzu-Kung asked, "Is there any single saying that one can act upon all day and every day?" The Master said, "Perhaps the saying about consideration; never do to others what you would not like them to do to you." (XV: 23)

Again the *Analects* show an understanding of psychology and the necessity for greater equality to eliminate crime:

> Chi K'ang-tzu was troubled by burglars. He asked Master K'ung what he should do. Master K'ung replied saying, "If only you were free from desire they would not steal even if you paid them to." (XII: 18) [In other words, if K'ang-tzu did not accumulate so many valuables, he would not tempt people to rob him.]

In my opinion, the most outstanding value of the Analects, as opposed to the Bible, is their emphasis on the search for knowledge and the rejection of reliance on blind faith:

> One who studies wisely with set purpose, who questions earnestly, then thinks for himself about what he heard, such a one will incidentally achieve goodness. (XIX: 16)

> From a gentleman consistency is expected, not blind fidelity. (XV: 36)

> He who learns but does not think is lost. (II: 15)

The *Analects* even recognized the dual impact of heredity and environment in forming personality:

> Culture is just as important as inborn qualities, and inborn qualities no less important than culture. (XII: 8)

It is especially sad that after three thousand years of the Judeo-Christian tradition we have not come to recognize this simple moral truth advanced by Confucius:

> Putting men to death without having taught them [the right]; that is called savagery. (XX: 2)

I could go on—the *Analects* discuss culture, conduct of affairs, responsibilities, effective leadership, loyalty to superiors, and much more. One could argue with some of the teachings. For example, they lean heavily on tradition and, in my opinion, give too much credence to the pronouncements of Chinese rulers of antiquity. However, Confucianism manages to maintain a sense of balance even here, and also displays a sense of humor completely absent in the biblical writings. The story is related of how one of the disciples of Confucius continually chanted an analect which he thought to be particularly profound. Rather than being congratulated he was gently chided by the Master: "Come now, the wisdom contained in them is not worth treasuring to that extent" (IX:26). In my opinion, the world needs more wit and wisdom such as that offered in Confucianism, and less of the damning dogmatism of Christianity.

Ironically, there is an inherent dilemma in teaching moderation in all things, of abstaining from extremes. By definition, extremism either produces or elicits strong emotion from people. So there will always be those anxious to spread some extreme doctrine, even at the risk of their lives. The danger may even add spice to the desire to convert others. On the other hand, how can a doctrine of moderation elicit strong emotion? Confucianism tried to answer this need through reliance on ritual. Ritual becomes the way of breathing life into the otherwise rather dry teachings of moderation. Confucius believed so strongly in the powers of ritual, that he felt the government could rely more effectively on the power of ritual than penalties to enforce its laws. As in all ritualistic teaching, however, the number of rules began to expand exponentially. Although breaking the rituals didn't carry the threat of eternal damnation or the terrible temporal punishments associated with Judeo-Christian religions, attempting to learn 3,300 "injunctions" became an end unto itself for the elite classes.

Important contributions to ethical practice were also made by many of the successors to Confucius. In the *Works of Mencius* we find one of the first conceptual links made between economics and morality. Mencius recognized that "a constant mind without a constant livelihood is impossible," and so it becomes the purpose of government "to produce the necessities of life in sufficient quantity."[10] Another important contributor to the Confucian tradition was Hzün Tzu, who taught that even though by their nature humans were evil, by education and moral training people could become good. Most importantly, Hzün Tzu held that the human mind was central to understanding the universe. His emphasis on human understanding led to a naturalistic view of religion. His conclusion was not much different than that of today's behaviorists: "By perfect understanding of nature, people can control their environment and universe."[11]

Finally, there was Mo Tzu, who rejected mystical intuition, authority, and precedent as the basis for morality. Like Aristotle, Mo Tzu arrived at his axioms deductively and then proceeded to argue inductively from those premises. While this methodology is flawed (it ignores the essential element of validation), it led Mo Tzu to essentially the same utilitarian conclusions postulated two centuries later by Jeremy Bentham and John Stuart Mill. Mo Tzu started with the premise that if people were adequately educated as to what is most conducive to their benefit, they would all wish universal love and the common good. The consensus of the common good led Mo Tzu to his two axioms: "the commonweal (the greatest benefit to the greatest number), and the common accord (the theory that the policy producing the greatest benefit must be acceded to by all)."[12]

It is important to recognize that these philosophical positions are far more sophisticated and viable than those of modern Western religions, which ground their propositions on the specious reasoning of revealed truth. Moreover, because they did not make the claim to divine inspiration, they were amenable to reason and evidence. It is to be hoped that after their disastrous experiment with the "religion" of Maoism, the Chinese people will again embrace the ancient principles that, although modified to meet today's needs and problems, reflect the pragmatic approach of their early philosophers.

Hinduism

Farther west, in India, another ethical system was established long before the time of Confucius. The Sanskrit writing known as the *Rig-Veda* was the basis for Hinduism in its myriad forms. As explained earlier, it appears that either much of Judeo-Christian mythology originated in India, or perhaps the Hindu legends were also derived from earlier Assyrian and Sumerian myths. Although Hindu pantheism gradually degenerated into mysticism, one of the central doctrines of the *Rig-Veda* is central to Hinduism even today. Hindus are supposed to say "Tat twom asi" (This thou art) to every living thing with which they come in contact. In so doing, they recognize the oneness and mutual interdependence of all life. All distinctions among religions, races, and nationalities are considered artificial and divisive. In this belief we can recognize a basis for environmentalism and humanism. Unfortunately, as Hinduism became vulgarized into a popular religion the concept of caste distinction crept in along with the commensurate evils such a concept is bound to spawn.

A second major contribution of the *Rig-Veda* was its shift of emphasis away from the death of the individual to the immortal life of nature. Feuerbach picked up on this theme when he stressed the immortality of humanity. It is in the continued evolution of human institutions and culture that a person's deeds live on long after their individual identity has disappeared.

At its purest, Hinduism is a vague form of transcendentalism, which can be added to or blended with scientific knowledge.[13] However, it is rarely found in this benign form. Like so many other religions, there is a huge gulf between the philosophical basis for Hinduism and the popular practice of the religion. One of the major dangers of Hinduism was the belief that Divine grace flowed through the guru, who linked himself through the chain of past gurus to God (not unlike the claim of the pope). The result was that the followers of the guru were to practice total surrender to his dictates as if they were direct from God (again, not unlike the pope).

The dangerous absurdity of this belief was evidenced not long ago in our country with the creation of the town of Rajneeshpuram in Oregon by the devotees of Bhagwhan Shree Rajneesh. Followers had to irrevocably turn over all their personal wealth to Rajneesh. Later, in order to control local politics, the cult recruited the down and out from all over the nation to relocate to their community, thus gaining their votes to swing the local elections. Of course, since they were considered a religion they paid no taxes on the fortune being amassed by the guru. Finally, when Rajneesh began to arm his little feudal kingdom to the teeth, secular authorities decided to step in for fear that another Jonestown disaster might be brewing. Eventually, this would-be divine emissary was sent packing, without his dozens of Rolls-Royces.

The Hindu caste system is another obnoxious consequence of their theology. We have seen by the riots in recent years how difficult it will be to eliminate this anachronistic belief. It is considered by orthodox Hindus to be absolutely just because the virtues and sins of a former life determine a person's birth in a particular caste. Hence, it is by reconciling one's self to the present caste and behaving accordingly that the caste of one's next life will be determined. That this has been a successful means of social control is obvious by its longevity. That it has any place in the twenty-first century is more than a little questionable.

At the beginning of this book I mentioned the worldwide resurgence of fundamentalist religions. India has not escaped this phenomenon. In its most disgusting manifestation, some Hindu sects have reinstated the horrifying custom of throwing the wife of the deceased onto the funeral pyre. Religious belief also is responsible for the continuing intermittent bloodshed between Hindus and Moslims as well as Moslems and Sikhs in India.

Buddhism

Long ago, with the corruption of Hinduism into many segmented religious sects, it was inevitable that class bigotry (such as the caste system) and divisiveness should develop. It was only natural, then, that a reformer arise to establish a new way. Thus, Siddhartha Gautama, the first Buddha, found a ready following for his new, more humane teachings.

Most Westerners are ignorant of the fundamentals of Buddhism and tend to think that its followers worship Buddha as a god. This mistake has been fostered by Western religious leaders who try to create the impression that theism is a worldwide concept. Although the devotion of the peasants to Buddha may appear close to worship of a deity—due in part to the influx of Christian and Hindu theism—the teachings of Buddha have no concept of God as a First Cause, Creator, or Almighty Father. Nor do his teachings urge his followers to seek personal salvation by following some rigid code of moral behavior. Rather, Buddhism preaches a morality based upon rationality, human equality, and brotherhood.[14]

To the Buddhist, all things are one, all divisions are an illusion. Therefore, to be desirous of anything is simply to fail to recognize that you already are that thing. Buddhism is a more subtle doctrine than pantheism, yet it comes close to that concept.

The Buddhist seeks, but does not strive, to attain Nirvana, which is not a place like heaven; personal immortality is simply one more delusion. Rather, Nirvana is total escape from all desire, all wants, all feelings; it comes from subverting the individual consciousness with the oneness of the absolute—the "All." The word English translators frequently use for this state is the Void; but this word doesn't do justice to the concept. This "nothingness," as it has also been translated, is not simply a negative state but a return to the cosmic "All." I think "Devoid" is a better idea—devoid of all personal identity.

Obviously, I cannot begin to explore this unique worldview. What is important for our purposes is not the metaphysical underpinning of Buddhism, which is quite fuzzy anyway, but the way of life resulting from its application. Buddhism—particularly the Zen form, with its emphasis on personal enlightenment through everyday living and meditation, can lead to a more peaceful and tranquil mental state than can be attained by Western religious belief. In Buddhism there is no attempt to view nature as a hostile, alien force that must be conquered. Different races, religions or nationalities are not held to be superior or inferior since their distinctions are recognized as arbitrary artifacts of unenlightened minds, a view carried over from the *Rig-Veda*. War becomes absolutely absurd because it can only occur between at least two people, and for the Buddhist the distinction of personality is an illusion.

Regrettably, despite its positive aspects, Buddhism has serious drawbacks. It should be apparent that it is very easy to slide from a position of nonstriving to pure escapism. The Buddhist monk, like his Christian counterpart, has often opted to escape from any meaningful social involvement. This can mean turning one's back on injustice, rather than combating it. However, this was far from true for those Vietnamese monks who set themselves ablaze to focus world attention on U.S. efforts to determine the future of Vietnam. The best recommendation for Buddhism is that, like Confucianism, this belief system has existed for twenty-five centuries without a single Crusade, Inquisition, or imperialist attempt to invade and destroy the culture of another people.

Greek Naturalism

A more naturalistic basis for morality began with the early Greeks. I use the term "naturalism" rather than rationalism to avoid confusion with the specific philosophical school bearing the latter name, but in a broad sense they are similar. The hallmark of naturalism was to rely upon observation and/or logic to develop moral judgments, rather than mere acceptance of allegedly divine commands of self-proclaimed prophets. The skepticism of the Greek philosophers challenged the popular notion of the gods five centuries before the rise of Christianity. Xenophanes understood the principle of anthropomorphism and poked fun at the worship of idols by saying that if they could, oxen would make similar idols of oxen. Anaxagoras denied the divinity of the sun, declaring it to be a red hot stone bigger than the Peloponese. Euhemerus speculated that the gods had their origin in popular heroes who gradually became the object of common veneration. Democritus developed the philosophy of Atomism which posited a materialistic basis for the universe.

As early as 600 B.C.E. the Greeks had moved from the notion of divine kingship to an understanding that all government was created by humans for humans. One of the most profound assessments of a "good" government was offered by the lawgiver Solon, whose goal was to establish a moderate democracy. Solon defined the ideal government as, "that where the least injury done to the meanest individual is considered as an insult on the whole constitution."[15]

Anaxagoras provided one of the earliest attempts at working out a reasoned basis for understanding human nature. He held that any theory must be judged in terms of its harmony with the world. But it was the Sophists, such as Protagoras and Gorgias, who recognized that "man is the measure of all things." In a sense, this concept is the basis for the modern philosophy of humanism. The assertion that all morality was relative to human needs and social interactions earned them the condemnation of Socrates, Plato, and Aristotle, all of whom believed that morality was an absolute set of unchanging principles. Over the centuries, ignorant and/ or deliberate misrepresentation of the Sophists' position resulted in the term "sophistry" being equated with attempts to twist the truth through clever, self-serving arguments. However, the original Sophistic teachings simply recognized the absurdity of searching for the meaning of life in terms of a cosmic perspective. Moreover, the Sophists denied the existence of metaphysical absolutes. It took philosophy over two thousand years to recognize the wisdom of this latter perspective.

There appears little of value for matters of morality in Aristotle's metaphysics. However, his *Nicomachean Ethics* is a masterpiece. Aristotle doesn't really provide an adequate basis for why a person should behave morally, but he does develop an excellent set of guidelines for ethical behavior. His concept of distributive justice is still the philosophical basis of much of today's system of common law. One group of Aristotle's followers, the Peripatetics, taught that love toward all humanity was based not on a particular religion but on natural principles. The secular humanist readily embraces this view.

Another Greek philosopher, Epicurus, has been much maligned by Christian apologists, but his teachings have much to commend them. Centuries later the Roman Stoic Seneca, who professed to be totally opposed to the Epicurean tradition, quoted Epicurus in almost every one of his *Letters to a Friend*. Among the more noble tents of Epicurus was his belief that all divisions were arbitrary and divisive. The Epicurean position, as expressed by one of his students, was that the whole earth should be viewed as "just one country, the native land of all, and the whole world is just one household."[16] This was a much broader and more enlightened perspective than any offered by the teaching of Jesus and comes closer to the Buddhist position. Would that it had gained dominance over the narrow religious and nationalistic views that plague our world today!

Epicurus spoke frankly against the myth about gods interfering in human affairs. Like Gorgias, Epicurus held that humankind was the center of all things. This is not the same as saying that an individual should view the world as if he or she were the center of it. This important distinction was (deliberately?) overlooked by his detractors. The view of Epicurus was shared by the poet Menander: "I am a man; I deem nothing that concerns mankind to be a matter of indifference to me."[17]

In the worldview of Epicurus, the idea of immortality was not only dismissed as a myth, but actually considered a form of selfishness: "But the wise man finds his life span sufficient to complete the full circle of attainable pleasures, and when the time of death comes, he will leave the table of life, satisfied, freeing the place for others." Certainly, this is a more humane and considerate sentiment than that of those who expect society to divert resources that could benefit hundreds of people, by adding a few months or years to the lives of people who have lived far beyond the average of their fellow human beings.

The obligation of each of us to all of humanity was also recognized by the Greek and Roman Stoics, who taught that "man was not born for his own sake but for the sake of others, i.e., for love."[18] This view may be a little extreme, but is better than believing humans are born either to serve God or gain salvation through being good—both of which lead to narrow-minded self-righteousness.

Around 175 B.C.E., the Academic Skeptics Arcesilaus and Carneades, attempted to work out a reasonable basis for justifying actions and beliefs. Carneades showed the difficulty of knowing anything with certainty and proposed that all knowledge involves different degrees of probability.*

For almost a thousand years, from 600 B.C.E. to 400 C.E., art, philosophy, and science flourished. However, with the rise and spread of Christianity it was not long before true philosophical thought was being challenged by antirational theology. The death knell for intellectual discussion was sounded when Cyril instigated a Christian mob to murder the philosopher Hypatia of Alexandria in 415 C.E. With the silencing of the philosophical community in Alexandria, the Western world was plunged into an intellectual abyss that lasted a thousand years.

The Enlightenment and Later

The light of reason could not be completely extinguished, however. The embers of human intellectual reawakening were fanned into a flame during the Renaissance by such luminaries as Averroës, Francis Bacon, Roger Bacon, Copernicus, Erasmus, Galileo, Montague, and William of Ockham. The flame became a roaring blaze with the brilliant essays of René Descartes, Thomas Hobbes, Gottlieb Leibniz, Issac Newton, and Baruch Spinoza However, as significant as the contributions of these men were, it was the much less well known Italian philosopher Giambattista Vico (1668–1744) who first set a new course for philosophy, and consequently ethics, by stating that to know anything about the world human beings must adopt the empirical approach of experimentation and observation. With this heretical idea Vico laid the foundation for the edifice of British Empiricism. For John Locke, George Berkeley, and David Hume, experience became

---

*I have also considered how one can actually estimate the probability of a person's belief in God—not the probability of the correctness of the belief as Carneades attempted, but the probability of belief itself. Given a quantification of such variables as proximity to death, education, strength of parents' belief, life experiences, career success, and the like, I think a correlation of the data could yield a fairly accurate prediction of the strength of an individual's belief in God. Such a study would not be easy, since it is doubtful that such extensive information could be gained by a simple questionnaire. It would require in-depth psychological evaluations, with extensive controls to guard against the biases of the study administrators and participants. Nevertheless, I believe it would pose an interesting avenue for investigation despite the predictable objections of religious institutions.

the basis for all knowledge. From Hume, it is easy to trace this philosophical approach through the works of Jeremy Bentham, John Stuart Mill, Karl Marx, C. S. Peirce, William James, John Dewey, G. E. Moore, and finally to the Vienna Circle and the logical positivists: Moritz Schlick, Rudolf Carnap, Otto Neurath, A. J. Ayer, Bertrand Russell, Ludwig Wittgenstein, and others.

In their pursuit of understanding via a rigorous scientific method, these courageous thinkers had to constantly battle the ignorance and superstition fostered by organized religions seeking to cloud our minds with their soporific mysticism and anti-intellectual dogmas. But the diligence of these philosophical explorers has yielded a rich cornucopia of wisdom and ethical observations far superior to and more fruitful than the primitive teachings of the Judeo-Christian tradition. In fact, it is apparent that Judeo-Christian teachings have adopted much of their legacy, although always after many years of opposing the advance of truth. Throughout this volume we have reviewed many of the insights of the philosophers since the Enlightenment. Let's consider a few additional ethical gems uncovered by these miners of wisdom.

Hume defined personal merit as "the possession of mental qualities, useful or agreeable to the person himself or to others."[19] Religious belief and practice are not relevant given such a definition. Immanuel Kant taught the "equality of all rational beings whatever their rank, with respect to the claim of being an end in himself, respected as such by everyone, a being which no one might treat as a mere means to ulterior ends."[20] Persons become an end in themselves, not mere tools to serve the gods.

To be happy, man requires more than merely to be free from pain, injustice, and inequality. There must be a positive aspect to existence as well. Although he makes no reference to Epicurus, Jeremy Bentham echoed this philosophy in that he considered pleasure not to be the evil which religion tried to make of it, but a good. Bentham worked out a felicific calculus the end of which was to promote the most pleasure for all.

The American social thinker Thomas Paine suggested that "to be happy in old age it is necessary that we accustom ourselves to objects that can accompany the mind all the way through life."[21] What sound advice! Paine doesn't merely reject crass pecuniary materialism but, like Arthur Schopenhauer, offers meaningful substitutes—art, philosophy, and culture.

Friedrich Nietzsche recognized the value of art in even more dramatic terms: "Art and nothing but art, . . . we have art in order not to die of the truth."[22] To some extent, I will admit that the invention of religious ritual performs the same function as art in this regard. The French philosopher and novelist Albert Camus concurred with Dostoyevsky, who expressed the same opinion: "Man simply invented God in order not to kill himself. That is the summary history of mankind down to this moment."[23]

Psychologist Rollo May is also convinced that myths are essential for people to find meaning in their lives.[24] He may be right for those at the bottom of the economic and social ladder, or for those faced with death or insurmountable adversity. But it is difficult for me to see how reliance upon myth will provide the factual foundation for the citizens of a democracy to make the informed decisions required if our ever more complex culture is to survive. Moreover, today, with adequate leisure time to enjoy the arts (and sports and hobbies), most people can do better than rely on myths to make life bearable.

Auguste Comte, the founder of sociology, attempted to work out a secular religion complete with its own rituals, but one founded on science rather than metaphysics, and dedicated to the worship of humanity rather than gods. For Comte the new norm (which actually harks back to the Greeks and Chinese) was love of one's fellow man. Comte called for a reformation of the social order and a seeking after the ultimate goal of human progress. Unfortunately, in replacing priests with scientists, Comte invested them with the same infallibility that the Church had claimed for itself. Ultimately, Comte's secular religion took on an increasingly dogmatic tone in his later writings until it sounded just like so many other religious systems. The unfortunate result of Comte's philosophy would be a totalitarian statism based on science rather than faith.

Most recently, Bertrand Russell viewed his life as devoted to three passions: "the longing for love, the search for knowledge, and the unbearable pity for the suffering of mankind."[25] Not a bad set of values; think of the potential for social progress that could occur if those values could be shared by all persons.

The contention, therefore, that belief in God is necessary to ensure morality and attain happiness is simply not true. Humankind has been developing its system of ethics for thousands of years. Religions oftentimes have borrowed the work of some of the more profound thinkers throughout the ages, but more often than not (as shown in earlier chapters) religion has backed the established authority and sought to impede human progress, whether ethical or cultural. Hans Küng admits that with regard to ethical development, "it is pointless to look for a distinguishing Christian feature in any kind of abstract idea or principle, in any kind of sentiment, generally in a horizon of meaning, in a new disposition or motivation."[26]

Then Küng goes on to make the same mistake that Kant did. He assumes that without a divine source of values, there can be no values; consequently, man will fall prey to nihilism. Like Hume, Kant held that an "ought" cannot logically be derived from an "is." In other words, from a cosmic perspective, we can never determine what human beings should do simply from the fact of their existence, since, cosmically speaking, all situations—whether leading to human sorrow or happiness—are a matter of indifference. Nothing is good of or for itself. Kant takes it a step further and claims that "there is not the slightest ground in the moral law for a necessary connection between the morality and proportional happiness of a being."[27] From this point Kant goes on to conclude that the only justification for morality is to "assume the existence of God."[28] This line of reason has caused much confusion down to the present day.

The reason for this confusion is twofold. First, while it is true that from a cosmic perspective it is irrelevant that we are happy—or even that we exist—the cosmic perspective itself is an irrelevant abstraction. On the other hand, from our perspective as individual humans, it is very important that we be happy. Second, Kant incorrectly assumes that because the existing moral law of his day seemed to have little relevance to happiness, morality could never be directly related to happiness. However, morality is itself a mere creation of man in an attempt to gain happiness. Although you cannot derive an "ought" from either the cosmic perspective or that of an individual, you can determine what others should do to make you happy: for example, they should refrain from injuring you. Hence, there will be certain moral rules to which all persons could agree since all would benefit from them. Human "rights" are those moral principles that humans have decided are basic to their happiness. As such, even moral principles must be organic, changing to reflect new knowledge or to meet new human needs.

To define a principle as a "God-given right" is an attempt to universalize the principle to be applicable to all times and circumstances. It also, in effect, removes the principle from examination and validation in terms of its impact on human welfare. The danger here is that when an authoritative religion is vested with the infallible authority to determine what constitutes a moral right or moral obligation, it will structure the rules of morality to serve the interests of the religious institution itself before the interests of humankind. When morality becomes controlled and defined by an elite, whether an authoritarian state or religion, it is structured primarily to serve those in power.

Humankind probably devised some rudimentary moral laws long before it created organized religions. William James recognized that moral behavior could be explained by purely natural means: "Instinct and utility between them can safely be trusted to carry on the social business of punishment and praise."[29] James may have been overly simplistic and optimistic in this view, but he was on the right track.

According to Paul Beattie, the origins of morality can be traced primarily to the role model of the family. Parenthood, which originally was largely instinctive, by virtue of the nurturing of infants and care of young children, provided a role model, not in terms of what was taught, but in the relationships involved. Seeing the benefits of mutual dependence and harmony existing in successful families generated the idea that society could benefit if this selfless relationship could be extended to the "family of man."[30]

Social custom was the device used to transmit moral codes which stood the test of time. Customs prevent each individual from acting in a socially destructive way and facilitate the transmission of values from one generation to the next. While customs are not fluid, they are sufficiently plastic to permit remolding if the needs of the day demand it. Religion, on the other hand, rigidly formalizes moral structures, thus inhibiting further evolution. Nevertheless, sociobiologists such as E. O. Wilson caution that it would be wrong to reject all the moral values and rules of religion out of hand, since the real origin of those values is not a mythical God or religious institutions per se, but rather the genetically transmitted disposition to altruism (or at least reciprocity). Therefore, religions can be of some benefit if they effectively reinforce certain moral values even if the theological basis for accepting those values is erroneous. Still, as I've said, each moral value and rule must be periodically reviewed for appropriateness and relevance, and this is where religions usually fail.

Additionally, there is little doubt that man is a social animal. According to psychologists such as Alfred Adler, the communal feeling is the natural human moral state. For Adler, alienation is the cause of immoral behavior. Many years earlier, Feuerbach also expressed the belief that alienation caused much human misery and cruel behavior. Feuerbach reflected a distinctive eastern flavor in his thinking—although he may not have intended to—when he discussed the need for unity of the species and unity of nature: "Love can only be founded on the unity of the species, the unity of intel-ligence—on the nature of mankind."[31] Moreover, "Only by uniting man with nature can we conquer the supernatural egoism of Christianity."[32]

Although nature plays an important part in formulating human morality, today we recognize the equally important role played by the environment—both physical and emotional. Behaviorism—which is often misunderstood and unfairly maligned—shows that through suitable conditioning a subject can be taught to react to a given stimulus. The reaction is not totally predictable, because the genetic makeup of each individual is different and the conditioning is never totally controlled like a laboratory experiment. However, the guilt experienced by a Catholic who ate meat on Fridays (years ago when it was forbidden) or the ecstasy felt on receiving Communion, are excellent examples of conditioned responses.

Now, what does all this mean? Simply that not only may humans possess a biological predisposition to behave morally, but that we are capable as a species of creating moral laws that further our collective interests.

Furthermore, when a person's genetically determined character traits are in harmony with those thought desirable by a given culture, and when that person's social conditioning reinforces those socially acceptable behaviors, the individual is deemed to be behaving morally. Consequently, given the absence of physical problems or sudden tragedy, such individuals will probably be reasonably happy. However, in the long run, society itself must develop values and an ethic in harmony with its environment or the resultant discord will destroy the accepted value system of the society. To take an extreme example, if destruction of the environment places severe limitations on the water or food supply, people will be forced to compete for existing supplies of food and perhaps kill or be killed in the process.

To summarize:

1. To be happy, people must live in harmony, at least to a limited extent, with their conditioning and genetic characteristics.

2. The conditioning must be in harmony with the values of the culture in which they live.

3. The societal norms and values must be in harmony with the realities and limitations of the natural environment.

4. Morality is the attempt to determine the proper behavior which ensures the reciprocal harmony between the individual and his society, and between society and nature.

5. The earliest attempts at morality were modeled upon the family and have been refined through the reflections of philosophers.

6. Some of these philosophers were members of organized religions, but it was the heritage of human intellectual progress handed down through the ages, not divine inspiration, which determined the development of moral thought.

7. The primary failing of all religions is the stagnation of moral thought into doctrine and dogma which prevents further evolution and refinement. When there are major shifts in societal needs, this stagnation can threaten the welfare of the human race. For example, today's population explosion threatens to destroy the ecology of the world and force much of humanity into a death struggle over shrinking resources. Yet the Catholic Church is still responding to a doctrine appropriate to a time when there were high mortality rates and no effective contraception or safe abortion.

At some future time I will develop the theoretical basis for establishing moral guidelines that are founded upon the three harmonies I've just touched upon. I wish to close this chapter with a brief discussion of a modern alternative to theistic religion which meets the needs of all human beings more fully than today's religions and does not suffer from their fatal flaws. This viable alternative to religion is a form of secular humanism which places humanity in its proper perspective vis-à-vis the environment, and rejects all forms of theism as ignorant and dangerous superstitions.

Secular Humanism

The roots of humanism can be traced back to the ancient Greeks. It's a philosophical perspective based upon the most realistic conceptions of human nature as developed by the finest minds of the past 2,500 years. It is rooted not in mythological gods, but human beings themselves. "To be radical means to grasp something at its root. The root of mankind is man."*[33] Humanism was implicit in the view of Feuerbach: "What we really need: love of man, finally instead of love of God, man's faith in himself instead of belief in God, complete involvement in this world instead of concern for the next."[34] The consequence of such a worldview is a strategy for living which, as stated by H. J. Blackman, is " 'adopt and adapt,' not 'obey' or 'conform.' "[35] Although the concept of humanism, like any philosophical school, is broad and viewed somewhat differently by its many adherents, a commonality of perspectives was outlined by Paul Kurtz and a broad spectrum of humanist philosophers, writers, psychologists and educators. Their proposal, *A Secular Humanist Declaration,*[36] lists ten ideals of humanism:

(1) **Free Inquiry**—The touchstone of the humanist movement. The free exchange of ideas is the basis for all human progress. Humanists reject all dogmatic constitutions whether religious, political or social.

(2) **Separation of Church and State**—James Madison and Thomas Jefferson were the prime movers in founding the world's first secular state. Their legacy has kept the United States free from the terrible religious wars that have wracked virtually every country. Today, religious groups are again attempting to tear down this separation by seeking state subsidies for their religious institutions and insinuating their beliefs into our schools, our government, [and] into the very constitution itself. All who value freedom will reject this blatant attempt to institute a state religion.

(3) **The Ideal of Freedom**—The objective of free inquiry, if it is to be realized, obviously requires a system of participatory democracy. But it

---

*Today we would substitute the nonsexist term "human" for "man."

extends further than the simple-minded "freedom to starve" of the libertarians. Mathelde Niel further defines humanism as "a way of thinking and acting which aims, on the one hand, at the liberation of the individual from the authoritarian, absolute and segregationist spirit, and which attempts on the other hand, to transform economic and social systems which encourage his alienation."[37]

(4) **Ethics Based on Critical Intelligence**—Philosopher Paul Kurtz best expressed this idea: "Humanists share . . . a concern for humanity, a belief that moral values must be removed from the worth of theological dogma, and a conviction that our moral ideas must be constantly reexamined and revised in the light of present needs and social demands."[38]

Although there are objective standards, there are no absolute standards given from on high. Rather, all standards must have as their common goal human happiness and, as such, are discoverable through reason and require verification to establish their validity: "[moral principles] need to be hammered out of the anvil of reason, not fed by the fires of neoprimitive passion."[39]

(5) **Moral Education**—It is a major failing of the public school system that to avoid a source of possible controversy, it fails to teach any morality. If, indeed, ethics is a legitimate subject for scientific analysis, it certainly deserves to be treated as such in our school system. Although recognizing the necessity for moral education, a weakness of *The Secular Humanist Declaration* is, in my opinion, its failure to recognize that morality requires the nurturing and development of social instincts. Without this broad perspective, morality can degenerate into a simplified code of conduct— "being good rather than doing good"—which characterizes so many religious moralities. On the other hand, if educated properly, persons will be con- ditioned to think always in terms of the effects of their actions upon other human beings. Such a social "conscience" should cause people to develop the "good habits" described by Aristotle, to ensure greater social harmony and happiness for all.

(6) **Religious Skepticism**—If this volume serves no other purpose, it should raise a degree of skepticism in even the most devout theist—assuming the person is not totally incapable of using the faculties of reason. But here again, I would push humanism a step further and urge a universal (but not radical) skepticism. By this I mean simply that all "truths" or scientific "facts" should be considered as tentative. The degree of confidence attached to a fact should be a function of the degree of verification. Since there can be no absolute verification, there can be no absolute certainty. However, simply because one cannot be 100 percent certain does not mean that one

cannot be committed to action. Radical skepticism, which denies that we can know anything or draw even tentative conclusions, leads to the paralysis of indecision. What I am suggesting is that we act in accordance with the evidence; if new evidence arises that throws the weight of argument toward a new hypothesis, we must shift course accordingly.

(7) **Reason Rather Than Faith**—Enough has been said of the role of scientific reason as the surest way of reaching tentative truth. It is obvious that this criterion excludes from the secular humanist movement popes, priests, ministers, rabbis, and all those who have substituted faith for reason. As for those who believe, like Küng, that faith and reason can live side by side, they are only deluding themselves. As I have shown, these two approaches to truth are fundamentally irreconcilable.

(8) **Science**—Although recognizing both the potential abuses of science and its limitations, the evidence supports the humanist contention that the scientific method is still the most reliable method for understanding the world. Comte contended that there were three stages in the development of society. The first was the theological, dominated by prejudice and superstition. The second was metaphysical, which relied on reason but required no validation. The result was mere speculation. The third stage, which Comte termed "positive" is characterized by knowledge based upon experience, i.e., the basis of the scientific method.

Nowhere can the fruits of scientific inquiry be seen better than in the conquest of disease. For thousands of years humankind prayed to its gods for protection from pestilence. Despite such entreaties the average life expectancy was forty years or less. It is only in the last century that science has unlocked the secrets of bacteria and viruses. In so doing, it has extended the life expectancy for theist and nontheist alike in the developed nations to seventy years or more. Just look at some of "God's curses" that science has virtually eliminated where modern medicine is available: bubonic plague, typhus, smallpox, diptheria, polio, cholera, hydrophobia, hookworm, malaria, sleeping sickness, whooping cough, and measles, to name just a few. And it is science, not supplication of the gods, that will eventually cure or prevent multiple sclerosis, muscular dystrophy, and a host of birth defects. Science can also provide adequate food and energy, without which a secure and happy life is impossible. But science will succeed only if ignorant religious beliefs do not nullify its efforts by promoting unconstrained population growth.

I should add that although humanism recognizes the invaluable contribution of science, it also recognizes the need to fulfill the aesthetic appetites of humans through the arts: music, drama, painting, and so on.

(9) **Evolution**—It probably should be unnecessary that evolution be explicitly itemized as a principle of humanism. However, Kurtz undoubtedly felt compelled to do so since it has become the focal point for the intrusion of a religious doctrine—creationism—into the classroom under the guise of science. The attempt to legislate the teaching of a religious belief in public schools is a serious threat to academic freedom. Like the efforts to legislate prayer, it is a bald-faced attempt to break down the protective wall between church and state and poses a serious threat to the freedom of all.

(10) **Education**—One of the primary functions of education is to develop critical thinking. The mass media should also seek this goal. In the United States today, however, the media are devoted almost exclusively to entertainment, oftentimes pandering to the grossest human impulses, particularly violence and greed. The pro-religious bias in the media is also cause for alarm. Instead of educating the population to recognize arcane and superstitious beliefs, the media reinforce them. Instead of being the vanguard of human knowledge and understanding, the media often act as a drag on scientific, social, and cultural advances.

The public school system in the United States has been accused of teaching secular humanism. Moreover, the fundamentalists argue, secular humanism is a religion. Therefore they conclude that the schools are guilty of violating the constitutional separation of church and state. Like all fundamentalist arguments, this one is comprised of so many fallacies I hardly know where to begin.

Humanism is not being taught in any public schools; would that it were. The moral collapse in our society today is due in part to the fact that no ethical system is being taught in the public schools. Many educators are beginning to recognize this as a major deficiency. A basic system of nonsectarian ethics has been developed by a group in San Antonio, Texas: the American Institute of Character Education. It stresses courage, honesty, generosity, kindness, truthfulness, cooperation, and respect for others. Where it has been tried it resulted in reduced vandalism, better behavior, and improved test scores. It has received high marks from teachers, students, and parents. It is humanistic in its values. It is secular since it doesn't mention God. No one thinks of it as a religion, and it would be absurd to do so. It does not discuss things like evolution or the role of reason. However, even if these elements were taught as part of other subject matters such as science, it still would not comprise a religion.

Webster's Dictionary gives four definitions of "religion." The first and most common use of the term refers to "the service and worship of God or the supernatural." Obviously, secular humanism is not a religion in the accepted usage of the term since it professes no belief in a transcendental reality. The other definitions refer to "institutionalized . . . beliefs and practices," and a "system of beliefs and practices," and a "system of beliefs held to with ardor and faith." As I have explained, secular humanism is not a set of beliefs. It specifically rejects all belief systems *a priori,* arguing that the scientific method has proven to be much more reliable for ascertaining the truthfulness of a hypothesis. Secular humanism is a philosophy holding that human beings, not gods, are responsible for solving the problems of humankind. It has no doctrines or dogmas as to the nature of those solutions. It has no churches or officials whose proclamations must be followed, and no membership rites, rituals, or duties.

Some theologians have attempted to extend the meaning of religion so broadly and vaguely as to rob the term of all meaning. Paul Tillich has sought to identify religion with "ultimate concerns." This is simply a semantic trick to make the definition so all-inclusive as to make it unassailable by those who oppose religion. The fundamentalists also make a disingenuous effort to distend the definition of religion to encompass any philosophical or ideological systems. If religion can be defined so broadly as to include all accepted ideological or philosophical systems then capitalism, democracy and even vegetarianism are religions. Earlier I showed the similarities between the organization of the Catholic Church and many Communist societies. But would anyone really want to call Communism a religion? If so, they are entitled to the same tax-free status and protections extended to any other religion. Clearly to include philosophical positions and secular organizations under the rubric "religion" is to render the term devoid of all meaning. Such a clumsy effort serves only one purpose: to force religious instruction into the public school system.

The *Secular Humanist Declaration* does not promote the "religion" of secular humanism because there is no such religion. Rather, the *Declaration* is a statement of philosophy designed to promote those conditions necessary for attaining a more humane world. Of course, religions would agree that this is exactly their goal as well. But that they have all failed is evident from a cursory glance at the world situation today. Yet many persons would agree with A. James Reichley that religion still offers a better foundation for democratic values than humanism. Reichley worries that basing morality on either the self or society will fail. If it is based on "the self, a rational individual will honor only those social values that serve his fairly immediate selfish interest. . . . If [based on] society, personal freedom and the rights of individuals are left at the mercy of established secular authority."[40] What Reichley fails to recognize is that it is the *balance* between the interests of society and the self that must be the basis for morality. Moreover, it is the whole purpose of democracy to try to balance these two requirements. Democracy is not an end in itself but the most effective means yet established to the end of balancing competing self-interests.

Reichley is still locked into the old transcendental notion that there is an ultimate source of value outside of human beings. He assumes that there is a God in the first place. Take away that unsubstantiated assumption, and the source of all value must be with humans. Given that the source of value is human, only human institutions can ascertain those values from knowledge of basic human nature, and then devise means of persuading people to adopt those values. After several thousand years of experimentation with the human institution of religion, we can conclude that it is not effective for determining moral values. Religions would appear fatally flawed both because they are very undemocratic, usually serving the needs of a small elite, and because they invariably ignore scientific analysis, preferring to base their moral dictums on ancient laws and metaphysical speculation.

I would be the first to admit that there have been men and women of great insight who have contributed significantly to the field of ethics and the social advancement of humanity in general, while at the same time being devoutly religious. That they were religious is unfortunate because their brilliant analysis has oftentimes become so mixed with their fallacious religious beliefs, that when we are forced to discard the latter there is the chance of overlooking the value of the former as well. This must not be allowed to happen. Religion must always be seen in the perspective articulated by H. L. Mencken:

> Religion was invented by man just as agriculture and the wheel were invented by man, and there is absolutely nothing in it to justify the belief that its invention had the aid of higher powers, whether on this earth or elsewhere. It is, in some of its aspects, extremely ingenious and in others it is movingly beautiful, but in yet others, it is so absurd that it comes close to imbecility.[41]

Even worse, as I have demonstrated, by inflaming and justifying the worst of human instincts as the will of God, theistic religions have resulted in countless millions of people being tortured and murdered. It continues today. Efrain Rios Montt was the military ruler of Guatemala in 1982 and 1983, whose death squads executed thousands of Indians. In attempting to raise money for his New Right missionary organization he proclaimed "a Christian has to walk around with his Bible and his machine gun."[42] Such is the dim legacy of thousands of years of religious belief.

19

Conclusion

Some philosophers in the past have contended that since, by definition, God is inherently unknowable, the only proper intellectual position for an individual is that of agnosticism. Others have reached the same conclusion on the basis that the existence of God can be neither proved nor disproved.

I have presented the position that since there is no evidence or logic to support the belief in a god, the only supportable intellectual attitude is that of nontheism, i.e., atheism. I have argued that humanity must adopt a method of separating truthful propositions from falsehoods or else every absurdity must be accepted with equal credibility. This state of intellectual anarchy would have resulted in the human race never developing beyond the knowledge level of the Neanderthal. In effect, human progress has been achieved primarily by adopting the scientific method, which demands that we accept as tentatively true the proposition most supported by the weight of evidence.

A review of today's fastest-growing religious sects reveals certain common factors contributing to their success. They were founded and promoted by charismatic pretenders who claimed that they had direct communication with God. The fundamentalist and evangelical ministers today follow that same tried and true scheme, either claiming direct revelation or using the myriad vague and conflicting biblical injunctions to support their demagoguery. They prey on the fear, misery, ignorance, and prejudice of their followers. The great danger of these religious charlatans lies in their unremitting attack on the separation of church and state in an effort to legislate their theological beliefs. Whether they are motivated from the desire for personal aggrandizement and greed, or sincere but misplaced superstition, they pose a very real danger to the liberties of all Americans.

In recent years, the hierarchy of the Catholic Church has joined forces with the fundamentalist Christian sects in promoting this mischief. In March

1993 Cardinal John J. O'Connor and TV evangelist Pat Robertson issued a 25-page manifesto, "Evangelicals and Catholics Together: The Christian Mission in the Third Millennium." Among other aims the new coalition seeks to outlaw abortion, obtain state funding for parochial schools and introduce religious education in public schools. In essence it seeks to further erode the separation of church and state.

Under the leadership of the ex-actor and consummate showman, Pope John Paul II, the Catholic Church has reversed the liberal trend initiated by Pope John XXIII, and is trying to reassert its political muscle in an effort to regain control over its straying flock. In tune with neoconservativism which is inevitable in an aging population, the Church hierarchy is making a last-ditch effort to defend the papal supremacy on moral issues. They have launched a no-holds-barred lobbying effort to press for government support of Church schools, while attacking family planning and abortion.

The history of the Catholic Church shows just how dangerous religious institutions can become when they gain political power. Millions of people have been persecuted, tortured, and murdered during the millennium when the papacy dominated European politics. It is essential to recognize that this was no unfortunate religious historical aberration, but the logical consequence of vesting belief and power in people who claim to speak for God.

Many parallels can be drawn between the establishment of more recent Christian sects and the founding of early Christianity. Its founders (perhaps a man named Jesus, certainly Paul) were charismatic zealots who appealed to downtrodden and ignorant masses. Every form of deceit, demagoguery and, ultimately, raw power was used by their successors to establish their religion.

In an investigation of the proposition that Jesus was a god, the evidence shows the claims made concerning Jesus are no more than those made concerning dozens of other ancient heroes and demigods, some of whom are historical, while others are purely mythical. Moreover, there is no more evidence to support the belief in the stories of Jesus than in the legends of Zoroaster, Krishna, Mithras, or a dozen other alleged gods. Whether a historical Jesus actually existed is a matter of some conjecture; there is very little historical support for his existence. He left no writings and there are only problematical references by contemporary historians regarding various personages who might have been the Jesus of the Bible. In any case, we know virtually nothing about a historical person named Jesus.

The gospel accounts of Jesus were written by unknown men who had not known Jesus personally, but were interested in spreading the new religion. Many of the teachings of this new religion were admirable and some were not; none was unique or revolutionary. The initial success of the spread of Christianity was due to the emphasis on the promised new world order and immortal life for all believers. The eventual dominance of the new faith was due to its establishment as a state religion, a ruthless persecution of all dissent, and a militant missionary alliance with European imperialism.

In discussing belief in God, I showed that the syllogistic proofs were all invalid since they are tautalogies that invariably assume their conclusions in their first premise. Moreover, reason alone cannot be used to prove any physical fact. Just as Euclid could develop a geometry based on an assumption that only a single line could be drawn through a point parallel to a given straight line, the Russian mathematician Nikolai Lobachevski (1792–1856), developed an equally consistent and valid geometry by assuming the contrary position: that two lines could be drawn through a point parallel to a given straight line. All metaphysical systems and proofs are of the same nature: even if internally consistent, they offer no necessary reference to the real world.

Not only is there no evidence for the existence of a god or gods but the classic definition of God is fraught with contradictions that would make the existence of such a being as impossible as a square circle. After thousands of years of using the term "God," and the sacrifice of millions of lives to support one conception of the term over another, we humans are still no closer to providing a meaningful definition.

It is not difficult to trace the origins of myths concerning the gods. Early man needed a simple explanation for the mysteries of nature. Positing a being with human qualities not only explained the capriciousness of nature but offered primitive peoples the opportunity of swaying the intentions of the gods and, hence, the opportunity of controlling nature. It is equally easy to understand the psychological motivations which refined the myths and continue to sustain them today. People will always fear death, attempt to rationalize their hostility to others, and seek to escape loneliness. Belief in God and religious affiliation fills these needs. There are also potential penalties for opposing such beliefs, such as social ostracism.

While the promoters of theism have powerful motivators, both psychological and monetary, to assist them, there is no profit to be made by promoting nontheism. It's like forming a society of those who have neither seen nor believe in UFOs. Few people care passionately about what they don't believe.

On balance, theism is neither beneficial nor even neutral to human beings. Like a placebo, theism can effect cures. It can also act as a drug to alleviate the pain associated with existence. But in the long run it is an addiction that slows our efforts to understand human nature and hampers progress toward universal peace and happiness.

Theism has always led to organized religions. Religions have provided another source of arbitrary human division and divisiveness. Their primary goal is to propagate a particular set of doctrines that protect and strengthen their organizations. The advancement of human happiness is never seen as a goal for its own sake. Since science threatens to discover natural causes for all natural phenomena, including human behavior, science is a threat to religion. Furthermore, the behavioral sciences—psychology and psychiatry—offer the distant prospect that people might be happy without the delusions of religion. If this were attained, religious belief would be seriously undermined. For these reasons organized religion must forever be opposed to true science. History has shown this to be the case.

Religious warfare has cost millions of lives. Religions invariably attempt to persuade people to place their blind trust in authority figures, often with disastrous consequences. Such a danger was thought to be remote in the United States just a few years ago. However, recent history has witnessed the rise of Christian fundamentalism, which offers the specter of evangelicals such as Pat Robertson running for President. The prospect of a President who contends that he speaks for God is indeed frightening. Some of the most inhumane, barbaric periods in history have occurred when religions have usurped the powers of the state: consider the Catholic Church in the Middle Ages, the rise of Muhammadanism, or the reign of the Ayatollahs in Iran.

In a 1992 lecture to the National Planning Forum, former U.S. Secretary of State Henry Kissinger stated that following the fall of the Soviet Union one of the primary roles for the United States was to prevent Moslem fundamentalism from becoming the dominant force in Asia.[1] His focus was too narrow: fundamentalism anywhere in the world is a threat to peace. In the United States, Christian fundamentalism is the most serious threat to our freedom and social progress.

There is little evidence that religion fosters moral behavior. Recent polls have shown that the United States is the most religious of the developed nations, yet it has by far the greatest incidence of violent crimes such as murder, robbery, and rape.

This book was written for those people who still, despite the tremendous amount of propaganda and social pressure aimed at making true believers of us all, have managed to retain an open mind. From discussions with friends, especially younger people, I believe that there are still those who can be persuaded by reason and evidence. Their problem is simply a lack of time to survey the evidence. I have attempted to provide a cursory overview of some of that evidence in this volume. In so doing I had to be more concerned with the breadth rather than the depth of the subject matter. For the serious student, I urge you to read some of the books listed in the bibliography. The works by Bertrand Russell and George H. Smith, along with an *Anthology of Atheism and Reason* and *Critiques of God*,

I think are especially discerning. To keep current on the subject, I also strongly recommend obtaining the catalog of Prometheus Books, one of the few publishers dedicated to publishing works of the highest quality on skepticism, rationalism, and ethical issues.

In a sense, it is unfortunate that most works on the subject of theism are written by professors, scientists and learned men. They are of high intellectual caliber, but what is needed is to drive the message home viscerally. People need to internalize the message. This is where the artist could play such a valuable role. By graphically demonstrating the atrocities caused as a result of archaic religious belief systems, he or she could stem the decline of a civilization that I perceive to be slipping to a more primitive, barbaric level.

In future volumes I will analyze the needs of humankind today, to forge a new, verifiable ethic to serve as a foundation for social policy. I will propose new social and economic policies based on that ethical framework and designed to meet the individual, societal, and environmental needs of the twenty-first century. Such a task would obviously be beyond my capabilities if I tried to construct it out of whole cloth. However, as in the present work, I can follow a trail blazed by those courageous men and women who have dared all in their search for truth. Even then, I recognize the potential futility of my efforts. I am tempted to adopt the attitude of Harrison Starr who, when informed by Kurt Vonnegut that Vonnegut intended to write an antiwar novel said, "Why don't you write an anti-glacier book instead?"[2] However, I will not adopt a defeatist attitude toward the intractable grip of religious superstition. Instead, I hold as my inspiration the efforts of the French Resistance fighters as described by one of them, the philosopher Albert Camus, in his book *The Plague.* Even though one person cannot hope to win the battle against disease, any more than against a tyrant with overwhelming forces, at least a person can maintain his dignity and give his life a legitimate purpose—that meaningfulness which true believers seek from their imaginary gods.

I close with the words of a man who has written two sentences that have strongly touched my life. His name is David Tribe and, after studying the legacy of freethinkers of the past in terms of such social advances as free, secular, and compulsory education; family planning; the role of women, and the like, he wrote:

> The influence of Freethinkers is not to be seen in the numbers that have joined their organization or stood up on the fringe to be counted. . . . It is the way people's vital secondary beliefs have been affected, whatever their views of ultimate reality, whether they stay inside or leave the churches.[3]

End Notes

Chapter 1

    1. This section is a summary of an article by Lois Randle, "The Apocalypticism of the Jehovah's Witnesses," *Free Inquiry* (Winter 1984/85): 19.

    2. "Life Everlasting in Freedom of the Sons of God," Watchtower Publication, cited by Randle, "The Apocalypticism of the Jehovah's Witnesses," p. 20. The title is illustrative of intellectual content in Witnesses publications.

    3. "Make Sure of All Things," Watchtower Publication, cited by Randle, "The Apocalypticism of the Jehovah's Witnesses," p. 21.

    4. "Let God Be True," Watchtower Publication, cited by Randle, "The Apocalypticism of the Jehovah's Witnesses," p. 22.

    5. "Kingdom Ministry." Watchtower Publication, cited by Randle, "The Apocalypticism of the Jehovah's Witnesses," p. 22.

    6. "Is Their Danger In Occult Charms?" Watchtower Publication, Dec. 1, 1974. Cited by Randle, "The Apocalypticism of the Jehovah's Witnesses," p. 23.

    7. John Spencer as reported in *British Journal of Psychiatry,* June 1975. Cited by Randle, "The Apocalypticism of the Jehovah's Witnesses," p. 23.

    8. Randle, "The Apocalypticism of the Jehovah's Witnesses," p. 22.

    9. *Free Inquiry* (Spring 1984): 7.

    10. This section is a summary of an article by Rita Swan, "Christian Science, Faith Healing and the Law," *Free Inquiry* (Spring 1984): 5.

    11. Ibid., p. 5.

    12. Ibid., p. 4.

    13. Ibid., p. 6.

    14. Ibid.

    15. Ibid.

    16. Douglas Hackleman, "Suppression and Censorship in the Seventh Day Adventist Church" (Introduction), *Free Inquiry* (Fall 1984): 15.

    17. This section is a summary of an article by Douglas Hackleman, "Ellen White's Habit," *Free Inquiry* (Fall 1984): 16–22.

18. Ibid., p. 17.
19. Ibid.
20. Ibid., p. 18.
21. Ibid.
22. Ibid.
23. Ibid., p. 19.
24. Ibid.
25. Ibid., p. 20.
26. Walter Rea, *The White Lie* (Turlock, Calif.: M & R Publications, 1982).
27. Lucy Smith, "Biographical Sketches of Joseph Smith the Prophet and His Progenitors for Many Generations" (Liverpool, England). Cited by George D. Smith "Joseph Smith and the Book of Mormon," *Free Inquiry* (Winter 1983/84): 22. George D. Smith is a Mormon and a president of Signature Books, which publishes works of authors in the Mormon community.
28. Leonard J. Arrington and Davis Britton, *The Mormon Experience,* pp. 10–11, cited by Ed Decker and Dave Hunt, *The God Makers* (Eugene, Oreg.: Harvest House Publishers, 1984), p. 94. Sworn affidavit by Wesley P. Walters, Oct. 28, 1971, that he and Fred Poffarl found the records of Judge Albert Neely and Constable Philip M. DeZang concerning the arrest and conviction of Joseph Smith for fraud.
29. *Book of Mormon* 1 Nephi 12:23; 2 Nephi 5:21-24; Jacob 3:5-9; Alma 3:6-10.
20. George D. Smith, "Joseph Smith and the Book of Mormon," p. 25.
31. Lucy Smith, cited by George D. Smith, "Joseph Smith and the Book of Mormon," p. 25.
32. Eber D. Howe, *Mormonism Unveiled* (Plainsville, Ohio: Eber D. Howe, 1834), pp. 270-72. Cited by George D. Smith, "Joseph Smith and the Book of Mormon," p. 23.
33. *History of the Church,* vol. 5, p. 372. Cited by George D. Smith, "Joseph Smith and the Book of Mormon," p. 23.
34. Decker and Hunt, *The God Makers,* p. 100.
35. Ibid., p. 103.
36. Dr. Wrl, *Mormon Portraits,* 1886, pp. 70–72, and Orson F. Whitney, *Life of Herbert C. Kimball,* pp. 333-35, 339. Cited by Decker and Hunt, *The God Makers,* p. 166.
37. Decker and Hunt, *The God Makers,* p. 166.
38. Fawn M. Brodie, *No Man Knows My History,* p. 466. Quoted by Decker and Hunt, *The God Makers,* p. 166.
39. *History of the Church,* vol. 6, p. 361. Cited by Decker and Hunt, *The God Makers,* p. 153.
40. Decker and Hunt, *The God Makers,* pp. 153-54.
41. *Journal of Discourses,* vol. II, p. 128. Cited by Decker and Hunt, *The God Makers,* p. 151.
42. Decker and Hunt, *The God Makers,* p. 151.
43. S. Dilworth Young, BYU Fireside Meeting, May 5, 1974, from "Saints

Alive in Jesus, The Mormon Plan for America," asst. notes. Cited by Decker and Hunt, *The God Makers*, p. 44.

44. Decker and Hunt, *The God Makers*, p. 110.

45. *Journal of Discourses*, vol. 7, p. 53. Cited by Decker and Hunt, *The God Makers*, p. 210.

46. *The History of the Church*, vol. 1, pp. 498–99. Cited by Decker and Hunt, *The God Makers*, p. 223.

47. Letter dated July 22, 1844, from Sarah Scott cited in "Among The Mormons," pp. 152–53. Cited by Decker and Hunt, *The God Makers*, p. 220.

48. *Doctrine of Salvation*, vol. 1, pp. 184–90. Cited by Decker and Hunt, *The God Makers*, p. 41.

49. *American Universal Encyclopedia*, 1884, p. 219. Cited by Decker and Hunt, *The God Makers*, p. 235.

50. Decker and Hunt, *The God Makers*, pp. 116–19.

51. Oliver B. Hunington, "The Young Women's Journal," 1892, vol. 3, p. 263. Cited by Decker and Hunt, *The God Makers*, p. 79.

52. *Doctrines and Covenants*, 9:8. Cited by Decker and Hunt, *The God Makers*, p. 28.

53. Decker and Hunt, *The God Makers*, p. 9.

54. *Journal of Discourses*, vol. 6, p. 32. Cited by Decker and Hunt, *The God Makers*, p. 43.

55. *The Improvement Era*, Ward Teacher's Message, "Sustaining the General Authorities of the Church," June 1945, p. 1. Cited by Decker and Hunt, *The God Makers*, p. 48.

56. *Journal of Discourses*, vol. 3, p. 247. Cited by Decker and Hunt, *The God Makers*, p. 232.

57. Decker and Hunt, *The God Makers*, p. 238.

58. "Utah: Inside the Church State," *Denver Post*, Special Reprint, Sunday Supplement, Nov. 21–28, 1982, from introductory comments by Will Jarrett, Executive Editor. Cited by Decker and Hunt, *The God Makers*, p. 19.

59. Decker and Hunt, *The God Makers*, p. 19.

60. Ibid.

61. Jerald and Sandra Tanner, *Mormonism: Shadow or Reality?* pp. 415–16. Cited by Decker and Hunt, *The God Makers*, p. 255.

62. James Randi, *The Faith Healers* (Buffalo, N.Y.: Prometheus Books, 1987). See also James Randi, "Peter Popoff Reaches Heaven Via 39.17 Megahert," *Free Inquiry* (Summer 1986): 6.

63. Randi, "Peter Popoff Reaches Heaven Via 39.17 Megahert," p. 7.

64. James Randi, "Be Healed in the Name of God, An Expose of the Reverend W. V. Grant," *Skeptical Inquirer* (Spring 1986): 9.

65. Philip Singer, "Grant's 'Miracles': A Follow-up," *Skeptical Inquirer* (Spring 1986): 22–23.

66. Paul Kurtz, "W. V. Grant's Faith Healing Act Revisited," *Free Inquiry* (Summer 1986): 12.

67. Randi, "Be Healed . . . ," p. 18.

68. Ibid., p. 12
69. Henry Liborsat, "Sister Briege McKenna, Healer," *Catholic Digest* (Dec. 1986): 40.
70. Paul Kurtz, "Does Faith-Healing Work?" *Skeptical Inquirer* (Spring 1986): 31.
71. As quoted by Randi, "Be Healed . . . ," p. 10
72. Joseph E. Barnhart, "On the Relative Sincerity of Faith-Healers," *Skeptical Inquirer* (Spring 1986): 27.
73. Quoted by Edd Doerr, "Madison's Legacy Endangered," *Free Inquiry* (Spring 1983): 6.
74. Ibid.
75. Gerard T. Straub, "Salvation for Sale. An Inside View of Pat Robertson's Organization," *Free Inquiry* (Summer 1986): 22.
76. Ibid., p. 19.
77. A. James Reichley, *Religion In American Public Life* (Washington D.C.: The Brookings Institution, 1985), p. 331.
78. Ibid.
79. Ibid.
80. Sonia L. Nazario, "Crusade Vows to Put God into Schools Using Local Elections," *Wall Street Journal,* July 15, 1992.
81. Frederick Edwords and Stephen Cabe, "Getting Out God's Vote," *The Humanist,* May/June 1987, p. 9.
82. See Edd Doerr's discussion, "Madison's Legacy Endangered," p. 6.
83. Justice Louis Brandeis, quoted by Richard Taylor, "Religion vs. Ethics," *Free Inquiry* (Summer 1982): 53.
84. Robert Johnson, "Heavenly Gifts," *Wall Street Journal,* December 11, 1990, p. A1.
85. Lowell Streiker, "Ultrafundamentalist Sects and Child Abuse,"*Free Inquiry* (Spring 1984): 10–16.
86. Jim Castelli, "License to Heal," *Common Cause Magazine,* January/February, 1991, p. 8.
87. Streiker, "Ultrafundamentalists Sect and Child-Abuse," pp. 10–16.
88. Delos Banning McKown, *With Faith and Fury* (Buffalo, N.Y.: Prometheus Books, 1985), p. 190.
89. Lynn Ridenhour, "Academic Freedom at Liberty Baptist College," *Free Inquiry* (Winter 1983/84): 16.
90. Ibid., p. 17.

Chapter 2

1. John Paul Sartre, *The Reprieve,* trans. by Eric Sutton (New York: The Modern Library 1967), p. 318.
2. J. M. Robertson, "The Crusades," in *Classics of Free Thought,* ed. by Paul Blanshard (Buffalo, N.Y.: Prometheus Books, 1977), p. 141.

3. Geoffrey Parrinder, ed., *World Religions* (New York: Facts on File, 1971), p. 424.

4. Ignatius, *Magnesians* 6.1, *Ephesians* 5.3, Quoted by Elaine Pagels, *The Gnostic Gospels* (New York: Vintage Books, 1981), p. 42.

5. Clemens Romanus, I Clement 3.3, 1.1, Quoted by Pagels, *The Gnostic Gospels,* p. 40.

6. Ibid., p. 41.

7. "Apocalypse of Peter" 79.20–32, Nag Hammadi Library (NHL), 69, quoted by Pagels, *The Gnostic Gospels,* p. 48.

8. Joseph Campbell, *The Masks of God: Occidental Mythology* (New York: The Viking Press, 1964), p. 499.

9. David Roberts, *Smithsonian Magazine,* May, 1991, pp. 40–51.

10. Bertrand Russell, *Religion and Science* (London: Oxford University Press, 1961), p. 95. See also W. E. H. Lecky, "The Horror of Witchcraft," *Classics of Free Thought,* pp. 107–108.

11. James A. Haugt, "Murder in the Name of Religion," *Free Inquiry* (Summer 1990): 45.

12. *Wall Street Journal,* Nov. 2, 1992, p. 2.

13. For a discussion of the St. Bartholomew's Day massacre and the Thirty Years' War, see Joseph McCabe, *History's Greatest Liars* (Austin, Tex.: American Atheist Press, 1983), pp. 175ff.

14. Ibid., p. 27.

15. Marie Mendez-Acosta, "Belief and Unbelief in Mexico," *Free Inquiry* (Winter 86/87): 28.

16. Avro Manhattan, *Vietnam—Why Did We Go?* (Chino, Calif.: Chick Publications, 1984), p. 28.

17. Ibid., p. 28.

18. As reported in *Osservatore Romano & World Press Inc.* (Oct. 14–16, 1951), Quoted by Manhatten, *Vietnam,* pp. 39–40.

19. Manhatten, *Vietnam,* p. 126.

20. Reichley, *Religion in American Public Life,* p. 223.

21. Ibid., p. 224.

22. Gordon Beadle, "The Life and Times of the 'Real' Cardinal Spellman," *The Humanist* (Sept./Oct. 1985): 17. For a thorough examination of the influence of Spellman on American politics see John Conney, *The American Pope: The Life and Times of Francis Cardinal Spellman* (Times Books).

23. Ibid., p. 18.

24. Manhatten, *Vietnam,* p. 63.

25. Ibid., p. 64.

26. Ibid., p. 35.

27. Ibid., p. 183.

28. Hans Küng, *Does God Exist?* translated by Edward Quinn (New York: Vantage Books, 1981), p. 176.

29. Alfred Loisy, "My Duel with the Vatican." Cited by Joseph L. Blau, "New Thoughts (and Old) on Science and Religion," *Free Inquiry* (Summer 1982): 67.

30. Michael Baigent and Richard Leigh, *The Dead Sea Scrolls Deception* (New York: Summit Books, 1991), p. 111.

31. Antony Flew, "Scientific Humanism," in *The Humanist Alternative,* edited by Paul Kurtz (Buffalo, N.Y.: Prometheus Books, 1973), p. 110.

32. *Time,* Sept. 1, 1986, p. 65.

33. Joseph McCabe, *History's Greatest Liars* (Austin, Tex.: American Atheist Press, 1983), p. 85.

34. Robert T. Francoeur, "A Positive Humanist Statement on Sexual Morality," *Free Inquiry* (Winter 1986): 16.

35. *Free Inquiry* (Winter 1986–87): 13.

36. *The Economist,* Nov. 15, 1986, p. 24.

37. *Time,* Sept. 2, 1986, p. 65.

38. McCabe, *History's Greatest Liars,* p. 7.

39. Jim Buis and Joseph L. Conn, "The Bishops and The Ballot Box: Facing Dissent," *Church and State* (November 1984): 6.

40. *Chicago Tribune,* "Catholics, Evangelists Find New Common Ground," March 30, 1994, Sect. 1, p. 2.

41. Pius IX "Syllabus of Errors," as quoted by Manhatten, *Vietnam,* p. 83.

42. Ibid., p. 24.

43. James Hastings Nichols, *Democracy and the Churches* (Westminster, 1951), pp. 58,86. Quoted by Reichley, *Religion in American Public Life,* p. 184.

44. Ibid., p. 286.

45. Hennesey, *American Catholics,* pp. 302–303, as quoted by Reichley, *Religion in American Public Life,* p. 286.

46. Ibid., p. 288.

47. Watter J. Burghardt, *Religion Freedom, 1965 and 1975* (Paulist Press, 1977), p. 69. Quoted by Reichley, *Religion in American Public Life,* p. 288.

48. *Church and State* (October 1985): 6–7.

49. Buis and Conn, "The Bishops and the Ballet Box," p. 6.

50. Homer Smith in a lecture delivered at the University of Richmond, "Biblical Ethics and Contemporary Society," October 31, 1986.

51. Bertrand Russell, *Religion and Science* (New York: Oxford University Press, 1980), p. 106.

52. *Everson* v. *Board of Education,* 330 U.S. 22-28 (1947); quoted by Sam Erving, Jr. "The Constitution and Religion," *Free Inquiry* (Summer 1983): 19.

53. Andrew M. Greeley, *The American Catholic: A Social Portrait* (New York: Basic Books, 1977), p. 149. Quoted by Reichley, *Religion in American Public Life,* p. 291.

54. Adrienne Knox, "Facts of Life on Abortion," *Sunday Star Ledger,* August 30, 1992.

55. Melcom Potts, *World Population News Service,* May 1986, p. 6.

56. Ibid.

57. Edd Doerr, "The Suppression of NSSM 2000," *The Humanist* (Sept./ Oct. 1992): 25.

58. *Chicago Tribune,* September 16, 1992, Section 2, p. 2.

59. Alan Murray, "Alternative Agenda for Rio Summit," *Wall Street Journal,* June 8, 1992, p. 1.

60. Doerr, "The Suppression of NSSM 200," p. 26.

61. Albert Camus, *The Fall,* trans. Justin Obrian (New York: Alfred A. Knopf, 1969), p. 127.

62. *Chicago Tribune,* August 31, 1986, Sec. 1, p. 5.

63. James W. Prescott, *The Humanist* (Sept./Oct. 1986): 10–11

64. Betty McCollister, "Anti-Abortion and Religion," *Free Inquiry* (Winter 1986–87): 14.

65. Joseph Fletcher, "Why Ethics Should Avoid Religion," *Free Inquiry* (Summer 1982): 52.

66. Küng, *Does God Exist?* p. 253.

Chapter 3

1. G. A. Wells, *The Historical Evidence for Jesus* (Buffalo, N.Y.: Prometheus Books, 1982), p. 13.

2. Ibid., p. 8.

3. Ibid., p. 13.

4. Pagels, *The Gnostic Gospels,* Introduction, p. xvi.

5. Ibid., p. xix.

6. Ibid., p. 87.

7. "Gospel of Philip," 63.32–64,5 Nag Hammadi Library (NHL) 138. Quoted by Pagels, *The Gnostic Gospels,* Introduction p. xiv.

8. "Gospel of Thomas," NHL 32.10–11. Quoted by Pagels, *The Gnostic Gospels,* p. xiii.

9. Pagels, *The Gnostic Gospels,* pp. xv–xvi.

10. "Apocalypse of Peter," 79.22–30 NHL 343. Quoted by Pagels, *The Gnostic Gospels,* p. 48.

11. "Teachings of Silvanus," 85.24–106.14 NHL 347–56. Quoted by Pagels, *The Gnostic Gospels,* p. 156.

12. Pagels, *The Gnostic Gospels,* p. 138.

13. "Teachings of Silvanus," 88:24–92.12 NHL 349—350. Quoted by Pagels, *The Gnostic Gospels,* p. 153.

14. Pagels, *The Gnostic Gospels,* p. 149.

15. "Testimony of Truth" 69:18 NHL 414. Quoted by Pagels, *The Gnostic Gospels,* p. 134.

16. "Gospel of Thomas," 42.7–51.18 NHL 123–130. Quoted by Pagels, *The Gnostic Gospels,* p. 155.

17. Tertullian, "De Praeser," 41. Quoted by Pagels, *The Gnostic Gospels,* p. 50.

18. *Pistis Sophia* 36.71. Quoted by Pagels, *The Gnostic Gospels,* p. 78.

19. Pagels, *The Gnostic Gospels,* p. 111.

20. Ibid., p. 179.

21. R. Joseph Hoffmann, "The Origins of Christianity: A Guide to Answering Fundamentalists" *Free Inquiry* (Spring 1985): 51.

22. Ibid., pp. 50–56.

23. Drawn in part from Hoffmann, "The Origins of Christianity," pp. 50–56.

24. Randel Helms, "How the Gospels Tell a Story," *Free Inquiry* (Summer 1982): 20ff.

25. Ibid., p. 21.

26. Thomas Paine, *The Age of Reason,* Introduction by Philip S: Foner (Secaucus, N.J.: Citadel Press, Inc., 1948).

27. Ellen G. White, "Early Writings 1854." Cited by Douglas Hackleman, "Ellen White's Habit," *Free Inquiry* (Fall 1984): 16.

28. John M. Allegro, *The Dead Sea Scrolls and the Christian Myth* (Buffalo, N.Y.: Prometheus Books, 1984).

29. Wells, *The Historical Evidence for Jesus,* p. 15. A good example of this "theologizing" is given in Well's discussion of John's gospel pp. 130ff.

30. George H. Smith, *Atheism: The Case against God* (Buffalo, N.Y.: Prometheus Books, 1979), p. 210.

Chapter 4

1. W. R. Cassels, "Supernatural Religion," in *An Anthology of Atheism and Rationalism,* ed. Gordon Stein (Buffalo N.Y.: Prometheus Books, 1980), p. 173.

2. James George Frazer, *The Golden Bough* (Chicago: The Macmillan Company, 1951), p. 378.

3. T. W. Doane, *Bible Myths and Their Parallels in Other Religions* (New Hyde Park, N.Y.: University Books, 1971), p. 285.

4. J. P. Lundy, *Presbyter Monumental Christianity* (New York: J. W. Bouton, 1876) p. 151. Cited by Doane, *Bible Myths,* p. 286.

5. Ibid., p. 286.

6. T. W. Rhys-Davids, *Buddhism: Being A Sketch of the Life and Teachings of Gautama Buddha* (London: Society for Promoting the Christian Knowledge) p. 184. Cited by Doane, *Bible Myths,* p. 303.

7. Doane, *Bible Myths,* pp. 112–28.

8. Charles Guignebert, "The Birth of Jesus," in *The Origins of Christianity,* ed. R. Joseph Hoffmann (Buffalo, N.Y.: Prometheus Books, 1985), p. 246.

9. Ibid., p. 251.

10. Justin Martyr, *Apology to the Emperor Hadrian* 1, ch. XXII, cited by Doane, *Bible Myths,* p. 124.

11. Joseph Wheless, "Genealogies of Jesus," in *Classics of Free Thought,* ed. Paul Blanshard (Buffalo, N.Y.: Prometheus Books, 1977) pp. 182–83.

12. Allegro, *The Dead Sea Scrolls and the Christian Myth,* p. 156.

13. Geoffrey Higgins, *Anacalypsis: An Enquiry into the Origin of Languages, Nations and Religions* (London: Longman, Rees, Orne, Brown and Longman), vol. 1, p. 561. Cited by Doane, *Bible Myths,* p. 143.

14. Tacitus, *Annals,* 14.22, quoted by Gerald Larue, "Astronomy and the 'Star of Bethlehem,' " *Free Inquiry* (Winter 1982/83): 26.

15. Doane, *Bible Myths,* p. 156.

16. Viscount Amberly, *An Analysis of Religious Belief* (New York: D. M. Bennett, 1879), p. 226. Cited by Doane, *Bible Myths,* p. 157

17. Ibid., pp. 151–52.

18. Thomas Thorton, *A History of China* (London: William H. Allen & Co., 1844), vol. 1, p. 152. Cited by Doane, *Bible Myths,* p. 152.

19. Higgins, *Anacalypsis,* p. 130, cited by Doane, *Bible Myths,* p. 167.

20. John Allegro, *The Dead Sea Scrolls and the Christian Myth,* lists several of the references to the number seven: seven spirits of God (Zech. 4:5), seven angels (Rev. 19:7–9), stone with seven facets (Zech. 3:9), seven hours and seven eyes (Apoc. 5:29), seven pillars (Wisdom 9:1). The magic of the number seven originates from the astronomical observation of the seven visible planets.

21. *Science News,* January 17, 1987, p. 40.

22. F. C. Conybeare, "The True Jesus," in *The Origins of Christianity,* p. 262.

23. Allegro, *The Dead Sea Scrolls and the Christian Myth,* p. 145.

24. Justin Martyr, "Quaest. XXIV," quoted by C. W. King, *The Gnostics and Their Remains, Ancient and Mediaeval* (London: Bell & Dunley, 1864), p. 242. Cited by Doane, *Bible Myths,* p. 264. See Doane, pp. 261-264 for more of the miracles of Apollonius which rivaled those of Jesus.

25. Albert Barnes, "Lectures on the Evidences of Christianity." Cited by Doane, *Bible Myths,* p. 271.

26. Cassels, "Supernatural Religion," pp. 168–69.

27. Paul Kurtz, "The Miracle at Lourdes," *Free Inquiry* (Spring 1986): 33.

28. James Randi, "Lourdes Revisited," *Skeptical Inquirer* (Summer 1982): 4.

29. Wrey Herbert, "An Epidemic In The Works," *Science News* 122 (September 18, 1982): 188. Herbert describes how under conditions of stress or strong emotion, the symptoms of disease can spread through a group of people. Examples are given of groups of women in sewing factories and children in classrooms who experienced nausea, fainting, fever, and even false symptoms of pregnancy, when one of their number was afflicted.

30. Harry Houdini, *Miracle Mongers and Their Methods* (Buffalo, N.Y.: Prometheus Books, 1981).

31. James Randi, *Film-Flam!: Psychics, ESP, Unicorns and Other Delusions* (Buffalo, N.Y.: Prometheus Books, 1982). Randi shows how even reasonably intelligent people like Sir Arthur Conan Doyle, the creator of the master detective Sherlock Holmes, have been taken in by schoolgirl tricks.

32. Paul Kurtz, "Does Faith Healing Work?" *Free Inquiry* (Spring 1986): 35.

33. Bertrand Russell, *Religion and Science* (New York and London: Oxford University Press, 1980), p. 83.

34. Charles Guignebert, *Jesus,* translated by S. H. Hooke (New York: University Books, 1956) p. 43. Quoted by Joseph Campbell, *The Masks of God: Occidental Mythology* (New York: The Viking Press, 1964), vol. 4, p. 355.

35. George Bernard Shaw, *Saint Joan, Major Barbara, Androcles and the Lion* (New York: The Modern Library, 1952), p. 348.

36. James B. Wilbur and Herold J. Allen, *The Worlds of Hume and Kant* (Buffalo, N.Y.: Prometheus Books, 1982), p. 54.

37. Paine, *Age of Reason*, p. 95.

38. Smith, *Atheism: The Case against God*, p. 213.

39. Doane, *Bible Myths*, p. 182.

40. Frazer, *The Golden Bough*, p. 341.

41. Doane, *Bible Myths*, pp. 188–205.

42. Paine, *Age of Reason*, p. 67.

43. Doane, *Bible Myths*, p. 207.

44. Edward Gibbon, *The History of the Decline and Fall of the Roman Empire* (Philadelphia: Claxton, Remsen and Hoffelfinger, 1876), vol. 1, pp. 589–90. Cited by Doane, *Bible Myths*, p. 209.

45. Eduard Lohse, "The Political History of Judaism," in *The Origins of Christianity*, p. 31.

46. Doane, *Bible Myths*, p. 215–32. See also Frazer, "The Myth and Ritual of Attis," in *The Golden Bough*, p. 403.

47. Elaine Pagels, *The Johannine Gospel in Gnostic Exegesis* (Nashville, 1973). Cited by Pagels in *The Gnostic Gospels*, p. 12.

48. "Gospel of Mary" 10.17–21 in NHL 472. "Gospel of Peter" 83.8–10, in NHL 344. Pagels, *The Gnostic Gospels*, p. 13. See also her footnote.

49. John K. Naland, "The First Easter," *Free Inquiry* (Spring 1988): 10–20. Naland provides an insightful summary of the many discrepancies in the gospel accounts.

50. Pagels, *The Gnostic Gospels*, p. 50.

51. J. K. Elliott, "The Story of the First Easter," in *The Origins of Christianity*, p. 323.

52. Justin Martyr, *Dialogue against Typho* 108, as quoted by Thomas James Thorburn in *The Resurrection Narratives and Modern Criticism* (London: Kegan, Paul, Trench, Trubner & Co. Ltd., 1910). Cited by Josh McDowell, *Evidence That Demands a Verdict* (San Bernardino, Calif.: Here's Life Publisher's, Inc., 1979), p. 236.

53. McDowell, *Evidence that Demands a Verdict*, p. 238.

54. Dupuis, *The Origin of Religious Worship* (New Orleans, 1872). Cited by Doane, *Bible Myths*, p. 228.

55. McDowell, *Evidence That Demands a Verdict*, p. 198.

56. J. M. Robertson, "The Crucifixion Legend," *The Origins of Christianity*, p. 325.

57. Wells, *The Historical Evidence for Jesus*, p. 194.

58. Guignebert, *Jesus*, p. 247.

59. Frazer, *The Golden Bough*, p. 417.

60. Ibid., p. 418.

61. Baronius, *Annales Ecclesiastici* 36. Cited by Doane, *Bible Myths*, p. 409.

62. John Kendrick, *Ancient Egypt under the Pharaohs* (London: B. Fellows,

1850). This and many other references to pagan Madonna and child pictures are discusssed by Doane, *Bible Myths*, pp. 336ff.

63. Rhys Davids, *Buddhism*, p. 183. Cited by Doane, *Bible Myths*, p. 326n.

64. James Borwick, *Egyptian Belief and Modern Thought* (London: C. Kegan Paul & Co. 1878), p. 241. Cited by Doane, *Bible Myths*, p. 405.

65. Gerald Massey, "The Historical Jesus and Mythical Christ," in *An Anthology of Atheism and Rationalism*, p. 234.

66. H. L. Mencken, *Treatise on the Gods* (New York: Alfred A. Knopf, 1946), p. 122.

67. "Denarius," in *Chambers' Encyclopaedia*, American rev. ed. (Philadelphia: J. Lippincott & Co., 1877). Cited by Doane, *Bible Myths*, p. 345

68. J. W. Draper, *History of the Conflict between Religion and Science* (New York: D. Appleton & Co., 1876). Cited by Doane, *Bible Myths*, p. 411.

69. Doane, *Bible Myths*, p. 316–25.

70. Max Weber, *Economy and Society*, ed. by Guenther Roth and Claus Wittich (Berkeley: University of California Press, 1978), p. 461.

71. Frazer, *The Golden Bough*, pp. 574ff.

72. Ibid., p. 577.

73. Ibid., p. 567.

74. Ibid., p. 556.

75. Parrinder, *World Religions*, pp. 181 and 187.

76. Mencken, *Treatise on the Gods*, p. 28.

77. Doane, *Bible Myths*, p. 305.

Chapter 5

1. Massey, "The Historical Jesus and Mystical Christ," pp. 231ff.

2. John M. Robertson, "The Historical Jesus," in *An Anthology of Atheism and Rationalism*, p. 227.

3. T. H. Robinson, "The Hope for a Messiah," in *The Origins of Christianity*, p. 104.

4. Justin, *Cum Typho*; Tertullian, *De Baptismo*. Cited by Doane, *Bible Myths*, p. 221.

5. Doane, *Bible Myths*, p. 410.

6. Hans Küng, *Does God Exist?* p. 161.

7. Parrinder, *World Religions*, p. 377.

8. Maruim M. Mueller, "The Shroud of Turin: A Critical Appraisal," *Skeptical Inquirer* (Spring 1982): 26.

9. Richard Walters, "The Shroud Controversy Goes On," *Catholic Digest* (Nov. 1990): 72.

10. Edward Greenly, "The Historical Reality of Jesus," in *An Anthology of Atheism and Rationalism*, p. 187.

11. Josephus, *Jewish Antiquities*, book 18. Quoted by Gordon Stein, "Historicity of Jesus," in *An Anthology of Atheism and Rationalism*, pp. 178ff.

12. Stein, "Historicity of Jesus," in *An Anthology of Atheism and Rationalism*, pp. 179–80.

13. Ibid., p. 180.

14. Ibid.

15. Greenly, *The Historical Reality of Jesus*, p. 6.

16. Voltaire, "The Important Examination of the Holy Scriptures," in *An Anthology of Atheism and Rationalism*, p. 161.

17. Quoted by McDowell, *Evidence That Demands a Verdict*, p. 116.

18. Ibid., p. 117.

19. Massey, "The Historical Jesus and Mystical Christ," p. 232.

20. Ibid., p. 233.

21. Ibid.

22. Paine, *Age of Reason*, p. 172.

23. Mencken, *Treatise on the Gods*, p. 230.

24. Eusebius, *Praeparatio Evangelica*, bk. xii, chap. 31. Cited by Doane, *Bible Myths*, p. 565.

25. Mencken, *Treatise on the Gods*, pp. 231.

26. Doane, *Bible Myths*, p. 434.

27. Voltaire, "The Important Examination of the Holy Scriptures," p. 166.

28. Küng, *Does God Exist?* p. 685.

29. Cassels, "Supernatural Religion," p. 173.

30. Alfred Loisy, "The Origins of the New Testament," Trans. by L. P. Jacks, pp. 10–11 (New Hyde Park, N.Y.: University Books, 1962). Quoted by George H. Smith, *Atheism: The Case against God*, p. 205.

31. Hugh J. Schonfield, *The Passover Plot* (New York: Bantam Books, 1965).

32. Shaw, "Preface to *Androcles and the Lion*," *Saint Joan*, p. 415.

33. Higgins, *Anacalypsis*, vol. 1, p. 747. Cited by Doane, *Bible Myths*, p. 423.

34. Doane, *Bible Myths*, p. 426.

35. Ibid., p. 424.

36. Higgins, vol. 2, p. 34. Cited by Doane, *Bible Myths*, p. 423.

37. Michael Baigent and Richard Leigh, *The Dead Sea Scrolls Deception* (New York: Summit Books, 1991), p. xv.

38. Wells, *The Historical Evidence for Jesus*, p. 204.

39. Weber, *Economy and Society*, p. 617.

40. Baigent and Leigh, *The Dead Sea Scrolls Deception*, p. 38.

41. Allegro, *The Dead Sea Scrolls and the Christian Myth*, p. 132–33.

42. "The Messianic Rule II," in G. Vermes, *The Dead Sea Scrolls in English*, 3rd ed. (Sheffield, 1987). Cited by Baigent and Leigh, *The Dead Sea Scrolls Deception*, p. 136.

43. Baigent and Leigh, *The Dead Sea Scrolls Deception*, p. 186.

44. Allegro, *The Dead Sea Scrolls and the Christian Myth*, p. 192.

45. J. M. Robertson, "The Crucifixion Legend," in *The Origins of Christianity*, p. 292.

Chapter 6

1. Gibbon, *The Decline and Fall of the Roman Empire,* vol. 2, p. 274. Cited by Doane, *Bible Myths,* p. 447.

2. Thomas Taylor, *Taylor's Mysteries; A Dissertation on Eleusinian and Bacchic Mysteries.* (Amsterdam). Cited by Doane, *Bible Myths,* p. 447.

3. Julian, Epistol. 52, p. 436. Quoted by Gibbon, *Decline and Fall,* vol. 2, p. 360. Cited by Doane, *Bible Myths,* p. 448.

4. Bertrand Russell, *Wisdom of the West* (New York, N.Y.: Crescent Books, Inc., 1961), p. 133.

5. Reichley, *Religion in American Public Life,* p. 63.

6. Socrates, *Ecclesiastical History,* bk. VII, chap. 15. Cited by Hypatia Bradlaugh Bonner, "Christianity and Conduct," in *An Anthology of Atheism and Rationalism,* p. 272. See also Doane, *Bible Myths,* pp. 440–41.

7. Reichley, *Religion in American Public Life,* p. 63.

8. McCabe, *History's Greatest Liars,* p. 19. McCabe refers to the work of Father Delehaye, Bishop J. A. F. Gregg and Msgr. Duchesne.

9. Ibid., p. 27.

10. Ibid., p. 101.

11. Quoted by Rev. Robert Taylor, *Syntagma of the Evidence of the Christian* (Boston: J. P. Mendum, 1876), p. 52. Cited by Doane, *Bible Myths,* p. 437.

12. Augustine, *The City of God* (Chicago: Encyclopedia Britannica Inc., 1952), vol. 18, pp. 562–64. Cited by Smith, *Atheism: The Case against God,* p. 107.

13. "Letters from Rome." Quoted by C. Middleton, *The Miscellaneous Works of Conyers Middleton D.D., Principle Librarian of the University of Cambridge in 4 Volumes* (London: Richard Manby, 1752), p. 4. Cited by Doane, *Bible Myths,* p. 438.

14. Alvin M. Josephy, Jr., *The Indian Heritage of America* (New York: Alfred A. Knopf, 1970), p. 286.

15. Christopher Davis, *North American Indians* (New York: The Hamlyn Publishing Group Limited, 1969), p. 18.

16. Josephy, *The Indian Heritage of America,* p. 293.

17. John Upton Terrell, *The Navajos* (New York: Weybright and Talley, 1970), p. 26.

18. Ibid., p. 27.

19. Ibid., p. 48.

20. Josephy, *The Indian Heritage of America,* p. 287.

21. Ibid., p. 294.

22. Ibid., p. 279.

23. *Wall Street Journal,* October 2, 1985, p. 12.

24. Davis, *North American Indians,* p. 35.

25. T. C. McLuhan, *Touch the Earth: A Self-Portrait of Indian Existence* (New York: Pocket Books, 1972) p. 61.

26. Ibid., p. 63.

27. Ibid.

28. Josephy, *The Indian Heritage of America,* p. 287.

29. Ibid., p. 294.

30. *Native American Rights Fund Legal Review* (Winter 1988): 3

31. Reichley, *Religion in American Public Life,* p. 56.

32. Perry Miller, ed., *The American Puritans: Their Prose and Poetry* (Double-day, 1956), p. 98. Quoted by Reighley, *Religion in American Public Life,* p. 56.

33. Reichley, *Religion in American Public Life,* p. 57.

34. Quoted in Irwin H. Polishok, *A Controversy in New and Old England* (New York: Prentice Hall, 1967), pp. 34, 78. Cited by Reichley, *Religion in American Public Life,* p. 66.

35. Donald R. Boles, *The Bible, Religion, and the Public Schools* (Iowa City: Iowa State University), pp. 115–19, and Albnese, *Son of the Fathers,* p. 56. Quoted by Reichley, *Religion in American Public Life,* p. 100.

36. Reichley, *Religion in American Public Life,* pp. 89–90.

37. Ed Doerr, "Madison's Legacy Endangered," *Free Inquiry* (Spring 1983): 6.

38. As quoted by Sam J. Erwin, Jr., "The Constitution and Religion," *Free Inquiry* (Summer 1983): 12. Former North Carolina Senator Erwin, who may be remembered for his role in the Watergate hearings, was a recognized expert on constitutional law. His review of the history of the legal battles to separate church and state is required reading for anyone trying to understand the debate on this subject.

39. Editorial, *Church & State,* January 1987.

40. Ibid.

41. Robert S. Alley, "The Founding Fathers and Religious Liberty," *Free Inquiry* (Spring 1983): 5.

42. W. E. H. Lecky, "The Horrors of Witchcraft," in *Classics of Free Thought,* pp. 107–108.

43. Bertrand Russell, *Why I Am Not a Christian,* ed. with an appendix by Paul Edwards (New York: Simon and Schuster, 1957), pp. 209ff. My account doesn't do justice to Russell's persecution. The appendix should be read to appreciate the degree to which organized religions will go to eliminate intellectual opposition.

44. Ibid., p. 210.

45. Ibid., p. 215.

46. Ibid., p. 221.

47. Küng, *Does God Exist?* p. 304.

48. Quoted by Joseph Lewis, *Lincoln the Freethinker,* 1924, reprinted as *Lincoln the Atheist* (Austin: American Atheist Press, 1979), p. 16.

49. Ibid., p. 17.

50. Ibid.

51. Hennesy, *American Catholics,* pp. 145–46. Quoted by Reichley, *Religion in American Public Life,* p. 184.

52. Ibid.

53. Ray H. Abrams, *Preachers Present Arms* (Wellesley, Mass.: Round Table Press, 1933), p. 69. Quoted by Reichley, *Religion in American Public Life,* p. 2154

54. Reichley, *Religion in American Public Life,* p. 80.
55. Ibid., p. 220.

Chapter 7

1. Arthur Waley, translator and annotator, *The Analects of Confucius,* bk. XII:2 (New Yord: Vintage Books, 1938).
2. *Mahabharata,* quoted by Doane, *Bible Myths,* p. 415.
3. Professor Andrew Drews, "The Teachings of Jesus," in *The Origins of Christianity,* pp. 267ff.
4. Quoted by Donne, *Bible Myths,* p. 415.
5. Clarence Darrow, "Absurdities of the Bible," in *Classics of Free Thought.*
6. Drews, "The Teachings of Jesus," p. 279.
7. The New Testament, Confraternity Edition, p. 100. *New Catholic Edition of the Holy Bible* (New York: Catholic Book Publishing Company, 1949).
8. Smith, *Atheism: The Case against God,* p. 324.
9. Ibid., p. 321.
10. G. A. Wells, *The Historical Evidence for Jesus* (Buffalo, N.Y.: Prometheus Books, 1982), p. 105.
11. Origen, *Contra Celsum,* 1.9–10. Cited by Doane, *Bible Myths,* p. 275.
12. Reichley, *Religion in American Public Life,* p. 218.
13. Küng, *Does God Exist?* p. 87.
14. William B. Murphy et al., *God and His Creation* (Dubuque, Iowa: The Priory Press 1958), p. 99.
15. Harry Elmer Barnes, "The Jesus Stereotype," in *Classics of Free Thought,* p. 3.
16. As quoted by Sam Erwin, Jr., "The Constitution and Religion," p. 13.
17. Howard V. and Edma Hong, eds., *Søren Kierkegaard's Journals and Papers,* vol. 4 (Bloomington: Indiana University Press, 1975), #4583. Cited by John Donnelly in "Suffering: A Christian View," in *Infanticide and the Meaning of Life* (Buffalo, N.Y.: Prometheus Books, 1978), p. 168.
18. Kendrick Frazier, "Quackery: A Massive and Growing Problem," *Skeptical Inquirer* (Winter 1984–85): 109–111.
19. George H. Smith, *Atheism: The Case against God,* pp. 299–300.
20. Havey David Thoreau, "Walden," in *Walden and Other Writings of Henry David Thoreau,* ed. and intro. by Brooks Atkinson (New York: The Modern Library, 1959), p. 194.
21. *Thus Spake Zarathustra,* in *The Philosophy of Nietzsche* (New York: The Modern Library, 1950), p. 94.
22. W. Somerset Maugham, *The Moon and Sixpence* (Garden City, N.Y.: Doubleday & Company, Inc., 1919), p. 80.
23. Shaw, "Preface to *Major Barbara,*" *Saint Joan,* p. 209.

Chapter 8

1. Küng, *Does God Exist?* p. 615.

2. George William Foote, "Bible Romances," in *An Anthology of Atheism and Rationalism,* pp. 113ff.

3. George Smith, *The Chaldean Account of Genesis* (Minneapolis: Wizards Book Shelf, 1977).

4. McDowell, *Evidence That Demands a Verdict,* p. 68.

5. Gerald Larue "Creationism: 500 Years of Controversy," *Free Inquiry* (Summer 1982): 13.

6. George Smith, *The Chaldean Account of Genesis,* p. 62: "The chaos (or water) Tiamet (the sea) was the producing-mother of the whole of them."

7. Ibid., p. 86.

8. Ibid.

9. Ibid., p. 91. In an early Babylonian pictograph, the Sacred Tree is shown with a figure on each side and the serpent in the background.

10. Ibid., p. 165.

11. Ibid., p. 269.

12. Ibid., p. 272.

13. *Aristeas to Philocrates,* trans. Mose Hadas (New York, 1951), p. 302. Cited by John Priest, "The Bible and Authority," *Free Inquiry* (Summer 1982): 16.

14. Bruce Metzger, *Chapters in the History of the New Testament Textual Criticism* (Grand Rapids, Mich.: William B. Eerdmans Publishing Co., 1963). Quoted by McDonnell, *Evidence That Demands a Verdict,* p. 43.

15. "Explorers Find Boat Formation in Noah's Territory," *Chicago Tribune,* August 6, 1984, sec. 1, p. 3.

16. Robert Jastrow, *God and the Astronomers* (New York: Warner, 1980), p. 116. Cited by David A. Conway in his book review "Jastrow and Genesis," *Free Inquiry* (Winter 1981): 32.

17. Isaac Asimov, "Science and the Mountain Peak," *Skeptical Inquirer* (Winter 1980–81): 48.

18. Jastrow, *God and the Astronomers,* pp. 114–15.

19. Doane, *Bible Myths,* pp. 19–32.

20. Ibid., p. 24.

21. Smith, *Chaldean Accounts of Genesis,* p. 299.

22. S. F. Dunlap, *Vestiges of the Spirit History of Man* (New York: D. Appleton & Co., 1858), p. 40, and J. C. Pritchard, *An Analysis of the Historical Record of Ancient Egypt* (London: Sherwood, Gilbert & Piper, 1838), p. 74. Cited by Doane, *Bible Myths,* p. 52.

23. Ian Wilson, *Exodus: The True Story behind the Biblical Account* (San Francisco: Harper & Row, Publishers, 1980).

24. *The History of Cornelius Tacitus,* trans. by Arthur Murphy (London: Jones & Co., 1831), bk. II, chap. III. Cited by Doane, *Bible Myths,* p. 53.

25. Ibid.

26. George William Foote, "Bible Romances," in *Anthology of Atheism and Rationalism*, p. 118.

27. Doane, *Bible Myths*, p. 57n.

28. Voltaire, "The Important Examination of the Holy Scriptures," in *An Anthology of Atheism and Rationalism*, p. 155.

29. *Secular Humanist Bulletin* 4, no. 2 (September 1988).

30. Paine, *Age of Reason*, p. 114.

31. Pope Leo XIII, *Providentissimus Deus* (1893), quoted by Gerald Larue, "Creationism: 500 Years of Controversy," *Free Inquiry* (Summer 1982): 13ff.

32. S. F. Dunlap, *Vestiges of the Spirit History of Man.* Quoted by Doane, *Bible Myths*, p. 54.

33. A. Eustace Haydon, "Yahweh," in *The Origins of Christianity*, p. 76.

34. Ibid., p. 81.

35. McDowell, *Evidence That Demands a Verdict*, pp. 267–321.

36. Peter W. Stoner, *Science Speaks: An Evaluation of Certain Christian Evidences* (Chicago: Moody Press, 1963), p. 96. Quoted by McDowell, *Evidence That Demands a Verdict*, p. 272.

37. McDowell, *Evidence That Demands a Verdict*, p. 287.

38. Küng, *Does God Exist?* p. 297.

Chapter 9

1. For a further discussion, see R. Travers Herford, "The Law and the Pharisees," in *Origins of Christianity*, p. 149.

2. Ludwig Feuerbach, *The Essence of Christianity*, trans. by George Elliot (New York: Harper and Row, 1957), p. 114.

3. Weber, *Economy and Society*, p. 495.

4. Joseph Wheless "Is It God's Word?" in *Classics of Free Thought*, p. 181.

5. J. M. Wheeler, "Sixty Years of Freethought," in *An Anthology of Atheism and Rationalism*, p. 339.

6. Küng, *Does God Exist?* p. 661.

7. Max Müller, *Lectures on the Origin and Growth of Religion, as Illustrated by the Religions of India* (London: Longmans, Green, and Co., 1878), p. 130. Cited by Doane, *Bible Myths*, p. 59.

8. Küng, *Does God Exist?* p. 468.

9. Charles Watts, "The Death of Christ," in *An Anthology of Atheism and Rationalism*, pp. 214–15.

10. Feuerbach, *The Essence of Christianity*, p. 210.

11. George H. Smith, *Atheism: The Case against God*, p. 164.

12. Thomas Aquinas, *Summa Theologica*, second part, pt. II, Q.10, A.3. Cited by Smith, *Atheism: The Case against God*, p. 4.

Chapter 10

1. Quoted by Paul Blanshard, ed., *Classic of Free Thought,* p. 119.

2. Peter Gay, *The Bridge of Criticism* (New York: Harper & Row, 1979), p. 22. Cited by Joseph Blau "New Thoughts (and Old) on Science and Religion," *Free Inquiry* (Summer 1982).

3. I. I. Rabey, *Chicago Tribune,* September 28, 1986, sec. 6, p. 2.

4. Konrad Lorenz, *On Aggression* (San Diego: Harcourt Brace Jovanovich, 1963), p. 288.

5. Paul Kurtz, *Exuberance: An Affirmative Philosophy of Life* (Buffalo, N.Y.: Prometheus Books, 1985), pp. 59ff.

6. Rudolf Carnap, "The Elimination of Metaphysics Through Logical Analysis of Language," trans. Arthur Pap, in *Logical Positivism,* A. J. Ayer, ed. (New York: The Free Press, 1959), p. 72.

7. Smith, *Atheism: The Case against God,* p. 102.

8. Sigmund Freud, "The Future of an Illusion," in *Critiques of God,* ed. Peter Angeles (Buffalo, N.Y.: Prometheus Books, 1976), p. 152.

9. J. B. Wilbur and H. J. Allen, eds., *The Worlds of Hume and Kant* (Buffalo, N.Y.: Prometheus Books, 1982), p. 120.

10. "The Categories," from Immannuel Kant, *Critique of Pure Reason,* trans. and ed. Norman Kemp Smith (New York: St. Martins's Press, Inc., and Macmillian & Co., London, 1929). Quoted by Wilbur and Allen, *The Worlds of Hume and Kant,* p. 119.

11. Richard Robinson, "Religion and Reason," in *Critiques of God,* p. 123.

12. Ludwig Wittgenstein, *Philosophical Investigations,* trans. by G. E. M. Amcombes (Oxford: Basil Blachwell, 1968). Quoted by Küng, *Does God Exist?* p. 504.

13. Martin Heidegger, "Zeit und Sein," in *Zur Sachs des Denkens, Tübingen* (1969), p. 21. Quoted by Küng, *Does God Exist?* p. 497.

14. Richard Kroner, in a paper delivered to the Third Conference on Science, Philosophy and Religion. Cited by Earnest Nagel in his notes to "Malicious Philosophies of Science," in *Critiques of God,* p. 366.

15. Smith, *Atheism: The Case against God,* p. 182.

16. Erich Fromm, *Escape from Freedom* (Chicago: Holt, Rinehart and Winston, 1969).

17. Augustine, *Contra epistolam Manichaei quam vocant fundamenti,* ch. 5 in CSEL 25/1, p. 197. Cited by Küng, *Does God Exist?* p. 66.

18. Augustine, "Sermo 43, 9" in CC 41. Cited by Küng, *Does God Exist?* p. 66.

19. Quoted by Walter Kaufman, *Critique of Religion and Philosophy* (New York: Harper Torch books, 1972), pp. 305-307. Cited by Smith, *Atheism: The Case against God,* p. 100.

20. Martin Luther, *The Bondage of the Will,* trans. by J. I. Parker and O. R. Johnson (London: J. Clark, 1957), II, 7. Quoted by Antony Flew, "Divine Omnipotence and Human Freedom," in *Critiques of God,* p. 237.

21. George Jacob Holyoake, "English Secularism," in *An Anthology of Atheism and Rationalism,* p. 300.

22. Ernest Nagel, "Malicious Philosophies of Science," in *Critiques of God,* p. 323.

23. Horkheimer and Adorno, *Dialektik der Aufklärung Philosophische Fragmente* (Amsterdam: 1947, new ed. Frankfort 1969.) Cited by Küng, *Does God Exist?* p. 328.

24. F. Heiler, *Das Gebet* (Munich, 1918; 5th ed., 1923). Quoted by E. T. Prayer, *A Study in the History and Psychology of Religion* (New York: Oxford University Press, 1932; Galaxy Books, 1958), pp. 148–49. Cited by Küng, *Does God Exist?* p. 606.

25. Smith, *Atheism: The Case against God,* p. 111.

26. J. L. Austin, "Other Minds" in *Philosophical Papers,* ed. J. O. Urmson and G. J. Warnock (London: Oxford University Press, 1961), p. 66. Cited by Smith, *Atheism: The Case against God,* p. 135.

27. Robert M. Pirsig, *Zen and the Art of Motorcycle Maintenance* (New York: Bantam Books, 1974), p. 237.

28. Michael Scriven, "God and Reason," in *Critiques of God,* pp. 95ff.

29. B. C. Johnson, *The Atheist Debator's Handbook* (Buffalo, N.Y.: Prometheus Books, 1983), p. 12.

30. Smith, *Atheism: The Case against God,* p. 120.

31. *Schopenhauer Selections,* ed. Dewitt H. Parker (New York: Charles Scribner's Sons, 1928), pp. 14, 15.

32. Russell, *Religion and Science,* p. 83.

33. Ibid., p. 78.

34. Ibid., p. 37.

35. Mencken, *Treatise on the Gods,* p. 244.

36. Gallup Youth Survey, Gallup Organization Inc., cited by Kendrich Frazier, "New Gallup Youth Poll Finds Decline in Supernatural Belief," *Skeptical Inquirer* (Spring 1987): 229.

37. Kendrich Frazier, "Mainlining of Mysticism: Poll Shows New Popularity," *Skeptical Inquirer* (Summer 1987): 333. Kendrich reports from a poll taken by Andrew Greeley of the University of Chicago's National Opinion Research Council and reported in *American Health,* Jan.–Feb. 1987.

38. William E. McMahon and James B. Griffis, "Further Reflections on Ernest Angley," *Free Inquiry* (Summer 1986): 16.

Chapter 11

1. Küng, *Does God Exist?* p. 651.

2. Aldous Huxley, *Doors of Perception,* cited by McKown, *With Faith and Fury,* p. 344.

3. Wayne Proudfoot, *Religious Experience* (Berkeley, Calif.: University of California Press, 1985), p. 100.

4. William James, *Varieties of Religious Experience* (New York: Longmans, Green, 1902). Cited by Proudfoot, *Religious Experience,* p. 103.

5. Walter N. Pahnke, "Drugs and Mysticism," in B. Aaronson and H. Osmond, eds., *Psychedelics: The Uses and Implications of Hallucinogenic Drugs* (New York: Doubleday, 1970), pp. 145–65. Cited by Proudfoot, *Religious Experience,* p. 105.

6. Proudfoot, *Religious Experience,* p. 111.

7. Barry L. Beyerstein, "Neuropathology and the Legacy of Spiritual Possession," *Skeptical Inquirer* (Spring 1988): 252.

8. Ibid., p. 258.

9. Robert A Baker, "The Aliens among Us: Hypnotic Regression Revisited," *Skeptical Inquirer* (Winter 1987–88): 150.

10. Sheryl C. Wilson and T. X. Barber, "The Fantasy-Prone Personality: Implications for Understanding Imagery, Hypnosis, and Parapsychological Phenomena," in *Imagery: Current Research and Applications,* ed. A. A. Sheikh (New York: Wiley, 1983). Quoted by Baker, *The Aliens among Us,* p. 152.

11. Walter Kaufman, "The Core of Religion," in *Critiques of God,* p. 131. Kaufmann does an excellent job of demonstrating the fallacy of mysticism as an approach to knowing.

12. Richard Swinburne, *The Existence of God* (Oxford: Clarendon Press, 1991), p. 266.

13. James Bisset Pratt, *The Religious Consciousness* (New York: Macmillian, 1940), p. 410. As quoted by Walter Kaufmann, "The Core of Religion," in *Critiques of God,* pp. 130–31.

14. Kaufmann, "The Core of Religion," p. 136.

15. Theresa of Avila, *Life,* chap. 40, as quoted by L. B. Brown, *The Psychology of Religious Belief* (New York: Academic Press, 1987).

16. Bertrand Russell, *Religion and Science,* p. 188. Russell also provides a strong refutation of mysticism in his essay of that same name, chap. 7, p. 171. See also William James, *Varieties of Religious Experience.*

Chapter 12

1. *First Vatican Council, Dogmatic Constitution on Catholic Faith, 1870, DS 3026.* Cited by Küng, *Does God Exist?* p. 510.

2. William B. Murphy et al., *God and His Creation* (Dubuque Iowa: The Priory Press, 1958), p. 75.

3. Kurt E. M. Baier, "The Meaning of Life," in *Critiques of God,* p. 300.

4. V. Caterus, "Objectiones Primae," in ATVII p. 99. Cited by Küng, *Does God Exist?* p. 34.

5. Johnson, *The Atheist Debater's Handbook,* p. 67.

6. John A. T. Robinson, *Honest to God* (Philadelphia: The West Minister Press, 1963), p. 29. Cited by Smith, *Atheism: The Case against God,* p. 35.

7. Quoted in Frank Swancara, *The Separation of Religion and Government*

(New York: Truth Seeker Co., 1950), p. 140. Cited by Smith, *Atheism: The Case against God,* p. 33.

8. Murphy, *God and His Creation,* p. 82.

9. Thomas Aquinas, *Summa Theologica,* First part Q. 2, Art. 3. Quoted by Murphy, *God and His Creation,* p. 84.

10. Ibid., p. 84.

11. *Schopenhauer Selections,* p. 92.

12. Richard Morris, *Time's Arrows* (New York: Simon and Schuster, 1984), p. 132.

13. Roger Penrose, *The Emperor's New Mind* (Oxford: Oxford University Press, 1989), pp. 325–26.

14. Morris, *Time's Arrows,* p. 215.

15. R. Cowen, "Nearby Galaxy Sheds Light on Dark Matter," *Science News* (June 12, 1993): 374–75.

16. C. Ezzell, "ROSAT Data Hint at a Closed Universe," *Science News* (January, 9, 1993): 20–21.

17. L. D. Landau and Lifshitz, *Statistical Physics* (London: Pergamon Press Ltd., 1958), p. 29. Cited by Smith, *Atheism: The Case against God,* p. 256.

18. For a complete discussion of the origins of the universe, see Victor J. Stenger, *Not by Design* (Buffalo, N.Y.: Prometheus Books, 1988).

19. Morris, *Time's Arrows,* p. 216.

20. Aquinas, *Summa,* First Part, Q2. Art. 3. Quoted by Murphy, *God and His Creation,* p. 89.

21. Paul Edwards, "The Cosmological Argument," in *Critiques of God,* p. 47.

22. Nathaniel Branden, *The Objectivist Newsletter* 1, no. 5 (May 1962): 19. Cited by Smith, *Atheism: The Case against God,* p. 240.

23. Baier, "The Meaning of Life," in *Critiques of God,* p. 307.

24. Antony Flew, *God and Philosophy,* p. 193. Cited by Smith, *Atheism: The Case against God,* p. 232.

25. Johnson, *The Atheist Debater's Handbook,* p. 64.

26. Ibid., p. 62.

27. Bertrand Russell, *Wisdom of the West,* edited by Paul Foulker (London: Crescent Books, 1959), p. 159.

28. Santayana, *The Birth of Reason and Other Essays,* p. 72.

29. Aquinas, *Summa,* First Part, Q.2, Art. 3. Quoted by Murphy, *God and His Creation,* pp. 91–92.

30. Bertrand Russell and F. C. Copleston, "A Debate on the Existence of God," in *The Existence of God,* edited by John Hichs (New York: Macmillan, 1964), pp. 168–69. Quoted by Smith, *Atheism: The Case against God,* pp. 248–49.

31. Edwards, "The Cosmological Argument," p. 56.

32. Smith, *Atheism: The Case against God,* p. 238.

33. Aquinas, *Summa,* First Part, Q.2, Art. 3. Quoted by Murphy, *God and His Creation,* pp. 93–94.

34. Stephen Nathanson, "Nihilism, Reason, and the Value of Life," in *Infanticide and the Value of Life,* edited by Marvin Kohl (Buffalo, N.Y.: Prometheus Books, 1978), p. 199.

Chapter 13

1. Aquinas, *Summa*, First Part, Q.2, Art.3.

2. Ernest Nagel, "Philosophical Concepts of Atheism," in *Critiques of God*, p. 10.

3. William James, *Pragmatism* (New York: Longmans, Green, and Co., 1907), p. 114.

4. Smith, *Atheism: The Case against God*, p. 260.

5. E. M. Macdonald, "Design Argument Fallacies," in *An Anthology of Atheism and Rationalism*, p. 95.

6. Stenger, *Not by Design*, p. 19.

7. Charles Bradlaugh, "A Plea for Atheism," in *An Anthology of Atheism and Rationalism*, p. 16.

8. Tom Stoppard, *Rosencrantz and Guildenstern are Dead*, in *Nine Plays of the Modern Theater*, edited by Harold Clurman (New York: Grove Press, 1981), p. 686.

9. Macdonald, "Design Argument Fallacies," p. 95.

10. Pierre Lecomte DuNoüy, *Human Destiny* (New York: Signet, 1949), bk. 2, pt. 3, pp. 35–37. Cited by Wallace Matson, "The Argument from Design," in *Critiques of God*, p. 71.

11. DuNoüy, *Human Destiny*, p. 31. Cited by Matson, "The Argument from Design," p. 73.

12. Matson, "The Argument from Design," p. 73.

13. Chapman Cohen, "Theism and Atheism," in *An Anthology of Atheism and Rationalism*, p. 65.

14. As described by Chris McGowan, *In the Beginning . . . : A Scientist Shows Why Creationists Are Wrong* (Buffalo, N.Y.: Prometheus Books, 1984), pp. 48–51. See also R. E. Dickenson, "Chemical Evolution and the Origin of Life," *Scientific American* 239 (1978): 70–86.

15. R. Pollie, "Sex and the Celibate Fruit Fly," *Science News* 122 (October 2, 1982): 212.

16. McGowan, *In the Beginning*, pp. 110–26.

17. Charles Cazeau, "Geology and the Bible," *Free Inquiry* (Summer 1982): 33.

18. C. Simon, "Fossils Span Evolutionary Gap," *Science News* (February 2, 1982): 119.

19. McGowan, *In the Beginning*, p. 150.

20. "Evolution at a Snails Pace," *Science News* 120, no. 19 (November 7, 1981): 292.

21. McGowan, *In the Beginning*, p. 127.

22. Ibid., p. 68.

23. Ibid., pp. 94 and 156.

24. Ibid., p. 121.

25. Ibid., p. 26.

26. Ibid., p. 20.

27. Ibid., p. 29.

28. Ibid., p. 20.

29. Antony Flew, "Darwin, Evolution and Creationalism," *Free Inquiry* (Summer 1982): 48.

30. McGowan, *In the Beginning,* p. 61.

31. Ibid., p. 55.

32. J. Greenberg, "Fossils Trigger Questions of Human Origins," *Science News* (February 6, 1982): 84.

33. J. A. Miller, "Human Evolution: Chromosomes as Legacy," *Science News* (March 20, 1982): 196.

34. George Santayana, "Harmony," in *The Birth of Reason and Other Essays,* edited by Daniel Cory (New York: Columbia University Press, 1968).

35. Küng, *Does God Exist?* p. 533.

36. Ibid., p. 534.

37. Ibid.

38. Ibid.

39. Ibid., p. 535.

40. Ibid., p. 575.

41. Immanuel Kant, *Critique of Judgement,* trans. J. H. Bernard (Hafner Publishing Co., 1950), pp. 285–86. As reprinted by Wilbur and Allen, *The Worlds of Hume and Kant,* p. 187.

42. Küng, *Does God Exist?* p. 541.

43. Kant, *Critique of Judgment,* p. 145.

44. Ibid.

45. Küng, *Does God Exist?* p. 571.

46. Ibid., p. 573.

47. Ibid., p. 574.

48. Ibid., p. 658.

49. Ibid., p. 185.

50. Richard Swinburne, *The Existence of God* (Oxford: Clarendon Press, 1979).

51. Ibid., p. 7.

52. Ibid., pp. 120–32.

53. Ibid., pp. 56–69.

54. Ibid., p. 254.

55. Ibid., p. 272.

Chapter 14

1. Søren Kierkegaard, "Fear and Trembling." Cited by Sidney Hook, "Modern Knowledge and the Concept of God," in *Critiques of God,* p. 37.

2. Ibid., p. 37.

3. Ibid.

4. Archibald MacLeish, *J.B.* (Boston: Houghton Mifflin Company, 1958), p. 14.

5. Küng, *Does God Exist?* p. 155.

6. Ernest Nagel, "Philosophical Concepts of Atheism," in *Critiques of God,* p. 14.

7. John Gardner, *Grendel* (New York: Ballantine Books, 1971), p. 115.

8. John Donnelly, "Suffering: A Christian View," in *Infanticide and the Meaning of Life,* p. 164.

9. Smith, *Atheism: The Case against God,* p. 85.

10. John Stuart Mill, "Growing Up without God," in *Classics of Free Thought,* p. 125.

11. Baier, "The Meaning of Life," in *Critiques of God,* p. 319.

12. Luther Burbank, "Our Savior, Science," in *Classics of Free Thought,* p. 23.

13. Robert Ingersoll, "Questions for God," in *Classics of Free Thought,* p. 89.

14. Swinburne, *The Existence of God,* p. 185.

15. H. J. McCloskey, "God and Evil," in *Critiques of God,* pp. 203–24.

16. Antony Flew, "Divine Omnipotence and Human Freedom," in *Critiques of God,* pp. 227–37.

17. Ibid., p. 233.

18. Swinburne, *The Existence of God,* p. 202.

19. Murphy, *God and His Creation,* p. 228.

20. Ibid., pp. 236–37. "Yet God's will not to sustain man in the performance of good is not an evil act, because the human will has no claim to such continuous divine support . . . , nor does God have any obligation so to sustain man's will."

21. Flew, "Divine Omnipotence and Human Freedom," p. 233.

22. Küng, *Does God Exist?* p. 623.

23. Feuerbach, *The Essence of Christianity,* p. 55.

24. Smith, *Atheism: The Case against God,* p. 73.

25. Santayana, "Ultimate Responsibility," *The Birth of Reason,* p. 76.

26. David Hume, "Treatise On Human Nature," bk. 1, part III, sections II & III, ed. Selby and Brige (Oxford: Clarendon Press), pp. 270–74. Cited by Wilbur and Allen, *The Worlds of Hume and Kant,* p. 29.

27. Bradlaugh, "A Plea for Atheism," in *Anthology of Atheism and Rationalism,* p. 18.

28. Stanislaw Lem, "Non Serviam," in *The Mind's I,* edited by Douglas R. Hofstaden and Daniel C. Dennett (New York: Basic Books, Inc. Publishers, 1981), p. 341.

29. Annie Besant, "Why I Do Not Believe In God," in *An Anthology of Atheism and Rationalism,* p. 32.

30. Reichley, *Religion in American Public Life,* p. 48.

31. As quoted by Smith, *Atheism: The Case against God,* p. 65.

32. Ibid., p. 52.

33. Feuerbach, *The Essence of Christianity,* p. 15.

34. Smith, *Atheism: The Case against God,* p. 56.

35. Rudolph Carnap, "The Elimination of Metaphysics through Logical Analysis of Language," in A. J. Ayer, ed., *Logical Positivism* (New York: Macmillan Publishing Co., Free Press, 1959), p. 66.

36. Smith, *Atheism: The Case against God,* p. 43.
37. Gordon Stein, ed., *An Anthology of Atheism and Rationalism,* p. 5.
38. Smith, *Atheism: The Case against God,* p. 66.
39. Ibid., p. 88.
40. David Brooks, "The Necessity of Atheism," quoted by Smith, *Atheism: The Case against God,* p. 219.

Chapter 15

1. William James, *Pragmatism* (London: Longmans, Green and Co., 1907), p. 204.
2. Alfie Kohn, "Do Religious People Help More?" *Psychology Today* (December 1989).
3. M. Argyle and B. Beit-Hallahmi, *The Social Psychology of Religion* (London: Routledge and Kegan Paul, 1975). Cited by Brown, *The Psychology of Religious Belief,* p. 118.
4. L. B. Brown, *The Psychology of Religious Belief* (New York: Academic Press, 1987), p. 118.
5. T. W. Adorno et al., *The Authoritarian Personality* (New York: Harper and Row Publishers, 1950), pp. 844ff.
6. H. Hartshore and M. A. May, *Studies in Deceit* (New York: Macmillan, 1982). Cited by Brown, *The Psychology of Religious Belief,* p. 50.
7. E. J. Shoben, "Moral Behavior and Word Learning," *Religious Education* 58 (1963): 137–45. Cited by Brown, *The Psychology of Religious Belief,* p. 196.
8. C. D. Batson et al., "Brotherly Love or Self-Concern? Behavioral Consequences of Religion," in L. B. Brown, ed., *Advances in the Psychology of Religion* (Oxford: Pergamon Press, 1985). Quoted by Brown, *The Psychology of Religious Belief,* p. 201.
9. D. Wright, "Religious Education from the Perspective of Moral Education," *Journal of Moral Education* 12, no. 2 (1985): 111–15. Quoted by Brown, *The Psychology of Religious Belief,* p. 201.
10. Gordon W. Allport, *The Nature of Prejudice* (Garden City, N.Y.: Doubleday Anchor Books, 1958), p. 420.
11. Adorno et al., *The Authoritarian Personality,* p. 209.
12. Ibid., p. 68.
13. G. W. Allport and J. M. Ross, "Personal Religious Orientation and Prejudice," *Journal of Personality and Psychology* (1967): 432–43. Cited by Brown, *The Psychology of Religious Belief,* p. 68.
14. Wade Clark Roof, "Religious Orthodoxy and Minority Prejudice: Causal Relaionship or Reflection of Localistic World View?" *American Journal of Sociology* 80, no. 3: 643.
15. Allport, *The Nature of Prejudice,* p. 417.
16. Francis Galton, *Hereditary Genius: An Inquiry into its Laws and Consequences* (New York: Appleton & Co., 1887). Cited by Brown, *The Psychology*

of Religious Belief, p. 1.

17. C. R. B. Joyce and R. M. C. Welldon, "The Efficacy of Prayer: A Double Blind Clinical Trial," *Journal of Chronic Disease,* no. 18 (1965): 367–77. Cited by Gary P. Posner, "God in the CCU?" *Free Inquiry* (Spring 1990): 44–45.

18. P. J. Collipp, "The Efficacy of Prayer: Triple Blind Study," *Medical Times,* no. 97 (1969): 201–204. Cited by Posner, "God in the CCU?" pp. 44–45.

19. Randolph C. Byrd, M.D., "Positive Therapeutic Effects of Intercessory Prayer in a Coronary Care Unit Population," *Southern Medical Journal* (July 1988). Cited by Posner, "God in the CCU?" pp. 44–45.

20. T. A. Wills, "Supportive Functions of Interpersonal Relationships," in S. Cohen and L. Syme, eds., *Social Support and Health* (New York: Academic Press, 1984). Cited by Brown, *The Psychology of Religious Belief,* p. 155.

21. A. E. Bergin, "Religiosity and Mental Health: A Critical Re-evaluation and Meta-analysis," *Professional Psychology: Research and Practice* 14, no. 2 (1983): 170–84. Cited by Brown, *The Psychology of Religious Belief,* p. 72.

22. Argyle and Beit-Hallahmi, 1975, as cited by Brown, *The Psychology of Religious Belief,* p. 211.

23. C. D. Batson and W. L. Ventis, *The Religious Experience: A Social-Psychological Religion* (New York: Oxford University Press, 1982). Cited by Brown, *The Psychology of Religious Belief,* p. 211.

24. J. E. Dittes, "Psychology of Religion," In G. Lindzey and E. Aronson, eds., *The Handbook of Social Psychology,* vol. 5 (Reading, Mass.: Addison Wesley, 1969), pp. 602–59. Cited by Brown, *The Psychology of Religious Belief,* p. 211.

25. Farig Ismail, "Humanism in Modern India: An Interview with M. Tarkunde," *Free Inquiry* (Summer 1986): 51.

26. Ibid.

27. Henry David Thoreau, *Civil Disobedience,* in *Walden and Other Writings of Henry David Thoreau,* edited and intro. by Brooks Atkinson (New York: The Modern Library, 1950), p. 637.

28. Brown, *The Psychology of Religious Belief,* p. 117.

29. Thomas Paine, "Letter to Erskine," *The Age of Reason,* p. 50.

30. Quoted in Niebuhr, *Nature and Destiny of Man,* vol. 2, p. 221. As cited by Reichley, *Religion in American Public Life,* p. 35.

31. Tom Stoppard, *Rosencrantz and Guildenstern Are Dead,* p. 706.

32. Feuerbach, *The Essence of Christianity,* p. 162. According to Feuerbach this statement was quoted approvingly by Martin Luther.

33. Ibid., p. 16.

34. Robert Ingersoll, "The Christian Heaven," in *Classics of Free Thought,* p. 90.

35. Shaw, "Preface to *Major Barbara,*" *Saint Joan,* p. 197.

36. Albert Camus, "Summers in Algiers," in *The Myth of Sisyphus and Other Essays* (New York: Vintage Books, 1955), p. 113.

37. Quoted by Chapman Cohen, *Essays in Free-Thinking* (London: Pioneer Press, 1928), p. 19. Cited by Corliss Lamont, "Illusions of Immortality," in *Critiques of God,* p. 273.

38. William Osler, *Science and Immortality* (New York: Houghton Mifflin, 1904), p. 19. Cited by Lamont, "Illusions of Immortality," p. 257.

39. Allport, *The Nature of Prejudice*, p. 413.

40. Radio Advertisement on WNIB, Summer 1987.

41. Reichley, *Religion in American Public Life*, p. 40.

42. Feuerbach, *The Essence of Christianity*, p. 253.

43. Lorenz, *On Aggression*, p. 269.

44. Koran, 2nd Surah, verses 94 and 154. *The Holy Qur'an*, trans. by Abdullah Vusus Ali (Elmhurst, N.Y.: Tahrike Tarsile Qur'an, Inc., 1988).

45. Aquinas, *Summa*, Pt. II, Q.10, A.3. Cited by Smith, *Atheism: The Case against God*, p. 4.

46. J. H. Newman, *Certain Difficulties Felt by Anglicans in Catholic Teachings* (1918). Cited by Joseph Fletcher, *Situation Ethics* (Philadelphia: Westminister Press, 1966), p. 20.

47. Quoted by Reichley, *Religion in American Public Life*, p. 33.

48. Robert G. Ingersoll, "Some Mistakes of Moses," in *Anthology of Atheism and Rationalism*, p. 147.

49. Quoted by William James in *Pragmatism*, p. 26.

50. Peter Lombard, 1. iv. dist. 50, c.4. Quoted by Feuerbach, *The Essence of Christianity*, p. 257.

51. Russell, *Religion and Science*, p. 135.

52. Arthur Schopenhauer, "The World as Will and Idea," *Schopenhauer Selections*, ed. DeWitt H. Parker (New York: Charles Scribner's Sons, 1928), p. 259.

53. Russell, *Religion and Science*, p. 106.

54. Quoted by Mencken, *Treatise on the Gods*, p. 270.

55. Erich Fromm, "An Analysis of Some Types of Religious Experience," in *Critiques of God*, p. 163.

56. Quoted by Mencken, *Treatise on the Gods*, p. 244.

57. Russell, *Religion and Science*, p. 101.

58. Ibid., p. 104.

59. Feuerbach, *The Essence of Christianity*, p. 193.

60. Quoted in Adorno et al., *The Authoritarian Personality*, p. 733.

61. Ibid.

62. Clarence Darrow, "Absurdities of the Bible," in *Classics of Free Thought*, p. 35.

63. Hypatia Bradlaugh Bonner, "Christianity and Conduct," in *An Anthology of Atheism and Rationalism*, p. 271.

64. Feuerbach, *The Essence of Christianity*, p. 274.

65. Timothy J. Cooney, *Telling Right from Wrong* (Buffalo, N.Y.: Prometheus Books, 1985), p. 125.

66. Kai Nielson, *Ethics without God* (London: Pemberton Books, 1973), p. 13.

67. Ibid., p. 10.

68. Feuerbach, *The Essence of Christianity*, p. 184.

69. G. E. Moore, *Principia Ethica* (Cambridge, England: Cambridge University Press, 1903), p. 82.

70. T. H. Huxley, "Agnosticism versus Christianity," in *Classics of Free Thought*, p. 84.

71. James Madison, "Memorial and Remonstrance Against Religious Assessments," in *Classics of Free Thought*, p. 113.

72. Manly P. Hall, *Locked Keys of Freemasonry*, p. 48. Quoted by Decker and Hall, *The God Makers*, p. 137.

73. George Bernard Shaw, "Preface to *Androcles and the Lion*," in *Saint Joan*, p. 335.

74. Reichley, *Religion in American Political Life*, p. 355.

Chapter 16

1. N. Scott Momaday, *House Made of Dawn* (New York: New American Library, 1968), p. 120.

2. John M. Allegro, *The Sacred Mushroom and the Cross* (Garden City, N.Y.: Doubleday & Co., 1970), p. 24.

3. Weber, *Economy and Society*, pp. 427–28.

4. Sigmund Freud, "The Future of an Illusion," in *Critiques of God*, p. 145.

5. Frazer, *The Golden Bough*, see especially chapters 4 and 5.

6. Russell, *Religion and Science*, p. 83.

7. Joseph Campbell, *Primitive Mythology*, p. 467. Quoted by Reichley, *Religion in American Public Life*, p. 40.

8. C. G. Finney, *Lectures on Revival of Religion*, Leavitt (New York: Lord and Co., 1835). Quoted by Brown, *The Psychology of Religious Belief*, p. 7.

9. W. G. McLoughlin, *Modern Revivalism: Charles Grandison Finney to Billy Graham* (New York: Ronald Press, 1959). Quoted by Brown, *The Psychology of Religious Belief*, p. 7.

10. Weber, *Economy and Society*, vol. 12, p. 455.

11. Quoted by R. Payne Knight, *The Symbolical Language of Ancient Art and Mythology* (New York: J. W. Bouton, 1876), p. 114. Cited by Doane, *Bible Myths*, p. 47.

12. E. G. Squire, *The Serpent Symbol and the Worship of the Reciprocal Principles of Nature in America* (New York: George P. Putnam, 1851), p. 38. Cited by Doane, *Bible Myths*, p. 562.

13. Albert Reville, *History of the Dogma of the Deity of Jesus Christ* (London: Williams and Norgate, 1870), p. 29. Cited by Doane, *Bible Myths*, p. 373.

14. George Smith, *Chaldean Account of Genesis*, pp. 86–87.

15. Cunningham Geikie, D.D., *Life and Works of Christ* (New York: D. Appleton & Co, 1880), vol. 1, p. 151. Cited by Doane, *Bible Myths*, p. 502.

16. King, *The Gnostics and Their Remains*, p. 68: "There can be no doubt that the head of Serapis, marked as the face is by a grave and pensive majesty, supplied the first idea for the conventional portraits of the saviour." Cited by Doane, *Bible Myths*, p. 501.

17. Charles Guignibert, "Hellenistic Culture," in *The Christ* (Secaucus, N.J.: University Books, 1968). Cited in *The Origins of Christianity,* p. 55.

18. Julius Caesar, *De Bello Gallico* G. 13–18. Trans. by J. J. Edwards, Loeb Classical Library (Cambridge: Harvard University Press). Quoted by Joseph Campbell, *Masks of God: Occidental Mythology* (New York: Viking Press, 1964), p. 225.

19. D. S. Russell, "The Resurrection of the Dead: A History," in *The Origins of Christianity,* p. 111.

20. Irenaeus, *Against Heresies,* bk. iii, chap. XI, sect. 8. Quoted by Doane, *Bible Myths,* p. 459.

21. Middleton, *The Miscellaneous Works of Conyers Middleton,* p. 19. Cited by Doane, *Bible Myths,* p. 273.

22. Eusebuius, *Praeparatio Evangelica,* bk. xii, chap. 31. Cited by Doane, *Bible Myths,* p. 565.

23. Mencken, *Treatise on the Gods,* p. 231.

24. Ibid., p. 231.

25. Charles Bradlaugh, quoted by Paul Blanshard, in *Classics of Free Thought,* p. 18.

26. John Gardner, *Grendel* (New York: Ballantine Books, 1971), p. 139.

27. Joseph Campbell, *The Masks of God: Occidental Mythology* (New York: The Viking Press, 1964), p. 378.

28. Parrinder, *World Religions,* p. 375.

Chapter 17

1. Erich Fromm, *Escape from Freedom* (New York: Holt Rinehart and Winston, 1941), p. 65.

2. Feuerbach, *The Essence of Christianity,* p. 121.

3. Ibid., p. 14.

4. Ibid., p. 73.

5. Theodore Gaster, "Biblical versus Secular Morality," lecture delivered at Free Inquiry's Fifth Annual Conference, University of Richmond, October 31, 1986.

6. Edward O. Wilson, *On Human Nature* (Cambridge, Mass.: Harvard University Press, 1978; rpt. Bantam Books, 1982), p. 5.

7. John Steinbeck, *Pastures of Heaven* (New York: Viking Press, 1932; rpt. New York: Bantam Books, 1951). p. 43.

8. Argyle and Beit-Hallami, *The Social Psychology of Religion,* p. 198. Cited by Brown, *The Psychology of Religious Belief,* p. 139.

9. Schopenhauer, "The World as Will and Idea," *Schopenhauer Selections,* p. 289.

10. Winifred Kirkland, *The New Death* (New York: Houghlin Mifflin, 1918), p. 9. Cited by Corliss Lamont, "The Illusion of Immortality," in *Critiques of God,* p. 279.

11. Shaw, "Preface to *Androcles and the Lion,*" *Saint Joan,* p. 401.

12. Kurt Vonnegut, *Palm Sunday* (New York: Dell Publishing Co., 1981), p. 215.

13. Quoted by Andrew Greeley, *The Denominational Society: A Sociological Approach to Religion in America* (1972), p. 21. Cited by Brown, *The Psychology of Religious Belief,* p. 119.

14. Feuerbach, *The Essence of Christianity,* p. 63.

15. There is conflicting evidence in this regard. A study by O. J. Strunk found a "close similarity between father and the concept of God," while M. O. Nelson concluded that the concept of God was more closely related to that of a mother figure. Another study by Vergote and Tamayo failed to discover any relationship between a God image and a parental image. These conflicting results can perhaps be explained. The image of God is a projection of desirable attributes of both mother and father qualities. The earliest forms of the gods were depicted alternately as father and mother images (e.g., father sun and mother earth). It is not surprising that the studies yielded different results, since it may be only a few unusual cases where people consciously make the association. On the other hand, subconscious associations are much harder to detect. For further discussion see: O. J. Strunk, "Perceived Relationships between Parental and Deity Concepts," *Psychological Newsletter* 10 (1959): 222, 226; M. O. Nelson, "The Concept of God and Feelings toward Parents," *Journal of Individual Psychology* 27 (1971): 46–49; and A. Vergote and A. Tamayo, *The Parental Figures and the Representation of God* (Mouton: Hague, 1980).

16. R. Stark, "On the Incompatibility of Religion and Science: A Survey of Graduate students," *Journal for the Scientific Study of Religion* 3 (1963): 13–21. Cited by Brown, *The Psychology of Religious Belief,* p. 86.

17. R. M. Dreger, "Some Personality Correlates of Religious Attitudes as Determined by Projective Techniques," *Psychological Monographs* 66, no. 3 (1952). Cited by Brown, *The Psychology of Religious Belief,* p. 86. See also J. G. Ranck, "Religious Conservatism—Liberalism and Mental Health," *Pastoral Psychology* 12 (1961): 34–40. Cited by Brown, *The Psychology of Religious Belief,* p. 86.

18. J. E. Dittes, "Religion Prejudice and Personality," In M. P. Strommon, ed., *Research on Religious Development: A Comprehensive Handbook. A Project of the Religious Education Association* (New York: Hawthorne Books, 1971), pp. 355–90. Cited by Brown, *The Psychology of Religious Belief,* p. 86.

19. L. J. Francis, "Personality and Religion: Theory and Measurement," in L. B. Brown, ed., *Advances in the Psychology of Religion* (Oxford: Pergamon Press, 1985), pp. 171–84. Cited by Brown, *The Psychology of Religious Belief,* p. 86.

20. Erich Fromm, "An Analysis of Some Types of Religious Experience," in *Critiques of God,* p. 173.

21. Feuerbach, *The Essence of Christianity,* p. 249.

22. Nathaniel Branden, *The Psychology of Self-Esteem* (New York: Bantam Books, 1969), p. 192.

23. Ibid.

24. John T. Omhundro, "Von Daniken's Chariots: A Primer in the Art of Cooked Science," *The Zetetic* 1, no. 1 (Fall 1976): 58.

25. C. Ward and M. H. Beunbbuan, "Spirit Possession and Neuroticism in West Indian Pentecostal Community," *British Journal of Clinical Psychology* 20 (1981): 295–96. Cited by Brown, *The Psychology of Religious Belief*, p. 176.

26. Quoted in Chapman Cohen, *Essays in Free Thinking* (London: Pioneer Press, 1928), p. 26. Cited by Corliss Lamont, "The Illusion of Immortality," in *Critiques of God*, p. 285.

27. Shaw, "Preface to *Androcles and the Lion*," *Saint Joan*, p. 418.

28. Schopenhauer, "The World as Will and Idea," *Schopenhauer Selections*, p. 228.

29. Saul Bellow, *The Dean's December* (New York: Harper & Row, 1982), p. 242.

30. E. Haldeman-Julius, "The Mental Disease Called Religion," in *Classics of Free Thought*, p. 73.

31. Fromm, "An Analysis of Some Types of Religious Experience," p. 177.

32. Ibid., p. 163.

33. Morris R. Cohen, "The Dark Side of Religion," in *Classics of Free Thought*, p. 31.

34. Richard Wright, *Black Boy—A Record of Childhood and Youth* (New York: Harper and Row Publishers, 1937), p. 170.

35. Ibid.

36. Isaac Asimov, "Asimov's Corollary," *Skeptical Inquirer* (Spring 1979): 58–67.

37. Burnham P. Beckwith, "The Effect of Education on Religious Faith," *Free Inquiry* 2, no. 1 (Winter 1981/82): 31.

38. Burnham P. Beckwith, "Effects of Intelligence on Religious Faith," *Free Inquiry* (Spring 1988): 46–56.

39. R. H. Thoules, "The Tendency to Certainty in Religious Belief," *British Journal of Psychology* 26 (1935): 16–31, and L. B. Brown, "A Study of Religious Belief," *British Journal of Psychology* 53, no. 3 (1962): 259–72. Both cited by Brown, "A Study of Religious Belief," p. 116.

40. C. Rogan, H. N. Maloney, and B. Beit-Hallahmi, "Psychologists and Religion: Professional Factors and Personal Beliefs," *Review of Religious Research* 21 (1961): 208–17. Cited by Brown, "A Study of Religious Belief," p. vi.

41. Larry A. Jackson, "Keeping the Faith—Western Religion's Future," *The Futurist* (October 1985): 26.

42. Barry Singer and Victor A. Benassi, "Fooling Some of the People All of the Time," *Skeptical Inquirer* 5, no. 2 (Winter 1980–81): 17–24.

43. James Randi, "The Project Alpha Experiment: Part 1. The First Two Years," *Skeptical Inquirer* 7, no. 4 (Summer 1983): 24ff.

44. Schopenhauer, "The World as Will and Idea," *Schopenhauer Selections*, p. 290.

45. M. D. Goulder, "Midrash and Lection in Matthew," *The Speaker's Lecture in Biblical Studies, 1969–1975* (London: SPCK, 1974), p. 650.

46. L. B. Brown, *The Psychology of Religious Belief*, pp. 193–94. Brown cites the following studies: J. N. Kotre, *The View from the Border* (Dublin: Gill and

MacMillain Ltd., 1971); B. E. Hunsberger and L. B. Brown, "Religious Socialization, Apostacy and the Impacts of Family Background," *Journal for the Scientific Study of Religion* 23, no. 3 (1984): 239–51; and L. J. Francis, *Monitoring the Christian Development of the Child* (Abingdon: Culham College Institute, 1954).

47. Denis Diderot, "Missionaries, Atheists and Marriage," in *Classics of Free Thought*, p. 53.

48. Schopenhauer, "The World as Will and Idea," *Schopenhauer Selections*, p. 286.

49. Charles Darwin, "De-Censoring Darwin's Religion" from *The Autobiography of Charles Darwin*, edited by Nora Barlow (Harcourt Brace Jovanovich); *Classics of Free Thought*, p. 47.

50. Felix Frankfurter, "*McCollum* vs. *Board of Education*," in Classics of Free Thought, p. 62.

51. Robert S. Alley, "The Founding Fathers and Religious Liberty," *Free Inquiry* 3, no. 2, (Spring 1983): 4.

52. Branden, *The Psychology of Self-Esteem*, p. 142.

53. Gordon Stein, "Why Atheists Are Feared," *Free Inquiry* (Winter 1985/86): 53.

54. M. Argyle, "Seven Psychological Roots of Religion," *Theology* 67, no. 530 (1964): 1–2. Cited by Brown, *The Psychology of Religious Belief*, p. 174.

55. Brown, *The Psychology of Religious Belief*, p. 115.

56. Edmund D. Cohen, "The Psychology of the Bible Believer," *Free Inquiry* (Spring 1987): 22–27.

57. Albert Ellis, *The Case against Religion: A Psychotherapist's View and the Case against Religiosity* (Austin, Tex.: American Atheist Press).

58. Paul Kurtz, *The Transcendental Temptation* (Buffalo, N.Y.: Prometheus Books, 1986).

59. Karl Marx, *Economic and Philosophical Manuscripts*, trans. from *Karl Marx: Selected Writings*, edited by David McLellan (Oxford University Press, 1977). Quoted by Raya Dunayevskaya, in Paul Kurtz, ed., "Humanism and Marxism," in *The Humanist Alternative* (Buffalo, N.Y.: Prometheus Books, 1973), p. 153.

60. Karl Marx, *Introduction to the Critique of Political Economy* (New York: Lawrence and Wishart, 1970). Quoted by Raya Dunayevskaya, "Humanism and Marxism," in *The Humanist Alternative*, p. 153.

61. Albert Schweitzer, *The Quest for the Historical Jesus: A Critical Study of Its Progress from Reimarus to Wredo* (New York: MacMillan, 1948).

62. Robert G. Ingersoll, "Some Mistakes of Moses," in *An Anthology of Atheism and Rationalism*, p. 151.

Chapter 18

1. Küng, *Does God Exist?* p. 469.

2. W. R. Cassels, "Supernatural Religion," in *An Anthology of Atheism and Rationalism*, p. 178.

3. *The American Heritage Dictionary of the English Language* (Boston: Houghton Mifflin, 1982), p. 948.

4. Harold W. Wood, Jr., "Modern Pantheism as an Approach to Enviornmental Ethics," *Environmental Ethics* 7, no. 2 (Summer 1985): 151–63.

5. Chief Luther Standing Bear of the Oglala Band of Sioux, as quoted in *Touch the Earth, A Self-Portrait of Indian Evidence,* compiled by T. C. McLuhan (New York: Pocket Books, 1972), p. 45.

6. Queen of All Saints Church Newsletter.

7. Barbara Ruben, "A New Green Gospel—Preaching for the Planet," *Environmental Action* (January/February 1991): 23.

8. *The Analects of Confucius,* trans. by Arthur Waley, p. 130.

9. Ibid.

10. *The Works of Mencius,* 7b:12. Cited by Parrinder, *World Religions,* p. 322.

11. Parrinder, *World Religions,* p. 325.

12. Ibid., pp. 325–26.

13. M. P. Rege, "Religious Belief in Contempoary Indian Society," *Free Inquiry* 6, no. 3 (Summer 1986): 41–48.

14. Ibid., p. 47.

15. Paine, *Age of Reason,* footnote by author, p. 184.

16. Norman Wentworth Dewitt, *Epicurus and His Philosophy* (New York: Meridian Books, 1967), p. 30.

17. Ibid.

18. Feuerbach, *The Essence of Christianity,* p. 267.

19. David Hume, "Enquiry Concerning the Principles of Morals," Selection XXIV: Sec IX, Pt.1 (Oxford: Clarendon Press; rpt. Wilbur & Allen), p. 80.

20. Immanuel Kant, *Conjectural Beginnings of Human History,* edited by Lewis Beck (New York: Bobbs Merrill Co., Inc., 1982; rpt. Wilbur & Allen), p. 99.

21. Paine, *Age of Reason,* p. 137.

22. As quoted by Albert Camus in "Absurd Creation," from *The Myth of Sisyphus and Other Essays,* trans. by Justine O'Brian (New York: Vintage Books, 1955), p. 69.

23. Dostoevsky, *The Possessed,* quoted by Camus, "Absurd Creation," p. 80.

24. Rollo May, *The Cry for Myth* (New York: W. W. Norton and Company), 1991.

25. Bertrand Russell, *Autobiography* (London: Allen and Unwin, 1967), vol. 1, p. 13. As Quoted by Küng, *Does God Exist?* p. 99.

26. Küng, *Does God Exist?* p. 692.

27. Immanuel Kant, *Critique of Judgement,* trans. by J. H. Bernar (Riverside, N.J.: Hafner Publishing Co., 1951; rpt. Wilbur & Allen), p. 147.

28. Ibid.

29. James, *Pragmatism,* p. 118.

30. Paul Beattie, "How Are Ethics Related to Religion?" *Free Inquiry* (Summer 1982): 60.

31. Feuerbach, *The Essence of Christianity,* p. 266.

32. Ibid., p. 270.

33. Karl Marx, quoted by Dunayeuskaya, "Humanism and Marxism," p. 158.

34. Küng, *Does God Exist?* p. 203. Küng does not profess this position; rather he was attempting to summarize the argument of Feuerbach.

35. H. J. Blackman, "A Definition of Humanism," in *The Humanist Alternative,* p. 34.

36. *A Secular Humanist Declaration,* drafted by Paul Kurtz and endorsed by 58 prominent scholars and writers (Buffalo, N.Y.: Prometheus Books, 1980).

37. Mathelde Niel, "Contribution to a Definition of Humanism," trans. by Henry Darcy, in *The Humanist Alternative,* p. 146.

38. Paul Kurtz, "Humanism and the Moral Revolution," in *The Humanist Alternative,* p. 49.

39. Ibid., p. 55.

40. Reichley, *Religion in American Public Life,* p. 348.

41. Mencken, *Treatise on the Gods,* p. 7.

42. Dennis Bernstein and Connie Blitt, "Onward Christian Soldiers," *The Progressive,* July 1985, p. 18.

Chapter 19

1. Henry Kissinger, Speech to Planning Forum International Strategic Planning Conference in New Orleans, May 1992.

2. Kurt Vonnegut, Jr., *Slaughterhouse-Five or The Children's Crusade* (New York: Seymour Lawrence Book/Delacorte Press, 1969), p. 9.

3. David Tribe, "Our Freethought Heritage: The Humanist and Ethical Movement," in *The Humanist Alternative,* p. 25.

Bibliography

Allegro, John M. *The Dead Sea Scrolls and the Christian Myth.* Buffalo, N.Y.: Prometheus Books, 1984.
———. *The Sacred Mushroom and the Cross.* Garden City, N.Y.: Doubleday & Company, Inc., 1970.
Alley, Robert S. "The Founding Fathers and Religious Liberty." *Free Inquiry* 3:2 (Spring 1983): 4–5.
Angeles, Peter, ed. *Critiques of God.* Buffalo, N.Y.: Prometheus Books, 1976.
Ayer, A. J., ed. *Logical Positivism.* New York: The Free Press, 1959.
Baigent, Michael, and Leigh, Richard. *The Dead Sea Scrolls Deception.* New York: Summit Books, 1991.
Beckwith, Burnham P. "The Effect of Education on Religious Faith." *Free Inquiry* 2:1 (1981): 26–31.
Blau, Joseph L. "New Thoughts (and Old) on Science and Religion." *Free Inquiry* 2:3 (1982): 67–70.
Branden, Nathaniel. *The Psychology of Self-Esteem.* New York: Bantam Books, 1969.
Brown, L. B. *The Psychology of Religious Belief.* San Diego, Calif.: Harcourt Brace Jovanovich, 1987.
Camus, Albert. *The Fall.* Translated by Justin O'Brien. New York: Alfred A. Knopf, 1969.
Campbell, Joseph. *The Masks of God: Occidental Mythology.* New York: The Viking Press, 1964.
Davies, Paul. *God and the New Physics.* New York: Simon and Schuster, 1983.
Davis, Christopher. *North American Indian.* New York: The Hamlyn Publishing Group Limited, 1969.
Decker, Ed, and Hunt, Dave. *The God Makers.* Eugene, Ore.: Harvest House Publishers, 1984.
DeWitt, Norman Wentworth. *Epicurus and His Philosophy.* New York: The World Publishing Co., 1954.

Diamond, Sara. *Spiritual Warfare—The Politics of the Christian Right.* Boston: South End Press, 1989.

Doane, T. W. *Bible Myths and Their Parallels in Other Religions.* New Hyde Park, N.Y.: University Books, 1971.

Doerr, Edd. "Madison's Legacy Endangered." *Free Inquiry* 3:2 (1983): 6.

Dunlap, S. F. *Vestiges of the Spirit History of Man.* New York: D. Appleton Co., 1858.

Eisenman, R. H. *James the Just in the Habakkuk Pesher.* Leiden, 1986.

———. *Maccabees, Zadokites, Christians and Qumran.* Leiden, 1983.

Ellis, Albert. *The Case against Religion: A Psychotherapist's View.* Austin, Tex.: American Atheist Press.

Ervin, Sam J., Jr. "The Constitution and Religion." *Free Inquiry* 3:3 (1983).

Feuerbach, Ludwig. *The Essence of Christianity.* Translated by George Eliot. New York: Harper and Row, 1957.

Frazer, James George. *The Golden Bough.* Chicago: The Macmillan Co., 1951.

Fredricksen, Paula. *From Jesus to Christ—The Origins of the New Testament Images of Christ.* New Haven and London: Yale University Press, 1988

Friedman, Richard Elliot. *Who Wrote the Bible?* New York: Summit Books, 1987.

Fromm, Erich. *Escape from Freedom.* Chicago: Holt Rinehart and Winston, 1969.

Gardner, John. *Grendel.* New York: Ballantine Books, 1971.

Gleick, James. *Chaos.* New York: Viking Press, 1987.

Greenberg, J. "Fossils Trigger Questions of Human Origins." *Science News,* February 6, 1982.

Hackleman, Douglas. "Ellen White's Habit." *Free Inquiry* 4:4 (Fall 1984): 20.

Helms, Randel. "How the Gospels Tell a Story." *Free Inquiry* 2:3 (1982): 20–23.

Herbert, Wray. "An Epidemic in the Works." *Science News,* September 18, 1982, pp. 188–90.

———. "Melancholy Genas." *Science News,* February 13, 1982, p. 108.

Hoffmann, R. Joseph, ed. *The Origins of Christianity.* Buffalo, N.Y.: Prometheus Books, 1985.

Houdini, Harry. *Miracle Mongers and Their Methods.* Buffalo, N.Y.: Prometheus Books, 1981.

James, William. *Pragmatism.* New York: Longmans, Green, and Co., 1907.

Johnson, B. C. *The Atheist Debater's Handbook.* Buffalo, N.Y.: Prometheus Books, 1983.

Josephy, Alvin, M., Jr. *The Indian Heritage of America.* New York: Alfred A. Knopf, 1970.

Kreyche, Robert J. *First Philosophy.* New York: Holt, Rinehart and Winston, 1959.

———. *Logic for Undergraduates.* New York: The Dryden Press, 1957.

Küng, Hans. *Does God Exist?* New York: Vintage Books, 1975.

Kurtz, Paul. *A Secular Humanist Declaration.* Buffalo, N.Y.: Prometheus Books, 1980.

———. *The Transcendental Temptation—A Critique of Religion and the Paranormal.* Buffalo, N.Y.: Prometheus Books, 1986.

Larue, Gerald. "Astronomy and the Star of Bethlehem." *Free Inquiry* 3:1 (1982/83): 25ff.

Lekachman, Robert. *Greed Is Not Enough, Reaganomics.* New York: Pantheon Books, 1982.

MacLeish, Archibald. *J.B.* Boston: The Houghton Mifflin Co., 1958.

McCabe, Joseph. *History's Greatest Liars.* Austin, Tex.: American Atheist Press, 1983.

McCrone, Walter. "Shroud Image Is the Work of an Artist." *The Skeptical Inquirer* 6:3 (1982): 35–36.

McDowell, Josh. *Evidence That Demands a Verdict.* San Bernardino, Calif.: Here's Life Publishers, 1979.

McKown, Delos. *With Faith and Fury.* Buffalo, N.Y.: Prometheus Books, 1985.

Manhattan, Auro. *Vietnam, Why Did We Go?* Chino, Calif.: Chick Publications, 1984.

Mencken, H. L. *Treatise on the Gods.* New York: Alfred A. Knopf, 1946.

Menninger, Karl. *The Vital Balance.* New York: The Viking Press, 1963.

Miller, J. A. "Human Evolution: Chromosomes as Legacy." *Science News,* March 20, 1982, p. 196.

Morris, Richard. *Time's Arrows.* New York: Simon and Schuster, 1984.

Mueller, Marvin M. "The Shroud of Turin: A Critical Appraisal." *The Skeptical Inquirer* 6:3 (1982): 15–33.

Murphy, William B.; Donlon, Thomas C.; et al. *God and His Creation.* Dubuque, Iowa: The Priory Press, 1958.

The New Catholic Edition of the Holy Bible, Confraternity Edition. New York: Catholic Book Publishing Co., 1949.

Paine, Thomas. *The Age of Reason.* New Jersey: Citadel Press, 1948.

Parker, DeWitt H. *Schopenhauer Selections.* New York: Charles Schribner's Sons, 1928.

Parrinder, Geoffrey, ed. *World Religions from Ancient History to the Present.* New York: Hamlyn Publishing Group Limited, 1971.

Pirsig, Robert M. *Zen and the Art of Motorcycle Maintenence.* New York: Bantam Books, 1974.

Pollie, R. "Sex and the Celibate Fruit Fly." *Science News,* October 2, 1982, p. 212.

Proudfoot, Wayne. *Religious Experience.* Berkeley and Los Angeles: University of California Press, 1985.

Randi, James. *The Faith Healers.* Buffalo, N.Y.: Prometheus Books, 1987.

———. *Flim-Flam! Psychics, ESP, Unicorns and Other Delusions.* Buffalo, N.Y.: Prometheus Books, 1982.

Randle, Lois. "The Apocalypticism of the Jehovah's Witnesses." *Free Inquiry* 5:1 (Winter 1984/85).

Rea, Walter. "Who Profits from the Prophet?" *Free Inquiry* 4:4 (Fall 1984).

———. *The White Lie.* Turlock, Calif.: M&R Publications, 1982.

Reichley, A. James. *Religion in American Life.* Washington D.C.: The Brookings Institution, 1985.

Renan, Ernest. *The Life of Jesus*. Buffalo, N.Y.: Prometheus Books, 1991.

Ridenhour, Lynn. "Academic Freedom at Liberty Baptist College." *Free Inquiry* 4:1 (Winter 1983/84).

Roof, Wade Clark. "Religious Orthodoxy and Minority Prejudice: Causal Relationship or Reflection of Localistic World View?" *American Journal of Sociology* 80:3.

Russell, Bertrand. *Religion and Science*. New York: Oxford University Press, 1980.

———. *Why I Am Not a Christian*. New York: Simon and Schuster, 1957.

———. *Wisdom of the West*. New York: Crescent Books, 1961.

Rutland, Robert A. "James Madison's Dream: A Secular Republic." *Free Inquiry* 3:2 (1983): 8-11.

Santayana, George. *The Birth of Reason and Other Essays,* edited by Daniel Cory. New York and London: Columbia University Press, 1968.

Schafersman, Steven D. "Science, the Public, and the Shroud of Turin." *The Skeptical Inquirer* 6:3 (Spring 1982): 37-56.

Schonfield, Hugh J. *The Passover Plot*. New York: Bantam Books, 1965.

Schuster, Lynda. "The Biblical Jesus Is the God of the Sun in Southern Mexico." *Wall Street Journal,* June 9, 1983.

Shaw, George Bernard. *Saint Joan; Major Barbara; Androcles and the Lion*. New York: The Modern Library, 1952.

Simon, C. "Fossils Span Evolutionary Gap." *Science News,* February 20, 1982, p. 119.

Singer, Barry, and Benassi, Victor A. "Fooling Some of the People All of the Time." *The Skeptical Inquirer* 5.2 (1980-81): 17-24.

Skinner, B. F. *About Behaviorism*. New York: Alfred A. Knopf, 1974.

Smith, George. *The Chaldean Account of Genesis*. Minneapolis: Wizards Book Shelf, 1977.

Smith, George D. "Joseph Smith and the Book of Mormon." *Free Inquiry* 4:2 (Winter 1983/84).

Smith, George H. *Atheism: The Case against God*. Buffalo, N.Y.: Prometheus Books, 1979.

Stein, Gordon, ed. *An Anthology of Atheism and Rationalism*. Buffalo, N.Y.: Prometheus Books, 1980.

Stengler, Victor J. *Not by Design—The Origins of the Universe*. Buffalo, N.Y.: Prometheus Books, 1988.

Streiker, Lowell. "Ultrafundamentalist Sects and Child Abuse." *Free Inquiry* 4:2 (Spring 1984).

Sutherland, Charles W. *Disciples of Destruction*. Buffalo, N.Y.: Prometheus Books, 1987.

Swan, Rita. "Christian Science, Faith Healing and the Law." *Free Inquiry* 4:2 (Spring 1984).

Swinburne, Richard. *The Existence of God*. Oxford: Clarendon Press, 1991.

Taylor, Richard. "Religion vs. Ethics." *Free Inquiry* 2:3 (1982): 53-57.

Terrell, John Upton. *The Navajos*. New York: Weybright and Tally, 1970.

Twain, Mark. *Letters From the Earth,* edited by Bernard De Vot. New York: Harper and Row Publishers, 1974.

Waley, Arthur. *The Analects of Confucius.* New York: Vintage Books, 1938.

Watts, Alan W. *The Way of Zen.* New York: Vintage Books, 1957.

Weber, Max. *Economy and Society,* edited by Guenther Roth and Claus Wittioch. Berkeley: University of California Press, 1928.

Wells, G. A. *The Historical Evidence for Jesus.* Buffalo, N.Y.: Prometheus Books, 1982.

Wells, H. G. *The Outline of History.* Garden City, N.Y.: Garden City Books, 1940.

Wilbur, James B., and Allen, Harold J. *The Worlds of Hume and Kant.* Buffalo, N.Y.: Prometheus Books, 1982.

Wolf, Fred Alan. *Taking the Quantum Leap.* New York: Harper and Row Publishers, 1981.

Index